CORNELL STUDIES IN CIVIL LIBERTY

FREEDOM'S FETTERS:

The Alien and Sedition Laws

and American Civil Liberties

The Institute of Early American History and Culture is sponsored jointly by the College of William and Mary and Colonial Williamsburg, Incorporated.

Freedom's Fetters

THE ALIEN AND SEDITION LAWS
AND AMERICAN CIVIL LIBERTIES

James Morton Smith

Published in Co-operation with the Institute
of Early American History and Culture

CORNELL UNIVERSITY PRESS

ITHACA, NEW YORK

FOR MY WIFE

The Power behind the Drone

If we advert to the nature of Republican Government, we shall find that the censorial power is in the people over the Government, and not in the Government over the people.—JAMES MADISON

Preface

IF, as Professor Parrington has suggested, the eighteenth century was a *saeculum politicum,* the Federalist-Republican controversies of 1798–1800 provided an altogether appropriate climax to an Age of Politics. One of the chief concerns during the last years of the century was with civil liberties. The problem of balancing freedom and order over a century and a half ago may seem a simple one when compared with reconciling liberty and security today, but the early discussion and actions clearly outline the basic alternatives in a free society.

Recent historians have protested that the events of the 1790's have been overpersonalized and overdramatized. I have tried to avoid both pitfalls, but there is no use denying that this book deals with a dramatic struggle in which the white-hot issue of individual rights was hammered out on the anvil of American political experience. In his *History of the American People,* Woodrow Wilson declared that the Sedition Law of 1798 "cut perilously near the root of freedom of speech and of the press." It was in 1941 that I first became seriously interested in finding out just how close to the root the Federalist laws actually did cut. At that time I was writing a master's dissertation on a criminal syndicalism, or state sedition, act which had been passed after World War I. The fact that no one had made a detailed study of the Alien and Sedition Laws intrigued me, and I decided then to undertake such a study as my next research topic. Three years of war service and two years of teaching delayed the project, but I have worked on it with some degree of regularity since 1948. This work was undertaken without any particular regard for present-day implications. I wanted to discover why a society which generally agreed on the necessity of state and federal bills of rights should have differed so violently on the meaning of those guarantees. As my research progressed, I discovered more and more modern parallels—arguments over presumptive guilt and protests against anonymous informers are prime examples—but I have resisted any temptation to belabor them.

This first of two volumes on the Alien and Sedition Laws, therefore, concentrates as exclusively as possible on the enactment and enforcement of the Federalist measures of 1798 and attempts to assess their influence in shaping the development of the political process of republicanism, with its dual goals of majority rule and individual rights. A second volume, on the Kentucky and Virginia Resolutions, will deal with the opposition to this repressive legislation, the issues which this opposition raised concerning fundamental rights, and the significance of the Resolutions as an exposition upon the nature of the American constitutional system. Together they will form an integrated investigation of the relationship between liberty and authority in a popular form of government, thus constituting a chapter in the evolution of the American civil liberties tradition. I hope that they will be something more than studies of differing ideas of fair play and constitutionalism, for the questions involved go to the very heart of the concept of intellectual freedom.

It has often been pointed out that Federalists and Republicans had many commonly shared convictions, but there were also crucial differences. During the formative years preceding the Jeffersonian "Revolution of 1800," the constant clash between these parties revealed sharply divergent attitudes toward the democratic heritage of the American Revolution. The years between 1798 and 1801 afford the first instance under the Constitution in which American political leaders faced the problem of defining the role of public criticism in a representative government. Part I, "Retreat to Repression," is a detailed account of the Federalist solution to this problem; it is a critical chronicle of the internal security program adopted by the Adams administration during the Half War with France. Part II, "The Pattern of Enforcement, 1798–1799," surveys the use of the Alien Friends Act and the Sedition Law and then traces in detail the early prosecutions of seditionists. As its title suggests, Part III, "The Reign of Witches," is devoted to the accelerated use of the Sedition Law as a political weapon during the election of 1800, a campaign which culminated in the peaceable overthrow of constituted authority for the first time under the Constitution. Except for the tragic upheaval following Lincoln's election, this peaceful process of democratic change has proved the rule.

I am grateful to all of the many persons who have assisted me in this study, but two were notably helpful. First and foremost is Curtis P. Nettels, to whom I owe a special acknowledgment not only for his generous counsel and encouragement during the research and writing stages, when his criticism and craftsmanship aided me most, but also for his continued interest in this volume as it progressed toward publication. I am also obligated to Robert E. Cushman in a special sort of way. It was through his help that arrangements for final publication were made possible, and his constant kindness and continual assistance deserve far more than this brief appreciation. Discussions with Bradley Chapin, Allan J. McCurry, Freeman W. Meyer, Jerome S. Ozer, Robert A. Rutland, and Robert A. Silsby helped me to clarify my thoughts and formulate my opinions on complicated questions. To Lester J. Cappon, Director of the Institute of Early American History and Culture, I express my gratitude for careful criticisms and for his kind and sympathetic consideration throughout the preparation of the book for the press.

I have one other group of people to thank. Early training with C. H. Cramer, Alfred B. Sears, and the late H. C. Peterson sharpened my desire to pursue historical studies, and my parents and brother helped make that desire and this book a reality. Finally, a word of thanks to M. P. Catherwood and Maurice Neufeld, at the School of Industrial and Labor Relations of Cornell University, who made it possible for me to stay in the academic profession when history jobs were scarce.

No one knows better than I the inadequacy of the method by which authors acknowledge their debt to the personnel of historical societies and research libraries. Perhaps the people at the following institutions will know that my thanks are sincere: the Cornell University Library in Ithaca; the American Antiquarian Society in Worcester; the Massachusetts Historical Society, the Boston Public Library, and the Boston Athenaeum in Boston; the Houghton Library of Harvard University in Cambridge; the Connecticut Historical Society in Hartford; the New York Public Library, the New York Historical Society, and the Columbia University Library in New York; the New York State Historical Association in Cooperstown; the Historical Society of Pennsylvania in Philadelphia; the Rare Book Room and the Manuscripts Division of the Library of Congress and the National Archives in Washington; the University of Virginia Library in Charlottesville; the Virginia State Library and the Virginia Historical Society in Richmond; the Ohio Historical Society in Columbus; and the Missouri Historical Society in St. Louis.

It is a pleasure to acknowledge the grants-in-aid assistance which I received from the Institute of Early American History and Culture and the Social Science Research Council.

I wish to express my grateful acknowledgment to Appleton–Century–Crofts Company, Incorporated, of New York, for permission to quote from *A History of the American People*, by John Bach McMaster; to the Mattabesett Press of Middletown, Connecticut, for permission to quote from *Richard Alsop, a Hartford Wit*, by Karl Pomeroy Harrington; and to The Tuttle Company of Rutland, Vermont, for permission to quote from *Anthony Haswell, Printer—Patriot—Ballader*, by John Spargo. Permission to quote from the Adams Papers has been granted by the Adams Manuscript Trust of Boston, Massachusetts.

Parts of this book have appeared in the following journals and I wish to thank the editors for granting me permission to use this material: *The Historian, The Huntington Library Quarterly, The Journal of Southern History, Journalism Quarterly, The Mississippi Valley Historical Review, The New England Quarterly, The New-York Historical Society Quarterly, New York History, The Pennsylvania Magazine of History and Biography, The Quarterly Journal of Speech, The Review of Politics,* and *The William and Mary Quarterly.*

If I could think of a person or an organization to whom I could shift responsibility for the errors of fact and judgment, I should gladly do it here. The most careful research has failed to turn up such a scapegoat, so I must grudgingly accept full blame for the faults of the book.

JAMES MORTON SMITH

Williamsburg, Virginia
October, 1955

Contents

Part One

RETREAT TO REPRESSION: THE ENACTMENT OF THE ALIEN AND SEDITION LAWS

CHAPTER I

Background for Repression: America's Half War with France and the Internal Security Legislation of 1798

High Stations, Tumult, but not bliss create.—ABIGAIL ADAMS

THE unheralded arrival of John Marshall in the United States in June, 1798, climaxed one of the most dramatic diplomatic missions in American history. When he accepted the post of envoy extraordinary to the French Republic a year earlier, Marshall could not have foreseen that he would return to the United States as a great national hero. Yet the nation's capital seldom has witnessed such an enthusiastic reception as his welcome. Despite the oppressively hot weather which made Philadelphia's streets nauseous, hundreds of curious people marched a distance of six miles to escort the Virginian into the city. Acclaimed as "the man whom his country delights to Honor," he was greeted by an official delegation, headed by Secretary of State Timothy Pickering, accompanied by three corps of Philadelphia cavalry in full regalia, and followed by "a concourse of citizens in carriages, on horseback, and on foot." [1] Forming a

[1] Abigail Adams to Mary Cranch, Phila., June 23, 1798, Stewart Mitchell, ed., *New Letters of Abigail Adams, 1788–1801* (Boston, 1947), 194; *Gazette of the United States* (Philadelphia), June 20, 25, 1798.

This chapter appeared in substantially the same form in *The Huntington Library Quarterly*, 18 (1954), 37–58.

cavalcade, Marshall's "applauding fellow-citizens" paraded from the Jolly Post Tavern in Frankfort to Philadelphia's fashionable and famous City Tavern, "by much the largest and most elegant house occupied in that way in America." [2] All along the route, immense crowds thronged the streets, the windows, and even the tops of houses in many instances, to catch a glimpse of the man who "at the hazard of his life had displayed the most eminent talents and fortitude in support of the interest and honour of his country." Amid the firing of cannon, "the ringing of bells and shouts of the exulting multitude," the rather disconcerted hero had returned, somewhat surprised "at the unexpected pleasure of his Reception." [3]

The crowds were not the only admirers of Marshall. President John Adams sent a special message to Congress, announcing the arrival of the envoy at "a place of safety, where he is justly held in honor." [4] Senators, congressmen, and numerous "respectable citizens" visited the Virginian's hotel to congratulate him on his safe return, and Federalist members of both houses of Congress made arrangements for a formal dinner at O'Eller's Hotel as a tribute of "affection, approbation and respect." Over one hundred and twenty men gathered to praise "the patriotic firmness with which he sustained the dignity of his country, during his important mission." Included at this celebration were Secretary Pickering and other Cabinet members, the judges of the United States Supreme Court—soon to be headed by the man they were honoring, Speaker of the House Jonathan Dayton and many congressmen and senators, the presiding officer of the Senate of Pennsylvania, officers of the army, the Right Reverend Bishops Carroll and White, "and several other worthy and distinguished gentlemen." [5] Of the sixteen toasts greeted with "unbounded plaudits," the thirteenth—"Millions for defense, but not

[2] Elias Boudinot to his wife, Rose Hill, June 21, 1798, J. J. Boudinot, ed., *The Life, Public Services, Addresses and Letters of Elias Boudinot, Ll.D., President of the Continental Congress* (Boston and New York, 1896), II, 141; Carl and Jessica Bridenbaugh, *Rebels and Gentlemen: Philadelphia in the Age of Franklin* (New York, 1942), 21.

[3] Jefferson to James Madison, June 21, 1798, Paul Leicester Ford, ed., *The Writings of Thomas Jefferson* (New York, 1892–99), VIII, 439–440; *Porcupine's Gazette* (Philadelphia), June 20, 1798; *Gazette of the United States*, June 20, 1798; E. Boudinot to his wife, June 21, 1798, J. Boudinot, *Elias Boudinot*, 141.

[4] James D. Richardson, *A Compilation of the Messages and Papers of the Presidents, 1789–1897* (Washington, 1896), I, 266.

[5] *Gazette of the United States*, June 21, 22, and 25, 1798; *Porcupine's Gazette*, June 22 and 25, 1798. The committee on arrangements was composed of five Federalists.

a cent for tribute"—was encored with the greatest enthusiasm.[6]

Opposition to "the terrible Republic" reached its zenith in the summer of 1798, culminating in what President Adams called "the half war with France." [7] Ever since President George Washington's Proclamation of Neutrality in 1793, the United States had maintained a precarious impartiality between England and France, despite its economic dependence on the former and its treaty obligations to the latter. By refusing to side with either party, America incurred the enmity of both. British seizures of American neutral shipping made war appear almost inevitable in 1794, but Jay's Treaty had warded off that threat. This success, however, gave offense to the French, who became increasingly belligerent toward the United States. Not without some reason, the French Directory viewed this treaty as evidence of an American-British entente, for the United States, by acceding to the English view of neutral rights, was required to permit the capture of provision ships bound for France, and to order French privateers out of American ports. Claiming that the treaty with Great Britain violated America's Revolutionary alliance with her, France began an aggressive campaign against American shipping in 1796, and the raids of her corsairs soon eclipsed the British depredations of 1793. When President Washington recalled James Monroe and appointed Charles Cotesworth Pinckney as American ambassador to the French Republic, that country refused to recognize the new minister, thus breaking off diplomatic relations. By the time Pinckney's dispatches reached the State Department, John Adams had become chief executive of the United States.

Writing on the day that her husband became the second president of the United States, Abigail Adams made the prophetic observation that "High Stations, Tumult, but not bliss create." [8] After his inauguration, John Adams faced a more critical situation with France than Washington had with Great Britain three years earlier. Because of this diplomatic crisis, the new president called a special

[6] *Gazette of the United States*, June 25, 1798. Also see Albert J. Beveridge, *The Life of John Marshall* (Boston and New York, 1916), II, 343–355, especially 348–349.

[7] Adams to Benjamin Rush, Sept. 30, 1806, *Old Family Letters, Copied from the Originals for Alexander Biddle* . . . , ser. A (Philadelphia, 1892), 85. For a discussion of Anglo-American collaboration during America's undeclared naval war with France, see Bradford Perkins, *The First Rapprochement: England and the United States, 1795–1805* (Philadelphia, 1955), 92–115.

[8] Abigail Adams to Mercy Warren, Quincy, March 4, 1797, *Warren-Adams Letters, Being Chiefly a Correspondence among John Adams, Samuel Adams and James Warren*, Massachusetts Historical Society, *Collections*, 73 (1925), 332.

session of Congress to convene on May 15, 1797. In his speech to the national legislature, he asserted that France had treated the United States "neither as allies, nor as friends, nor as a sovereign state." Although he urged Congress to take adequate defense measures, he followed Washington's example and announced that he would attempt further negotiations. Accordingly, he picked John Marshall of Virginia and Elbridge Gerry of Massachusetts to join Pinckney, the ousted minister.[9]

Even before the commissioners arrived in Paris in 1797, Congress had empowered the president to call out 80,000 militia, provided for harbor fortifications, and authorized the completion of three frigates which had been started at the time of difficulties with the Barbary Coast pirates. To prevent the war spirit from forcing the United States into hostilities before the envoys had a chance to negotiate a settlement, however, President Adams issued an executive order forbidding the arming of merchant ships, and Congress prohibited the fitting out of privateers.

For six months the American envoys attempted to deal with Talleyrand, the French foreign minister, but their efforts were rebuffed. Unofficial agents made it clear that negotiations could not proceed without the promise of an American loan to France, which would be used to finance her war effort, and a bribe of one quarter of a million dollars for the Executive Directory. To this demand, the envoys gave a concise answer: "No, no; not a sixpence." [10] Two months later, in March, 1798, Talleyrand signaled the failure of the mission by proposing that Gerry remain to negotiate alone. Although his colleagues advised against it, Gerry felt compelled to accept this invitation in order to avoid a complete diplomatic break. He notified Talleyrand, however, that he remained only in a private capacity. Marshall demanded his passports and sailed for America on April 24, but Pinckney received permission to take his daughter to southern France on a short trip for her health.

Not until March 4, 1798, did President Adams receive coded dispatches from his envoys covering the period from October, 1797, to January, 1798; these declared that there was no hope of their being received officially. Without waiting for a complete decoding of the dispatches, Adams notified Congress of this opinion on March 5. Two weeks later, after weighing the full contents, he advised Congress that a settlement with France seemed unlikely and called for

[9] The speech is given in Richardson, *Messages*, I, 322–329.

[10] Arthur Burr Darling, *Our Rising Empire, 1763–1803* (New Haven, 1940), 247–292, gives an excellent summary of the negotiations.

hasty defense measures. On March 23 the chief executive sent orders recalling Pinckney, Marshall, and Gerry, unless they had been received officially and were engaged in negotiations with authorized agents of the Directory.

Vice-President Thomas Jefferson labeled Adams' message of March 19 as "insane," and the Republicans demanded that the president lay before Congress the envoys' dispatches on which he based his call to arms. In this they were joined by the extreme Federalists who thought that the revelations of the reports would strengthen rather than weaken the impulse toward war. When Adams communicated the dispatches to Congress on April 3, he withheld the names of the French agents who served as Talleyrand's go-betweens, referring to them only as X, Y, and Z. These papers revealed that the American envoys had been refused an official audience with accredited officials and had been treated with contempt by Talleyrand's agents. Congress immediately ordered their publication, and an anti-French feeling swept the nation.[11] As later dispatches arrived from France, Adams sent them on to the Congress with special messages on May 4, and June 5, 18, and 21. In the last he announced General Marshall's arrival, and then vowed: "I will never send another minister to France without assurances that he will be received, respected, and honored, as the representative of a great, free, powerful, and independent nation." [12]

The XYZ revelations "really electrified all classes," and the nation began immediate preparations for war.[13] Even before the dispatches were laid before Congress, a special appropriation was passed to speed construction on the three frigates authorized in 1797. Between April and Marshall's return, Congress voted to prohibit the exportation of arms, appropriated funds for the procurement of cannon, arms, and ammunition, and expanded harbor defenses. A Department of the Navy was established, twelve armed vessels and ten galleys were added to protect American trade, and the president was authorized to instruct American naval vessels to capture foreign

[11] The Philadelphia *Aurora*, April 10–12, 1798, reprints the dispatches. Secretary of State Pickering wrote that one good effect of their publication was that there was now "little opposition by Democrats in the House, and French worship is subsiding outside." Pickering to George Washington, April 14, 1798, *Historical Index to the Pickering Papers*, Mass. Hist. Soc., *Collections*, 6th ser., 8 (1896), 538.

[12] Richardson, *Messages*, I, 266.

[13] Fisher Ames to Christopher Gore, July 28, 1798, Seth Ames, ed., *Works of Fisher Ames with a Selection from His Speeches and Correspondence* (Boston, 1854), I, 238.

armed ships which committed depredations against the American merchant marine. Congress also established an additional regiment of the regular army and empowered the president to raise a provisional army of 10,000 and to accept volunteer companies on a standby basis. These preparedness measures were accompanied by an embargo which suspended commercial intercourse with France and her dependencies.

Marshall's dramatic return in mid-June gave new impetus to congressional action. A prominent Federalist observed that his "arrival will be of eminent service at this moment, [as] it will tend to urge on energetick measures," and the president's wife predicted that it would "hasten the business" of Congress.[14] Renouncing all treaties with France, both the Revolutionary alliance of 1778 and the commercial and consular agreements of 1788, the administration took drastic steps which carried the United States into a virtual state of undeclared war with France. Congress re-established the Marine Corps, scheduled three more ships for the navy, and expanded the growing army by adding twelve new regiments of infantry and six troops of light dragoons. Quasi-naval warfare was inaugurated by an act which allowed armed merchantmen to repel French searches and depredations and by another which authorized the United States Navy to seize French armed vessels whether they were engaged in depredations or not.[15] Finally, General Washington was recalled from the shade of his fig tree at Mount Vernon to command the augmented army, which was placed under the field direction of the inspector general, Major General Alexander Hamilton. To meet the expenses of these warlike measures, Congress laid a two-million-dollar direct tax and authorized the president to borrow the amount at not more than 6-per-cent interest in anticipation of the tax revenues.

John Adams rode the crest of popular enthusiasm stirred up by the XYZ affair. "Millions for defense, but not a cent for tribute" became the pugnacious motto of the day, and new patriotic songs, such as "Adams and Liberty" and "Hail Columbia," received wide popular acclaim. Written by Joseph Hopkinson, a prominent Philadelphia lawyer of the Federalist party, "Hail Columbia" was sung to the tune of the "President's March" and served unofficially as the national

---

[14] E. Boudinot to his wife, June 21, 1798, J. Boudinot, *Elias Boudinot*, 141; Abigail Adams to Mary Cranch, June 19, 1798, Mitchell, *New Letters*, 194.

[15] Naval operations are described in *Naval Documents Relating to the Quasi-War between the United States and France*, 7 vols. (Washington, 1935–38):

anthem until 1931.[16] On the evening of its first performance, the president's wife attended the Philadelphia theater incognito "to see for myself the Effect." "The House was very full"—crowded with "the most respectable people in the city," she informed her sister— "and at every Choruss, the most unbounded applause ensued. In short it was enough to [have] stund one." Six times the new song was sung, "and the last time, the whole Audience broke forth in the Chorus whilst the thunder of their Hands was incessant, and at the close they arose, gave 3 Huzzas, that you might have heard a mile—My Head," the first lady concluded, "aches in consequence of it." [17]

The most popular method by which the Federalists indicated their patriotic support of the administration's measures was the presentation of addresses praising the president's policies. "A spirit of warm and high resentment against the rulers of France has suddenly burst forth in every part of the United States," an eminent Federalist informed the American ambassador to Great Britain, "and addresses from all bodies and descriptions of men are pouring like a torrent upon the President and both Houses of Congress." "I suppose the fact to be," he continued in a somewhat exaggerated vein, "that since man was created and government was formed no public officer has stood higher in the confidence and affection than our present President does." [18] Mrs. Adams acknowledged that the testimonials in approbation of the administration's policies were "indeed an incourageing, and gratefull reward" to the president for his exertions.[19] "In short," she wrote, "we are now wonderfully popular except with Bache & Co who in his paper calls the President old, querilous, Bald, blind, cripled, Toothless Adams." She thought that this "wretch" Bache, however, was so out of step with public opinion that "the wrath of an insulted people will by & by break upon him." [20]

Mrs. Adams' reference to Benjamin Franklin Bache, grandson of Benjamin Franklin and editor of the Philadelphia *Aurora,* leading Republican paper in the United States, indicates that political passions had been fanned to such heights following the XYZ affair that

[16] "Adams and Liberty," written by Robert Treat Paine, a Federalist editor, was sung to the tune later used for the "Star-Spangled Banner."

[17] Abigail Adams to Mary Cranch, Philadelphia, April 26, 1798, Mitchell, *New Letters,* 165. Also see the *Gazette of the United States,* April 25–26, 1798.

[18] Robert Troup to Rufus King, New York, June 3, 1798, Charles R. King, ed., *The Life and Correspondence of Rufus King* (New York, 1894–1900), II, 329.

[19] Abigail Adams to Mercy Warren, June 17, 1798, *Warren-Adams Letters,* 340.

[20] Abigail Adams to Mary Cranch, April 28, 1798, Mitchell, *New Letters,* 167.

Republican criticism of the president and the Federalist measures was extremely unpopular. The year 1798, however, was not an isolated one. Party charges had been flung and returned ever since American political parties had appeared during Washington's first administration. Federalists and Republicans had first split on domestic economic policy. The political divisions of the United States, therefore, were not the product of differences over European friends. They stemmed from ancient disagreements between commercial and agrarian forces, creditors and debtors, and New Englanders and Virginians.

Both the Federalist and Republican parties were antimonarchical, but they differed in their attitude toward popular government. Fearing anarchy, the Federalists thought in terms of authority and stressed the responsibilities of the constituted authorities to govern. To them republican government could operate only if ruled rather energetically by a governing elite. Their chosen basis, therefore, was an oligarchy of wealth and talent. Believing in the basic wisdom of the wealthy, they favored control by "the good, the wise, and the rich." [21] To this trinity of virtues, they added fear of a constantly threatening evil in a republic—rule by the "mass of the people," as Alexander Hamilton phrased it. Fisher Ames wrote at the time of the XYZ affair that introducing the sovereign people into public affairs was too much like playing government "as it were in the street." [22] Convinced that passions and prejudices dominated human nature, they emphasized the need of a government strong enough to check these propensities of the people. Essentially antidemocratic, the Federalists were the philosophical descendants of the Puritan John Cotton, who had raised a well-known rhetorical question: "If the people be governors, who shall be governed?"

The chief ends of government, according to the Federalists, were political stability and the security of society, or, as one of their leading spokesmen put it, the protection of "the rights of property, and the tranquillity of society." Thus, power and property were wedded in Federalist theory and practice. Hamilton, for instance, had long been convinced that there should be a union of "the interest and credit of rich individuals with those of the State." [23]

By Federalist definition therefore, Federalism was an amalgam of

[21] See Dixon Ryan Fox, *The Decline of Aristocracy in the Politics of New York* (New York, 1918).

[22] Ames to Gore, July 28, 1798, *Ames's Works*, I, 238.

[23] Fisher Ames, "Eulogy on Washington," Feb. 8, 1800, *ibid.*, II, 81; Hamilton to Robert Morris, 1780, Henry Cabot Lodge, ed., *Works of Alexander Hamilton* (New York, 1885–86), III, 79.

"the natural aristocracy of the Union." Supported by the lawyers, the clergy, the merchants and the wealthy, the large landowners of the Middle states, and the great planters of the South, they banded together against their increasingly numerous internal foe, the Democratic-Republicans.[24]

The Republicans, headed by Jefferson, retained the republican faith in popular government, dedicated to the proposition that all men are created equal. Fearing tyranny, they stressed liberty and the pursuit of happiness rather than authority and security, demanding a government responsive to public opinion, without the guidance of an elite ruling class. Consisting largely of the planting-farming-mechanic group, they preferred an agrarian republic of equal opportunity and mild legislation, a refuge for the oppressed, and a symbol of liberty to the world. Like Jefferson, they distrusted commerce and finance as speculative ventures, stressing three ends of government: simplicity, frugality, and equality.

After 1793 the party cleavage was widened not only by growing differences over domestic issues, but also by fundamental disagreements on foreign policy, the sympathies of the Federalists tending to the British and those of the Republicans to the French side in the European war. Federalists generally were admirers of English society, the English common law, the British constitution, and British finance. Moreover, the Federalist financial system was grounded on revenues collected from commerce with Great Britain.

After the French Revolution went through the Terror, conservatives who had supported the American Revolution came to fear revolution as a menace to established order. To them the issues involved in the French Revolution were anarchy versus order, licentiousness versus authority, the masses versus the classes, and atheism versus religion. The odious connotation of the word "revolution" was also transferred to the word "republican," since both were identified with the newly proclaimed French Republic, whose Terror had rendered revolution repulsive. One of the addresses to the president illustrated the Federalist fear of "modern innovations." "We abhor," it read, ". . . that word 'reform,' which in the fond credulity of our imaginations, we believed to be for the amelioration of the situation of man; we now shun it as we would a monster ready to engulph all

---

[24] Edward Channing, *A History of the United States* (New York, 1905–25), IV, 164, says that the Federalists were "aristocratic from the start to finish and became more reactionary and more aristocratic with each successive year." Also see Richard Hildreth, *The History of the United States of America* (New York, 1856), IV, 346–347.

social order, annihilate civil government, and subvert the heretofore approved course of things." [25] To the Republicans, on the other hand, the issues involved in the French Revolution pitted liberty against oppression, republicanism against monarchy, and democracy against a decadent aristocracy. The Jeffersonians became, therefore, doubly offensive to the Federalists: to their faith in the capacity of the people for responsible government was added their sympathy for the revolutionary movement in France. "It suffices for a man to be a philosopher," Jefferson wrote, "and to believe that human affairs are susceptible of improvement, and to look forward, rather than back to the Gothic ages, for perfection, to mark him as an anarchist, disorganiser, atheist, and enemy of the government." [26]

Indeed, each party feared that its opponent was so identified with Old World influences that it constituted a threat to American institutions. The Republicans feared that Federalist sympathy for England denoted a secret desire to maintain monarchical forms and class distinctions. The Federalists feared that the sympathy of the Jeffersonians for France indicated a desire to plunge the United States into confusion, institute the Terror, destroy government, uproot religion, and seize private property. To the Republicans, their opponents were aristocrats, Tories, Monocrats, or the British party; to the Federalists, their political enemies were democrats, disorganizers, Jacobins, anti-Federalists, or the French party. The use of European designations, however, should not obscure the fact that American issues, not British or French sympathies, were always uppermost in the thinking of both parties. "Each party," a French observer pointed out, simply used "foreign influence as it needs, to dominate." [27] An acute English visitor corroborated this comment. "The Federalists," he wrote, "accuse the other party of being Democrats, the Antis accuse their opponents of being Aristocrats. The Feds. say the Antis wish to introduce Anarchy & plunder & the French, the other party say that the Federalists are contending for Monarchy Aristocracy & *British influence* which they alledge to be too great already." "Federalist & Anti-Federalist," he concluded,

[25] Militia Officers and Inhabitants of Guilford County, North Carolina, to the President of the United States, *A Selection of the Patriotic Addresses, to the President of the United States. Together with the President's Answers. Presented in the Year One Thousand Seven Hundred and Ninety-Eight, and the Twenty-Second of the Independence of America* (Boston, 1798), 331.

[26] Jefferson to T. M. Randolph, Phila., May 3, 1798, Jefferson Papers (Mass. Hist. Soc.).

[27] Quoted in Samuel Eliot Morison and Henry Steele Commager, *The Growth of the American Republic* (New York, 1942), I, 352.

". . . does not mean those for & against a Federal form of government, but in fact ins & Outs, tho' it is not confessed. . . ." [28]

Adams had early antagonized the Republicans by a phrase in his special message to Congress in May, 1797. At that time he criticized the Directory's address on the departure of the recalled Republican, Monroe, who was to be replaced by the Federalist Pinckney. The remarks by the French executive, the president declared, evinced "a disposition to separate the people of the United States from the Government; to persuade them that they have different affections, principles, and interests, from those of their fellow-citizens, whom they themselves have chosen to manage their common concern; and thus to produce divisions fatal to our peace." [29] This use of the phrase "separating the people from their government" gave to those Federalists who failed to distinguish between the government and the men who administered it an opportunity to denounce Republican opposition to Federalist measures as opposition to the government itself. The Republicans not unnaturally objected to this contention. The result was that the special session became more acrimonious than ever, and congressional halls resounded with "the roar and tumult of bulls and bears." Thomas Jefferson, leader of the Republicans who was presiding over the Senate for the first time as vice-president, wrote Edward Rutledge in June, 1797, that

the passions are too high at present, to be cooled in our day. You and I have formerly seen warm debates and high political passions. But gentlemen of different politics would then speak to each other, and separate the business of the Senate from that of society. It is not so now. Men who have been intimate all their lives, cross the street to avoid meeting, and turn their heads another way, lest they should be obliged to touch their hats.[30]

When the president notified Congress on March 19, 1798, that it seemed unlikely that the mission to France could succeed, he exhorted that body to make defense preparations not only with "promptitude and decision" but with "unanimity." [31] This plea for

[28] D. M. Erskine to Lord Erskine, Phila., Jan. 1, 1799, Patricia Holbert Monk, "D. M. Erskine: Letters from America, 1798–1799," *William and Mary Quarterly,* 3d ser., 4 (1949), 257.

[29] *Debates and Proceedings in the Congress of the United States,* 5th Cong. (1797–98), 3346. This volume is cited hereafter as the *Annals.*

[30] Jefferson to Edward Rutledge, June 24, 1797, Andrew A. Lipscomb and Albert Ellery Bergh, eds., *The Writings of Thomas Jefferson* (Washington, 1903–04), IX, 411.

[31] *Annals,* 5C, 2S, 1271–1272.

unanimity, however, was thwarted by Republican opposition to measures which they thought might lead to war. The Federalists had a ready explanation for this opposition. Included among the XYZ papers communicated to Congress was the boast by Monsieur Y that France had a party in America. Indeed, he had claimed that the ministers would fail if they returned to the United States in an attempt to unite the American people in resistance to France's demands for money. "The diplomatic skill of France," he bluntly asserted, "and the means she possesses in your country, are sufficient to enable her, with the French party in America, to throw the blame which will attend the rupture of the negotiations on the Federalists, as you term yourselves, but on the British party, as France terms you." [32]

Although the envoys replied that France miscalculated on the party situation in America, the Federalists at home took advantage of the foreign crisis to strike at their domestic political opponents. Their first move was to identify the Republican party with the French, and then to treat opposition to administration measures as nearly traitorous. Jefferson became the chief target of the Federalist fusillade. "More and more," wrote Federalist Senator Theodore Sedgwick, the vice-president was becoming "an object of abhorrence & detestation" among "the well disposed." [33] *Porcupine's Gazette*, an ultra-Federalist journal, denounced Jefferson as "the head of the democratic frenchified faction in this country," and the New York *Commercial Advertiser* claimed that in case of a French invasion an American Executive Directory would be established, headed by Jefferson, James Madison, James Monroe, and Aaron Burr.[34] Contrasting the patriotism of President Adams with the infidelity of Vice-President Jefferson, a Federalist rally raised glasses to this Fourth of July toast: "John Adams. May he, like *Samson*, slay thousands of Frenchmen with the *jawbone* of Jefferson." [35]

When Albert Gallatin, Republican leader in the House, proposed that a bill authorizing the construction of armed vessels be amended to prohibit their use as convoys in peacetime, his argument was attacked as an invitation to surrender American rights and independence to a foreign nation. Representative John Allen, Federalist from Connecticut, quickly claimed that Gallatin was a tool of the "diplo-

---

[32] *Ibid.*, 3355.

[33] Sedgwick to King, Phila., July 1, 1798, *King's Correspondence*, II, 352–353.

[34] *Porcupine's Gazette*, June 27, 1798; *Commercial Advertiser*, quoted in the *Aurora*, June 11, 1798. Also see "Pliny," Phila., July 26, 1798, *Gazette of the United States*, June 27, 1798.

[35] *Columbian Centinel* (Boston), July 14, 1798.

matic skill of France." "Were France herself to speak through an American mouth," Allen said, "I cannot conceive what she would say more than what we have heard from certain gentlemen to effect her purposes." "I believe there are men in this country, in this House, whose hatred and abhorrence of our Government leads them to prefer another, profligate and ferocious as it is." Allen added that the "vile incendiary paper" published by Bache was no contemptible engine in the business of sowing discord, dissension, and distrust of the government; it constantly teemed with the most atrocious abuse of all the measures and administrators of the government. "A flood of calumny is constantly poured forth against those whom the people have chosen as the guardians of the nation." He claimed that it was well known that the *Aurora* always spoke the sentiments of the Republicans in the House and was supported by them. Such were the fruits of "the diplomatic skill of France" and the efforts of "her party in this country," he concluded.[36]

The Federalist newspapers immediately took up the cry against the Republican "traitors." "To be lukewarm after reading the horrid scenes" reported in the XYZ dispatches, said a New York paper, "is to be criminal—and the man who does not warmly reprobate the conduct of the French must have a soul black enough to be *fit* for *treasons strategems* and *spoils.*" [37]

The defense of American sovereignty and independence, and the protection of American commerce, wrote another journal, "are points in which all but traitors must agree; and traitors must be silent." It remained for the nation's number-one Federalist newspaper, Philadelphia's *Gazette of the United States,* to coin their political slogan: "*He that is not for us, is against us.*" "May all party spirit," echoed a group of Federalist militia on Independence Day, "be lost in the common cause of national independence." Few Federalists, however, were so outspoken as the Independent Rangers, one of New York City's military companies, who toasted "one and but one party in the United States," although the Sons of St. Tammany came close when they expressed this desire in Philadelphia: "May the delirium of Democracy, never revisit America." [38]

The president's wife was convinced that "those whom the French boast of as their Partizans" were "very wicked men" who would be

[36] *Annals,* 5C, 2S (April 20, 1798), 1482, 1485. For the complete speech, see 1476–1488.

[37] *New York Gazette,* April 12, 1798.

[38] *Commercial Advertiser,* April 20, 1798; *Gazette of the United States,* June 20 and July 7, 1798; *Daily Advertiser* (New York), July 10, 1798; and *Claypoole's American Daily Advertiser* (Philadelphia), May 4, 1798.

"adjudged traitors to their country." She wrote that "the Common People say if J[efferso]n had been our President, and Madison & Burr our negotiators, we should all have been sold to the French." "All our trouble, and all our difficulty" she ascribed to the vile emissaries of the French and abjured her native state of Massachusetts to cleanse itself of its three Republican congressmen. Connecticut was the only state free from such "abominations," she noted; "Virginia has but two Federilists [sic], North Carolina but one. Can we expect such measures to be adopted as the safety and security of the Country require?" [39]

President Adams also joined in this denunciation of France and its "diplomatic skill." In his answers to the addresses presented to him, he was often as vehement as the most outspoken Federalists, condoning their charge that the Republicans were a French faction. Replying to an address which condemned France's "diplomatic skill" and the attempts to defame the Adams administration, he informed a Massachusetts group that "the agents of a foreign nation have had too much color for boasting of their intriguing talents, and of having a party in this country, devoted to their interest." [40] Advising the youth of New York to "beware of contaminating your country with the foul abominations of the French revolution," the chief executive declared that the United States had been insulted by the "imperious claims of a foreign power, professing to confide in our disunion, and boasting of the means of severing the affections of our citizens from the government of their choice." [41] It was now the part of every citizen to join with the government in opposition to France's insults. "It is indeed high time," read one of his answers, "for the friends of government and good order to exert themselves, and declare their opinions, or in a short time, there might have remained, neither government nor order." In another he asserted that if the American people were, as represented, in opposition to the government of their choice, "it would show them ripe for *military despotism under foreign influence.*" [42] He did not wonder that American blood boiled at these ideas. [43]

Like his wife, the president bewailed the existence of "disor-

[39] See Abigail Adams to Mary Cranch, April 7, 13, 22, and Jan. 20, 1798, Mitchell, *New Letters*, 154, 156, 161, 124–125.

[40] President Adams to the Inhabitants of Wells, Mass., Phila., May 28, 1798, *Gazette of the United States*, June 27, 1798.

[41] See the addresses of June 2, 1798, and an undated one placed before July 14, 1798, Charles Francis Adams, ed., *The Works of John Adams* (Boston, 1850–56), IX, 199, 207.

[42] See the *Gazette of the United States*, May 2, July 3, and May 15, 1798.

[43] Answer of May 8, 1798, *Adams' Works*, IX, 191.

ganizers" in his native state and suggested that the Federalist ticket was the salvation of the country. To the citizens of Weston, Massachusetts, he sent sincere congratulations "on their signal felicity, in having no disorganizers. Two or three of this description of characters are sufficient to destroy the good neighborhood, interrupt the harmony, and poison the happiness of a thousand families. A town that is free from them," he concluded, "will ever prove their federalism in elections, be firm in the cause of their country, and ready to defend it in all emergencies." [44]

As a student of political science, however, Adams recognized the inevitability of party divisions. In one answer, he expressed his belief that the distinction of aristocrat and democrat, however odious and pernicious it might be rendered by political artifice at any given time, would never disappear as long as some men were taller and others shorter, some wiser and others sillier, some more virtuous and others more vicious, some richer and others poorer. It was a distinction grounded on unalterable nature and intended for the order of society and the benefit of mankind. Like the sexes, parties ought to be mutually beneficial to each other. He thought that human wisdom could do no more than reconcile the parties "by equitable establishments and equal laws, securing, as far as possible, to every one his own." To this dispassionate appraisal of the political scene he added one note of warning: "And woe to that country, which supinely suffers malicious demagogues to excite jealousies, ferment prejudices, and stimulate animosities between them [the parties]." [45]

Yet in this same message, Adams expressed his "infinite satisfaction" that the prospect of a just and necessary war had silenced all essential differences of opinions. He had confessed in an earlier message, however, that "Republics are always divided in opinion concerning forms of government, and plans and details of administration —these divisions are generally harmless, often salutary and seldom very hurtful, except when foreign nations interfere and by their arts and agents excite, and ferment them into parties and factions; such interference and influence must be resisted and exterminated or it will end in America, as it did anciently in Greece, and in our own time in Europe, in our total destruction, as a republican government and independent power." Party divisions were acceptable then, so long as they did not "enlist under foreign banners." [46]

Since the president's answers often reflected the attitude of his

[44] *Columbian Centinel,* Aug. 15, 1798.

[45] To the Inhabitants of Harrison County, Va., Aug. 13, 1798, *Adams' Works,* IX, 217.

[46] *Gazette of the United States,* May 4, 1798; *Adams' Works,* IX, 215.

addressers, his replies varied in party intensity. On some occasions he absolved the opposition from any general imputation of foreign influence and disloyalty, and at other times he seemed to countenance the charge that a French party existed in America. In the former vein, he wrote that so far as he knew the opposition to the federal government, in all the states, was too small to merit the name of division. "It is a difference of sentiments in public measures," he added, "not an alienation of affection to their country." As for the Southern states, where the Republican strength was concentrated, he was confident that they would join "with all their fellow-citizens, with equal spirit, to crush every attempt at disorganization, disunion, and anarchy. The vast extent of their settlements, and greater distance from the center of intelligence, may require more time to mature their judgment, and expose them to more deceptions by misrepresentation; but in the end, their sensations, reflections, and decisions, are purely American." [47] He was certain that Virginians were true Americans—or almost certain. It depended, he said, upon Virginia, stronghold of the Republicans, "to say whether this country has in it a Faction to crush, a faction to be humbled in dust and ashes, before the indignant frowns of their injured, insulted, and unoffending country." [48]

On the other hand, Adams' letters to his addressers often fell into a line of argument which seemed to characterize all opposition to administration policy as the work of designing French partisans who opposed the government. He confessed that he, like a group of Vermont memorialists, had long seen foreign influence prevailing and endangering the peace and independence of the country. Dangerous and restless men, he added, had long misled the understanding of well-meaning citizens and prompted them to measures which "would sink the glory of our country and prostrate her liberties at the feet of France." While he hoped this spell had been broken, he feared that the veil had not been removed from the eyes of all citizens. "The snare is not yet entirely broken, and we have not yet escaped." [49] "These Lovers of themselves," he noted on another occasion, "who withdraw their confidence from their own Legislative Government, and place it on a foreign nation, or Domestic Faction,

[47] To the Legislature of New Hampshire, June 29, 1798, and To the Inhabitants of Hartford, Conn., June 29 and May 10, 1798, *Adams' Works*, IX, 203, 192.

[48] To the Field Officers of the 81st Militia Regiment in Bath County, Va., *Albany Centinel*, Aug. 28, 1798.

[49] June 25, 1798, *Adams' Works*, IX, 202. Also see the address to Plymouth, Mass., *ibid.*, 195.

or both in alliance, deserve all our contempt and abhorrence." [50]

To a Massachusetts group, he wrote that political misinformation had been especially active there. Too many believed that France, though crushed under the iron hand of a military despotism, enjoyed liberty. He was confident, nonetheless, that "all Americans by birth, except perhaps a very few abandoned characters," had always preserved a superior affection for their own country.[51] At once this seemed to proscribe citizens who had not been born in America, as well as the few "abandoned characters" whom the president mentioned. At least the Republicans gave his remarks this interpretation.

They saved their most bitter protests, however, for his answer to the militia of New Jersey. The soldier-citizens had declared: "Let our enemies flatter themselves that we are a divided people.—In New Jersey, Sir, with the exception of a few degraded and a few deluded characters, to whose persons, and to whose services the invading foe shall be welcome, from the moment of their arrival, and whom we shall engage to convey in safety to their lines.—In New Jersey, Sir, there is but *one voice*.—" To this bombastic address, the president replied that "the degraded and deluded characters may tremble, lest they should be condemned to the severest punishment an American can suffer—that of being conveyed in safety *within the lines* of an invading enemy." The Republicans interpreted this address as applying to their whole party, which would be treated as traitors in case of invasion.[52] Even Hamilton was disturbed by this blunt statement of the president. "It is not for us," he wrote his Federalist successor as secretary of the treasury, "particularly for the government, to breathe an irregular or violent spirit." To him, Adams' statement was both intemperate and revolutionary; there were limits to what should be said, and Hamilton was apprehensive that the president might run into indiscretion. If he did so, it would do harm "to the government, to the cause, and to himself." Hamilton therefore requested Wolcott to give some hint to the president, "for we must make no mistakes." [53]

[50] To the Inhabitants of Chester County, Pa., Phila., May 4, 1798, *Claypoole's American Daily Advertiser*, May 29, 1798.

[51] To the Inhabitants of Dedham, Mass., July 14, 1798, *Adams' Works*, IX, 207.

[52] *Columbian Centinel*, May 25, 1798; *Aurora*, June, 1798, *passim*.

[53] Hamilton to Oliver Wolcott, June 5, 1798, John C. Hamilton, ed., *Works of Alexander Hamilton* (New York, 1851), VI, 294. Although Hamilton believed that there were limits to what should be said publicly, he earlier expressed sentiments similar to those in the president's answer. Frankly admitting his conviction "that the powerful faction which has for years opposed the government,

Aside from this single criticism, the temper of Adams' addresses received the highest praise from the Federalists. Hamilton wrote that he had been well pleased with the answers because they were calculated to animate and raise the public mind. Another Federalist wrote that whenever an address deviated from the sentiments of freemen alive to the honor and sovereignty of their country, the president undertook "to whip the addressers." As a matter of fact, President Adams' answers were of fundamental importance in shaping the climate of opinion which nurtured the alien and sedition legislation. "The answers of the President," wrote Fisher Ames, "have elevated the spirit, and cleared the filmy eyes, of the many. The people have risen *gradatim;* every answer was a step up stairs." [54] Collected and published as a book in 1798, the president's pronouncements were hailed by the Federalists as "the scriptures of Political Truth." Their general diffusion, said Boston's *Columbian Centinel,* "would enlighten the misinformed—convert the misguided —instruct the ignorant—confirm the wavering—and establish the firm." [55] Writing at a later time, Secretary of State Pickering, most high-toned of the Federalists around the president, noted that "Mr. Adams, in his vigourous answers to the numerous addresses presented to him, enforced by the weight of his official station, as president of the U. States contributed, doubtless, more than any other man to elevate the temper of the nation" to its resistance of France and French influence.[56]

This tendency to identify the Republicans with the French set the stage for congressional action not only against the external foe, but

---

is determined to go every length with France," he concluded that the Republicans would aid a French invasion directly or indirectly. Hamilton to Washington, New York, May 19, 1798, *Hamilton's Works* (Lodge ed.), VIII, 483. The new army, therefore, was created not only to meet the French, but also for internal policing; see the observations of Fisher Ames on the use of military force against Jefferson's "faction." Ames to Wolcott, Dedham, Jan. 12, 1800, in George Gibbs, ed., *Memoirs of the Administrations of Washington and John Adams, Edited from the Papers of Oliver Wolcott, Secretary of the Treasury* (New York, 1846), II, 320. For the conclusions of the most recent investigator, see Manning J. Dauer, *The Adams Federalists* (Baltimore, 1953), 210, 215–216.

[54] Hamilton to Wolcott, June 5, 1798, *Hamilton's Works* (Hamilton ed.), VI, 294; Troup to King, July 10, 1798, *King's Correspondence,* II, 363; and Ames to Timothy Pickering, Dedham, July 10, 1798, *Ames's Works,* I, 232.

[55] Nov. 17, 1798.

[56] Memorandum, Pickering Papers, XLVI, 75 (Mass. Hist. Soc.). For an important article about Washington's attitude on these problems, see Marshall Smelser, "George Washington and the Alien and Sedition Laws," *American Historical Review,* 59 (1954), 322–334.

what the Federalists chose to call the "internal foe." The Federalists attempted to discredit the Republicans and to reduce them to political impotence by associating them with "foreign influence" and by attacking their loyalty, ideology, and morality. While these charges had been made before 1798, the crisis with France gave the Federalists an opportunity to equate opposition to the government's policy with sedition and near treason. Hamilton, for instance, was convinced that "many of the leaders of faction will . . . take ultimately a station in the public estimation like that of the Tories of our Revolution." [57] By trumpeting their charges against the Republicans, the Federalists tried to win popular support at the same time that they repressed popular opposition. Rallying their forces behind the banners of national defense and political orthodoxy, they hoped to entrench themselves in power and to continue their dominance in politics, economics, religion, and society.

The XYZ affair was not so much the cause, as the occasion, for striking at political opposition.[58] When Senator Theodore Sedgwick, Federalist whip in the Upper House, first heard of the XYZ fiasco, his response, though laconic, was immediate: "It will afford a glorious opportunity to destroy faction. Improve it." [59] Under the guise of patriotic purpose and internal security, the Federalists enacted a program designed to cripple, if not destroy, the Jeffersonian party. In the face of the emergence of an effective grass-roots democratic opposition to their domestic and foreign policies, they retreated to repression as a means of retaining political power. The authoritarian alien and sedition system was the logical culmination of Federalist political philosophy.

[57] Hamilton to King, June 6, 1798, XLI (New York Hist. Soc.).

[58] Federalist Senator William Bingham of Pennsylvania wrote that as a result of the XYZ affair "the Friends of the Government have improved the opportunity of cloathing the Executive with additional Energies." Bingham to King, Sept. 30, 1798, *King's Correspondence*, II, 425. For two interesting discussions of this theme, see Alfred Young, "The Federalist Attack on Civil Liberties," *Science and Society*, 17 (1953), 59–64, and Marshall Smelser, "The Jacobin Phrenzy: Federalism and the Menace of Liberty, Equality, and Fraternity," *Review of Politics*, 13 (1951), 457–482. For an excellent survey of the whole period, see John C. Miller, *Crisis in Freedom: The Alien and Sedition Acts* (Boston, 1951).

[59] Sedgwick to ———, Phila., March 7, 1798, Sedgwick Papers (Mass. Hist. Soc.).

CHAPTER II

Nativism, Politics, and Naturalization

Let us no longer pray that America may become an asylum to all nations.—W. S. Shaw to Abigail Adams

THE Federalist system of political intolerance was inaugurated by the Naturalization Act of 1798. Like the subsequent Alien and Sedition Laws, this measure coincided with the Gallophobia which followed the publication of the XYZ dispatches. Indeed, it was signed on the day that John Marshall returned to the nation's capital from his unsuccessful mission to France. Despite its close association with these diplomatic events, this legislation was the result of a move directed against domestic dissension and disaffection rather than foreign danger. Naturalization had always opened the gate to political participation for immigrants, and the Democratic-Republicans had long attracted the majority of the foreign vote. For that reason the Federalists hoped to deprive foreign-born citizens of their right to engage in political activity. Unable wholly to prevent the Jeffersonians from recruiting former aliens into their ranks, the Federalists slowed down the process of enlistment by nearly tripling the time required for immigrants to become citizens.

Originally the Federalists had raised no weighty objections to speedy naturalization. The first Congress passed a liberal act in 1790 which granted citizenship to newcomers after they had resided in the United States for two years. After the Revolution in France spilled over into international war in 1792, however, the European opponents of the French struck at reformers, republicans, radicals, and pro-French sympathizers. The neutral United States immediately became the haven of refugees. To its shores came discontented Englishmen, aristocratic Frenchmen, German pietists fleeing forced military service, French planters escaping from West Indian uprisings led by Toussaint l'Ouverture, and Irishmen in flight from British repression.

Because of this influx of aliens, Congress revised the Naturalization Law in 1795, stipulating that foreigners must reside in the United States for five years before they were entitled to citizenship. This change had the support of both parties, the Federalists dreading the democratic "disorganizers" who came to America, and the Democratic-Republicans fearing the antirepublican principles of the "aristocratic" immigrants.[1]

The Naturalization Act of 1798, however, was a political maneuver by the Federalists designed to cut off an increasingly important source of Republican strength. Congressman Oliver Wolcott had manifested the Federalist fear of foreigners as early as 1794, when he expressed his apprehensions over "the great numbers of violent men who emigrate to this country from every part of Europe." [2] The Irish, especially, became obnoxious to the administration. In 1798 Ireland was again seething with revolt. When military measures under General Cornwallis finally quelled the rebellion, the proscription of Irish patriots forced the emigration of many as the only alternative to long prison terms or the gallows.[3] Their anti-British attitude and their contempt for the party of conservatism and privilege turned most of those who came to the United States from the Federalists, who distrusted democracy and feared insurrection against constituted authority. Many newcomers had extensive political experience, and they soon added their criticism of the Adams administration to that of other Democratic-Republicans.[4]

In the special session of Congress in May, 1797, the Federalists freely admitted their alarm over the alliance between "the Democracy" and the immigrants and proposed to levy a tax of twenty dollars on certificates of naturalization. When Republicans objected that this plan aimed not to raise revenue but to restrict immigration,

[1] Marcus Lee Hansen, The Atlantic Migration, 1607–1860, A History of the Continuing Settlement of the United States (Cambridge, 1945), 65.

[2] Wolcott to Oliver Wolcott, Sr., May 3, 1794, Gibbs, Administrations of Washington and John Adams, I, 136.

[3] Hansen, Atlantic Migration, 65.

[4] John Spencer Bassett, The Federalist System, 1789–1801 (New York and London, 1906), 252.

Harrison Gray Otis defended the policy of proscription in his "Wild Irish Speech." The tax, he said, would tend to eliminate "the mass of vicious and disorganizing characters who cannot live peaceably at home." While he respected those persons who had already become citizens, he urged that the United States should not invite "hordes of wild Irishmen, nor the turbulent and disorderly of all parts of the world, to come here with a view to disturb our tranquillity, after having succeeded in the overthrow of their own Governments."

Despite Otis' eloquence, this attempt failed. But he continued to reflect the apprehension of the Federalists. "If some means are not adopted to prevent the indiscriminate admission of wild Irishmen and others to the right of suffrage," he wrote his wife, "there will soon be an end to liberty and property." [5] A letter from Uriah Tracy, a Federalist senator from Connecticut, made his attitude plain. "I have seen many, very many Irishmen," he wrote of a trip through Pennsylvania, "and with a very few exceptions, they are United Irishmen, Free Masons, and the most God-provoking Democrats on this side of Hell." It remained for youthful William Smith Shaw, the president's nephew who became his private secretary late in 1798, to push the nativist argument to the limit. "The grand cause of all our present difficulties," he wrote the first lady, "may be traced . . . to so many *hordes of Foreigners* imigrating [sic] to America." "Let us no longer pray," he concluded, "that America may become an asylum to all nations." [6]

Federalist antipathy for the political proclivities of the Irish was well expressed in a poem written by one of the Hartford Wits:

> "True Whigs of '76," a goodly store,
> Imported fresh from Erin's peaceful shore,
> Time serving changelings, faction's desperate band,
> And all the *virtuous* refuse of our land,—
> Thick as the flies that round some carcass pour,
> Or lice that punish'd Pharoah's [sic] sins of yore;
> And kindly give Us through their *patriot* cares,
> In our own way to *gest* our own affairs. [7]

In the diplomatic field, Rufus King, American minister in London, prevented Great Britain from banishing Irish political prisoners to

[5] Samuel Eliot Morison, *The Life and Letters of Harrison Gray Otis, Federalist, 1765–1848* (Boston and New York, 1913), I, 107–108.

[6] Tracy to Wolcott, Aug. 7, 1800, Gibbs, *Administrations of Washington and Adams*, II, 399; Shaw to Abigail Adams, Cambridge, May 20, 1798, Adams Papers, VIII, no. 48 (Mass. Hist. Soc.).

[7] Karl P. Harrington, *Richard Alsop, "A Hartford Wit"* (Middletown, Conn., 1939), 68.

the United States. The British had figured that the United States was a logical destination by reason of its sympathy with the Irish rebellion, an event similar to the American war for independence. King notified the British, however, that America wanted none of these leaders of the "wild Irish." "I certainly do not think," he wrote the Duke of Portland, "they will be a desirable acquisition to any nation." To Secretary of State Timothy Pickering he expressed his fear that the disaffected Irish would disfigure "our true national character," which was purest in untainted New England.[8] Massachusetts-born John Quincy Adams agreed that the United States had "too many of those people already." [9]

To one of his correspondents, King pointed out the political objections to Irish immigrants; most of them, he complained, arrayed themselves on the side of the Republicans. Senator William Bingham of Pennsylvania expressed the same opinion. The Irish, he wrote King, "will join the party in opposition to the Government, & will vent their Resentments against Great Britain, by attacking those disposed to be on friendly Terms with her. They will be discontented, & therefore disorganizing Characters, whose Residence amongst us cannot be otherwise than injurious, in the present Moment of political agitation." [10]

The XYZ mania gave the Federalists an opportunity to return to their attack on immigrants and at the same time strike a blow at the Republicans. Public reaction to the insults suffered by American agents in France made war seem imminent. Abusive aliens were immediately labeled as agents of France. *Porcupine's Gazette*, edited by William Cobbett, himself a British subject, laid down a barrage against aliens, especially the Irish, and their political mentors, the Democratic-Republicans. In May he described a purported conspiracy for the destruction of the American government by the French and "that restless, rebellious tribe, the emigrated United Irishmen." The pro-Federalist editor was convinced that the infernal Irish had infiltrated every public department of the government and would rise up against the United States as soon as France launched an in-

[8] King to Portland (private), Margate, Eng., Sept. 13, 1798, *King's Correspondence*, II, 640; King to Pickering, London, July 19, 1798, *ibid.*, 638.

[9] Adams to King, Aug. 27, 1798, King Papers (Huntington Library).

[10] King to Henry Jackson, Brighton, Eng., Aug. 28, 1799, and Bingham to King, Phila., Dec. 8, 1798, *King's Correspondence*, II, 646, 481–482. Secretary of State Pickering notified King, "Your timely interference to prevent the emigration of the Irish traitors to this Country is extremely acceptable to the President. . . ." Feb. 5, 1799, *ibid.*, 644.

vasion against the American coast. In these sentiments Porcupine but echoed the views of Otis, who had earlier accused the Republicans and their alien allies of sabotaging American negotiations for the settlement of disputes with France. This misguided and desperate party, Otis added, was in league with other bad citizens in France and was sending instructions regularly to influence the decisions of the Directory.[11]

This tendency to identify foreign influence with domestic faction is perhaps best illustrated by the warning of "A Friend to America and Truth" to President Adams that resident Frenchmen and domestic traitors were plotting a massacre in Philadelphia on May 9, set aside by presidential proclamation for fasting and prayer. But the "grandest of all grand Villains," according to this anonymous author, was not a foreigner; it was "that traitor to his country—that infernal Scoundrel Jefferson," the vice-president of the United States.[12]

In preparing defense measures against France, therefore, the Federalists did not overlook what they regarded as a pernicious domestic danger—political opposition.[13] Their first move against the Republicans, however, was oblique. Acting on the assumption that the American "Jacobins" were allied with France, they took advantage of the anti-French feeling to strike at aliens. On April 17, Joshua Coit, Federalist representative from Connecticut, proposed that the House Committee on the Defense of the Country and for the Protection of Commerce should determine whether the Naturalization Act of 1795 ought to be suspended or amended. The acute Jefferson was quick to discern the political implications of this move:

One of the war party, in a fit of unguarded passion, declared some time ago they would pass a citizen bill, an alien bill, and a sedition bill; accordingly, some days ago, Coit laid a motion on the table of the House of Representatives for modifying the citizen law. Their threats point at Gallatin, and it is believed they will endeavor to reach him by this bill.[14]

[11] *Detection of a Conspiracy Formed by the United Irishmen, with the Evident Intention of Aiding the Tyrants of France in Subverting the Government of the United States of America*, William Cobbett, *Porcupine's Works* (London, 1801), VIII, 220–225; Morison, *Otis*, I, 70.

[12] See "A Friend to America and Truth" and "An unfortunate mislead Man, but a real friend to America" to John Adams, April 18, 1798, Adams Papers, XIX, 184, 186 (Mass. Hist. Soc.).

[13] Frank M. Anderson, "The Enforcement of the Alien and Sedition Laws," American Historical Association, *Annual Report for 1912*, 115. This pioneering article is the starting point for all later work in this field.

[14] Jefferson to Madison, Phila., April 26, 1798, *Jefferson's Writings* (Ford ed.), VII, 244.

Outlining the alien legislation which Congress subsequently enacted, the Defense Committee's report on Coit's resolution listed three major recommendations. It condemned the policy of promiscuous reception and residence of aliens, which had made it possible in the past for foreigners to be admitted to citizenship when there was not sufficient evidence of their attachment to the laws and welfare of the United States to entitle them to such a privilege. The committee therefore proposed that the naturalization laws should be amended in order to prolong the term of residence required before an alien could become a citizen of the United States or of any state. Moreover, it urged legislation providing for the removal of aliens suspected of hostile intentions. As a final precaution, the report suggested that provision should be made for apprehending and removing enemy aliens whose country had declared war against the United States.[15]

When this report was referred to Congress, Congressman Samuel Sewall, chairman of the Defense Committee, suggested that the residence requirement of five years should be doubled at the very least. Mere prolongation of the term of residence, however, was much too mild for the two most outspoken Federalist leaders in the Fifth Congress, Robert Goodloe Harper and Harrison Gray Otis. "The time is now come," Harper asserted, "when it will be proper to declare that nothing but birth shall entitle a man to citizenship in this country." He contended that the United States had fallen into the error of admitting foreigners to citizenship when it first began to form constitutions, both state and federal. Arguing that this policy had produced great evils, he insisted that the United States could prevent these in the future by curing itself of "the folly of believing that the strength and happiness of the country would be promoted by admitting all the congregations of people from every part of the world to the rights of citizenship." The South Carolinian's extreme proposition was rejected without discussion, when the Speaker ruled it out of order.[16]

Otis then proposed to amend the committee report in order to bar aliens naturalized in the future from holding any federal office "of honor, trust, or profit." To this Harper tried to add another restriction that would have prevented such persons from voting for public officials. The rights of American citizenship, he repeated, should be enjoyed only by persons born in the United States. The views and attachments of "strangers" could not be the same as those of native

[15] *Annals,* 5C, 2S (May 1, 1798), 1566. The report contained the germ of all subsequent alien legislation.
[16] *Ibid.* (May 2, 1798), 1567–1568.

citizens. Not that he objected to foreigners living in the United States, he hastened to assure the House—far from it. He favored giving them every facility for raising their families, acquiring property, and holding it or transferring it to their relatives. But he was convinced that an essential principle of civil society required that none but persons born in a country should be permitted to take part in its government. Had Harper's proposal been adopted, it would have achieved its object of destroying the Republican party's "foreign vote." Because of constitutional objections, however, he was forced to withdraw his amendment for further study.[17]

In urging the reversal of the national policy which allowed former aliens to hold public office, Congressman Otis pointed out that citizenship did not always confer this right. In Great Britain, for example, naturalized citizens were excluded from all places of honor, profit, or trust.[18] Such a policy should be imitated by the United States. It was fast becoming such an important nation that foreign governments soon would attempt to gain an influence in its councils. Speedy action was necessary, Otis urged, for if any considerable number of ex-foreigners were elected to Congress, a motion to exclude them would be odious.

Otis supported his political intolerance with an elaborate constitutional argument. Congress, he observed, has the power to establish a uniform rule of naturalization. Such a rule could extend the residence period to the life of the alien, thus excluding him from citizenship forever. If Congress could prevent foreigners from becoming citizens, it followed that any modification of the rights of citizenship short of total exclusion was within its power. "Where an absolute power may be exercised," he contended, "a conditional

[17] *Ibid.*, 1568. Harper withdrew his amendment to study whether or not the Constitution would allow the federal government to restrain the states in their admission of citizens; the move seems to have been based on the concept that the power vested in Congress to establish a uniform rule of naturalization was exclusive as regards admission to federal citizenship only. The question of dual citizenship was not settled until the ratification of the Fourteenth Amendment in 1868.

[18] Otis used the word "aliens" to refer to alien-born persons who became naturalized citizens. The British law provided that no person born outside the kingdom, except of English parents, even though naturalized, should be capable of holding any office under the king, or of receiving grants; see 12 and 13 William III, ch. ii. During George I's reign a statute stipulated that no future naturalization should be valid without a clause declaring such disability. This remained the law until the British Naturalization Act of 1870. See 13 George II, ch. vii, and 20 George II, ch. xliv. Also see *Blackstone's Commentaries* (Gavit ed.), 157–158.

power may also be exercised." Moreover, Otis concluded, any policy short of total exclusion, such as his own, would be a generous exercise of governmental power for which aliens ought to be grateful.[19]

Two types of citizenship would have been established by Otis' amendment. Naturalized citizens would not have gained all the rights and privileges of native citizens. Although they would have been allowed to vote, they would have been barred from holding public office. By condemning foreigners to second-class citizenship, the Otis plan would have prevented the Republicans in the future from drawing political leaders, such as Albert Gallatin, from the ranks of naturalized citizens.

The Republican attack on the Otis amendment was short but decisive. Abraham Venable of Virginia denied that distinctions could be made between naturalized and native citizens. Congress does not have the power to say that men who are entitled to hold offices by the Constitution shall not hold them, he said. Nathaniel Macon of North Carolina agreed that if a man is a citizen he is eligible to office if he meets the constitutional requirements. These cannot be altered by law, he added. If the people elected a former alien to Congress, and if he had been a citizen seven years, Congress could not say that he was ineligible. The Republicans contended that second-class American citizenship is not possible under the Constitution.[20]

These constitutional objections convinced Samuel Sitgreaves of Pennsylvania that the Otis proposal was not the best device for barring aliens from political activity. He urged, instead, a term of residence so long that aliens would never become citizens. Such a term would effectually exclude them from political participation, he said, and no inroads would be made upon the rights of citizens. Since Otis had indicated earlier that he would be satisfied if the House preferred to extend the residence requirement rather than adopt his amendment, he withdrew his drastic proposal. The Committee of the Whole then reported favorably on all three of the Defense Committee's resolutions without amendment.[21]

The naturalization bill was drafted by a Federalist-dominated

[19] Annals, 5C, 2S, 1568–1572. This argument that Congress has the power to exclude all foreigners from citizenship seems obviously fallacious. That aliens were meant to be allowed to become citizens through the process of naturalization is evident from the inclusion of that clause in the Constitution.

[20] Ibid., 1571.

[21] Ibid., 1572–1573. Although Otis withdrew his plan because of constitutional objections, his native state backed his nativism three months later when it proposed to circumvent constitutional disapproval with an amendment to exclude foreign-born citizens from Congress.

committee. Since the extreme views of Harper and Otis had been
dropped as unconstitutional, the Defense Committee presented a
bill which called for a declaration of intention by an alien at least
five years before he could be naturalized and for a total residence of
fourteen years before he could become a citizen. The *Annals of Congress* record but a slight debate on this drastic change, which nearly
tripled the residence requirement. Joseph McDowell, a North Carolina Republican, was the only opponent who expressed his views. He
had no objections to an increase of the five-year stipulation to seven
years, or even to nine years if the committee thought that better.
But to discourage respectable foreigners from emigrating to this
country by barring them from the rights of citizenship was to alter
the traditional American policy entirely. "When persons come here
from foreign countries," he argued, "it was our interest to attach
them to us, and not always to look upon them as aliens and strangers."
McDowell's dissent failed to alter the fourteen-year requirement,
which was adopted by a vote of 41 to 40.[22]

The only important debate on the bill came when Albert Gallatin,
Swiss-born floor leader of the Republicans, proposed to abolish its
retroactive features. As the bill stood, the extension of the term of
residence applied to aliens who were then living in the United States
as well as to newcomers. Those persons who were residents of
the United States prior to the act of 1795, Gallatin declared, should
be allowed to qualify for citizenship under the five-year requirement
of that act. He also urged exemption from the longer period for
those who had arrived since 1795 and had declared their intention
of becoming citizens.[23]

Samuel Sewall, chairman of the drafting committee, reported that
his group opposed any alteration. The foreigners to whom Gallatin
alluded had failed to become citizens of the United States, not
through ignorance, but because they placed no high value upon
American citizenship. The Massachusetts Federalist thought it especially imprudent to make Irishmen eligible to hold seats in the
government after a residence of five years because of the "present dis-
tracted state of the country from whence they have emigrated." The
longer Sewall argued the further he got from his committee's plan for
naturalizing foreigners within a given time limit, and the closer he
approached Harper's position that citizenship should derive only

[22] *Annals,* 5C, 2S (May 21, 1798), 1776. The *Annals* do not report a single
roll-call vote on the naturalization bill.
[23] *Ibid.,* 1776–1778.

from birth. The alien-born, the chairman declared, should be ineligible for office. Why let naturalized foreigners participate in government when most of them could not have done so in their home countries? Was not their situation vastly improved by the change they made? He supposed they came not with a view of getting into the government, but "to acquire property, and to enjoy peace and happiness, and this they might do independent of citizenship." If Gallatin's proposal to exempt resident aliens from the bill's retroactive provisions were adopted, Sewall concluded, it would endanger the country.[24]

James A. Bayard, the Delaware Federalist, agreed that there was no reason why the restrictions should not extend to aliens already resident in the United States as well as to those who might come in the future. The one had no greater claim than the other. He believed that "as many Jacobins and vagabonds have come into the United States during the last two years, as may come for ten years hence." The bill, he argued, was specifically aimed at such persons; without it, they would become citizens and might be elected to office.

Despite the opposition to his proposal, Gallatin had struck successfully at the Federalists. Even Otis had agreed that exceptions to his proposed ban on office-holding should be made if a person had given notice that he intended to become a citizen.[25] Federalists who represented districts containing numerous aliens now came forward to support Gallatin's amendment. Maryland's William Craik had no objection to barring from citizenship such foreigners as might arrive in the future, but he thought that it would be unjust to attack all foreigners then residing in the United States. Nor would it be proper to favor emigrants from any particular country. Many persons in his district either had been naturalized under the state law only, or they had not been naturalized at all. Most of them were Germans who neglected to become American citizens by reason of their ignorance of the American language and laws. But, the Federalist congressman insisted, they were entitled to every privilege that could be given them.[26]

The Republican line of argument was set forth by Nathaniel Macon of North Carolina and W. C. C. Claiborne of Tennessee. Macon argued that if persons had given notice of their intention to become citizens, they had complied with the laws in part, and that it would not be right to prevent their complying in full. He feared that some of the House would go too far in proscribing aliens in general in

[24] *Ibid.*, 1778.   [25] *Ibid.*, 1568–1572.   [26] *Ibid.*, 1779.

order to reach obnoxious individuals. He assumed that the politically minded aliens had already become naturalized. But, he added, many persons had never become citizens because they lived in distant parts of the country or were ignorant of the language.

Claiborne assured the nativists that there were many aliens in the frontier country who had not taken advantage of the laws of 1790 or 1795. At the time of the passage of the earlier statutes, such people could not easily learn of the actions of Congress. They lived "in a country in which there was no post road, and where, of course, they had no newspapers to give them information of what was going on at the seat of Government." The Tennessean asserted that many unnaturalized aliens had given the strongest proofs of attachment to the country. "They have fought and bled in the service of the United States," he concluded, "and are as much wedded to the Government of the United States as any man born on American soil." If Gallatin's amendment should fail, the frontier folk would be deprived of their rights under the existing law.

The arguments of this backwoods Republican were seconded by the frontier Federalist from up-state New York, John Williams. He believed that resident aliens who held land and behaved well should not be prevented from becoming citizens. "It was an acknowledged principle," he said, "that representation and taxation ought to go together." Such would not be the case if the naturalization bill were passed without Gallatin's amendment.

Supported by the Republicans and dissident Federalists, the proposal abolishing the retroactive features of the bill was adopted by the House. It provided that aliens who were residents before 1795 had to take advantage of their exemption from the fourteen-year period within a year after the passage of the new law. Those who had given notice of their intention to become citizens under the act of 1795 had to complete their naturalization within four years after making the declaration, or they would be subject to the longer requirement. After approving these limitations, the House sent the bill to the Senate.

Soon after the amended version passed the House, James A. Bayard, who had supported the original bill, changed his views. Congress, he declared, was in danger of carrying restrictions against aliens too far. He therefore proposed that Congress suspend the Naturalization Act of 1795 for an indefinite time, rather than pass any new regulations. Bayard's belated concern for foreigners was not as disinterested as it appeared. By barring further naturalization proceedings as long as the Federalist majority desired, his move would have eliminated Gallatin's exemptions. Apparently, Bayard thought it more urgent to bar aliens from politics immediately than to extend the residence requirement. The plea that restrictions might be carried too far served to justify restraints more drastic than any previously suggested.[27]

The Senate's only sharp contest over the bill occurred when the Republicans attempted to cut the proposed residence term in half. "We were within one vote . . . in the Senate," Jefferson wrote, "of striking out 14 years and inserting 7. Langdon who would have been for it had previously declined voting on the bill at all, because he had just taken his seat." His vote, of course, would have divided the Senate evenly and given the vice-president an opportunity to vote for the shorter term.[28] Although this major alteration was defeated by the Federalist majority, the Senate passed minor amendments, which the House agreed to on June 13. President Adams signed the measure on June 18.

Praising the adoption of the new law, the Federalist *Gazette of the United States* declared that "every native American must observe with pleasure the great change in the public mind relative to the admission of aliens to the rights of citizenship." Those who had lived under despotic governments, the editor continued, formed the habit of censuring them: "Among this class, and Americans who have formed their political opinions abroad, are to be found the most violent declaimers against our government." [29] Fortunately, Senator Bingham wrote, the new naturalization law would "deprive them of the power of influencing Elections" in the future.[30]

The Naturalization Law of 1798 provided that an alien must prove that he had lived in the United States for fourteen years, five of which had been spent in the state or territory where he was being naturalized. At least five years before his citizenship could be granted, he must declare his intention of becoming a citizen. However, aliens residing in the United States before 1795 were given one year in which to take advantage of the more liberal provisions of the act of

[27] *Ibid.*, 1780–1784. For Bayard's opposition to the "Jacobins and vagabonds" excepted from the bill by Gallatin's amendment, see above. For the best book on the Delaware congressman, see Morton Borden, *The Federalism of James A. Bayard* (New York, 1955).

[28] Jefferson to Madison, June 14, 1798, Jefferson Papers, CIV, 17794 (Lib. Cong.). The Senate vote is given in the *Annals*, 5C, 2S (June 12, 1798), 574.

[29] *Gazette of the United States,* June 28, 1798. Also see the New York *Commercial Advertiser,* Sept. 3, 1798.

[30] Bingham to King, Bellevue, Jersey Shore, Sept. 30, 1798, *King's Correspondence,* II, 426.

that year. Immigrants who had made a declaration of intention under this law might be admitted to citizenship within four years after such declaration. Alien enemies were barred from citizenship by this measure.

The act also subjected all white aliens to a system of national surveillance. Newcomers were to register with the clerk of the district court, or with an authorized registrar of aliens, within forty-eight hours of their entry, and resident aliens were to report within six months after the bill became law. Each registrant was to be given a certificate of report and registry, and a centralized record of all naturalizations was to be maintained by the secretary of state.[81]

Under the hot sun of diplomatic crisis and party animosity, nativism flowered profusely in the political greenhouse of 1798. The attempt by Harper to restrict the rights of citizenship to the native-born was a rigorous proposal unauthorized by the Constitution, as was Otis' proposition to exclude naturalized citizens from the right to hold public office. Although Congress did not enact these efforts to destroy the Republicans' foreign vote and to bar naturalized politicians from engaging in conduct inimical to Federalism, the Federalists adopted an act which established the longest residence requirement for citizenship in the history of the United States. At the same time, this restriction on the enfranchisement of immigrants dealt the Democratic-Republican party a heavy blow by robbing it of an important element of its support. Ironically, the only ameliorating feature of the Federalist policy of partisan proscription—the exemption of aliens already resident in the United States from the extended residence requirement—was the work of foreign-born Albert Gallatin, the leader of the opposition party in the House and the chief target of the original bill.

[81] *The Statutes at Large of the United States, 1789–1873* (Boston, 1845–1873), I, 566. Hereafter cited as *Stat. at L.*

CHAPTER III

Biography of a Bill:
The Alien Enemies Act

Whenever there shall be a declared war between the United States and any foreign nation . . . , all natives, citizens, denizens, or subjects of the hostile nation . . . shall be liable to be apprehended, restrained, secured and removed, as alien enemies.—ALIEN ENEMIES ACT

THE two alien laws passed by Congress in 1798 were further manifestations of that feeling of anti-alienism which had motivated the enactment of the Naturalization Law. The first of these, the Alien Friends Act ("An Act Concerning Aliens") was a Federalist measure designed only for the temporary crisis with France; it was limited to two years and could be exercised in peace or war. The Alien Enemies Law, on the other hand, was a permanent wartime statute passed with bipartisan support. The Republicans had no objections to a well-drawn bill governing the control of alien enemies, but they did oppose vesting such dictatorial powers in the hands of the president that he might establish a policy which could be directed against American citizens as well as enemy aliens.

The question of the control of aliens had been tied to that of naturalization almost as soon as that topic had been broached by Representative Coit. Samuel Sitgreaves, the Pennsylvania Federalist, suggested on April 19 that the committee reporting on naturalization should also investigate the status of aliens in the United States. Fearful of a war with France, he urged that measures should be taken against resident French citizens. They might be placed under regulations, he said, or sent out of the country. Although his recommendation did not differentiate between alien enemies and friends, Sitgreaves' fear of imminent war indicated that the measures should deal with enemy aliens.

That such a permanent wartime statute would receive Republican backing was demonstrated when Congressman Thomas T. Davis of Kentucky agreed that some regulation was necessary. He cited the case of a Frenchman residing in his state who was constantly setting the people against their government. This Republican support clinched the argument, and the resolution was referred to the Defense Committee.[1] When that group reported on changes in the naturalization law, it also recommended a bill to deal with alien enemies. In case of war, invasion, or predatory incursion, the committee suggested, the president should issue a proclamation prescribing such conditions for apprehending or expelling alien enemies as the public safety might require. If an enemy alien were not personally chargeable with actual hostility, a reasonable period should be allowed for his departure, with all his effects. Aliens whose exception from these provisions was consistent with the public safety might be granted passports or licenses of residence.[2]

The extreme Federalists attacked these proposals as vigorously as they had assailed the committee's resolutions on naturalization. Otis again led the attack, joined by Nathaniel Smith and John Allen of Connecticut and Samuel Sitgreaves of Pennsylvania. Smith claimed that a foreign government might commit an act tantamount to war without a declaration of war. Yet the wording of the resolution would not allow the United States to deport citizens of the hostile nation. He therefore moved to provide for their removal in the event that their government "shall be at war with the United States." This change was unnecessary, Sewall replied, because Congress alone had the power of deciding on the question of war. He could not see how it could be determined whether any nation was at war with the United States until the declaration was made by that nation, or by Congress.

Although it was Smith who first criticized the report, it was Otis who again led the attempt to batter down the constitutional safeguards erected by the bill. He proposed an amendment which provided that aliens should be removed if their government "shall authorize hostilities against the United States." To confine the power

---

[1] *Annals*, 5C, 2S (April 19, 1798), 1453. It was adopted unanimously.
[2] *Ibid.* (May 1, 1798), 1566–1567.

of deportation to narrow limits seemed to Otis to undermine the whole system of national defense. Formalities and safeguards such as the bill prescribed should not hamper the government. When an enemy authorized hostilities, the United States should "take up that crowd of spies and inflammatory agents which overspread the country like the locusts of Egypt, and who were continually attacking our liberties." He insisted that something ought to be done which would strike these people with terror. At a time of danger, the United States should not "*boggle* about slight forms." It should seize these persons, wherever they could be found carrying on their seditious and malignant purposes. If the United States failed to take these steps against its enemies, it would cripple its own defense efforts.

In the present crisis with France, said John Rutledge of South Carolina, the United States need not wait for a declaration of war before expelling French agents and intriguing spies. France would never declare war so long as her agents were allowed to remain in America. Their residence, he said, was of greater consequence to her "than the lining of our seaboard with privateers, or covering our coasts with men."

Sitgreaves, who had first suggested protective measures against aliens, backed Otis' amendment as an essential feature of the defense system against the dangers threatening the nation. Confining defense operations to land and naval forces would not "destroy the cankerworm which is corroding in the heart of the country," he exclaimed. The United States should take advantage of its knowledge of France's hostile intentions. Frenchmen could not now be considered as alien friends. Such emissaries had not only fomented the difficulties between America and France, but they had endeavored to set the American people against its government. Measures of defense and protection for present exigencies should be the most particular duty of Congress because the president needed wide powers to meet this enemy. Aliens of reputable character would be in no danger from this proposal, he assured the House. Only factious and bad men would be deported. Otis had given this same assurance, but had concluded that Congress should not bother with safeguards. In this Sitgreaves seemed to agree.

The man who was least concerned with formalities and safeguards, however, was John Allen of Connecticut. Only his respect for Mr. Sewall, he informed the House, kept him from suspecting that some latent and mischievous design lurked in the Defense Committee's lenient resolution. Even Otis' amendment did not go far enough. To Allen's suspicious mind, the power of deportation should not depend upon any contingency, be it war, invasion, or a state of hostility. Nor should it be limited to alien enemies. The resolution should be extended to all aliens in the United States. Allen's chief concern arose from the fact that aliens, once they were naturalized, could participate in elections. Recent naturalizations in Philadelphia, he said, had just preceded the election and had increased Republican strength. To deal with this threat to Federalist supremacy he proposed that the president should have the power to remove any alien at any time for any reason.

Furthermore, he hinted at the need for some sort of legislation to deal with American citizens. "He believed there were citizens in this country who would be ready to join a foreign Power in assisting to subjugate their country. What passed before our eyes, and every day offended our ears, were so many proofs of it." [3] Allen remained the most suspicious and the most extreme of the Federalists.

The only Republican to refute the extremists was Joseph McDowell of North Carolina. He challenged Otis to point out the spies and seditious persons who swarmed over the country. If this could be done, he would be glad to join in measures against them. The French commissions, about which Representative Davis of Kentucky had complained, probably had been granted under the authority of Genêt, but McDowell believed that none had been issued since 1793. The North Carolinian also denied Otis' contention that privileges formerly allowed foreigners might be withdrawn on the theory that the nation's population was sufficient. He informed the city-bred Otis that some parts of the country still sought inhabitants. Furthermore, the "hostility" amendment would distress the minds of foreigners who had been induced to come to America with a view of becoming citizens. They might be treated as enemy aliens even though no war existed.

As a matter of fact, Otis' observations made it appear that hostilities had already commenced between America and France. If this was the case, McDowell asked, why did not the House say so, and act accordingly? Otis confessed he was ready to vote for war if the North Carolinian would introduce a proposition for that purpose. If Otis wanted war, McDowell retorted, he could offer his own resolution. Even if there should be a war with France, McDowell did not think it proper to give the president power to send all French-

---

[3] *Ibid.*, 1573–1578. Since the *Annals* were compiled several years after the congressional debates from accounts contemporary with those proceedings, all speeches are reported in the third person.

men out of the country, "however peaceably they might be residing here."

Chief defender of the resolutions was Samuel Sewall, chairman of the committee which had drafted them. He opposed Otis' amendment by arguing that the United States could not be considered in a state of war unless Congress had constitutionally declared it or unless war had been declared against this country. The provisions for apprehending, securing, or removing aliens should be as well guarded and definite as possible. This was to be long-range legislation, formulating American policy for the future as well as for the present difficulties with France. Therefore, its powers should be confined to cases that were particularly dangerous. Foreigners guilty of crimes against the United States should be apprehended and punished according to existing laws. The proposed regulation was not pointed at them.

Sewall agreed with McDowell that Otis' motion would render national policy too indefinite and would give the president an improper power. The chief executive might send aliens from America, and the foreign country involved would reciprocate. Thus, American citizens might be deported, or imprisoned, and their property confiscated at a time when Congress did not judge it expedient to go to war. Unlike the North Carolina Republican, however, Sewall did not think that the resolution as reported proposed too wide a power for the president.

Conversely, Sewall denied Allen's assertion that the resolve was too narrow. Allen's fears were based on a mental defect or a disease of his body, Sewall said, rather than on any real ground for alarm. The Defense Committee contemplated neither excluding all aliens nor granting a power that would make it possible to place every alien in the country in a dungeon. Aliens guilty of seditious practices should be restricted, but not placed under an arbitrary authority. Civil policy distinguished between alien enemies and alien friends. This distinction Allen would abolish. Therefore, Allen's regulation could not be adopted unless the United States were inclined to assume the character of the absolutism of the Turks or Arabs. He noted that the resolution under discussion recommended a bill regulating alien enemies. But if the House was determined to arrest every alien, it should bring forward a resolution for that purpose.[4]

Shaken by these blasts from his fellow Federalist, the leading extremist withdrew his proposal, and the House then voted down the

[4] *Ibid.*, 1573, 1580.

Otis amendment, 55 to 27. Although Sewall attempted to appease the extreme Federalists by amending the resolution to provide for the removal of aliens who came from a country "between which and the United States shall exist a declared state of war," Otis thought this no great concession because it still allowed deportation or apprehension of alien enemies only in time of war. No matter what was said about the need for permanent regulations, he said, the immediate problem was to provide against the residence of alien enemies already in the United States. They were the cause of the crisis with France—"the root of all the evil." Sitgreaves attempted to unite the Federalists by combining elements of Otis' and Sewall's amendments. This led to a suggestion that aliens might be removed if their country should "declare hostility against the United States." [5]

Objections now came from the Republicans. Davis, who had seconded Sitgreaves' motion for the original resolution, asked for a postponement to consider the constitutionality of this amendment. Gallatin, in seconding the move, summed up the arguments to that point. They had pivoted on the words "hostility" and "war," and he maintained that the Constitution made a distinction between them. Since this was so, there was a difference in the relation between alien subjects of a nation with which the United States was at war and those of a nation with which there was a state of actual hostility. In war, alien subjects could be removed as enemy aliens under the law of nations. The only pertinent question, therefore, was: Could citizens of a nation in actual hostility with the United States be considered as alien enemies? If they could not, then Congress might be barred from action, since it could not prohibit, prior to 1808, the migration of such persons, including aliens, as any of the states thought proper to admit. At least, this constitutional doubt ought to be explored, especially since the term "actual hostility" was vague in its nature. Gallatin then asked for and obtained a postponement of further discussion on this resolution. [6]

When the House again considered the resolution on May 8, it authorized a bill based on Sewall's amendment, providing for the deportation of aliens from a country with which the United States was in a declared state of war. The first section instructed the presi-

[5] *Ibid.*, 1580–1581. Otis was attempting to give a new meaning to the words "alien enemy." As Sewall had pointed out, civil policy distinguished between alien enemies and alien friends. The status of alien enemy is created by war. Yet Otis insisted on speaking of the French in America as alien enemies, although he readily admitted that there was no declared war between France and the United States.

[6] *Ibid.*, 1581–1582. See the Constitution, Art. I, Sec. 9.

dent to direct American policy toward enemy aliens. Whenever he issued a proclamation, alien enemies were "liable to be apprehended, restrained, secured, and removed." Similar action could be taken against them in case of an attempted or threatened invasion of American territory. The president could proclaim the manner and degree of their restraint, determine who among them could be permitted to continue their residence here and upon what security, make provisions for the removal of those who were refused permission to reside within the United States, and "establish any other regulations which shall be found necessary in the premises, and for the public safety." These almost unlimited powers were subject only to the regulations which Congress might establish subsequently.

Alien enemies not chargeable with actual hostility or other crime against the public safety were to be allowed the full time stipulated in any treaty between the United States and the hostile nation for their departure and for the recovery, disposal, and removal of their goods and effects. If there was no such treaty the president or Congress was to determine a reasonable time which would be "consistent with the public safety, and according to the dictates of humanity and national hospitality." The bill also subjected enemy aliens, with their goods and effects, to a just retaliation for any unusual severities, restraints, and confiscations that the warring country laid on Americans resident there. The power of the president was limited in these cases to the end of the next ensuing session of Congress and was also subject to any subsequent law which Congress should enact.

Congress thus proposed to delegate extensive powers to the chief executive, subject only to their subsequent regulation. In short, the bill was an enabling act, directing the president to frame, proclaim, and enforce American policy toward alien enemies in time of war. He was to lay down the rules and directions for the enforcement of his proclaimed policy. All justices and judges of the states and of the United States, all justices of the peace having criminal jurisdiction and authority for the securing of offenders, and all marshals, sheriffs, and other officers were required to discharge, enforce, and execute the duties assigned them by the proclamation or other public act of the president.

The bill enjoined the American people to be "obedient and assisting" to such rules and directions. If a person should knowingly harbor or conceal any alien enemy, or if anyone should willfully hinder, obstruct, or oppose any officer in the exercise and discharge of the authorities and duties which had been assigned in the president's directions, he was to be punished "as by law is or shall be declared." Leaving the penalty open to later definition meant that a crime would be established for which there would be no punishment until either Congress subsequently laid down the penalty or the president established the penalty in his proclamation. Moreover, this section applied not only to aliens but to American citizens.[7]

This last section drew immediate fire, both from Republicans and Federalists. The most telling blow was struck by Bayard in committee, and his work was defended on the floor by Gallatin. Bayard declared that the last section contained a principle contrary to all maxims of American jurisprudence. It provided that after a crime had been committed a law would be passed punishing it. Moreover, the crime was not even defined. Whether it would amount to treason, misprision of treason, or only a misdemeanor was left uncertain. It would be impossible for a person to know what crime he had committed or to what punishment he was liable. To make the law definite, he proposed that the crime be made a misdemeanor punishable by fine and imprisonment.

Sewall admitted that this section contained a good deal of uncertainty, but his committee saw no way of remedying the evil without making the law too mild in its operation. He opposed making such offenses uniformly misdemeanors because in some cases the crime might amount to high treason, and carry the death penalty, and in others it might only be a misprision of treason, which was punishable by imprisonment not exceeding seven years and a fine not exceeding $1,000. He cited this example:

If an alien should have resided here for a number of years, and he should turn out to have been a spy, and a citizen of the United States should have harbored and concealed the said alien, knowing him to have been a spy, he would be chargeable with high treason for aiding and abetting the enemies of the United States within its territory, or at least a misprision of treason.[8]

An offender would not be tried and punished by a law passed after the offense was committed, Sewall assured Bayard, because Congress would enact such a law between the passage of the present bill and the time that the offense might be committed. This explanation was so weak that the Committee of the Whole adopted Bayard's amendment by a vote of 44 to 25, fixing the maximum fine at $1,000 but leaving the prison term undetermined. The bill was then reported to the House.

[7] *Ibid.* (May 8, 1798), 1631; (May 22, 1798), 1785.
[8] *Ibid.*, 1786–1787. This example contains no reference to a state of war.

The proponents of the sliding-scale system of punishments renewed their attacks on Bayard's amendment on the floor of the House. Nathaniel Smith condemned a uniform punishment as inflexible. Sewall agreed that offenders should be punished by progressive penalties, according to the degree of their offense. The bill defined the offense as harboring an alien enemy. Anyone committing this offense became a "suspected person." But the crime and punishment had to be ascertained by other laws.

Bayard, who had already defeated this view in committee, was quick to defend his amendment. Section three referred to an offense of a definite nature—harboring and concealing an alien enemy after a presidential proclamation. Therefore, a definite punishment ought to be prescribed. If Sewall and others wanted to define punishments in exact conformity to the degree of offense, they should prepare the scale of punishments now, and not leave it till some future time. The offense could not amount to treason, he said, because that crime is defined by the Constitution and cannot be varied by any law of Congress.

Albert Gallatin pointed out that the whole field of "constructive treason" would be opened up by the ambiguity of section three. For a bill to define certain circumstances which would render a man a suspected person, without establishing and punishing the offense of which he was guilty, seemed altogether new legislation to the Republican leader. If a man commits an offense, he should be punished, Gallatin acknowledged, but he refused to consent to punish a man on mere suspicion. This bill would establish a new crime—that of being a suspected person. Evidence of that crime would be the overt act of harboring and concealing an alien enemy. The punishment would be apprehension and imprisonment until it was discovered what law the prisoner had violated. Such a procedure was contrary to the constitutional provision that no person shall be deprived of life, liberty, or property without due process of law. Under this law persons might be deprived of their liberty not only without any process, but also without being guilty of any crime.

Instead of deciding what the law would be, Gallatin continued, the bill gave the president the power of legislation. Federal and state officers, and the people of the United States, were not to execute any law, he said, but to carry into effect the proclamation or other public act of the president. They were to be obedient to the will of the president, instead of being obedient to the laws. While he favored a permanent enemy alien act, the Pennsylvanian wanted Congress to declare what the offense and punishment should be. He therefore moved to recommit the bill. If it were not revised, he thought Congress might just as well boil the bill down to these words: "The President of the United States shall have the power to remove, restrict, or confine alien enemies and citizens whom he may consider as suspected persons." [9]

In an attempt to beat off Gallatin's move for recommittal, Sewall and Otis disregarded the Republican leader's arguments against the section penalizing American citizens for harboring alien enemies and shifted their attention to the section dealing with alien enemies. The intention of the bill, said Sewall, was to provide for the public safety. In the United States that power is lodged in Congress. The alien enemies bill was designed to share this power, giving the president the power of judging what is proper to be done, subject to subsequent approval by Congress. In the event of a war with France, all her citizens here would become enemy aliens. But it would be unnecessary to remove or restrict many of them.[10] Therefore, it would be impossible for Congress to describe the cases in which aliens or citizens ought to be punished. These matters the president could determine by his proclamation.

Otis joined Sewall in defending the discretionary power vested in the president by the bill. If the conduct of alien enemies was extremely suspicious, they ought to be taken into custody, even though no positive crimes could be proved. In case of an invasion by the French army, some alien enemies might show a disposition which would warrant their imprisonment. How such dispositions could be defined by law Otis did not know. Congress should delegate to the executive the power to restrain such men from doing injury. Otherwise they would carry on a correspondence "with their countrymen and our enemy." They would constitute a band of spies ready to join an invading enemy in their attack and plunder. The president should have the power of judging in these cases, because punishment "ought not to depend upon the slow operations of a trial."

Since neither Sewall nor Otis discussed the points raised by Gallatin, he withdrew his motion to recommit the whole bill and moved to commit the third section only. When Macon insisted on recommitting the whole bill, his suggestion was voted down, 37 to 36. Gallatin's motion to recommit the third section resulted in a 38-to-38 tie. When Speaker Dayton voted with Gallatin's opponents, how-

[9] *Ibid.*, 1787–1789.

[10] *Ibid.*, 1790. One of the anomalies of the third section, therefore, was that it would penalize citizens for harboring alien enemies who might not be offenders.

ever, the proposed bill, intact after a day's debate, was ordered engrossed for its third reading.

The closeness of the vote on recommittal led the Republicans to make a final effort to postpone the bill. After it was read the third time, Robert Williams, congressman from North Carolina, moved for recommitment. He objected not so much to the provisions respecting aliens as to those conferring power on the president to issue proclamations which would affect American citizens.

Gallatin then summarized the grounds for recommittal in a closely reasoned speech. There was every good reason for a bill to control alien enemies, he said, but it should not be in such a general and vague form as the proposed statute. That measure was founded upon the principle "that the President of the United States shall have the power to do by proclamation what ought to be done by law." This delegation of power by Congress to the president became the front line of Gallatin's attack, and from it he made successive sorties to show the bill's weaknesses and vagueness.

First, he observed that the president would be allowed to determine in his proclamation when alien enemies could be apprehended, restrained, secured, and removed. Gallatin understood the meaning of all these terms except "restrained." It was not defined, nor was it a legal phrase.

In the second place, he pointed out that alien enemies would not only be subject to indefinite restrictions, but also that they, together with their goods and effects, would be exposed to a just retaliation for any unusual severities, restraints, or confiscations levied on Americans in the enemy nation. What was meant by "unusual severities," Gallatin wanted to know? If it was other than apprehending, restraining, or removing a person or confiscating his goods, he thought that, upon American ideas of government, the United States could not retaliate. Neither propriety nor justice would warrant America's committing a disgraceful act against citizens of another nation because that nation had committed an atrocious act upon American citizens.[11]

Perhaps, Gallatin continued, the words were to be held *in terrorem* over France. If so, he thought it was not a very creditable proceeding. It was doubtful that the president could exercise such severities

[11] *Ibid.*, 1791–1794. When Sewall rose to explain, the Speaker ruled him ineligible; the Federalists had voted on May 18 to allow a member to speak but once on a question. This had been directed originally against Gallatin, the most effective Republican spokesman against the alien legislation then under discussion, but it also worked to the disadvantage of the Federalists.

constitutionally in view of the express prohibition against cruel and unusual punishments. Furthermore, the words would carry no threat to France. Ninety-nine out of a hundred Frenchmen in America were *émigrés*, and it would be immaterial to the French nation how such exiles were treated.

In the third place, Gallatin objected to the provisions of the bill concerning confiscations. Jay's Treaty, he pointed out, expressly declared that sequestrations were impolitic and unjust in every case. He did not deny that it might be necessary to resort to sequestrations and confiscations on some occasions by way of indemnification. But he insisted that it ought to be done by law, not by the president.

Continuing his argument, Gallatin proposed that Congress should pass the law itself and not leave every regulation relative to this subject with the president. He cited the second section, which provided that "where no treaty exists, a reasonable time shall be allowed for aliens not chargeable with hostility to depart, which shall be ascertained . . . by the President, or by the congress of the United States." This kind of double legislation was new to him. Why should not this bill specify the length of time allowed these aliens before departure? He urged that now was the time, and that Congress was the proper body, to do it. The basic objection, then, was that the bill was devoid of legislation. Even if the first two sections were unchanged, Congress ought to define the duties of citizens.

Gallatin next considered the features of the bill that pertained to enforcement. If justices and judges were to have anything to do with the removal of aliens, Congress should define their spheres of action. This would be better than leaving the thing to the decision of one man. His final objection was directed against one of the criminal provisions which was applicable to citizens. Under the third section, a person could be imprisoned up to seven years and fined up to $1,000 if he was found guilty on the hazy charge of "harboring and concealing" an alien enemy. Surely Congress could do better than this two-word definition of a crime. At least it should distinguish between cases of misdemeanor and those which might arise from ignorance, in which case no offense at all might exist. If this were not done, the only function of a jury would be to decide the fact of harboring and concealing. The court, not the jury, would then judge the criminality of the act and fix the punishment.[12]

---

[12] *Ibid.*, 1794–1796. If a citizen harbored for one night, however undesignedly, an alien enemy, he was guilty under the third section. For arguments against the Sedition Act over the jurisdiction of the jury and the court in libel trials, see Chapter VII.

These arguments prevailed, and the House by a vote of 46 to 44 sent the bill to a special committee.[13] The alien enemy measure languished in committee for over a month. During that time the Federalists became more bellicose and pushed through a temporary alien act to cope with the emergency created by the diplomatic impasse with France. This law dealt with both alien friends and alien enemies and vested vastly greater powers in the hands of the president than did the proposed alien enemy legislation.

Thus, when Samuel Smith, only Republican on the select committee to which the wartime alien bill was returned, asked for a discussion of that measure on June 25, Otis tried to postpone consideration until the next session of Congress. The emergency alien bill which had been passed satisfied him that the president would have sufficient power over aliens in wartime as well as in peacetime. Therefore, there was no immediate necessity for another bill.

Gallatin, who had never opposed a well-defined alien enemies bill, now insisted on the necessity of such a measure. Otis' move, he noted, made it seem that the Federalists wished more to guard against alien friends than against alien enemies. The Republican leader admitted that if the bill was not passed the president would have the power to remove any alien if he thought it necessary and proper, whether such a suspect was an alien enemy or an alien friend. In case of war, however, it would be impossible for the president to remove all dangerous alien enemies. Congress, therefore, should describe the way in which they might be laid under restraints by way of security.

Otis hastily withdrew his motion to postpone the bill, as he had no basic objection to it. Although the measure was passed the next day and sent to the Senate, the *Annals* record no debate in either house.[14] The Senate passed the bill on July 3, and President Adams' approval made the law effective on July 6.

Section one of the Alien Enemies Act was based on the first two sections of the original bill. In case of war, invasion, or predatory incursion against the United States, the president was to issue a proclamation of the event. Male citizens of the hostile nation then residing in the United States became alien enemies who could be apprehended, restrained, secured, and removed. The president was to direct American policy toward such enemies, deciding whether they should be permitted to reside in the United States and on what se-

[13] Five of the six members on the committee were Federalists.

[14] *Annals*, 5C, 2S, 2034, 2050. The National Archives has the manuscript copy of the bill passed by the House on June 26; see Senate Records, 5C, 2S, RG 46.

curity, and designating the method of removal of those not permitted to remain should they refuse or neglect to depart. The statute also authorized any other regulations of alien enemies which the president deemed necessary for the public safety.

Another provision specified that alien enemies not chargeable with actual hostility should be allowed the full time stipulated by treaty for the recovery, disposal, and removal of their goods and effects and for their departure. If no treaty existed between the hostile nation and the United States, the president was to declare a reasonable time that would be consistent with the public safety, the dictates of humanity, and national hospitality.[15]

Section two of the statute followed Gallatin's suggestion that the duties of enforcement officers should be defined by law, rather than left to the discretion of the president. It required the courts of the United States, and the state courts having criminal jurisdiction, to give a full examination and hearing to complaints against any alien residing within their jurisdiction "to the danger of the public peace or safety, and contrary to the tenor or intent of such presidential proclamation." Upon a showing of sufficient cause, the court could order sureties for his good behavior. In addition, the alien enemy could be restrained in conformity with the regulations laid down in the presidential proclamation. In all cases, the court could imprison or otherwise secure the offender until the performance of its order.

Although the *Annals* contain no debates on the Alien Enemies Law during its final stages of passage, it appears to have been virtually a Republican measure. The bill was called from committee by Samuel Smith, the only Jeffersonian in that group, and the only speech demanding its enactment came from Albert Gallatin. Moreover, the final bill incorporated five of the six suggestions laid down by Gallatin in his formidable speech which had led to the recommitment of the original bill. The fundamental objection of the Republicans had been that the proposed bill was lacking in legislation. Congress now set forth the law, rather than leaving it to the president's discretion or to subsequent congressional enactment. The only objection not heeded was that against the word "restrained" in the first section; that undefined term was retained in the law. But the definition of the other parts of the bill, which treated it as a

[15] *Annals*, 5C, 2S, 3753; also see *Stat. at L.*, I, 577. It should be noted that this provision, allowing aliens time to depart as provided for by treaty, was nullified next day so far as Frenchmen were concerned. On July 7 the American treaties with France were abrogated.

declaratory word, did not confer a wide grant of discretionary power. This was partially accomplished by lopping off that part of section one which would have subjected alien enemies to a retaliation for any unusual severities committed by the enemy nation on Americans resident there. Furthermore, the act omitted references to the regulation of American policy by subsequent congressional action.

The original provisions dealing with confiscations and sequestrations disappeared from the final law. The "double legislation" proviso, which would have authorized the president or Congress to define a reasonable time for the departure of alien enemies not chargeable with hostility, was changed to allow the president to exercise this power. Congress, however, established the duties of officers who were to carry out the removal of alien enemies in conformity with the presidential proclamation. Finally, section three of the original bill was eliminated completely. To the Republicans this had been the most objectionable part of the Federalist bill because of its criminal sanctions against citizens. As finally passed, the Alien Enemies Law raised no controversial constitutional questions.[16] The Federalists, of course, had no objection to a permanent wartime enemy alien measure, once they had enacted their emergency alien law giving stringent control over all aliens.

Thus there was an overlapping of the legislation affecting aliens. Intent upon striking at any foreigner obnoxious to them, the Federalists first passed the temporary "Act concerning Aliens" which was enforceable in peacetime as well as wartime. This legislation, however, was limited to two years. The Alien Enemies Law, on the other hand, was a permanent measure which has remained a fundamental part of American wartime policy.

[16] Andrew C. McLaughlin, *A Constitutional History of the United States*, 267, says: "Possibly we might criticize the act because no provision was made for the proper protection of those persons who were alleged to be enemy aliens but asserted they were citizens; but on the face of the act itself one cannot find the assignment of unconstitutional authority." Also see *Ng Fung Ho* v. *White*, 259 US 276, 284 (1922).

CHAPTER IV

Aliens in Peace and War: "An Act Concerning Aliens"

> And if a stranger sojourn with thee in your land, ye shall not vex him. But the stranger that dwelleth with you shall be unto you as one born among you, and thou shalt love him as thyself.—Leviticus 19:33–34

FROM the Federalist point of view, an Alien Enemies Act was not sufficient to meet the national crisis; it was a wartime measure, applicable only against enemy aliens. Whether or not war came with France, they wanted a statute empowering the government to deal with objectionable immigrants, such as the "Wild Irish" refugees and English radicals. To meet this demand the Federalists enacted their most drastic legislation against foreigners, the "Act Concerning Aliens," or the Alien Friends Law.[1] It made every alien in the United States liable to arbitrary arrest and deportation in peace or war, and it climaxed the upsurge of nativism set off in Federalist quarters by the revelations in the XYZ dispatches. It was an extension of the antiforeignism which had motivated the Naturalization Law; it was both a political weapon and an attempt to attain a greater "purity of national character."

Unlike the other alien acts, this measure originated in the Senate, long the stronghold of aristocratic Federalism.[2] On April 25, less than a week after the House had started on the naturalization and alien

[1] *Stat. at L.*, I, 570.
[2] Bassett, *Federalist System*, 259.

enemy bills, Senator James Hillhouse of Connecticut called for the appointment of a committee to draft a bill authorizing the removal of any alien from the United States who might be "dangerous to its peace and safety," the issuance of permits to aliens who were allowed to remain, and the enumeration of all newcomers landed in American ports.[3] Jefferson wrote Madison that the motion called "for giving power to send away suspected aliens," adding that the bill was meant for the Comte de Volney and General Victor Collot, two prominent Frenchmen then in the United States.[4]

The Senate appointed an all-Federalist committee on April 26 to draft the alien bill. On May 4 this group reported a lengthy measure containing thirteen sections. It not only authorized the president to remove all aliens whom he judged dangerous to the peace and safety of the United States, but, as Jefferson had predicted, it allowed the deportation of suspected aliens. The president could expel any foreigner if he had reasonable grounds to believe that a suspect was "concerned in any treasonable or secret machinations against the government." In neither case was there to be a trial by jury. Nor did the order of removal have to specify the findings on which it was based.[5]

If any alien who was sent out or deported from the United States should return, he was to be tried and, if convicted, banished for life or fined and confined to hard labor for a specified number of years. If the alien was found at large after the sentence of banishment had been pronounced, he was to be seized, imprisoned without trial, and "kept to hard labour for and during life." [6]

In addition to setting forth the grounds for expulsion, the bill proposed a national registration and surveillance system for all aliens permitted to reside in the United States. No alien would be allowed to remain in the country without a special permit issued by a presidential agent. To obtain a permit the alien had to submit an ap-

[3] *Annals*, 5C, 2S (April 25, 1798), 548. Also see the *Aurora*, April 28, 1798. The motion asked that "permits be granted to such aliens as shall be suffered to reside" in the United States. Residence by sufferance became the new theme of Federalist references to aliens.

[4] Jefferson to Madison, Phila., April 26, 1798, *Jefferson's Writings* (Ford ed.), VII, 244.

[5] Although the bill is not given in the *Annals*, the *Aurora*, May 8, 1798, prints the complete text. The original manuscript copy of the bill is filed in Senate Records, 5C, 2S, RG 46 (National Archives).

[6] The Senate refused to ratify an amendment requiring the entry of the deportation order "in a well-bound book, to be kept in the office of the Secretary of the Department of State, for the inspection of Congress." See *Annals*, 5C, 2S, 566.

plication to the issuing agent, with supporting proof that his conduct during his residence had conformed to the Constitution and laws of the United States. If the agent accepted this proof, he would issue a permit describing the "town, place or places within the United States" where the registrant was to remain. The agent also could require a surety bond for the good behavior of the alien.

If any alien should fail to obtain a permit, he could be apprehended, tried, and, if convicted, sentenced to imprisonment during the life of the act or fined and assessed court costs. If fined, he was to be imprisoned until the fine was paid. If any permit-holding alien should violate its provisions by traveling out of his defined zone, or if he should disturb or intermeddle with the government of the United States "by any seditious writing, printing or speaking or in any other way," he was to be tried, and imprisoned or fined. The president could order the deportation of aliens imprisoned under the act if he thought it necessary for the public safety.

Reversing the burden of proof in all these proceedings, the bill specifically placed that burden on the alien. He had to prove that he had conformed to the law and the Constitution in order to obtain a permit; in all cases involving his compliance with the permit he had to prove that he had not violated it. The government need not prove that he had. This section, which applied to all alien-born persons whose residence commenced after March 3, 1798, went even further. In all cases involving the question of an applicant's right to citizenship, the burden of proof was placed on the alien.

The only "strangers" exempted from obtaining permits or from arbitrary removal were foreign ministers and consuls, their secretaries and servants, any sailor whose ship was in port, and any alien merchant conforming to regulations prescribed by the president. The chief executive also might grant a passport or safe-conduct permit exempting aliens from the provisions of the act. All other aliens, whether they held permits or not, could be deported if the president suspected or judged them of being dangerous.

Buried in the heart of this bill was a bold attempt to purify the national character by isolating all aliens from American society and from each other. It stipulated that no person could "harbour, entertain or conceal any alien" without first giving written notice to a federal district judge or Supreme Court justice several days in advance. This was to apply to all aliens, with or without permits. Every offending "entertainer," citizen or alien, would have been subject to an unspecified fine. The whole bill was to continue in force until December, 1799.

The draconic measure was immediately printed in the Philadelphia *Aurora,* which labeled it, with great sarcasm, "a memorable speciman of the knowledge and liberality of the *wisest* and *most enlightened* Senate in the world." It was so infamous, Bache wrote, that it could not pass the Senate, and if it did, it would be defeated in the House. As an example of the bill's vehemence, he singled out the section forbidding any person to entertain, harbor, or conceal an alien "under God knows what penalty." One of his correspondents lived on a main traveled road in Virginia and entertained on the average of one hundred aliens a year. Although he lived about one hundred and thirty miles from a federal judge, it would be necessary, under this bill, for him to dispatch a courier that distance "before he durst give a dinner to a visitor from Europe." [7] The alien bill, Bache asserted, was a "statutory monster now squeaking for existence" which "completely unmasked the principles and plans of the federal, aristocratical, six per cent friends of *order.* A numerous body of people are to be subjected to ruin at the arbitrary mandate of the President." [8] Vice-President Jefferson thought the alien bill "a most detestable thing"—"worthy of the 8th or 9th century," [9] and Madison called the original measure "a monster that must forever disgrace its parents." [10] The wife of the chief executive, however, thought that "in times like the present, a more careful and attentive watch ought to be kept over foreigners. This will be done in future," she wrote her sister, "if the Alien Bill passes, without being curtailed and clipt until it is made nearly useless." [11]

On June 1 the alien bill was ordered back to committee where it was "curtailed and clipt" but not made useless. Although the simplified version dropped the proposed system of national surveillance of aliens, it retained many drastic features from Hillhouse's original draft. The first section repeated the two grounds for expulsion: the president's suspicions and his judgment that the alien was dangerous. Senator Stevens T. Mason, Republican from Virginia, successfully moved an amendment which directed that the order should

[7] *Aurora,* May 9, 1798.

[8] *Aurora,* May 11, 1798.

[9] Jefferson to Madison, Phila., May 31, 1798, *Jefferson's Writings* (Ford ed.), VII, 261; Jefferson to Thomas Mann Randolph, Phila., May 9, 1798, Jefferson Papers, CIV, 17758 (Lib. Cong.). Congressman Richard Sprigg of Virginia labeled it "the furious alien bill." Sprigg to Richard Sprigg, Jr., Phila., May 16, 1798, Mercer Papers (Va. Hist. Soc.).

[10] Madison to Jefferson, May 20, 1798, Gaillard Hunt, ed., *Writings of James Madison* (New York, 1900–10), VI, 320.

[11] Abigail Adams to Mary Cranch, May 26, 1798, Mitchell, *New Letters,* 179.

be served on an alien "by delivering him a copy . . . or leaving the same at his usual abode." But the Senate again refused to require that the order specify the cause of removal.

The revised bill also completely reorganized the permit system. Instead of being issued to all aliens permitted to remain, licenses were to be granted only to those aliens who, having been ordered to depart, should prove to the president or one of his agents that their continued residence involved no injury or danger to the United States. The license, which was revocable at the president's pleasure, would specify the length of time the alien might remain in the country and the place where he was to reside. If a person who had been ordered to depart should fail to obtain a license or should violate his permit, he could be deported on apprehension, or he could be tried, imprisoned up to three years, and barred from citizenship forever. Any alien imprisoned under the law could be deported at any time the president deemed it necessary. If any person who had been removed should return to the United States voluntarily, he could be imprisoned for life and kept at hard labor.

The new bill also incorporated from the original those provisions which required captains of incoming ships to report the number of aliens on board his vessel. The courts of the United States were to be given cognizance of offenses against the act, and the enforcement was placed in the hands of "all marshals and other officers of the United States." A temporary measure, the bill was to expire two years after its enactment.[12]

In a much-quoted letter, Alexander Hamilton cautioned his fellow Federalists not to be cruel or violent in framing their alien policy. Although this letter to Secretary of State Pickering is invariably cited as evidence of Hamilton's opposition to the Alien Friends Law, the Federalist leader did not suggest that the Senate's rigorous bill should be dropped. Instead, he assumed that an anti-alien measure would be adopted and asked the president's leading adviser, "What policy in execution is likely to govern the *Executive?*" He personally favored a vigorous enforcement policy. "My opinion," he informed Pickering, who became the chief enforcement officer of the Alien and Sedition Laws, "is that the mass [of aliens] ought to be obliged to leave the country." He suggested two exceptions, however, to his proposed policy of mass removal. "The provisions in

---

[12] Although the text of the revised bill is not given in the *Annals,* it and the original manuscript bill are preserved in the Senate Records, 5C, 2S, RG 46 (National Archives). For Mason's amendment, see *Annals,* 5C, 2S (June 8, 1798), 575.

a Treaty in favor of Merchants," he wrote, "ought to be observed and there ought to be *guarded* exceptions of characters whose situations would expose them too much if sent away and whose demeanor among us has been unexceptionable. There are a few such. Let us not be cruel or violent." [13]

This letter gives an excellent insight into the Federalists' views of cruelty and violence as applied to aliens. Hamilton did not object to the section in the Senate bill which provided that any alien could be deported without trial by jury or to the one which stipulated that any alien who returned to the United States in violation of a removal order might be imprisoned for life at hard labor without trial by jury. His sole remedy for the cruelty of the bill was protection for merchants and for the "few" aliens whose demeanor had been "unexceptionable." Hamilton, himself alien-born, apparently thought that it would be neither cruel nor violent to uproot the mass of peaceable aliens in the United States and deport them.[14]

When the Senate alien friends bill was sent down to the House on June 8, that body was considering similar legislation of its own. The earliest advocate in the House of a policy directed against alien friends as well as against alien enemies was Senator Hillhouse's Connecticut colleague, Congressman John Allen. On May 3, a day before the Senate committee reported its measure, Allen proposed that the House alien enemy bill should be altered in order to allow federal action against any and all aliens. Denouncing the Connecticut extremist as sick in the head, Sewall denied the need for such strong action. At the same time, however, he pointed out that the Defense Committee had reported only in part, and he promised further action against American citizens as well as aliens.

In the discussion of the naturalization and alien enemy legislation which followed, Allen's extremism gained support from the two rising leaders of the Federalist party, Harper and Otis. Their demands for ever more restrictive measures goaded the Defense Committee to ask the House to approve the consideration of measures against "the danger which may result by means of aliens and other

[13] Hamilton to Pickering, June 7, 1798, Pickering Papers, XXII, 196. This text of the original varies slightly from that given in *Hamilton's Works* (Lodge ed.), VIII, 490.

[14] Nearly a month earlier, John Jay, governor of New York and former chief justice of the United States Supreme Court, had approved the Senate's original alien act. Jay to Pickering, May 13, 1798, Henry P. Johnston, ed., *The Correspondence and Public Papers of John Jay* (New York and London, 1890–93), IV, 241. Hamilton's letter, however, dealt with the Senate's revision of the even more drastic original bill.

disaffected or seditious persons residing within the United States."
On May 18 this grant of power was agreed to without debate or
division.[15]

The administration party was now in a position to carry out the
program which one of the "war" Federalists had outlined as early as
April. With the passage of the Naturalization Law on May 22 and
the recommitment of the alien enemies bill the next day, the House
Defense Committee turned its attention to implementing its new
power over "aliens and other disaffected or seditious persons." On
June 4 the committee reported an omnibus alien and sedition bill "for
the prevention and restraint of dangerous and seditious practices."
The first section proposed that an alien might be apprehended and
deported as a dangerous person if he had been convicted of a felony or other infamous crime in his native country or in the United
States, if he was a notorious fugitive from justice in any foreign
country upon any charge of treasonable or seditious practices, or if
the president thought that his continued residence was injurious to
the public peace and safety. Penalties also were proposed for both
aliens and citizens guilty of seditious words or actions. The ever-
watchful Jefferson informed Madison that this bill and the Senate's
alien bill were both "so palpably in the teeth of the Constitution as
to show they mean to pay no respect to it." [16]

The assignment of these powers was certain to awaken public
alarm and arouse intense opposition. A correspondent of the *Aurora*
wrote that he had seen an American medal in Peale's Museum with
the motto "Liberty and Security" on one side and another maxim on
the milled edge: "*An asylum for the oppressed of all nations.*" "The
gilding of this coin," he wrote, "is a little worn off and evidently shows
base metal beneath." Another writer inserted an ironical paragraph
addressed to the Irish emigrants who had fled from "the British
bayonet and halter." To such refugees the correspondent gave this
advice: instead of coming to the United States with its restrictive
alien legislation, you ought to consider moving to a place "where
your love of country and a hatred to tyranny, will not subject you
to transportation without a trial by jury." He suggested that aliens
might escape the bill by forming a colony on the coast of Africa.
"The Hottentots," he concluded sarcastically, "are a hospitable people." At least, Bache wrote a few days later, aliens would not be
punished because they were suspected of being suspicious.[17]

[15] *Annals*, 5C, 2S, 1725, 1771.

[16] *Ibid.*, 1868; Jefferson to Madison, June 7, 1798, *Jefferson's Writings* (Ford
ed.), VII, 266–267.

[17] *Aurora*, May 29, June 8, 14, 1798.

When the House omnibus bill came up for discussion on June 16, the Republicans fought its alien provisions because they feared that the deportation features of the bill would be made applicable later to any citizen whom the Federalists might consider "dangerous." All the Federalists backed the bill except Allen. Although this was the toughest control bill yet introduced in the House, the Connecticut extremist did not think that it went far enough. There was no need, he argued, to clutter up the statute books with so many laws dealing with aliens. This bill aimed at alien friends, while another bill dealt with alien enemies. Provisions should be made for the removal of these persons, but he preferred his proposal of May 3 which would give the president control over "aliens of every description, without distinction." The new bill was of a confused nature, he argued, authorizing the president to expel aliens but not specifying the role of the courts. Would they make the removal? If so, in what manner would it be done? Although the Constitution guaranteed to all persons a right to trial by jury, this bill seemed to authorize summary action. How would the government determine whether aliens had been felons or notorious fugitives from justice in a foreign country? How would the persons of these aliens be identified?

Allen's solution for these difficulties made it clear that his objections to the bill came not from its lack of personal safeguards. He feared that the discretionary power which the bill granted to the president might be hampered by such procedural and constitutional niceties as trial by jury and by interminable delays in determining whether an alien had been a felon. This bad bill, which conferred upon the president powers of "an unlimited, confused nature," could become a good bill by eliminating the elements of confusion and leaving the president with unlimited power over all aliens. Allen therefore proposed that Congress should simply authorize "the Executive of this country, as in all other countries, to remove all aliens, of whatever country, who he deemed dangerous to the peace of the country." This could best be done, he concluded, by replacing the House seditious practices bill with the Senate alien friends bill.

Once again Chairman Sewall defended the Defense Committee's work. Stressing the distinction between alien friends and alien enemies, he urged that the arrest of aliens, merely because they were aliens, would be an act unworthy of any civilized nation whatever. His committee had kept this distinction in mind in framing separate legislation for alien enemies and alien friends. He conceded, however, that both bills were designed to deal with aliens when they became dangerous to the public peace and safety. Thus, alien enemies who were not suspected of being inimical to the interests of the country would not be removed, while alien friends whose residence would be likely to be injurious to the safety of the country might be deported. Agreeing with Sewall, the House adjourned without substituting the Senate's measure for its own omnibus bill.[18]

A singular series of circumstances, however, conspired to cause the House to reverse this stand and follow Allen's suggestion rather than Sewall's. On the same day that Allen recommended the substitution of the Senate bill for the House measure, the *Aurora,* most influential of the Democratic newspapers, published a letter from Talleyrand to the State Department before the government released a copy of its text.[19] The Federalists viewed this as proof of a direct pipeline between the French Directory and its American "agents." When the House reconvened on June 18, it postponed its omnibus bill and went into a committee of the whole on the Senate's more drastic alien friends bill. Before debate got under way, however, the House received a message from President Adams transmitting the eighth dispatch from the special envoys to France. This document, claimed the Federalists, was an incontrovertible answer to Talleyrand's letter and should be published to the people to counteract the machinations of the Directory and its agents in the United States. After some debate, ten thousand copies of the whole of the XYZ dispatches were ordered printed for public distribution.[20]

Marshall arrived in Philadelphia on the same day that Adams communicated the envoys' messages. These events of the eighteenth spurred the House into speedy action against aliens. It promptly substituted the Senate's bill for its own and, after debates on June 19 and 20, passed the act on June 21. This action coincided with President Adams' announcement that he would never send another minister to France without assurances of his proper reception. On June 22 the Senate approved the House amendments, and with the president's approval on June 25 the Alien Friends Act became the law of the land, exactly one week after the Naturalization Law. From the fateful weekend of June 16–18, the Federalist extremists held control of the House until the end of the session.

Yet the Federalists in the House were not as tough as those in the more aristocratic Senate. Perhaps this was because they had more able opponents, who were better led and greater in numbers. Nonetheless, the Republicans fought a losing battle against the bill. Gallatin failed in his attempt to strike out the section which gave the

[18] *Annals,* 5C, 2S (June 16, 1798), 1970–1971.   [19] *Aurora,* June 16, 1798.
[20] *Annals,* 5C, 2S (June 18, 1798), 1972–1973.

president discretionary power to order the deportation of aliens whom he suspected of being dangerous to the public safety or of being engaged in treasonable machinations against the government.

Although the Republicans failed in this frontal attack, the Federalists in the House made two important alterations in the Senate bill. Harper suggested that aliens who returned to the United States after having been removed should not be "confined to hard labor for and during life" but should be imprisoned only "during the pleasure of the United States." He thought it improper to treat suspected aliens as common felons, sentenced to life imprisonment at hard labor.[21] After considerable debate, Harper agreed to amend his motion so as to strike from the bill only those references to hard labor, while leaving the length of the sentence at life. The president, it was argued, could always shorten it by using his pardoning power.

Thomas Claiborne agreed that the American code of justice should not be stained with the hard labor provision as it stood in the Senate bill. The Virginia Republican therefore favored Harper's amendment as a means of ameliorating the punishment which otherwise would be "fitter for the code of Algiers than of America." He thought it sufficient if enemies of the country were either removed or confined. So did most of the House which accepted Harper's amendment.

Otis, the other cosponsor of the bill in the House, also proposed a new section. He moved a declaratory provision to affirm that it would be lawful for any alien ordered out of the country "to take any part of his goods with him, and if he leaves any property behind him, that it shall be subject to his order as much as if he remained in the country." He had information from the president of the Bank of the United States and from several merchants that aliens had "withdrawn their money from that and other banks . . . [in Philadelphia] to a considerable amount." These persons, he said, had been led to believe that if the government did not now seize their property, it would do it later. "As he looked upon all laws which went to a seizure of the property of aliens, as barbarous, he wished to introduce a section into this bill which shall show to this class of men that it is not the intention of the Legislature of the Union to touch their property."

Despite the opposition of the most nativistic of the Federalists,[22]

[21] *Ibid.*, 1973–1983, 1998.

[22] *Ibid.*, 1999–2002. Nathaniel Smith of Connecticut claimed that the amendment was unnecessary because the federal government could seize the property of "peaceable aliens" in time of peace, "anything in this law notwithstanding." *Ibid.* Just where he got this idea is difficult to say; the government could not confiscate the property of friendly aliens even in time of war.

Otis' amendment received strong backing in the Committee of the Whole. Harper, Bayard, and John Rutledge led the Federalists, with Gallatin and Samuel Smith speaking for the Republicans. Samuel Smith thought it a proper measure to quiet the minds of aliens, "for, when power is given to the president to seize and send out of the country any alien whom he pleases, they may reasonably be afraid of their property, as well as their persons." Since aliens could be deported without a moment's notice, they would have no time to look after their property.

Although Harper thought the fears of these aliens were unfounded, he had no objection to tying the hands of the government in this respect because "it never could be good policy for Government to lay its hands arbitrarily upon the property of individuals." He was certain that aliens would be perfectly safe without the declaration, but if they would be better satisfied with it, he wished to gratify them. Bayard agreed that the almost unlimited power conferred on the president made it necessary to incorporate the guarantee, "for what alien could say, however good his intentions may be, that the President may not be imposed upon, and that he may not be subject to the operations of this law, and sent out of the country." With the leaders of the Federalists conceding the need of some curb on executive authority over aliens, the issue could not long remain in doubt. Otis' amendment became section five of the alien friends bill passed by the House.[23]

After being reported from the Committee of the Whole, these amendments were accepted by the House, and one new amendment was added on the floor. Robert Williams, North Carolina Republican, proposed to change the length of the sentence from life to "so long as, in the opinion of the President . . . the public safety shall require it." This had been a part of Harper's original motion, but his amended proposition eliminated only the references to hard labor, thus leaving the length of the sentence at life. Williams was one of the leading opponents of the discretionary power which the bill vested in the president, but he swallowed his objections because the change which he proposed actually reduced the rigor of the bill, even though it increased the discretionary power of the president. The House's adoption of the Williams amendment tempered the severity of the Senate bill, by reducing the sentence against aliens who returned to the United States without the permission of the president. Instead of

[23] The *Annals* erroneously report that Otis' motion was negatived, 43 to 32. *Ibid.*, 2002.

being imprisoned for life at hard labor, they would be confined only as long as the public safety required.[24]

The Alien Friends Law was a temporary peacetime act designed to give the president extraordinary power over aliens. So far as they were concerned, it established the concept of guilt by suspicion for a two-year period. The chief executive could order the deportation of any foreigner who he judged was dangerous to the peace and safety of the United States or who he had reasonable grounds to suspect was concerned in any treasonable or secret machinations against the government. He could condemn any alien without hearing any evidence in his behalf and without setting forth the reasons for his finding. His order, however, was to specify the amount of time to be allowed an alien to depart. If the person was apprehended within the United States after the expiration of that time, he was to be forcibly deported or tried for violation of the president's expulsion order. If convicted, he could be imprisoned up to three years and barred from citizenship forever.

Not until the alien had been notified that he must leave the country could he present evidence in his behalf. If the prospective deportee could prove to the president's satisfaction that no injury or danger to the United States would result from his continued residence, the chief executive could issue him a license to remain in the United States. This meant, as the New York Republican, Edward Livingston, pointed out, that the alien would have to prove that the president had been wrong when he first decided that the alien was dangerous. If the license was issued, the president had discretionary power to determine how long, and at what place of residence, the licensed alien might remain in the United States. He could also direct the alien to post bond and obtain sufficient sureties for his good behavior during his residence under the license. A violation of the permit subjected the offender to a prison term not exceeding three years and a perpetual ineligibility for American citizenship. Finally, the license was revocable at the president's pleasure.

Section four of the act made an interesting distinction between crimes and offenses. Aliens were guilty of an "offense" if they gave reasonable grounds for suspicion or were judged dangerous by the president; the penalty was deportation. If they left as ordered, they were not "punished"; their departure resulted from their "offense" of being suspected or dangerous. If they did not leave when ordered

[24] The bill passed the House by a vote of 46 to 40. *Ibid.*, 2028–2029. It became law on June 25, 1798.

to do so, they committed a "crime" and upon apprehension could be forcibly deported or tried and imprisoned. Another provision stipulated that if any deportee should return voluntarily to the United State without the president's permission, he could be tried and, if convicted, sentenced to imprisonment "so long as, in the opinion of the president, the public safety may require." [25]

Although the Naturalization Act had been on the lawbooks but a week, the Alien Law tightened up its registration provisions by requiring ship masters to report the number of aliens brought into the United States. After July 1, 1798, commanders of incoming vessels were to make a written report to the customs officer immediately upon their arrival. These officials were to forward copies of the reports to the secretary of state's office, thus furnishing a master list which could be used to check whether or not the incoming aliens had registered within forty-eight hours of their arrival, as the Naturalization Act required.

[25] See *Stat. at L.,* I, 570. Although the act provided that the alien was to receive a trial for the offense of returning without the president's permission, it allowed the president, not the courts, to determine the length of the sentence. If the president thought it necessary for the public safety, he also could order the deportation of aliens who were in prison for violating the act.

CHAPTER V

Xenophobia: The Debates on the Alien Friends Law

A stitch in time saves nine.—Old Proverb

THE debates on the Alien Friends Act consumed less than two days of the House's time. From the beginning they concentrated on the technical issue of whether the Constitution delegated control over aliens to the federal government or whether that power had been retained by the state governments. The overbearing attitude of the Federalist majority, especially after June 18, soon made it apparent that they meant to pass the law, no matter what kind of arguments were raised against it.[1]

During the discussion, the Federalists attempted to reverse the burden of argument. Instead of forcing the proponents of the bill to defend its constitutionality, James A. Bayard declared, the opponents of the bill should show that the bill was not necessary for the safety of the country. Not only was the proposed action constitutional; emergency measures were absolutely necessary to cope with the national crisis. "The times are full of danger," Otis urged, "and it would be the height of madness not to take every precaution in our power." Gordon agreed that uncommon circumstances made action mandatory. Uncommon measures therefore were justifiable. The government need not await open action by dangerous aliens; potential subversives should be expelled upon suspicion. "Persons who come here with a view of overturning the Government," he con-

[1] Henry Adams, *The Life of Albert Gallatin* (Philadelphia, 1880), 206.

tinued, "will not commit any overt act which shall bring them under the laws of the country." [2]

Otis readily admitted that no proof "positive and direct" existed of any danger from alien friends, but he agreed that aliens of suspicious character should be deported before they had a chance to do harm.[3] The French system of espionage, he reiterated, was the cause of her victories and her facility in revolution-making. The crisis called not for nice and unnecessary arguments, but for the most active war preparations, including decisive measures against dangerous aliens. Thus the Federalists set forth two diametrically opposed challenges to the Republicans: (1) Bayard asked them to show that the alien bill was unnecessary, and (2) Otis claimed that the crisis was so pressing that arguments on the necessity of the bill were unnecessary.

The Republicans naturally chose Bayard's alternative. If anyone possessed facts which demonstrated the necessity of the use of arbitrary means against aliens, Gallatin asserted, he should lay them before the House. But if no evidence were produced, the Republicans had a right to say that no necessity existed for the alien bill. The Federalists must have facts unknown to him, the Republican leader continued, or they would be unjustified in creating a groundless alarm. But their failure to produce any evidence of plots led the Republicans to fear the worst. Nothing was more common, Williams pointed out, than for a government to institute an alarm of some sort of danger whenever it wanted "to make inroads upon the liberties of the people." The Constitution would be a very slender security to the rights of the people if, on the cry of there being a danger here or seditious persons there, it was violated in order to meet the hypothetical evil. He hoped that "vain and idle insinuations" of dangers and seditions would not alarm the House into a violation of the Constitution which they were sworn to support. The stories about secret plots and conspiracies, the existence of a French press in the United States, and a dangerous correspondence between American citizens and the French Directory, said McDowell, were "founded in that spirit of alarm which had been so long kept up, and . . . trumped up for the purpose of assisting the passage of this bill." Men who were guilty neither of treason nor sedition would probably be banished under the Alien Friends Act.[4]

[2] *Annals*, 5C, 2S (June 19, 1798), 1985–1986.

[3] *Ibid.*, 1987–1989. This action, Otis added, would be "in the nature of a punishment for supposed offences." This contradicts another Federalist argument that deportation was not punishment.

[4] *Ibid.*, 1980, 1995, 1964, 2021.

From the complexion of the alien bill, Livingston added, one would be led to believe that "a number of aliens, enjoying the protection of our Government, were plotting its destruction; that they are engaged in treasonable machinations against a people who have given them asylum and support, and that there is no provision for their expulsion and punishment." Were these the circumstances which brought the bill into existence?

To this rhetorical question, Livingston replied that the Federalists had failed to prove any danger. Even if they had, "the wise laws . . . upright judges and vigilant magistrates" of the United States would be competent to punish every treasonable or seditious attempt whether committed by alien friends or by citizens.[5] Gallatin pointed out that if the present laws were insufficient to reach every case, they might be amended. If it became necessary to send persons out of the country because of their offenses, he believed that laws would be framed for the purpose of punishing them. But all crimes and punishments should be accurately defined; offenders should not be left without trial, subject to the arbitrary control of one man. Moreover, if the Federalists could give reasons for an alien law, the states would be as ready to take the new action as would the general government. This was peculiarly so in view of the fact that it was the duty of the states rather than the United States.[6]

If spies or foreign agents could be pointed out, McDowell agreed that he would favor a law defining their crime and punishment, although he believed imprisonment afforded as much protection to the United States as did banishment. He traced the bill to "a strong aversion which at present exists against France and Frenchmen." But Samuel Smith, Maryland Republican, pointed out its wider applicability. He fully expected war with France in less than a month; then all French immigrants would become enemy aliens. The Alien Friends Act, therefore, "would fall upon German, English, and Irish emigrants." Most of these had become state citizens, but had not yet become citizens of the United States. They usually became very useful citizens, and to subject them to deportation without trial, even though they might have completed nearly all of their five-year residence term, seemed unfair to Smith. Yet this could be done "on the information of any evil disposed person."[7]

The Federalists also made extensive use of historical arguments to support the need of taking steps to nip the alien danger in the bud. Otis cited the countries overthrown by revolutionary France

[5] *Ibid.*, 2006–2007. It should be noted that Livingston distinguished between criminal attempt and mere suspicion of danger.
[6] *Ibid.*, 1980, 1983.   [7] *Ibid.* (June 20, 1798), 2021–2023.

since 1793, and asserted that "French apostles of sedition" had laid
the groundwork for the fall of Holland and Switzerland. "Do we
not know, said he, that the French nation have organized bands of
aliens as well as their own citizens, in other countries, to bring
about their nefarious purposes. . . . By these means they have over-
run all the republics in the world but our own. . . . And may we
not expect the same means to be employed against this country? We
certainly might," Otis concluded. The fate of the fallen furnished
"sufficient reason to be alarmed" with French espionage and intrigue. If the American people were strongly attached to their government, so too had been the Dutch and the Swiss. While he did not
expect that the people would be lured into any revolutionary projects
to increase their liberty, he was not so sure what they would do in
response to the efforts of French agents to foment a fear that they
might lose what liberty they already enjoyed.[8]

The Federalists' fears of a conspiracy to overturn the government
and place it under a foreign yoke, Gallatin replied, seemed to be
based more on what had taken place in other countries than on any
existing danger in the United States. Their frequent appeal to the
fate of Holland, Switzerland, and Venice meant that the Federalists
had been "led away by imaginary fears, or wished to improve the
temporary alarm they had themselves created, for the purpose of
assuming and exercising arbitrary power over a few obnoxious persons." In the first place, neither the revolution in Holland nor that
in Switzerland had been engineered by resident alien friends, as the
Federalists claimed. In both, an invading enemy and citizens of the
revolutionized country had carried out the overthrow. But the act
being debated applied not to aliens as enemies; the House was
remodeling another bill for that purpose. In the second place, when
the Federalists reasoned from analogy, they had to do more than
argue that merely because certain events had happened in another
country they would take place in the United States. Had they proved
that resident aliens caused the downfall of foreign countries, Livingston noted, they would have had to "show that we are in the same
situation; or that any such plots have been detected, or are even
reasonably suspected here." [9]

The Federalists had pushed their argument by analogy one step
further. England, they claimed, had not been overthrown by the

[8] *Ibid.* (June 19, 1798), 1988–1989.

[9] *Ibid.* (June 20, 1798), 2006, 2027. For a recent scholarly confirmation of
Gallatin's historical summary, see R. R. Palmer, "Much in Little: The Dutch
Revolution of 1795," *Journal of Modern History*, 26 (1954), 15–35.

domineering spirit of France because she had passed anti-alien laws. "Unless we follow their example," Harper urged, "we shall not, like them, escape the scourge which awaits us." [10]

Samuel Smith replied that while the Republicans might admit that this action "was wise conduct in Great Britain (which he was far from doing) what was wise in their situation would not apply to ours." The proceedings of societies and individuals who favored a change in the British constitution to allow parliamentary reform, Gallatin conceded, gave England at least some pretext for her alien and sedition laws. But that was no reason why the United States should imitate Great Britain's legislative example at the outbreak of her war with France. In the United States "no change in the Constitution was desired by any set of men, no symptoms of disaffection had appeared anywhere." Instead, the administration seemed to have gained ground, and their measures had never been supported by "stronger symptoms of approbation." Moreover, added Samuel Smith, the United States had needed no laws against aliens to get through the Revolution, and foreign influence "was much more to be dreaded at that time than at the present." [11]

The Federalists, Livingston concluded, had used two arguments to demonstrate the necessity of the law. The first was the "plot" which Harper had referred to on June 18; the other was the foreign examples cited by Otis. The Republican spokesman asserted that neither of these arguments was sufficient to sustain the necessity of the proposed legislation. No plot had been detected, nor was any reasonably suspected. Indeed, Harper had done no more than promise to follow up his clue in an attempt to "destroy this monster of sedition." Yet he had failed to reveal the hiding place of that lurking beast. Legislation, the New Yorker insisted, should be based "upon facts, not on surmises," "on evidence, not vague suspicions." The alien friends bill, he concluded, was based on nothing more sub-

[10] *Annals*, 5C, 2S (June 19, 1798), 1992. For an interesting analysis of the close connection between American and British policy on internal security measures, see Dauer, *The Adams Federalists*, 157–159. The influence of *The French Revolution in English History* is discussed by Philip A. Brown (London, 1918).

[11] *Annals*, 5C, 2S, 2022–2027. Gallatin, unlike the Federalists, made the vital distinction between the Constitution and the administration which ran the government under its authority. When the Federalists spoke of the government, they failed to distinguish between the form of government as ordained by the Constitution and the administration of that government. Thus when they spoke of the "overthrow" of the government, they meant the defeat of the administration at the polls, as well as the possible change in the form of government. As a matter of fact, they feared that the former would bring the latter.

stantial than individual suspicions, private fears, and overheated imaginations.[12]

The Republican challenges to the bill set the limits of the debate. Their approach to the problem of control over aliens led them to focus their discussion on this basic constitutional question: Does the federal government, Gallatin asked, have any power to deport alien friends? They denied federal power on four grounds. First, they objected that the power to expel alien friends was neither delegated to Congress nor implied by any delegated power. By the Tenth Amendment it was reserved to the states or to the people. In the second place, even if this power had been delegated, it could not be exercised before 1808 because of the ban on congressional action against migration until that time. Moreover, even if Congress could remove aliens before 1808, the alien friends bill violated personal guarantees of the Constitution by its arbitrary procedures. Finally, the Jeffersonians condemned the bill as inexpedient, unwise, and unnecessary.

All the Federalists agreed that the proposal was a necessary and proper preparedness measure, but there was considerable variation in their reasons as to just where the government got its power over immigrants. Since all the alien bills were introduced into the House by the Committee on the Defense of the Country and for the Protection of Commerce, it was not unusual that the arguments in favor of congressional power should reflect the concerns of the committee drafting the legislation. Rephrasing Gallatin's inquiry, the Federalists asked whether Congress did not have the power to provide for the common defense and the general welfare. If the proposed bill served these purposes, then it was within the power of Congress. They did not deny that Congress had not been delegated the power to remove alien friends, but they argued that this authority was implied in various grants of power, ranging from the inherent right of every sovereign nation to preserve itself to the right to regulate commerce. If Congress did not have the power of restraining seditious persons and of expelling dangerous aliens, the Federalists strenuously contended, it did not have the power to promote the general welfare by preserving peace and to provide for the common defense through an efficient prosecution of a war.[13]

Some Federalists cited the Preamble to the Constitution as the

[12] *Annals*, 5C, 2S, 2006–2007.
[13] *Ibid.* (June 16, 1798), 1955, 1959–1960.

source of federal power over aliens. Sewall quoted it at the start of his argument:

We, the People of the United States, in Order to form a more perfect Union, establish Justice, insure domestic Tranquility, provide for the common defence, promote the general Welfare, and secure the Blessings of Liberty to ourselves and our Posterity, do ordain and establish this Constitution for the United States of America.

These words established the sovereignty of the United States, Sewall said, "and that sovereignty must reside in the government of the United States." Congress therefore had the power to provide for the general welfare and internal tranquillity, and if the residence of any aliens in the United States would be likely, in the opinion of Congress, to endanger the public peace and tranquillity, Congress could take such measures respecting them as they thought fit.[14]

That the Preamble should be interpreted as a grant of power to the federal government was a proposition too far-reaching not to provoke an instant rebuttal from the Republicans. If it conferred any power, they maintained, it would swallow up the rest of the Constitution. Congress, said Williams, would be all-powerful, and the state governments would have no power at all.[15] Several of the general provisions in the Preamble had been contained in the Articles of Confederation, Gallatin pointed out, including the right to provide for the general defense. Because the general powers relating to the common defense were nearly similar under the Articles and the Constitution, Gallatin thought that the opinion of the old Congress, in relation to their authority, was applicable to the claims of the present Congress under the authority of the Preamble of the Constitution. Although the old Congress could have claimed, as the Federalists were now doing, that its general defense powers gave it a power over aliens, it had not legislated on this subject of alien control, but instead had requested the states to act.

In asserting that the Preamble established national sovereignty and

[14] *Ibid.*, 1957–1958. Note that the Federalists, at least on this occasion, argued that sovereignty resided not in the people but in Congress. Speaker Dayton, the only Federalist in the House who had participated in the Constitutional Convention, agreed that the great object of the Constitution had been to provide for the general welfare and common defense, and he said that this would have been considered so even if the Preamble had not declared it. *Ibid.*, 1994.

[15] *Ibid.*, 1962. In *Jacobsen* v. *Massachusetts*, 197 US 11 (1905), the Supreme Court ruled that the Preamble confers neither governmental power nor private right.

that that sovereignty resided in Congress, the Federalists overlooked
the basic fact set forth in the Preamble—the fact that the Constitution is ordained and established by "We, the people of the United
States." Sovereignty, a word not mentioned in the Constitution, resides not in Congress but in the people. Furthermore, the Federalists,
by concentrating their attention on those portions mentioning only
the common defense, the general welfare, and domestic tranquillity,
also overlooked two other important objects of the Constitution as
set forth in the Preamble, "establish Justice" and "secure the Blessings of Liberty to ourselves and our Posterity." Measures to insure
domestic tranquillity could be pushed so far as to snuff out liberty
and create grave injustices.

Of the six purposes mentioned in the Preamble, Otis and his Federalist colleagues designated the defense clause as the most important function of the Constitution; it alone dealt with the "sacred
and superior duty of providing for the safety of the country." If
anything in the Constitution appeared to bear a different construction—and this Otis denied—it ought to be reconciled to this supreme
power. Without this power, he contended, all efforts against France
would prove vain and futile. If the individual states claimed any
specific power, such as control over dangerous aliens, which was inconsistent with this general power of the nation, their claim must
vanish before the obligation of the general government to provide
for the common defense.[16]

"If we find men in this country," Otis continued, "endeavoring to
spread sedition and discord; who have assisted in laying other countries prostrate; whose hands are reeking with blood, and whose
hearts rankle with hatred towards us—have we not the power to
shake off these firebrands?" If the states, rather than Congress, exercised control over aliens, they might retain a number of men
whose residence had been provably dangerous to the safety of the
United States. Under such a system of control, these persons,
"stamped with infamy in their own country, and plotting treasons
against ours, must remain in some part of the territory of the United
States, while congress has not the power to get rid of them until
all the States concur in the same object." He argued that a government which could not exercise an authority which might be necessary to its existence was little better than no government at all. The
Constitution, he concluded, would not be worth a farthing if it prevented Congress from restraining and banishing suspected aliens.

"What power is reserved by the Constitution to the States," said

[16] *Annals*, 5C, 2S (June 19, 1798), 1986.

Dana, ". . . is for reasons which are applicable to those States," but "what relates to the Union generally must be done by the Government of the United States." [17] The common defense and general welfare clauses, he said, relate to the Union generally. Therefore, the state governments, which had no knowledge of foreign relations, nor of the common defense of the Union, could not act in these fields. Otis agreed that the Constitution was designed to embrace all exterior relations. "The provisions of the Constitution," said Otis, "were plain and adequate to all the exigencies of the nation." [18]

Several of the Federalists transcended the Constitution and sought the power to expel aliens in the sovereign power of self-preservation. "There is one power," Dana declared, "inherent and common in every form of Government. . . . The power of preserving itself . . . implies the necessary power of making all laws which are proper for this purpose." He thought that a law for removing dangerous aliens was consistent with that power, and Harper agreed that the federal government could not exist without it. He did not think that "though we see the knife of the traitor held to our throats, we are to wait until the States Governments come and snatch it away." [19]

The Republicans did not deny the Federalists' major premise that every nation possessed an inherent right to permit or exclude aliens from entering their society, but they did deny that the Constitution granted that power to the federal government. Instead, they insisted that the exclusive control over aliens belonged to the individual states. Thus both sides sent their forces foraging among the clauses of the Constitution to bring back arguments which would buttress their position. The Federalists were hard put because none of the delegated powers of the general government touched upon the control of alien friends. The Republicans, however, relied heavily on the Tenth Amendment, which said that all rights not delegated to the federal government, nor prohibited to the states, were reserved to the states or to the people. They claimed that under the federal system devised by the Constitution the provisions of the alien friends bill were unconstitutional. The power to banish or remove aliens was not delegated to Congress, and the states were not prohibited from regulating or restraining the residence of aliens. All the Federalist spokesmen had tried to show that Congress possessed its power by implication. The Republicans did not deny the doctrine of implied powers, but they reminded their opponents that they had to

[17] *Ibid.*, 1987; 1969 (June 16, 1798).   [18] *Ibid.* (June 19, 1798), 1986.
[19] *Ibid.*, 1970, 1983, 2025–2026, 1990, 1969.

prove the law was necessary and proper for carrying into effect some specific power expressly given by the Constitution.[20]

Gallatin launched a vigorous attack on the Federalist position that Congress possessed a right to expel alien friends because its right to provide for the common defense was superior to and absorbed all other powers and because it had inherent general powers which made it equal to any possible exigency which might arise. Did Otis and his colleagues really mean that if the nation's power of providing for the common defense or for its self-preservation was limited, the Constitution would not be worth having, as Otis had said? Did they like it only for the powers it gave, and not for the restraints it put on power? Their claim was so general that the Republican leader could not understand it unless they defined it more closely. If they meant that all powers should be vested in the general government because something might possibly occur which might call for the exercise of them, he denied it. The Constitution set limits to the powers of the government. Congress could not suspend the right of habeas corpus except in cases of rebellion or invasion. But what if it were thought necessary to suspend that right even though neither an invasion nor a rebellion had taken place? He observed that Great Britain had claimed in 1793 that a dangerous conspiracy existed against the government and had justified the suspension of its habeas corpus act as necessary to meet the situation effectively. If Otis argued on the same ground, he could claim, as Harper had, that a dangerous conspiracy existed in the United States. But if Otis moved a suspension of the right of habeas corpus as necessary to meet this "conspiracy," Gallatin continued, the Constitution would block such a motion because it stipulated that "it shall not be suspended, but in cases of actual rebellion or invasion." If this was what Otis meant, Gallatin concluded that the government could not do everything which the Federalists might suppose necessary.

If Otis' general statement meant that Congress ought to exercise all the powers that might be vested in government, Gallatin continued, the Constitution rejected this view by recognizing a division of powers between the federal and state governments. In the case of regulations dealing with aliens, Congress possessed the power to declare war and to punish persons guilty of treasonable practices, but it had no cognizance over aliens as suspicious characters. This matter, he maintained, remained with the state governments, and he had no doubt that they would pass a law on the subject if one were necessary.[21]

The Federalists, however, continued to argue that if Congress had

20 *Ibid.*, 1974. Also see Williams' remarks, *ibid.*, 1995.   21 *Ibid.*, 1977.

the right to defend the Union, it also had a right to prepare for defense by ejecting suspicious aliens without awaiting a declaration of war. This time Otis went into the body of the Constitution instead of relying on the Preamble or an extraconstitutional inherent power. He referred to the taxation clause which gives Congress the "Power to lay and collect Taxes . . . to pay the debts and provide for the common Defense and general Welfare of the United States." Wars, he said, were waged "for the common defence and general welfare." The ends to be served by the taxation clause, therefore, were defense and welfare; the taxing power was merely the means to promote these ends. Moreover, all the other powers given to Congress were equally for the promotion of the general welfare and common defense. "From the whole section," he argued, "it appeared clear that congress has a right to make war for the common defence and general welfare, and of course to do everything which is necessary to prepare for such a state." Thus a federal law for the expulsion of dangerous aliens in time of peace was justified as a preparedness measure.[22]

In citing the taxation clause as the source of Congress' power over aliens, Harper and Bayard elaborated Otis' argument. Their interpretation, however, dropped all references to taxation and concluded that the general power "is expressly given to Congress to provide for the common defence and general welfare." To this Bayard added the elastic clause so that his final proposition held that "Congress has the power to do what is necessary for the common defence and general welfare." Harper agreed that the general government had a right to pass all necessary laws in pursuance of the common defense and welfare of the United States. "If any of these laws should require certain aliens to be sent out of the country, what has appeared to be necessary for the general welfare cannot be carried into effect if the States have a right to insist upon keeping their aliens." [23]

Thus, the Federalists appealed not only to the nation's inherent right to self-preservation, a special form of "common defense," and to the Preamble of the Constitution, but finally to the powers listed in the Constitution. The common defense and general welfare clauses, not only in the Preamble but also in the taxation clause, were construed as grants of power which Congress could properly implement with an alien friends bill.

The Republicans could no more acquiesce in this interpretation

---

[22] *Ibid.*, 1986.

[23] *Ibid.*, 1965–1967, 1991. It is worth noting that only one of the Federalists made any reference to the word "proper" from the necessary and proper clause. They seemed to assume that anything was proper which they deemed necessary.

of the taxation clause than they could in the Federalist construction of the Preamble. Abraham Baldwin of Georgia, one of the two signers of the Constitution then in the House, and Robert Williams of North Carolina now joined Gallatin in a rebuttal to those relying on the common defense and general welfare clauses as the constitutional props with which to support the punitive alien legislation. Baldwin pointed out that these words never had been considered as a source of legislative power. They had been introduced to limit and describe the other parts of the sentence dealing with the taxing power. The first instance in which Congress had decided that they created no substantive power occurred when the abolition societies petitioned the national legislature claiming that the constitutional power to abolish slavery was derived from the general welfare clause. A lengthy consideration at that time led the House to decide by a large majority that these words could not be relied upon as giving any separate power from that contained in the other part of the sentence. In another instance, Baldwin recalled, Congress had refused to agree that the clause authorized the establishment of "manufactories" for the general welfare.

Gallatin agreed that the "obvious and universally received meaning" of the general welfare and common defense clauses was to define the purpose for which taxes should be laid. If the Constitutional Convention had intended that Congress should have a separate power to provide for the general welfare, aside from the taxation clause, the power would have been given in a separate paragraph. The Pennsylvanian asserted that he had been informed that these words had been inserted in the Constitution as a limitation to the power of laying taxes. After the convention had completed the Constitution, Gouverneur Morris of the Committee on Style had attempted to put these words into a separate paragraph, "so as to create not a limitation, but a distinct power." This trick, however, had been defeated by the vigilance of Roger Sherman of Connecticut. As the words stood in the Constitution, he concluded, they were a limitation and not an extension of powers.[24]

[24] *Ibid.*, 1967–1968, 1976. For this attempt by Morris, see George Mason's account in the *Documentary History of the Constitution* (Washington, 1894–1905), V, 246–247. Max Farrand, *The Records of the Federal Convention of 1787* (New Haven, 1911–37), III, 379, reprints the above speech of Gallatin and says that the episode he refers to "is quite probably" the one related by Mason. For an example of Morris' thinking on the general welfare clause as a separate grant of power, see his remarks to James McHenry on Sept. 6, 1787, Farrand, *Records*, II, 529–530. There is a recent attack on the arguments of Gallatin and the Jeffersonians in William Winslow Crosskey, *Politics and the Constitution in the History of the United States* (Chicago, 1953), I, 395, and II, 1326.

To say that the general welfare requires a thing to be done, said Williams, is not enough to give Congress the power to do it. If it were a subject within the limits of the Constitution, Congress could do it. But if it were a subject which belonged to the states, Congress could not do it no matter how necessary it might be. The general welfare covered much ground, and if the general government had all power to promote it, the state governments and the people would have none. This, however, was a claim that no one could maintain, because it was not denied that state governments and the people retained the powers not delegated to the general government.[25]

Baldwin agreed that the Federalist's interpretation would

do away with all ideas of this being a Federal Government, and that there are State Governments in existence who have their portion of power; for if all the power which is necessary to "provide for the common defence and general welfare," be possessed by the Federal Government, all the State Governments must fall prostrate before it as there will be no power left for them to exercise.

If the taxation clause were to be interpreted so as to give Congress these extensive powers, then the rest of the Constitution was superfluous.[26]

Only once did the Federalists venture to cite a specifically delegated power as implying federal control over aliens. Sewall, chairman of the Committee on Defense and Commerce, left the "common defense" arguments to others and traced Congress' power over aliens to the commerce clause. Since Congress had the right to regulate foreign commerce, and since foreigners generally came here for commercial purposes, he urged that Congress had the power to regulate all foreigners, unless this power was canceled by the migration clause. This article, however, did not interfere with Congress' right to regulate foreigners because it gave Congress a power to impose a tax upon immigrants. Thus it was merely a commercial regulation and came within the powers of Congress to regulate commerce.[27]

[25] *Annals*, 5C, 2S, 1962, 1994–1995. Also see Gallatin's remarks, *ibid.*, 1975.

[26] *Ibid.*, 1968. For a penetrating analysis of the convention's proceedings on the meaning of the terms "common defense and general welfare" as used in the taxation clause, see Madison to Andrew Stevenson, Montpelier, Nov. 17, 1830, *Letters and Other Writings of James Madison* (Congress ed., Philadelphia, 1867), IV, 77; the memorandum Madison drew up at this time (*ibid.*, 131–133); and a supplement to the letters to Stevenson (*ibid.*, 134–137). Also see *Madison's Writings* (Hunt ed.), IX, 413.

[27] *Annals*, 5C, 2S, 1957. This clause, of course, does not give Congress power to tax immigration. Congress' power to impose a tax under this clause was restricted to "imported" persons—that is, slaves.

Both Williams and Gallatin assailed Sewall's argument. That all immigrants should be considered as articles of commerce was not only inconsistent with the Constitution, said Williams, but was inconsistent with any meaning of the word "commerce" that he had ever heard of. Gallatin argued that the bill was of a political, not a commercial, nature and did not relate to aliens as merchants. Any power which Congress might have over alien merchants would have to be exercised as a commercial regulation; it would have to relate to them as merchants—"to their professions, not to their existence as men." Moreover, any commercial power of this sort could not be applied to aliens other than merchants. Nor would this law be necessary for carrying into effect the power to regulate commerce. Its regulations, he concluded, would in no way determine how trade should be carried on with foreign countries or from one state to another.[28]

The Federalists advanced one other line of reasoning almost as tenuous as that based on the commerce clause. On one occasion Sewall traced the power to remove alien enemies not to the power to make war, as he had done in discussing the alien enemies bill, but to Congress' "sovereign power to preserve peace and tranquillity." Moreover, he claimed that this power was so broad that it allowed "Congress to authorize the President to take whatever measures are necessary with respect to aliens, which are not inhuman and improper in themselves." This argument eliminated any distinction between alien friends and alien enemies and opened the way to the most arbitrary action against aliens at any time, provided only that it was not "inhuman and improper." [29]

Gordon, whose nativism rivaled that of John Allen, led the Federalists a step farther in this fancy bit of legerdemain by classifying all aliens as potential enemies. He shifted the discussion of dangerous aliens to a wholly new plane by asserting that aliens were dangerous not in their individual capacity but because they were numerous. He feared that aliens from a nation with whom the United States was at peace might enter through one state, settle all over the country, organize themselves against the government, and "overturn" it. Fortunately, Gordon argued, the general government could regulate these potentially dangerous aliens, even though they came from a friendly country. He based his conclusion on Congress' power to declare war. Since the United States was about to make war on France, Congress had the power to send the "natives of the enemy-country" out of the United States. This could be done even before

[28] *Ibid.*, 1962, 1975.   [29] *Ibid.*, 1959.

the declaration of war, Gordon contended, because if Congress had the power of war, it had the power to do a less hostile act. He then posed this problem:

Suppose, at some future time, there shall be as many aliens of various nations as citizens in the United States; and suppose the United States should be engaged in war with any one of the nations of Europe, might not such a band of men, if suffered to remain, prove the destruction of the country? They certainly might, and no nation would act so unwisely as to give them an opportunity of becoming so.[30]

In other words, a war between the United States and any one of the nations of Europe would be not only a signal for action against alien enemies but would also authorize action against "aliens of various nations." To Gordon there was no such thing as an alien friend. All aliens were potential enemies and therefore could be treated as enemy aliens in time of war, even though they were not from the enemy nation. Moreover, since he had already argued that "natives of the enemy-country" could be deported even before a declaration of war, it followed that any alien could be removed before such a declaration. Since it was within the realm of possibility that at some time in the future the United States might go to war with "any one of the nations of Europe," Gordon's argument meant that the United States government might take steps to remove aliens at any time as potential saboteurs. Deportation was less hostile than war and was therefore authorized by the war power.

The rebuttal of the Republicans to this tortuous line of reasoning was short and to the point. They readily agreed that Congress had the power to remove alien enemies. This resulted from the power to make all laws necessary to carry into effect the specific power of declaring war, including the right of making prisoners of war and of making regulations with respect to alien enemies, who might be treated as prisoners of war. Moreover, Congress could dispose of the persons and property of alien enemies as it thought fit, so long as it followed the laws of nations and its own treaties. But the war power did not give Congress the right to remove alien friends, as Gordon had argued. Nor did the lack of the power to remove alien friends deprive Congress of the right to regulate alien enemies, as Sewall had claimed.

The Republicans got in one last word against Congress' power to

[30] *Ibid.*, 1984. Like Otis and Sewall, Gordon did not cite Congress' specific power to declare war, but claimed that the right to make war was founded on the principle that the safety of the community must be provided for.

enact alien friends legislation, which the Federalists left unanswered. Gallatin claimed that the bill was in conflict with treaty provisions with Holland, Sweden, and Great Britain. Although the alien enemies bill contained a clause allowing enemy aliens a reasonable time for the disposal of their effects, "agreeably to treaty or the law of nations," the alien friends bill provided for the instant expulsion of suspects. Jay's Treaty with Great Britain, the Dutch-American Convention, and the Swedish Treaty provided that in case of a rupture between the signatories nine to twelve months would be allowed for citizens of the enemy country to depart. But the alien friends bill did not allow a suspected person a period of time for preparing to remove. Instead of being a step less hostile than war, it allowed more stringent procedures in peacetime than would have been authorized if there had been a rupture between the United States and these countries.[31]

It was not unusual that the Federalists should have sought their constitutional justifications for the Alien Friends Act in the "common defense" and the commerce clauses. This was to be expected inasmuch as the House committee which shaped all the alien legislation was the Committee on the Defense of the Country and the Protection of Commerce. From their expansive arguments, however, emerged the threat of a centralized state capable of doing anything which the administration in power might think necessary for self-defense. Limitations on federal power were construed into new grants of power, and prohibitions became authorizations. According to Gordon, war powers could be exercised in the absence of war, and all alien friends could be treated as alien enemies even in time of peace. Otis claimed that the broad power to promote the general welfare was so inclusive that it embraced every other power; all powers of the federal government were but means to this general end. Well might the Republicans protest that this power, coupled with the "necessary and proper" clause, would have destroyed the federal system and established an all-powerful centralized nation. As Gallatin pointed out, this construction of the Constitution would have nullified the Tenth Amendment. If all power were delegated

[31] *Ibid.*, 1979–1980. For the provisions of Jay's Treaty, see Article 26 of the Treaty of 1794, *Treaties and Conventions Concluded Between the United States of America and Other Powers Since July 4, 1776* (Washington, 1889), 392–393. Samuel Flagg Bemis, *Jay's Treaty, A Study in Commerce and Diplomacy* (New York, 1923), discusses the treaty's provisions in Chapter XIII, but makes no reference to this article. The other provisions cited by Gallatin are Article 18 of the Treaty with the Netherlands (1782), and Article 12 of the Treaty with Sweden (1783), *Treaties and Conventions*, 754, 1049.

to Congress, then none could be reserved to the states or to the people. Congress would indeed have been sovereign, as Sewall and Dana contended, and the people would have been the creatures of Congress rather than Congress the creation of the people. Congress would have become the master rather than the servant of the people because its field of action would have been all-embracing. Congress, instead of having delegated powers in specified spheres of action, would have extended its sovereignty to all spheres of action that could have been justified by reference to the congressional majority's concept of the general welfare and the common defense.

The Migration or Importation of such Persons as any of the States now existing shall think proper to admit, shall not be prohibited by the Congress prior to the Year one thousand eight hundred and eight, but a Tax or duty may be imposed on such Importation, not exceeding ten dollars for each Person.—Constitution of the United States

The Republicans had tried to show in their basic arguments that Congress was altogether prohibited from passing an alien law because such a power was neither delegated nor implied. After exhausting their ammunition from this front line, they fell back to their second defensive position, claiming that the "migration or importation" clause expressly barred congressional action against alien friends for the time being. The bill, said the Jeffersonians, would give the president the power to remove any alien whom he pleased, and this would amount to the same thing as prohibiting "the migration . . . of such persons as any of the States shall think proper to admit." [32] Thus they claimed that even if federal control over migration and expulsion of aliens could be derived by implication from any of the specific powers of Congress, "whether that of regulating commerce, or declaring war, or of any other, or if it be included in a supposed general power of providing for the common defence and general welfare, even, in that case, its exercise is prohibited to Congress, . . . till the year 1808, and, on this ground, the present bill is also unconstitutional." They could see no difference between a power to expel aliens as soon as they arrived and a power to prevent their admittance upon arrival.

The Federalists first attempted to meet this argument by asserting that the migration clause applied solely to slaves and therefore could not bar congressional action against aliens. While none of

[32] Gallatin, *Annals*, 5C, 2S, 1979–1980; Williams, 1963; Livingston, 2008.

the Republicans denied that the chief concern of the provision was the slave trade, they denied that this was its only purpose. Gallatin and Livingston from the Middle states and Samuel Smith, Robert Williams, and Baldwin from the Southern states argued that it applied to immigrants also. The word *migration,* Gallatin said, as distinguished from the word *importation,* could only apply to free immigrants. The act of migration was a free act of the will. The voluntary arrival of free persons coming to the United States could not be the same act as the arrival of slaves who were brought into the United States without their consent. The word *importation* related exclusively to slaves. Furthermore, the word *persons* in this clause was general and did not exclude free immigrants. Thus, both the words "migration" and "importation" had appropriate meanings and were included to secure the interests of the different quarters of the Union, according to the Republicans. States desiring inhabitants, especially the Middle states, wished to provide against any federal laws which might impede the immigration of settlers, while the Southern states did not want to see the prohibition of the importation of slaves.[33]

The question of encouraging immigration, Gallatin continued, was of local consequence, especially to states with large, thinly populated areas. Their policy had always been to encourage immigration, and he had thought that was the general policy of the United States. "He believed it had only been the violence of party which had created any difference of opinion on the subject." States which attracted few immigrants should be little concerned about immigration unless they sought to check the growth of population in other states in order to keep representative preponderance in their hands. If the bill should pass, ten times as many people in Pennsylvania would be under the arbitrary power of the president as would be "in all the New England States put together." The bill "was not only a refusal to encourage migration, it was a bill to prevent migrations."[34]

Abraham Baldwin, the only Republican then in the House who had helped frame the Constitution, agreed that the clause applied to immigrants as well as slaves. When the 1808 clause was introduced at the Constitutional Convention, he recalled, an objection to the use of the word "slaves" had led to the substitution of this clause that "the migration or importation of such persons as the several

[33] Gallatin, *ibid.,* 1979; the italics are his. Also see Baldwin, 1978–1979; Livingston, 2009; Samuel Smith, 2023, 1964.

[34] *Annals,* 5C, 2S, 1983. Also see McDowell, 2021.

states shall think proper to admit." When some of the delegates observed that this expression would extend to persons other than slaves, he concluded, this was not denied, but neither was any alteration made.[35]

Although they were somewhat confused as to what line of argument to adopt in order to counter the Republican claim that the migration clause prohibited congressional action against aliens prior to 1808, the Federalists denied that it deprived Congress of its power to order the removal of dangerous aliens. The speeches of Sewall and Otis on June 16 illustrate the confused and contradictory arguments advanced by the Federalists. Sewall agreed with the Republicans that the clause applied both to aliens and to slaves, while Otis contended that it applied to slaves only. Sewall also admitted that Congress could not prohibit the migration of aliens before 1808, but he argued that this restriction on congressional power implied that "Congress had some power over aliens." Although Congress could not prohibit migration, they could restrict it. The migration clause, he said, authorized Congress to tax immigrants admitted by the states and the power to tax admission was the power to restrict admission.[36] Thus, a clause expressly forbidding Congress to prohibit migration implied legislative power to regulate aliens in every other respect except admission, and it could restrict that. It followed, according to Sewall, that Congress had the power to regulate the expulsion of aliens. Moreover, once an alien had been admitted by a state, the power of Congress to provide for the general welfare and internal tranquillity gave it the right "to take cognizance of everything which relates to aliens." Drawing a line of distinction between the control of the admission of aliens into the United States and their control once they had been admitted, Sewall concluded that the states could admit aliens, but that Congress could expel those deemed dangerous.

Otis, the chief advocate of the Alien Friends Law in the House, at first denied this distinction, claiming that the migration clause applied solely to the slave trade and therefore did not deprive Congress of control over the migration of aliens. If Congress could not exercise control over the migration of aliens generally, it could no more prevent the "migration" of a French invasion army into the

[35] *Ibid.*, 2003–2004.

[36] *Ibid.*, 1958. Sewall's argument here was inaccurate, as the taxation portion of the clause applied only to slaves. He also had misinterpreted this clause earlier when advancing his claim that the power to regulate commerce included the power to regulate aliens.

United States than it could the landing of other aliens. Congress had not been delegated the power to prevent an invading army from "migrating" into the United States, he claimed, but no one doubted that it possessed that power. Nor had Congress been delegated the power to prevent the migration of other "dangerous" aliens, but it could do so. This latter power was more necessary than the former, he concluded, because "an army of spies and incendiaries scattered through the continent" would be more dangerous to the country than an armed invasion.

Otis must have thought this a pretty weak argument, for he reversed himself in the same speech and conceded that the migration clause applied to aliens as well as to slaves. Although he did not give up his claim that Congress had the general power of admitting aliens, he conceded that this power was reserved temporarily to the states. This reservation, however, implied that Congress might prohibit the migration of foreigners after 1808; hence it was merely an exception from Congress' general power over aliens and should be interpreted strictly. The New Englander then construed the word "admit" in such a restricted sense that he managed to salvage an area for federal action before 1808 from a clause which, by his own admission, barred Congress from acting until 1808. Unless the Republicans could point to a state law which specifically called for the admission of dangerous aliens, they could not prove that any state had thought it proper to admit these persons. Until one of the states passed this legislation, Congress could act against dangerous aliens.[37]

This novel interpretation of the word "admit," said the Republicans, gave rise to a curious principle. The claim that Congress could act so long as the states failed to act meant that any state could pass a law to contravene or repeal the federal alien act if the state thought that the act violated its right to admit immigrants. The power of admitting aliens, said Williams, belonged to the states, and they retained the right to use it or let it alone. Congress had no right to lecture the states. They could not say to the states, "You have been backward in your duty, and therefore we will do it for you."[38]

By his own argument, Otis conceded to the states a power greater than the one the Republicans contended for, because his argument would have allowed the invalidation of a federal law by a state statute. Gordon tried to extricate his colleague from this embarrassing position by denying that the interests of any of the states could be served by admitting "dangerous" aliens. Hence, none of

[37] *Ibid.*, 1958–1961, 1988.   [38] Gallatin and Williams, *ibid.*, 1978, 1985.

them would have any reason for contravening a federal act against such characters.

Falling back in confusion, the Federalists retreated from their exposed position, and Otis redirected their arguments by returning to the distinction made earlier by Sewall: "Can the right of expulsion be exercised by the United States, without infringing the right of admission, which is reserved to the individual States?" By distinguishing between the right to admit aliens and the right to expel them, the Federalists came up with their answer to the Republican interpretation of the migration clause. The states could admit whom they pleased, and the federal government could expel whom it pleased, if it was necessary for the general welfare. Banishment, said Harper, had nothing to do with migration.[39]

The debate over the migration clause again emphasized the difference between the two parties in their theories of congressional power. The Democratic-Republicans, whose main line of argument was that Congress could exercise only those powers delegated or implied, cited the migration clause as a prohibition on the power of the federal government. By no stretch of the imagination, much less of the Constitution, could this prohibition authorize federal action in an area reserved to the states. The Federalists, on the other hand, construed the prohibition as an implied grant of federal power which was reserved temporarily to the states. The states controlled admission of aliens until 1808, they finally admitted, but this interpretation of the migration clause posed no obstacle to the power of Congress to deport aliens. As a matter of fact, the Federalists had been consistent in their main conclusion. Whether they argued that the migration clause gave the states control over the slave trade only, or whether they conceded that it granted control over the migration of aliens to the states as well, they all concluded that it did not bar the federal government from sending out of the country those aliens who were deemed dangerous to the welfare of the United States.

Figuring that a good offense made the best defense, the Republicans laid down a third basic objection to the alien friends bill. Even if Congress had power over aliens, it would have to be exercised constitutionally. But the alien bill subjected men to arbitrary actions and was therefore unconstitutional. The Republicans denounced the bill as an open, wanton, and undisguised attack on the guaranties of civil rights in the Constitution. In defiance of the Fifth and Sixth Amendments, the suspected stranger could be removed without a presentment of a grand jury, without a speedy and public trial by

[39] *Annals,* 5C, 2S, 1986–1987, 1991. Also see Bayard, 1967, and Otis, 1961.

an impartial jury, without being informed of the nature and the cause of the accusation, without confrontation and examination of witnesses against him, without compulsory process for obtaining witnesses in his favor, and without counsel. In short, he would be deprived of his liberty without due process of law.

Moreover, the Republicans contended, the bill violated the separation-of-powers feature of the Constitution. By concentrating legislative, judicial, and executive powers in the hands of the president, men could be removed from the United States on the unproven suspicions of one man. So far as aliens were concerned, said the Republicans, the bill amounted to a suspension of the right of habeas corpus. Nor were the faults of the bill confined in applicability to aliens. They feared that the line of reasoning advanced by the Federalists to justify this measure could be used to rationalize similar bills to remove citizens or slaves.

The Federalists, as Gallatin pointed out, had come full circle since their arguments on the Naturalization Law less than a month before. At that time they had asserted that they wished to give security to the persons and property of aliens. The alien bill, however, related not to the political rights of aliens, as did the naturalization measure, but to their personal liberty, their civil rights, and their property. All the bulwarks, said Livingston, which the Constitution opposed to encroachments upon personal liberty would fall before "this engine of oppression . . . thus are all the barriers which the wisdom and humanity of our country had placed between accused innocence and oppressive power, at once forced and broken down." [40]

Livingston's brilliant speech against the bill on the day that it passed the House pointed up the arbitrary nature of the law. The new crime, he claimed, was defined as exciting the suspicions of the president. This law would remain unknown to all but the chief executive because no man could know what would arouse his suspicions.

A careless word, perhaps misrepresented, or never spoken, may be sufficient evidence; a look may destroy, an idle gesture may insure punishment; no innocence can protect, no circumspection can avoid the jealousy of suspicion; surrounded by spies, informers, and all that infamous herd which fatten under laws like this, the unfortunate stranger will never know either of the law, or of the accusation, or of the judgment, until the

[40] *Ibid.*, 1983, 2010. For a protest that "trial by Jury and the Sovereignty of the respective States appeared to be prostrated" by "the late most extraordinary Acts of Congress," see Thomas McKean to John Dickinson, Phila., June 24, 1798, McKean Papers, III (Hist. Soc. Pa.).

moment it is put in execution; he will detest your tyranny, and fly from a land of desolators, inquisitions, and spies.[41]

All these invasions of personal rights, said Gallatin, added up to a violation of the Fifth Amendment, which provides that "no person shall be deprived of life, liberty, or property, without due process of law." He denied that Congress could give the president the power to deprive either an alien or a citizen of his liberty or property. The mere act of giving that power by law was not "due process of law." His argument followed the same line when he claimed that the act virtually abolished the writ of habeas corpus for aliens. The Federalists had argued that since the bill described the cases in which a man was liable to arrest and imprisonment it was not a suspension of the right of habeas corpus. Gallatin maintained, however, that under such an interpretation the age-old privilege was being done away with by a legal distinction. The fact that Congress gave the president by law the power of arbitrary imprisonment did not make the imprisonment less arbitrary.

Livingston saved his most vitriolic thrusts at the unconstitutionality of the bill for his argument that it violated the separation of powers. The principle which distinguishes a free constitution and a despotic power, he declared, is the distribution of the legislative, executive, and judiciary powers into several hands, as is done by the first three articles of the Constitution. In all free governments, the New Yorker continued, these powers are exercised by different men; their union in the same hand "is the peculiar characteristic of despotism." Yet this law conferred all three functions upon the president. He made the law by fixing in his mind what acts, words, thoughts, or looks would constitute the crime of being "suspected to be dangerous to the peace and safety of the United States." Moreover, he could vary the law at pleasure, "as every gust of passion, every cloud of suspicion, shall agitate or darken his mind." He then applied the law to those whom his own suspicions, "or the secret whisper of a spy," designated as its object. In case of disobedience to his order, the president could execute the sentence by imprisonment during his pleasure. In short, Livingston concluded, the bill was "a refinement upon despotism." By failing to establish an ascertainable standard of guilt, the bill created a law whose formulation, application, and execution were vested in the "private interests or passions" of one man.[42]

According to the Republican arguments, therefore, one of the bill's

[41] *Annals,* 5C, 2S, 2008.   [42] *Ibid.,* 2007–2008.

chief defects was that it made no provisions for a public trial before removal. Instead, the accused would be judged by "a secret and worse than inquisitorial tribunal," said Livingston, where "all is darkness, silence, mystery, and suspicion." The only provision calling for a jury trial was that which dealt with a deportee who returned contrary to the president's order. Although Gordon had claimed that this provision would give the accused person a trial, he obviously misinterpreted the provision. There was no trial provided for on the initial deportation of a dangerous alien. Even if a person returned, Williams protested, he would be tried because he did not obey the mandate of the president, even though his original offense was created by the suspicion of the chief executive that he was dangerous.

There was one ameliorating feature in the bill—that which allowed suspected aliens to obtain a license to stay if they could convince the president that his suspicions were unfounded—but Livingston lambasted this as a "miserable mockery of justice!" How could the accused remove these suspicions if he did not know what he had done to arouse them? It was like telling the victim, he said sarcastically, that "you need only disprove facts that you have never heard —remove suspicions that have never been communicated to you; it will be easy to convince your Judge . . . that he is tyrannical and unjust; and, having done this, we give him the power he had before, to pardon you if he pleases." [43]

The Federalists shrugged off all these objections to the arbitrary nature of the bill. The hypothesis that aliens are parties to our Constitution, Otis argued, was a very erroneous one. "We, the people of the United States" were the only parties concerned in the making of that instrument. Since it was not made for the benefit of aliens, they could not claim equal rights and privileges with American citizens. Foreigners could not complain of "any breach of our Constitution" until they had become citizens on the terms laid down by Congress in its naturalization laws. Gordon also contended that constitutional limitations on the powers of government did not apply to aliens. This implied that the government of the United States and of the individual states possessed unlimited power over aliens. Otis agreed with this, but he tempered it somewhat. Every nation, he said, could forbid the entrance of foreigners, prescribe the conditions of admission, the duration of their residence, and even the part of the country where they might reside. The powers of regulating commerce, of making war, and of defending the country gave

[43] *Ibid.*, 1995, 2010.

this power in its fullest extent to the national government, but it was limited temporarily by the Constitution to allow the states to control the admission of aliens. Even so, the people had vested in Congress the remainder of this sovereign authority.[44]

Thus, the Federalists did not deny that the provisions of the bill were arbitrary. They merely argued that Congress had unlimited power over aliens, except as regarded their admission into the states.

Aliens would not be deprived of any rights by the bill, because they had no rights under the Constitution, except those extended as a matter of courtesy. Second, those that had been extended included only judicial guarantees in criminal proceedings. Since they would not be accused of a crime, they could not demand a trial by jury. Deportation was no punishment; the bill was a preventative measure. By becoming dangerous to the public peace, the alien would demonstrate that he did not have the qualifications necessary for citizenship. The rights of hospitality which had been extended to him would be revoked by his own action. He had no right to complain. Even though he were deported, his property would not be confiscated; it was not affected in any way by the law.[45]

Livingston led the Republican attack on the view that the Constitution applied only to citizens. He asserted that that document made no distinction between citizens and aliens when it referred to all "persons accused," "all trials for crimes," all "judicial power," and all "criminal prosecutions." These provisions were general and applied to aliens as well as to citizens. Moreover, the courts uniformly extended them all to aliens. "We never," he said, "hear it inquired whether the accused is a citizen, before we give him a public trial by jury." Alien friends owe a temporary allegiance to the United States and in turn are protected by American laws.

The New Yorker doubted if the Federalists had read the bill. Not only did it penalize those "suspected of being dangerous to the peace and safety of the United States," but it was also directed at those "concerned in any treasonable or secret machinations against the Government thereof." It was absurd to say that "treason is no crime, and plotting against our Government is no offence." This absurdity, said Livingston, was compounded when the Federalists were forced to argue that since there was no crime the penalty was no punishment—that deportation was only a precautionary measure. To Liv-

[44] *Ibid.*, 1984–1985, 2018.
[45] The chief arguments were advanced by Otis. *Ibid.*, 1960, 1988, 2019–2020. Also see Sewall, 1958, and Gordon, 1985.

ingston, deportation seemed a severe punishment for a man who had dissolved his former connections with his native country to seek his fortune in this one. This would be especially so if, while the man was awaiting his residence period to end before becoming a citizen, he should be ordered out because the suspicions of the president had been aroused by "the tale of a domestic spy, or the calumny of a secret enemy." [46]

In their final attacks on the arbitrary character of the bill, the Republicans stressed two points; first, that it would be directly applicable to slaves as well as aliens and, second, that the arguments which the Federalists had used to defend the bill against aliens could be equally effective in supporting a similar bill against citizens. If aliens could be sent out of the United States despite the ban on congressional action against migration before 1808, Williams feared that Congress could send slaves out of the country despite the importation clause.[47] Otis quickly denied that the Federalist interpretation of the "migration and importation" clause would justify a law to authorize the president to export slaves. They were neither aliens nor citizens; "they were merely property, which it was the shame and misfortune of the country to possess, but which the Government could not touch or invade."

Gallatin objected that arguments used to defend this bill could be employed to support a bill of a similar nature against citizens. The Federalist contention that the alien bill was necessary and proper to regulate commerce could certainly be applied to a citizen bill because Congress had power not only to regulate commerce with foreign countries, but among the several states, and with the Indian tribes. If an alien could be removed under the power to regulate foreign commerce, then by the same line of reasoning citizens could be removed under the power to regulate domestic commerce. The Federalists had also claimed that deportation of dangerous aliens could be justified as a legitimate exercise of the power to provide for the common defense and the general welfare. They could argue equally well that "seditious and turbulent citizens might be as dangerous to the peace of the country, as aliens of a similar description," and therefore should be banished. If the Federalists mauled the

---

[46] *Ibid.*, 2011–2012.

[47] The Southern states, said the North Carolinian, readily granted that slaves were dangerous property and an evil in the United States. Furthermore, said Livingston, slaves could be regarded as aliens on their first importation. If the president thought them "dangerous to the peace and safety," the New Yorker concluded, he would be obliged to order them removed. *Ibid.*, 1963, 2009. For Otis' rebuttal, see *ibid.*, 2020.

Constitution in this way to get at aliens, Gallatin had no doubt that they would give a repeat performance against citizens whenever they wanted to do so.[48]

Livingston contended that being dangerous to the peace and safety of the United States either was a crime or it was not. If it was, the Constitution provided that both aliens and citizens should be tried by jury. If it was not, the logic of the Federalist argument allowed the transportation of both. But if Congress could dispense with the law toward the one, Gallatin insisted, they could do it with respect to the other.

The Federalists had made continual reference to "plots and conspiracies" against the government, but Livingston denounced these as "frightful images that were necessary to keep up the present system of terror and alarm." Nonetheless, these mysterious allusions and dark hints had implicated American citizens, not aliens. If the Federalists were convinced that laws were necessary to protect the United States against dangerous persons, their own arguments led to the conclusion that it was more necessary to move "against our own citizens than against strangers; and I have no doubt," Livingston added, "that either in this, or some other shape, this will be attempted." The proposed measure amounted to "a sacrifice of the first-born offspring of freedom . . . by those who gave it birth." He warned that the American people, "though watchful against foreign aggression, are not careless of domestic encroachment." To "excite a fervor against foreign aggression only to establish tyranny at home" would awaken them to "a sense of their danger." It would be absurd to call Americans *free and enlightened* when Congress established "a code, compared to which, the ordeal is wise, and the trial by battle is merciful and just." The fundamental principles of freedom were in danger, the Republican spokesman concluded; the arguments which had been advocated in support of the alien bill "would have disgraced the age of Gothic barbarity." [49]

Otis and Harper denied that the Federalists would proceed against dangerous citizens as they proposed to proceed against dangerous aliens. For the Republicans to make this charge amounted to an accusation that Congress would exercise its new powers over aliens in an atrocious manner by perfidiously turning it against their

[48] *Ibid.*, 1980–1981. Although the Sedition Law did not authorize transportation or banishment of offenders, the constitutional arguments advanced by the Federalists to support legislation against seditious citizens duplicated many of their arguments on the alien bill.

[49] *Ibid.*, 2013–2021; the italics are his. Also see 1981.

fellow citizens. Neither of the Federalist leaders, however, denied that steps would be taken against their fellow citizens whose "treasonable correspondence" with the Directory implicated them in the newly found "plots and conspiracies." But these "internal enemies" and "domestic traitors" would be punished under a strong sedition bill. Citizens would not be banished; they would be brought to "legal punishment," said Harper. For its self-defense, the country could restrain not only a foreign enemy through an alien bill, but also domestic traitors by means of a sedition bill modeled on the house seditious practices bill, which, Harper said, had been recommitted because its provisions had been too indefinite.[50]

The Republican stand against the alien friends bill represented a defense in depth consisting of four prepared positions of argument. First, they denied that Congress had any delegated power over alien friends, nor could it be implied. Second, even if that power could be implied, Congress was specifically prohibited from exercising this control until 1808. In either event, the legislature did not have the power to enact the bill in 1798. Third, they argued that even if they conceded that Congress had power over aliens, the bill was so arbitrary as to be unconstitutional. And finally, the bill was unnecessary.

The Republicans opposed the bill on their chosen ground. Against these positions, the Federalists unleashed far-reaching counterarguments. They held that Congress could do anything not prohibited to promote the general welfare and common defense; the power to pass the alien bill was both implied and inherent. The migration clause allowed action against aliens before 1808; although the states could admit aliens, the United States otherwise possessed unlimited power over them. The rigorous bill was not unconstitutional, because aliens had no claims to constitutional safeguards against arbitrary proceedings. Claiming that the bill was both necessary and proper, the Federalists defended it as an emergency measure designed to nip a national danger in the bud.

The turning point in the arguments came on June 18, when the House sidetracked its omnibus bill in favor of the Senate's bill. From that moment until the end of the session, the more extreme elements of the Federalist group guided legislative action. The transition from the moderate approach is epitomized by the shift in leadership and sponsorship of the alien friends bill in the House.

[50] *Ibid.*, 1991, 2024–2025. See 1989 for Otis' remarks about "treasonable correspondence" and 2016 for Kittera's references to "internal enemies."

Although Otis' biographer observes that "the responsibility for this legislation has not been fixed upon any one individual or group in the Federal party," [51] the task of assigning responsibility is not difficult. Until the weekend of June 16–18, Sewall had been the House leader of the Federalists in all legislation bearing on national defense. At the beginning of the second session of the Fifth Congress, Gallatin had characterized him as "the first man of that party." [52] As chairman of the Defense Committee, he had watched over the passage of the naturalization bill and guided the debates on the alien enemy legislation before it had been recommitted. He had beaten off the attempts by Harper, Otis, and Allen to tighten up these measures, and as late as June 16 he had prevented Allen from sidetracking his committee's seditious practices bill for the Senate's alien bill. But the weekend of June 16–18 was decisive in the thinking of the Federalists. When the House took up the Senate measure on June 18, Sewall made no objections. Instead he and all the rest of the Federalists followed the lead of the extremists.

The high priests of the new dispensation were Harper, Otis, and Allen, the three most outspoken advocates of repressive measures. Although Allen had moved the replacement of the House bill with the Senate proposal, he did not participate in the debates on the latter measure. Instead, Otis and Harper alternated in their new roles of party whip. The only other Federalists to enter the debate were William Gordon, a New Hampshire representative, Speaker Dayton, and John Wilkes Kittera, a Pennsylvania congressman. An analysis of the reported speeches shows that Otis had the floor nearly half the time that the Federalists were defending the bill. His arguments formed the framework upon which the Federalists built, and they included the widest claims of federal jurisdiction. Moreover, Otis had made the longest speech in favor of the alien provisions of the House seditious practices bill before it was replaced by the Senate alien bill. Although he received able support, especially from Harper and Gordon, Otis was the chief Federalist spokesman for the alien friends legislation discussed in the House.[53]

Responsibility for the act can now be assigned. Hillhouse, a Connecticut senator, suggested the act, and a thoroughly Federalist Senate sent the bill down to the House. Allen, a Connecticut represen-

---

[51] Morison, *Otis*, I, 111.

[52] Gallatin to his wife, Dec. 19, 1797, Adams, *Gallatin*, 188.

[53] Otis spoke 42 per cent, and Harper 30 per cent, of the time. Dayton, Gordon, and Kittera also spoke at length.

tative, moved its discussion in the House, and a combination of events brought this about. Otis and Harper then guided the bill through that chamber, supported by the enthusiastic votes of the whole Federalist party. Although Harper became the acknowledged captain of the extremists, his first lieutenant, Harrison Gray Otis, was the man most responsible for the rapid passage of the alien friends bill by the House.[54]

Nor should President Adams' role be overlooked. Although he later wrote that he believed the Alien Law "to have been constitutional and salutary, if not necessary," he also disclaimed any liability for that measure.[55] Writing to Jefferson in 1813, he protested that he was no more responsible for it than Jefferson had been; neither "was concerned in the formation" of the measure. In justification of the law, however, he recalled that "we were then at war with France. French spies then swarmed in our cities and our country; some of them were intolerably impudent, turbulent, and seditious." The Alien Law, he declared, was designed to check these persons. "Was there ever a government which had not authority to defend itself against spies in its own bosom—spies of an enemy at war?"[56]

It is obvious that the ex-president did not distinguish here between the Alien Friends and the Alien Enemies Laws. Congress did not declare war against France, so the Alien Enemies Law was never in effect during the Adams administration. The argument that he was no more responsible for the law than Jefferson is also mistaken. Adams' answers to the hundreds of addresses did as much as any single thing to bring about the passage of drastic laws not only against aliens but citizens as well. Moreover, the vice-president's signature on legislation which passed the Senate was a mere formality. Jefferson possessed no vote except in case of ties. The president, on the other hand, is the validating officer for all legislation, and his approval made the bill law. Had Adams opposed that law, he could have exercised his veto. Thus his statement that Jefferson's signature to the law made him as responsible for it as Adams does not hold up under analysis. As a matter of fact, Adams' letter was written because Jefferson had called the Alien Friends Act "a libel on legislation."[57] Adams' only ground for disowning responsibility

[54] William O. Lynch, *Fifty Years of Party Warfare, 1789–1837* (Indianapolis, 1931), 76, says that "Harrison Gray Otis, a nephew of James Otis, was the chief defender of an anti-alien policy, while Harper led the fight for the sedition bill."

[55] Adams to Benjamin Rush, Quincy, Dec. 25, 1811, *Adams' Works*, X, 10.

[56] Adams to Jefferson, Quincy, June 14, 1813, *Adams' Works*, X, 42.

[57] Jefferson to Joseph Priestley, March 21, 1801, *Jefferson's Writings* (Ford ed.), VIII, 22.

for the law lies in the fact that none of his messages to Congress called for such a measure. His public addresses, however, often expressed anti-alien sentiments, and once Congress passed the act, he promptly approved it. Although no alien was actually deported under the law's provisions, President Adams signed several blank warrants for that purpose, in case offenders should be seized.

CHAPTER VI

The Sedition Law and the Right of Political Opposition

The genius of the Constitution, and the opinions of the people of the United States, cannot be overruled by those who administer the Government.—JOHN MARSHALL, C. C. PINCKNEY, and ELBRIDGE GERRY to Talleyrand

THE Alien and Sedition Laws have been described as "an effective weapon against what was deemed an especially pernicious and dangerous form of domestic opposition in time of war." [1] Only the Alien Enemies Law, however, was made contingent upon a declaration of war. The rest of these ill-fated acts were designed to deal with domestic political opposition in time of peace. Congressional action against sedition, therefore, supplemented the Federalists' measures against foreigners. Both the Naturalization and Alien Friends Laws represented a growing distrust not only of aliens but of the people in general. The capstone of the internal security program of the Federalist party was the Sedition Law.

The first section punished conspiracies and combinations to impede the operation of federal laws and set the penalty at not more than five years' imprisonment and a fine of not more than $5,000. The second penalized any person, citizen as well as alien, for any "false, scandalous and malicious" statements against the presi-

[1] Anderson, "Alien and Sedition Laws," Amer. Hist. Assoc., *Annual Report for 1912*, 115.

dent, either house of Congress, or the government, made with intent to defame them, or to bring them into contempt or disrepute, or to excite against them the hatred of the good people of the United States. The maximum penalty was two years' imprisonment and a $2,000 fine.[2]

The Sedition Act was not the first attempt by the Federalists to strike at domestic political opposition during the crisis with France. As early as May 22, 1797, less than three months after Adams' inauguration, the federal grand jury at Richmond, Virginia, handed down a presentment which denounced the Republican representative from Albemarle district for criticizing the Adams administration in letters to his constituents. Jefferson, then vice-president, labeled this presentment as the perversion of a legal institution into a political one, and the Virginia House of Delegates condemned it as a "violation of fundamental principles of representation . . . an usurpation of power . . . and a subjection of a natural right of speaking and writing freely."[3]

Although Congressman Cabell was never brought to trial, the XYZ hysteria led the Federalists to renew their attempts to strike at Republican critics. The aims of the majority were so ill concealed that Jefferson outlined them only three weeks after Adams had communicated the envoys' XYZ dispatches to Congress. After watching the introduction of the naturalization and the alien bills, he notified his friend Madison that "there is now only wanting, to accomplish the whole declaration before mentioned by the Federalists, a sedition bill, which we shall certainly soon see proposed. The object of that, is the suppression of the Whig presses. Bache's had been particularly named."[4] When Fenno's Federalist *Gazette* was the only paper to reach Madison a week later, he feared the worst. "I hope," he wrote Jefferson, "the bridle is not yet put on the press."[5]

Although the "bridle" had not yet been put on the press, the

---

[2] *Stat. at L.*, I, 596.

[3] Adrienne Koch and Harry Ammon, "The Virginia and Kentucky Resolutions: an Episode in Jefferson's and Madison's Defense of Civil Liberties," *William and Mary Quarterly*, 3d ser., 5 (1948), 152–153.

[4] Jefferson to Madison, April 26, 1798, *Jefferson's Writings* (Bergh ed.), X, 31–32. Beveridge, *Marshall*, II, 382, says, "When Jefferson first heard of this proposed stupid legislation, he did not object to it, even in his intimate letters to his lieutenant Madison. Later, however, he became the most ferocious of its assailants." He claims that Jefferson's first harsh word was on June 7, 1798, thus completely overlooking this letter of April 26, the first one to mention the alien and sedition bills.

[5] Madison to Jefferson, May 13, 1798, *Madison's Writings* (Cong. ed.), 141.

Federalists were "chafing at the bit" to do just that. No one was more insistent upon the need of a sedition law to suppress criticism of the government and the president than President Adams' wife.[6]

As early as 1796 she had condemned the Republican press as "the offspring of faction . . . nursed by sedition, the adopted bantling of party." At that time, however, she did not think a sedition law necessary, because she admitted that she felt "perhaps too keenly the abuse of the party." Instead, she concluded that a public figure could afford to let his actions and his integrity stand as his shield against calumny. Even the great Washington, who "had the support of the people and their undiminished confidence to the hour of his resignation," had been reviled and abused, but he had endured it. Guided by his predecessor's example, Mrs. Adams wrote, her husband would have to be "armed as Washington was with integrity, with firmness, with intrepedity. These must be his shield and his wall of brass; and religion too or he never will be able to stand sure and steadfast." [7]

As the crisis with France grew worse, however, the president's wife discarded these early views. After the publication of the XYZ dispatches, she consistently labeled the Republicans as the "French party." The emissaries of this powerful party, she wrote, "are scatterd through all parts of this extensive union, sowing the seeds of vice, irreligion, corruption, and sedition." This party had substituted sophistry for argument, and personal reflections had replaced "National Dignity and Decorum." It was her belief that they also used the same weapons of calumny and abuse that the French terrorists had used in France to overturn one set of rulers for another. Although the good sense of the American people generally directed them to the right decisions where they had access to information and could judge for themselves, Mrs. Adams wrote, the liberty of the press had degenerated to licentiousness. In distant and remote parts of the nation, therefore, "this continued abuse, deception, and falshood [sic] is productive of great mischief, and tends to destroy

---

[6] The editor of Mrs. Adams' letters observes that "they are full of references to current politics . . . [and] probably reflect the private thoughts and feelings of her husband." Mitchell, New Letters, xxv. Charles Francis Adams has noted that "her opinions, even upon public affairs, had at all times great weight with her husband, who frequently marked upon her letters his testimony to their solidity." Adams, Familiar Letters of John Adams and His Wife Abigail Adams, during the Revolution (Boston, 1875), xxvii–xxviii.

[7] Abigail Adams to Thomas Boylston Adams, Quincy, Nov. 8, 1796, Adams, Letters of Mrs. Adams, the Wife of John Adams (Boston, 1841), II, 231–232.

that confidence and Harmony which is the Life Health and Security of a Republick." [8]

On the same day that Jefferson wrote Madison of his alarm, Mrs. Adams informed her sister that vile Republican incendiaries dared to keep up "the most wicked and base, violent and caluminiating abuse" against the president in Bache's paper. Republican criticism was not only an insult to the executive and the government but also to "the Majesty of the Sovereign People." She presumed that Congress would pass a sedition bill because every issue of the two leading Republican journals, the Philadelphia *Aurora* and the Boston *Chronicle,* contained statements which "might have been prossecuted [sic] as libels upon the President and Congress." [9]

Although Adams never recommended that Congress pass a law against sedition, his answers to public addresses placed him in agreement with the Federalist sentiment which produced the Alien and Sedition Laws, all of which he signed willingly. The first of the addresses which flooded the president after the XYZ affair contained a denunciation of those

characters in the United States who call themselves Americans, and who, with patriotism on their lips, and professions of regard for the Constitution of our Country, are endeavoring to poison the minds of the well-meaning citizens and to withdraw from the government the support of the people. . . . They are instruments of disorganization and sedition, many of whom are probably employed by that nation, whose rulers seek the destruction of America.

In his reply Adams did not mention disorganization or sedition, but he remarked that if there were such perverse characters they were not so numerous as those who were "merely erroneous[ly] deceived by partial information, and transported by too ardent a zeal." [10]

In another of his early addresses, however, Adams slapped directly at the Republicans. While thanking his correspondents for

[8] Abigail Adams to Mercy Warren, Phila., April 25, 1798, *Warren-Adams Letters,* Mass. Hist. Soc., *Collections,* 73 (1925), 338.

[9] Abigail Adams to Mary Cranch, Phila., April 26, 1798, Mitchell, *New Letters,* 165. For additional examples of Mrs. Adams' views, see her letters to Mrs. Cranch, May 26 and June 23, 1798, *ibid.,* 179, 195–196.

[10] For the address of "The Grand Inquest of the United States, for the district of Pennsylvania, to the President of the United States," April 13, 1798, and the president's answer of April 14, see *Claypoole's American Daily Advertiser,* April 16, 1798. Private letters to the president, as well as public addresses, counseled passage of punitive "measures for preventing the sowing of sedition." See Rev. Cotton Tufts to John Adams, Weymouth, May 2, 1798, Adams Papers, XIX, no. 193 (Mass. Hist. Soc.).

their confidence in his administration, the president called attention to the "agitations of the human species which have affected our people, and produced a spirit of party which scruples not to go all lengths of profligacy, falshood and malignity in defaming our government." [11] This sentiment was to be echoed repeatedly by the Federalists during the debates on the sedition bill.

In May, President Adams declared to the citizens of Easton, Pennsylvania, that "the spirit of disunion is much diminished, more however by an event which no man could have foreseen, than by our own wisdom—but unless the spirit of libelling and sedition shall be controlled by an execution of the laws, that spirit will again increase." [12] To another group he went further in denouncing calumny and calling for conformity of opinion. "If the designs of foreign hostility and the view of domestic treachery are now fully disclosed," he wrote, linking the internal political opponents of his administration with the hostile French, "if the moderation, dignity, and wisdom of government have awed into silence the clamors of faction, and palsied the thousand tongues of calumny; if the spirit of independent freemen is again awakened, and its force is combined, I agree with you that it will be irresistable." [13]

Other remarks during this period followed the same line of argument. When the young men of Boston pledged themselves to sacrifice their "youthful prospects in unnerving the arm of sedition, and repelling the inroads of oppression," the president observed that he "ought not forget the worst enemy we have"—worse even than the French menace which led the chief executive to exhort: "To arms, then my young friends—to arms . . . let us resort." The greatest danger facing the nation, Adams insisted, was "that obloquy, which you have observed, is the worst enemy to virtue, and the best friend to vice; it strives to destroy all distinction between right and wrong, it leads to divisions, sedition, civil war, and military despotism." [14]

[11] Answer to the mayor, aldermen, and citizens of the city of Philadelphia, April 23, 1798, *ibid.*, April 24, 1798. This address is given in *Adams' Works*, IX, 182.

[12] Answer of May 11, 1798, *Columbian Centinel*, May 26, 1798. Adams apparently refers to the need to execute state libel laws as no federal sedition bill had yet been introduced into Congress. However, he might have referred to federal proceedings at common law; three Republican editors were arrested for sedition by federal authorities before the Sedition Law was passed.

[13] Answer to the inhabitants of the town of Hartford, Conn., May 10, 1798, *Adams' Works*, IX, 192.

[14] The address of the young men of Boston is in the *Aurora*, June 14, 1798. The president's answer of May 22 is in *Adams' Works*, IX, 194.

Jefferson was particularly disturbed by the president's threats against his fellow citizens in an answer to a Newark address. "The delusion and misrepresentations which have misled so many citizens," Adams wrote, "must be discountenanced by authority as well as by the citizens at large." The vice-president viewed this as an allusion to the circular letters written by congressmen to their constituents, and he feared that the Federalists would again try to hedge in this right with legal restrictions, as they had attempted in Cabell's presentment. Legal action, of course, would be directed only at Republican representatives, Jefferson predicted, even though the letters by Federalist congressmen to their constituents "are ten times more numerous, and replete with the most atrocious falsehoods and calumnies." He thought that Adams' address "may look to the sedition bill which has been spoken of, and which may be meant to put the printing presses under the *imprimatur* of the executive." [15]

Whether or not Adams' remarks were intended as endorsements of legislation then being discussed in Congress, they came from the president whom the nation looked to for leadership and did much to establish the climate of opinion which paved the way for the Federalist program in Congress. In an address to the inhabitants of his home town of Braintree, Adams agreed with them that the tongues and pens of slander were instruments "with which our enemies expect to subdue our country," and he assured the students of New Jersey College that libels against the government were as odious as those against persons. "Reputation is of as much importance to nations, in proportion," he said, "as to individuals. Honor is a higher interest than reputation. The man or the nation without attachment to reputation, or honor, is undone. What is animal life, or national existence, without either?" [16]

These sentiments, re-enforced by the demands of such extremists as Harper, Otis, and Allen, goaded Sewall's Defense Committee on May 16 into requesting authority to take action against "the danger which might result by means of aliens and other disaffected or seditious persons residing within the United States." On May 18 the House granted this power and the committee reported on June 4 an omnibus alien and sedition bill "for the prevention and

[15] The president's remarks are given in the *Gazette of the United States,* May 2, 1798. For Jefferson's comments, see his letter to Madison, Phila., May 3, 1798, *Jefferson's Writings* (Bergh ed.), X, 33–36. He again predicted that Bache was a main object of any sedition bill.

[16] *Adams' Works,* IX, 197, 205–206.

restraint of dangerous and seditious practices." The first part provided for the deportation of dangerous aliens, but the second portion was a full-blown sedition act which applied to citizens as well as aliens. This section stipulated that a person was guilty of a seditious practice if he secretly or openly joined a combination or conspiracy with an intention of opposing any measures of the government of the United States which were directed by proper authority, or to defeat the operation of any law of the United States, or to discourage or prevent any officeholder in the federal government from undertaking or executing his trust or duty.[17] Although these provisions dealt with seditious practices, others dealt with seditious utterances and seditious libels. The bill provided penalties for any person who, by any writing, printing, or advised speaking, should threaten danger to the character, person, or property of any government officeholder. It also would have penalized any person who counseled, advised, or attempted to procure any insurrection, riot, or unlawful assembly or combination, whether the combination or conspiracy had the proposed effect or not. Violators could be fined and either bound with sufficient surety for good behavior or imprisoned.[18]

This bill would have virtually stifled any opposition, no matter how constitutional, to actions by the federal government. Persons engaging in an open combination, such as a political party, which proposed the repeal of a federal statute could have been snared under several provisions of the measure. The most obvious provision would have been the one which punished "any person, whether alien or citizen, who shall . . . openly combine . . . with an intention of opposing any measures of the Government of the United States, which are or shall be directed by the proper authority." The bill did not specify opposition by force or violence but applied to any opposition, especially singling out that by any writing, printing, or advised speaking. Thus a petition for the repeal of an obnoxious act—perhaps this proposed act should it become law— might have become criminal, because those favoring repeal must oppose the law. Moreover, an attempt to repeal a law might be interpreted as an effort to defeat its operation; if so, this action

---

[17] *Annals,* 5C, 2S, 1771, 1868.

[18] The complete text of the bill is given in the *Aurora,* June 6, 1798, and in the *Annals,* 1868. Alien offenders could not only be fined, but could be banished or removed from the territory of the United States in lieu of the surety or imprisonment.

would have been criminal. If a proponent of repeal accused a legislator of voting for an "unconstitutional" law, would this not impute bad conduct on the part of the congressman, and would not such an imputation "threaten danger to his character"? Under this proposed law a responsible party leader would have been guilty of a crime if he attempted to procure an assembly of his party members to oppose peaceably and constitutionally a measure of the government by urging its repeal. Such an assembly would have been unlawful because the intent of the leader was to oppose a measure of the government. Moreover, the meeting would have been criminal whether the move for repeal had the proposed effect or not.

On June 6 the *Aurora* printed without comment the text of the bill after quoting the First Amendment in full. Three days after its introduction, Jefferson notified Madison that the Federalists "have brought into the lower house a sedition bill, which among other enormities, undertakes to make printing certain matters criminal, tho' one of the amendments to the Constitution has so expressly taken religion, printing presses &c out of their coercion. Indeed this bill and the alien bill," the vice-president concluded, "are so palpably in the teeth of the Constitution as to show they mean to pay no respect to it." [19]

A singular series of events occurred during the weekend of June 16–18, giving the Federalists an opportunity to demand even more drastic action against the Republicans. On June 13 Dr. George Logan, a Republican leader in Philadelphia and an ardent Quaker, sailed for France on a one-man peace mission. He made his departure something of a mystery, however, and this gave the Federalists an opportunity to put the worst possible interpretation on his unofficial attempt to restore amicable relations between France and America. "Recollect his connections," warned *Porcupine's Gazette*, whose readers did not need to be told that Logan was an "opposition man":

Recollect that seditious Envoys from all the Republics that France has subjugated first went to Paris and *concerted measures* with the *despots;* recollect the situation of this country at this moment, and *tremble for its fate!* The whole of this business is not come to light yet. We shall soon know it. In the mean time, watch Philadelphians, or the fire is in your houses and the *couteau at your throats.* . . . Take care; or, when your

[19] Jefferson to Madison, June 7, 1798, *Jefferson's Writings* (Ford ed.), VII, 266–267.

blood runs down the gutters, don't say you were not forewarned of the danger.[20]

Not to be outdone by Cobbett, the *Philadelphia Gazette,* another Federalist newspaper, added its warning of doom. "There cannot be the least question, but the Doctor, from his *inordinate* love of *French liberty,* and hatred to the *sacred constitution* of the United States, has gone to the French Directory, fraught with intelligence of the *most dangerous tendency* of this country." The "infernal design" of this Quaker, "a noted and violent democrat," could only be "the introduction of a French army, to *teach us the genuine value of true and essential liberty* by re-organizing our government, through the blessed operation of the bayonet and guillotine." [21]

Even more sensational was the treatment given a letter published by Bache. On June 16 a communication from Talleyrand to the American envoys at Paris appeared in the *Aurora* two days before President Adams notified Congress of its receipt by the government. The Federalists immediately claimed that the letter had been printed in the "French paper" by order of the Executive Directory and that French agents were taking extraordinary means to spread it. When the president transmitted the letter and the envoys' answer to Congress on June 18, the majority ordered that the whole of the XYZ dispatches be printed and distributed to counteract the machinations of the French and their agents in America.[22] That they had no other evidence for their accusations against the Republicans than their suspicions, the Federalists freely admitted. Representative Thatcher of Massachusetts, who accused Bache of being an agent of the Directory, said that "he hoped soon to lay before the House satisfactory evidence of the fact." Harper did not wait for evidence, but made the flat charge that France had secret agents in America. "Every means," he gravely charged, "had been

[20] June 18, 1798. For an excellent discussion of this peace mission, see Frederick Tolles, "Unofficial Ambassador: George Logan," *William and Mary Quarterly,* 3d ser., 7 (1950), 3–25.

[21] Cited by Deborah N. Logan, *Memoir of Dr. George Logan of Stenton* (Philadelphia, 1899), 59–60n. Also see the *Gazette of the United States,* June 18, 1798.

[22] *Annals,* 5C, 2S, 1973. The Senate concurred with the House, and on June 22 a joint resolution directed Secretary Pickering to order the printing of ten thousand copies "to be distributed, gratis, throughout the United States, and particularly in such parts thereof, wherein the dissemination of information, through the medium of newspapers, is the most obstructed." See *ibid.,* 3794. This marked the beginning of government publication of documents for public distribution. See Hildreth, *History of the United States,* V, 217.

made use of to excite resistance to the measures of our Government, and to raise a spirit of faction in the country favorable to the views of France." The publication of Talleyrand's letter was only one of the ramifications of the scheme. Without naming Logan, he earnestly announced that an event of the past few days would lead to the discovery of "a treasonable correspondence, carried on by persons in this country with France, of the most criminal nature." He pledged that he would probe this mystery; he had got hold of some of the threads of it, and he hoped soon to unravel the whole mischievous proceeding so as to bring its authors to "condign punishment." [23]

Marshall's arrival in Philadelphia on the same day that these statements were made only added fuel to the conflagration. It signified the failure of the three-man mission to secure peace with honor, and many now expected war with France at any moment. Three days later President Adams announced that he would never send another minister to France without proper assurances that he would be received.

The publication of Talleyrand's letter in the *Aurora*, the Federalist alarm at Logan's peace mission, the terrific impact of Marshall's return at that precise moment, and President Adams' belligerent message of June 21 set the stage for the introduction of a stringent anticitizen sedition measure. First, however, the House postponed its omnibus alien and sedition bill to push through the Senate's alien bill. During the debates on this measure, continued references to seditious practices made it evident that the Federalists would return to a sedition bill as soon as they had passed the alien act. Harper, Otis, and Allen led the forces in the House most insistent upon action against seditious citizens and referred continually to this "plot" against the interests of the United States, tying it in with their attacks on the "great opposition" to the alien act. The Republicans, Harper charged, favored the residence of aliens who were plotting against American security. Their arguments were designed "to completely stop the wheels of Government, and to lay it prostrate at the feet of its external and internal foes." He condemned all opponents of Federalist-sponsored defense bills as traitors who were working effectively to bind the government for its enemies. Although he did not possess enough evidence to link up the Jeffersonians directly with the treasonable corre-

[23] *Annals*, 5C, 2S, 1972. Bache went before the mayor of Philadelphia and took an oath that the Talleyrand letter came into his possession not from France but from a gentleman in Philadelphia. See the *Aurora*, June 21 and 25, 1798.

spondence "plot," Harper insinuated that the opponents of the alien bill were parties to that conspiracy. Its ramifications were so visible "that he should deem himself the worst of traitors and assassins to his country, if he did not resist those attempts which are made to bind us hand and foot, until our enemy comes upon us."

He supposed it was for this reason that this bill met with so much opposition, and that such means were used to excite prejudices against it. Because it puts a hook into the nose of persons who are leagued with the enemies of this country. The zeal shown in this House, and in other places, against this bill, evidences the deadly hatred of certain persons towards it.

Harper's insinuations amounted to a charge that the Republicans in the House were creatures of France, and he bluntly warned that "no traitors should be left in the country to paralyze all our efforts for its defence, and when the enemy appeared, give him possession of it." [24]

The political nature of these and other Federalist innuendoes stung the usually cool Gallatin into a retort. The Federalists, he replied, worked on the assumption that they had an exclusive claim to purity of intention, while they assigned the worst of motives to the Republicans. Since the alien bill had not been the subject of discussion outside Congress, Gallatin could only surmise that the Federalists were attempting to circulate "an insinuation to the public that there is a party in this House who wish to abandon their country" to an invading French army. Not only were Harper's vague generalizations totally unsubstantiated, but his insinuations were incapable of proof. They deserved no other appellation than calumny; they were grossly "indecent and improper." "Might I not," the Republican leader continued, "if I chose to preserve as little regard for decency as that gentleman, charge him at once with a willful intention to break the constitution, and an actual violation of the oath he has taken to support it?"

Gallatin added that Harper's assertion that Great Britain had been preserved by an alien bill might have been answered by showing his subservience to the British government whose measures he followed with "perfect servility." If he used the Federalist line of reasoning, he could claim that England's adoption of an alien bill was the only reason why such a measure had been introduced in the United States. [25]

Harper's reply reflected not only his attitude toward political opposition, but also that of the Federalists whose leadership he and

[24] *Annals*, 5C, 2S, 1991–1992.   [25] *Ibid.*, 1996–1997.

Otis had assumed. He expressed surprise that the Republicans should be so "extremely sore" on statements about motives, and then denied that he had said anything on that score. "When a gentleman," he added, "who is generally so very cool, should all at once assume a tone of passion, as to forget all decorum of language, it should seem as if the observation had been properly applied to that gentleman." Thus, while he disavowed any insinuations about the motives of the Republicans, Harper continued to subject their spokesman to innuendoes.

The Federalist leader confessed that he wished to imitate the British government's internal security policies. The situations confronting the United States and Great Britain were similar; both were equally threatened by a formidable foe, he added, which openly professed its reliance upon "an internal support in each country. Was there anything extraordinary, then, that the measures taken in the two countries are in some degree alike?" To his mind it only proved that "the persons entrusted with the management of the Government in both countries have vigor and sense enough to discover the danger, and courage to resist it." Harper was willing to "go further and say he wished the measures taken in this country might be really successful in effecting their object, and equally resist our external enemies and domestic traitors." [26]

The Federalists had no apologies for their unproven accusations against the Democratic-Republicans; nor were they ashamed of the model for their legislative policies. They were in the saddle and meant to run down any opposition that got in their way. [27]

During the debates on the Alien Friends Act, therefore, Federalist arguments shifted increasingly from aliens to "domestic traitors" and foreshadowed the introduction of a separate sedition bill as soon as they had enacted adequate alien laws. Edward Livingston, the outstanding opponent of the alien act, predicted that an anti-citizen measure would be next:

You have already been told of plots and conspiracies. . . . But who were implicated by these dark hints—these mysterious allusions? They were our own citizens, sir, not aliens. If there is then any necessity for the system now proposed, it is more necessary to be enforced against our own citizens than against strangers; and I have no doubt, that either in this, or some other shape, this will be attempted. [28]

Harper confirmed this prediction; since citizens could not be restricted as easily as aliens, they might be more dangerous to the

[26] *Ibid.*, 1997. England passed a stringent alien act in 1794.
[27] Adams, *Gallatin*, 205.   [28] *Annals*, 5C, 2S, 2013.

peace and safety of the country than aliens, whose rights he had denied. Dangerous citizens, however, could be curbed by laws against seditious practices. Harper repeated his belief that "there existed a domestic—what, said he, shall I call it?—a conspiracy, a faction leagued with a foreign Power to effect a revolution or a subjugation of this country, by the arms of that foreign Power. . . . He must hope, for the good of his country . . . that the projectors, and others concerned in it, may be brought to justice." [29]

Congressman Kittera, Federalist from Pennsylvania, agreed that the alien measure should be followed by a strong sedition bill; together they might preserve the United States from "the dangers with which we are threatened from internal enemies. . . . He never, in his opinion, heard a doctrine more fraught with heresy, and inconsistent with reason, than the doctrine opposed to this [alien] bill." [30]

It remained for Otis, however, flatly to accuse the Republicans of sedition. Not only were their arguments "fraught with heresy," as Kittera claimed; they were open evidence of the seditious disposition in the United States. Otis singled out Livingston's speech against the alien bill as proof of the need of a sedition law:

That gentleman had just preached up the duty of insurrection in this place; he had called upon the people to resist the laws. Never had he expected to hear this French doctrine enforced as orthodox upon that floor. He could hardly believe his own ears. Good God! exclaimed he, what society has that gentleman frequented? What books has he read? He could not believe that the gentleman was himself ready to resist the laws or join in an insurrection. These were not his own principles; they were, however, evidence of the contagion of the French mania. When a mind like that of the gentleman is so easily infected, no better evidence need be required of the necessity of purifying the country from the sources of pollution.[31]

The House, however, was not so speedy as the Senate in moving to purify the country of its pollution. On the fateful weekend of

---

[29] *Ibid.*, 2024–2025. Commenting on Harper's speech, Chief Justice Francis Dana of Massachusetts cautioned that "untill the threads are wrought into halters, and actual Traitors are seized instead of being denounced, there can be no safety for our Country." Dana to Abigail Adams, Ipswich, June 23, 1798, Adams Papers, VIII, no. 74 (Mass. Hist. Soc.).

[30] *Ibid.*, 2016. Kittera claimed that it was inconsistent to assert at one time that the government was so strong as to be dangerous to liberty and at another to say that the government did not have constitutional power "to prevent imminent danger to the Government from seditious persons."

[31] *Ibid.*, 2017–2018.

June 18, Senator James Lloyd of Maryland predicted the passage "of a strong act to punish Sedition," and five days later he received permission to introduce a bill "to define more particularly the crime of treason, and to define and punish the crime of sedition." [32] After considerable opposition, the Senate gave the bill its first reading three days later.[33] In a letter to former President George Washington, General Lloyd acknowledged that the actions of the Republicans, Bache and Logan, were chiefly responsible for his drafting of the law. Although incensed by Bache's publication of Talleyrand's letter, he was especially disturbed by Logan's mission and the absence of a "law by which he could be laid hold of." [34]

In defining treason, Lloyd designated the government and the people of France as enemies of the United States and declared that adherence to them or giving them aid and comfort was treason. This was the first and only time in American history that a legislative attempt has been made to establish by law the concept of treason in peacetime. The death penalty was prescribed for violators of this section. Misprision of treason was defined in section two as failure to divulge any knowledge of "any of the treasons" described in section one. Violators were to be fined and imprisoned. The third section seems to have been modeled on section one of the House's earlier seditious practices bill, which had been postponed. Like that provision, it penalized seditious conspiracies and combinations of persons who banded together with the intention of opposing any measures of the United States or intimidating or preventing any federal officeholder from executing his duty. It also specified that if any person should "by any writing, printing, or speaking threaten such officer or person in public trust, with any damage to his character, person or property, or shall counsel, advise, or attempt to procure any insurrection, riot, unlawful assembly or combinations, whether such conspiracy . . . advice or attempt shall have the proposed effect or not," he would be guilty of a high misdemeanor. Fine and imprisonment were the penalties.[35]

Another provision of Lloyd's bill was aimed at any person who

[32] James Lloyd to George Washington, Phila., June 18, 1798, Washington Papers, CCLXXXVIII (Lib. Cong.); *Annals*, 5C, 2S, 588.

[33] *Annals*, 5C, 2S (June 26, 1798), 589–590. Also see the *Aurora* and *Porcupine's Gazette*, June 27, 1798.

[34] Lloyd to Washington, Phila., June 18, 1798, Washington Papers, CCLXXXVIII (Lib. Cong.).

[35] If the person was an alien, the court also might banish him. For the complete text of this measure, see the *Aurora*, June 28, 1798. The bill is mentioned in *Porcupine's Gazette*, June 27, 1798.

attempted to defame or weaken the government and laws of the
United States or to defame the president or any court of justice
by writing, printing, publishing, or speaking. The bill branded as
"seditious or inflammatory" any declarations or expressions tending
to produce a belief among the citizens that the federal government
had been led to pass any law by motives "hostile to the constitution, or liberties and happiness of the people." Expressions which
tended to justify the hostile conduct of the French government
toward the United States were also punishable. Fine and imprisonment awaited any person who attempted to defame the president
or any federal court by declarations "directly or indirectly tending
to criminate their motives in any official transaction." Thus, the most
stringent sedition measure, like the most rigorous alien bill, originated in the aristocratic Senate "where Federalism was most ram-
pant." [36]

Such Republican papers as the Boston *Chronicle*, the New York
Argus, and the Philadelphia *Aurora* immediately attacked the Senate's measure as a gross violation of the First Amendment. "If I
know," the *Argus* editor wrote, that "a member is actuated by
motives hostile to the constitution, as they must be on the present
occasion, have I not a right to say so, and if I now have this right
can such freedom of speech be abridged? Certainly not," he argued.
From the trend in Congress, Bache feared that "to laugh at the cut
of a coat of a member of Congress will soon be treason." And would
it not be treason punishable by death to board or lodge a Frenchman whom the bill declared to be an enemy of the United States?
Would this not be giving "aid and comfort" to the declared enemy?
The *Aurora* asked if Senator Lloyd considered himself exempted
from his oath to support the Constitution, and the Boston *Chronicle*
advised the Federalists that sedition bills only served to show the
impotence of the cause they were intended to sustain.[37]

When the nation's capital was moved from New York to Philadelphia, a Boston humorist had advocated a glass dome on the
building where the congressmen assembled in order to *"throw a
better light on their proceedings."* The *Chronicle* now observed
that any restraint by an administration on critical observations
argued that it feared such light because it had "insufficient confidence in its own integrity." Denouncing the sedition bill as the last
gasp of an "expiring Aristocracy," the editor predicted that liberty

[36] Bassett, *The Federalist System*, 259.

[37] New York *Argus*, quoted in the *Aurora*, July 3, 1798; *Aurora*, June 29,
1798; Boston *Independent Chronicle*, quoted in the *Aurora*, July 6, 1798.

would "eventually arise with renovated lustre," so that citizens could speak openly of their government.[38]

Upon seeing the text of the Senate's treason and sedition bill, Hamilton scratched an urgent note to Secretary of the Treasury Oliver Wolcott advising further consideration of the measure. Some of the provisions seemed to him so highly exceptionable as to threaten civil war. "I hope sincerely," he wrote, "the thing may not be hurried through. Let us not establish a tyranny. Energy is a very different thing from violence." His objection to the bill, however, was not based upon its restrictions on freedom of speech and of the press. Fearing that the vigorous measure would make the Republicans martyrs to an obviously tyrannical act, he objected to it solely because he considered it to be politically inexpedient. "If we push things to an extreme," he wrote his successor, "we shall then give to faction *body* and *solidity*." In short, Hamilton urged further consideration of the bill because it threatened to strengthen, rather than weaken, the Republican "faction." He did not oppose a sedition law as such, nor did he urge the Federalists to kill their bill. He only hoped they would not hurry it through in its original form.[39]

Although the Federalist senators did alter their drastic bill, Hamilton's letter did not influence their action. On June 27, two days before Hamilton saw the measure, the Senate referred it to an all-Federalist committee headed by Lloyd. The revised version omitted the portions prescribing the death penalty for Americans adhering to the government or people of France, or giving them aid or comfort. By dropping the first two sections of the original proposal, the Federalists gave up their attempt to define the crime of treason more precisely than is done in the Constitution, and concentrated on drafting a sedition law. They simply retained sections three and four of the original bill.[40]

The revised draft deleted all references to France but repeated the provision punishing libelous or scandalous writings, whether they were true or false. So long as the words tended to censure the motives of the president or of a federal judge or tended to induce the belief that the government passed any of its laws from motives hostile to the Constitution or the happiness of the people of the United States, they were punishable. The *Aurora* condemned

[38] *Boston Gazette*, Oct. 18, 1790; *Independent Chronicle*, July 5, 1798.

[39] Hamilton to Wolcott, June 29, 1798, *Hamilton's Works* (Hamilton ed.), VI, 307.

[40] *Annals*, 5C, 2S, 596.

the bill for "making it criminal to expose the crimes, the official vices or abuses, or the attempts of men in power to usurp a despotic authority." [41]

Fourth of July toasts also illustrated the opposition of the Jeffersonians. At the celebration in Easton, Pennsylvania, glasses were raised to these words: "May the friends of the Gag-bill sleep in oblivion until the angel Gabriel sounds his last trumpet." [42] In Dutchess County, New York, however, the Democratic Society hoped that Senator Lloyd would not escape so easily. "May the man who first suggested the sedition bill," they said, "be the only sufferer under it." [43] The Tammany Society of New York City celebrated the Fourth by drinking a toast to freedom of speech and the liberty of the press: "May every wanton and unjust abridgement of them be deemed High Treason against the majesty of a free People." In Philadelphia the Democratic-Republicans in Congress were abjured to die in the last ditch rather than consent "to a prostitution of the constitution or to a prostration of the freedom and happiness of the people." [44]

On July 4 Senator Lloyd again wrote to George Washington, commenting upon Bache's activities, and "the few wicked men who, for base & selfish purposes, wish to subject our Country to foreign domination." He then traced the progress of his bill, which the Senate passed that day:

Your Excellency has probably seen in the papers a bill which was introduced into the Senate, to define and punish the Crimes of Treason and Sedition.

This bill after having been *amended,* as some of my friends think, by striking out that part which relates to Treason, and having afforded much ground for declamation to the lovers of Liberty, or, in other words, the Jacobins, passed the Senate yesterday, 18 to six, and will certainly pass the Ho. of Representatives. I enclose the bill as amended.

I fear Congress will close the session without a declaration of War, which I look upon as necessary to enable us to lay our hands on traitors, and as the best means that can be resorted to, to destroy the effect of the skill of the Directory in their transactions with Mr. Gerry. [45]

[41] July 3, 1798.

[42] *Aurora,* July 12, 1798. This issue reported similar toasts from Fredericksburg, Va.; Morristown and Patterson, N.J.; Dover, Del.; Georgetown, S.C.; and Dutchess County and New York City, N.Y.

[43] *Albany Centinel,* Aug. 7, 1798.   [44] *Aurora,* July 6 and 13, 1798.

[45] Lloyd to Washington, Phila., July 4, 1798, Washington Papers, CCLXXXIX (Lib. Cong.).

The passage of the Lloyd bill on the Fourth was accompanied by verbal clashes delivered with "more violence than ever." Stevens T. Mason, Republican senator from Virginia, reported that

there seemed to be a particular solicitude to pass it on that day. . . . The drums Trumpets and other martial music which surrounded us, drown'd the voices of those who spoke on the Question. The military parade so attracted the attention of the majority that much the greater part of them stood with their bodies out of the windows and could not be kept to order. To get rid of such a scene of uproar and confusion an attempt was made at adjournment and then of a postponement of that question. These were both overruled and the final decision taken.[46]

Lloyd's measure passed by a straight party vote. After dropping its attempt to define treason, the Senate changed the title of its bill, designating it as "an act in addition to the act, entitled 'An act for the punishment of certain crimes against the United States.'" Although less vicious than the original measure, the second Senate bill was nonetheless an "energetic" act designed to suppress criticism of elected and appointed officials. "Its passage thro the Senate," remarked Senator Tazewell of Virginia, "is an unauspicious event to have happened on the 4th of July." [47]

[46] Mason to Jefferson, Phila., July 6, 1798, Jefferson Papers, CIV, 17825 (Lib. Cong.).

[47] Tazewell to Jefferson, Phila., July 5, 1798, *ibid.*, 17823.

CHAPTER VII

Trumpets and Alarms: Preliminary Debates on the Sedition Law

From all sedition, privy conspiracy and rebellion; from all
false doctrine, heresy, and schism; from hardness of heart
and contempt of Thy Word and Commandment, Good
Lord, deliver us.—*The Book of Common Prayer*

AFTER replacing its omnibus alien and sedition bill with the Senate's Alien Friends Act, the House marked time on sedition measures until July 5, when it received Lloyd's bill. When Otis moved
that it should be given its first two readings on the same day, Republican Representative Carter B. Harrison of Virginia called for
a reading of the Bill of Rights in an effort to set up the First and
Tenth Amendments as defenses against a sedition act. Speaker
Jonathan Dayton informed the House that the only objection that
could be made at that stage of the proceedings would be a motion
to reject the bill; Livingston then made that proposal.[1] The debates
which followed placed the Republicans and Federalists in para-
doxical positions. Since the Republicans viewed the sedition bill
as an attempt to stifle free criticism of the administration, they
tried to protect the right of free comment by rejecting the bill without further discussion. The Federalists, who wished to regulate
speech, argued for free debate on the bill.

[1] *Annals*, 5C, 2S, 2093.

This preliminary discussion dealt with a technical point of House procedure—should the Senate's sedition bill be rejected without a second reading? Any discussion of details of the bill which were susceptible of amendment was out of order. The speakers, therefore, had to confine their remarks to the general question of the need of sedition legislation. The question was best phrased by Gallatin:

Does the situation of the country, at this time require, that any law of this kind should pass? Do there exist such new and alarming symptoms of sedition, as render it necessary to adopt, in addition to the existing laws, any extraordinary measures for the purpose of suppressing unlawful combinations, and of restricting the freedom of speech and of the press? For such were the objects of the bill whatever modifications it might hereafter receive.[2]

The Federalists, led by John Allen and Samuel Dana of Connecticut and Robert Goodloe Harper of South Carolina, answered with a big yes, while the Republican leaders, Nathaniel Macon of North Carolina and Albert Gallatin of Pennsylvania, demurred.

In those hot July days, tempers grew short and arguments hotter. "Long John" Allen, leading advocate of restrictive measures against aliens, headed the forces defending Lloyd's bill in the House. Six feet five inches tall, a lean 230 pounds, this formidable Connecticut Yankee's "whole appearance was calculated to inspire dread rather than affection," one of his friends later wrote. "For neutral ground, either in morals or politics, he had no taste, and but little less than absolute abhorrence." As in his earlier pronouncements against foreigners, Allen presented the most extreme of the Federalist arguments. Based on a handful of newspaper clippings, his speech may be divided into three parts. He first claimed that a treasonable combination existed against the government, and then charged that this combination consisted of Republican newspapers, congressmen, and others. To deal with this dangerous conspiracy, he demanded that Congress enact a sedition law. "If ever there was a nation which required a law of this kind," he said, "it is this."

Let gentlemen look at certain papers printed in this city and elsewhere, and ask themselves whether an unwarrantable and dangerous combination does not exist to overturn and ruin the Government by publishing the most shameless falsehoods against the Representatives of the people of all denominations, that they are hostile to free Governments and genuine liberty, and of course to the welfare of this country; that they ought,

[2] *Ibid.*, 2107.

therefore, to be displaced, and that the people ought to raise an *insurrection* against the Government.[3]

As evidence of this combination Allen quoted from the *Aurora:* "It is a curious fact," the editor had written, "that America is making war with France and *not* treating, at the very moment the Minister for Foreign Affairs fixes upon the very day for opening a negotiation with Mr. Gerry. What think you of this, Americans!"[4] The intention of this paragraph, Allen concluded, was to persuade the people that peace with France "is in our power . . . but that we reject her offers, and proceed to plunge our country into a destructive war."[5]

Nor was the House itself free from men motivated by seditious intentions, the Connecticut Yankee continued. On July 2, Livingston had proposed a resolution requesting the president to instruct Gerry to conclude a treaty with France, even though Marshall and Pinckney had returned.[6] Branding the proposal as malicious, Allen condemned it for following the same line of reasoning as that of the *Aurora.* Livingston's motion had been based on his contention that Gerry had ample powers to negotiate alone because the commission of the three envoys had been "joint and several." Here, said Allen, was a false idea which Livingston was attempting to impress on the public mind. Livingston, however, was more than a liar, according to Allen;[7] his motion was additional evidence of an extensive *"combination against the Government,* in attempts to persuade the people of certain acts, which a majority of this house, at least, and of the people at large, I believe, know to be unfounded."

Livingston's speech against the alien bill was also denounced as a seditious attack on President John Adams because the New York

[3] *Ibid.,* 2093–2094. For Allen's plea that his ungovernable temper should excuse some of his harsh remarks, see *ibid.* (April 20, 1798). The biographical information comes from a sketch by David S. Boardman in "Bench and Bar," *History of Litchfield County, Connecticut with* . . . *Biographical Sketches of Its Prominent Men and Pioneers* (Philadelphia, 1881), 16–17. Boardman roomed with Allen and shared his law office after 1793.

[4] *Aurora,* June 28, 1798. Talleyrand's letter of the 14th Germinal (April 3, 1798) had fixed April 5 or 7 as the date for a conference with Gerry for a resumption of communications. Gerry informed the foreign minister, however, that he could only confer informally and in an unaccredited capacity. See the letters in *Annals,* 5C, 2S, 3460–3461.

[5] *Annals,* 5C, 2S, 2094.

[6] *Ibid.,* 2084. Livingston's resolution was defeated on July 3 by a vote of 51 to 30. *Ibid.,* 2086.

[7] *Ibid.* (July 5, 1798), 2094. Allen said Livingston and his colleagues could not and did not believe that Gerry had power to treat alone, "let them say what they will."

Republican had said that aliens would be judged by a "secret tribunal where jealousy presides, where fear officiates as accuser, and suspicion is the only evidence that is heard," whereas the law said *the President* shall determine." The whole speech was either a foul calumny on the good people of the United States, Allen asserted, or Livingston had a more intimate acquaintance with treasons and traitors than he had ever been in the habit of ascribing to him. The Federalist spokesman then dissected Livingston's speech paragraph by paragraph to prove that the Republican was trying to stir up revolution and insurrection. In the course of his speech, Livingston had posed the hypothetical question of what the American people would do if Congress passed a tyrannical anti-citizen law modeled on the alien act which banished persons without trial by jury:

I now ask, sir, whether the people of America are prepared for this? . . . Whether they are ready to submit to imprisonment, or exile, whenever suspicion, calumny, or vengeance, shall mark them for ruin? Are they base enough to be prepared for this? No, sir, they will, I repeat it, they will resist this tyrannic system! The people will oppose, the States will not submit to its operation. They ought not to acquiesce, and I pray to God they never may. My opinions, sir, on this subject are explicit, and I wish they may be known; they are, that whenever our laws manifestly infringe the Constitution under which they were made, the people ought not to hesitate which they should obey. If we exceed our powers we become tyrants, and our acts have no effect. Thus, sir, one of the first effects of measures such as this, will be disaffection among the States; and opposition among the people to your Government; tumults, violations, and a recurrence to first revolutionary principles. If they are submitted to, the consequences will be worse. After such manifest violation of the principles of the Constitution, the form will not long be sacred.

Allen interpreted this statement as an attempt to set up the doctrine that every man has the right of deciding for himself which laws are constitutional and, further, that all who agree that a law is unconstitutional have a right to combine and oppose it by force. This was Allen's first mention of opposition to laws by force, but in his next sentence he reverted to his more usual phraseology. If the people oppose the law, he said, without distinguishing between forcible opposition and verbal protests, "they are insurgents and rebels." The intention and tendency of Livingston's oral statements, Allen concluded, was to produce "divisions, tumults, violence, insurrection, and blood." [8]

[8] *Ibid.,* 2095–2096. Allen read Livingston's speech as reported in the *Aurora.* For the original speech, see the *Annals,* 2005–2015.

The Federalist spokesman claimed that Livingston was a party to a revolutionary conspiracy against the Constitution, the government, and the peace and safety of the United States. Again he resorted to articles in Republican newspapers to prove his charge of conspiracy. Had not the *Aurora* written that "the period is now at hand when it will be a question difficult to determine, whether there is more safety and liberty to be enjoyed at Constantinople or Philadelphia"? [9] Here, he added, was obviously an attempt to induce the poor, deluded readers of the factious prints to believe that the country was rapidly approaching Turkish slavery.

A final charge against the *Aurora* was based on a letter written to the editor protesting against the alien friends bill while it was before Congress. The writer had suggested that aliens should ask any recruiting officers who might try to get them to join the provisional army if it was reasonable that aliens should fight in defense of a country which unjustly proscribed them. Proceeding upon the principle that "he who is not with us is against us," Allen concluded that the letter writer and the editor were "vile assassins of our country's peace" who were attempting to inflame the passions of Irish aliens against the United States and its government. More than that, Bache's intention could only have been to persuade aliens to join the ranks of an invading French army once it had landed.[10]

Nor was the *Aurora* the only offender, Allen continued. The New York *Time Piece* was guilty of a heinous offense in its characterization of President Adams as a "mock Monarch," "a person without patriotism, without philosophy, without a taste for the fine arts." This was but another evidence of what Allen called "a conspiracy against Government and people." All these newspaper items, he continued, were "awful, horrible" examples of "the liberty of opinion and freedom of the press." He did not think they should be allowed. "The freedom of the press and opinions was never understood to give the right of publishing falsehoods and slanders, nor of exciting sedition, insurrection, and slaughter, with impunity. A man was always answerable for the malicious publication of falsehood; and what more does this bill require?" [11] Livingston's motion

---

[9] This statement appeared in the *Aurora*, June 29, 1798.

[10] *Annals*, 5C, 2S, 2099. The letter, dated June 14, 1798, and signed "A Republican," appeared in the *Aurora* on July 4, 1798. It was addressed "To Irish Emigrants and Particularly That Class Denominated Aliens."

[11] *Annals*, 5C, 2S, 2097. It should be noted that the bill did not then require that the words be false. The Senate's sedition bill would have continued the British common law precept of "the greater the truth the greater the libel." Allen obviously misread the bill when he said that it was directed at the malicious

to reject the sedition bill, he implied, was but a maneuver by the American Jacobins to help the Republicans keep their presses by raising a hue and cry for the safety of the freedom of speech and of the press. Allen finally abandoned his argument that the bill was directed at presses emitting falsehoods, and blurted out the political object of the bill. Since the Republicans sought to keep the weapon of the press in their hands, he concluded, it was the business of the Federalists "to wrest it from them."

At one point Allen came close to contending that criticism of the proposed sedition bill was itself seditious. Because the *Aurora* had urged resistance to the passage of Lloyd's bill while it was before the Senate, Allen accused its editor of speaking "the tocsin of insurrection." He observed, however, that the "infamous printer" was merely parroting Representative Livingston, who had counseled resistance.

A question by W. C. C. Claiborne, Republican representative from Tennessee, cleared up any ambiguities which Allen might have left unexplained in his attack on the Republicans and their press. Claiborne asked if Allen were not a supporter of the *Aurora* through his subscription to it. The Connecticut Federalist admitted that he took the paper at public expense, but he hastened to add that he did so only to see what abominable things could actually issue from a genuine Jacobinic press. He neither supported it with his name nor his influence, as the Republicans did. In an innuendo understood by all, he slapped at Vice-President Thomas Jefferson, leader of the Republicans. *Porcupine's Gazette,* one of the leading anti-Republican journals, had accused the vice-president of close consultation with Bache. Now Allen repeated the charges, leaving Jefferson unnamed: "I do not walk the streets arm-in-arm, I hold no midnight conference, I am not daily and nightly closeted with the editor." [12] From innuendo, he then jumped to accusation:

I say, sir, this paper must necessarily, in the nature of things, be supported by a powerful party; I do not say of whom that party is composed. The

---

publication of falsehood. It was directed at words, true or false, which tended to question the motives of governmental actions or which tended to damage the reputation of the president or federal judges.

[12] Of this charge, Jefferson wrote that he was occasionally visited by Bache, the grandson of his old friend, Benjamin Franklin: "If the receipt of visits in my public room, the door continuing free to every one who should call at the same time, may be called *closeting,* then it is true that I was *closeted* with every person who visited me; in no other sense is it true as to any person." Jefferson to Samuel Smith, Monticello, Aug. 22, 1798, *Jefferson's Writings* (Bergh ed.), X, 55.

anonymous pieces and paragraphs it contains, evince the talents and industry employed to give it currency; and it is perfectly well understood, by all parties and persons, to contain the opinions of certain great men, and certain gentlemen in this House. This inflammatory address to the Irishmen, is, therefore, understood by them to come clothed with high authority. This is the work of a party; this paper is devoted to party; it is assiduously disseminated through the country by a party; to that party is all the credit due; to that party it owes its existence.

Thus, Allen finally spelled out his concept of the nature of the internal threat to the nation. He had started out by calling for a sedition law to get at newspapers which he said published falsehoods, preached insurrection, and sought the overthrow and ruin of the government. The paragraphs which he cited were condemned as "horrible" examples of the liberty of the press. Words which urged constitutional opposition to the passage of bills of questionable constitutionality were denounced as criminal "acts practiced against the repose of our country," and newspaper articles were referred to as "deadly thrusts at our liberty . . . , approaches to revolution and Jacobinic domination." [13] But the real source of pollution was not the papers; they were merely the "engine" through which the treasonable conspiracy functioned. The archconspirators were the Republican members of the House.

As if he had not made himself explicit enough in accusing the Republicans of attempting to overthrow the government by argument and newspaper articles, Allen turned to another kind of writing "calculated to excite the deeds of death." Following the line of thinking set forth by the grand jury in the Cabell presentment, Allen accused Republican congressmen of writing to their constituents "things which they cannot justify." The sedition bill was intended to prevent or punish this sort of treasonable calumny, Allen averred. For an example of this evil type of writing, he quoted from an "interesting letter from a Member of Congress from Virginia to his constituents." After comparing the American and British governments, the representative had expressed a fear that there were tendencies in the conduct of the American government which might lead to abuses of the executive power, pointing to the fund-

---

[13] *Annals*, 5C, 2S, 2110. Allen's zeal to suppress this treasonable combination to overthrow the government led him to a position which established himself as a likely recruit for such a conspiracy. If the federal government could not make a law to regulate such papers as the *Aurora*, he was ready to dissolve it. "Away with such a Government," he insisted; "it is not worth preserving; it cannot stand; it contains the seeds of a swift and sudden dissolution." *Ibid.*, 2099–2100.

ing of the national debt and the establishment of the Bank of the United States:

The nature of these institutions, and their political effects, already discernable in this country, and brought to full form and maturity in England, plainly prove their great fitness and agency in producing a dangerous preponderance of Executive power; the Executive is regularly supported by a party in both Houses of Congress on every questionable case respecting its powers or projects for expense.

That this seemingly innocuous letter was evidence of an aim to overthrow the government, Allen had no doubt. Here was a seditious member of Congress misinforming constituents. Allen implied that the congressman who wrote the letter was guilty of a deliberate lie: "How could a member of this House seriously inform his constituents that 'the public debt has been studiously augmented'?" The writer, Allen added, knew the reverse to be true, and how he could say anything that the letter contained was more than the Connecticut Federalist could imagine. But Allen exercised his imagination enough to conclude that the intent of the writer was "to inflame his constituents against the Government, though at the expense of all truth." The letter was obviously "calculated to excite the deeds of death." Dispatched to the Southern states, these letters led to opinion adverse to the government and its administration, thus contributing to the possibility of a civil war.[14] Allen argued that the government could not exist without the power to punish these outrageous misrepresentations of the national authority. Nor did the government lack the power to remedy these evils with a well-drawn sedition law. "It is inherent in every Government," he said, "because it is necessary to its preservation." [15]

On Eagle's wings immortal Scandals fly
While virtuous actions are but born and die.—JOHN DRYDEN

Allen's strictures received the backing of the leader of the House Federalists, Robert Goodloe Harper. Unlike his colleague, however,

[14] *Ibid.*, 2100–2101. This letter appeared in the *Aurora*, June 28, 1798. Note that Allen did not mention French or foreign influence in this attack on Republican criticism of the Federalist administration. The banking system, which the Republicans had opposed since 1790, was the object to be protected from adverse criticism.

[15] *Annals*, 5C, 2S, 2101. Although Allen claimed to have no doubts on the extent of governmental power, he contradicted himself in the very same sentence by saying, "If it be determined we have not this power, the people will certainly vest it in Congress for no Government can exist without it."

Harper did not claim that Republican newspapers, by themselves, formed a dangerous combination to overthrow the government. Newspaper calumnies, he admitted, did not bother him much. "He had always despised the base calumniators, believing that a man's propriety of conduct would always be sufficient to shield him against slanders. When he saw the President of the United States and the Government of the Union defamed, he still despised them, and he believed also that the people were not affected by them, because he saw they did not rise in insurrection against the Government." [16]

Why then did Harper believe a law was necessary to restrict seditious writing and speaking? What catalytic agent converted the newspapers into a dangerous conspiracy? Harper readily admitted that the Republican representatives in Congress were the agents:

Whilst this abuse was confined to certain newspapers in the United States, it excited in him, therefore, no alarm; but, when he heard a gentleman on the floor of this House, whose character and connexions gave him weight with the people, pronouncing an invective against the Government, and calling upon the people to rise against the law, the business put on a very serious appearance; he thought so, not because he should wish to have that gentleman muzzled (for he knew he had the liberty of uttering as much treason as he pleased, and that if his own sense of propriety and decorum was not sufficient to check him, there was no other check upon him,) but because this speech may have a very different effect from the filthy streams of certain newspapers; it may gain a credit with the community, and produce consequences which all former abuse has failed to do. It is time, therefore, for the Government to take alarm.

Thus it was not newspaper defamation as such that Harper feared. Only when the seditious spirit raised itself in respectable quarters, especially in Congress, did it become necessary for the government to take action. Congressional immunity, however, protected all statements made in either branch of Congress. How, then, could the government strike at seditious congressmen?

Harper had a ready answer to this question. The evil of seditious speaking and writing was not confined to speeches delivered in the House. Other sources of pollution were letters written by representatives and senators. He had recently seen a private letter [written by Congressman McDowell of North Carolina],[17] he said, which

---

[16] This speech is reported in the *Aurora*, July 7, 1798.

[17] *Annals*, 5C, 2S, 2102. When Harper claimed that he knew the signature on the private letter, Representative McDowell challenged the Federalist leader to state "where he saw the signature to know it." The Republican congressman said that he had seen a letter in the leading Federalist paper, Fenno's *Gazette*

had given administration measures the most vile coloring and had imputed to members the most abominable motives, which were contrary to what the writer knew to be the truth at the time. When members signed their names to such falsehoods, what effect might they not produce? Harper queried. Other countries had been turned upside down by such vile practices; he hinted that this letter was an attempt "to excite those insurrections, which had heretofore been excited by other means." The most daring attempts to sow discontent among the people had proved ineffectual in the past, and he now trusted that the good sense and patriotism of the people would be their shield. Since he was not sure that this would be the case, however, Harper wanted to play things safe by passing an energetic sedition law which, by suppressing such inflammatory letters, would prevent the deplorable effects the letters aimed at.

This is a near-classic statement of the nip-revolution-in-the-bud philosophy; it is based on the premise that words must be punished for a tendency which someone supposes will lead to unlawful action. But the words must be punished long before there is any probability that they will lead to such actions. Harper did not quote from the letter which he claimed made a sedition law necessary; only his suspicions about its tendency were presented to the House.

The "rational" liberty of the press, he continued, would not be restricted by a well-defined law if the accused was given a fair trial by jury. He had often heard harangues on the liberty of the press, as if it were to swallow up all other liberties. Its true meaning, however, was much more modest, he assured the House. "It is no more than that a man shall be at liberty to print what he pleases, provided he does not offend against the law, and not that no law shall be passed to regulate this liberty of the press."

When Livingston claimed that the bill was designed not only to restrict the liberty of the press but to restrain freedom of speech on the House floor as well, Harper broke in to deny any intention of restricting congressional debate. He conceded, however, that the sedition bill was meant to restrict "the consequences of it out of doors." This could be done in only one of two ways, Livingston pointed out—either by restricting members from speaking or by preventing the people from knowing what was said. The Federalists could achieve their objective, Livingston charged, only by "schack-

---

of the United States, which was signed "McDowell." He admitted this letter was his, but he denounced the insinuations contained in the editor's analysis. Harper confessed that McDowell's letter was the one he had referred to, but he denied breaking the seal or writing the strictures upon it in Fenno's paper.

ling [*sic*] newspapers, and preventing that free communication of sentiment which has heretofore been expressed on public topics." This was an accurate summary of Harper's argument, and he did not deny it. Nor did he deny the assertion by John Nicholas of Virginia that the Federalists' bill sought to prevent the publication of the views of the Republican representatives to their constituents and to the world.[18] Newspapers printing these letters could be prosecuted for sedition. Thus, Harper's proposals would have isolated the political opposition from the public which elected them. When election time rolled around, the anti-administration campaigners would have been subject to prosecution for any denunciation of the administration or of its personnel, policies, or motives.

Four Republican spokesmen backed Livingston's move to reject Lloyd's bill in this preliminary round of general argument. Gallatin was joined by Macon and McDowell of North Carolina and John Nicholas of Virginia. It was Gallatin who went to the heart of the matter for the Republicans. He argued that the Federalists had failed to prove their case; they had proved the existence neither of any criminal combinations against the government nor of any new and alarming symptoms of a seditious disposition among the American people. "The only evidences brought by the supporters of this bill," he charged, "consist of writings expressing an opinion that certain measures of Government have been dictated by an unwise policy, or by improper motives, and that some of them are unconstitutional." Was the administration afraid to leave these questions open to argument? The American government, he pointed out, had been formed, had acquired strength, and had been supported by the people without the assistance of a sedition law; thus far "it had been able to repel opposition by the single weapon of argument." Was the administration now afraid that error could not be successfully opposed by truth? Did it require "the help of force to suppress the limited circulation of the opinions of those who did not approve all their measures?"

These questions Gallatin answered in the affirmative. The sedition act, he contended, was designed to coerce the administration's political opposition. "This bill and its supporters suppose, in fact that whoever dislikes the measures of Administration and of a temporary majority in congress, and shall, either by speaking or writing, express his disapprobation and his want of confidence in the men now in power, is seditious, is an enemy, not of Administration, but of the Constitution, and is liable to punishment." To place the

18 *Annals*, 5C, 2S, 2102–2104.

press under any restraint in its reporting on the measures of the members of the government would be to seal the conduct of representatives from the scrutiny of the people. The sedition bill, the Republican leader asserted, could be considered only as a Federalist weapon "to perpetuate their authority and preserve their present places."

Gallatin particularly thought Harper's support of the measure was based on unusual grounds. The Federalist leader had asserted that he had no apprehension from licentiousness of the press until he had heard Livingston's speech against the Alien Friends Law. A sedition law, however, could punish only the licentiousness which Harper did not fear; it could not extend to congressmen for speeches made on the floor of the House. Nonetheless, Gallatin was not surprised that Harper should make that attempt. His charge that Livingston spoke seditious sentiments was the first attack ever made upon a speech delivered in the House of Representatives, he reminded his colleagues. He confessed, moreover, that he had expected such a move by the South Carolina Federalist for some time, "for, in his career, after having grossly attacked members first for writing circular letters, and then on account of their private correspondence, the next step must be to make their speeches the foundation of a sedition law." [19]

The Republican leader vigorously denied the Federalist charges hurled at Livingston's speech. It had been neither an invitation to the people to oppose, nor an opinion that they should oppose, the Alien Act. Instead, Livingston had set forth the general proposition that the people have a right to resist, and would resist, unconstitutional and oppressive laws. This doctrine, Gallatin believed, was neither seditious nor treasonable. Only the day before, America had celebrated the Fourth of July—a monument to the right of resisting unconstitutional laws. This right should never be exercised lightly; it was a delicate question "to be decided by motives of prudence and by principles of morality." But the Alien Law, which he thought unconstitutional, was not sufficient to justify resistance and opposition, even if no redress could be obtained in the courts.

Most of the Republicans concentrated their attention on the Federalist attack on the press, rather than on their assault on circular letters to constituents. To restrict the use of speaking and writing, Nicholas claimed, would strike at the root of free republican gov-

[19] *Ibid.*, 2108–2110. For Harper's attack on Congressman William Findley for writing circular letters to his constituents, see *Claypoole's American Daily Advertiser*, April 14, 1798.

ernment. The people of the United States were competent judges of their own interests, and the press should remain perfectly free to furnish them with information on those interests. If the press were restricted, the people would surmise that "there is something in our measures which ought to be kept from light." Because of the crisis with France, he was willing to give liberal support to Federalist defense measures, especially if war came, but he was not ready "to create a *domestic tyranny*."

Livingston denied Harper's argument that the liberty of the press could not be infringed so long as the sedition law was clear and well defined and guaranteed a trial by jury to offenders. If this were true, Livingston said, Congress might restrict all printing at once; "We have . . . nothing to do but to make the law precise, and then we may forbid a newspaper to be printed, and make it death for any man to attempt it!" If Congress passed such a bill, it would more than abridge the liberty of the press; it would annihilate that freedom which the Constitution said should not be abridged. Livingston therefore insisted that a vote should be taken on his motion to reject the Senate's sedition bill; if he were to withdraw this motion against such an unconstitutional measure, he would consider himself guilty of treason.

At a time when national unity was most necessary, Macon added, a sedition law would add nothing to American strength. Instead, it would "produce more uneasiness, more irritation, than any act which ever passed the Legislature of the Union." To go abroad for precedents was to overlook an essential difference between American political conditions and those of Great Britain and Europe. In America the people would discern any encroachment upon their liberty much sooner than in Europe, where the great bulk of the people did not participate in government. A bill modeled on such precedents would boomerang against its sponsors. He pleaded that the people could be trusted with free discussion as safely as could their representatives. "They know," Macon insisted, "that truth is not afraid of investigation"; they would suspect that something was wrong if the government feared free discussion.[20]

Branding their Republican opponents as "heralds of calumny and

---

[20] *Annals*, 5C, 2S, 2104–2106. As for Allen's criticism of the *Aurora*, Macon believed if anything appeared in that newspaper which was unfounded it would always be contradicted in another journal. There were papers on both sides of the political fence. Although he praised no paper, he thought there were two other gazettes which contained at least as many lies as did the *Aurora*. He referred to Fenno's *Gazette of the United States* and to *Porcupine's Gazette*, edited by William Cobbett.

apostles of insurrection," the Federalists brushed aside all arguments against a law establishing the political crime of seditious libel. Allen's Connecticut colleague, Samuel Dana, said the bill had but two objectives: the punishment of calumnies and conspiracies against the federal government. Freedom of speech and of the press conferred no "license to injure others or the Government, by calumnies, with impunity." These liberties would not be abridged by the bill; it merely restrained the liberty of lying and the privilege of vice. "Let it be remembered," he cautioned, "that the uttering of malicious falsehoods, to the injury of the Government, is the offence which it is now intended to restrain; for, if what is uttered can be proved true, it will not, according to this bill, be punished as libellous."

As a matter of fact, the Senate bill was directed not against "malicious falsehoods" but at "libelous or scandalous" utterances. Despite Dana's statements to the contrary, the bill was designed to suppress true statements as well as false ones, as the bill contained no provision that the truth of an utterance should be a defense against the charge of libel. Dana confessed as much two sentences later when he said that freedom of language meant nothing more "than the right of uttering . . . what is not injurious to others." According to this view true statements would be punishable if they were "injurious" to others.[21]

All the rest of the Federalists who spoke against Livingston's motion to reject the sedition bill supported their position by calling for further debate of the measure which the Republicans claimed would stifle free discussion. William Craik of Maryland asserted that he would vote against the bill if it hindered congressmen from communicating freely with their constituents or restrained the publication of the House debates. He did not believe, however, that it restrained any of these things, so he wished to hear its merits discussed further, rather than to reject it without a second reading.

Otis believed that the bill contained nothing contrary to the common law of the several states. If this were true, said Kittera, the bill should pass. All governments should inform the people about crimes based on common law principles. Moreover, some of the judges in the federal courts had decided recently that there was no federal common law jurisdiction in criminal cases. To cover the possibility that there was no common law crime of sedition, a sedition bill was mandatory. In a straight party vote, the Federalists carried the day, defeating Livingston's motion by a vote of 47 to 36. By keeping

[21] *Annals,* 5C, 2S, 2112.

alive the Senate's sedition bill, they had won the first round in the House.[22]

On July 6, the day after this Federalist victory, Harper suggested that the bill should be referred to a select committee for "considerable alteration." When this motion was turned down for another which proposed continued discussion of the bill by the Committee of the Whole House, Harper submitted to that committee a lengthy list of resolutions applicable to seditious writers.[23] Although only the first was incorporated into the final sedition law, these seven resolutions deserve attention because they represent the high-water mark of Federalist efforts to suppress political opposition. In them the majority's party whip spelled out the proposals which he thought necessary to cope with the internal crisis. Together they would have eliminated all criticism of the Federalist administration and its majority in Congress.

The first resolution provided for the punishment of persons printing or uttering any "false, scandalous, and malicious writing" against the government of the United States, either house of Congress, or the president, with the intent to defame them or bring them into contempt or disrepute, or to excite against them the hatred of the good people of the United States, or to stir up sedition within the United States. It also made such writings illegal if made with intent to excite any unlawful combinations for opposing or resisting any law of the United States, "or to resist, oppose, or defeat any such law or act." This last clause made the writings punishable in the absence of "unlawful combinations." If the intent of the writer was to oppose any law or act of the United States, either individually or through lawful combinations and assemblies, by petition or repeal, he was to be punished, provided his writings were false, scandalous, and malicious. A final clause punished such writings made with the intent to aid, encourage, or abet any hostile designs of any foreign nation against the United States, their people, or government.

The second resolution stipulated exactly the same provisions for persons who uttered or published any false, scandalous, and malicious "words or expressions" by "public and advised speaking or discourse." It stipulated, however, that it was not to apply "in cases

[22] Otis' statement about the common law of the states is in the *Annals*, 2105. The debates and the vote are on 2113–2114.

[23] *Ibid.*, 2114–2116. Gallatin asked whether the House seditious practices bill which had been recommitted on June 23 was going to be reported on. He suggested that, if it were, perhaps the Senate bill should also be recommitted so that both could be reported together. Sewall said that since the bills were so similar, the committee would drop the House's bill if the Senate measure passed.

where freedom of speech is expressly allowed by the Constitution of the United States or of any State." The only place where freedom of speech is expressly allowed by the Constitution is the floor of Congress. The First Amendment protects not only speech but the press; moreover, it is not an express allowance but a negative provision which prohibits congressional action. Harper's resolution, therefore, was directed against congressmen for utterances made outside the halls of Congress. A public and advised discourse, such as a letter to their constituents or a campaign speech, would be penalized if it contained the forbidden words or expressions with the requisite intent.

Harper also proposed that punishment should be meted out to persons assembling, convening, or attending any public or secret meeting with intent to form, or assist in forming, any "plot" against the peace of the United States or against the execution of any law of the United States. This resolution also struck at what Harper had earlier condemned as "treasonable correspondence" by punishing persons attending any such public or secret meeting "with intent to establish, hold, or carry on any correspondence with any foreign nation, its agents or people," for any of the purposes listed in the resolution.

Persons were also to be penalized, even though they did not attend a public or secret meeting, if they carried on individually, or caused to be carried on, "any correspondence with any person or persons whatsoever, with intent to form any plot against the peace of the United States, or to aid any hostile designs of any foreign nation against the United States, their people or government." This provision, unlike the previous one, was not restricted to correspondence with a foreign nation, but applied to that with any person whatsoever. Unless the letter were revealed by the recipient or was voluntarily produced by the author, the only possible way in which this provision could have been enforced would seem to be by postal censorship. Neither of the resolutions relating to correspondence defined a "plot" against the peace of the United States. Presumably Harper meant these provisions to apply to the sort of "plot" which he had accused Logan and Bache of participating in.

To these proposals, Harper added a curious proviso. Nothing in them, read the sixth resolution, ought to extend "to abridge the freedom of speech and of the press, or the right of the people to peaceably assemble and to petition the Government for a redress of grievances," as established by the Constitution. Here was a most sophisticated view of the First Amendment. After striking at the

rights of speech, press, and assembly and at individual or joint
action, whether public or secret, Harper added the pious disclaimer
that his resolutions ought not to infringe these basic guarantees of
individual liberty.[24]

Two days' debate was sufficient to hammer out the final version
of the Sedition Law. Most of the debate of July 9 was devoted to
amending the Senate bill, while that of the tenth centered around
the constitutionality of the measure. Although four important alterations changed Lloyd's bill considerably in detail, the House left
the declared purposes of the act virtually untouched. Section one
was the only portion of the Senate bill to survive the House debates.
Section two was replaced by the first of Harper's resolutions.[25]
This altered the bill in two important respects. Lloyd's measure
would have protected Congress, the president, and all federal
judges from utterances which traduced or defamed them. Harper's
section, however, covered the government of the United States,
Congress, and the president. By eliminating federal judges from
the charmed circle of privileged officials, Harper narrowed the
scope of the law. Second, his resolution changed the definition of
seditious utterances. The Senate had specified that "libellous or
scandalous" words would constitute sedition, but Harper stipulated
that the words must be "false, scandalous, and malicious" and must
be spoken or written with a "bad intent."

Under the original bill, observations about the conduct of Congress could have been punished if the words had been spoken with
the intent of creating a belief among the people that Congress,
in passing a law, acted from motives hostile to the Constitution or
to the liberties and happiness of the people. The charges might be
true, but if the speaker harbored the forbidden intent, he was guilty.
More startling, though, had been the provision which related to
government officials personally. Any statement, no matter how true,
which tended to censure the motives of the president or of any
federal judge in any official transaction would have been punishable as seditious. In this instance, the speaker could have told the
truth with the best of intentions, but if his words tended to censure

[24] Harper's proposals are printed in the *Annals*, 2115–2116, and in the *Gazette
of the United States*, July 7, 1798. Harper proposed to limit his resolutions to
one year. They were referred to the Committee of the Whole, which was then
considering Lloyd's bill.

[25] *Annals*, 5C, 2S, 2133–2138, especially 2134. In the Committee of the Whole,
Harper's amendment barely squeezed through by a 35-to-34 vote. The House
itself accepted only after Speaker Dayton voted to break a 40-to-40 tie.

motives, he would have come within the purview of the law. If his
charges really were true, they could not help having a bad tendency.
Harper's amendment, on the other hand, provided that if the accusation of the government, Congress, or the president was true it was
not seditious. His definition was theoretically broad enough even
to allow false accusations to go unpunished if they were spoken
with good intentions. Moreover, Bayard proposed a section which
allowed any person prosecuted under the act to give evidence of
the truth of his statements as justification for any alleged libel.

These changes, however, should not obscure the fact that both
the Senate and House versions of the bill established criticism of
the government or some of its officials as the test of the criminality
of the utterances. Harper's and Bayard's amendments apparently
exempted deserved criticism—that is, true criticism—from prosecution, thus tightening the test somewhat. Harper's test also made
the "bad intent" of the speaker an ingredient in the crime, whereas
the Senate test had required "bad intent" only if the remarks were
leveled against Congress but did not require it if the criticism was
aimed at the motives of the president or federal judges. The tendency of the words and the intent of the speaker thus became the
basic tests of seditious utterances.

After deciding on the standard of guilt to be used in gauging
the criminality of words, the House turned to the question of who
should apply the test. In normal criminal procedure, both in the
United States and in England, the jury was allowed to decide the
fact and apply the law—they first decided whether or not the alleged act had been committed, and if it had, they decided whether
or not it was a violation of the law. But in criminal libel cases,
especially in seditious utterances, this procedure had been perverted so as to allow the jury to decide only whether or not the
accused had written or published the allegedly seditious words.
The judge then decided on their criminality. This common law
practice remained the rule during the American colonial period,
and was not altered in England until Parliament passed Fox's Libel
Act in 1792. This statute restored the jury to its normal function
of judging the fact and applying the law.[26]

Claiborne of Tennessee called attention to this alteration of the
common law by Great Britain and proposed a similar proviso in
the sedition bill. Unless it was added, judges might turn to the

[26] Sir Thomas Erskine May, *Constitutional History of England* (New York,
1889), II, ch. ix; Sir James Fitzjames Stephen, *A History of the Criminal Law of
England* (London, 1883), II, ch. xxiv.

common law precedents of colonial times and adopt Lord Mansfield's doctrine that the law respecting libels could be determined only by the courts. Prosecutions for libel had been rare in the United States, Claiborne continued, but since they seemed destined to increase, he wanted to prevent any misunderstandings. Juries should be allowed to return general verdicts of guilty or not guilty of the accused crime. Otherwise, the courts might restrict them to a finding that the accused was guilty of publishing the words and arrogate to itself the task of determining their criminality. Although proposed by a Republican, this amendment was concurred in by most of the Federalists.[27]

Samuel Smith, a Maryland Republican, also succeeded in altering section one of the bill so as to limit that part to seditious conspiracies and combinations. The Senate measure had provided that any person using words which threatened damage to the character, person, or estate of any federal officeholder could be fined $5,000 and imprisoned up to five years. This provision, of course, was more drastic than section two; the penalties would have been two and a half times as severe, and the coverage would have extended not only to the president and Congress but to any federal officer. It was dropped, however, by a close vote.[28]

A final alteration stressed the political nature of the bill. Although Harper's resolutions of July 6 had proposed a one-year limit on any sedition law, the House voted to extend the act until March 3, 1801, the expiration date of Adams' administration. Instead of being restricted to the duration of the external crisis with France, it was to coincide with a political term of office.

[27] *Annals,* 5C, 2S, 2135–2138. The vote was 67 to 15.

[28] The *Annals* give an inaccurate report on the House's action to strike out this clause, stating that Smith's motion was lost by a 43-to-29 vote. The tabulated vote, however, gives 43 votes for the motion to delete and 39 against it. The clause, therefore, was dropped from the bill.

CHAPTER VIII

Congressional Crucible: The Forging of the Sedition Sword

> If by the Liberty of the Press were understood merely the
> Liberty of discussing the Propriety of Public Measures
> and Political opinions, let us have as much of it as you
> please.—BENJAMIN FRANKLIN

IN 1798 a pervasive political plague—suspicion—swept over the
young republic. Fear of foreigners soon gave way to distrust of
democrats, and the Federalist party, sure of a majority, easily
jammed through their final measure to repress Republicanism. Indeed, the only important debate on the constitutionality of the
sedition bill was confined to half a day. Considering the importance
of the subject, even these arguments are sketchy. This, of course,
is partially due to the inadequate report contained in the *Annals*,
but there are other reasons.[1] Perhaps the most important reason
was the certainty of a Federalist victory. Once they had marshaled
a majority for the Alien Friends Act, the most arbitrary of their
measures, the vote on the sedition bill was a foregone conclusion.
It had been mentioned as a part of their internal program as early
as April. The administration party was so confident of victory that
Otis apologized to his colleagues for having to take up so much

---

[1] The discussion between Nicholas and Harper (*Annals*, 5C, 2S, 2141) indicates that Bayard spoke on the bill, but his arguments are not given. In one instance, material is omitted which "would occupy too much room." *Ibid.*, 2151.
Both Harper and Gallatin pleaded the lateness of the hour as a reason for cutting
short their arguments. *Ibid.*, 2164.

time in order to reply to the Republicans. To him the need of the law and the meaning of the First Amendment appeared self-evident, but he thought it necessary to answer the opposition, whom he accused of attempting to deceive the people into thinking that they were being deprived of a "darling privilege."

The Federalist argument for constitutionality consisted of two simple propositions: first, that the original Constitution had given Congress jurisdiction over sedition, and, second, that the Bill of Rights had not removed that cognizance. In support of their first point, Otis and Harper claimed that the federal government had inherent power to protect itself from sedition and libels. "Every independent Government," Otis declared, "has a right to preserve and defend itself against injuries and outrages which endanger its existence." The offenses listed in section one—provisions against unlawful combinations formed to oppose governmental measures, to intimidate federal officers, to excite insurrection, or to counsel or advise these deeds—were acts tending directly to the destruction of the Constitution. By reasoning along lines of indirect causation, the Massachusetts Federalist then justified section two, arguing that "all means calculated to produce these effects, whether by speaking, writing, or printing, were also criminal."

Although the Constitution had not delegated to Congress the power to pass a law against sedition, Otis and Harper said that Congress had the power to make all laws necessary and proper for carrying into execution its powers. They claimed that the government could not function "if sedition for opposing its laws, and libels against its officers, itself, and its proceedings, are to pass unpunished."

But the Federalists did not rest their case wholly on the inherent power of Congress and the necessary and proper clause. Otis also claimed that the Constitution granted the federal courts common law jurisdiction over criminal cases, including sedition. The Constitution had been formed to establish justice. Since justice, by common law standards, affords redress for every crime that threatens to disturb the lawful operations of government, the mention of the word "justice" in the Preamble constituted an implied grant of power to the national government, through its judicial system, to protect itself against such outrages as sedition.

Otis did not rely solely on implication. He added that Article III of the Constitution definitely conferred common law jurisdiction on the federal courts. In defining the powers of the federal judiciary, this article distinguished between cases in law and equity arising under the Constitution and cases arising under the laws of the United States. Otis contended that since the clause, "cases arising under the constitution," did not refer to cases arising under the statutes of the United States, it must refer to cases arising under the common law, "that legal discretion which had been exercised in England since time immemorial, and is to be learnt from the books and reports of that country." To buttress this argument, he turned to such constitutional terms as "trial," "jury," and "impeachment"; these, he said, could only be defined by common law standards. He concluded, therefore, that the original Constitution gave the federal courts common law jurisdiction over sedition.[2]

Otis' contention, the Republicans were quick to point out, largely answered itself. If the federal courts had common law jurisdiction over seditious libel as Otis contended, why was it necessary for Congress to pass a law conferring that jurisdiction on them? The efforts of the Federalists to obtain a sedition law, Gallatin argued, showed that they did not believe their own claims about the jurisdiction of the federal courts. It proved that they thought these courts could not act against libels without the assistance of a statute.

The Republicans flatly denied that there was a common law of the United States. Although they admitted that the common law of England had been received in each colony, they called attention to the fact that it had been modified in every one according to the needs of each. The Constitution, therefore, could not have adopted the common law of all the states because it varied from state to state. Nor could it have adopted the common law of England, because that had been so modified in the states that the Constitutional Convention could not have rejected these American improvements without comment. On the other hand, if the common law had been adopted by the Constitution and was part of it as Otis contended, it was alterable only by a constitutional amendment and not by a law.[3]

Gallatin also rejected Otis' argument that Article III included

[2] *Ibid.*, 2145–2157. For a recent defense of the Federalist views on the common law jurisdiction of federal courts, see Crosskey, *Politics and the Constitution;* for his discussion of the Sedition Law, see 767–768.

[3] *Annals*, 5C, 2S, 2141. Otis' biographer contends that the common law argument was not raised by Otis, but by Gallatin. See Morison, *Otis*, I, 121n. Otis' claim, however, was advanced in the same speech which Morison describes as "one of the best" Otis ever made in Congress, "a defense of the jurisdiction of the federal government over seditious libel; a speech distinguished by careful preparation and documentation, and by sound and statesmanlike interpretation of the Constitution."

federal jurisdiction of common law crimes. Instead, it excluded them by declaring that judicial authority extended only to cases of admiralty, those affecting public ministers, suits between states, citizens of different states, and foreigners, and to cases arising under the Constitution, laws, and treaties "*made* under the authority of the Constitution." If a law or treaty did not cover an offense, Gallatin continued, the federal courts had no jurisdiction. He denied Otis' claim that the clause which conferred jurisdiction over "cases arising under the constitution" was meant to include jurisdiction over offenses not arising under the laws of the United States. It referred only to such cases as might arise from any doubtful construction of the Constitution itself or from any specific power given or prohibition enjoined by the Constitution.[4]

Nor did the technical common law expressions used in the Constitution, such as trial, writ of habeas corpus, and others, prove the jurisdiction of the federal courts over common law crimes. Gallatin agreed that the courts recognized and used common law terms in cases where they had jurisdiction, but this recognition did not extend their jurisdiction beyond the limits defined in the Constitution. Otis had simply confused the principles of the common law and the jurisdiction over cases arising under it. The Federalist spokesman had forgotten what he had set out to prove, Gallatin concluded. The question was not, as Otis ended up arguing, whether federal courts had power over seditious utterances without a sedition law, but whether the Constitution vested Congress with the power of conferring this jurisdiction on the courts.

This the Republicans denied. Neither the original Constitution nor the Bill of Rights gave Congress power to pass a law against sedition. At the time of the ratification of the Constitution no one understood that prosecutions for libels could take place under the jurisdiction of the federal government rather than in the state courts. Not a single member in any of the state ratification conventions had argued that Congress had the power to pass such a law; instead, it had been universally denied. The people of the United States, Gallatin reminded the Federalists, were under the authority not of a single government but of two distinct governments—that of the state in which they lived and that of the United States. The

---

[4] *Ibid.*, 2157. As an example of a case arising under the Constitution, but not under the laws or treaties made under its authority, Gallatin cited the instance of a federal court having to declare a retrospective law of a state to be null and void because unconstitutional.

Constitution had not established a consolidated union, but a federal one, which possessed only those powers defined by the Constitution. Though it seemed evident that Congress had only enumerated powers, Nicholas agreed, the people had added the Tenth Amendment so that no one could mistake that principle. If any power was not delegated to the United States, nor prohibited to the individual states, it remained respectively with the states or with the people.[5]

Since no one contended that the Constitution specifically delegated to Congress the right to pass a sedition act, the examination turned on whether it was included in, or implied by, any of the other powers delegated to the national legislature. The Federalists claimed that Congress had the inherent power—a sort of undefined general legislative power—to punish offenses against government, but the Republicans denied this emphatically. If this accommodating principle were true, Livingston asserted, the powers of the Constitution would extend to every possible case. Under such a power, Gallatin added, federal officials might label any act which might be obnoxious to them as an offense against government and make it a punishable crime. Instead of granting Congress this general power, the Constitution listed the cases in which Congress could define and punish offenses.

Since sedition was not one of those enumerated, Gallatin continued, the only clause which could possibly justify the Federalist claim was the necessary and proper clause. But this clause did not give Congress the power either arbitrarily to create offenses against the government or to take cognizance of cases which were exclusively under the jurisdiction of the state courts, the Pennsylvanian said. Before the Federalists could claim that a sedition law was necessary and proper, they had to show the specific power given to Congress or to the president by some other part of the Constitution, which would be carried into effect by a law against seditious libels. Although the Federalists had declared that the law was necessary, the Republican leader concluded, they had failed to point out the distinct power which it was designed to carry into execution.[6]

[5] *Ibid.*, 2139. The Virginia convention had declared that the liberty of conscience and of the press were essential rights which could not be "cancelled, abridged, restrained, or modified, by any authority of the United States."

[6] *Ibid.*, 2159. Morison, *Otis,* I, 120, calls this the only weak part of Otis' argument.

Congress shall make no law respecting an establishment of religion, or prohibiting the free exercise thereof; or abridging the freedom of speech, or of the press; or the right of the people peaceably to assemble, and to petition the government for a redress of grievances.—First Amendment

The Federalists, who had argued that the original Constitution gave Congress the power to pass a sedition law, denied that the First Amendment deprived the government of this power. Freedom of speech and of the press, Otis argued, were terms which could be defined only by the English common law. Indeed, the First Amendment merely codified the definition set forth in Blackstone's famous *Commentaries*.[7] This freedom, he continued, "is nothing more than the liberty of writing, publishing, and speaking one's thoughts, under the condition of being answerable to the injured party, whether it be the Government or an individual, for false, malicious, and seditious expressions, whether spoken or written; and the liberty of the press is merely an exemption from all previous restraints." Subsequent punishment of words, therefore, was no violation of this freedom.[8]

Otis claimed that states which had constitutional guarantees similar to the First Amendment had given judicial and legislative interpretations of those guarantees in accordance with Blackstone's common law definition. They all agreed that freedom of the press meant freedom from censorship prior to publication and not freedom from prosecution for defamatory and seditious libels. If the proposed sedition law was a violation of the federal Constitution, he concluded, then the states which he had cited infringed their constitutions as well.[9]

Liberty of speech and of the press, Harper added, stood on precisely the same legal footing as the liberty of action. Every man

[7] *Annals*, 5C, 2S, 2148. Blackstone's definition is found in Book IV of his *Commentaries*. These observations were published before the American Revolution. For an analysis of their applicability to the United States, see Chapter XVIII.

[8] *Annals*, 5C, 2S, 214. Otis quoted Blackstone to prove that the expiration of the law requiring parliamentary licensing of the press automatically established freedom of the press in 1694.

[9] *Ibid.*, 2148–2149. Otis did not mention the wide police powers possessed by the states or contrast these with the relatively small powers of the federal government in such matters. Neither did he distinguish between civil and criminal libels or between defamatory, blasphemous, and seditious libels.

had the liberty of action to do what he chose to do, but if he abused this liberty by attacking people or destroying their property, he could be punished. In the same way, every man might publish what he pleased, but he became subject to punishment, if he abused this liberty by publishing slanders against his neighbors, or false, scandalous, and malicious libels against officeholders or the government.

To support this argument, Harper attempted to show that Benjamin Franklin, grandfather of the editor of the Philadelphia *Aurora* and long an advocate of the liberty of the press, agreed that a law against false, scandalous, and malicious libels would not abridge the First Amendment. In one of his last writings Franklin had discussed the abuses of the press and agreed that up to 1789 there had been no check. But after the adoption of the federal Constitution, there had been so much discussion of the necessity of checks and balances that he suspected that some check might be proper to place on the abuses of the press which might not be construed as an "infringement on the sacred liberty of the press."

Franklin proposed to leave the freedom of the press untouched, but he urged the "liberty of the cudgel to go with it." Writing in an obviously facetious vein, he offered this advice to his fellow citizens:

If an impudent writer attacks your reputation . . . break his head. If he conceals himself behind the printer, and you can nevertheless discover who he is, you may, in like manner, waylay him in the night, attack him from behind, and give him a drubbing. If your adversary hires better writers than himself to abuse you more effectually, you may hire brawny porters, stronger than yourself, to assist you in giving him a more effectual drubbing.

Franklin added a last sentence to this advice: "But if the Government should ever happen to be affronted, as it ought to be, with the conduct of such writers, I would not advise proceeding immediately to these extremities, but that we should, in moderation, content ourselves with tarring and feathering and tossing them in a blanket."

After this literary horseplay, Franklin concluded seriously by contending that if "it should be thought that this proposal of mine may disturb the public peace, I would then humbly recommend to our legislators to take up the consideration of both liberties, that of the press, and that of the cudgel: and, by an explicit law, mark their extent and limits; and, at the same time that they secure the person of a citizen from assaults, they would likewise provide for the security of his reputation." Harper therefore claimed that the great authority of Franklin supported his contention that the liberty of the press would not be abridged by an explicit federal sedition law to curb its licentiousness.[10]

It is unfortunate that the Republicans did not get a chance to reply to Harper's observations, because he grossly misinterpreted the advice of a noted defender of the freedom of the press. In the first place, Franklin's essay was directed to the legislators of Pennsylvania in an effort to get, not a national sedition law, but a state libel act. He called for a specific law to define libel so as to provide for the security of a citizen's personal reputation. Harper not only shifted Franklin's argument so as to apply to the jurisdiction of the federal government rather than to that of the states, but he expanded Franklin's recommendations to apply not only to personal reputations but to official reputations as well.

Although Franklin did mention affronts to the government in his facetious prefatory remarks, he confined his serious proposals to personal libels—"private resentments"—not to public functions and functionaries of the government. On this question the old newspaperman had definite ideas.[11] In his attempt to line up Franklin as a supporter of sedition laws, Harper overlooked or deliberately omitted the only remarks in the pamphlet which bore on this question. "If by the *Liberty of the Press*," Franklin had written, "were understood merely the Liberty of discussing the Propriety of Public Measures and Political opinions, let us have as much of it as you please." In short, Franklin called for a state civil defamatory libel law rather than a federal or even a state criminal seditious libel statute.[12]

In citing Franklin's references to the cudgel and the press, Harper also tried to strengthen his argument that the liberty of action and the freedom of the press stood on the same legal footing. The First Amendment, he argued, no more allowed violent abuse of the presi-

[10] *Ibid.*, 2169–2170. Entitled "An Account of the Supreme Court of Judicature in Pennsylvania, viz. The Court of the Press," Franklin's pamphlet first appeared in the *Federal Gazette* (Philadelphia), Sept. 12, 1789. It is reprinted in Albert Henry Smyth, ed., *The Writings of Benjamin Franklin* (New York and London, 1905–07), X, 36–40.

[11] When Franklin was sixteen his brother was jailed in Boston for a "high affront" to the colonial government of Massachusetts Bay. When the General Court ordered James Franklin's arrest for contempt, the editor escaped from punishment by listing his younger brother, the apprentice Benjamin Franklin, as publisher of the paper. The grand jury later refused to indict James Franklin. See Clyde Augustus Duniway, *The Development of the Freedom of the Press in Massachusetts* (New York, 1906), 99–103.

[12] *Franklin's Writings* (Smyth ed.), X, 38.

dent and Congress than the liberty of action implied the freedom of assault, trespass, or assassination.[13]

According to Harper's analogy, there could be no legal difference between a physical assault and a verbal attack—between saying "I'll punch him in the face" and actually striking a person. The analogy placed the spoken word on the same footing with the fatal finality of assassination and made shooting off at the mouth a crime equivalent to that of shooting off a gun in order to murder a person. Harper completely overlooked the fact that whatever damage is inflicted by physical action cannot be undone but only punished, while erroneous and even false views propagated by speech and the press can be rebutted by similar methods. Insults may be rectified by apology, and in the last resort, civil, and even criminal, libel suits can be instituted in the state courts.

The sole purpose of the sedition law, according to its defenders, was to enact the common law of seditious libel into a law of the United States. The original Constitution, they claimed, had given Congress power to pass a law against sedition. The First Amendment, instead of altering this power, had reaffirmed it. Otis also argued that the federal courts had jurisdiction to punish sedition as a common law crime in the absence of a federal statute. The law, therefore, would be no innovation upon the immemorial laws and customs of the United States. Instead of creating a new offense, it re-enacted what had always been the common law. At the same time, it spelled out the common law meaning of the First Amendment. Rather than abridging the freedom of speech and of the press, the law would merely stifle its licentiousness.[14]

In rejecting the Federalist definition of the First Amendment, the Republicans first raised this question to determine its meaning: What danger in the existing law did the people of the United States wish to remedy by adding this new safeguard to the original Constitution? Certainly the Federalist contention that the amendment

[13] *Annals*, 5C, 2S, 2167–2168. Harper had tried to write this interpretation of the First Amendment into the Sedition Law by a proviso specifying that "nothing in this law shall be construed to abridge the freedom of speech and of the press, as secured by the Constitution of the United States." See *ibid.*, 2134. He withdrew this motion, however.

[14] *Ibid.*, 2151. This is the same line of argument advanced by Mansfield's successor, Lord Kenyon, during the French Revolution. It so exasperated the leading British writer on criminal law that he commented: "Hobbes is nearly the only writer who seems to me capable of using the word 'liberty' without talking nonsense." See Sir James Fitzjames Stephen, *History of the Criminal Law of England*, II, 348n.

changed nothing could not explain why the people in the thirteen states had gone to all the trouble between 1789 and 1791 to push through the Bill of Rights. The Republican explanation of these exertions was that the people feared some existing power of Congress and wished to correct it. Since the Constitution did not specifically delegate to Congress any power over the press, the only possible source of this power was the necessary and proper clause. Although the Republicans denied that this clause implied any power to pass a sedition law, Gallatin agreed that its very generality might afford some frail foundation for claims that it empowered Congress to regulate the press. The First Amendment, therefore, had been added to remove any shadow of doubt. It was an express exception to any pre-existing power which the original Constitution might possibly have given Congress over the press. If the First Amendment meant anything, it had to restrict powers granted to Congress by the Constitution, since Congress has no other powers.

Blackstone's definition did not go far enough, said the Republicans. The First Amendment sought not only to preserve the pre-Revolutionary victory abolishing censorship prior to publication, but to achieve a new victory guaranteeing free discussion of public men and measures. It not only rejected the English common law concept of libels against the government but also prohibited Congress from adding any restraint, either by previous restrictions, by subsequent punishment, or by an alteration of jurisdiction or mode of trial. One of the all-important changes which a federal law would make would be the transfer of jurisdiction over the offense of libel from state to federal courts. This transfer, Gallatin contended, would alter the mode of procedure to the injury of the accused. Not only would he be deprived of the benefits of a trial by a jury of his vicinity but in some states the jury would be selected by a federal marshal who owed his tenure to the president. Since a libel against the administration constituted sedition, Gallatin queried, what chance would a citizen have of a fair trial, if the jury was picked, and possibly packed, by "a creature of the Executive"? [15]

Moreover, Nicholas added, the presiding judge would owe his appointment to the president and would be so interested in the case as to make the trial of truth or falsehood unsafe in his hands. Editors would soon not only refrain from publishing anything which might be offensive to the powers-that-be; they would be afraid to publish the truth because they might not always be able to establish the

[15] *Annals*, 5C, 2S, 2160–2163. Robert A. Rutland has written an excellent account of *The Birth of the Bill of Rights, 1776–1791* (Chapel Hill, 1955).

truth to the satisfaction of a court of justice. The sedition bill, he concluded, would lead "to the suppression of every printing press in the country, which is not obsequious to the will of Government." [16]

Harper readily agreed that the bill proposed to transfer the trials from state courts to the courts of the United States, but he denied that Gallatin's objections to the method of selecting a jury should prevent the enactment of the law. By implication, however, he admitted that the shift in jurisdiction would work to the disadvantage of the accused. He claimed that there was as much danger that the jury selected by state or local officials would be inclined in favor of the accused as there was that a jury chosen by a federal marshal would be inclined against the accused.[17] In short, the Federalists did not want to run the chance that a state court, especially in a Republican state, would not convict critics of the administration. They preferred to rest the verdict for this political crime in the hands of federal tribunals, presided over by federally appointed officers.[18]

Even if the Republicans conceded that the First Amendment did not prevent Congress from passing laws punishing the licentiousness of the press, Gallatin said, the bill's supporters would have to recur to the original provisions of the Constitution and show why the bill was now necessary to carry some of its powers into operation. The government, said the Republican leader, had executed its powers for nine years without the assistance of such an act. Therefore, a sedition law was not necessary at all times. Even this measure was limited to less than three years. What danger which had not formerly existed now threatened that the laws would not be executed? Neither Harper's unproven "plot" nor Allen's entertaining "newspaper scraps" offered any proof that a "wonderful, yet unknown change" had altered the situation of the United States so as to render a sedition law necessary. There was nothing novel or alarming about paragraphs blaming or attacking government officials and measures. Why, asked Gallatin, should the present administration fear newspaper abuse more than Washington's administrations or other men? It appeared to him that at no time had there been less to fear from anti-administration publications.

Newspaper paragraphs and invisible plots were not enough to prove the necessity of a sedition law, Gallatin continued; its advocates "must prove that the President dare not, cannot, will not execute the laws, unless the abuse poured upon him from certain

[16] *Ibid.*, 2140–2141. [17] *Ibid.*, 2166.
[18] See James Schouler, *History of the United States of America* (New York, 1880–1913), I, 412.

presses is suppressed." The Republican leader could see no reason for a sedition law other than the fact that the Federalists, riding the wave of public feeling created by the XYZ affair, felt that they were strong enough to overpower their opposition and pass it. Yet this very strength—the fact that they expected to be supported by the people in a flagrant attack on the Constitution, said Gallatin— showed that they did not need the assistance of a sedition law to execute the laws of the United States.[19]

The past nine years of peace, Harper replied, should not lull the nation into a sense of false security. Times had changed, and legislative needs had changed with them. A sedition law was necessary to serve as a sword of defense to the United States when it was on the point "of being driven into a war with a nation which openly boasts of its party among us, and its 'diplomatic skill,' as the most effectual means of paralyzing our efforts, and bringing us to its own terms." The "French party" in America, the Federalist leader insisted, sought to stop the wheels of government as the nation was shifting from peace to war.

Again Harper offered no proof of these accusations. Instead, he finally admitted that he had no proof of his much-mentioned "plot" of treasonable correspondence with France. "Legal proof," he said laconically, "was one thing, and he did not know that he should ever be able to produce it." But he was personally convinced that France "is not without a party in this country, engaged in a most criminal correspondence with her agents, devoted to her service, and aiding . . . the efforts of her 'diplomatic skill.'" Although it was small, it was active, artful, determined, and capable of doing much mischief because it operated through corrupt partisans and hired presses. The purpose of the sedition law, he concluded, was to "repress the enterprises of this party." Harper then repeated his charge that the Jeffersonian party constituted "the French faction," which aimed at reducing the American government to a "single representative democracy."

This did not deter the Republicans from advancing a final argument against the sedition bill. They gave three additional reasons why a law was unnecessary to suppress abuse of the liberty of the press. Since falsehoods depreciate the press, they contended, newspapers will attempt to tell the truth. Moreover, the sound under-

[19] *Annals,* 5C, 2S, 2161. Macon said that he knew of but three or four papers of any consequence that were open "to any animadversions on Government, written with ever so much decorum." See *ibid.,* 2143.

standing of the people is the greatest check on any calumny of this sort. Finally, if members of the legislature are charged falsely, they are in the best possible position to refute the charges. The press is open to the government. Counterargument, not coercion, was the Republican answer for calumny. Livingston summed up this position in four words: "Let the public judge."

The heart and soul of a free government—its main support, said Nicholas—is a free press. The people have no other means of examining the conduct of their elected officials. Gallatin bluntly accused the Federalists of trying to suppress a free circulation of opinion in the hope that they could deceive the people with one-sided accounts and thus perpetuate themselves in power. The sole intent of the sedition bill, he charged, was to punish writings of a political nature—libels against the government, the president, or either branch of Congress. The pious assertions by Otis and Dana that the bill could affect only the authors of false publications did not disprove its political bias. Laws against political writings critical of administration policies had always been used by tyrants "to prevent the diffusion of knowledge, to throw a veil on their folly or their crimes, to satisfy those mean passions which always denote little minds, and to perpetuate their own tyranny." The principles of the law of political libels, Gallatin concluded, were to be found in the rescripts of the worst emperors of Rome and in the decisions of the Star Chamber. Identifying the Federalists with these historical tyrants, Gallatin flung a final charge at them. Governments actuated by pure motives, although despising the slanders of malice, had always listened to the criticisms of their conduct, knowing that to resort to repression of writings attacking their measures was to confess that these could be defended by no other means. Unlike the Federalists, they knew that "the proper weapon to combat error was truth." [20]

On July 10 the House enacted the Sedition Law of 1798 by a vote of 44 to 41.[21] Two days later a little-noticed provision passed Congress as a supplement to the sedition statute. It authorized all federal judges to bind persons to good behavior in cases arising under the laws of the United States. Thus an offender against the Sedition Act could be required to post bond in addition to being fined and imprisoned. This would deter offenders from repeating their criticisms, because such action might lead to the forfeiture of the bonds. Since federal judges exercised discretionary power over the amount

[20] *Ibid.*, 2164.　　　　　　[21] *Ibid.*, 2171.

of the surety and the length of the binding, this legislation amounted
to an economic enjoining action against further criticism by the
person bound.[22]

Denouncing the Federalists as "the majority of three," the *Aurora*
warned Americans that they "had better hold their tongues and
make tooth picks of their pens." Deploring the new measure, the
New York *Time Piece* ridiculed it as a "harmonizer of parties" in
view of the fact that "they must all sing to the same tune!" The
Boston *Independent Chronicle,* on the other hand, insisted on the
right of citizens to express their opinions on public men and measures. When the independent citizens of the United States considered
public measures as leading to an annihilation of their constitutional
liberties, no terrors could intimidate or deter them from a manly
censure of their servants. In a free country, it was the duty of citizens to speak their sentiments, "and may the hand be palsied,"
the editor continued, "that shrinks back from its duties let the
threats of the SERVANTS OF THE PEOPLE become ever so
vociferous to controll it." [23]

On July 14 President John Adams signed the statute which was
to expire with the end of his term in office. On the same day, the
following "Advertisement Extraordinary!!!" appeared in the defiant
Aurora:

Orator Mum takes the very orderly method of announcing to his fellow
citizens that a thinking Club will be established in a few days at the sign
of the *Muzzle* in *Gag* street. The first subject for cogitation will be:
"Ought a Free People to obey the laws which violate the constitution
they have sworn to support?"
N. B. No member will be permitted to think longer than fifteen minutes.[24]

In every case involving freedom of speech and of the press, there
is one basic question which overshadows all others: What standard
is to be used to test the criminality of the utterance? Another important question, though of less importance, is this: Who shall
apply the test? The two legal rules incorporated in section three
of the sedition statute dealt with the question of who shall judge.
By admitting truth as a defense and by entrusting criminality to
the jury rather than to the judge, the law made important proce-

[22] *Stat. at L.,* I, 609.
[23] *Aurora,* July 14, 1798; *Time Piece,* July 13, 1798; *Independent Chronicle,*
quoted in the *Aurora,* July 11, 1798.
[24] *Aurora,* July 14, 1798.

dural changes in the common law. A twelve-man jury was less likely to convict a person for criticizing the government, especially if the government were unpopular, than was a judge appointed by that government, and the threat of suppression was further weakened by allowing the truth of the remarks to prevent a conviction.

But it was section two which laid down the test of criminality. This section in effect transferred the English common law "bad tendency" test to the legal code of the United States. It made blame of the government, Congress, or the president the test by which to determine the criminality of utterances. Although this portion also listed the "bad intent" of the speaker as a necessary ingredient of the crime, it made no reference to any intent of the offender to cause violence. It was only necessary to prove that the defendant intended to write the words in order to defame or bring into contempt or disrepute the government, Congress, or the president. Moreover, the Federalists had made it clear in the debates that the "bad intent" of the writer would be inferred from the "bad tendency" of his words. If the words placed the government in a bad light, they tended to its overturn, according to Harper, and the writer would be presumed to have intended this consequence. Both Harper and Allen claimed that letters by Republican congressmen to their constituents gave administration measures "the most vile coloring." Allen claimed that the circular letter written by an unidentified Virginia congressman was "calculated to excite the deeds of death." From this supposed bad tendency of the words he concluded that the "bad intent" of the writer "must be to inflame his constituents against the Government." Although Harper failed to quote from the letter which he condemned, he claimed that its effect (that is, its tendency) was to turn the country upside down. It followed that the intent of its author was "to excite those insurrections, which had heretofore been excited by other means."

The Sedition Law which emerged from the congressional crucible of heated debate was a two-edged sword with the motto "Truth is a defense" written on one side of the blade and "The jury shall decide" inscribed on the other.[25] When a sword swings into action, however, there is a strong probability that no eye will be swift enough to read the engraving. What matters most, therefore, is not the inscriptions, but the sword. Section two forged the sword and

[25] Harper called the law a sword. I am also indebted to Chafee's use of this analogy in his *Free Speech in the United States*, 467.

made the "bad tendency" test the blade with which to cut down political opposition to the government. Section three merely wrote the inscriptions.

This controversy over freedom of speech and liberty of the press pointed up the fact that the conflict pivoted on the concept of the relation of the people to the government. The Federalist and Republican positions boiled down to antagonistic views of this problem. The Federalists asserted the principle that the rulers, by the nature of their positions as the chosen leaders of the people, were the wise and good guides of the country. If the rulers were mistaken, their errors might be pointed out respectfully, but the people should not make adverse criticism, especially of the legislator's motives, in conversation or in newspapers. If they did not know their "place," they ran the risk of prosecution. The only lawful way to present their grievances was through their lawfully chosen representatives in Congress and in the state legislatures, who should be petitioned in an orderly way so as not to upset what Mrs. Adams called the "National Dignity and Decorum." Even though the constituted authorities were mistaken, no censure should be leveled against them which tended to diminish their authority.

An important source of Federalist precedent was the course of action pursued by the British in combating the political and social forces unleashed by the French Revolution.[26] Harper claimed that America could be saved from these insidious forces only by imitating the British example of alien and sedition laws. As early as 1796 Fenno's *Gazette of the United States* commented favorably on the British sedition law:

The Jacobins of this country have been looking forward with the most eager anticipation to riots insurrection and revolutions in England from the Sedition bills lately passed. But alas! All these hopes are blasted by the late intelligence; the bill had passed, had been in operation two months, and *all was quiet*. And what is not a little wonderful, the Jacobins of that country, after making such a tremendous warning before the bills passed, and exclaiming that liberty would be destroyed by them, and the freedom of speech and deliberation annihilated, now whine out that their great object of reform can be as lawfully pursued as before they passed.[27]

[26] In 1794 and 1795 England passed a stringent Alien Act, an "Act Suspending Habeas Corpus in Certain Cases," a Treasonable and Seditious Practices Act, a Seditious Assemblies Act, and a new Treasons Act. The marked similarity between these laws and the Federalist program is discussed in Dauer, *The Adams Federalists*, 157–159.

[27] *Gazette of the United States,* March 25, 1796.

By relying on the Blackstonian view that the government was master, the Federalists accepted the pre-Revolutionary definition of free speech and liberty of the press. This constant harking in Congress to British examples carried the Federalists close to the House of Commons' claim to omnipotence [28]—to the days when debates were secret, voting lists unpublished, and "insults" to constituted authorities were crimes. Republican complaints were viewed not as manifestations of legitimate political criticism but as evidences of disobedience, disloyalty, and the hand of French "diplomatic skill."

The debates over the Sedition Law formed a part of the unending discussion of the relationship between the liberty of the individual and the security of the state. The Federalists were so interested in providing for the security of the state, which they identified with their administration, that they were willing to run the risk of suppressing the liberties of the individual. Arguing that unusual circumstances called for unusual measures, they moved to penalize verbal opposition as well as forcible opposition to the nation's laws. Wishing to eliminate political heresy, they decided to stamp out any criticism which had even a remote tendency to undermine the authority of their administration and lead to an "overthrow" of their party at the polls.

These contentions by the Federalists led a Republican wit to submit a new definition of the term "administration." According to this lexicographer, the word referred to "a set of men placed at the helm of government, to direct its movements. It is said they are the peculiar favorites of heaven, and partake of the divine essence. It is a sacrilege to look askance at them, and to wound their hallowed ears with the recital of unpleasant truths, is to arraign the wisdom of Providence, whence they derive an indefeasible divine right to rule uncontrolled over the mighty multitude." [29]

The Republicans asserted that the people and not the government were the sovereign power in the United States. They denied that Blackstone's *Commentaries*, written on the eve of the American Revolution by an antirepublican Tory, were the guide to the meaning of the liberties of Americans. The Revolution, the American political ideal it realized, and the Constitution and the First Amendment adopted by the people had abolished Blackstone's

[28] For Federalist claims that "the sovereignty of the country is vested by the Constitution in Congress" rather than in the people, see Dana's and Sewall's speeches, *Annals*, 5C, 2S, 1580, 1957–1958.

[29] *Norfolk Epitome of the Times*, quoted in the *Aurora*, Feb. 16, 1799.

limitations and reversed the relation of the people to the government. The rulers were but the elected agents of the people.

The Republicans have been condemned by some writers as hypocritical states'-righters who defended the right of the states to punish seditious utterances at the same time that they denounced the exercise of that power by the federal government as fatal to liberty. They were not so interested, so the charge runs, in defending the general concept of the liberty of the press as they were in restricting the powers of the general government. This conclusion that the Republican argument was strictly a states'-rights discourse does not square with the evidence.[30]

The debates on the Sedition Law turned on two points, the jurisdiction over libels and the nature of free speech. One of Otis' arguments was that since the states had jurisdiction over libels, the federal government must have also. The Republicans readily agreed that the states' police power gave them jurisdiction over libels. As a matter of fact, until the Sedition Act was brought forward no one had questioned the fact that cognizance of libels belonged exclusively to the state courts, either at common law or under state statutes.[31] Livingston went so far as to concede that if it were merely a matter of jurisdiction, seditious utterances against the federal government could be punished in state courts. But it did not follow that because the states had a given power the federal government had a concurrent power. On the question of jurisdiction, the Republicans pointed to the division of powers set forth in the Constitution. As a final defense against federal action against libels, they relied on the Tenth Amendment. The federal government had only delegated powers, and since the power to pass a law punishing political libels was neither enumerated nor necessary and proper to carry any delegated power into execution, it followed that this power was reserved to the states or to the people. Thus, even when the Republicans advanced a "states'-rights" argument, they were on solid constitutional ground by denying an all-embracing criminal jurisdiction to the federal government. At the same

[30] Hildreth, *History of the United States,* V, 302, concludes that "the opposition argued, not like liberal statesmen and wise legislators, but only like violent anti-Federal politicians." He then lists a series of arguments which he thinks wise congressmen could have used in opposing the Sedition Law. An analysis of the debates demonstrates that the Republicans utilized every issue suggested by Hildreth's hindsight.

[31] Gallatin, *Annals,* 5C, 2S, 2163; Macon, *ibid.,* 2151; Livingston, *ibid.,* 2154. Gallatin referred not to seditious libels, which he claimed could not exist under a free government, but to defamatory libels against personal reputations, obscenity, etc.

time, this argument was a realistic defense of free speech and a free press because the immediate threat to civil liberties came from the proposed federal statute.

When the Republicans left the question of jurisdiction, however, and moved on to a discussion of the nature of free speech, they argued for unpunishable criticism of officials and laws, both state and federal. This was best illustrated by the argument of Livingston, who in his discussion of jurisdiction had been the only Republican to assert that state courts could punish libels against the federal government. When he dealt with the concept of speech in a free and independent government, however, he denied that there was any such thing as slanders against the government. Governments, he said, may protect their characters by disproving charges leveled against them and letting the people decide. One of the most important purposes of society and government is the discovery and spreading of truth on subjects of general concern. This is possible only through unlimited discussion, for, as Livingston pointed out, once force is thrown into the argument, it becomes a matter of chance whether it is thrown on the false side or the true, and truth loses all its natural advantages in the contest. To appeal to a law to crush criticism is to admit that it can be met in no other way. Censure then is combated by force or arms, not by force of reason, he concluded.[32]

The Republicans phrased their defense of freedom of speech and of the press in general terms; they pointed out that all popular governments rest on public opinion, not force. Their arguments which labeled as tyrannical any government punishing political libels applied to state governments as well as the federal government. Viewed as a whole, their argument, despite the meager character of the reported debates, was a vigorous defense of the principle of free speech and a free press in a free republican form of government. They made clear their belief that political libels had been withdrawn from the realm of prosecution by either the state or federal government. Their arguments indicate that in a free and elective government the people retain the right to criticize their representatives without being charged criminally with stirring up sedition and disaffection or with bringing these representatives into disrepute. To the Republicans the First Amendment prohibited the punishment of words for their supposed injurious tendencies. The people could decide for themselves whether criticisms were deserved or undeserved; they needed no elite ruling group to point out which words were insidious and which were not.

[32] *Annals*, 5C, 2S, 2153–2154.

In this debate over liberty and authority, the Republicans were willing to support laws directed against actions by force and violence in opposition to the laws of the land. They agreed that when beliefs and opinions are put into action, they are liable to the limitations which apply to other actions. Although section one of the Sedition Law was worded vaguely and aroused some Republican opposition, they conceded that it was directed against "seditious practices"—not against words, beliefs, and opinions, but against forcible opposition to the law. They nevertheless opposed this section of the law as useless, claiming that the nation already had laws which punished this offense. Even so, they launched no vigorous protests against any provisions of section one except that which related to speech, and this clause was eliminated in the final law. Instead, they concentrated their attacks on section two, which dealt with opposition not by force and violence but by speaking, printing, writing, and publishing. In short, the Republicans did not oppose laws which they thought would promote the security of the state, but they drew the line when those measures encroached upon the constitutional liberties of the people.[33]

Who was responsible for this audacious attempt by the "majority of three" to suppress minority political opinion? No one denies that an arrogant Federalist party pushed the bill through Congress. But as Samuel Eliot Morison has observed, "the responsibility of this legislation has not been fixed upon any one individual or group in the Federal party." [34] Indeed, as another writer has pointed out, "every biographer has endeavored to clear the fame of his own hero from any complicity in the sorry business." Thus "it has come to pass that, if all the evidence that has been adduced can be believed, these statutes were foundlings . . . for whom no man was responsible." [35] Yet this was an age of personalities, when public acts often took the names of their sponsors; references to Jay's Treaty, Harrison's Land Law, and Hamilton's financial program illustrate this tendency.

The task of fixing responsibility for the Sedition Law is not a difficult one. The statute contained two basic sections. The first was a part of Lloyd's treason and sedition bill, and the second was

[33] For a thoughtful article on balancing the interest of the state with the individual's interest in free political belief and expression, see Roscoe Pound, "Interests of Personality," *Harvard Law Review*, 28 (1915), 454.

[34] Morison, *Otis*, I, 111.

[35] John T. Morse, *John Adams* (Boston and New York, 1884), 283.

a part of Harper's resolutions. The logical name for the Sedition Act, then, would be the "Lloyd-Harper Law." These were the men immediately responsible for the provisions of the statute; they were the sponsors. In addition, they herded the law through their respective houses. Lloyd not only drafted the original bill but also headed the Senate committee which revised it. In the House, Harper, the acknowledged leader of the Federalists, became the act's strongest supporter, although Otis and Allen sustained him to the limit.[36]

These leaders received the enthusiastic support of the other Federalists both in Congress and out, with the possible exception of John Marshall. In his political platform during the congressional election of 1798, Marshall announced that he would have opposed the Alien and Sedition Laws had he been in Congress. They were both "useless" and "calculated to create unnecessary discontents and jealousies." Although his return from the XYZ mission had done much to prompt "energetic measures" in the summer of 1798, the future chief justice opposed the Sedition Law as inexpedient.[37] For this act of party "disloyalty," Marshall was severely censured by the New England extremists, who branded him a half-Federalist.[38] Condemning the Virginian's stand, Fisher Ames wrote that "no correct man,—no incorrect man, even,—whose affections and feelings are wedded to the government, would give his name to the base opposers of the law. . . . This he has done. Excuses may palliate,—future zeal in the cause may partially atone,—but his character is done for. . . . The moderates [such as Marshall] are the meanest of cowards, the falsest of hypocrites." [39]

Marshall, however, did not oppose the Sedition Law on grounds of constitutionality. Instead, when the Virginia legislature passed its famous resolutions against the Alien and Sedition Laws, Marshall penned the Federalist reply which defended their constitutionality. Thus, the only known Federalist opponent of the Sedition Law supported it as constitutional.[40]

Every other Federalist who is on record favored the passage of

[36] Lynch, *Fifty Years of Party Warfare*, 76.

[37] See his letter to "Freeholder" in the *Times and Virginia Advertiser* (Alexandria), Oct. 11, 1798. Beveridge, *Marshall*, II, 575–577, reprints the complete letter.

[38] Beveridge, *Marshall*, II, 390–394.

[39] Ames to Christopher Gore, Dec. 18, 1798, *Ames's Works*, I, 245–247.

[40] Theodore Sedgwick to Rufus King, March 20, 1799, *King's Correspondence*, II, 581, calls the report "a masterly performance for which we are indebted to the pen of General Marshall." Also see Sedgwick to Hamilton, Feb. 7, 1799, *Hamilton's Works* (Hamilton ed.), VI, 392. The report is in the *Journal of the*

the law and its execution. This included President Adams, whose answers to incoming addresses did so much to incite anti-Republican sentiment. Although he neither recommended nor fathered this law, Adams approved it willingly, and later he specifically authorized its use against his critics. Only five days after he signed the measure, the president hinted that it might moderate the verbal attacks upon the government. "Until lately," read one of his addresses, "licentiousness has been too little restrained." [41] It took little imagination to see that he believed that the law directed against such "licentiousness" would restrain it. "I cannot but be of the opinion," he wrote to the citizens of Boston, "that the profligate spirit of falsehood and malignity, which has appeared in some, and the unguarded disposition in others, to encourage it, are serious evils, and bear a threatening aspect upon the Union of the States, their Constitution of Government, and the moral character of the Nation." [42]

Ten years later Adams attempted a defense of his support of the Alien and Sedition Laws. In a letter to the *Boston Patriot* he claimed that this legislation was part of Hamilton's secret instructions to congressional leaders and cabinet members. Adams denied that he had adopted Hamilton's idea of an alien and sedition law. "I recommended no such thing in my speech," he said; "Congress, however, adopted both these measures." Although Adams tried to throw the responsibility on Hamilton, he wrote: "I knew there was need enough of both, and therefore I consented to them. But as they were then considered as war measures, and intended altogether against the advocates of the French and peace with France, I was apprehensive that a hurricane of clamor would be raised against them, as in truth there was, even more fierce and violent than I had anticipated." [43] By his own admission, then, Adams supported the Sedition Act because he thought there was a need for it. Nor did his apprehensions prevent his approving its energetic enforcement against the critics of his administration.

Virginia House of Delegates, Dec. 1798, 88–90. Beveridge, *Marshall,* II, 405, says that "in no writing or spoken word, before he became Chief Justice of the United States, did Marshall so extensively state his constitutional views as in this unknown paper."

[41] To the officers and men of Colonel Romyen's militia regiment in Montgomery County, N.Y., dated Phila., July 19, 1798, *Albany Centinel,* Aug. 7, 1798.

[42] Answer dated Quincy, Aug. 7, 1798, *Columbian Centinel,* Aug. 19, 1798.

[43] *Adams' Works,* IX, 290–291. There is no indication in Hamilton's writings or papers that he recommended these laws, although he supported them vigorously.

The attempt by Adams to shift responsibility for the Sedition Law to Hamilton raises the question of that leader's attitude. Hamilton's biographers have been almost unanimous in absolving him of supporting the law. Some go even further and portray him as a defender of civil liberties who, along with Marshall, stood against the whole Federalist party.[44] These writers base their conclusions on the hastily written letter which Hamilton dashed off to Wolcott on June 29. This letter was directed solely against Lloyd's first draft of the Sedition Law, a version which the Senate itself recommitted two days before Hamilton wrote his letter.[45] When the Senate reported an energetic sedition bill in place of its violent treason and sedition measure, Hamilton did not register any complaint or advise any mitigating amendments. Although this new measure was more restrictive of free speech than was the final Sedition Law, he wrote no urgent letters opposing it. Nor did he protest when President John Adams signed the bill.

After the enactment of the Alien and Sedition Laws, Hamilton became a leading advocate of their enforcement. Early in 1799, following his appointment as a major general in the provisional army raised against France, he bemoaned the failure of President Adams to execute the laws more vigorously. "What avail laws which are not executed?" he asked the Speaker of the House. He claimed that many incendiary presses were edited by renegade aliens who engaged in their "destructive labors" in "open contempt and defiance of the [Alien and Sedition] Laws." "Why are they not sent away?" the general demanded. "Are laws of this kind passed merely to excite odium and remain a dead letter?" Vigor seemed to him as neces-

[44] For examples of these views, see Henry Jones Ford, *Alexander Hamilton* (New York, 1931), 323–324; David Loth, *Alexander Hamilton, Portrait of a Prodigy* (New York, 1939), 255; Schouler, *History of the United States*, 407; Charles A. and Mary R. Beard, *The Rise of American Civilization* (New York, 1930), 376–377; Miller, *Crisis in Freedom*, 73; Bowers, *Jefferson and Hamilton*, 376–377; Beveridge, *Marshall*, 382. In the most recent biography, the author does not discuss Hamilton's response to these laws. See Nathan Schachner, *Alexander Hamilton* (New York, 1946), 386–387. But in *The Founding Fathers* (New York, 1954), 467–468, Schachner portrays Hamilton as an opponent of the alien and sedition system. For a detailed discussion of Hamilton's attitude, see J. M. Smith, "Alexander Hamilton, the Alien Law, and Seditious Libels," *Review of Politics*, 16 (1954), 305–333.

[45] Henry Cabot Lodge, "Alexander Hamilton," *Studies in History* (Boston, 1885), 163–164, is almost the sole exception to the general run of historians on Hamilton's attitude. He observes that "the idea . . . that Hamilton opposed those measures is quite erroneous since, as a matter of fact, he was one of their strongest supporters."

sary in the enforcement of the laws by the executive branch as in their enactment by the legislative. "If the President requires to be stimulated," he suggested to the Speaker, "those who can approach him ought to do it."

Rigorous enforcement of the laws, however, was not enough for Hamilton. In his letter to the Speaker, he proposed even more drastic laws against criticism of government officials. The "internal situation of the United States" made it necessary to pass additional "laws for restraining and punishing incendiary and seditious practices." To counteract factional opposition to the government, which he feared would erupt into violence, Hamilton suggested that all writings which were libels at common law should be prosecuted in federal courts as sedition "if levelled against any officer whatsoever of the United States." If federal officials were to perform their duties properly, it was essential to maintain public confidence in them "by preserving their reputations from malicious and unfounded slanders." Hamilton thought that this could best be done in the federal courts: "They ought not to be left to the cold and reluctant protection of State courts, always temporizing, and sometimes disaffected." [46]

Since he did not explain whether these new provisions should be incorporated into the Sedition Act or should replace that law altogether, Hamilton's remarks are open to two interpretations. First, he could have meant exactly what he said—that all writings which at common law were libels should be regarded as seditious if leveled against federal officials. If Congress had passed a new act based on this concept, the truth of the statements about the officials would not have been a defense against the charge of seditious libel. The criticism might have been ever so truthful, but if it had tended to damage the reputation of the government, the administration, or the official, it could have been punished as sedition by common law standards. These specified that "the greater the truth, the greater the libel." Such an act would have outlawed all political opposition.

Second, Hamilton might have meant that the Sedition Act itself should be expanded in order to define as seditious all writings which were libels at common law. If this had been done, truth would have remained a defense, but the scope of the act would

[46] Hamilton to Dayton, 1799, *Hamilton's Works* (Lodge ed.), VIII, 517–522. The only date on this letter is 1799, but it is inserted between letters of Dec. 27, 1798, and Jan. 6, 1799. For an interesting comparison of Hamilton and Adams' political philosophy, see Adrienne Koch, "Hamilton, Adams and the Pursuit of Power," *Review of Politics*, 16 (1954), 37–66, especially 62.

have been widened to allow prosecution not only of critics of the president or of Congress but also of "any officer whatsoever of the United States." In either event, Hamilton was in favor of protecting the reputations of all federal officers from political criticism by enacting an even tougher sedition act than that of 1798. Moreover, any new law modeled after this suggestion would have shielded Hamilton from Republican criticism of his administration of the army. If he meant what he said, then, Hamilton backed a more drastic restriction of freedom of speech and of the press than the act which his biographers picture him as opposing.

Responsibility for the Alien and Sedition Laws rests on the whole Federalist party. Although this party openly split into the Adamite and Hamiltonian wings in the election of 1800, not a single Federalist questioned the constitutionality of the Sedition Law, and only John Marshall doubted its wisdom. With this sole exception, every Federalist favored its subsequent enforcement against Republican spokesmen, whether they were congressmen, editors, or less influential citizens.

Part Two

THE PATTERN OF
ENFORCEMENT
1798-1799

CHAPTER IX

The Hunters and the Hunted

Would to God the immigrants could be collected and
retransported to the climes from whence they came.
—*Gazette of the United States*, 1798

THE test of the effectiveness of an act presumably lies in the extent
to which it was invoked and enforced. Thirteen years after the expiration of the Alien Friends Act, former President Adams wrote
that he had not applied it in a single instance.[1] Although the arbitrary measure was never officially invoked, it was not without effect.
Adams' statement left out of consideration two important things:
first, the effect which the discussion and passage of the law had
in bringing about the departure of numerous foreigners who might
otherwise have run afoul of its provisions; and second, the persistent
efforts of some of the officials in the Adams administration to obtain
action against other foreigners who had not departed and whose
activities made them especially objectionable to the Federalists.

Dangerous Aliens: The Enforcement of the Alien Friends Act

Shortly after the introduction of the alien bills in Congress, apprehensive Frenchmen began scheduling passage from the United
States. In May, 1798, nearly two months before the law was passed,

[1] Adams to Jefferson, Quincy, June 14, 1813, *Adams' Works*, X, 42.

The first part of this chapter was published in the *Mississippi Valley Historical
Review*, 41 (1954), 85–104.

Jefferson wrote that "the threatening appearances from the Alien bills have so alarmed the French who are among us, that they are going off. A ship, chartered by themselves for this purpose, will sail within a fortnight for France, with as many as she can carry. Among these I believe will be Volney, who has in truth been the principal object aimed at by the law." [2] This reference to the Federalist attitude toward Constantin François Chasseboeuf, Comte de Volney, French scientist and author, was strikingly confirmed when, on June 22, *Porcupine's Gazette*, edited by the English expatriate William Cobbett, published a letter which charged that the country had become the resort "of abominably seditious foreigners of every distinction." Using the pseudonym "An American," this correspondent singled out Volney as an especially dangerous "French democrat," an atheist, and a disciple of French revolutionary thought.

It is a fact not to be controverted at this day [the letter continued], that the French have done more toward the destruction of the government of Europe, by their political emissaries, preaching the vile doctrine of infidelity and atheism, and by their spies sent to creat[e] divisions among the people, and distinction between them and their government; they have done more by this means of intrigue, than by the combined strength of their armies or the bravery of their military force.—With this truth we cannot be too strongly impressed. Americans! Beware—at this moment beware of the diplomatic skill of the French republic.[3]

Shifting his attack to Jefferson, the writer suggested that since the vice-president did not seem to consider an infidel and an atheist as dangerous to society, the continued presence of Volney was even more dangerous to the people of the United States.

To avoid expulsion, however, Volney had sailed for France aboard the *Benjamin Franklin* on June 7, nearly three weeks before the alien bill became law, and Jefferson, who had feared that those Frenchmen leaving to avoid the law would go "under irritations calculated to fan the flame," was relieved to find that Volney, at least, harbored no such animosity. "He is most thoroughly impressed with the importance of preventing war," he reported, "whether considered with reference to the interests of the two countries, of the cause of republicanism, or of man on the broad scale." [4]

[2] Jefferson to Madison, May 3, 1798, *Jefferson's Writings* (Ford ed.), VII, 248. Also see Jefferson to Monroe, May 21, 1798, *ibid.*, 257.

[3] *Porcupine's Gazette*, June 22, 1798, as quoted in Gilbert Chinard, *Volney et l'Amérique d'après des documents inédits et sa correspondance avec Jefferson* (Baltimore, 1923), 97–99.

[4] Jefferson to Madison, May 31 and June 7, 1798, *Jefferson's Writings* (Ford ed.), VII, 262, 267.

Also sailing on the *Franklin* was Victor Marie DuPont, the newly appointed consul general of the French Republic to the United States, who had arrived in May and, on finding that the government refused to accept his credentials, had decided to return to France with Volney and the other fleeing Frenchmen.[5] These departures met with administrative approval, and Secretary Pickering promptly requested free and unmolested passage for their ship en route to France. A similar permit was issued a month later to guarantee safe passage for a shipload of Frenchmen bound for Bordeaux; and in July and August, directly after the adoption of the Alien Friends Act, more than a dozen additional shiploads of anxious Frenchmen sailed for France or Santo Domingo.[6] The departure of Volney was hailed as "good riddance" by at least one New York newspaper, and so strong did the anti-alien feeling run in June that the *Aurora* soberly reported that "Cremona fiddles are to be ordered out of the kingdom under the *Alien Bill*," on the ground that their tones were "calculated to bring the *constitutional* music of *organs* and *kettle-drums* into contempt."[7] Although violins were not ousted, anti-French sentiment reached such heights in July that the first lady predicted that if a new French minister were to arrive he would not find the United States a resting place for twenty-four hours.[8] The nativist pressure became so pervasive that the rhymed review of the year's political events by one of the "Hartford Wits" included the observation that

> Each factious alien shrinks with dread
> And hides his hemp-devoted head.[9]

The Federalist press made every attempt to uncover the hidden heads of factious aliens and clamored for the enforcement of the

[5] Samuel E. Morison, "DuPont, Talleyrand, and the French Spoliations," Mass. Hist. Soc., *Proceedings*, 49 (1915), 64–65, citing a letter from Volney to Louis Marie de la Révellière-Lépeaux.

[6] Fifteen ships sailed in two months. Although most of the passengers were French merchants forced to leave because of the suspension of commercial intercourse between France and America, many of them left because of the passage of the Alien Act. For the official correspondence see Domestic Letters, XI (1798–99), 11–35, General Records of the Department of State, RG 59 (National Archives). Also see Frances S. Childs, *French Refugee Life in the United States, 1790–1800* (Baltimore, 1940), 190–191.

[7] New York *Daily Advertiser*, July 4, 1798; *Aurora*, June 23, 1798.

[8] Abigail Adams to Mary Cranch, July 17, 1798, Mitchell, *New Letters*, 205–206.

[9] Richard Alsop, *The Political Green-House for the Year 1798* (Hartford, 1799).

Alien Law. The *Gazette of the United States* claimed that the source of all political evils and misfortunes in the nation was "the facility with which foreigners acquire the full and perfect right of citizenship." This was the fountain from which defamation, falsehood, and sedition "so plenteously flowed." [10] A New York paper asked how a sound American could read with cold indifference

the vile incendiary publications of foreign hirelings among us. . . . Such abominable miscreants deserve no place on the American soil. When the state is in danger and strong remedies are necessary . . . none but an ENEMY can resist their use. Such remedies have been provided by the late Session of Congress; and however long the partisans of France may declaim against them, every good citizen rejoices in the provision, and will aid in giving it efficacy.[11]

In a letter to the New York *Commercial Advertiser* on Christmas Eve, "Marcus Brutus" questioned the value of immigration in general. He confessed that many foreigners had quickly imbibed American principles, but denounced many others as "turbulent and disaffected zealots . . . the commodious instrument of the agents of France." Another New York correspondent had earlier opposed the "false sentiment" that America was an asylum for the oppressed. He called for the blanket enforcement of the Alien Law in a classic statement of an oft-repeated nativist sentiment: "Would to God the immigrants could be collected and retransported to the climes from whence they came." [12]

Although President John Adams did not go this far, he traveled a long way down the same road in his answer to a New York address. It was exceedingly regrettable, he wrote, that any marks of disaffection had appeared in New York. If this was due to "the influx of foreigners, of discontented characters, it ought to be a warning. If we glory in making our country an asylum for virtue in distress and for innocent industry, it behoves us to beware, that under this pretext it is not made a receptacle of malevolence and turbulence, for the outcasts of the universe." [13]

Despite Adams' claim of nonexecution, then, his administration did not refrain on principle from enforcing the Alien Law. As a matter of fact, Secretary Pickering early complained that the law was so weak that the administration might be embarrassed in its enforce-

[10] *Gazette of the United States*, reprinted in the *Albany Centinel*, Aug. 3, 1798.

[11] *Albany Centinel*, Aug. 7, 1798. This story bears a New York dateline of Aug. 2, 1798.

[12] *Commercial Advertiser*, Dec. 24, 1798; *Daily Advertiser*, Sept. 2, 1798.

[13] To the Grand Jury of the County of Dutchess, N.Y., Sept. 22, 1798, *Adams' Works*, IX, 223.

ment efforts. Two omissions aroused his apprehensions: the law did not require aliens to post sureties pending their departure, and the president was not authorized to seize and confine them while waiting for their departure or deportation.[14]

These drawbacks, however, did not prevent the secretary from proposing a vigorous enforcement policy. Since President Adams was spending the time between sessions of Congress at his home in Massachusetts, Pickering hoped to expedite action by having the chief executive delegate his power over aliens to the Cabinet. The heads of the departments could then confer and decide by majority vote which aliens to expel; the president would have only to sign blank arrest warrants which would be filled in by the Cabinet.[15]

On October 11, therefore, Pickering mailed some blank deportation orders to the president.[16] On the same day, however, the secretary sent a second letter proposing an alternative method of handling cases against undesirable aliens. Lest Adams should have any doubt about the legality or expediency of delegating his powers under the Alien Act to the decision of the Cabinet, Pickering suggested three aliens whom he was sure that the president would agree were dangerous and asked him to sign the blank warrants for use against this trio.[17] Although the president did not question the legality of delegating his powers, he was convinced that the law's broad powers ought to receive "a strict construction." Adams therefore wrote his secretary that he preferred to make the decisions himself.[18]

Nonetheless, it was Pickering who became the chief enforcement officer. As the leading official in the Cabinet, he carried on an extensive correspondence with important Federalists in the Middle states, traditionally the most liberal in their immigration policies. Philadelphia and New York, the nation's leading ports of debarkation, received most of his attention, and the United Irishmen were most often mentioned as a dangerous group. On August 23, 1798, the United States district attorney for Pennsylvania, William Rawle, wrote Pickering about some unidentified "secret projects" of the United Irishmen. On the next day Richard Peters, United States district judge, notified the secretary that Philadelphia and vicinity

14 Pickering to the President of the United States, Trenton, Aug. 28, 1798, Pickering Papers, XXXVII, 325 (Mass. Hist. Soc.).

15 Pickering to the President, Oct. 4, 1798, ibid., IX, 426.

16 Pickering to the President, Oct. 11, 1798, Adams' Works, VIII, 607n.

17 Pickering to the President, Oct. 11, 1798, Pickering Papers, IX, 453 (Mass. Hist. Soc.).

18 Adams to Pickering, Quincy, Oct. 17, 1798, ibid., XXIII, 241. This letter is printed in Adams' Works, VIII, 606–607, under the date of Oct. 16.

contained "some Rascals . . . both Aliens and infamous Citizens" whom he wanted to handle if he could do it legally. He promised to send a full account of the "Alien Scoundrels" to Pickering if he could obtain one.[19]

Since both men were concerned about "the same discontented characters which infest our country," Pickering suggested that the judge talk with the district attorney about the steps necessary to cope with the dangerous aliens. He promised Rawle that he would "do anything to aid the measures you think proper respecting them," and "cheerfully" engaged to reimburse any expenses incurred in detecting the Irish "villains . . . who you have reason to apprehend are plotting mischief against your country." Later in the year John Jay, former chief justice of the United States Supreme Court and then governor of New York, sent Pickering an extract from an original letter which he claimed proved the existence of American societies of United Irishmen and of a design to increase their number.[20]

As early as August 18, less than two months after Adams signed the Alien Law and nearly two months before he decided not to delegate his authority to the Cabinet, Pickering informed the president that he was considering the use of the law. Ten days later he mentioned persons who "were objects of the alien law and ought to be sent out of the country." It was not until October, however, that Pickering launched his most concerted effort at enforcement. On October 4 he suggested that the French general, Victor Collot, and "some other foreigners ought to be ordered to depart from the United States." [21]

[19] Pickering to Rawle, Aug. 28, 1798, Pickering Papers, XXXVII, 326 (Mass. Hist. Soc.), acknowledges Rawle's letter of Aug. 23; Peters to Pickering, Belmont, Pa., Aug. 24, 1798, *ibid.*, XXIII, 71.

[20] Pickering to Peters, Aug. 28, 1798, Peters Manuscripts, X (1792–1807) (Hist. Soc. Pa.); Pickering to Rawle, Aug. 28, 1798, Pickering Papers, XXXVII, 326 (Mass. Hist. Soc.); and Jay to Pickering, Albany, Dec. 21, 1798, *ibid.*, XXIII, 372. That Rawle kept close tab on foreigners in Philadelphia is shown by this extract from a letter to Pickering: "I am also told there is in Philadelphia a Madame D'Autrement the mother of the present confidential secretary to Talleyrand which as foreign letters sometimes pass through your office it may be well to remember— She lately received a very large basket from Paris—." See his letter of Oct. 31, 1798, *ibid.*, XXIII, 275.

[21] Pickering to the President, Aug. 28 and Oct. 4, 1798, *ibid.*, XXXVII, 325, and IX, 426. In August, Adams had sent Pickering a copy of a letter from a Mr. Barnes who referred to these persons. Barnes's letter has not been located, and Pickering does not identify the aliens.

Like Volney, and perhaps for better reasons, Collot had been one of the targets of the Federalists in the passage of the Alien Act; but unlike Volney he did not leave the country because of its threats. While serving as the French governor of Guadeloupe he had surrendered that island to the British in 1794 with the understanding that he would be permitted to return to France. In order to avoid involvement in the Reign of Terror, however, he later persuaded the British officials to let him come to the United States on parole as a prisoner of war. Acting under a commission from the French minister to the United States, he made a trip in 1796 along the Ohio and Lower Mississippi, from Pittsburgh by way of St. Louis to New Orleans, and aroused the suspicions of both the Federalists and the Spanish authorities because of the thoroughness of his examination of the topography, the resources, and the military establishments in the American West and in Spanish Louisiana.[22] In the course of his journey he was arrested and temporarily detained by the American commander at Fort Massac on the Ohio and by the Spanish governor in New Orleans. Following his return to Philadelphia early in 1797, administration agents kept close track of his activities. In November of that year Secretary Pickering received a report that Collot was connected with a French project for the seizure of Louisiana and the western part of the United States, and in February, 1798, Secretary of War James McHenry was given similar information, which he turned over to Pickering after the passage of the Alien Act.[23]

[22] For an excellent account of this mission, see George W. Kyte, "A Spy on the Western Waters: The Military Intelligence Mission of General Collot in 1796," *Mississippi Valley Historical Review*, 34 (1947), 427–442. Collot's own detailed notes on the expedition were published after his death as *Voyage dans l'Amérique septentrionale* (2 vols. and Atlas; Paris, 1826). For a statement from the French minister to his home government, see Pierre Auguste Adet to Minister of Foreign Affairs, June 21, 1796, Frederick J. Turner, ed., "Correspondence of the French Ministers to the United States, 1791–1797," Amer. Hist. Assoc., *Annual Report for 1903*, II, 928–929; and for the official American attempt to hamper Collot's mission, see James McHenry, secretary of war, to Arthur St. Clair, May, 1796, William H. Smith, ed., *The St. Clair Papers: The Life and Public Services of Arthur St. Clair* (Cincinnati, 1882), II, 395–396.

[23] J. J. Ulrich to Pickering, Nov. 29, 1797, Pickering Papers, XXI, 368 (Mass. Hist. Soc.); McHenry to Pickering, Sept. 10, 1798, quoting a report from Colonel Francis Mentges to McHenry, Feb. 13, 1798, *ibid.*, XXIII, 137. Mentges had received his information from Joseph Anthony Mercier, a French brick mason, who had conversed with Collot at his lodgings on the Schuylkill, near Philadelphia. Also see Durand Echeverria, "General Collot's Plan for a Reconnaissance of the Ohio and Mississippi Valleys, 1796," *William and Mary Quarterly*, 3d ser., 9 (1952), 512–520.

It was apparently on the basis of these reports that Pickering now decided to act. On October 11, a week after he had first suggested that Collot and other foreigners be ordered to depart, he submitted several blank orders and requested Adams to sign three of them for use against Collot, one of his associates named Sweitzer, and the French scientist, Pierre Samuel DuPont de Nemours, if he should arrive in the United States. At the same time he communicated the recommendation of Secretary of the Treasury Wolcott that the secretary of state should be designated as the proper officer to take evidence from aliens living in the vicinity of the nation's capital who wished to prove their innocence in order to obtain a license to remain in the United States. In cases such as Collot's, Pickering added, allowing an alien permission to offer these proofs would be a mere formality "in compliance with the *letter* of the law: for it is impossible for him to offer a good reason for staying here, or any facts to prove that he is not a French intriguer and bitter enemy to this country." Even though Adams favored a strict interpretation of the law, he not only signed blank warrants to be filled out for the arrest of Collot and Sweitzer, and for DuPont de Nemours, "if he is to be found," but he also authorized Pickering to issue licenses to aliens "within a reasonable distance from the seat of government." [24]

Instead of moving against Collot and Sweitzer immediately, Pickering engaged Colonel Francis Mentges, Secretary McHenry's informant of the preceding February, to keep check on Collot and to get information on Sweitzer. When the colonel informed Pickering that General Jean M. P. Serurier was in the United States in disguise, the secretary launched a search for him and other Frenchmen, postponing the arrest of Collot and Sweitzer so as not to tip off the new suspects. [25]

While Pickering was trying to implicate additional aliens, General Collot decided to take advantage of the 1794 Articles of Capitulation. A change in the administration in France and an intensification of the anti-French mood in the United States led the general to apply to Robert Liston, British minister to the United States, for a passport to protect him on his return to France. When Liston informed Pickering of Collot's desire to depart, the secre-

[24] Pickering to the President, Oct. 11, 1798, Pickering Papers, IX, 453 (Mass. Hist. Soc.); Adams to Pickering, Oct. 17, 1798, *ibid.*, XXIII, 241. The letter is endorsed on the back by Pickering: "received 26th with three Orders relative to Aliens."

[25] Pickering to the President, Aug. 1, 1799, *ibid.*, XI, 525. See also *Adams' Works*, IX, 6.

tary, who had earlier favored the general's immediate expulsion, now opposed his departure.[26] The British minister therefore refused to issue the passport, and the agents of the secretary of state continued to check on Collot in the hope that he would reveal the whereabouts of General Serurier and other suspects. After months of suspense, Pickering concluded that Serurier was not in the United States. By that time, he confessed to the president, "so many months had elapsed, and the session of Congress commenced, when other business pressed, the pursuit of these aliens was overlooked." [27]

On June 21, 1799, a Federalist paper reported that Collot was preparing to leave the United States.[28] A little later Colonel Mentges advised Pickering that Sweitzer was ready to depart for Hamburg. On August 1, 1799, nearly a year after Adams had authorized the expulsion of these aliens, Pickering relayed this information to the president but claimed that Collot, contrary to the press reports, remained in the country. Moreover, he added, the general was as much disposed as ever to do all the mischief in his power. Because of the reiterated observations that the Alien Law was a dead letter, the secretary of state suggested a new method of handling Collot as an alternative to deportation. Inasmuch as he was still a British prisoner of war, the United States might compel him to place himself under British jurisdiction, "where he can do no harm." [29]

President Adams, however, preferred to try the Alien Law against Collot. Although he feared it would prove "inadequate to the object intended," he asserted that he had always been ready and willing to execute it against the French general. The fact that the United States was about to enter a second negotiation with France did not alter the situation; the president was satisfied that Collot

[26] See George W. Kyte, "The Detention of General Collot: A Sidelight on Anglo-American Relations, 1798–1800," *William and Mary Quarterly*, 3d ser., 6 (1949), 628–630. Liston wrote that Pickering opposed Collot's removal because he feared that the general would turn over to the French government the valuable military information which he had obtained concerning the West and would seek French authorization for an attack on the United States from that quarter with himself in command. While these reasons are plausible, they were as applicable at the time Pickering favored Collot's removal as when he opposed it. It seems more probable that Pickering opposed the removal of Collot because he considered him as the key man who would lead government agents to a round-up of many other suspects.

[27] Pickering to the President, Aug. 1, 1799, Pickering Papers, XI, 525 (Mass. Hist. Soc.).

[28] *Gazette of the United States*, June 21, 1799.

[29] Pickering to the President, Aug. 1, 1799, Pickering Papers, XI, 525 (Mass. Hist. Soc.).

was "a pernicious and malicious intriguer." It was therefore more necessary than ever "to remove such an instrument of mischief from among our people, for his whole time will be employed in exciting corrupt divisions, whether he can succeed or not." [30]

Again Collot was not arrested immediately, although a close watch was kept on his activities. Elisha Boudinot, one of the justices of the New Jersey Supreme Court, notified Pickering on August 7, 1799, that the general was residing at Newark incognito. "He cannot be here for any good," the vigilant judge wrote, "and if sufficient cause could be obtained to send him off, I suppose it would be but doing what the public voice says ought to have been done long ago—hither to the *Alien bill* as to any good it has done is a meer [*sic*] dead letter—"

To buttress his suggestion that Collot should be deported, the New Jersey Federalist reported several bits of derogatory information, which he thought worthy of communication even though they might be "of no moment." For one thing, the general subscribed to the leading Republican journal, the Philadelphia *Aurora,* thus proving that he was a dangerous democrat. Moreover, Collot took the opposition paper under an assumed name. And, wrote the judge, this was not all. One of his informants had mentioned Collot's "intriguing spirit," and another had heard him criticize the government. Finally, he reported, he knew a Frenchman who knew a lady who lodged where Collot was staying, and this lady, the judge assured Pickering, thought that the general was "very inquisitive of the character of every frenchman in . . . the neighborhood— and also of the principal inhabitants. . . ." [31]

A week later Boudinot again pressed Pickering to authorize the arrest of Collot, assuring the secretary that "the business would be effectually done." If the law would justify the seizure of papers, the judge was certain that some of importance could be obtained by a prudently managed raid.

In his effort to have Collot expelled, Boudinot sought information from a Mr. Boisobier, who had already testified to having heard Collot criticize General Washington and the American government "in a very virulent manner." Boisobier now declared that Collot was "a very dangerous character in this country"; the general, he declared, had once said "that if there was Warr between france

---

[30] Adams to Pickering, Aug. 13, 1799, *Adams' Works,* IX, 13–14.

[31] Elisha Boudinot to Pickering, Aug. 7, 1799, Pickering Papers, XXV, 84–85 (Mass. Hist. Soc.).

and this Country, he would be one of the first to step forward and plunder the property of certain Individuals." [32]

Even as he relayed his new findings, however, the judge was apprehensive that his investigation might be futile. Boisobier was reluctant to appear as an informer against Collot, fearing that the general might exert influence in such a way as to cause trouble for his family in Guadeloupe. But this refusal to testify against Collot was not the only source of discouragement for Boudinot. He complained to Pickering that the reopening of negotiations with France might make the general's removal unnecessary. To the disgruntled New Jersey justice, these developments were regrettable: peace with France might mean that "this Spy may appear triumphant and in a capacity to take vengeance on his enemies." [33]

Despite the persistent attempts of top Federalists to deport Collot, the French general was never arrested, nor was he sent away under the Alien Law. Although there is no further reference to Collot in Pickering's papers after 1799, he remained in the United States, still a British prisoner of war, until about August, 1800. When Liston refused to give him a passport of safe conduct to France, the general applied to the French government. It turned his case over to the French agent in England in charge of the exchange of prisoners, who eventually obtained an order authorizing Collot's return to France. Upon receiving this order, Liston granted a passport to Collot who sailed about August, 1800. By that time, however, the Alien Friends Law had expired.[34]

Less fortunate than Volney in anticipating the adoption of the Alien Act and less resourceful than Collot in evading its enforcement was Médéric Louis Elie Moreau de St. Méry, a French scholar and a former member of the French Assembly, who had fled the Reign of Terror and had established a bookstore in Philadelphia in 1794. Here he enjoyed the friendship and patronage of the officials of the Washington administration, and Vice-President Adams, a frequent customer, even exchanged copies of his own writings

[32] Boudinot to Pickering, Aug. 15 and 26, 1799, with enclosures, *ibid.*, 102, 115–116. Collot was reported to have remarked in 1795 that in case of a disturbance in America, "he would make himself Chief of Walloons, and that the first house he would plunder or strip would be of his friend Mr. FitzSimmons." See the deputation of J. A. Mercier to Boudinot, Aug. 8, 1799, *ibid.*, 86.

[33] Boudinot to Pickering, Aug. 26, 1799, *ibid.*, 115.

[34] Kyte, "Detention of General Collot," *William and Mary Quarterly*, 3d ser., 6 (1949), 630.

for books written by Moreau de St. Méry.[35] Not until 1798 did this French bookseller become an object of Federalist suspicion, when, as he confided to his diary, "everybody was suspicious of everybody else: everywhere one saw murderous glances." [36] Realizing the seriousness of the swelling wave of anti-French sentiment, he had already decided to leave the United States when he received a warning from the French consul in New York that "all those who have no love for Robespierism had better get out and get out quick." [37] But he did not act quickly enough to avoid having his name included in the president's list of Frenchmen to be deported under the Alien Act. Curious as to why he was listed with Volney and Collot, Moreau de St. Méry asked Senator John Langdon of New Hampshire to question the president about the nature of the charge against him. "Nothing in particular," was Adams' laconic reply, "but he's too French." [38]

As the tension grew, some of Moreau's friends gave him keys to two shelters where he and his family could take refuge should their home be attacked. On the same day, July 14, he obtained passports for himself and his family, but it was to be more than a month before he could get out of the country. On August 3, three weeks after issuing the passports, Secretary Pickering gave him a letter of safe conveyance requesting all American ships of war or private armed vessels to allow him and his family to make their trip to France "without any hindrance or molestation whatsoever" and to furnish any assistance or protection that he might need during the voyage. After receiving similar guarantees from the British and Spanish ministers, Moreau de St. Méry sailed for France on August 23, 1798.[39]

Not always as helpful as in the Moreau case, Pickering requested the use of the Alien Law in three other types of cases—against incoming aliens, against diplomatic personnel, and against alien writers who criticized the administration too vigorously. When he first recommended proceedings against Collot and Sweitzer, Picker-

[35] Moreau de St. Méry's Diary, entry of July 18, 1798, Kenneth and Anna M. Roberts, eds., *Moreau de St. Méry's American Journey, 1793–1798* (New York, 1947), 253.

[36] Diary entry of June 27, 1798, *ibid.*, 252.

[37] Jean-Antoine B. Rozier to Moreau, June 27, 1798, *ibid.*

[38] Diary entry of July 14, 1798, *ibid.*, 253.

[39] See diary entries of July 14, 18, and Aug. 1, 3, 18, and 23, 1798, *ibid.*, 253–255, 364. A copy of Pickering's letter of safe conveyance is in Pickering Papers, IX, 139 (Mass. Hist. Soc.), and Dept. of State *Domestic Letters*, XI (1798–99), 35, RG 59 (National Archives).

ing also mentioned DuPont de Nemours.[40] In July, 1798, the American minister to England, Rufus King, wrote Pickering that DuPont and a delegation of French philosophers from the National Institute had applied for passports from the English government after the Directory had given them passports to go to the United States to improve and extend the sciences. King understood that the group planned to settle on the Upper Mississippi out of the limits of the United States and within the boundaries of Spain, but he expressed doubt that either the American or English government would "give any encouragement to this mission of the Directory." [41]

When Pickering relayed this information to the president, Adams replied that King had judged correctly of the American government; he hoped that he had conjectured equally well of the English. The president was not willing to grant passports to DuPont or any other French philosopher "in the present situation of our country. We have had too many French philosophers already," Adams continued, "and I really begin to think, or rather to suspect, that learned academies, not under the immediate inspection and control of government, have disorganized the world, and are incompatible with social order." [42]

It was a foregone conclusion, then, that the president would agree with Pickering that if DuPont "should arrive in the United States and be discovered, he ought if possible, not to be allowed even to breathe the air of the United States." Exactly one month after he vowed not to grant passports to DuPont's group, Adams signed a blank arrest warrant to be used against the French scientist, "if he is to be found." [43] This warrant was never executed because DuPont did not arrive in the United States until after the expiration of the Alien Law.

President Adams did not always approve Pickering's proposals.

[40] Pickering to the President, Oct. 11, 1798, Pickering Papers, IX, 453 (Mass. Hist. Soc.).

[41] Rufus King to the Secretary of State, July 14, 1798, King's Correspondence, II, 368.

[42] Adams to Pickering, Sept. 16, 1798, Adams' Works, VIII, 596. Even after the expiration of the Alien Act in June, 1800, President Adams refused to grant passports to aliens whom he considered undesirable. Writing in August, 1800, to Pickering's successor as secretary of state, he said: "The German letter proposing to introduce into this country a company of schoolmasters, painters, poets, &c., all of them disciples of Mr. Thomas Paine, will require no answer. I had rather countenance the introduction of Ariel and Caliban, with a troop of spirits the most mischievous from fairy land." Adams to John Marshall, Aug. 11, 1800, ibid., IX, 73.

[43] Adams to Pickering, Oct. 16, 1798, ibid., VIII, 606–607.

When the secretary suggested that the Alien Law might be utilized against French diplomatic personnel in the United States, the president forbade it. Before the passage of the act, the United States had refused exequaturs to French consuls in America in retaliation for France's rejection of the American negotiators. The government also refused to accept Victor Marie DuPont in May as a replacement for Letombe as consul at Philadelphia. Nevertheless, the French consuls who were already resident in the United States were allowed to remain.

In October, 1798, Pickering called the president's attention to the arrival of a new consul at Boston and suggested that he and any other new ministers ought to be ordered away as soon as they arrived. "Perhaps," he added, "the old French consuls should not much longer be permitted: nothing but the actual charge of numerous French people who need their pecuniary assistance can countenance their remaining among us." [44] There is no indication, however, that Adams took any action against either new or old French consuls, except in the case of Victor Marie DuPont.

Nearly a year later Pickering was still trying to obtain the removal of Letombe. He wrote the president that the French consul not only exercised his usual functions but also that he used the title of Consul General of the French Republic, even though his exequatur had been withdrawn. Moreover, Pickering charged, Letombe "held the pursestrings of the republic in this country, and paid the bribes ordered by the French Minister Adet; the minister being gone, he is probably vested with powers adequate to the object. With much softness of manners, he is capable of submitting to, and doing, anything corruptly which his government directs." [45]

Remembering the French minister's exertions against him in the election of 1796, Adams replied that if Pickering could prove that Letombe had paid the bribes ordered by Adet, or anything like it, the consul ought to be sent away. Even in that case, however, the president thought it would be better to inform him that he was expected to go rather than to order him out at first by proclamation under the Alien Act. "There is a respect due to public commissions," wrote the president, who had spent several years in the diplomatic service, "which I should wish to preserve as far as may be consistent with safety." [46]

[44] Pickering to the President, Oct. 11, 1798, Pickering Papers, IX, 453 (Mass. Hist. Soc.).

[45] Pickering to the President, Aug. 1, 1799, Adams' Works, IX, 6–7.

[46] Adams to Pickering, Aug. 13, 1799, ibid., 13–14.

A final type of case in which the administration contemplated using the Alien Law was that of alien writers who were critical of the Federalists. Less than two weeks after Congress passed the Alien Act and a week before Adams signed the Sedition Law, John D. Burk, co-editor of the New York *Time Piece*, was arrested for seditious statements against the president and the government of the United States. Burk had fled Ireland in 1796 in order to avoid arrest for sedition. In New York he headed the local lodge of United Irishmen. This made him doubly offensive to Pickering, who wrote the New York district attorney: "If Burk is an alien no man is a fitter object for the operation of the alien law. Even if Burk should prove to be an alien it may be expedient to punish him for his libels before he is sent away." [47]

Eventually the Adams administration decided to expel Burk rather than to prosecute him for sedition; it made a deal with him, offering to waive legal proceedings if he should promise to leave the country. Although Burk agreed to this bargain, he violated it by going into hiding in Virginia until the Alien and Sedition Laws expired.[48]

In an effort to suppress the Philadelphia *Aurora,* the Federalists attempted to utilize both the Alien and Sedition Acts. William Duane, the paper's editor, was indicted several times for his continued invective against the administration, but Pickering thought that the best way to deal with the offensive editor was to deport him. In 1799 he wrote Adams that Duane pretended "that he is an *American citizen*, saying that he was born in Vermont." But the secretary thought that Duane had left America before the Revolution and had returned only recently; he therefore concluded that the editor was really a British subject who might be banished from the United States under the Alien Law. President Adams agreed with this analysis and authorized the execution of that statute. This permission was never used, however, either because the editor claimed to be a native-born citizen or because Pickering thought it would be easier to prosecute the sedition case against him rather than try to prove that he was an alien.[49]

In only one instance did the president overrule the secretary of state in a decision to use the Alien Law against an alien writer. Pickering suggested that it might be used against Dr. Joseph

[47] For the arrest, see the New York *Time Piece,* July 9, 1798; *Aurora,* July 10, 1798. Pickering's instructions of July 7, 1798 to Richard Harison are in Pickering Papers, XXXVII, 315 (Mass. Hist. Soc.).

[48] The Burk case is discussed fully in Chapter X.

[49] For a detailed account of the proceedings against Duane, see Chapter XIII.

Priestley for his part in circulating an anti-administration article written by Thomas Cooper, the Republican publicist who was later tried for sedition.[50] The president had known Priestley in England as an eminent scientist and a liberal theologian. When the latter fled the repression of liberal groups in Great Britain in 1794, he settled in Pennsylvania. In 1796 he preached a series of sermons in Philadelphia which Vice-President Adams attended faithfully. When these lectures were published, the Unitarian minister dedicated them to Adams.[51]

After Adams became president, Priestley wrote him in August, 1797, recommending Cooper, a fellow immigrant, for a political appointment. Adams failed to answer because of his practice of never replying to letters of solicitation, and by the spring of 1798 a coolness had developed between the two men politically.[52] When Pickering reported that Priestley was involved in the circulation of Cooper's anti-administration view, therefore, he must have been confident that the president would agree that Priestley ought to be removed from the United States as a measure "of maintaining our internal tranquility." But this was too much for Adams. In the same letter in which he authorized the use of the Alien Law against Collot and the Sedition Law against Cooper, he notified Pickering that he did not think it wise to execute the Alien Law "against poor Priestley at present. He is as weak as water, as unstable as Reuben, or the wind. His influence is not an atom in the world." Although this view was hardly flattering to one of the most influential scientists of that day, it was enough to forestall his deportation by the zealous secretary of state.[53]

[50] Pickering to the President, Aug. 1, 1799, Pickering Papers, XI, 524 (Mass. Hist. Soc.). The secretary of state observed that Priestley's dangerous political prejudices were indicated by the fact that he "was at the *democratic* assembly on the 4th of July at Northumberland [Penn.]."

[51] For Adams' association with Priestley in England, see *Adams' Works*, III, 396–397, 420. The dedication of the sermons is in Priestley, *Discourses Relating to the Evidences of Revealed Religion* (Philadelphia, 1796), iii–vii.

[52] The letter is in *An Account of the Trial of Thomas Cooper* (Philadelphia, 1800), 5–7. Adams' reason for not answering this letter is in Adams to Pickering, Aug. 13, 1799, *Adams' Works*, IX, 13. Priestley mentions the growing political split with Adams in his letter to the Reverend T. Belsham, Jan. 11, 1798, in Joseph Torvill Rutt, *Life and Correspondence of Joseph Priestley* (London, 1831), II, 391.

[53] Pickering to the President, Aug. 1, 1799, Pickering Papers, XI, 524 (Mass. Hist. Soc.); Adams to Pickering, Aug. 13, 1799, *Adams' Works*, IX, 13–14. For Priestley's defense of his action, see his *Letters to the Inhabitants of Northumberland and Its Neighbourhood, on Subjects Interesting to the Author and to Them* (2d ed.; Philadelphia, 1801), 11–16; 44–49; and 68–71.

Adams contemplated the use of the Alien Law against one other alien writer. The vehement "Porcupine" broke with the administration in February, 1799, after the president decided to send a second peace commission to France. Charging that Adams had sold out to the French-loving Republicans, Cobbett's denunciations of the president reflected the extreme Federalist point of view and were as bitter as any writings which the Republican papers leveled at Adams when he signed the Alien and Sedition Laws. Indeed, Adams confided to his wife that Cobbett merited the Alien Law, and one Federalist journal erroneously reported Porcupine's expulsion, but the president never followed up this threat.[54] Instead, Cobbett lost a libel suit to Dr. Benjamin Rush in Philadelphia, retreated to New York to edit the *Rush Light,* a paper which concentrated on his controversy with Dr. Rush about the practice of bloodletting, and finally returned to his native England in June, 1800, the same month in which the Alien Law expired.

Despite repeated demands by the Federalist press, there was not a single deportation under the arbitrary statute which Congress had justified as a measure of national defense against dangerous aliens.[55] The chief reason for the record of nonenforcement was the determination of John Adams to give the law a much stricter interpretation than the Federalist extremists desired. Refusing to become a rubber stamp to the zealots in his Cabinet, two of whom he subsequently dismissed, he preferred to retain the power of final decision rather than to sign blank warrants which Pickering and his colleagues might use as they pleased. Yet he was always willing to enforce the law against aliens whom he deemed dangerous and gladly signed warrants for the seizure of Collot, Sweitzer, and DuPont.

Another explanation of the administration's failure to deport any aliens was, of course, the mass exodus of frightened foreigners even before the passage of the law. Moreover, both Adams and Pickering were convinced that even the arbitrary Alien Act was too weak to be effective; both bemoaned the fact that the law would not allow the confinement of an alien until his departure or deportation.

Paradoxically enough, the administration's most persistent enforcement effort failed because of the zeal of Timothy Pickering.

[54] Adams to Abigail Adams, Feb. 22, 1799, quoted by C. F. Adams, *Life and Works of John Adams,* I, 545. See the *Massachusetts Mercury* (Boston), March 5 and 8, 1799, for reports of Cobbett's arrest under both the Alien Friends and the Sedition Laws.

[55] For a demand that the Alien Act should be used against immigrants from France, Ireland, and the West Indies, see the *Columbian Centinel,* May 8, 1799.

His anxiety to implicate and track down additional suspects allowed Collot to remain in the United States until the expiration of the Alien Law. When the French general departed, therefore, he left at his leisure rather than under duress. In the only instance where the administration made a deal to avoid using the law, moreover, the offender did not leave the United States but went into hiding.

Inaction by President Adams, overzealousness by Secretary Pickering, and evasion of the law by John D. Burk combined to thwart the most strenuous efforts to enforce the Alien Friends Law, making it a dead letter from enactment to expiration. Only the *Columbian Centinel* in Boston noted the death of the law with regret. Its short epitaph observed that "not one of the numerous alien incendiaries which have infested, and now infest, the *United States,* have suffered any of the penalties of it,—and as they will attribute the forbearance of government to scar[e], not clemency, we cannot but add, more's the pity." [56]

The Press and Freedom of Political Opinion: A Survey of the Enforcement of the Sedition Law

It is patriotism to write in favor of our government—it is sedition to write against it.—Boston *Columbian Centinel,* October 5, 1798

Although the Alien Law became something of a dead letter, the Sedition Act was not neglected by the administration. In the famous XYZ papers which President Adams communicated to Congress during the diplomatic difficulties with France in 1798, the French negotiators boasted of their ability to separate the American people from their government. Although the American envoys bluntly replied that this was mere braggadocio,[57] the Federalists in Congress accepted the French assertion as a statement of fact and concluded that it could be refuted only by presenting to the world a united front free from dissent. When the Democratic-Republicans, long their opponents on political and economic programs, refused to co-operate in the new "unanimity"—especially if it meant unqualified support of the Federalist war program—the Federalists enacted the Sedition Law to intimidate or silence their domestic critics and thus to force a united front.[58]

[56] *Columbian Centinel,* July 2, 1800.

[57] Envoys to the French Minister of Exterior Affairs, *Annals,* 5C, 3355.

[58] A typical toast of the Federalists was given by the New York Society of the Cincinnati: "The Congress: Unanimity and vigor to their councils." *Gazette of the United States,* July 7, 1798.

Although some historians have asserted that the law was passed in a moment of panic and was little enforced during its lifetime,[59] most agree that the Federalists executed it in a vigorous and systematic manner, directing it exclusively against their Jeffersonian opponents. During the debates on the law, the Federalists openly avowed their intentions of repressing "licentious" Republican criticism.

The same animus which marked the congressional debates characterized the Federalist enforcement policy. By identifying their administration with the government and the government with the Constitution, the Federalists construed criticism of the administration as opposition to the government and an attempt to subvert the Constitution.[60] The most insistent pressure for execution of the law came from the Federalist newspapers, which constantly clamored for action against their Republican competitors. The stronger the Federalist control of an area, the stronger was the demand for strict enforcement of the law. In Pennsylvania the *Gazette of the United States* led the chorus; in New York it was the *New York Gazette*, the New York *Commercial Advertiser*, and the *Albany Centinel*; and in New England it was the *Columbian Centinel* and *J. Russell's Gazette* in Boston and the *Connecticut Courant* in Hartford. All agreed with the Fourth of July toast offered by the Federalists of Dedham, Massachusetts: "Freedom of speech—let the revilers of our government have *rope* enough. For honest men of all parties the cord of friendship; for traitors and foreign spies the hangman's cord." [61]

Even before the XYZ affair, there were complaints against the pressures for conformity of political opinion. "Anything opposed to the ideas of the Administration," one writer complained, was branded as "Jacobinism," a scare word intended to denote the anarchy in France in 1793–1794. "To be true Federalists," he lamented, "we must be at once deaf, dumb and blind; we must hear nothing—say nothing—see nothing." Yet the editor who allowed the insertion of these remarks in 1797 announced after the passage of the Sedition Law that "his Paper now is, and henceforth shall be,

[59] Channing, *History of the United States,* IV, 222, says that although its passage was regrettable, "there were a few prosecutions under the Sedition Act, but not many." He deemed the law and its enforcement so unimportant that he did not discuss a single one of the trials, although he defended the sedition statute. *Ibid.,* 231–232.

[60] Marshall Smelser, "The Jacobin Phrenzy: Federalism and the Menace of Liberty, Equality and Fraternity," *Review of Politics,* 13 (1951), 457–482.

[61] *Columbian Centinel,* July 11, 1798.

completely, positively, and absolutely FEDERAL." Since the crisis with France called for "decided and unequivocal support of Government, order and Laws," he resolved that his paper would no longer accept any writing "whose direct or covert tendency, is to villify your own administration, and to justify the conduct of foreign and internal foes." [62]

Less than three weeks after the XYZ papers were given to Congress, the *Gazette of the United States,* edited by the printer to the United States Senate, called for more drastic steps than the exclusion of anti-administration views in Federalist newspapers; it urged the repression of Republican presses. On the Fourth of July the Boston *Independent Chronicle,* the leading Republican paper in New England, was burned at a Federalist celebration in Newburyport, Massachusetts. After the passage of the Sedition Law, an upstate New York printer urged that a conflagration be made of such "seditious papers" as the Philadelphia *Aurora* and the New York *Argus.* A New Hampshire writer declared that "certain gazettes are industriously disseminated, each paragraph a scandalous libel, each line a malicious lie. To 'fat headed' fools, to flagitious . . . and desperate disappointments and to scooling envy, the trumpet of sedition 'discourses sweet music.'" In charging the Republicans with being seditious, the *Albany Centinel* defined sedition as an attempt "to weaken the arm of Government, by undermining the confidence of the community in its measures." [63]

The Boston *Centinel* flatly stated that "whatever American is a friend of the present administration of the American Government is undoubtedly a true republican, a true Patriot. . . . Whatever American opposes the Administration is an Anarchist, a Jacobin and a Traitor." The administration represented the majority of the people and all honest men should support it, "exercising only the constitutional mode of changing men and of course measures." Since the constitutional mode of changing men was by electing different ones, this assertion limited political participation to voting and eliminated oral or written opposition to men and measures. Nor did the *Centinel* deny this limitation. "It is patriotism to write

[62] For the earlier comments, see the *Oracle of the Day* (Portsmouth, N.H.), Oct. 7, 1797, quoted in William Robinson, *Jeffersonian Democracy in New England* (New Haven, 1916), 23. The editor's later views are expressed in the issue of July 28, 1798, reprinted in the *Albany Centinel,* Aug. 7, 1798.

[63] *Gazette of the United States,* April 24, 1798; *Albany Centinel,* Aug. 3, 10, 1798; "The Lay Preacher," *Farmers Weekly Museum* (Walpole, N.H.), reprinted in the *Albany Centinel,* Aug. 21, 1798.

in favor of our government," it said tersely; "it is sedition to write against it." [64]

As decisive evidence that the nation contained "internal enemies and foreign mercenaries," the *New York Gazette* cited newspapers which defamed the national administration and the Federalist-dominated Congress. Although it agreed that opposition to bad government was justifiable, the paper declared that all resistance and opposition to a "really legitimate government is treason against the People, and deserves the severest punishment." Yet the Republican papers were "indiscriminately defaming the Legislature and Administration—of course openly vilifying that very PEOPLE for whom they profess so deep a respect." Although it did not think every opposition journal was supported by French money, the Federalist paper nevertheless accused the leading Republican papers of deriving assistance from sources other than their subscription lists.

Whether they were supported by foreign money or not, however, the Republican papers were real evils. "They are the greatest curse to which free governments are liable," the New York paper charged. They circulated falsehoods about men chosen by the people, thus promoting the anarchical and despotic principles of France, America's deadliest enemy. "Whoever does this is a foe—whoever countenances it is a traitor,—the PEOPLE should watch him with a jealous eye, and consider him ripe for 'treason stratagems and spoils.' . . . They should be ferreted out of their lurking places, and condemned to the punishment merited by every patricide from the days of Adam to our own." [65] With the Federalists in this state of mind, the wonder is not the number of Republicans prosecuted, but that more were not seized.

Not only was it seditious and treasonable to write against the administration; Republican papers were suspect even if they remained quiet. The *Connecticut Courant* warned that when the Jacobins were silent it was "ominous of evil. The murderer listens to see if all is quiet, then he begins. So it is with the Jacobins." [66] Warning against these "incorrect" papers, the correct *Courant* suggested that the least they deserved was contempt.

[64] *Columbian Centinel*, Oct. 5, 1798, quoted in the *Albany Centinel*, Oct. 12, 1798.

[65] *Gazette and General Advertiser*, Nov. 13, 1798.

[66] *Connecticut Courant* (Hartford), Aug. 13, 1798, quoted in Robinson, *Jeffersonian Democracy in New England*, 24.

And lo! in meretricious dress,
Forth comes a strumpet called "The Press,"
Whose haggard, unrequested charms
Rush into every blackguard's arms,
Ye weak, deluded minds, beware!
Nought but the outside, here is fair!
Then spurn the offers of her sway
And kick the loathsome hag away.[67]

In a plea for the enforcement of the Sedition Law, the *New York Gazette* ran a series of articles on "The Crisis" and called for vigilante groups to prosecute not only newspaper editors but other enemies of the country. "Your country was never more in jeopardy than at the present moment," "Plain Truth" asserted. The danger, however, was no longer from a foreign foe. "The long knives of Kentucky, the whiskey boys of the woods of Pennsylvania, the United Irishmen of Virginia are all cock a top . . . for insurrection and confusion."

To Americans he propounded this question: "Why do you not form associations to prosecute the enemies of your country, until that country is rid of them, and they are safe in the arms of their *beloved* France?" [68] The way to deal with the domestic danger facing them was for Americans "in deed, as well as in words, to rally round our government, and swear to bring every man to punishment, who vilifies the men of your choice, or strives to weaken the barrier of your country's independence." Americans ought to make one last struggle to destroy its internal enemies, and "Plain Truth" thought the time had come. The number of internal enemies were "as the opposition of a knat [sic] to an Elephant." The pointed moral of this series of articles was—strike at the Republicans while they are weak.[69]

In denouncing the Democratic-Republicans as factious seditionmongers, *J. Russell's Gazette* singled out several Republican congressmen as likely victims of the Sedition Law. If the American people wished to build up the kingdom of Satan, the *Gazette* an-

[67] New Year's Address of 1801, *Connecticut Courant.*

[68] *Gazette and General Advertiser,* Dec. 15, 1798. This policy had been followed in England, where, after the French Revolution, extralegal bodies formed associations for the purpose of suppressing political reform and prosecuting "seditious utterances." The parent group was called the "Society for the Protection of Liberty and Property against Republicans and Levellers." See Sir Thomas Erskine May, *The Constitutional History of England* (New York, 1889), II, 144, who says that "such associations were repugnant to the policy of our law."

[69] *Gazette and General Advertiser,* Dec. 19, 1798.

nounced, "let them chuse [*sic*] democrats to Congress." But if they
wanted to purify Congress and perpetuate purity in elections, they
would have to "set their faces against the French pharisees, who
would have delivered up our widows, houses and our country too,
to the Directory to be devoured." Gallatin, Findley, and Lyon were
fitter subjects for the execution of the Sedition Law than for the
framing of statutes.[70] The New York *Commercial Advertiser,* another administration defender, evolved a rule of thumb whereby
to judge the seditious: "When a man is heard to inveigh against
the Sedition Law, set him down as one who would submit to no
restraint which is calculated for the peace of society. He deserves
to be suspected." [71]

*Most High God . . . withhold us from unreasonable discontent,
from disunion, faction, sedition, and insurrection.*—PRESIDENT
ADAMS, Proclamation of Day of Fasting, March 6, 1799

These papers need not have clamored so much, because John
Adams' administration had every intention of enforcing the Sedition
Law. Indeed, the most powerful of all the Republican editors,
Benjamin Franklin Bache of the Philadelphia *Aurora,* was indicted
even before the law was passed. His arrest under the common law
for seditious libels against the president and the government was
a forerunner of the trials that followed. A common law indictment
was also returned against the New York *Time Piece* while the sedition bill was before Congress.

Once the law was on the books, leaders of the administration,
from the president to the district attorneys, took an active interest
in its enforcement. Although President Adams did not initiate any
legal proceedings against his critics, his correspondence shows that
he personally approved of two of the major trials against Republican editors in 1799–1800. Whereas he gave the provisions of the
Alien Friends Law a strict interpretation, the vague language of
the Sedition Law was enforced against the most trivial writings and
oral statements. In no instance did he veto any prosecution under
the act, nor did he take any action on petitions for pardon which
he received from offenders against the Sedition Law.[72]

[70] J. *Russell's Gazette* (Boston), reprinted in the *Commercial Advertiser,*
Sept. 3, 1798.
[71] *Commercial Advertiser,* Dec. 29, 1798.
[72] Although Adams pardoned one offender, he did so not on the prisoner's
petition but on the recommendation of the government attorney who had prosecuted the case. See Chapter XVII.

As in the proceedings under the Alien Friends Law, the chief enforcement officer was Secretary of State Timothy Pickering. More than any other official, he "typified extreme Federalism of the purest and most rigid kind." One of his biographers has described him as one who believed so firmly that he was right that he denied there could be any honest difference of opinion. "To him the maxim that there are two sides to every question seemed an insult to the understanding. There was right and wrong, and the eternal battle between them; there could be nothing else." [73]

Pickering scanned Republican newspapers systematically. Even before the passage of the Sedition Law he wrote letters directing the New York district attorney to institute common law proceedings against the Mount Pleasant, New York, *Register,* and the New York *Time Piece.* After the passage of the law he not only continued his attentive reading of the opposition press, but, according to an *Aurora* report, he assigned a special State Department clerk "to search the *obnoxious papers* for suitable matter to cut them up at law." [74] He also received volunteer reports from faithful Federalists calling his attention to items that he or his agents might have overlooked.[75]

Before any case had been tried under the law, Pickering received an address to President Adams from Prince Edward County, Virginia, which urged the repeal of the Alien and Sedition Acts. Not only did the secretary refuse to forward the petition to the president, but he also issued a public letter severely censuring the Virginians and strongly supporting the constitutionality and necessity of the laws. The Sedition Act, he said, prescribed punishment only for "pests of society, and disturbers of order and tranquillity," and could not be considered as an attack on freedom of speech and of the press.

The president thought this answer "concinnate and consummate" and Mrs. Adams was delighted with it. She thought it worth all the answers that had ever been written in response to impudent petitions. The reply was so excellent, Adams assured Pickering, that he wished the secretary had to answer all the "saucy addresses"

[73] Lodge, "Timothy Pickering," *Studies in History,* 183, 200–201.

[74] *Aurora,* Nov. 9, 1798.

[75] Parker Campbell sent a "highly inflamatory and prejudicial" Kentucky newspaper to William Rawle, district attorney for Pennsylvania, who forwarded it to Pickering. See Campbell to Rawle, Washington [Penn.], July 12, 1798, Pickering Papers, XXV, 22 (Mass. Hist. Soc.), and Rawle to Pickering, July 21, 1798, *ibid.,* 45. For other examples, see the letters of Charles Hall in Chapter XIV, and those of John B. Walton in Chapter XV.

which he received.[76] The Federalist press also praised Pickering's comments as just but feared that "with determined oppositionists, and rancourous Jacobins, not any thing will have a good effect." It was fortunate, therefore, that the Sedition Law existed, because the Jacobins would "pursue the beaten path of clamor, and their railings against wholesome restraint, till their villainies successively come within the cognizance of the law." [77]

Pickering saw no reason to restrict the Sedition Law to public utterances. When his vigilant eye noted a statement in a Richmond paper that Congressman John Clopton wrote not only circular letters to his constituents but also "*private* ones 'too violent to be made circular,'" the secretary immediately ordered the examination of the Republican representative's private letter with a view to prosecuting him for sedition. Clopton, who was then running for Congress against John Marshall, was reported to have written that the president was a traitor, grasping at absolute power by bribing a majority of the House. Since the original was in the possession of a Federalist, William Pollard, "a very worthy man of Hanover," Pickering suggested that the letter be authenticated by him so that Clopton's infamous and mischievous lies would not pass unnoticed.[78]

Federalist district attorneys and federal marshals, of course, cooperated closely with Pickering. Nor were the justices of the United States Supreme Court remiss in their attention to the enforcement of the Sedition Law. Although Judge Samuel Chase was the leading judicial advocate of prosecutions against the seditious, it was the uniform practice of federal judges, and especially Supreme Court justices on circuit, to charge grand juries with the duty of inquiring into all offenses against the Sedition Law.[79]

Over a year before the law was passed, a federal grand jury, after receiving a charge from Judge James Iredell, brought in a present-

[76] Pickering to P. Johnson, Sept. 22, 1798, *Albany Centinel,* Oct. 16, 1798; and Adams to Pickering, Oct. 15, 1798, *Adams' Works,* VIII, 605–606. C. F. Adams observes that Adams' "praise appears to savor too much of partisan feeling. The sharp reply to the address placed Mr. Adams . . . in the attitude of combat with the opposition." See *ibid.,* 606n.

[77] *Albany Centinel,* Oct. 16, 1798.

[78] Pickering to Edward Carrington, Oct. 23, 1798, Pickering Papers, IX, 512. No action was taken in this case. Clopton was defeated by Marshall for Congress. For a report on the campaign, in which Marshall opposed the Alien and Sedition Laws, see Beveridge, *Marshall,* II, 375–431.

[79] Answer and Pleas of Judge Samuel Chase, *Report of the Trial of Hon. Samuel Chase . . . before the High Court of Impeachment* (Baltimore, 1805), 36.

ment against Congressman Samuel J. Cabell for his circular letters to his constituents. In turn, the representative claimed that it had been

a regular practice of the federal judges to make political discourses to the grand jurors throughout the United States. They have become a band of political preachers, instead of a sage body to administer the law:— They seem to be making use of their power and influence both personally and politically to control the freedom of opinion, and these things excite a suspicion that the time will come when men of different political and religious sentiments from the judges will not find that easy access to justice which different opinions may expect.[80]

The most striking example of judicial prosecution was that which Chase conducted against James T. Callender, correspondent of the Richmond *Examiner* and a pamphleteer whose talent for vituperation was a match for the most vindictive Federalist writer. The judge not only charged the jury to bring an indictment, but furnished them with a copy of the writing in which the offensive passages had been marked. On his return trip to Philadelphia after presiding at this trial, Judge Chase held court in New Castle, Delaware, where he detained the grand jury an extra day in his attempt to secure an indictment against a "seditious printer" in Wilmington. District Judge Gunning Bedford, who sat with Chase at this session, later testified that the Supreme Court justice had observed "in a public and in a jocular way" "that it was hard he could not get a single man indicted in Delaware, while he could in every other place." [81]

During the Federalist "reign of witches," [82] newspapers reported a number of arrests under the Sedition Law which I have been unable to track down beyond the mere mention of arrest. During the Pennsylvania gubernatorial contest in 1799, a German-language newspaper in Reading printed an attack on the Federalist candidate, Senator James Ross, who had voted for the Sedition Act. Branding that law as "a dreadful, shameless, and destroying attempt" against the Constitution, Editor Schneider urged the defeat of Ross, one of the "political murderers of our liberty"; he should

[80] *Aurora*, May 31, 1797. For one of Iredell's charges under the Sedition Law, see his instructions to the Philadelphia grand jury, Griffith J. McRee, ed., *Life and Correspondence of James Iredell* (New York, 1857), II, 551, 570.

[81] See the *Report of the Trial of Hon. Samuel Chase*, 22, 44, 63–64, 219, 223.

[82] This is Jefferson's phrase; see his letter to John Taylor, Phila., June 1, 1798, *Jefferson's Writings* (Ford ed.), VII, 265.

not be "rewarded for having tied our tongues, and gagged us." This attack upon a prominent Federalist and the laws of the land led Pickering to instruct the district attorney to prosecute Schneider, but there is no indication that a sedition charge was brought.[83] The co-editors of the *Harrisburger Morgenrothe,* however, were charged with publishing seditious statements against the laws and government of the United States. Benjamin Mayer and Conrad Fahnestock were arrested in August, 1799, and posted bail for their appearance before the federal circuit court in Philadelphia.[84]

Judah P. Spooner, a printer in Fairhaven, Vermont, was reported under arrest both in 1798 and 1799. There seems to be no evidence that he was indicted in 1798, but a charge apparently was filed the next year, although Spooner was discharged without being tried.[85] Another Vermont case on which there is little evidence should be mentioned. Newspaper reports listed Dr. Shaw of Castleton as being arrested in 1799, tried in 1800, and acquitted.[86] If these reports are true, the doctor was the only victim of the law who was not fined or imprisoned.[87]

Federalist enforcement machinery ground out at least seventeen verifiable indictments. Fourteen were found under the Sedition Act, and three were returned under the common law, two before and one after the passage of the statute. Although most of the prosecutions were initiated in 1798 and 1799, the majority of the cases did not

[83] *Aurora,* July 30, 1799; Pickering to Rawle, July 5, 1799, Pickering Papers, XI, 390 (Mass. Hist. Soc.).

[84] *Bee* (New London, Conn.), Sept. 18, 1799; *Palladium* (Frankfort, Ky.), Oct. 3, 1799. There is no indication that the editors were tried.

[85] For the report of the alleged indictment of Spooner and James Lyon at the time of Congressman Lyon's arrest, see the *Vermont Gazette* (Bennington), Oct. 12, 1798, and the *Independent Chronicle,* Oct. 22, 1798. In 1799 Spooner was reported under arrest in the New York *Spectator,* Oct. 19, 26, 1799; *Aurora,* Oct. 24, 1799; *Gazette of the United States,* Nov. 6, 1799. The *Spectator,* Oct. 26, 1799, reports his release.

[86] Shaw's arrest is mentioned in the *Spectator,* Oct. 19, 26, 1799. His trial and acquittal is reported briefly in *Spooner's Vermont Journal* (Windsor), May 13, 1800; the *Connecticut Gazette and Commercial Intelligencer* (New London), May 21, 1800; and the *Connecticut Courant,* May 26, 1800.

[87] For references to other arrests and attempted prosecutions, see the *Independent Chronicle,* July 30, 1798, which reports the arrest of James Bell in Carlisle, Pa., for "treasonable expressions"; Charles P. Polk to James Madison, Fredericktown, Md., June 20, 1800, Madison Papers, XXI, 89 (Lib. Cong.), for the attempted prosecution of Dr. John Tyler; and Dr. John Vaughn to Jefferson, Wilmington [Del.], Jan. 10, 1801, Jefferson Papers, CVIII, 18605 (Lib. Cong.), for the attempted prosecution of the doctor "under the *ignoble* Sedition law."

come to trial until April, May, and June, 1800. Indeed, the chief enforcement effort was tied directly to the presidential campaign of 1800. As the contest between Adams and Jefferson approached, Pickering laid systematic plans for action against the leading Jeffersonian journals in the United States. The opposition press was led by five papers—the Philadelphia *Aurora*, the Boston *Independent Chronicle*, the New York *Argus*, the Richmond *Examiner*, and the Baltimore *American*. Because of their strategic geographical location and their able editorial direction, these gazettes circulated widely. Nor was their influence confined to their subscription lists. In those days before the communications revolution, the smaller newspapers consisted largely of material reprinted from the important journals. Thus, a blow at any of the "big five" Republican presses would be a severe setback to the Democratic-Republican party in 1800.

In the summer of 1799 Pickering launched a campaign to prosecute every one of the leading Republican papers which either had not been prosecuted under the Sedition Law or which had no cases pending against it. He took personal charge of the proceedings against William Duane, editor of the *Aurora*, and received the approval of President Adams. The secretary wrote identical directives to the district attorneys in New York, Richmond, and Baltimore instructing them to scrutinize the Republican papers issued in their cities and to prosecute them for any seditious libels against the president or any federal official.[88] Since the *Chronicle* had been chastised, Pickering did not send a directive to Boston.

The timing of these communiqués is important. They were written early in August, 1799, so that the district attorneys would have time to bring indictments at the September or October term of circuit court. Even if the trials had to be postponed until the April or May term in 1800, as was the case against the New York *Argus*, they would still come in time to silence the papers or their editors during the campaign of 1800. As a result of Pickering's efforts, suits were brought against every one of the "big five" Republican journals except the Baltimore *American*. Moreover, the editors of four other Democratic newspapers of lesser importance were indicted, and two of these gazettes ceased publication. In New York, the *Time Piece* and the *Mount Pleasant Register* folded as a result of sedition proceedings. In New England, the New London, Con-

[88] For Pickering's instructions to the district attorneys, see his letters to Zebulon Hollingsworth, Aug. 12, 1799; to Richard Harison; and to Thomas Nelson, Aug. 14, 1799, Pickering Papers, XI, 602–603, 599, 611 (Mass. Hist. Soc.).

necticut *Bee* suspended operation from April until August, 1800, while editor Charles Holt served his sedition sentence. Only the Bennington *Vermont Gazette* continued to appear regularly while its editor was in federal prison for criticizing the authorities.

The fact that the most prominent Republican papers were assailed through prosecutions of their proprietors, editors, chief writers, or foremen, combined with the attacks on less important journals, affirmed the Federalist assertions and the Republican fears that the Sedition Law was passed to silence or intimidate the opposition press. In addition to the proceedings against major and minor Republican newspapermen, there were prosecutions launched against individual Republicans, some of state and national stature and others, of local, or indeed little, political significance. The first group was headed by the initial victim of the act, Congressman Matthew Lyon, who criticized President Adams in a letter to the editor of a Federalist newspaper. This group also included Republican publicist Dr. Thomas Cooper and New York State Assemblyman Jedidiah Peck. In the latter category were the victims of panicky localities. One of these prosecuted a man in his cups for expressing a desire that the shot from a cannon had lodged in the president's posterior. "That there should have been any such cases," Professor Anderson concludes, ". . . illustrates the possibilities of oppression which lay in the sedition law." [89]

Strictest enforcement of the law came in areas that were either thoroughly Federalist, as in New England, or in states where Federalist supremacy was threatened by the rising Republicans, as in New York and Pennsylvania. All the indictments in 1798–1799 were returned in the New England or Middle states—three in Massachusetts, three in New Jersey, and one each in Vermont, New York, and Pennsylvania. All the proceedings in 1800, except the one against Callender in Virginia, also were instituted in New England and the Middle states—three in New York, two in Pennsylvania, and one each in Vermont and Connecticut. Thus sixteen of the seventeen federal proceedings against sedition were concentrated in the Federalist-dominated New England and Middle states. The only Republican state in which a sedition trial occurred was Virginia, and Callender's case there was the final one to go to a jury. Symbolically enough, his sentence was to end on March 3, 1801, the same day on which the Sedition Law was to expire.

[89] Anderson, "The Alien and Sedition Laws," Amer. Hist. Assoc., *Annual Report for 1912*, 122. Once again I have relied heavily on Professor Anderson's work for this summary.

CHAPTER X

Anticipation:
Common Law Indictments

One of the first rights of a human is to speak or to publish his sentiments.—BENJAMIN FRANKLIN BACHE

DURING the debates on the Sedition Law of 1798, two Republican newspapers were singled out as the most horrible examples of the licentiousness which the Federalists hoped to suppress with that law. One of these—the Philadelphia *Aurora*—was the nation's leading opposition newspaper; the other—the New York *Time Piece*—was the most rapidly growing anti-Federalist journal in the United States in 1798. Even before Congress could enact a sedition statute, however, administration officials brought charges against Benjamin Franklin Bache, editor of the *Aurora*, and John Daly Burk, editor of the *Time Piece*. These proceedings were based on the concept that, despite the absence of a specific law, the federal government possessed common law jurisdiction over the crime of seditious libel.

Benjamin Franklin Bache, the Philadelphia Aurora, and Seditious Libel

As Jefferson had predicted, Bache was the chief target of the Sedition Law. The tottering circulation of Bache's *Aurora* and Carey's *Recorder* so alarmed Jefferson that he solicited Republicans to exert themselves to procure subscriptions. "If these papers fail," he wrote Madison at the height of the XYZ fever, "republicanism will be entirely brow beaten. . . . At present, the war hawks talk of septembrizing, Deportation, and the examples of quelling sedition set by the French Executive. All the firmness of the human mind is now in a state of requisition." [1]

The Federalists were so anxious to bring Bache to "condign punishment" that they anticipated the passage of a sedition statute with a preliminary proceeding designed to silence his criticism. On June 26, 1798, the day that Senator Lloyd introduced his treason and sedition bill and nearly three weeks before President Adams signed the Sedition Law, the Republican editor was arrested to answer a federal common law indictment for seditious libels against the president and the executive branch of the government. [2]

The Federalists had plenty of reasons for wanting to move against the leader of the opposition press. Bache had founded his paper in 1790, when he was only twenty-one, building it into the leading Republican journal by 1798. [3] In his brief career he directed a constant fire against the Federalists, hitting every prominent leader of that party from Washington down. An ardent democrat and a defender of the French Revolution, he opposed Washington's domestic and foreign policies with vigor. In 1795 he disclosed an important state paper by printing the complete text of Jay's Treaty while the Senate was discussing it behind closed doors. [4] Late in 1796 he reprinted letters which the British had forged in 1777 to discredit Washington. [5]

During the embroglio with France which followed the signing of Jay's Treaty, Bache consistently opposed war, urging that difficulties should be settled by diplomacy rather than by an appeal to arms. For his advocacy of this policy, he was condemned by the

[1] Jefferson to Madison, Phila., April 26, 1798, *Jefferson's Writings* (Ford ed.), VII, 245–246.

Much of this section appeared as an article in the *Pennsylvania Magazine of History and Biography*, 77 (1953), 3–23.

[2] *Aurora*, June 27, 1798.

[3] The only study of Bache is by Bernard Faÿ, *The Two Franklins: Fathers of American Democracy* (Boston, 1933). Faÿ also has a short article on "Benjamin Franklin Bache, A Democratic Leader of the Eighteenth Century," in American Antiquarian Society, *Proceedings*, n.s., 40, pt. II (Oct. 1930), 277–304.

[4] *Aurora*, June 30, 1795. Senator Stevens T. Mason of Virginia gave a copy of the treaty to Bache.

[5] One of the last official acts of President Washington was to deposit in the Office of the Department of State a statement "to the present generation and to posterity" that these letters were "a base forgery." See his letter to the secretary of state, Phila., March 3, 1798, in John C. Fitzpatrick, ed., *The Writings of George Washington from the Original Manuscript Sources, 1745–1799* (Washington, 1931–44), XXXV, 414–416.

Federalists as "a dull-edged, dull-eyed, hagard-looking hireling of France." [6] *Porcupine's Gazette*, edited by William Cobbett, claimed that

The most infamous of the Jacobins is
BACHE
Editor of the *Aurora*, Printer to the French Directory, Distributor General of the principles of Insurrection, Anarchy and Confusion, the greatest of fools, and the most stubborn sans-culotte in the United States. [7]

Bache's anti-administration views did nothing to endear him to the majority leaders in Congress, who barred him from the House floor in 1797. The editor condemned Speaker Jonathan Dayton's actions as an "act of tyranny" which injured his press at the same time that it kept "a free and firm statement of the proceedings" from the public. [8] When the Republicans sought to establish uniform rules for stenographers and reporters attending the House, the Federalists decided that newspapermen were admitted by the indulgence of the Speaker, who could revoke the privilege at any time. Speaker Dayton agreed and accused the Republicans of pandering to the public with their remarks in favor of widely reported debates. Throughout the 1797–1798 session of Congress, therefore, Bache was barred from the House. [9]

When the *Aurora* showed some sympathy for President Adams after his conciliatory inaugural address in March, 1797, the new executive was wary. To his wife he predicted that he would "soon be acquitted" of that paper's criminal praise. [10] Following Adams'

[6] *Porcupine's Gazette*, July, 1797, reprinted in *Porcupine's Works*, VI, 329n.

[7] *Porcupine's Gazette*, cited by Faÿ, *The Two Franklins*, 338. For an analysis of the great favor which this paper won with the Federalists, see William Reitzel, "William Cobbett and Philadelphia Journalism: 1794–1800," *Pennsylvania Magazine of History and Biography*, 59 (1935), 223–244. The president's wife was a great admirer of Peter Porcupine's efforts. To her sister she wrote that "Peter says many good things, and he is the only thorn in Baches side." Abigail Adams to Mary Cranch, Phila., March 13, 1798, Mitchell, *New Letters*, 143–144.

[8] Benjamin Franklin Bache, *Truth Will Out! The Foul Charges of the Tories against the Editor of the Aurora Repelled by Positive Proof and His Base Calumniators Put to Shame* (Philadelphia, 1798), "Prefactory Remarks."

[9] *Annals*, 5C, 2S (March 21, 1798), 1293–1294. For the preliminaries to this debate, see *ibid.*, 1036, 1044, and 1068. Also see the *Aurora*, Feb. 27, 1798. For one of Bache's complaints against his exclusion, see the *Aurora*, June 14, 1798.

[10] John Adams to Abigail Adams, Phila., April 24, 1797, C. F. Adams, ed., *Letters of John Adams Addressed to His Wife* (Boston, 1841), 254.

warlike message which urged the special session of Congress to adopt an accelerated defense program against France, Bache stopped lauding the president. By June, Mrs. Adams was deploring the *Aurora*'s impudence, fearing that the common people would be misguided by its stories about her husband's administration.[11] In a near classic statement of the "bad tendency" test of words, she wrote: "Scarcely a day passes but some such scurrility appears in Baches paper, very often unnoticed, and of no consequence in the minds of many people, but it has, like vice of every kind, a tendency to corrupt the morrals of the common people. Lawless principles naturally produce lawless actions."[12]

As the crisis with France grew worse, the president's family became increasingly insistent upon the need for legal action to suppress criticism of the government and the chief executive. Mrs. Adams branded "this lying wretch of a Bache" and all Republicans as agents of the French: "There is no end," she wrote, "to their audaciousness, and you will see that French emissaries are in every corner of the union sowing and spreading Sedition. We have *renewed information* that their System is, to calumniate the President, his family, his administration, until they oblige him to resign, and then they will Reign triumphant, *headed by the Man of the People* [Thomas Jefferson]. It behooves every pen and press to counteract them," she concluded, "but our Countrymen in general are not awake to their danger."

The president's wife was convinced that "not a paper from the Bache press issues . . . but what might have been prosecuted as libels upon the President and Congress." So "wicked and base" was the *Aurora*'s "violent and calumniating abuse" of her husband that she thought it ought "to be Presented by the grand jurors." Indeed, she finally concluded that if Bache's press and other Republican newspapers were "not surpressd, we shall come to civil war."[13]

Federalist bitterness against Bache was so intense that Cobbett suggested that no man should pay the slightest respect for his feelings. The Republican editor, he observed, "has outraged every prin-

[11] Abigail Adams to Mary Cranch, Phila., June 8, 1797, Mitchell, *New Letters*, 96.

[12] Abigail Adams to Mary Cranch, Dec. 12, 1797, *ibid.*, 117. For a discussion of the Sedition Law and the "bad tendency" test of words, see Chafee, *Free Speech in the United States*, ch. i.

[13] Abigail Adams to Mary Cranch, Phila., March 20; April 21, 26; and May 10, 1798, Mitchell, *New Letters*, 146–147, 159, 165, and 172.

ciple of decency, of morality, of religion and of nature." Sharpening his quills, Porcupine advised his readers always to treat Bache "as we should a TURK, A JEW, A JACOBIN, OR A DOG."

Charging that the French intended to overturn the American government through the agency of the Democratic-Republican newspapers, Cobbett urged the government to "regenerate" the press. Unless opposition newspapers were dealt with immediately, he continued, a set of villainous Republican editors, "most unquestionably in the pay of France," would continue to distribute their corroding poison throughout the Union. Although he agreed with one of his correspondents that strict postal control might be utilized to prevent the circulation of Republican journals, he suggested that as a more immediate step all Federalist merchants should withdraw their advertising from the opposition press in an effort to force it to the wall.[14]

This economic pressure was not without its effect on the *Aurora*. Although Bache claimed that the paper was profitable enough to support itself, he admitted that the withdrawal of support rendered the paper less lucrative than it might have been.[15] Jefferson, however, reported that its circulation was tottering.[16]

Economic coercion was not the only method of intimidation practiced against Bache in 1798 when political passions ran highest. Twice in that year Bache's house was attacked by mobs and twice the editor was personally assaulted. On May 7 twelve hundred young men paraded to martial music through the streets of Philadelphia, finally halting before President Adams' home to offer their services against France. When the president appeared to address them, he wore full military uniform, including a sword at his side. After the youths had heard the chief executive's remarks, they marched off and continued their celebration with a dinner. In the evening a group of the intoxicated enthusiasts left the party and mobbed Bache's home, but his friends drove them off.[17] Two nights later, on a day proclaimed by the president as one of fasting and

[14] *Porcupine's Gazette*, March 17, 1798, quoted by Faÿ, *The Two Franklins*, 344–345; *Porcupine's Gazette*, May, 1798, reprinted in *Porcupine's Works*, VIII, 194.

[15] Bache, *Truth Will Out!* "Prefactory Remarks."

[16] Jefferson to Madison, April 26, 1798, *Jefferson's Writings* (Ford ed.), VII, 245–246. This letter "leaked" to the *Gazette of the United States*, June 4, 1798. For Bache's statement that his circulation was at a peak, see the *Aurora*, June 5, 1798. This assertion was probably bravado.

[17] *Porcupine's Gazette*, May 7, 1798; *Aurora*, May 9, 1798; Bache, *Truth Will Out!* "Prefactory Remarks"; *Time Piece*, May 14, 1798.

prayer, another mob in the City of Brotherly Love smashed the windows in Bache's house. The Republican editor viewed these assaults as an attempt to awe him into "a base dereliction of his duty." [18]

While visiting a Philadelphia shipyard, Bache was brutally assailed by Abel Humphreys, son of the builder of the frigate *United States*. For this attack "the champion of the faction," as Bache called his assailant, was prosecuted, convicted, forced to pay damages, and bound over to keep the peace. Shortly thereafter this "friend of order" was appointed by President Adams to a diplomatic mission to Europe. Later in the year Bache was assaulted by John Ward Fenno, son of the editor of the chief Federalist organ, the *Gazette of the United States*.[19] None of these tactics, however, silenced the *Aurora* or its youthful editor. On June 16, 1798, Bache disconcerted the administration by printing a secret state paper two days before Congress received a copy of it from President Adams. This action set in motion a series of events which enabled the Federalists to strike a legal blow at the editor and his paper. The embarrassing document which he published was Talleyrand's offensive yet conciliatory letter to the American envoys in France— offensive because it virtually disregarded John Marshall and Charles Cotesworth Pinckney as proper negotiators, conciliatory because it offered to discuss all outstanding issues with the remaining plenipotentiary, Elbridge Gerry. Although Talleyrand's letter had reached the secretary of state only two days before it appeared in the *Aurora*, Bache defended his publication of the "scoop" on the ground that the administration was withholding it in an effort to embroil the United States in an unnecessary war with France.[20]

On the day that the much-discussed letter appeared, *Porcupine's Gazette* declared that it was certain that Bache had received it from France or from some French agent in America "for the express purpose of *drawing off the people from the Government*, of exciting discontents, of strengthening Republican opposition, and to procure a *fatal* delay *of preparation for war*." Ought not this "prostitute printer," he asked, "to be regarded as an organ of the *diplomatic skill* of France? And ought such a wretch to be tolerated at this

[18] *Gazette of the United States*, May 10, 1798; Bache, *Truth Will Out!* "Prefactory Remarks."

[19] Edmund Kimball Alden, "Benjamin Franklin Bache," in Allen Johnson, Dumas Malone, and Harris E. Starr, eds., *Dictionary of American Biography* (20 vols. and 1 supp. vol., New York, 1928–44), I, 462–463; Bache, *Truth Will Out!* "Prefatory Remarks"; *Gazette of the United States*, Aug. 9, 1798.

[20] *Aurora*, June 16, 1798.

time?"[21] President Adams' wife thought that Bache ought to be "seazed" immediately. The appearance of the French foreign minister's letter in the *Aurora,* she wrote, should convince "the most unbelieving of the close connection between the Infernals of France & those in our Bosoms."[22] When Congress met on Monday, June 18, the leading Federalist spokesman, Robert Goodloe Harper, and George Thatcher of Massachusetts acted on the same conviction and branded Bache as an agent of the French Directory who was in an open and treasonable correspondence with Talleyrand.[23]

The *Gazette of the United States* also joined in the accusations against its old antagonist, claiming to have proof of Harper's and Thatcher's charge. It announced that John Kidder had arrived in Philadelphia only the week before with dispatches from the Directory to Bache. These he innocently delivered to the editor of the *Aurora* and Bache printed one of them on June 16. Here was an open and shut case of treason proved by the courier. The *Philadelphia Gazette,* however, gave a different version. On March 18 a clerk from Talleyrand's office had handed two packets to William Lee of Boston, one of Kidder's fellow passengers bound from France to America. One envelope was addressed to Bache and bore the seal of the French Foreign Affairs Office. The *Gazette* claimed that Lee left the ship before it reached Philadelphia, but it did not say whether he or Kidder had charge of the letters to Bache at that time.[24]

In an attempt to correct these stories and to prove his innocence of complicity in the "treasonable plot," Kidder published a statement in *Claypoole's American Daily Advertiser* which contradicted all the previous stories. He declared that his traveling companion Lee had begged him to take charge of a number of letters addressed to Bache, Genêt, and other American citizens. He said that after he landed, he had put the letters in the New York post office, without suspecting their contents. Thus, he denied handing the letters directly to Bache as the *Gazette of the United States* claimed. Kidder's statement, said Porcupine, nevertheless proved

[21] *Porcupine's Gazette,* June 16, 1798.

[22] Abigail Adams to Mary Cranch, June 19, 1798, Mitchell, *New Letters,* 193.

[23] This charge is discussed in Chapters IV and VI. One of the president's correspondents also cited Bache's publication of the letter as proof that the editor was "an agent of the French Directory." See Tristram Dalton to B. Bartlett, Washington, June 21, 1798, Adams Papers, XIX, 236 (Mass. Hist. Soc.).

[24] *Gazette of the United States,* June 18, 1798; *Philadelphia Gazette,* June 18, 1798.

that "the infamous Lightning-rod, jun. was a *hireling* of, and *in correspondence with* the despots of France." [25]

The Federalists hailed such evidence as proof of the claims of Harper and Thatcher. The *New York Gazette* printed Kidder's statement as a handbill. Another of Lee's traveling companions, however, feared that Kidder's story portrayed Lee as a French courier. Samuel M. Hopkins therefore hastened to explain how Lee, a man of "respectable character," came into possession of the papers. According to Hopkins' story, he had sailed from France with Kidder and Lee. Because the time of Lee's intended departure had been known for some time before he left Paris, many letters were entrusted to him for delivery in America, as was customary. When these were sorted, those bearing the seal of the French minister of foreign affairs attracted Lee's attention, since they were addressed to Bache, James Monroe, Citizen Genêt, and "some other persons of the same description." Lee therefore decided to send these letters to Secretary of State Pickering rather than to drop them into the post office. Hopkins and Lee had left the ship while it was still off the American coast, and Hopkins presumed that in Lee's hurry to sort the letters for their different destinations, he had left some with Kidder.

Administration officials were eager to probe to the bottom of the allegedly treasonable plot. After a hasty trip from the nation's capital, Secretary Oliver Wolcott arrived in New York on June 19 for a personal interview with Lee. In their discussions, which took place at the home of Samuel Hopkins, the secretary indicated that he was not so much interested in the letters to Bache, Monroe, and Genêt as in those which Hopkins had said were addressed to "other persons of the same description." He made it clear that he was after the leader of the "traitors" by asking repeatedly *"if there were any letters for Mr. Jefferson."* The invariable answer was "No." Failing to implicate the vice-president in the plot, Wolcott settled for lesser game. He accepted the letters which Lee offered, gave a receipt to the interceptor, and mailed them to Secretary of State Pickering. These letters included a packet for Bache, sealed with the official stamp of the French Office of Foreign Affairs.[26]

[25] *Porcupine's Gazette,* June, 1798, reprinted in *Porcupine's Works,* VIII, 245.
[26] *Diary of William Dunlap (1766–1839), The Memoirs of a Dramatist, Theatrical Manager, Painter, Critic, Novelist, and Historian* (New York, 1930), I, 294, entry of June 20, 1798. Dunlap was a friend of Hopkins and was present when Wolcott received the letters from Lee. Wolcott's attempt to obtain evidence of Jefferson's "treason" was not revealed at the time, nor is it mentioned

In a final effort to clear his name of any taint of treason, Lee also issued a public statement which elaborated on the details given by Kidder and Hopkins, but studiously avoided any reference to Wolcott's visit. Asserting that he did not recall who had handed the letters to him in France, he protested that he knew nothing of the contents of the one addressed to Bache or any of those bearing the French seal; indeed, he denied noticing them until he was at sea. In his hurry to leave the ship he had left some of them with Kidder by mistake. All the others, Lee now acknowledged, had been turned over to government officials.[27]

During these efforts of the administration to implicate him, Bache had not been idle. On June 20 he appeared before the mayor of Philadelphia and swore that he had not received the Talleyrand letter from France. He insisted that a man in Philadelphia had delivered it to him for publication. He added that he had not yet received the mysterious packet which Kidder claimed he had put into the post office. The Republican editor also pointed out that since his publication of Talleyrand's letter to the American envoys, the greatest effort had been made to divert public attention from its contents "by making noise about the *manner* in which it came into print." The Federalists had followed this plan of attack, he said, because the letter "had a tendency to counteract the system of alarm, which it has been the avowed object of the Tories to encourage." Bache also published an interview with Kidder in which the latter again stated that he had posted all the letters which had been entrusted to him. He was not sure, however, that the one addressed to Bache was among these.[28]

Bache was now ready to refute the alarming stories about treasonable correspondence. Denying that he was an agent of the French, he surveyed the discrepancies in the various stories advanced by the Federalists. First of all, the letter which he pub-

in Gibbs, *Administrations of Washington and Adams*. In listing the names of those whom he hoped Wolcott would implicate, Stephen Higginson placed Jefferson first, then added James Monroe, Edmund Randolph, Abraham Baldwin, Citizen Genêt, and Bache. See Higginson to Wolcott, June 29, 1798, Gibbs, 68–70.

[27] *Gazette and General Advertiser*, June 21, 1798. Also see William Lee to James Monroe, Boston, Feb. 10, 1801, Monroe Papers (N.Y. Pub. Lib.); William Lee to Oliver Wolcott, July 10, 1798, and Stephen Higginson to Wolcott, Boston, July 11, 1798, Wolcott Papers, XIV, 107, and VI, 39 (Conn. Hist. Soc.); George W. Erving to Monroe, Phila., April 9, 1801, Monroe Papers, VI, 1108 (Lib. Cong.).

[28] *Aurora*, June 21, 1798.

lished had not been received from France. Second, the elusive
packet from France had not yet been received. Fenno's story that
Kidder had delivered it punctually had been repudiated by Kidder,
who first said that he had dropped it into the post office, but later
said he was not sure that it was among those posted. It was on
this contradictory evidence, Bache continued, that the two mouthpieces of the administration, Harper and Thatcher, had made their
insinuating accusations; he now called on them for proof. For his
part, he offered written testimony that he had not received any
such letters from France.

The editor then challenged the administration to inform him
where he could find his delayed letter, which was "said to be sealed
with the seal of the French Department of Foreign Affairs." From
his interview with Kidder he suspected that it was a pamphlet
by Pichon, a personal friend, formerly an attaché at the French
Legation in Philadelphia, who was now in the Office of Foreign
Affairs in France. Bache ridiculed the idea that Pichon was carrying on a treasonable correspondence. It hardly seemed likely, he
said, that a conspirator would identify his letters with the seal
of the Foreign Office. Nor was it likely that he would entrust his
correspondence to Lee, a man whom he did not know. The editor
concluded by requesting the federal authorities to surrender the
delayed packet immediately. He asserted that even if it were returned with the seal broken or defaced he would attribute it to
accident and never suspect that the authorities had done either.[29]

Two days later a messenger from Secretary Pickering delivered
the missing packet to the *Aurora* office. Keeping the sealed envelope
in the view of the messenger all the time, Bache summoned two
other persons to witness the opening of the diabolical package. On
the outside the letter was addressed "Au Citoyen B. F. Bache
imprimeur à Philadelphie," and it was sealed with a stamp bearing
the words "République Française, Relations Exterieures." On the
back of the letter over the seal were two endorsements in which
Wolcott acknowledged receipt of the packet from Lee on June 20,
and Pickering noted that he had received it in the mail from New
York on June 22, 1798.[30]

[29] Signed statement of Frederick Woolbert and Michael Leib, June 19, 1798,
Aurora, June 21, 1798. Kidder deposited the mail from the ship on June 11.
The two witnesses above were present when Bache asked postal clerks whether
he had received any of the mail posted that day. The clerks replied in the
negative. See Bache's comments in *ibid.*, June 22, 1798.

[30] Certified statement by Matthew Carey and Joseph Clay, Phila., June 23,
1798, in "The Plot Unravelled," *Aurora*, June 25, 1798.

When the seals were broken and the letter opened, the "treasonable correspondence" proved to be two pamphlets on English affairs by Pichon. This, of course, exploded the Harper-Thatcher "plot." They had maintained that the Talleyrand letter which Bache published had been delivered by Kidder from France. This packet, which had sent the Federalists in search of Republican "traitors" and had kept the nation in a state of constant alarm for a week, contained not a single word on American relations with France.[31]

The story of what he thought had happened was then reconstructed by Bache. Lee, he said, probably informed the administration of the packet and asked whether he should turn it over to its addressee or to the government. Fearful of receiving another man's property without authority or law, the executive departments dispatched Wolcott to New York to inspect the suspected letter and decide "whether it was worth while to violate every principle of law and honor to get at their contents." At the same time, two administration mouthpieces, anticipating startling revelations against the editor, were instructed to accuse Bache of being a French hireling. Even if the charges were untrue, they would damage the editor, who would be hard put to disprove them. If the letter contained nothing damaging, it could be destroyed and the claim made that it had been seized by a boarding officer. The fact that there had been a packet would allow the calumnies against him to continue to circulate.[32]

This Federalist plot had been foiled, Bache continued, by Kidder's published statement in Claypoole's paper. In this Kidder made it appear that Lee was the go-between for Talleyrand. To clear himself of this suspicion, Lee admitted that he had turned the letters over to the government. After this revelation, Wolcott and Pickering finally decided to deliver the package rather than to face a prosecution for illegally detaining property not belonging to them. What right, Bache asked, had Wolcott to receive an editor's mail and then send it to a third person rather than to its proper addressee? He was sure that Wolcott would seek redress if an editor received a letter or any other property addressed to the secretary,

[31] One was entitled "Lettre d'un Francais a M. Pitt," and the other was "Seconde Lettre d'un Francais a M. Pitt." Both were directed to "B. F. Bache de la part du Cn. Pichon." The messenger from the State Department was present during these proceedings.

[32] Aurora, June 25, 1798. Captain Pender of the British navy boarded the ship in which Lee was a passenger and seized some letters from France.

detained it for a time, and then sent it to a third person. Yet here was a Cabinet official holding back proof that Bache was innocent of the charges assiduously circulated by Wolcott's friends in Congress. And where, he queried, had these legislators obtained the information on which to base their charges? It could only be from those government officials whom Lee had notified. They were Cabinet officers not even known to the Constitution, Bache continued; they were creatures of the president, "subject to his will and pleasure, and independent of the People." [33]

Shall these men, the editor persisted, be permitted to place themselves above the law with impunity, to intercept private correspondence, and to defame private character? He considered it unnecessary to bring them before courts of justice for defamatory libel because he thought that the tribunal of the press could counter their arrogant claims. Conceding that the charges which Harper and Thatcher made in the House were privileged, he nevertheless demanded that they do justice to "injured innocence" by withdrawing their thoroughly disproved accusations. If they remained silent, they would not only deprive him of plenary justice; they would also disgrace themselves.

Finally, Bache asked why his accusers had spread reports that he had been arrested, or had fled, or had been jailed. From an "almost official" source, he had learned that a warrant actually had been signed for his arrest. Was this done to intimidate him, to force him to flee? If it was, he replied, his enemies had miscalculated. He had not truckled before his accusers, nor was the spirit of his paper cowed:

Persecution shall only fan the flame of his detestation for those whom he considers the enemies of the best interests of his country. They shall not make him abandon his post for fear of a trial even before their tribunals. He will even prefer death, as a victim, to a flight that would render his innocence suspected. This is high language, it may be said. It is the language of injured and triumphant innocence. Perhaps administration may not understand it. [34]

[33] *Ibid.* The *Bee*, Aug. 1, 1798, observed that "we do not recollect the particular law that gives the secretary of state a right to stop and examine the letters of private citizens." Reprinted in the *Independent Chronicle*, Aug. 13, 1798.

[34] *Aurora*, June 25, 1798. On June 22 Bache claimed that if Thatcher had proof of his treason and failed to produce it, the representative would be guilty of misprision of treason for concealing the crime. Bache's articles in the *Aurora* of June 19, 21, 23, and 25 were published in pamphlet form, with a two-page preface, under the title *Truth Will Out!*

Bache's convincing proof of his innocence, the Boston *Independent Chronicle* declared, should be inserted by all the "Ministerial printers" who, along with official spokesmen, had subjected the editor to "very extraordinary treatment." If they had succeeded in fixing the charge of treason on Bache, "he would have been justly consigned to exemplary punishment, and his name to the execration of his fellow citizens, and of posterity." His defense against "the botched up charge of conspiracy," however, had defeated the malignant intentions of his traducers, and the Federalist papers could not honestly and honorably refuse it a place in their columns.[35]

According to the Republican newspapers, Bache's publication of Talleyrand's letter had stymied the Federalist warmongers by revealing France's willingness to negotiate with Gerry. The New York *Time Piece* contended that even if Bache had obtained the letter directly from Talleyrand, he would have committed no crime. The two countries were at peace, the editor argued, and even if they were at war, nothing would hinder an American editor from procuring from any person, "no matter whom, intelligence, useful to America. The re-taking of Toulon," he continued, "was announced ten days before the official account of it; consummate blockheads! insolent traitors, is it treason, to publish intelligence useful to America?" [36]

The administration appeared willing to concede that it had no evidence of Bache's treason. At least, the Republican editor was not prosecuted for printing the Talleyrand letter. It was clear, however, that the Federalists were in no mood to brook his criticism. Eager to crush its foe, the administration seized upon some of the remarks which he had made in his defense against the unfounded charge of treason. In these, of course, he not only had censured the conduct of Wolcott and Pickering; he also had implicated the president himself in words tending to bring his administration into disrepute. Despite the absence of a federal sedition law, the administration launched a sedition prosecution at common law instead of waiting until Congress acted.

Arrested on a warrant issued by District Judge Richard Peters, Bache was brought into court on June 26 and charged with "libelling the President & the Executive Government, in a manner tending to excite sedition, and opposition to the laws, by sundry publications and re-publications." [37] Alexander J. Dallas, secretary of Penn-

[35] *Independent Chronicle*, reprinted in the *Aurora*, July 7, 1798.
[36] *Time Piece*, June 22, 1798.
[37] *Aurora*, June 27, 1798. The words "Executive Government" in the indict-

sylvania, and Moses Levy, a leading radical Democratic lawyer, represented Bache. After obtaining a two-day delay, the editor was paroled to the district marshal until June 29.

Bache assured the public that the prosecution could not be supported in the federal courts if the opinion of Supreme Court Justice Samuel Chase was followed. In the case of the *United States* v. *Worrall,* argued in Philadelphia only three months earlier, Chase had declared that federal courts lacked common law jurisdiction in criminal cases.[38] Bache, however, thought that the ultimate decision would turn not on the question of jurisdiction but on that of liberty of the press. Apologizing for the scarcity of news in the *Aurora* of June 27, he attributed it to the novelty of his arrest the day before. "The faction," he wrote, "have, so far, only obtained a day's respite." The editor pledged that "prosecution no more than persecution, shall cause him to abandon what he considers the cause of truth and republicanism; which he will support, to the best of his abilities, while life remains." [39]

On June 29 Bache appeared with his counsel before Judge Peters at his chambers. District Attorney William Rawle represented the government and supported the validity of the warrant. The editor's lawyers denied that the federal courts were vested with common law jurisdiction in criminal cases and cited Judge Chase's ruling in the Worrall case. Since Judge Peters had expressed the opposite view in that case, they conceded that it was useless to emphasize this point, although they asserted that it was proper to present their objection to him. In the event that the charge was not dismissed for lack of jurisdiction, they had advised Bache to enter in

---

ment refer to Bache's statements about the Cabinet officials, Pickering and Wolcott. Pickering had instituted a personal libel suit against Bache as early as February, 1798, because of a letter which charged the secretary with "a shameful breach of the laws" in receiving gratuities from persons seeking passports which were supposed to be issued without cost. See the *Aurora,* Jan. 24, 1798; Pickering to Bache, Jan. 25, 1798, and Pickering to Rev. John Clark, Jan. 26, 1798, Pickering Papers, XXXVII, 264–266 (Mass. Hist. Soc.), and Rawle to Pickering, Feb. 27, 1798, *ibid.,* XXII, 48. An investigation revealed that gratuities had been accepted in the State Department office, and Pickering discharged the guilty clerks. There is no indication in Pickering's papers or in the *Aurora* that this suit ever came to trial.

[38] The trial of *United States* v. *Worrall* is reported in 2 Dallas 384–396, and in Francis Wharton, ed., *State Trials of the United States during the Administrations of Washington and Adams* (Philadelphia, 1849), 189–199.

[39] *Aurora,* June 27, 1798. In an article the day before his arrest, the editor had observed that the proceedings of the legislature "may be commented on in papers." *Ibid.,* June 25, 1798.

recognizance for his appearance at the next circuit court term. This move would give them time to arrange a mode of proceeding which would not only guarantee complete justice to their client, but, if possible, would avoid a collision between state and federal courts. The posting of bail, the defense counsel argued, in no way impaired either Bache's right to object to federal jurisdiction before a full panel of the United States Circuit Court or his right to any other legal proceedings, such as testing the legality of any imprisonment with a writ of habeas corpus returnable before a state judge or court.

Judge Peters agreed that it would be superfluous to discuss the question of jurisdiction before him because he had not changed his opinion as announced in the Worrall case. He therefore could not hesitate to take cognizance of the charge, especially since he had issued the arrest warrant. By posting bail, Bache did not waive the right to take exception to the court's jurisdiction when the case came up. The judge then set bail at $4,000 and required Bache to give security for $2,000 and two sureties for $1,000 each. The trial date was set for the October term.[40]

True to his word, Bache did not slacken his criticism of the administration's measures. Instead, he attacked them as warlike and singled out the Alien and Sedition Laws for special censure. In a pamphlet entitled *Truth Will Out!* he accused the administration of a studied attempt to suppress his press by official and unofficial action. This, he claimed, became necessary "when it was determined to enlist this country on the side of despotism and then to pass alien, treason and sedition bills, that have not a parallel even in the British code." He asserted that his persecution included attempts to deprive his paper of support, "a cowardly, premeditated and unprovoked attack" by Humphreys, arbitrary removal from the floor of the House of Representatives, attacks upon his home, and libelous attacks on his character by "the tools of faction connected with the administration." When all these efforts failed to ruin him and his paper, he concluded, a prosecution was instituted against him for a seditious libel on President Adams. Although Bache thought it improper to discuss the merits of the pending case, he assured his readers that it would furnish him another "cause of triumph" even if he were obliged to submit to the "assumed jurisdiction" of the federal courts.[41]

On July 16, two days after the president signed the Sedition Law, Bache wrote a penetrating paragraph discussing the question of

[40] *Aurora,* June 30, 1798.
[41] Bache, *Truth Will Out!* "Prefactory Remarks."

liberty and order in a republican form of government. He concluded that the attempt to safeguard the security of the state had
been pushed so far as to endanger the liberty of the individual.
"The efforts of the administration," he wrote, "seem to be to protect themselves." Declaring that the Constitution guarantees certain rights of the people as well as those of the government, he
observed:

It is as much the sworn duty of the administration to protect the one as
the other. . . . One of the first rights of a human is to speak or to publish
his sentiments; if any government founded upon the will of the people
passes any ordinance to abridge this right, it is as much a crime as if the
people were, in an unconstitutional way, to curtail the government of one
of the powers delegated to it.

In Turkey, the *Aurora* concluded, the voice of the government
rather than the voice of the people was law, and Turkey was called
a despotism. "Here the voice of the government is likewise the law
and here it is called *liberty*. We may next expect to hear the African
tyger, on being imported here, has been metamorphased into a
Lamb!" [42]

Although Federalist editors gloated over the prospect of Bache's
coming trial, they deplored the continued circulation of the *Aurora*.
"The Devil," said a Philadelphia paper, "is represented as coming
forth with wrath, because he had but a short time; so his emissaries,
by their rage and violence, appear to anticipate an arrest in their
career of villainy—since the passage of the Sedition Law, the scum,
filth and foam of the Aurora Cauldron has flowed more than ever."
Fashionable eating places, such as the Coffee House in Philadelphia
and the Tontine Coffee House in Albany, barred Bache's paper. [43]

The harassed editor continued to publish his paper despite these
discouragements. Nor did he leave his post when the worst yellow
fever epidemic since 1793 moved into Philadelphia in the late
summer of 1798. On September 5 Bache caught the fever. Five
days later death cheated the Federalists of their first victim of a
sedition prosecution. Although the Republican press agreed with
the Boston *Independent Chronicle* that "the real friends of their
country cannot but lament the loss of so valuable a citizen," [44] most

[42] *Aurora*, July 16, 1798.
[43] *Albany Centinel*, Aug. 14 and 24, 1798.
[44] *Independent Chronicle*, Sept. 17, 1798. The *Argus* published a "monody
on the death of Benjamin Franklin Bache," which the *Aurora* reprinted on
Nov. 8, 1798. The poem was written by John D. Burk, editor of the *Time
Piece*, then being prosecuted under the federal common law for a seditious
libel on President Adams.

Federalists echoed the epitaph of *J. Russell's Gazette:* "The memory of this scoundrel cannot be too highly execrated." [45]

Bache's death did not silence the *Aurora.* In an extra which was on the streets before dawn on September 11, his widow assured "the friends of civil liberty, and patrons of the *Aurora*" that she would continue the paper as soon as arrangements could be made. "In these times," she added in tribute to her husband, "men who see, and think, and feel for their country and posterity can alone appreciate the loss; the loss of a man inflexible in virtue, unappalled by power or persecution, and, who, in dying knew no anxieties but what were excited by his apprehensions for his country— and for his young family." [46]

On November 1, 1798, the *Aurora* resumed publication under the editorship of William Duane, who had been Bache's assistant. Pledging to continue his predecessor's "undeviating adherence to the principles of our Constitution, and an unwearied watchfulness against those eternal foes of republics, avarice, ambition, and corruption," Duane promised to publish the *Aurora* "with inflexible fidelity to the principles upon which it was founded and reared up." [47] Under his guidance Bache's paper continued as the leading journal of Republican opinion in the United States. Indeed, the new editor's criticism of the administration soon marked him out as successor to the Federalists' animosity for Bache, but the most concerted attempts to bring him to trial under the Sedition Law failed.

The Case of the Seditious Alien: John Daly Burk and His New York Time Piece

As in the proceedings against Bache, administration officials did not await the enactment of the sedition statute before indicting John Daly Burk, whose paper had been singled out in Congress by John Allen as a leading example of perverted licentiousness.[48] Established only nine days after the inauguration of John Adams as president of the United States, the *Time Piece* became a vigorous anti-administration semiweekly under the editorship of Philip

[45] *J. Russell's Gazette,* Sept. 20, 1798.

[46] *Aurora,* handbill, Sept. 11, 1798, cited by Faÿ, *The Two Franklins,* 356.

[47] *Aurora,* Nov. 3, 1798, reprinted in the *Bee,* Nov. 14, 1798.

[48] For a sketch of the *Time Piece,* see Clarence Brigham, *A History and Bibliography of American Newspapers, 1690–1820* (Worcester, 1947), I, 696.

This section appeared in much the same form in the *Journalism Quarterly,* 30 (1953), 23–36.

Freneau, former editor of the *National Gazette*.[49] When the poet-editor retired from journalism in March, 1798, he was succeeded by Mathew Davis, a protégé of Aaron Burr. Three months later the *Time Piece* received its most controversial editor when Davis was replaced by Burk, who now is best remembered for his multi-volume history of Virginia.[50]

Born in Ireland about 1775, John Daly Burk came to the United States in 1796 as a political refugee. Early in his career he outraged the authorities of the University of Dublin, who expelled him for his republicanism and deism. A short time later he fled his native land to avoid arrest for a sedition prosecution after participating in an attempt to rescue a political prisoner being led to execution.[51] Quickly identifying himself with his adopted land, he became editor of Boston's first daily newspaper, *The Polar Star and Boston Daily Advertiser*, and gained something of a literary reputation at the age of twenty-one by writing one of the first American plays based on a national historical theme, *Bunker Hill, or the Death of General Warren*.[52]

In both of these undertakings, the precocious editor dedicated

[49] S. E. Forman, *The Political Activities of Philip Freneau*, in *Johns Hopkins University Studies in History and Political Science*, ser. XX, nos. 9 and 10 (Baltimore, 1902), is the standard work. Freneau's editorship of the *Time Piece* is mentioned on pp. 82–83.

[50] For a brief discussion of Burk's historical works, see Michael Kraus, *A History of American History* (New York, 1937), 146–147. The best biographical sketch is by Edward A. Wyatt, IV, "John Daly Burk, Patriot-Playwright-Historian," *Southern Sketches*, 1st ser., no. 7 (Charlottesville, Va., 1936). Charles Campbell, ed., *Some Materials for a Brief Memoir of John Daly Burk, Author of a History of Virginia* (Albany, 1868), is useful. Also see the article by Walter Prichard Eaton in the *Dictionary of American Biography*, III, 278–280.

[51] Because of his articles in the Dublin *Evening Post*, a paper which supported the cause of the people against the Crown, Burk was tried before the university board on a charge of deism and republicanism, convicted, and expelled. While editing the *Polar Star*, he published an account of the trial and his defense. See Joseph T. Buckingham, *Specimens of Newspaper Literature: With Personal Memoirs, Anecdotes and Reminiscences* (Boston, 1850), II, 297–298. Burk gives a personal account of his departure from Ireland in his *History of the Late War in Ireland* . . . (Philadelphia, 1799), 43–50.

[52] The *Polar Star* was established on Oct. 6, 1796. Buckingham, *Specimens of Newspaper Literature*, II, 294–300, discusses the rising and setting of the *Star* under Burk's editorship. For an evaluation of Burk's dramatic works, see Arthur Hobson Quinn, *A History of the American Drama from the Beginning to the Civil War* (New York, 1923), 117–119, 126. The play was produced at Boston's Haymarket Theatre in 1797 and remained a popular patriotic play for Fourth of July celebrations for fifty years. It was reprinted, with an introductory essay by Brander Matthews, in Dunlap Society, *Publications*, no. 15 (New York, 1891).

himself to promoting liberty as best he could. Although not yet a citizen, he addressed his subscribers as "fellow citizens" because he felt as though

I too am a citizen of these states. From the moment a stranger puts his foot on the soil of America, his fetters are rent in pieces, and the scales of servitude, which he had contracted under European tyrannies, fall off; he becomes a free man; and though civil regulations may refuse him the immediate exercise of his rights, he is, virtually, a citizen.

Although he intensely opposed everything hostile to liberty, especially to freedom of speech and of the press, the youthful editor refrained from discussing personalities and steered clear of partisan politics while conducting the *Polar Star*. His sympathies in foreign affairs were naturally strong against the British government, royalty, and aristocracy and in favor of France and republicanism, but he abhorred "that gloomy and monastic system of politics" which condemned those who differed in opinion "to the Inquisition and Bastile." [53]

When Burk's experiment in daily journalism failed early in 1797, he moved to New York, where his patriotic play, *Bunker Hill*, was staged in September. Burk also wrote a tragic drama entitled *Female Patriotism, or the Death of Joan d'Arc*, which was produced in April, 1798, in New York's Park Theater. Although this play has been characterized as "one of the bright spots that reward the reader of our early drama," it coincided with the difficulties between the United States and France and did not meet with favor.[54]

The playwright then resumed his newspaper work, becoming editor of the *Time Piece* on June 13, 1798. He no longer avoided partisan politics in his new post. His predecessor, Philip Freneau, was a pioneer Republican and ally of Thomas Jefferson who had made the *Time Piece* an advocate of the Jeffersonian party's views. Burk's first issue appeared when political passions ran high—the Alien and Sedition Laws were pending before Congress—and he immediately sided with Jefferson and the Democratic-Republicans.[55] Moreover, he proposed to expand the influence of his paper by

[53] Buckingham, *Specimens of Newspaper Literature*, II, 295–297.

[54] Quinn, *History of the American Drama*, 117–119.

[55] Burk later wrote that Burr was both "a friend and father" to him during his stay in New York. Burk to Jefferson, Amelia County, Va. [1801], *William and Mary College Quarterly Historical Magazine*, 2d ser., 5 (1925), 100. The Federalists suspected that Burr was the security for the purchase money of the press when Burk and Dr. James Smith bought it from Davis. Robert Troup to Rufus King, July 10, 1798, *King's Correspondence*, II, 364.

converting it to a daily and by publishing for continental distribution a weekly edition to be called *The Friend of the People.*

The spirit of the new paper, Burk promised, would be wholly Republican. Although it would be a staunch supporter of the federal Constitution, "its Federalism will not be of that kind which displays itself in mere sycophantic compliance with every act of Administration, in clamouring for war, taxes, standing armies and a government of Terror, in efforts to suppress the liberty of speech and the press." He stated that the new daily "will love the constitution as it ought to be loved—for its excellence, for its republicanism; and will hold up to public abhorrence those who attempt to violate it, whatever be their professions.—This," Burk boldly concluded, "is our Federalism." [56]

At the same time, the new editor promised that the *Time Piece* would never attack private character. "The conduct of men in public stations," on the other hand, was "fair game," and he pledged himself to criticize advocates of royalty and aristocracy and to combat attacks on republican liberty. Even here he promised to abide by the honorable spirit of sportsmen: "The pursuit, however keen, shall be without perfidy or malice."

His paper, Burk declared, would be "Edited by its Editor"; it would not be "filled with the Lethargic, and sometimes Fanatic essays of correspondents." Although he retained long analytical articles and some poetry in the rejuvenated *Time Piece,* his most characteristic contributions were short editorial squibs against Federalist policies and politicians. Under his vigorous editing, circulation increased by 134 subscribers in nine days and passed that of Noah Webster's Federalist *Commercial Advertiser,* making it second only to New York's leading Federalist journal, the *Daily Advertiser.*[57]

Taking notice of the meteoric rise of the *Time Piece* under its new editor, the Federalist press also took advantage of the anti-foreignism stirred up during the Franco-American embroglio to call for drastic action against the alien editor of the Republican paper. Noah Webster denounced the *Time Piece* as contemptible and condemned Burk as "infamous for his turbulent, revolutionary Jacobin sentiments." The way to deal with this rival editor was to

---

[56] *Time Piece,* June 13, 1798. This proposal had been discussed as early as May but was not formally announced until June 13. See the *Aurora,* May 19, 1798.

[57] *Time Piece,* June 22 and 29, 1798. Burk claimed that his circulation would exceed that of the *Daily Advertiser* as soon as he converted to a daily.

run him out of town. "The most effectual means of ridding society of this pattern of wisdom, modesty, and excellence," the editor of the *Commercial Advertiser* suggested with a touch of irony, "would be that of placing him on horseback for in that case he would speedily ride to the devil." One of the *Advertiser's* correspondents raised this question: Is there ever a case in which the summary punishment of tar and feathers is justifiable? In case there was not, he had two suggestions for handling the editors of the *Time Piece*. Either the attorney general of New York should prosecute them for private and public libels, or they should be banished to Botany Bay.[58]

The Federalists also undertook a whispering campaign as a means of discrediting Burk. On June 27, two days after the passage of the Alien Friends Law, the editor denied a rumor that he had expressed a desire for France to invade America, and challenged his accuser to identify himself. Burk insisted that he was incapable of speaking such a villainous sentiment. He loved both the American and French nations, he said, and his attachment to republicanism made him view war between these two republics as "melancholy, ruinous and disastrous to Liberty." [59]

Writing under the name of "Themistocles," Burk's anonymous assailant replied that he had overheard Burk rejoice at the report of a French invasion of Ireland and express the hope that an invasion of America would follow so that "every scoundrel in favour of this government would be put to the guillotine." According to "Themistocles," Burk complained that he might be deported under the Alien Law. If the French landed in America, he was supposed to have boasted, "he would let them know who was the stronger party."

"Themistocles" also lodged another charge against the impetuous "editor of the seditious *Time Piece*." Had Burk not insulted the majesty of the American people by these critical remarks about their Chief Magistrate?

When such a character attempts by antiquated and exploded sophistry, by Jesuitical arguments to extinguish the sentiment of Liberty; TIS FIT the mask should be torn from this meaner species of Aristocracy than history condescended to record, where a person without patriotism, without philosophy, without a taste for the fine arts . . . is *jostled* into the chief magistry by the ominous combination of *old Tories with old opinions*,

[58] *Commercial Advertiser*, June 18, 1798; "One of the Young Men," *ibid.*, June 11, 1798, quoted in the *Time Piece*, June 13, 1798.
[59] *Time Piece*, June 27, 1798.

and old Whigs with new: TIS FIT this mock Monarch, with his *court* composed of tories and speculators should pass in review before the good sense of the world.

"How long, ye slumbering Americans, will you be thus insulted?" "Themistocles" queried. Calling for the deportation of Burk, he advised his readers to awake from their "deathlike stupor, and spurn from the society of freemen this wretch who is composed of that stuff of which the Spy, the Assassin and the Sycophant, is formed." [60]

Although Burk did not deny his criticism of President Adams, he wrote a letter to the *Commercial Advertiser* specifically refuting the rest of the charge and claiming at least seven witnesses who would testify on oath to its falsity. He also appeared before a notary and swore that he had stated no wish that the French should invade America. Nor had he made any sanguinary wish about Federalists being guillotined or any other wishes "so unfavourable to the public peace and happiness of America." Although he confessed that he had mentioned his hopes that the reported invasion of Ireland by France was true—in that case it would be unnecessary for the Federalists to use an alien or a sedition law against him, as he would return to Ireland on his own accord—he swore that he had not uttered the words imputed to him by his accuser.[61]

Burk's articles sustain this denial. Both before and after the rumor he repeatedly urged that "every man in this country should arm in defence of the American Republic," no matter what had been the conduct of the administration. On the Fourth of July he presided at the celebration of the United Irishmen in New York and drank toasts to the perpetuity of the Constitution and of American independence. "May Americans never be ashamed," ran another toast, "to celebrate this glorious anniversary, unless they permit their constitution to be violated." Nor did the Irishmen overlook the Alien Law. They concluded that "it must have been intended to operate only against royalists and aristocrats." [62]

At the same time that Burk vowed his attachment to the Constitution, he demonstrated his belief in the right of a free press by directing a steady attack on the administration's domestic and for-

---

[60] "Themistocles," *Commercial Advertiser*, July 3, 1798.

[61] Burk to the editor, *Commercial Advertiser*, July 6, 1798; sworn statement by Burk, *Time Piece*, July 6, 1798. William Stewart, printer for the *Time Piece*, swore that he did not hear Burk say that he wished France to land in America. Instead, he heard the editor say the exact opposite in a later conversation.

[62] *Time Piece*, July 2; *Aurora*, July 10, 1798.

eign policies. It was a short paragraph of July 2 which led to the sedition charge against him. When Talleyrand, the French foreign minister, broke off negotiations with John Marshall and Charles C. Pinckney, Elbridge Gerry remained behind in an effort to forestall a complete diplomatic rupture. He later wrote the president, however, that his stay was futile.[63] When President Adams communicated this letter to Congress, Burk printed it on the front page but intimated that certain passages had been altered "to promote certain ends in this country." [64] The editor claimed to have more than slight grounds for believing that Gerry was not a "political cipher" in France, that he had seen that channels for communication were still open, and that he had not wished to be recalled. In the same issue Burk questioned the sedition bill before Congress by asking if it was "Sedition to say the President is incorrect in a part of History?"

On the Fourth of July, Burk observed that only the wicked governors of men dread what is said of them. Since all public business is transacted for the people, the deeds of magistrates should be open to public examination. "The administration of government," he continued, "is nothing else but the attendance of the trustees of the people upon the interest and affairs of the people." Administrations are responsible to the people, who have every right to criticize their elected officials. It was deplorable, he concluded, that a situation should occur which made it possible for the Federalist administrators to charge their opponents with Jacobinism because the latter refused to acknowledge the "heaven born genius of an Adams." [65]

Deplorable or not, the administration had become so sensitive to Republican criticism that the Senate was considering a sedition law when Burk's blast against the president appeared. These remarks did not escape the watchful eye of Secretary of State Timothy Pickering, who was also a target of *Time Piece* criticism. He immediately called them to the attention of the federal district attorney in New York, Richard Harison, condemning the charge that the president had falsified Gerry's letter as itself "false," "inflammatory," and of a "seditious tendency." "It appears," he informed Harison, "that the Editor of the *Time Piece* is an Irishman and

---

[63] Elbridge Gerry to the President of the United States, Paris, April 16, 1798, *Annals*, 5C, 3459–3460. This letter was laid before Congress on June 21.

[64] *Time Piece*, July 2, 1798. Burk implied that these were either false or forged by saying some passages were "a F———."

[65] *Time Piece*, July 4, 1798.

alien," who had made a "treasonable speech" in the presence of "Themistocles." He therefore ordered the prosecutor to obtain an affidavit from Burk's accuser and to examine recent issues of the *Time Piece* for other seditious material.

Pickering also instructed the district attorney to ascertain the editor's citizenship status. "If Burke [*sic*] be an alien," he wrote, "no man is a fitter object for the operation of the alien act." Deportation, however, might be too lenient for a foreigner who edited "a vehicle of the most profuse & atrocious slander of the Government, & a ready instrument of sedition." It might be expedient to punish Burk for his libels before deporting him, Pickering suggested, unless allowing this dangerous alien to remain in the United States until the fall term of the federal court might prove a greater evil than leaving his seditious remarks unpunished. On the other hand, if Burk proved to be a citizen, Pickering instructed the government attorney to institute a sedition prosecution without awaiting the enactment of the sedition bill then pending in Congress. If Burk's "treasonable speech" was an offense against the laws and could be proved, the editor should be punished promptly.[66]

Harison needed no prompting from the secretary of state. On July 6, the day before Pickering sent his instructions, Burk was arrested in the name of the president of the United States on a charge of "seditious and libellous" utterances against President John Adams. Dr. James Smith, the other proprietor, also was arrested and charged with defamatory libel. Both proprietors appeared before District Judge John Sloss Hobart, who released them on $4,000 bail pending their trial before Supreme Court Justice William Paterson. Their sureties included such leading Republicans as Aaron Burr, Peter R. Livingston, and the wealthy Colonel Henry Rutgers.[67]

[66] Pickering to Harison, July 7, 1798, Pickering Papers, XXXVII, 315 (Mass. Hist. Soc.). See the *Time Piece*, July 2, 1798, for Burk's remarks on the secretary of state. In this issue, Burk asked if Pickering knew "such a man as Mitchel, an United Irishman. Let him answer this question, tis not material." Another squib called upon Philadelphia authorities "to search for the body of Mitchel, late clerk of William Cobbett, if it be not too late to ascertain whether his death *was or was not* produced by POISON." In a letter to the *Commercial Advertiser*, July 14, 1798, "Anti-Demagogue" asserted that these statements insinuated, "in a way not admitting of doubt or misconstruction, that Pickering murdered Mitchell by poisoning him."

[67] *Commercial Advertiser*, July 6, 1798; *Daily Advertiser*, July 7, 1798; *Argus*, July 7, 1798; *Time Piece*, July 9, 1798; *Aurora*, July 10, 1798. There is a memorandum of Burk's recognizance in E. E. Dunscomb, clerk of the court, to Pickering, May 24, 1799, Winthrop Sargeant Papers, Box 9, Item 46 (Ohio Hist. Soc.).

The Federalists rejoiced at this first blow struck against the rising Republican press in New York City. President Adams' wife called Burk's publication a "daring outrage which called for the Arm of Government." After the editor's arrest she noted that both Bache and Burk were in duress. "Let the vipers cease to hiss," she wrote approvingly. "They will be destroyed with their own poison." "Tho justice has been slow, perhaps dilatory in her progress," echoed Noah Webster in the *Commercial Advertiser,* "we hope she will not check her step till she has dragged the guilty to condign and *exemplary* punishment." Federal District Judge Robert Troup wrote that Burk had been arrested for that very purpose. "It is determined," the judge informed Rufus King, "to try whether we have strength enough to cause the constituted authorities to be respected." The administration had decided that it was necessary to protect "the character and conduct of its officers from the ribaldry and abuse uttered against them in certain papers," and Judge Troup had not even a fraction of a doubt that the "disorganizers" would be convicted.[68]

While Burk was out on bail, the *Time Piece* continued to appear regularly. Neither prosecution nor persecution, the editor confidently assured his readers, would awe him and Smith into "sycophancy or silence." Indeed, they were sure that their prosecution, whatever its issue, would be favorable to liberty. Burk insisted that he and Smith were victims of the prosecution because of their continual championing of freedom of the press. He had long published extracts from the *Letters of Junius* and he now added quotations from Erskine's and Curran's defense of liberty of the press.[69] On July 13 he devoted the entire front page to one of his essays on that vital freedom.

In discussing the arrests, the anti-Federalist newspapers pictured the Republican editors as martyrs to the cause of a free press. Although Bache was awaiting trial for seditious criticism of President Adams, he described the charge against Burk and Smith as an attempt by the Federalists to maintain their "alarm system." The editor of the New London *Bee* was more subtle. Without comment

[68] Abigail Adams to Mary Cranch, July 9, 1798, Mitchell, *New Letters,* 200; *Commercial Advertiser,* July 6, 1798; Troup to King, July 10 and Oct. 2, 1798, *King's Correspondence,* II, 364, 432.

[69] *Time Piece,* July 9, 1798. After his arrest, Burk dropped Junius "in compliment to a great law character"—John Adams. Burk's respect for Junius led him to name his only child after that advocate of liberty. On July 30 Burk reprinted Curran's defense of an Irish printer, noting that "at a time when the government of the United States thinks it expedient to prosecute for Libels, a publication of this nature is particularly well timed."

he contrasted the arrest of Burk, Smith, and Bache with the reply which the American envoys, Federalists to a man, had given to Talleyrand's demands that the American government discountenance anti-French pronouncements in Federalist newspapers. "In the United States," the commissioners had said, "no individual fears to utter what his judgment or his passions dictate, and an *unrestrained press* conveys alike to the public eye the labours of virtue and the efforts of particular interests." [70]

Interest in Burk's case was so great that when he received a letter under the frank of Congressman Edward Livingston a curious crowd gathered at the New York post office, where the letter was handed around from one person to another. Burk poked fun at these "patriotic gentlemen" who had handled the letter "with evident marks of inquietude and alarm, lest the sedition or treason should *ooze* out and convert them to the cause of democracy." The envelope contained nothing from Livingston to him, the editor informed the curious; it merely covered a letter from a Virginian who sent in two subscriptions to the *Time Piece*.[71]

The Federalists nevertheless attempted to use the congressman's letter to demonstrate another link between the Republican party and seditious and traitorous aliens. On the day that the *Daily Advertiser* ran Livingston's speech on the Alien Act, one of its correspondents attacked his arguments and asked if the Republican representative was in the habit of corresponding with "your protegee, the Irish fugitive," who only a week earlier had been arrested for a seditious libel on the nation's chief magistrate. Livingston must know that this suspicious character, who edited a paper "under the patronage of your party," used an assumed name after fleeing Ireland from a warrant for seditious practices.[72]

The *General Advertiser* also cited the letter as proof that the Republican party was a traitorous combination. The "base and unprincipled" Burk, wrote one of its correspondents, was the *"mouth piece* of traitors who lurk in the bosom of your country, the man whom EDWARD LIVINGSTON has declared, *must at all events be supported*—the man whose dedicatory incense having tickled the nostrils of a certain Colonel [Burr], is in return, by him, patronized and supported." [73] This "Seditious foreigner," the Federalist

---

[70] *Aurora*, July 9, 1798; *Bee*, July 18, 1798, reprinted in the *Aurora*, July 23, 1798. For the official text of this statement, see the *Annals*, 5C, 3445.

[71] *Time Piece*, July 11, 1798.

[72] Letter I by "C," *Daily Advertiser*, July 13, 1798.

[73] This refers to Burk's dedication of his play "Bunker Hill" to Burr, and to Burr's posting bail for Burk. For the playwright's praise of Burr's "courage and patriotism, talents and erudition," see Wyatt, *Burk*, 10.

paper concluded, was constantly employed in uttering "the most infamous falsehoods, defaming the most deserving characters, vilifying our Government and insulting our Country." [74]

Political animosity toward Republicans reached its peak in New York on July 21, when disturbances occurred at the home of Edward Livingston and the homes where Congressmen Albert Gallatin and Matthew Lyon were staying. Two nights later Burk was involved in "some confusion" at the old Coffee House. [75] As a warning to these "embryo heroes who designate themselves the friends of order and good government," "Citizen of the Sixth Ward" cautioned the Federalists to refrain from offering further insults to the representatives of the people. Livingston had just been re-elected to Congress, the correspondent wrote, so it was evident that the majority of citizens in New York approved his principles and conduct. Moreover, his constituents were ready to defend him "against any reptile Tory Faction," including the "unfledged, would be soldiers" who "preambulate [sic] the streets from 10 o'clock till midnight, vociferating God save the King, Hail Columbia, &c, using epithets and expressions which would disgrace a Porcupine—damning Livingston for a Jacobin, Democrat, Frenchman, &c, with several other phrases too indecent for publication." [76]

The most immediate result of the sedition proceedings against the *Time Piece* was the alienation of Dr. Smith from his volatile editor. Only a week after the arrest of the partners, the Federalist *Commercial Advertiser* gloated that the codefendants had quarreled on Friday the thirteenth, exactly a month after Burk assumed editorial control of their paper. According to "Observer," Burk wrote a violent invective against President Adams and read it to Dr. Smith, who thought it went too far. Fearful that the story might cause the forfeiture of the bond which they had posted with the court, Smith reportedly opposed publication of the piece. Burk replied that he thought it "would do a damn'd deal of mischief" toward bringing the president into utter contempt. When Smith continued to oppose its publication, the Federalist report added, Burk swore that he would insert it, no matter what his partner said. Smith then denounced Burk as "a damn'd rascal, and an unprincipled *alien*." Claiming that the editor's intemperate language had got them into their scrape with the government, Smith was reported to have ex-

[74] "A Citizen of New York," *Gazette and General Advertiser*, July 16, 1798.

[75] Paul Leicester Ford, ed., *The Journals of Hugh Gaine, Printer* (New York, 1902), II, 200, 203.

[76] *Greenleaf's New York Journal and Patriotic Register*, July 25, 1798.

pressed the wish that "he had been in Hell before he had ever seen" Burk. According to "Observer's" story, this assertion converted the dispute from a word-bandying into a type-throwing contest and a printer's devil finally had to separate the partners. The correspondent reported that Burk then departed for Philadelphia to complain to Livingston and surmised that Smith would be dismissed for lack of "*spunk* to go the necessary lengths." [77]

That there had been a disagreement between the partners became clear on July 20 when Dr. Smith disclaimed further responsibility for any debts contracted by Burk as editor. Moreover, he promised the subscribers that "no libelous or inflammitory [*sic*] matter shall be inserted in that paper, in future." Despite this internal dissension, Burk seems to have retained editorial direction of the paper. Subsequent issues displayed the vigorous style of the indicted editor, carrying blasts against Burk's personal enemy, "Themistocles," the pending prosecutions, and the newly enacted Sedition Law. Burk lamented that "the testimony of a contemptible informer" could brand as subversive an editor who had spent almost two years "in composing a Poem of the Epic kind, on the American Revolution, in which he has at least attempted to ennoble and immortalize that glorious event." The paper also denounced the indictment of the partners as political chicanery "which restrains a man by the terrors of prosecution and penalties, from uttering the calm and unclouded decisions of his understanding." [78]

The *Time Piece*'s attack on the Sedition Law also seems typical of Burk's writing. When Noah Webster defended the statute as "the fruit of opposition," the *Time Piece* replied that the British government had given the same excuse for abridging the rights of the subject in colonial times:

Upon these miserable pretexts the Boston port bill; the trials for treasons in Britain, committed in America; the bill for restraining the trade of America; the sending soldiers and foreign mercenaries to dragoon us; the employing "God and nature's instruments," the savages, whose known methods of conducting uncivilized war, was promiscuous carnage; the Jersey prisonship; the poisoning prisoners was justified by the advocates of Lord North's administration.

The Republican paper hoped that the American government was too wise to follow these examples. Endeavoring to shift odious labels from itself to its accusers, the *Time Piece* advised the government

[77] "Observer," *Commercial Advertiser*, July 16, 1798.
[78] *Time Piece*, July 20, 25, 30, 1798.

not to accept the counsel of Webster and "such seditious writers against the sovereign people." They were the real disorganizers, Jacobins and royalists who poisoned the minds of the people in endeavoring to divide them from the government.[79]

The Sedition Law, the editor contended, subjected printers to prosecution for every sentence "which the eye of a jealous government can torture into an offence. . . . Of course the law will tend to the suppression of every press, however congenial with the constitution, if it be not obsequious to the will of government." Under such a law, he asked, "who dare deny that truth is both libellous and seditious?" [80] In a sarcastic outburst, the *Time Piece* published a parody on "American Liberty; or, The Sovereign Right of Thinking":

> Since we are forbid to speak, or write
> A word that may our BETTERS bite,
> I'll sit Mum-chance from morn to night;
> But pay it off with THINKING.
>
> One word they ne'er shall fish from me,
> For *Master Rawle*, or *Charley Lee*; [81]
> Yet, if they'll let my thought be free,
> I'll pay them off with THINKING. . . .
>
> That still we're *sovereign* who'll deny?
> For though I dare not speak; yet I,
> One sovereign right will still enjoy,
> The sovereign right of thinking.[82]

Despite the paper's uncompromising stand, time was running out for the *Time Piece*. The animosity between the proprietors festered until they notified their readers on August 10 that a division of the partnership would be made as soon as it could be arranged. The Federalist prosecution and the dissension which it aroused between Burk and Smith thus combined to deal a death blow to the once-thriving newspaper. When Dr. Smith called a meeting of the subscribers in an effort to raise money to continue the Republican journal, the *Daily Advertiser* greeted the appeal as the "expiring groans of the *Time Piece*." This appraisal proved true; by September the *Time Piece* had run down completely. The Federalist press was exultant: "May such be the fate of every paper, that under the

---

[79] *Ibid.*, Aug. 8, 1798. [80] *Ibid.*, Aug. 25 and 28, 1798.

[81] Charles Lee was attorney general in President Adams' Cabinet, and William Rawle was federal district attorney for Pennsylvania.

[82] *Time Piece*, July 27, 1798.

hypocritical vizer of false patriotism and hallow-hearted professions of attachment to the people, aim at the subversion of our fair
fabric of law, government, individual security and domestic enjoy-
ment." Thus, even before the date of the scheduled trial of its editors, this anti-Federalist paper disappeared.[83]

Whether the administration was satisfied with the silencing of the
Republican journal or lacked confidence in its common law proceedings which antedated the Sedition Act, it seemed in no hurry
to prosecute Burk and Smith.[84] Indeed, the Federalists readily accepted Burk's offer to settle the case out of court. "Knowing the
moral certainty of force and imprisonment from the violence of
party spirit and the mode of packing juries," Burk decided it was
improbable that an alien would be acquitted of a charge of sedition. Even if he won his case, he would still be "at the mercy of the
President," who might deport him at any time. These reasons, combined with his desire to move sufficiently near to Ireland to assist
in any project for her emancipation from British rule, led him to
ask Burr to seek permission for his voluntary departure in return for
a dismissal of the case and a release from his bail recognizance.[85]

On December 28 District Attorney Harison transmitted Burr's
proposition to Secretary of State Pickering, who consulted President
Adams. On New Year's Day 1799, Pickering informed the government prosecutor that "all circumstances considered, the President
thinks it may be expedient to let him off, on the condition proposed
by Colonel Burr, his bail—that he Burke [sic] forthwith quit the
United States." The secretary specified, moreover, that this "turbulent mischievous person" ought to leave the Western Hemisphere.
If Burk remained on this side of the Atlantic, Pickering feared that
he would find his way to Spanish Florida or Louisiana "and finally
perhaps to some part of the United States, where the arm of the
Government may not easily reach him." He therefore ordered Hari-

[83] *Daily Advertiser*, Aug. 13, 1798. Brigham, *Newspapers*, I, 696, gives Aug.
30, 1798, as the last known issue.

[84] There is no indication that the case against Dr. Smith was ever tried. John
Henry Sherburne, ed., *The Suppressed History of the Administration of John
Adams from 1797 to 1801, as Printed and Suppressed in 1802, Written by John
Wood* (Philadelphia, 1846), 163, states that Smith's trial was not brought forward
because "the point which Mr. Adams wished to accomplish" was achieved when
the *Time Piece* ceased publication.

[85] Burk to Jefferson [1801], *William and Mary College Quarterly Historical
Magazine*, 2d ser., 5 (1925), 100. Although this letter is undated, it was written
in May or June, 1801; see Jefferson to John D. Burke [sic], Washington, June 21,
1801, *Jefferson's Writings* (Ford ed.), VIII, 66. Also see Pickering to Winthrop
Sargeant, May 22, 1799, Pickering Papers, XXXVII, 424 (Mass. Hist. Soc.).

son to ascertain the destination of the vessel in which Burk departed. Although Harison and Pickering originally proposed to suspend the prosecution in such a way that it could be resumed in case Burk violated the terms of the bargain, the district attorney finally agreed to dismiss the case.[86]

During these negotiations, Burk resided in New York, where he wrote a history of the recent revolt in Ireland.[87] Not until May, 1799, did he notify Pickering that he was ready to leave the United States. Since Burk proposed at that time to go by land to Charleston and then by ship to the Spanish port of New Orleans, Pickering immediately alerted Winthrop Sargeant, governor of the Mississippi Territory, and recommended that he inform the Spanish governor of Louisiana about this "turbulent, dangerous man." Despite Burk's avowed desire "to leave America and return to it no more," Pickering feared that he might try to re-enter the United States "where he might do more mischief than at New York." Confessing that he had never seen the obnoxious Irishman, Pickering promised to send Governor Sargeant a personal description of Burk, along with an authenticated copy of the indictment and proceedings against him, so that he might be prosecuted if he ever appeared in the Mississippi Territory.[88]

In June, 1799, Federalist newspapers reported that "the infamous *Burke* [sic], the United Irishman," had left the United States, and late in 1800 they circulated the story that he had been hanged in Ireland for sedition.[89] Both these stories were false. Burk did drop from view, but he did not leave the United States. Instead he went into hiding under an assumed name. Until the expiration of the Alien and Sedition Laws, he eluded Pickering's agents by serving as "Principal of a College" in Virginia.[90]

[86] Pickering to Harison, Jan. 1, 1799, Pickering Papers, XXXVII, 381 (Mass. Hist. Soc.). The costs of Burk's removal were to be borne by him or his bail. Pickering to Sargeant, May 22, 1799, *ibid.*, 424, states that Harison entered a nolle prosequi with the president's approval.

[87] *Aurora*, Dec. 11, 1798, reprints a New York story in which Burk requested material for his history of the war in Ireland.

[88] May 22, 1799, Pickering Papers, XXXVII, 424 (Mass. Hist. Soc.). On the same day the chief clerk in the State Department requested the clerk of the Circuit Court to forward copies of these documents to Governor Sargeant. Jacob Wagner to Edward Dunscomb, May 22, 1799, *ibid.*, 423. For Dunscomb's memorandum on the Burk case, see his letter to Pickering, May 24, 1799, Sargeant Papers, Box 9, Item 46 (Ohio Hist. Soc.).

[89] *Daily Gazette and General Advertiser*, quoted in the *Gazette of the United States*, July 1, 1799; *Otsego Herald* (Cooperstown), Sept. 18, 1800.

[90] Burk to Jefferson [1801], *William and Mary College Quarterly Historical*

After the defeat of the Federalists in the election of 1800 once more made it safe for him to appear in public, Burk wrote to President Jefferson reciting his activities in the cause of liberty, his persecution for a libel on Adams, his agreement to leave America, and his reasons for not leaving. In accordance with the agreement which Burr negotiated with the district attorney, Burk declared, he boarded a ship bound for Bordeaux. Two things, however, delayed his departure. Not only was he apprehensive that his movements were being watched by the spies of the British minister; he informed Jefferson that "an actual attempt" was made to seize him while aboard the ship. After that experience he was induced by "some of the best men in America" to postpone his sailing. "Want of means when I might perhaps have gone in safety," he added, "has since compelled me to remain. For more than two years have I by indirect exercise of the alien law been in fact exiled from society passing under a feigned name known only to a few confidential friends, rendered incapable of profiting by the exercise of my faculties, contracting debts the while dispirited allmost [sic] hopeless." [91]

Burk solicited Jefferson's recommendation as private secretary to some departmental officer. Although promising to mention him to the heads of the departments "with pleasure," the new president held out little hope for such an appointment.[92] Instead, Burk moved to Petersburg, Virginia, where he became a lawyer and the historian of his adopted state. That he bore no resentment against Jefferson is indicated by the dedication of his *History of Virginia* to the president, whom he praised for always finding "more satisfaction in abridging his authority, than other rulers have in aggrandizing themselves, at the expense of the liberty and happiness of their country." [93]

Magazine, 2d ser., 5 (1925), 100. For a reference to Burk as one of the incorporators of "The Trustees of Jefferson College in the County of Amelia," see Samuel Shepherd, *The Statutes at Large of Virginia . . . (New Series), Being a Continuation of Hening* (Richmond, 1835), II, 259–260.

[91] According to Burk, he chafed under these restrictions so much that he "made the Secretary of State acquainted with my place of residence and declared my readiness to take my trial." This letter, however, is not included in the Pickering Papers. For a mention of Burk as a candidate for the editorship of the Richmond *Press,* see William Brockenbrough to Joseph C. Cabell, Dec. 5, 1799, Cabell Papers (Univ. of Va.).

[92] Jefferson to Burke [sic], June 21, 1801, *Jefferson's Writings* (Ford ed.), VIII, 66.

[93] Burk, *The History of Virginia from Its First Settlement to the Present Day* (Petersburg, Va., 1804), I, preface.

Thus, neither of the two common law sedition proceedings brought by the Federalists against Republican newspaper editors came to trial. Death cheated the courts of Bache's case, and a deal negotiated by Aaron Burr, New York's leading Republican politician, led the administration to drop its case against Burk. Yet the prosecution against the New York paper was not without effect. Whereas the Philadelphia *Aurora* was revived after Bache's death, the *Time Piece*, deprived of its mainspring, ran no more.

CHAPTER XI

The Ordeal of the Critical Congressman: Matthew Lyon of Vermont

Licentiousness more endangers the liberties and independence of a free Government than hosts of invading foes.—SUPREME COURT JUSTICE WILLIAM PATERSON

DURING the congressional debates on the sedition bill, Representative Matthew Lyon of Vermont predicted to Senator Stevens Thomson Mason of Virginia that the bill was undoubtedly intended for Democratic-Republican congressmen "and very likely would be brought to bear on me the very first." [1] Less than three months after the passage of the Federalist measure, Lyon became its first victim.

While the law was pending before Congress, the Federalists openly declared that it was aimed at their opponents. Never fully accepting the emerging party system as a basic political concept, they had long denounced verbal opposition to their policies as "wrongheaded" and "factious." Lyon was a logical target for Federalist animosity. Almost from the moment that he took his seat at the special session of Congress in May, 1797, he was subjected

[1] Lyon to Mason, "In Jail at Vergennes," Vt., Oct. 14, 1798, *Independent Chronicle*, Nov. 22, 1798. This letter is also given in J. Fairfax McLaughlin, *Matthew Lyon, the Hampden of Congress, A Biography* (New York, 1900), 342–355.

to derisive remarks by the House majority. One of the few Republicans from New England, he was doubly offensive to the Federalists because of his Irish birth. He first aroused their ire when he opposed the appointment of a committee to visit the president to determine where and when he would receive the House's answer to his opening address. The nativist John Allen was disdainful of this un-American view and appealed to the better blood and accent of Americans to carry the question raised by the Irish-born Lyon.

The Vermont Republican replied that he had never before heard of congressmen boasting of their blood, but he had no objection to gentlemen of *"high blood"* going through with the "boyish piece of business" of carrying the answer to the president. Though he had no pretentions to "high blood" he thought he had as good blood as any Federalist, as he was born of a "fine, hale, healthy woman." He did not claim to be

descended from the bastards of Oliver Cromwell, or his courtiers, or from the Puritans who punished their horses for breaking the Sabbath, or from those who persecuted the Quakers, or hanged the witches. He could, however, say that this was his country, because he had no other; and he owned a share of it, which he had bought by means of honest industry; he had fought for his country. In every day of trouble he had repaired to her standard, and had conquered under it. Conquest had led his country to independence, and being independent, he called no man's blood in question.[2]

This outspoken reply in defense of his Irish ancestry outraged the Federalists. Harrison Gray Otis, whose denunciation of the "Wild Irish" had marked him as a leading xenophobe, suggested that since "the *Lyon* appeared to be in a savage mood" he should *"be locked up* while the House proceeded to the President." William Cobbett, English editor of *Porcupine's Gazette,* also sharpened a quill for *"The Lyon of Vermont."* On June 6 he penned a satirical article commenting on Otis' motion to cage this "singular animal" because of its uneasiness at *"going with the crowd."* Porcupine explained that Lyon was a "most extraordinary beast" who had been caught in the bog of Hibernia and, when a whelp, transported to America.

Curiosity induced a New Yorker to buy him, and moving into the country, afterwards exchanged him for a yoke of young bulls with a Vermontese. . . . His pelt resembles more the wolf or the tiger, and his gestures bear a remarkable affinity to the bear; this, however, may be

[2] *Annals,* 5C, 1S (June 2 and 3, 1797), 232–235.

ascribed to his having been in the habit of associating with that species of wild beast on the mountains: he is carnivorous, but not very ferocious —has never been detected in having attacked a *man*, but report says he will *beat women*.[3]

This was the beginning of a barrage of insults hurled at the Vermont Republican by the Federalists. Repeatedly referring to Lyon as "the greatest *beast* in nature," Porcupine denounced him and Albert Gallatin, Swiss-born Republican leader, as "two foreigners from the mountains." [4] Noah Webster's New York *Minerva* also assailed Lyon, claiming that he had distributed among his constituents a weekly newsletter. The Boston *Columbian Centinel* also charged that the congressman had franked hundreds of copies of the *Aurora*, "that Pandora box of anarchy," to his constituents. Lyon, concluded the *Minerva*, "is the redoubtable hero who, a few years before, was sold for his passage from Ireland, and who, for his cowardice in the American war, was condemned by General Gates to wear a *wooden sword*." [5]

It was not until January 30, 1798, however, that Lyon became a marked man. When Roger Griswold, a Federalist leader from Connecticut, made a disparaging remark about Lyon's military record in the Revolution,[6] the Vermont Republican replied by spitting in his face. Samuel Sewall of Massachusetts immediately proposed a resolution to expel Lyon for disorderly behavior. Although the Federalists condemned Lyon's action as "a personal outrage of the very grossest and most indecent nature . . . —an outrage which would not have been tolerated in any tavern in the country," they fell short of the two-thirds vote necessary to expel "the spitting

[3] *Porcupine's Gazette*, July, 1797, reprinted in *Porcupine's Works*, VI, 170–171; *Porcupine's Gazette*, June 6, 1797.

[4] *Porcupine's Works*, VI, 289, 327.

[5] *Centinel*, Jan. 24, 1798, quoted in Robinson, *Jeffersonian Democracy in New England*, 21n; *Minerva*, Aug., 1797, reprinted in *Porcupine's Works*, VI, 327.

[6] In 1774 Lyon organized an armed association which joined Ethan Allen in 1775, serving at Ticonderoga and in the early stages of the Canadian campaign. In 1776 the men in his command left their advance posts near the border because of their exposed position, and Lyon was cashiered by General Gates. This incident gave rise to the "wooden sword" story. Lyon's subsequent reinstatement in the Continental Army as a captain indicates that Gates's action was hasty and unjustified. After distinguished service in the campaigns against Burgoyne near Saratoga, Lyon resigned his continental commission for an appointment in the Vermont militia, becoming a colonel in 1780. See W. R. Robinson, "Matthew Lyon," *DAB*, XI, 532–534.

beast."[7] The Republicans viewed the expulsion attempt as a Federalist maneuver to get rid of an opposition vote in a nearly divided house.[8]

Porcupine continued to belabor Lyon as a supporter of the United Irishmen. "Matthew Lyon," the indignant English editor wrote, "came from Ireland. He not long ago drank 'Success to the United Irishmen,' then in open rebellion against their King, and he spit in the face of an American member of Congress." A Bostonian felt equally "grieved that the saliva of an Irishman should be left upon the face of an American & He, a New Englandman," and Mrs. Adams habitually referred to the spitting episode as "that dirty affair of Lyons."[9]

The Republican press ridiculed the Federalist members involved in the expectoration episode. One of its favorite jokes was about the country Irishman who read in a Federalist newspaper that Lyon had been traded for a couple of Connecticut oxen during his indenture. On a visit to Philadelphia, Patrick made a special trip to Congress to see Lyon, but was unable to distinguish him. However, he did witness Allen and Griswold of Connecticut speaking their minds "with great vehemence." At his boarding house, he was asked, "Did you see Mr. Lyon?" "No, by J——," cried Pat, "but I saw the two Conn. bullocks he was traded for."[10]

After the XYZ dispatches brought the diplomatic crisis with France to a climax, the Federalists denounced Lyon not only as a "wild Irishman" but also as a tool of France and an enemy of the United States. One Federalist newspaper denounced his congressional record as tending "to excite mobs and riots for the overthrow

[7] The discussions in Congress over Lyon's alleged breach of privilege may be followed from Jan. 30 to Feb. 12, 1798, in the *Annals*, 5C, 2S, 955–1029. The vote to expel was 52 to 44. See *ibid.*, 1008–1009. The quotation is Harper's. See *ibid.*, 979.

[8] Jefferson to Madison, Phila., Feb. 15, 1798, *Jefferson's Writings* (Ford ed.), VII, 202; also see Madison to Jefferson, Feb., 1798, *Madison's Writings* (Hunt ed.), VI, 310–311; and Gallatin to his wife, Feb. 13, 1798, Adams, *Gallatin*, 192–193.

Conversely, the Federalists asserted that the Republicans refused to vote for Lyon's expulsion "merely to avail themselves of his *vote* hereafter." To Harrison Gray Otis this was conclusive proof of Republican "disregard of all principle & decency, but as they have rope enough it is to be hoped they will hang themselves." Otis to his wife, Morison, *Otis*, I, 79.

[9] *Porcupine's Gazette*, Jan. 31, 1798; *Porcupine's Works*, IX, 336–338; Jonathan Mason, Jr., to Otis, Feb. 19, 1798, Morison, *Otis*, I, 87; Abigail Adams to Mary Cranch, June 23, 1798, Mitchell, *New Letters*, 194.

[10] *Carey's United States Recorder* (Philadelphia), Feb. 8, 1798.

of the government and the constitution." On his way home at the end of the session in July, 1798, the Republican representative passed through the Federalist strongholds of Trenton and New Brunswick, New Jersey. A band playing "The Rogue's March" serenaded him in Trenton, and a New Brunswick throng greeted him with insulting remarks. During his stay in New York City, a crowd demonstrated in front of his lodgings.[11]

In his home state of Vermont, Lyon also became the butt of Federalist jibes. When Lewis R. Morris, the Federalist representative from eastern Vermont, returned from Congress, a party in his honor contrasted his "integrity and federalism" with the "folly, indecorum and phrenzy of a *Lyon.*" Morris, they added, had supported the federal government and its interests against *"foreign tyranny and domestic faction."* [12]

Despite these Federalist denunciations of Lyon, he was a respectable man. He had come to America as a youthful indentured servant, had purchased his freedom, had fought in the Revolution, and then had founded the town of Fairhaven, Vermont. The wealthiest man in his part of the state, he established the first store in Fairhaven, built the first hotel, and started an iron works, a slitting mill, a sawmill, and a gristmill. In 1793 he launched a newspaper, which he published for two years. His marriage to the daughter of Governor Chittenden of Vermont symbolized his social standing. A leader in local politics and military affairs, he had served as secretary to the governor and council, as colonel and paymaster general of the Vermont militia, and as state assemblyman for nineteen terms. Thus, when the national party warfare of the 1790's began, he was an outstanding leader in Vermont. As he later wrote, he "had wealth, high political standing, an established character and powerful connections attached to me by long riveted confidence, as well as matrimonial affinity to throw in the scale." [13] In the campaign of 1796 the Green Mountain men of western Vermont chose him to represent them in Congress.

In 1798 Lyon was up for re-election. Even before he left Philadelphia in July to do his campaigning, he attempted to counter the stories circulated by his political adversaries. The Federalist

[11] *Albany Centinel,* July 31, 1798; *Porcupine's Gazette,* July 23, 1798; Ford, *Journals of Hugh Gaine,* II, 200.

[12] Letter from Brattleborough, Vt., July 17, 1798, to the *Albany Centinel,* Aug. 3, 1798.

[13] Andrew N. Adams, *A History of the Town of Fairhaven* (Fairhaven, Vt., 1870), *passim;* Robinson, "Matthew Lyon," *DAB,* XI, 523–524; Lyon to Armisted C. Mason, Jan. 16, 1817, McLaughlin, *Lyon,* 500–501.

papers in Philadelphia copied a violent attack on him from the *Vermont Journal* in Windsor. On June 20, twenty-four days before the passage of the Sedition Law, he wrote a vigorous reply to the editor of the Windsor paper.[14] Commenting on his refusal to accept the dogma of presidential infallibility, he wrote:

As to the Executive, when I shall see the efforts of that power bent on the promotion of the comfort, the happiness, and accommodation of the people, that executive shall have my zealous and uniform support: but whenever I shall, on the part of the Executive, see every consideration of the public welfare swallowed up in a continual grasp for power, in an unbounded thirst for ridiculous pomp, foolish adulation, and selfish avarice; when I shall behold men of real merit daily turned out of office, for no other cause but independency of sentiment; when I shall see men of firmness, merit, years, abilities, and experience, discarded in their applications for office, for fear they possess that independence, and men of meanness preferred for the ease with which they take up and advocate opinions, the consequence of which they know but little of—when I shall see the sacred name of religion employed as a state engine to make mankind hate and persecute one another, I shall not be their humble advocate.[15]

Lyon's pronouncement led a Federalist writer to conclude that *"a seditious foreigner* in our council may endanger us more than *a thousand Frenchmen* in the field." If Lyon could be replaced by a "Native American" in the coming election, another wrote, Vermont would no longer be under "obligations to Ireland, or any other foreign country, for the dregs and scum of their overburthened population"; at best Republicans were "worthless, degenerate, Frenchified citizens." [16] Only by suppressing the opposition could the Federalists expect to curb "the pernicious influence of that party." In short, the writer concluded, the Republicans should not only be defeated in the election; they should be exterminated.[17]

During his campaign for re-election, Lyon continued his attack on blind acceptance of executive policy, often quoting a letter from Joel Barlow, the American poet and land speculator then in France, to his brother-in-law, Abraham Baldwin, Republican representative

[14] Although Lyon mailed his letter that day, it was not postmarked until July 7, 1798. This was one week before President Adams signed the Sedition Law.

[15] *U.S. v. Lyon,* Wharton, *State Trials,* 333. This report is reprinted as Federal Case No. 8646, *The Federal Cases* (St. Paul, 1895), XV, 1183–1191. Lyon's letter was not published in the Windsor paper until July 31, 1798, over two weeks after the enactment of the Sedition Law.

[16] "Brutus" and "Observer," *Spooner's Vermont Journal* (Windsor), Aug. 28, 1798.

[17] "Observer," *ibid.,* Aug. 7 and 14, 1798.

from Georgia. Barlow warned that the misunderstanding between the United States and France was so alarming that President Adams should use the utmost caution in his every word and action if his object was to avoid hostilities. Yet, said Barlow, the president had made a "bullying speech" to Congress in November, 1797, while Pinckney, Marshall, and Gerry were on their way to Paris, and the Senate had responded with a "stupid answer."

Moreover, Barlow continued, Adams had borrowed the language of Edmund Burke to tell the world that "although he should succeed in treating with the French, there was no dependence to be placed on any of their engagements, that their religion and morality were at an end, that they would turn pirates and plunderers, and it would be necessary to be perpetually armed against them, though you were at peace." Barlow expressed his wonder that the answer of both houses to the president's speech had not been "an order to send him to a mad house. Instead of this the Senate have echoed the speech with more servility than ever George III experienced from either House of Parliament." [18]

Lyon's leading Federalist opponent in the elections of 1798 was the editor of the *Rutland Herald*, Stanley Williams, whose paper constantly flayed the "Vermont beast." When Lyon submitted a letter replying to these charges and outlining his stand on public issues, Williams refused to publish it. In the summer of 1798, therefore, Lyon established his own political organ, *The Scourge of Aristocracy and Repository of Important Political Truths.*

Edited by Lyon's eldest son, the first number of the *Scourge* appeared on October 1, 1798, boldly proclaiming its political creed:

When every aristocratic hireling from the English Porcupine, the summit of falsehood, detraction and calumny, in Philadelphia, down to the dirty Hedge-hogs and groveling animals of his race, in this and the neighboring States, are vomiting forth columns of lies, malignant abuse and deception, the Scourge will be devoted to politics, and shall commemorate the writings, essays and speeches of the ablest pens and tongues, in the Republican interest. Its great object shall be to oppose truth to falsehood, and to lay before the public such facts as may tend to elucidate the real situation of this country.[19]

The leading article in this first issue was Lyon's letter to his constituents which Williams had refused to publish. In it Lyon explained the technique by which the Federalists tried to discredit

[18] *U.S.* v. *Lyon*, Wharton, *State Trials*, 334. This pamphlet was published in Fairhaven on Sept. 1, 1798.

[19] *The Scourge of Aristocracy*, Oct. 1, 1798, quoted by McLaughlin, *Lyon*, 327.

their political opponents. Their chief weapon, he asserted, was to brand everyone who was not in favor of a "mad war" with France as "Opposers of the Government, Disorganizers, Jacobins, &c." This "new kind of jargon," he charged, was designed to confuse the people. He could not understand how an elected representative of the people could be called an opposer of the government simply because he did not agree to every proposition that came from the president. He had always supposed that representatives were sent by the people "to vote and support by arguments their own opinions, and that of their constituents, and to act for the interest of their country." To Lyon, this seemed to be nothing more than legitimate participation in the formulation of national policy.

When outvoted, Lyon continued, it was his duty to acquiesce and he did so. Yet he could not be expected in an election campaign to become the advocate of measures which he had opposed in Congress as injurious to the liberty and interests of the United States. His "opposition" to Federalist measures had been by the constitutional method of argument. He was bound by duty and by an oath to oppose any proposition which he thought injurious to his constituents and the Constitution. But opposition by argument was something quite different from forcible opposition by mob action or by riots and insurrections. Yet the "lying Tory papers printed in New York and Philadelphia," he declared, had equated his verbal opposition to administration measures with opposition to government by force and violence.

Moreover, Lyon's political enemies had accused him of wishing to see the United States subjugated by France. The Federalists, he replied, had accused every Republican congressman of being a traitor and often had added Vice-President Jefferson's name to the list. Such attacks Lyon branded as slanderous. His wishes for the welfare of any other nation had never interfered with his zeal for the United States. Indeed, he readily agreed that France was engaging in unwarrantable aggressions on American commerce. His aversion for the French had grown as their depredations on American merchants and commerce increased. By European standards, there could be no doubt "that the French have given us tenfold provocation for a declaration of war against them." Yet Lyon favored following the American example established at the time Jay's Treaty staved off war with England. Even after the XYZ revelations, he continued, he favored diplomatic negotiations rather than war. He would have readily assented to war against the French if it would have been an evil only to them or if he had thought it would have prevented further depredations. But war would not only be a calamity to the United States; it would do relatively little damage to France and would multiply its attacks.

In his election campaign Lyon also emphasized "war taxes." As the representative of a backcountry constituency, he could see no benefit to accrue to the nation in "an endless and useless contest concerning a commerce in which but a small part of the community were interested." It was to America's interest to remain at peace and to negotiate a settlement rather than to go into an offensive war whose cost would "fall on the landed interest, without the most distant prospect of retribution." For these reasons, he had opposed any measure which, in his opinion, might lead to war.[20]

Two days after the appearance of the *Scourge* on October 1, 1798, the federal Circuit Court for the District of Vermont convened in Rutland. In his charge to the grand jury, Associate Justice William Paterson of the United States Supreme Court discussed the yet-untried Sedition Law and recommended careful attention "to the seditious attempts of disaffected persons to disturb the government." Thanking the judge for his "solemn, momentous and invaluable charge," the grand jury commended its "pure principles of justice." "We solemnly feel," the jurors said, "what the Honorable Judge has so powerfully expressed, that licentiousness more endangers the liberties and independence of a free Government than hosts of invading foes." They lamented "that our liberties in some instances, are abused to licentiousness" and prayed for independence "without faction, and liberty without licentiousness." [21] Acting on the assumption that Lyon was a dangerous domestic enemy of the government, the federal grand jury indicted him for sedition on October 5, 1798.[22]

Lyon's biographer claims that the indictment of the Vermont representative "was really due and may be plainly traced" to the appearance of the *Scourge* only four days before the grand jury's action.[23] There seems little doubt, however, that Lyon would have

[20] "A letter from Matthew Lyon, Member of Congress from the Western District of Vermont to his Constituents," *ibid.*, 330–336.

[21] *Country Porcupine*, Oct. 22, 1798; *Rutland Herald*, Oct. 15, 1798.

[22] *Independent Chronicle*, Oct. 18, 1798. Although the Republican papers reported that indictments also were returned against James Lyon, the congressman's son, Anthony Haswell, editor of the Bennington *Vermont Gazette*, and Judah P. Spooner, Fairhaven printer, there seems to be no basis for these assertions. For the stories, see the *Independent Chronicle*, Oct. 22, 1798, and the *Vermont Gazette*, Oct. 12, 1798.

[23] McLaughlin, *Lyon*, 207.

been indicted had his newspaper not appeared. Indeed, he could hardly have been indicted for his article in the *Scourge*. In it he denied being an opposer of government. While he attacked the Federalists as Tories and aristocrats, he made no verbal attack on the president, either house of Congress, or on the government. When the grand jury indicted Lyon, therefore, they turned to his earlier publications. According to the Federalist press, these contained "artful and indirect accusations" against President Adams.[24]

Lyon's indictment contained three counts. The first charged that his letter to the *Vermont Journal* was scandalous and seditious. Branding Lyon as a malicious and seditious person of a depraved mind and a wicked and diabolical disposition, the grand jury reported that he had wickedly and maliciously contrived to defame the government and the president "with force and arms" by publishing his letter in the Windsor paper on July 31. His intent and design had been to bring them into contempt and disrepute, to excite against them the hatred of the good people of the United States, and to stir up sedition in the United States. The letter was a libel on John Adams as president and on the executive branch of the government of the United States. It contained "scurrilous, feigned, false, scandalous, seditious and malicious matters" which referred to the president's "continual grasp for power" and his "unbounded thirst for ridiculous pomp, foolish adulation or selfish avarice." The wicked publication of this scandalous and seditious writing, the first count concluded, had been made "in contempt of the good and wholesome laws of the United States, to the evil and pernicious example of others . . . and against the peace and dignity of the United States."

The second count charged that Lyon libeled the president and the Senate by publishing Barlow's letter on September 1, and the final accusation pertained to the aiding and abetting in the publication of this letter. Both charges were in the same form as the first one, imputing bad intentions to Lyon and asserting that he printed the letter "with force and arms" to the "great scandal and infamy" of the government, the president, and the Senate.[25]

It should be noted that all three counts of the indictment stipulated that Lyon published his writings "with force and arms." The Sedition Law contained no provision against the advocacy of force

[24] *Columbian Centinel*, Nov. 3, 1798.

[25] "*U.S.* v. *Lyon*, certified copy of the official court record, compiled . . . by Jesse Gove," *Annals*, 16C, 2S (Dec. 4, 1820), 478–485. This record of the case was prepared to support Lyon's petitions for the refund of his fine.

and violence; it was directed solely against criticism of the administration. The indictment's recital of the words, "with force and arms," had no real meaning as applied to the publishing of the forbidden words. Their appearance in the charge, however, along with the condemnation of Lyon as a man of a depraved mind and diabolical disposition, increased the chances of conviction for remarks made in the course of a campaign to retain his seat in Congress. If the harsh epithets of the indictment are disregarded, Lyon was charged with uttering political opinions critical of President Adams and the Federalist administration.

The nearly equal balance between the parties in the House of Representatives made the elections of 1798 extremely important. The prosecution of one of the best-known Republican leaders, while he was in the midst of his campaign for re-election, could not fail to attract national political attention. Indeed, this proceeding by the administration was doubly bold because the libel alleged in the first count had been written more than three weeks before the passage of the Sedition Law, although it had not been published until that law had gone into effect. Moreover, the Barlow letter had been reprinted by other newspapers, and Lyon's edition was plainly labeled "a copy." In these circumstances, a conviction was sure to raise political passions and fears to new heights.[26]

After the grand jury returned the indictment on October 5, the deputy marshal served a warrant on Lyon that evening at his home in Fairhaven. Lyon appeared at the Rutland Court House on Saturday morning, October 6, and pleaded not guilty. He told the court that he had sent to Bennington for two lawyers, but he did not expect them until Monday. The court replied that the trial might be postponed until the May, 1799, term, but Lyon elected to stand trial immediately, since he did not want to have the charge of sedition hanging over his head for eight months. Moreover, the next court would be held at Windsor in the eastern district, and Lyon feared that in Morris' district the Federalists would be sure "of having a unanimous jury, such as they want." His trial, therefore, was set for October 8 and he was admitted to bail till Monday.[27]

When the trial opened in Rutland before the presiding judge, Justice Paterson of the United States Supreme Court, and District Judge Samuel Hitchcock, Lyon requested a short delay because a stormy weekend had delayed the arrival of his lawyers. Before

[26] Wharton, *State Trials*, 339.

[27] *Albany Centinel*, Oct. 16, 1798; Lyon to Mason, Oct. 14, 1798, *Independent Chronicle*, Nov. 22, 1798.

noon, his messenger reported that neither lawyer could appear. Israel Smith, chief justice of the Vermont Supreme Court whom Lyon had succeeded in Congress the year before, consented to advise the defendant but declined to act as counsel because of insufficient time to prepare a defense. Lyon therefore served as his own lawyer.[28]

The jury was chosen from a panel of fourteen men who came from the same towns as the grand jury men. The government prosecutor challenged one of the panel who denied that he had ever formed or expressed an opinion as to Lyon's guilt or innocence. A deputy sheriff testified that he had heard the prospective juryman say that he thought the defendant would not, or should not, be condemned. Judge Paterson removed the name of this man from the jury list.[29] Lyon challenged two jurors for their known political opposition to him, but produced no evidence against one. When he showed that the other was the author of personal and political newspaper attacks on him during his election campaign, the presiding judge sustained the objection, ruling that a difference in political opinion was reason for disqualification in such circumstances. After the jury was sworn, Lyon entered a plea against the jurisdiction of the court, arguing that the Sedition Law was unconstitutional and therefore void. Although Judge Paterson struck this plea off, he informed Lyon that he might advance this argument during the trial.[30]

District Attorney Charles Marsh opened the government's case by producing Lyon's original letter of June 20 to Alden Spooner, the editor of the *Vermont Journal*. Although it bore the Philadelphia postmark of July 7, it had not been received in Windsor until after July 14, the date that the Sedition Act became law. Lyon admitted writing and mailing the letter and its subsequent publication on July 31 by the *Journal*.

On the second count, the government prosecutor proved that

[28] *U.S. v. Lyon*, Wharton, *State Trials*, 335. One of Lyon's lawyers was a member of the state legislature and was preparing to attend. The wife of the other was ill.

[29] *Ibid.*, 334. Lyon claimed that the deputy had begun a conversation with this juryman "on purpose to have something to swear." The latter suspected this was the case and avoided conversing with the deputy, according to Lyon. The juryman's removal, Lyon said, resulted in the withdrawal of the only member of the panel "that knew me enough to judge of my intentions." Lyon to Mason, Oct. 14, 1798, *Independent Chronicle*, Nov. 22, 1798.

[30] Wharton, *State Trials*, 334, says that there appears to have been no examination of one of the jurymen. See also Lyon to Mason, Oct. 14, 1798, *Independent Chronicle*, Nov. 22, 1798.

Lyon had read from Barlow's letter at public meetings in Vermont. Several witnesses testified that he used it for political purposes, employing language "highly disrespectful to the administration." [31] Attempting to tie this evidence in with the words "force and arms" contained in the indictment, District Attorney Marsh asked one of his witnesses, a young Federalist lawyer, if the reading of the letter had caused any tumult. The lawyer and an associate testified that they thought it had created a commotion at a political rally in Middletown. One of them had heard a person say there must be a revolution. Both agreed that there was some noise and tumult. Under cross-examination, however, they testified that there would have been no disturbance had they not attended the meeting; the tumult had been caused by the other people's dislike of their conduct.

The government attorney supported the third count by showing that Barlow's letter had been printed in Fairhaven from a copy written by Lyon and delivered to the printer by Lyon's wife. The youthful Federalist lawyer testified that Lyon had told him that not more than one or two passages in the letter could be called seditious.[32] Concluding the government's case, Marsh contended that the offensive remarks by Lyon violated the Sedition Law because they were libelous in themselves and uttered with the requisite bad intentions "which expressly come up to innuendos." [33]

When Judge Paterson started to give his charge to the jury without hearing any remarks in defense of Lyon, the representative asked why his testimony should not be heard. The judge "politely sat down" and directed Lyon to proceed.[34] In an address of nearly two and one-half hours, Lyon set up a three-point defense against the government charges. He asserted that the court had no jurisdiction over the offense since the Sedition Law was unconstitutional and therefore void; at least, it should not extend to writings composed before the law passed. Moreover, his writings were innocent, that is, they were not published with "bad intent." Finally, he declared that their contents were true.

Lyon offered no testimony on the first two points, but on the

[31] Cross examination brought out the fact that Lyon had tried to prevent the publication of the letter on one occasion. *U.S. v. Lyon,* Wharton, *State Trials,* 335. Lyon claimed that the evidence proved that he had always opposed the printing of the letter. Although he quoted from it, he had promised Congressman Baldwin, to whom Barlow's letter was addressed, that he would not allow its publication. Lyon to Mason, Oct. 14, 1798, *Independent Chronicle,* Nov. 22, 1798.

[32] Lyon to Mason, Oct. 14, 1798, *ibid.*

[33] *U.S. v. Lyon,* Wharton, *State Trials,* 335.

[34] Lyon to Mason, Oct. 14, 1798, *Independent Chronicle,* Nov. 22, 1798.

third he took the unusual step of asking Justice Paterson "whether he had not frequently dined with the President, and observed his ridiculous pomp and parade?" Almost as unusual as this question directed to the judge on the bench was the fact that the judge replied. He testified that he had sometimes, though rarely, dined with the president, but that he had never seen any pomp or parade; he had seen, on the contrary, a great deal of plainness and simplicity. When Lyon asked the judge whether he had not seen more pomp and servants at the president's than at the tavern in Rutland, the judge did not answer. Lyon then concentrated on denying that the evidence showed anything other than a legitimate political opposition.

In his charge to the jury, Judge Paterson emphasized the political issue. He declared that Congress had intended that the author and publisher of libels on the president, Congress, or the government should be punished. The validity of the statute could not be disputed until a competent tribunal had declared it null and void. Since the jury had nothing whatever to do with the constitutionality or unconstitutionality of the Sedition Law, they had but two points to decide. Had Lyon published the writings listed in the indictment? Had he done so seditiously, that is, with "bad intent"?

Since Lyon admitted the publications, the first question was undisputed. "As to the second point," the judge added, "you will have to consider whether language such as that here complained of could have been uttered with any other intent than that of making odious or contemptible the President and government, and bringing them both into disrepute. If you find such is the case, the offense is made out, and you must render a verdict of guilty." Thus the judge made the tendency of the words the test of intent.[35]

In one instance the judge openly assumed the role of advocate and insinuated that the Barlow letter which Lyon read from was a forgery. Let literary men read the letter, he said, and compare it with the poet's published works, and they would deny its authenticity.[36] At no time in his charge did Justice Paterson mention the concept of a legitimate political opposition, the fact that truth was a justification, or even the fact that acquittal was possible. His closest approximation to any of these was his reminder that Lyon

[35] *U.S.* v. *Lyon*, Wharton, *State Trials*, 335. For a discussion of tendency and intent in speech cases, see Chafee, *Free Speech in the United States*, 23–28.

[36] Lyon to Mason, Oct. 14, 1798, *Independent Chronicle*, Nov. 22, 1798. Also see Lyon's remarks on the floor of the House, Jan. 23, 1801, *Annals*, 6C, 2S, 973–974.

could not be guilty unless the jury was satisfied beyond all reasonable doubt that he was not innocent.[37]

After an hour's deliberation the jury returned a verdict of guilty. The judge then informed Lyon that he would have an opportunity to show cause why judgment should not be pronounced and to show his circumstances as to ability to pay. In sedition cases, said the judge, the greater the amount of property the defendant had, the greater the fine he should pay. Lyon replied, somewhat impertinently, that he doubted that anything he might say would influence the court, but the judge postponed the sentence until the next day to give Lyon time to think it over.

At nine o'clock on the morning of October 9, Lyon informed the judge that he had formerly valued his property at $20,000, but he doubted that it would bring half that in the depression days of 1798. He had recently mortgaged part of it for a debt of $1,700, but he still had property worth more than the legal limit of a fine under the Sedition Law, although he doubted that he could raise $200 in cash in view of the prevailing scarcity of money.

In sentencing Lyon, Judge Paterson proposed to make an example of him in order to show that abusive remarks against the administration or the government could not be made with impunity. The Republican's political rank only aggravated the crime. "Matthew Lyon," the judge lectured, "as a member of the federal legislature, you must be well acquainted with the mischiefs which flow from an unlicensed abuse of government, and of the motives which led to the passage of the act under which this indictment is framed. No one, also, can be better acquainted than yourself with the existence and the nature of the act." Lyon's offense, therefore, could not be allowed to slip through the court with only a nominal fine, because such leniency would be a conspicuous invitation for others to imitate Lyon's example in the expectation of complete impunity. The Federalist judge then sentenced the Republican congressman to four months in jail, imposed a fine of $1,000, and assessed court costs of $60.96. This sentence was magnanimous, the judge implied; what tended to mitigate it was the reduced condition of Lyon's estate. Nonetheless, the representative was to remain in prison until the fine and costs were paid.[38]

During the trial Lyon repeatedly charged that the jury was packed with men "who had been accustomed to speak ill" of him. He later

[37] Wharton, State Trials, 336.
[38] Ibid., 336–341. The amount of the court costs is given in Annals, 16C, 2S, 483.

claimed that both the grand jury and trial jury had been chosen from towns which were distinguished for their enmity toward him. The purpose of the trial, he concluded, was to crush him politically.[39]

The Federalist press greeted the sentence as "pleasing information to all friends of Government." "Justice though late, is sure," wrote Boston's *Columbian Centinel,* and the *Albany Centinel* added, "May the good God grant that this may be the case of every Jacobin."[40] In Connecticut the *Courant* crowed its approval in a couplet referring to

> Matthew Lyon, peeping thru' his grate,
> The fetter'd Delegate of Vermont state.

Noting that the beast was now caged and on exhibit in Vergennes, the *Courant* assured its readers that he was the same creature which had cavorted in Philadelphia "like a Monkey . . . where he was taken for an Ass for his braying, for a Cur by his barking, for a Puppy by his Whining, for a Hog for his eating, for a Cat by his spitting, and for a Lion, by nothing but his being the greatest of beasts."[41]

Alden Spooner, who had published Lyon's letter on July 31, rejoiced that the restraint of Lyon's licentiousness had vindicated the liberty of the press, "that guardian of American freedom." He was convinced "that if the people of America should be deprived of this invaluable birth-right, it would be by means of those who abused the sacred privilege of free discussion. The conviction of Mr. Lyon . . . ," he continued, "may prove in the end, a noble triumph of liberty and our equal laws over that unbridled spirit of opposition to government, which is, at the present moment, the heaviest curse of America."[42]

The report of a Vergennes correspondent was widely reprinted in the Federalist press. He characterized Judge Paterson's severe charge to the jury as "cool, candid and perspicuous," "a most illus-

---

[39] Lyon to Mason, Oct. 14, 1798, *Independent Chronicle,* Nov. 22, 1798.

[40] *Albany Centinel,* Oct. 12, 1798; *Columbian Centinel,* reprinted in *ibid.,* Oct. 23, 1798. On Nov. 13, 1798, the *Columbian Centinel* published an account of Lyon's trial for the amusement of its readers, condemning him as a man "whose name is companion with reproach;—whose fate excites no pity;—and his confinement no exultation."

[41] *Connecticut Courant,* Nov. 26, 1798, and Feb. 11, 1799.

[42] *Spooner's Vermont Journal,* Oct. 15, 1798. Under the Sedition Law, the Federalist editor was legally as liable to prosecution for publishing Lyon's letter as the congressman was for writing it.

trious specimen of the noble talents and judicial rectitude of that greatly admired and respected judge." According to this report, eleven of the jurors were ready to find a verdict of guilty as soon as they left the courtroom. After a recapitulation of the evidence, the one doubter concluded that "it was impossible to acquit him." There had been no attempt to impeach the court or jury of any partial or improper conduct, this report continued; on the contrary, the court, the district attorney, and the jury had received "unanimous approbation." [43]

Approbation may have been unanimous in Federalist circles, but the judgment was reprobated by all Republicans. The *Aurora* hailed Lyon as a martyr to the cause of free speech; his was the honor of being the first victim "of a law framed directly in the teeth of the Constitution of this federal republic." In New Jersey the *Centinel of Freedom* expressed regrets that "the *tory* and *aristocratic* levelers of *write* and *wrong* . . . exult at having caught the Lyon in their toils." The trial made a tremendous impression on Jefferson, who had drafted the Kentucky Resolutions in protest against the law even before its enforcement. "I know not which mortifies me most," he wrote after Lyon's conviction, "that I should fear to write what I think or my country bear such a state of things. Yet Lyon's judges, and a jury of all nations, are objects of national fear." [44]

The Lyon had hardly been caged before he began to roar. From his cell in jail, he wrote a long letter to Senator Mason of Virginia, publicizing the initial proceedings under the *"beloved* Sedition bill." His prediction that he would be the first victim of the law had come true. "Perhaps I," he added stoically, "who have been a football for dame fortune all my life, am best able to bear it." But he did not bear it in silence.

His letter, which appeared throughout the land, denounced the federal marshal for his savage treatment. Instead of being imprisoned at the federal jail in Rutland, the county seat where he was tried, Lyon was taken to the Vergennes jail, forty-four miles away, in the county where the marshal resided. The marshal refused to allow him to return to his lodgings to take care of his papers. Guarded by two armed troopers, Lyon left Rutland on October 9,

---

[43] After this story appeared in the *Albany Centinel*, Oct. 16, 1798, it was copied widely by the Federalist journals throughout the United States.

[44] *Aurora*, Nov. 1, 1798; *Centinel of Freedom* (Newark), Oct. 23, 1798; Jefferson to John Taylor, Nov. 26, 1798, *Jefferson's Writings* (Bergh ed.), X, 63. Also see Stephens T. Mason to Jefferson, Raspberry Plain, Nov. 23, 1798, Jefferson Papers, CIV, 17894 (Lib. Cong.).

stayed overnight near Middlebury, and arrived at Vergennes on the
tenth. By taking a circuitous route to the jail, the marshal paraded
the victim the whole length of the town where the state legislature
was meeting.

Lyon was then locked up in a twelve-by-sixteen cell, "the common receptacle for horse-thieves, money-makers, runaway-negroes,
or any kind of felons." An indoor toilet in one corner of the room
perfumed the air with a stockyardlike aroma. Light and air came
through a small open window, which was crossed by nine iron
bars. The cell had neither fireplace nor stove, Lyon observed, and
the iron bars failed to keep out the cold air of Vermont's October
nights.[45]

For four days the marshal refused him pen and ink unless his
letters were censored. But on the thirteenth his jailer rescinded
this ruling, and on the fourteenth and fifteenth the congressman
wrote Senator Mason to inform him of the outcome of the Vermont
elections. Morris, the Federalist representative from eastern Vermont, had been re-elected, and Lyon had outrun his nearest com-
petitor, Stanley Williams, by 3,482 votes to 1,554. But Lyon had
failed by a single ballot to obtain a majority of the 6,965 votes cast,
and a run-off election was scheduled for December while he was
in jail.[46]

For the first time in American history, a candidate for Congress
conducted his campaign from a federal prison. In answer to the
appeals which issued from Lyon's cell, local and national Federalist
leaders launched a terrific assault against him and his party, condemning them as saboteurs of the nation. Writing in the *Columbian
Centinel*, "Plain Truth" cautioned all true supporters of the government against "the insatiable Faction," which "mocks your wise
laws; and defies your magistrats." The writer was astounded that
Lyon, "the culprit who is now under punishment at *Vergennes*, is
styled a martyr" and that "his lies, issuing from his prison house,
find circulaters and believers." "Plain Truth" warned that Lyon and

[45] Lyon to Mason, Oct. 14, 1798, *Independent Chronicle*, Nov. 22, 1798.

[46] According to Lyon, his opponents received a total vote of 3,483 votes to his
3,482. There were also thirty votes for state representatives or for governor which
were deposited by mistake in the ballot box for congressman. If these are counted
in the totals, the vote for congressman is raised to 6,995, leaving Lyon thirty-one
votes shy of a majority. See Lyon to Mason, Oct. 14, 1798, *Independent Chronicle*,
Nov. 22, 1798.

Other sources, however, give the total vote as 6,989, leaving Lyon twenty-six
votes short of a majority. See *Spooner's Vermont Journal*, Oct. 29, 1798; *Independent Chronicle*, Nov. 8, 1798; McLaughlin, *Lyon*, 375.

the Republicans were "all cock a top for . . . *moody insurrection and confusions*"; they were America's "most vindictive and active enemy," and they were "on the march." [47]

At a Boston celebration of John Adams' birthday, the president's supporters toasted "the American Eagle" with the fervent plea that "the plots of Disorganizers [may] be pierced by his eye, and their opposition fall under his talons." [48] They also drank to Lyon's opponent in the run-off election: "Mr. Williams, the last Federal candidate in the second district of Vermont. May we always have Daniels whose virtues shall command respect even in the Lyon's den." [49] The *Columbian Centinel* declared that the "disciples of Folly and Bigotry" who had been convicted under the Sedition Law could never become martyrs. The fate of their "predecessors in iniquity," such as Robespierre of France and Daniel Shays of Massachusetts, should teach seditious Democrats that they would be remembered only as "infamous creatures." [50]

Only two days after Lyon was placed in his Vergennes den, the Vermont General Assembly appointed a committee, headed by Williams, to draft a laudatory address to President Adams. On October 20 the Assembly informed the president that although they were among the latest to address him they were among the foremost to approve his official conduct. They considered government as the association of "the honest, the pious, and the peaceable, to protect themselves from the wickedness of the dishonest, impious, and the unruly." If the designs of the former were effected, it was natural that the latter should complain "and attempt to break every barrier which protects society."

In an indirect reference to the Republican opposition to the administration, the Assembly warned that no government, however celebrated its excellency, had ever been spared the disgrace of opposition and frequent insurrections. The Federalist-dominated Assembly was sure that the president could "distinguish between the voice of your country and the clamour of party; we here offer you the genuine sentiments of our constituents, the freemen of Vermont, as delivered through their constitutional organ, the legislature." [51]

---

[47] *Columbian Centinel*, Nov. 24, 1798.   [48] *Ibid.*, Oct. 31, 1798.

[49] *Gazette of the United States*, Nov. 9, 1798.

[50] *Columbian Centinel*, Nov. 28, 1798.

[51] E. P. Walton, ed., *Records of the Governor and Council of the State of Vermont* (Montpelier, 1876), IV, 495. The address passed by a party vote of 129 to 23. See the *Journal of the Vermont Assembly for 1798, 75–80.*

Drafted by Lyon's Federalist opponent for Congress while the Vermont Assembly was in session in the town where Lyon was jailed, this partisan address was acclaimed by the *Columbian Centinel* as an "event which will totally crush the faction of the Lion, and all his whelps." [52] The Republicans in the Assembly quite naturally refused to endorse it because of its blanket approval of all the measures of Adams' administration. In a minority report to their constituents, they explained that although they were willing to go along with an Assembly address expressing veneration for the president's virtues and his zeal for the public welfare, they could not endorse every measure of his administration. Although they did not refer directly to Lyon's imprisonment, the Republican legislators asserted that the Federalist address was pointed at "distinguished characters who had always had their fullest confidence." [53]

The president's reply to the majority address echoed the views of the Federalists on opposition to the government. The true cause "of opposition and frequent insurrections" to good governments, the president wrote, was that while the honest and pious are always disposed to submit to a mild government, "the dishonest and impious take advantage of the feeble restraint, to commit mischief, because it can be done with impunity." These mischiefs lead to the necessity of severe curbs for the wicked, "and then the sordid animal becomes too tame under the curb, the lash and the spur." The chief executive, however, thought there was little danger from tumults so long as mild curbs showed "a tenderness of blood and a respect for human life." This maxim, he said, "preserved the Romans who for four hundred years never shed the blood of a man in sedition. An example worthy the contemplation and imitation of all other republics." [54]

In his answer President Adams also agreed with Judge Paterson's contention that the Sedition Law mitigated the rigors of the common law, which placed no limit on the penalty for sedition. He endorsed the Sedition Law as a necessary curb on the dishonest and impious who took advantage of the feeble restraints of a mild government. Like the Roman republic, he pointed out, the American nation respected human life while punishing sedition. Since

[52] *Columbian Centinel*, Oct. 31, 1798.

[53] *Vermont Gazette*, extra edition, Dec. 20, 1798, quoted in Walton, *Records of the Governor and Council*, 494n.

[54] President Adams to the Vermont Assembly, Phila., Nov. 30, 1798, *Vermont Gazette*, Dec. 27, 1798, quoted, *ibid.*, 495–496.

Representative Lyon was the only man who had been convicted under that law when the president wrote his address, these remarks applied directly to him. In short, President Adams' answer became a piece of campaign literature against Lyon's re-election; it placed the chief magistrate's stamp of approval on the conviction and imprisonment of "the sordid animal" because of the "mischief" created by his critical comments on the president's conduct.

Despite the efforts of the Federalists, Lyon was re-elected by a clear majority of nearly 600 over the rest of the field. His vote of 4,476 almost doubled that of Williams, who polled 2,444 votes. This news provoked only moans from the Federalist papers. One branded Lyon as an "animal who apes a monkey" and "talks and writes a gibberish between Wild Irish and vulgar American." In utter exasperation the New York *Commercial Advertiser* asked: "Must our national counsels be again disgraced by that vile beast?" [55]

After learning of his re-election, Lyon addressed a letter of thanks to the freemen of his district and dated it from his campaign headquarters, "Vergennes Goal [sic]." Calling his election a blow to the tyranny of the Sedition Law, he contrasted the action of his constituents with the address of the Vermont legislature to the president upholding the Alien and Sedition Laws. Although he did not mention the president's answer to this address, he reaffirmed his aversion to "pompous adulation and mean flattery." The real crime which had led to his punishment, he declared, was his refusal to sacrifice his sacred trust of representing his constituents "to the view of those who wish to see a luxurious court, crowded with shoals of military courtiers, speculators, and stock-jobbers, fattening on the labours of the farmer and the poor mechanic." While two judges and thirty jurymen had declared him guilty of bad intentions, Lyon concluded, 3,500 freemen had declared him not guilty. [56]

The triumphant majority received by Lyon should have been a warning to the Adams administration of the popular aversion to a law which forbade a candidate for Congress to express freely to his constituents his opinions on the public conduct of the president. His re-election certainly afforded strong evidence of the sym-

[55] McLaughlin, *Lyon*, 375; *Commercial Advertiser*, Feb. 8, 1799, and Dec. 28, 1798.

[56] Lyon to the Freemen of the Western District of Vermont, Vergennes, Goal, Jan. 12, 1799, *Aurora*, Feb. 8, 1799. Although Lyon gave his vote as 3,500, he received almost 4,500 votes.

pathy excited for him and might have been expected to deter a politically astute administration from action which created martyrs for the opposition party. Yet Lyon's case was to have two sequels.

Even before his constituents had expressed their indignation at the polls, they had demonstrated their resentment against his conviction in other ways. Several thousand Vermonters signed a petition asking the president to pardon Lyon. Vowing their love of America and its interest, they assured the president that they knew of no divisions among the American people in favor of a foreign nation or influence. Yet they were deprived of their representative. If Lyon were pardoned, the petitioners declared, the president would merit "the thanks, the prayers, and praises of millions." [57] When the Reverend John C. Ogden presented this petition to President Adams, the chief executive asked if Lyon himself had petitioned. When informed that he had not, the president refused to receive the petition on the ground that "penitence must precede pardon." [58]

For his role in seeking Lyon's release, the Reverend Ogden was marked out for Federalist vengeance. On his return from Philadelphia to Vermont, he stopped in his old home town of Litchfield, Connecticut, where he was arrested immediately and thrown into jail at the instigation of Secretary of the Treasury Wolcott, supposedly for an old debt of $200. The *Aurora* suspected that this action was taken because of Ogden's efforts in Lyon's behalf.[59] The *Connecticut Courant* consistently called Ogden "the Rev. Gaolbird," and the Boston *Centinel* chortled that once Lyon left his cell for Congress, he could sneak into Litchfield and take a petition from Ogden to the chief of the Republicans, Vice-President Jeffer-

[57] Petition from the Freemen of the Western District of Vermont, *Aurora*, Jan. 14, 1799.

[58] Jefferson to Madison, Phila., Jan. 3, 1799, *Jefferson's Writings* (Bergh ed.), X, 68. The *Aurora*, Jan. 4, 1799, denied that Lyon had petitioned the president for a pardon.

Reverend Ogden (1740–1800) was reputed to have been the first Episcopal minister ordained in Boston. From 1786 to 1793 he served as rector of St. John's Church, Portsmouth, New Hampshire. For a short sketch of Ogden, see James Grant Wilson and John Fiske, eds., *Appleton's Cyclopaedia of American Biography* (New York, 1888), IV, 561.

[59] *Aurora*, Feb. 16 and 19, 1799; *Connecticut Courant*, May 27, 1799. Ogden pelted prominent leaders with letters from the Litchfield jail. See Ogden to George Washington, Feb. 12, 1799, Washington Papers, CCXCIV (Lib. Cong.); and to Jefferson, Feb. 7 and March 5, 1799, Jefferson Papers, CV, 17959, 18010 (Lib. Cong.).

son.[60] When Ogden was finally released from jail four months later, a crowd of soldiers hounded him out of town as a "damned Democrat." Not until a group of "respectable gentlemen" rode to the rescue was he permitted to go on his way unmolested.[61]

Although the president refused to rescind Lyon's fine, the problem of payment was solved before his term expired. Senator Mason of Virginia proposed that since Lyon's sufferings were for the common cause of republicanism the fine should be paid by a common subscription among the enemies of political persecution.[62] Mason relied most heavily on such Republican leaders as Jefferson, Gallatin, Madison, Monroe, and Taylor whose contributions exceeded the fine and court costs.[63] Then in January, 1799, he rode from Philadelphia to Vergennes to secure the release of his friend, who had predicted only six months earlier that he would be the Sedition Law's first victim.

When this plan was first suggested, the Vermont Republican replied that he preferred a plan which would be less "uncertain, humiliating, and precarious." He therefore purchased a lottery grant and proposed to sell tickets for prizes. To publicize this lottery, he placed an advertisement in the leading Republican paper in the Green Mountain state, Anthony Haswell's *Vermont Gazette*.[64]

A third scheme for paying the fine was hit upon when some Republicans declared their fear that the federal marshal might refuse to take any money other than legal tender. This action, of course,

[60] *Connecticut Courant*, May 27, 1799; *Columbian Centinel*, Feb. 27, 1799. Ogden later wrote blistering attacks on the use of religion "to promote party, bigotry and error." See his anonymous publications, *A View of the New England Illuminati* and *A Short History of Late Ecclesiastical Oppressions in New England and Vermont* (Richmond, 1799). For a discussion of these works, see Vernon Stauffer, *New England and the Bavarian Illuminati* (New York, 1918), 348–354.

[61] *Aurora*, June 20, 1799. For Secretary Wolcott's role, see Frederick Wolcott to Wolcott, Litchfield, June 10, 1799, Wolcott Papers, Box 12 (Conn. Hist. Soc.), and Samuel Marsh to Wolcott, Norfolk, Nov. 13, 1799, *ibid.*, XV, 71.

[62] Pliny H. White, *The Life and Services of Matthew Lyon* . . . (Burlington, 1858), 21.

[63] President Adams' private secretary observed that "all the minority in Congress subscribed more or less." William Smith Shaw to Abigail Adams, Feb. 5, 1799, Adams Papers, VIII, No. 126 (Mass. Hist. Soc.). For one of his solicitations of a $50 or $100 contribution for Lyon, see Jefferson to Monroe, Jan. 23, 1799, *Jefferson's Writings* (Bergh ed.), X, 74.

[64] For the text of this advertisement, see *U.S. v. Haswell*, Wharton, *State Trials*, 684. Lyon offered as prizes a 500-acre farm near Whitehall, Vt., a house and farm in Fairhaven, and fifty $10 prizes. See Adams, *History of Fairhaven*, 111.

would have prolonged Lyon's imprisonment. Headed by Apollos Austin, a wealthy resident of Orwell, a group of Lyon's constituents raised $1,000 in silver dollars to assure the release of their representative. On February 9, 1799, the day Lyon's term expired, Austin and a large delegation of Republicans went to Vergennes with the silver,[65] but deferred to Senator Mason, who paid the fine with the gold which he had collected from the nation's Democratic-Republican leaders.[66]

At eight o'clock on the morning of February 9, 1799, Lyon was released from the Vergennes jail.[67] Before he stepped from his cell, he announced, "I am on my way to Philadelphia." This statement was a precautionary measure by the representative. He had heard that the marshal had summoned lawyers to examine the letters which he had written from jail. If they could ferret out more sedition, Lyon would be rearrested as he emerged from jail. Since congressmen are privileged from arrest enroute to Congress, Lyon made the announcement of his destination to forestall any Federalist attempts to rearrest him.[68]

Lyon's return to Philadelphia was a triumphant procession from prison to Congress. A huge crowd welcomed him as he stepped from jail. Forming a procession with the American flag at the head, they followed him for nearly twelve miles to Middlebury. In Tinmouth, the school children paraded for him, and one prospective Republican of school age delivered an oratorical welcome: "This day satisfies federal vengeance. Our brave representative, who has been suffering for us under an unjust sentence, this day rises superior to despotism." Three cheers for "The Victory of Liberty" capped the demonstration.[69]

In Bennington another large crowd cheered Lyon when he

[65] Roswell Bottom in the *Rutland Herald*, reprinted in Walton, *Records of the Governor and Council*, IV, 495.

[66] See the *Vermont Gazette*, March 28, 1799, for the letter of thanks to Senator Mason from the Democratic-Republicans of Vermont. Also see McLaughlin, *Lyon*, 376, and Walton, *Records of the Governor and Council*, 496n.

[67] Attested copy of the deputy marshal's release, *U.S. v. Lyon, Annals*, 16C, 2S, 486.

[68] *Connecticut Courant*, March 4, 1799; White, *Lyon*, 22. The leading Federalist newspaper later reported that "two other Bills for sedition were cut and dry for Mr. Lyon, on his return to Vermont." See the *Gazette of the United States*, May 10, 1799; *Spectator*, Oct. 19 and 26, 1799. I have not been able to locate any official account of Lyon's second indictment.

[69] White, *Lyon*, 22. Also see Rowland B. Robinson, *Vermont: A Study of Independence* (Boston and New York, 1899), 262.

stopped at the State Arms Tavern. Anthony Haswell, who was later charged with sedition for printing Lyon's lottery advertisement, delivered a welcoming address and congratulated the congressman on his new freedom and on his re-election. "You have suffered," he said to Lyon, "for admitting (without your consent) what your enemies were pleased to call sedition, to be printed, while the panders of power have scattered that identical publication in their prostituted papers with impunity, from north to south." [70] Praising the Constitution as the "glory of our land" and "the cement of our union," Haswell stressed the importance of the Bill of Rights which it had been necessary to add to the original charter. Yet even with those guarantees which had been advocated by "that revered sage," the "immortal Jefferson," the government had launched an "unprecedented and cruel persecution of our federal representative" as well as prosecutions against many Republican printers.

To commemorate Lyon's return to freedom, Haswell also wrote a poetic and "Patriotic Exultation on Lyon's Release from the Federal Bastile in Vergennes," which was sung at the Bennington celebration.

> Come let us raise the flowing strain,
> To bid our hero welcome,
> Our charter'd rights we will maintain,
> Tho' Fitch, or fiends [from] hell come. . . .
>
> The liberty of speech and press,
> Our sacred right by charter,
> Our constitution shall express,
> When Jacks are at low water. . . .
>
> Come take the glass and drink his health,
> Who is a friend of Lyon,
> First martyr under federal law,
> The junto dared to try [it] on.[71]

Thus the first victim of the Sedition Law, who had been serenaded with "The Rogue's March" on his way home, returned to Congress a political martyr. Typical of the toasts to the liberated Lyon was that at the Liberty Tree celebration in Bridgehampton,

[70] This refers to the publication of Barlow's letter by the Federalist papers, which held it up as an example of French influence.

[71] John Spargo, *Anthony Haswell, Printer—Patriot—Ballader* (Rutland, 1925), 53, 233–234. Fitch was the federal marshal who imprisoned Lyon at Vergennes.

New York, where glasses were raised to "Colonel Matthew Lyon, the martyr to the cause of Liberty and the Rights of Man: may his sufferings bring good out of evil, by arousing the people to guard their rights and oppose every unconstitutional measure." [72]

[72] *Independent Chronicle,* Jan. 17, 1799. In 1840 Congress refunded Lyon's fine to his family. See the *Congressional Globe,* 26C, 1S, 410–414, 478.

CHAPTER XII

The Massachusetts Cases and a Comic Footnote

> The great first principles of civil liberty . . . require that there should be a public and free examination of the doings of the government.—Boston *Independent Chronicle,* 1799

THE first four proceedings under the Sedition Act originated in Federalist New England. In the initial cases an important Republican congressman and a leading Democratic editor were indicted. The two trials in Dedham, Massachusetts, involving men of local significance only, indicated that the Sedition Law could be used as an effective instrument with which to suppress those who expressed opposition to that very act. But the classic illustration of the lengths to which panic-stricken politicians were willing to go in order to stamp out Jeffersonian criticism of Federalist policies was furnished by three minor trials in New Jersey in 1798–1799.

The Proceedings against the Boston Independent Chronicle

The leading Republican journal in New England, and second only to Bache's in the nation, was the Boston *Independent Chronicle.* Edited by Thomas Adams, this paper had shown some sympathy for President Adams after his inaugural address in 1797. Even in those halcyon days immediately following his inauguration, however, the president was suspicious of the attention which the

Republican papers gave him. "I warrant you," he wrote his wife before the special session convened, "I shall soon be acquitted of the crime of Chronicle, Argus and Aurora praise. Let it run its rig, however, and say nothing at present."[1]

This prediction proved true, and the *Chronicle,* along with the other Republican papers, soon criticized Adams for the vigorous defense program which he recommended in 1797. A consistent opponent of steps likely to lead to war, editor Thomas Adams favored diplomatic negotiations to settle American differences with France. Even after the XYZ revelations and the return of Marshall, the *Chronicle* advocated renewal of negotiations by Gerry, who had remained in France to avoid a complete rupture. The editor therefore launched an all-out opposition to the Federalist measures of 1798 and continued his criticism of President Adams.

As early as June, 1797, the *Chronicle* leveled a blast at the chief executive for the amount of money he would remove from the federal treasury in the form of pay vouchers over his four-year term. This insignificant comment particularly incensed the president's touchy wife. She even elevated the *Chronicle* above the *Aurora* as the worst of the opposition press. "I think impudent as Bache is," she confided to her sister, "the Chronicle has more of the true spirit of Satan, for he not only collects the Billingsgate of all the Jacobin papers but he add[s] to it the Lies, falshoods, calimny [*sic*] and bitterness of his own." While she thought that Bache would publish on both sides, she was convinced that Thomas Adams was devoted exclusively to a "wretched party." This aggravated his offense because "the mischief of these publications arises from their circulating amongst persons and in places where no inquiry is made into facts."[2]

When in 1798 the *Chronicle* repeated its remarks about the president's salary and added some statements about the pay of John Quincy Adams as diplomatic representative of the United States, Mrs. Adams could hardly restrain her pen. The amount of the president's salary, she said, was well known, and her son had "received exactly the same with other Ministers of the same rank from this Country." She surmised that the *Chronicle* writer, who

[1] John Adams to Abigail Adams, Phila., April 24, 1797, C. F. Adams, *Letters of John Adams Addressed to His Wife,* 254.

[2] Abigail Adams to Mary Cranch, June 8, 1797, Mitchell, *New Letters,* 96. For a brief discussion of the Adams' "touchiness" about their public life, see *ibid.,* 176n.

used the pseudonym of "Republican" to circulate his story, was in league with Republican Representative William Findley of Pennsylvania, whom she labeled a "vile liar" for similar charges made in a letter to his constituents. These "wretches" who deceived the people were nothing but hypocrites. "Perdition catch them," wrote the indignant first lady. "We had as good have no devil if he does not claim his own." [3]

These personal allusions were not the only cause for Mrs. Adams' concern over the Republican papers. When the *Chronicle* continued to oppose Federalist measures after the publication of the XYZ dispatches, she noted that "the Ethiopean cannot change his skin,[4] and the Emissaries were never busier or more active than the vile junto are at present." The Boston paper was nothing more than the "vile partner" of Bache's *Aurora*. Both were equally bad, rivaling "the malice & falshood of Satan." She was convinced, however, that "an abused and insulted publick" could not tolerate them much longer. "In short," she concluded, "they are so criminal that they ought to be Presented by the grand jurors." [5]

Three weeks later she apparently had decided that the devil had refused to claim Thomas Adams and Benjamin Bache as "his own," because she stated that it was time for government, state and federal, to take a hand. Nothing less than the complete suppression of the *Chronicle* and the *Aurora* could save the United States from a civil war. As a local weapon of suppression, she suggested that the Massachusetts Assembly enact a strong sedition law.[6]

The Federalists in and near Boston, however, first indicated their hostility to the *Independent Chronicle* by other than legal action. In Newburyport, Massachusetts, a Federalist picnic celebrated Independence Day by consigning copies of the *Chronicle* "to be cast into the fire and be reduced to ashes, which was immediately executed." Following the execution of this criminal, whose "confessions are too gross to be repeated," the Federalists spent the day

---

[3] Abigail Adams to Mary Cranch, Phila., April 21, 1798, *ibid.*, 159. The discrepancy between the *Chronicle*'s figures and those of Mrs. Adams arose over differing interpretations of expense-account money. Harper's attack on Findley's letter is in *Annals*, 5C, 2S (April 13, 1798), 1415. For a defense of the Adamses, see the letters from "Marcus" and "Detector et Flagellator," *Columbian Centinel*, March 21, 31, and April 4, 11, and 14, 1798.

[4] This is a Biblical reference; see Jeremiah 13:23.

[5] Abigail Adams to Mary Cranch, Phila., April 21, 1798, Mitchell, *New Letters*, 159.

[6] Abigail Adams to Mary Cranch, May 10, 1798, *ibid.*, 172.

"in harmony and good order, after a number of Federalist toasts had been given."[7]

Five days after the *Chronicle* was cast into the fire on the Fourth of July, its editor was cast out of Boston's New Relief Fire Society for conduct inimical to the independence, safety, and happiness of his country. The group resolved that by his Jacobin principles and conduct he had degraded American government and character while vindicating insults of a foreign country to the United States.[8] A Republican newspaper observed that the Fire Society must have meant the Adams administration when they referred to opposition to "the American government and character." There was a distinction, the editor pointed out: "the Constitution is the government, and the Administration mere agents under it, whose conduct every press ought to be free to scrutinize; otherwise the liberty of America, like that of France at the present moment, is nothing more than the 'shadow of a shade.' "[9]

Political pressure, paper-burning, and social ostracism did not intimidate the editor, even though his health was reported to be in a "precarious state." Nor did the passage of the federal Sedition Law cause him to soften his critical remarks. Instead he lashed at the alien and sedition system with all his vehemence and defied the government to prosecute him. He claimed that the Federalists had taken advantage of the foreign crisis "to further the work of injustice at home." This, then, was no time for a faithful sentinel on the walls of freedom to decline either the dangers of his post or to blow the trumpet of alarm with weak or equivocal sound. "Such," he vowed, "is not the spirit which actuates *this paper* nor such the reproaches by which it shall be stained. The hand of power may *suppress*, but never shall disgrace it," the editor continued defiantly, "and tho' it may be crushed by the lawless acts of violence, it shall never be intimidated by its threats."

Reserving his sharpest barbs for the Sedition Law itself, editor Adams asserted that under the pretexts of order and submission to the laws the Federalists had forged a system openly hostile to the spirit of freedom. Under the influence of a mischievous system of alarm, they passed measures "to screen from scrutin[y] the conduct

[7] Newburyport, Mass., story dated July 24, 1798, reprinted in the *Albany Centinel*, Aug. 3, 1798.

[8] New York *Daily Advertiser*, July 27, 1798. Also see the *Albany Centinel*, Aug. 3, 1798.

[9] "From an Albany paper, July 30, 1798," reprinted in the *Independent Chronicle*, Aug. 9, 1798.

of your own Government and to silence by an argument of force the remonstrances of reason; to wrest from your hands the weapon which conducted you to freedom, 'a right inestimable to freemen, and formidable to tyrants only!' " [10]

In a final italicized paragraph, the editor promised to pursue the practice of free inquiry despite the threat of the Sedition Act:

To that people we again pledge ourselves, that we will never sit quiet while their Liberties are invaded, or look in silence upon public oppression. We will use our exertions at whatever hazard to repel the invader and drag the criminal to justice, whoever may protect him in his transgression or partake of his crime. Our motto and principles are, an attachment to the Constitution, and we will pursue every legal measure to support it.

To the Federalists this open defiance was only additional proof of the seditiousness of Adams' paper. From nearby Dedham, Fisher Ames wrote that "the *Chronicle* wretches are despised and abhorred; but their malice is unchanged." [11] When a dozen copies of the Republican gazette were thrown into a store near the Boston Market, they were thrown out again. "What expedient," asked a Federalist paper, "will next be hit on to give currency to Sedition?" [12] From Lynn, Massachusetts, came the answer. There, copies of the *Chronicle* were reportedly found on the town roads. "This new mode of circulating poison," wrote "Truth-Liberty," "gives rise to various conjectures.—If it is expected, by thus sowing the seeds of sedition, to raise a crop here, the Editor is assured, that *the season has gone by;* and that in the soil of *Essex* sedition will not take root." [13]

Throughout August, September, and October, the *Chronicle* assailed its chief target, the Sedition Law. Reverting to the arguments advanced by Allen and Harper during the debates on the sedition bill, the *Hampshire Gazette* condemned the *Chronicle* as the "treasonable engine" through which the Republican party operated. In attacking General Thomson J. Skinner, Republican congressman from Massachusetts, for his political activities, the Northampton paper singled out his endeavors to get the *Chronicle's* editor, "Adams—a flaming minister of anarchy," to stir up trouble. By reason of the "hellish malice" of Adams and Skinner, the rabble in the town of Adams were erecting a liberty pole, or, as the writer

[10] *Chronicle*, reprinted in the *Aurora*, July 21, 1798.
[11] Ames to Christopher Gore, July 28, 1798, *Ames's Works*, I, 237.
[12] Boston story dated July 27, reprinted in the *Albany Centinel*, Aug. 3, 1798.
[13] "Truth-liberty," Lynn, July 26, 1798, to the *Columbian Centinel*, reprinted in *ibid.*, Aug. 10, 1798.

called it, a "standard of rebellion." The only just punishment for the instigators of this treason, the writer concluded, was a coat of tar and feathers. The same line of reasoning led the Berkshire grand jury to denounce the *Chronicle* as circulating "more infamous falsehoods and slanders than" any other Democratic paper.[14]

His reiterated denunciations of the Federalist administration and its alien and sedition legislation made Thomas Adams the first important editor to be indicted under the Sedition Law. Arraigned on October 23, 1798, he was brought before the federal Circuit Court in Boston presided over jointly by Judge William Paterson of the United States Supreme Court and by District Judge John Lowell.[15] Adams pleaded not guilty to the indictment on a charge of "sundry libellous and seditious publications . . . tending to defame the government of the United States." He was let to bail and ordered to stand trial in June, 1799. In announcing his arrest the editor asserted that he would defer comment until after his trial, "finding ourselves too INDEPENDENT in principle to attempt to prepossess the public mind on this interesting question." At the same time, however, he vowed that the *Chronicle,* "ever attached to a Republican system of Government, will always support the Rights of the People, and the Liberty of the Press, agreeable to the sacred charter of the Constitution." [16]

The pending trial did not mitigate the *Chronicle's* persistent attacks on the Federalists, who continued to writhe under the criticism of the Republican paper. Vouching that the Constitution would be his guide, the editor repeated the words written by John Adams during the American Revolution: a "Free Press will maintain the Majesty of the PEOPLE." This quotation, the newspaperman observed, had been written by President Adams for the patriot paper, the *Boston Gazette,* "when *British Excises, Stamp Acts, Land Taxes,* and Arbitrary Power, threatened this country with poverty and destruction." Yet by the Sedition Law, President Adams was protected from criticism while his adherents were at liberty to publish "the most indecent reflections" on Vice-President Jefferson and Republican congressmen. "In a free government," he asked, "can there be such a partial operation of Law?" [17] When a correspondent of the *Chronicle* attacked the Sedition Act, the *Massachusetts Mercury*

[14] *Hampshire Gazette* (Northampton, Mass.), Aug. 8, 1798, quoted by Anson Ely Morse, *The Federalist Party in Massachusetts* (Princeton, 1909), 223.

[15] *Chronicle,* Oct. 25, 1798. Also see diary entry of Nathaniel Ames, Oct. 24, 1798, Charles Warren, *Jacobin and Junto, or Early American Politics as Viewed in the Diary of Dr. Nathaniel Ames, 1758–1822* (Cambridge, 1931), 114.

[16] *Chronicle,* Oct. 25 and 29, 1798; *Aurora,* Nov. 3, 1798.

[17] *Chronicle,* Oct. 29 and Nov. 5, 1798.

demanded the indictment of "the seditious wretch whose vile dec-lamation is addressed merely to the passions of the uninformed—the tocsin of treason." [18]

Although this advice was not acted on immediately, the *Chronicle* was subjected to a second legal proceeding in February, 1799, four months before the scheduled trial of Thomas Adams. Again the Alien and Sedition Laws were the cause of the action. When the Massachusetts legislature rejected the Virginia Resolutions con-demning these laws, the *Chronicle* accused the assemblymen of violating their oaths of office. The legislators, Adams wrote from his sickbed, "deny to all other States in the Union, any right to decide on the constitutionality of any acts of Congress." [19] This attack on the General Court, inspired by the legislature's denial of its right to express an opinion on federal legislation, led directly to a state prosecution for seditious libel. On February 28, 1799, editor Adams and his older brother, Abijah, bookkeeper for the newspaper, were indicted by the Suffolk County grand jury after it had received a charge from Chief Justice Francis Dana. The Massachusetts jurist had earlier branded the Republican party as a French faction composed of apostles of atheism and anarchy, bloodshed and plunder. Although the Bay State had not passed a strong sedition bill as the president's wife had wished, the grand jury, acting in conformity with Dana's instructions, indicted the Adams brothers under the common law of England on the ground that all printing and publishing which had a direct and manifest tendency to stir up "uneasiness, jealousy, distrust and sedition" in Massachusetts or which had a tendency to turn the "affections, good will, and allegiance" of the citizens from the commonwealth was against the peace and dignity of the state and an evil example that others might imitate.[20] The president's wife and son promptly informed him of the state proceedings against the Adams brothers, and army officers stationed in Boston toasted "the Grand Jurors of Suffolk County: they have indicted the Printer of the *Chroni-cle*." [21]

By virtue of his severe illness, Thomas Adams was not brought

[18] *Massachusetts Mercury* (Boston), quoted by Warren, *Jacobin and Junto*, 101.

[19] *Chronicle*, Feb. 18, 1799, quoted by Buckingham, *Specimens of Newspaper Literature*, I, 257.

[20] Clyde Augustus Duniway, *The Development of Freedom of the Press in Massachusetts* (New York, 1906), 144–145.

[21] Abigail Adams to John Adams, Quincy, Feb. 25, 1799, Adams Papers, XXXI, 221 (Mass. Hist. Soc.); T. B. Adams to John Adams, March 1, 1799, *ibid.*, XX, 135; *Massachusetts Mercury*, Feb. 26, 1799.

to trial on this charge. On March 1, 1799, however, the bookkeeper went on trial for a seditious libel on the state legislature. James Sullivan, the state attorney general, argued that the English common law doctrine of libel applied, and he zealously upheld the maxim, "The greater the truth, the greater the libel." Defense counsel Benjamin Whitman and George Blake denied that the English common law of libels was the measure of American liberties after the Revolution: it was inconsistent with the republican principles of government established in the Constitution of Massachusetts. Prosecutions for public or "seditious" libel violated the nature and genius of free government, they argued, especially the guarantee of freedom of the press.[22] Defense evidence showed that Abijah Adams had nothing to do with the printing of the Chronicle; he was only the bookkeeper. The state prosecutor countered by asserting that since the bookkeeper generally handed out the papers to the customers he was to that extent engaged in its publication. During his charge to the jury. Chief Justice Dana announced that the English common law was the birthright of every American, and the jury tried to incorporate these diverse findings in its verdict. Refusing to find the bookkeeper guilty of printing the libel, the jury declared him guilty of publishing only. Under the direction of the court, however, this verdict was reduced to the usual finding of guilt as charged, and Abijah Adams was sentenced to serve thirty days in the county jail, to pay the costs of the prosecution, and to furnish a $500 surety bond as security that he would not commit a similar offense for one year.[23]

From his "bed of languishment," Thomas Adams assured his subscribers that, despite his illness and the imprisonment of the business agent, the Chronicle would appear regularly. "The CAUSE OF LIBERTY," he vowed, "will be supported amid these distressing circumstances." As for the bookkeeper, he endured his imprison-

---

[22] The freedom of the press clause in the state Constitution was largely the work of John Adams. In 1778 he recommended an article guaranteeing that "the people have a right to the freedom of speaking, writing and publishing their sentiments. The liberty of the press, therefore, ought not to be restrained." See Adams' Works, IV, 227. The Constitutional Convention revised this to read: "The liberty of the press is essential to the security of freedom in a State; it ought not, therefore, to be restrained in this Commonwealth." See Massachusetts Constitution of 1780.

[23] Duniway, Freedom of the Press, 145; Buckingham, Specimens, I, 259–260. For a full report of this state case, see the Chronicle, April 11–May 2, 1799. Also see a review of the case by Adams' attorney, George Blake, in the Chronicle, April 8–29, 1801.

ment "with that resignation and fortitude, which becomes a man who can appeal to his conscience for the rectitude of his conduct." Many leading citizens visited him at his cell. Foremost among these was former Governor Samuel Adams, whom the Federalists proscribed as the leading Jacobin in Massachusetts.[24] Upon his release, the bookkeeper thanked his friends for their attention to him during his confinement, and the *Chronicle* announced sarcastically that he was free "after partaking of an *adequate proportion* of his '*birth right*'" under the common law of England.[25]

Because the federal sedition trial of Thomas Adams was scheduled for June, a court-appointed physician visited the editor in May to determine whether he now could stand trial. His illness, however, was too serious to allow his appearance in court. Even though he reaffirmed his creed that he would always support the liberties and Constitution of his country, his severe illness and the pending federal and state sedition proceedings finally forced him to sell the *Chronicle* on May 2, less than a week after his brother's release. James White, a Boston bookseller whose store housed the *Chronicle* office, became the new publisher. Although nominally a Federalist, White was a close friend of Thomas Adams and hired as his new editor Ebenezer Rhoades, a young Republican printer whom Adams had chosen as foreman during his illness.[26]

As in the case against Bache, the leading Jeffersonian editor, death prevented the sedition trial of the number-two opposition newspaperman in the United States. Only a week after Adams disposed of his paper, and even before it reappeared under its new sponsors, the defiant editor died. "Heaven has thought fit," Rhoades observed, "to cancel the obligation by removing him from every earthly tribunal to those mansions where the righteous are at rest." [27] The Federalist sentiment was best expressed by Harrison Gray Otis, who later asserted that Adams had been "finally arrested, not by the Marshal of the district, but by that grim messenger whose mandate strikes terror to the heart of the false and malicious libeller." [28]

[24] Buckingham, *Specimens of Newspaper Literature*, I, 259.

[25] *Chronicle*, April 25, 1799, *ibid.*, 260.

[26] "Warned by great bodily indisposition," Adams sold the *Chronicle* on May 2, 1799. On May 13, 1799, it made its first appearance under new ownership. Evans, *American Bibliography* (1798–1799), Item 35654, XII, 335. Also see Brigham, *History and Bibliography of American Newspapers, 1690–1820*, I, 307. On May 15, 1800, White sold the *Chronicle* to Rhoades and Abijah Adams.

[27] *Chronicle*, May 16, 1799, reprinted in the New London *Bee*, May 29, 1799. Adams' death is reported in the *Chronicle*, May 13, 1799.

[28] *Annals*, 6C, 2S (Jan. 22, 1801), 955.

The Republicans, however, hailed Thomas Adams as another martyr. In a tribute to his predecessor, Rhoades declared that Adams had continued to express his warm attachment to the liberties of his country while confined to his sick room. "The principles advocated in the Chronicle he often dwelt upon with the most pleasing satisfaction, and seemed to feel a consolation in his dying moments, that his Press had been devoted to the propagation of those sentiments, which had a tendency to promote the blessings of peace and independence." The new editor promised that he would make every attempt to measure up to the motto which Adams had written for the paper: "Truth is its guide and Liberty its object." In his statement of policy, he pledged to carry on the fight for freedom of the press, making it clear that he objected to the Sedition Law, although circumspection kept him from referring to that act in his first issue.

The great first principles of civil liberty [he wrote] are, that all legislative power proceeds from the people;—that they have a right to inquire into the official conduct of their substitutes, the rulers;—to censure public measures when found to be wrong, and to use constitutional means to remove those, who violate the confidence reposed in them. These principles require, that there should be a public and free examination of the doings of the government. Information on these subjects can not be generally disseminated, but through the medium of newspapers. It is, therefore, necessary to the existence of civil liberty, that these should be open to writers, who discuss freely public measures, and even censure them when faulty.

Like Thomas Adams, Rhoades solicited his Republican friends to contribute remarks about the administration of the federal government. He presumed that the friends of the Adams administration would not object to this, "for poor indeed must that cause be, which cannot bear an examination." On the other hand, he promised not to refuse pieces defending the conduct of the administration. He stipulated only one requirement for such writings. They had to "contain reasoning instead of invective" and to answer the objections made against the administration "rather than exclaim *Jacobin* and *Traitor*." As the people were to exercise their sovereignty in judging the conduct of their rulers, he promised that diverse points of view would not be suppressed by the "noisy railings" of party zealots who wished to condemn their antagonists without a fair hearing. Thus men of opposite opinions were invited to express them in the *Chronicle* so that the public could weigh their merits. "By having both sides," he concluded, "the people will be able to get at the truth, and form a righteous judgement." [29]

This was the creed and the practice of the new *Chronicle*. Even Thomas Adams could not have said it better than his youthful ex-foreman.

The Federalist "Saints" versus "The Devil of Sedition": The Liberty Pole Cases of Dedham, Massachusetts, 1798–1799

One of the practices of the Revolutionary era which the Democratic-Republicans revived during the administration of John Adams was that of erecting liberty poles in protest against governmental actions which they thought tyrannical. This practice, which became especially prevalent in New England and the Middle states, stirred the Federalists to fury. Apprehensive that these "wooden gods of Sedition" would become the rallying points for disruptive forces and lead to insurrections, they either formed associations or called the authorities to cut down the "emblems of sedition." [30] Branding the erection of poles as an insult both to the federal government and to the American people, the Boston *Centinel* counseled immediate prosecutions against the Jacobins in order to "prevent the baneful consequences of civil commotion." [31]

Only at Dedham, Massachusetts, did the raising of a liberty pole lead to prosecutions and convictions under the Sedition Law of 1798. Dedham was the hometown of Fisher Ames, the Federalists' greatest orator who had retired from Congress in 1797, and of his older brother, Dr. Nathaniel Ames, an ardent Democratic-Republican.[32] Both men became involved in the proceedings against sedition in Dedham. Despite the weighty influence of Fisher Ames, Dedham had long been a Republican stronghold and possessed one of the few small-town Republican newspapers in Massachusetts.[33] The west end of town, commonly called "Clapboardtree's

[29] *Chronicle*, May 16, 1799, quoted in Buckingham, *Specimens*, I, 262.

[30] McMaster, *History of the People of the United States*, II, 401–403, has a description of the insults and violence occasioned by liberty poles.

This section is a slightly revised version of an article which appeared in *The New England Quarterly*, 28 (1955), 198–215.

[31] *Columbian Centinel*, Aug. 19, 1798.

[32] Samuel Eliot Morison, "Squire Ames and Doctor Ames," *New England Quarterly*, 1 (1928), 5–31.

[33] The irreverent editor of the Dedham *Columbian Minerva* reported, with tongue in cheek, that a man had been arrested "for calling the President's dog

Parish," was described by the younger Ames as the worst parish "in sin and Jacobinism." [34]

Long presided over by the Reverend Thomas Thatcher, a partisan preacher of Republican proclivities, this parish furnished responsive listeners to the words of David Brown, an itinerant Democratic speaker who came to Dedham in October, 1798.[35] A man between forty and fifty years of age, Brown was a native of Bethlehem, Connecticut, who had served in the Revolutionary army.[36] Although a common laborer who had received little schooling, he seems to have been "a man of considerable natural ability and of some reading." [37] He claimed to have been in all the states, where he had compiled information on land speculation by prominent persons. In a letter to Christopher Gore, Fisher Ames reported that Brown had informed the residents of Dedham of "my speculating connection with you, and how I made my immense wealth. I was not in this part of the country," Ames added; "otherwise, I should have noticed his lies,—not to preserve my reputation, but to disarm his wickedness." [38]

During the two years preceding his visit to Dedham, Brown had stumped the Bay State speaking and writing about politics and gathering information on over eighty towns.[39] In his writings he charged that an officeholding oligarchy controlled the federal government in its own interests to the detriment of the great body of citizens in the nation. By expanding their prerogatives as officeholders, he wrote, "our administration is . . . approaching to Lords and Commons as [fast as] possible." As an example of the few enriching themselves at the expense of the many, he cited the engrossment of western lands by speculators, asserting that "there is not an instance wherein the property of the Union is concerned but what the leaders of Government have ingroc'd [sic] the whole to themselves, and five hundred out of the union of five millions

---

a son of a b—h; but for want of sufficient proof was discharged!!!" See Warren, *Jacobin and Junto*, 100.

[34] Ames to Thomas Dwight, Dedham, Dec. 7, 1798, *Ames's Works*, I, 244.

[35] Ames to Christopher Gore, Dec. 18, 1798, *ibid.*, 247.

[36] *Chronicle*, June 17, 1799.

[37] Anderson, "Alien and Sedition Laws," Amer. Hist. Assoc., *Annual Report for 1912*, 122–125, first uncovered the Dedham cases. I have relied heavily on his excellent sketch. The highlights of the cases are given in Warren, *Jacobin and Junto*.

[38] Ames to Gore, Dec. 18, 1798, *Ames's Works*, I, 245.

[39] *Chronicle*, June 17, 1799.

receive all the benefit of public property and live upon the ruins of the rest of the Community."

In his unlettered way, Brown argued that

there all [always] has been an actual struggle between the laboring part of the community and those lazy rascals that have invented every means that the Devil has put in their hands to destroy the labouring part of the Community and those that we have chose to act as public servants, act more like the enthusiastic ravings of wild men than the servants of the people and are determined to carry their own measures by the point of a bayonet.

Brown also deplored the undemocratic tendency of the Sedition Law which shielded the administration from adverse criticism:

We . . . see our fellow Citizens crossing into a State of abject slavery, and do nothing to retrieve ourselves. . . . The language of the Government is reverence to the constitution, let the constitution be ever so corruptly administered, if it takes all their property with lives to support it, for the sake of one hundred out of the Union of five millions by teaching that a few men were cloth'd by God to govern in church and State, and that the rest were made for the express purpose to see how miserable he could make them both in things of time and futurity.

This semiliterate, though voluble, democrat told his audiences that seven-eighths of the people were opposed "to the measures of tyrants to enslave them." These policies would be defeated, he thought, because he "never knew a Government supported long after the confidence of the people was lost, for the people are the Government." According to Brown, the people opposed the Sedition Law, the land tax, and land speculation. If the petitions for redress of their grievances did not receive favorable action, he predicted that they would "break out like the burning mountain of Etna, and will have an unconditional redress of their grievances."[40]

It was Brown's appeal to the people, with its threat of political, or possibly apolitical, action that most alarmed Massachusetts Federalists. The federal district attorney in Boston, John Davis, promptly filled out a warrant for Brown's arrest on a charge of sedition, but the vagabond politician had moved out of Dedham

[40] U.S. v. David Brown, indictment in the archives of the United States Circuit Court, Boston, cited by Anderson, "Alien and Sedition Laws," Amer. Hist. Assoc., Annual Report for 1912, 123. Portions of the indictment are reprinted in Irving Mark and Eugene L. Schwaab, The Faith of Our Fathers (New York, 1952), 44–47. Also see the Chronicle, June 17, 1799.

before it could be served.[41] His charges had fired the imagination of his Republican listeners, however, and in October, 1798, they raised a liberty pole in Clapboardtree's Parish. To it they attached a sign which proclaimed:

> No Stamp Act, No Sedition, No Alien Bills,
> No Land Tax; downfall to the Tyrants of
> America, peace and retirement to the Pre-
> sident, Long Live the Vice-President and
> the Minority; May moral virtue be the basis
> of civil government.[42]

Alarmed over this "outbreak of sedition," the Federalist newspapers labeled the pole a "rallying point of insurrection and civil war." [43] The Federalists of Dedham viewed this symptom of Jacobin insurgency as a logical conclusion to the preachings of David Brown. According to Fisher Ames, this action was but a part of a general program formulated by the Republicans who had "sent runners everywhere to blow the trumpet of sedition." Brown, "a vagabond ragged fellow," had infected Dedham with the "poison" of sedition by discussing "the sins and enormities of the government." In short, Ames wrote, Brown had got the local democrats "ready to set up a liberty-pole, which was soon after actually done."

Spurred to action by "this insult on the law," Federal Marshal Samuel Bradford renewed his search for Brown.[44] Moreover, District Judge John Lowell directed him to proceed from Boston to Dedham and "to demolish the above mentioned Symbol of Sedition." [45] Before the marshal could carry out his mission, however, the Federalists from Dedham's south parish rallied their strength and invaded Clapboardtree's Parish to chop down the pole. In the melee that followed, the Republicans did not save the pole but did manage to seize one of the youthful Federalists who had to pay twenty dollars to his captors before he was set free.[46]

Fisher Ames was distraught over the boldness of the Democratic-Republicans and perturbed by "the tardiness and apathy, on the

---

[41] Ames to Christopher Gore, Dec. 18, 1798, *Ames's Works*, I, 247.

[42] *Chronicle*, Nov. 12, 1798. The indictment against Brown gives the same text, except that it omits the last clause.

[43] *Columbian Centinel*, Nov. 7, 1798; *Connecticut Courant*, Nov. 12, 1798.

[44] Ames to Christopher Gore, Dec. 18, 1798, *Ames's Works*, I, 247.

[45] *Massachusetts Mercury*, Nov. 7, 9, 1798, cited by Warren, *Jacobin and Junto*, 106.

[46] Ames to Pickering, Nov. 22, 1798, Pickering Papers, XXIII, 326 (Mass. Hist. Soc.).

part of the government, in avenging this insult on the law." "Though the liberty-pole is down," he lamented to the chief justice of New Hampshire, democrats abounded in Dedham. In a spirit of righteous indignation he asked, "What are we to do? The devil of sedition is immortal, and we, the saints, have an endless struggle to maintain with him." [47]

Ames need not have despaired, however, because the "saints" were not totally defenseless. After the destruction of the liberty pole, the government launched a campaign to track down the seditious culprits who had erected the "Dedham Jacobin pole." The first "imp" of the devil of sedition to be arrested was Benjamin Fairbanks, a wealthy farmer, a former selectman, and one of Dedham's leading citizens. The Boston *Centinel* exultantly reported that the marshal, accompanied by a posse of Federalists from a neighboring town, had seized the "deluded ringleader" on November 6 and taken him before Judge Lowell, who charged him with being "an accessory in erecting this rallying point of insurrection and civil war." When he was admitted to $4,000 bail, the paper hailed the action as evidence of "the leniency of the federal administration," pointing out that "in 1786 he would have been committed to close gaol." [48]

This comparison of the erection of a liberty pole with Shays' Rebellion illustrates how serious the panic-stricken Federalists viewed these peaceable actions of the Republicans. Fisher Ames was convinced that "the government must display its power *in terrorem*, or, if that be neglected or delayed, in earnest. So much irritable folly and credulity, managed by so much villainy, will explode at last; and the issue will be tried, like the ancient suits, by wager of battle." To Secretary of State Timothy Pickering, chief enforcement officer of the Alien and Sedition Laws, he wrote that the arrest of Fairbanks had awed the deluded, but that its effect had not been as great as their intemperance and folly merited. "The powers of the [sedition] law must be used moderately but with spirit and decision," he said; "otherwise great risk of disorders will be incur'd." [49]

The leading Republican journals saw no risk of disorders except

[47] Ames to Gore, Dec. 18, 1798; Ames to Jeremiah Smith, Nov. 22, 1798, *Ames's Works*, I, 247, 240.

[48] *Columbian Centinel*, Nov. 7 and 10, 1798. Also see Dr. Ames's diary entry for Nov. 6, 1798, *Dedham Historical Register*, 9 (1898), 26; 10 (1899), 27.

[49] Ames to Gore, Dec. 18, 1798, *Ames's Works*, I, 247; Ames to Pickering, Nov. 22, 1798, Pickering Papers, XXIII, 326 (Mass. Hist. Soc.).

those arising from the suppression of legitimate political protest. Harkening back to the days of the Revolution, Boston's *Independent Chronicle* condemned the Federalist action, asserting that during the Revolution

a flag-staff surmounted with the American standard was called a Liberty Pole and was approved and cherished by Government. Now they are called Sedition Poles and discountenanced and suppressed by Government. It is true, in '75, the British Government destroyed the poles as the rallying posts of sedition and rebellion; but they were tyrants for so doing. And it is true in '98, the American Federal Government did the same; but they were not tyrants for doing it, because the Sedition Law forbids our calling them so.[50]

These Republican protests did not slacken the hunt for the man who was most responsible for the raising of the liberty pole. It was not until March, 1799, however, that the "wandering apostle of sedition" was apprehended. At the time of his arrest in Andover, Brown was carrying a number of his manuscripts, which Federalist writers denounced as "malignant and perverse misrepresentations of the views and measures of the Government of the United States . . . designed to create discontent and to excite among the people hatred and opposition to their Government." Moreover, they charged that Brown had circulated these calumnies by every means which a "vicious ingenuity could suggest." "The main object of the writings," according to an Andover Federalist, "is to alarm the *Farmers, Mechanicks* and *Labourers* with an apprehension, that the *preservation* of the *liberty* and *property* depends on a *thorough Revolution.*" The general tendency of his remarks, another agreed, led his listeners "to inquire if all was going right in the Administration."[51]

These manuscripts, together with his instigation of the erection of the Dedham liberty pole, became the basis for the sedition charge against Brown. Since the "wandering apostle" was not as opulent as Fairbanks, he could not raise the $4,000 bail and was jailed at Salem.[52]

[50] *Chronicle,* Jan. 17, 1799.

[51] *Ibid.,* June 17, 1799; *Columbian Centinel,* March 27 and 30, 1799; *Salem Gazette,* March 29, 1799.

[52] The writings were alleged to have been composed with intent to defame the government, to stir up sedition, and to excite unlawful combinations "for opposing and resisting divers good and wholesome laws . . . and to aid, encourage and abet the hostile designs of the Republic of France against the United States."

A revealing letter to the *Salem Gazette* showed that the chief fear of the Federalists was that the Republicans might win the state elections if agitators such as Brown were not dealt with severely. "There is now on foot," the correspondent wrote, "a plan of the Jacobins, which they are pursuing everywhere with the most indefatigable industry, to have a majority in our next Legislature, who will favour the view of France, and the Virginia and Kentucky Resolutions calculated to that object. Already," he pointed out, "one Brown is now in our jail committed for seditious conduct to accomplish such purposes." Asserting that "the disorganizing agents in every county in the Commonwealth" were pursuing their plan to win the elections, the writer warned that there was reason to fear that the Republicans would "in many instances accomplish their ends." [53]

The Boston *Centinel* agreed that the opposition, finding it impossible to prostrate the country before France through the federal government, was attempting to achieve its ends through the state governments. It announced that the Republicans were making an organized effort to oust from the General Court of Massachusetts "every man of honesty, independence, and federalism." "Jeffersonian puppets" were the cause of the trouble, the *Centinel* claimed, labeling the vice-president himself as "the center of the circle. His myrmidons, faithful to their duty, act as he directs and bellow as he prescribes."

According to another alarmed Federalist, the Republican tactics were paying off. The Jacobins, he asserted, "know the weak side of the New-England farmers and Federalists to be a love of money and of course a dread of expense." By seizing with "art and avidity this string which leads directly to the heart" and, it might be added, to the pocketbook, the opposition had "created a division already." They had abandoned France and soft-pedaled calumnies on "the best patriots" in favor of attacks on the expenses incurred by a new navy and a standing army, on the enormity of an 8-per-cent loan, and on the land tax. This scheme, the writer warned, was both "the most politic and dangerous which they could have adopted." [54]

It was this fear that the Republicans were making headway which led that redoubtable publicist, Fisher Ames, to join the Federalist chorus in their "open avowal of contempt and detestation of jacobins." In a series of essays published in the *Boston Gazette*, he warned that the Republicans were plotting to subvert the govern-

[53] *Salem Gazette*, March 29, 1799.
[54] *Columbian Centinel*, April 6 and 17, 1799.

ment by winning control of its administration through the electoral process. Although he condemned the opposition party as a traitorous faction devoted to France, his articles were concerned almost exclusively with a denunciation of political democracy and the electioneering efforts of the Jeffersonians. The Federalist leader readily confessed that he was "terrified by the tendencies of democracy to anarchy"; the real sin of the Jacobins was their attempt to establish a "mobocracy." Warning that one of their "pestilent designs" was victory in the state election of 1799, Ames made an "unreserved exhortation to all friends of government" to defeat the Republicans in order "to repel the assault of the jacobins on law and liberty." "Now is the time and the occasion," he urged, for all friends of government to display the Federalist zeal that had "more than once saved the country." Already the Republicans had dispatched "bawlers and whisperers against government," such as Brown, as emissaries to stir up the people. "It is plain," he concluded, "that they intend to get the State governments into their hands. . . . In every State they are exerting themselves rather more like an armed force beating up for recruits, than a sect of political disputants."

The Republican conspiracy, however, aimed at more than the capture of the state governments in 1799; Ames charged that their real objective was the overthrow of the Federalists in the national election of 1800. The Jacobins, he asserted, were "everywhere in movement, preparing every engine of power and influence, to transfer the country, its liberty, its property, at the next election of president and vice-president, into the hands of men equally destitute of private virtue and of public spirit." If such men ever obtained a majority, they would "overturn, overturn, overturn, till property shall take wings, and true liberty and good government, find their graves." Gazing into the murky mist of the future, Ames shuddered and cried out an urgent warning to his fellow Federalists: unless they rallied round their banners and defeated the "weak and infatuated rabble," they would have to defend their cause with swords "within two years."

In a candid passage, Ames admitted that exhortation was not enough. "No nation," the anti-Democrat declared gloomily, "can rely on the sufficiently clear and early political discernment of its citizens, to discover and repel the danger to its liberty and independence; they may discover their danger too late. . . ." In short, the Federalists should not run the risk that the people might fail to discern the danger implicit in a Republican victory. Although he did not specifically single out the Sedition Law, Ames had obvious reference to it when he wrote that only "by arming our rulers with force enough, and appointing them to watch in our stead" could the people be protected from being duped by the Republican plot to defeat the Federalists at the polls.[55]

The sedition trials of the Dedham "insurgents" were open attempts by the Federalists to cope with the dangerous political activity of these followers of Jefferson. Both Fairbanks and Brown were bound over for trial before the June, 1799, term of the Circuit Court presided over by Associate Justice Samuel Chase of the United States Supreme Court. Although both defendants originally decided to stand trial, they later changed their pleas to guilty and threw themselves upon the mercy of the court. On June 7 Fairbanks readily confessed his presence at the erection of the liberty pole but pleaded that he had been misled. Declaring that he had not realized at the time "how heinous an offense" he had committed, the former selectman swore that he was now a reformed man. In his written pleas for a mitigated penalty, he assured the court that he was "a friend to my country, its liberty and independence" and vowed that his future conduct would be that of a good citizen.

This about-face by the "opulent farmer" touched his hometown foe, Fisher Ames. Although the former congressman refused to be Fairbanks' counsel on the grounds that it would be "unbecoming and improper" for a Federalist to defend a Jacobin, he nevertheless supported his fellow townsman's plea for clemency. After referring to the farmer's unblemished reputation, Ames explained that Fairbanks' involvement resulted from his "warm and irritable temperament." "Too credulous and too sudden in his impressions," he had mistakenly placed his confidence in his Jacobin neighbors. Ames flatly asserted that Fairbanks "was criminal in the affair of the Sedition Pole," but he claimed that "the men who had Mr. Fairbanks' confidence and abused it are more blameable than he." The real offender was David Brown, "that wandering apostle of sedition" who had disseminated such "bold falsehoods, and such artful and inflammatory sophistry" as to mislead "many pretty well informed and well disposed citizens" in Dedham. Moreover, Dedham's Republican newspaper had had "a very pestilent influence" in that town. Nor were the baneful effects of Jacobin propaganda

[55] "Laocoon," nos. I and II, *Boston Gazette*, April, 1799, in *Ames's Works*, II, 109–128. For a similar denunciation of Brown as an emissary promoting "the destructive principles" and subversive plans of the Republicans "to effect a change favorable to their views," see "Coriolanus," *Columbian Centinel*, March 30, 1799.

confined to newspapers; Ames charged that Republicans high in office had aggravated the bad opinion of the government and the laws which Brown had inspired.

Thus Fairbanks had been duped into his criminal attendance at the raising of the liberty pole. Ames observed, moreover, that the Dedham farmer had not participated in its erection. Nor had he attempted to flee when arrested. As a clinching argument, the Federalist orator pointed to Fairbanks' patriotic service during the Revolution and added, not without effect, that the former selectman was a man of substance.[56]

This plea by Ames, coupled with Fairbanks' complete confession of political indiscretion, led Judge Chase to hand out "the only lenient sentence in any of the sedition law convictions."[57] After observing that one object of punishment—reformation—had been accomplished, the judge let the defendant off with a sentence of only six hours' imprisonment, a fine of $5.00, and court costs of $10.50.[58] According to Chase, this was done in order to convince the deluded that the federal government was not arbitrary and unfeeling, "but mild, dispassionate and considerate; and exercised its authority with humane and liberal views."[59]

This leniency to the wealthy hometown culprit contrasted strikingly with the punishment meted out to the vagabond Brown. He was charged not only with the responsibility for erection of the liberty pole but also with publishing seditious criticism of the Adams administration. Although Brown pleaded guilty to these charges, Judge Chase was not to be denied this chance of demonstrating the seditious character of Brown's political utterances. Apparently agreeing with Ames's contention that Brown was the real criminal, Chase directed the government prosecutor to examine his witnesses in order to determine the degree of Brown's criminality. Testimony showed that the "stroling stranger" once had discussed Thomas Paine's *Age of Reason*, that he had read from manuscripts which criticized the administration, and that some of his severest invective appeared in a rhymed writing bearing the sinister title, *A Dagger for Tyrants*. One witness testified that Brown had hired a painter to copy the label which was attached to the

[56] *Chronicle*, June 20, 1799.

[57] Anderson, "Alien and Sedition Laws," Amer. Hist. Assoc., *Annual Report for 1912*, 122.

[58] Nathaniel Ames noted in his diary on June 7, 1799, that Fairbanks was sentenced to a fine of "5s, costs of 10s & 6 hours imprisonment." *Dedham Historical Register*, 9 (1898), 112.

[59] *Chronicle*, June 20, 1799.

"sedition pole," another claimed that Brown had held the ladder while a second Jacobin had nailed the sign to the pole, and a third swore that the Republicans had been "harsh in their expressions" to Federalists who heckled them while they were erecting the pole. To this derogatory information, too, should be added the denunciation of Brown made by Ames during his defense of Fairbanks.[60]

At no time during his hearing did Brown apologize for his actions as had Fairbanks, nor did he have a high Federalists to plead for clemency. Moreover, the itinerant Republican refused to become a party to the Federalist search for seditionmongers when he failed to divulge to Judge Chase the names of the persons who had prompted or aided him in his "mischievous and dangerous" political activities. Nor would Brown give the judge a list of the subscribers to an intended edition of his writings.

When he later came up for sentencing, however, Brown submitted to the court a written statement in which he expressed his sorrow "for uttering his *political* sentiments; more especially," he added, "in the way and manner I did utter them." His reason for refusing to reveal the names of his political friends was brief but eloquent: "I shall loose [sic] all my friends." Like Fairbanks, however, he promised that his future conduct would be that of a peaceable citizen.

This change of heart came too late to influence Judge Chase's decision. Indeed, he replied that Brown's statement disclosed nothing to mitigate the punishment which his "pernicious and dangerous practices demanded." Although the defendant requested that his punishment be limited to imprisonment because he lacked the resources to pay a fine, Judge Chase sentenced him to eighteen months in federal prison and a fine of $480 for "sowing sedition in the interior country." [61] Studiously avoiding any mention of the government's "humane and liberal views," the judge expounded at length upon the nature, malignity, and magnitude of Brown's offenses, particularly stressing the "vicious industry" with which

---

[60] *Ibid.*, June 17, 1799. Although this testimony placed Brown in Dedham at the time the pole was erected, it seems to be in error. Ames's letters, written shortly after the arrest of Fairbanks, state that Brown left Dedham before the raising of the pole. Moreover, Brown's indictment does not charge him with being present when the pole was raised. It should be noted that this testimony, which came eight months after the event described, was not subjected to cross examination.

[61] *Columbian Centinel*, quoted by Warren, *Jacobin and Junto*, 109. The *Chronicle*, June 17, 1799, lists the fine as $400. The $480 figure probably includes court costs.

Brown had circulated "his disorganizing doctrines and impudent falsehoods, and the very alarming and dangerous excesses to which he attempted to incite the uninformed part of the community." [62]

Although the Boston *Centinel* condemned Brown as an insurgent, it is clear that his real offense was his partisan political remarks to the less well-to-do people in Massachusetts. [63] His "disorganizing doctrines," as Chase called them, were confined to legitimate attempts to stir up discontent with the Adams administration, especially with the land and stamp taxes and the Alien and Sedition Laws.

Despite the relative insignificance of the charge against Brown, he received the most severe sentence imposed under the Sedition Law. Nor did the Federalists show any leniency when he petitioned for a pardon after sixteen months in jail. [64] In July, 1800, President Adams refused to grant a pardon. [65] Even when his term expired in December, 1800, Brown was not released because of his inability to pay his fine. As Brown had foreseen when he was sentenced, his poverty prolonged his confinement. In February, 1801, just a month before the Sedition Law expired, he addressed a second pathetic petition to Adams, setting forth the long period he had been in jail. Unless his fine was remitted, he asserted, his poverty eliminated any prospect that he would ever be released. [66] Although Adams had less than a month to serve as president, he did not pardon Brown, who then petitioned Jefferson shortly after his inaugural. This request by the prisoner was unnecessary, however, because Jefferson, the author of the Kentucky Resolutions, treated the Sedition Law as a nullity and granted full pardons to all offenders still in prison when he assumed office. [67]

[62] *Chronicle*, June 17, 1799.

[63] In his "Laocoon" essays, Ames, an acknowledged spokesman of the party which described itself as including "the good, the wise and the rich," attacked the Republicans because the large mass of its members were poor men. "In the resources of money," he wrote, "and that sort of credit which grows out of confidence in the virtues and morals of political men, the jacobins are weak indeed." They not only harbored "dangerous opinions" but also brazenly published them, including "printed threats . . . to demolish bank property and funded debt, and to wreak vengance on the aristocrats, meaning the possessors of property." See *Ames's Works*, II, 116–119.

[64] This included the time spent in the Salem jail while awaiting trial.

[65] Adams to Pickering, June 19, 1800, Miscellaneous Letters, 1800, Dept. of State, cited by Anderson, "Alien and Sedition Laws," Amer. Hist. Assoc., *Annual Report for 1912*, 124.

[66] Petition of Brown, *ibid.*

[67] For the decision of Jefferson and his Cabinet to pardon Brown, see "Notes

By that time, of course, the event which had called forth this extreme severity against Brown had occurred; the Republicans had "disorganized" the administration of the government by replacing the Federalists. For his participation in inciting the American people to this insurgency at the polls, David Brown served exactly two years in prison. Although his case has never been as widely publicized as that of the more prominent Democratic-Republicans, such as Congressman Matthew Lyon, he was assuredly "the most grievous sufferer from the penalties of the sedition law." [68]

Like Lyon's case, which led to a second sedition trial in Vermont, Brown's trial had a sequel. Dr. Nathaniel Ames, unlike his brother, was an outspoken Republican. Only a week after Adams signed the Sedition Law, the doctor noted in his diary that his friends feared for him because he exercised his right of speech and press "like an independent Republican." With some exaggeration, he recorded his belief that he was "in no danger of being hang'd for treason." Nevertheless, he became involved in the criminal proceedings against Brown under the sedition statute.[69]

In June, 1799, Dr. Ames was subpoenaed to testify in Brown's case but failed to attend on the ground that the summons was insufficiently served. Charged with contempt of court, Ames was arrested in October, 1799, and taken as a prisoner before District Judge Lowell and Associate Justice William Cushing of the Supreme Court.[70] The indignant doctor protested that he was "carried without warning to Boston before Circuit Court" after being seized "like a felon, for a pretended contempt of its process that I am not guilty of." Despite the doctor's claim, the court fined him the nominal sum of eight dollars to show that witnesses in sedition cases could not violate a court process.

After he was fined, Dr. Ames was taken to jail, where he requested copies of any papers in the court clerk's office relating to the proceedings against him. Although he offered to pay for these, the district attorney refused the request because, as Ames said, "he was

---

on Procedures on Prosecutions under Sedition Act," March 9, 1801, Jefferson Papers, CX, 18892 (Lib. Cong.). Brown's pardon of March 12, 1801, is recorded in the Book of Pardons and Remissions, no. I (1793–1812), 44–45, RG 59 (National Archives). Jefferson also contributed to Brown's fine. Jefferson to Monroe, July 12, 1802, Jefferson's Writings (Ford ed.), VIII, 167.

[68] Anderson, "Alien and Sedition Laws," Amer. Hist. Assoc., Annual Report for 1912, 125. The Maryland Gazette, March 26, 1801, reports Brown's pardon.

[69] Diary entry of Dr. Ames, July 20, 1798, Dedham Historical Register, 8 (1897), 138.

[70] Diary entries of June 8 and Oct. 22, 1799, ibid., IX, 112, and X, 26.

afraid I should make a bad use of them." This was but another
proof to the doctor "that Tiptoe novel Courts will become like the
Inquisition by secreting their process and dark arbitrary vexations
—the citizens ought to know how they proceed, but they yet fear
the public eye." Ames's pungent conclusion about the proceedings
against him was that the "pickpockets of the Bar" had "spunged"
him of eight dollars.[71]

It is impossible to avoid the conclusion that these proceedings
against Brown, Fairbanks, and Dr. Ames were part of the government's display of its power *"in terrorem,"* as Fisher Ames phrased it.
They are perfect illustrations of the Federalist campaign of intimidation against the Republican opposition in the crucial years before
the all-important election of 1800.

Low Comedy: Luther Baldwin's Comments on the President's Posterior

The case in which the enforcement of the Sedition Law hit bottom was that of Luther Baldwin, who was convicted because he
expressed a wish that a cannon shot had lodged in the president's
posterior. After Congress adjourned in July, 1798, President John
Adams made preparations for his usual retreat from the summer
heat of Philadelphia for the cool shade of his home in Quincy,
Massachusetts. On the twenty-seventh, he and Mrs. Adams passed
through Newark, New Jersey, which celebrated the event as a
festive occasion. Colors were displayed and "a number of respectable citizens" assembled to greet the chief executive's entourage.
"The Association of Young Men" manned an artillery piece and
paraded at the flagstaff while awaiting the president's arrival.

As the chief magistrate entered Broad Street about eleven o'clock,
he was greeted by the firing of the artillery piece, the ringing of
church bells, and, as he passed the flagstaff, a chant by the young
men who had fired the salute: "Behold the Chief who now commands." Three cheers followed, bells again pealed forth, and as
the president's party withdrew into the distance the cannon boomed
a sixteen-gun salute.[72]

There was one inebriated Republican, however, who took no de-
light in the festival. Luther Baldwin happened to be coming toward
John Burnet's dram shop when one of the tavern's plain-spoken

[71] Diary entry, Oct. 22, 1799, Warren, *Jacobin and Junto,* 111.

[72] New York *Commercial Advertiser,* Aug. 1, 1798.

This section is an expansion of a brief article published in *The Quarterly
Journal of Speech* 40 (1954), 284–287.

customers, noting that the cannon was firing after the president had passed, observed to Baldwin: "There goes the President and they are firing at his a—." According to the Newark *Centinel of Freedom*, this sequence of events then followed:

Luther, a little merry, replies, that he did not care if they fired thro' [*sic*] his a__: Then exclaims the dram seller, that is seditious—a considerable collection gathered—and the pretended federalists, being much disappointed that the president had not stopped that they might have had the honor of kissing his hand, bent their malice on poor Luther and the cry was, that he must be punished.[73]

Not until two months after these unguarded remarks did Supreme Court Justice William Cushing arrive in New Jersey to instruct the grand jury of the Circuit Court on the intricacies of the new sedition statute. After hearing his charge, the grand jury not only accused Baldwin but also indicted two of his tavern cronies, Brown Clark and a person identified only as Lespenard. On October 3 Lespenard pleaded not guilty, but later in the day he changed his plea to guilty and was fined forty dollars and costs. Baldwin and Clark pleaded not guilty, and their trials were postponed. Tried in 1799 before a Circuit Court presided over by Associate Justice Bushrod Washington of the United States Supreme Court and District Judge Robert Morris, these outspoken Republicans also retracted their pleas.[74] For speaking "sedicious words tending to defame the President and Government of the United States," both were fined, assessed court costs and expenses, and committed to federal jail until fine and fees were paid.[75]

[73] Newark *Centinel of Freedom*, reprinted in the *Aurora*, Oct. 12, 1799. This story was given wide circulation by Republican newspapers. See the New York *Argus*, Oct. 15, 1799, and the New London *Bee*, Oct. 16, 1799. An earlier account reported that Baldwin was arrested "for dropping an expression, in an unguarded moment, amounting, as it is said, to a *wish*, that the President of the United States was dead." *Chronicle*, Nov. 15, 1798, reprinting a Newark story dated Nov. 6, 1799.

[74] *Universal Gazette* (Phila.), Oct. 17, 1799; *Albany Centinel*, April 16, 1799; and the *Virginia Gazette* (Richmond), Oct. 18, 1799, asserted that Baldwin's indictment was brought under the federal common law, and Miller, *Crisis in Freedom*, 113, states that it was a common law indictment prosecuted by the State of New Jersey. All three New Jerseyites, however, were tried before a federal court, and it seems probable that they were indicted for violations of the Sedition Act, as Justices Cushing, Iredell, and Washington, all of whom presided in New Jersey in 1798–1799, pointedly instructed grand juries on the constitutionality of that statute.

[75] Baldwin was fined $150 and Clark $50. The court record is in the *Minutes of the U.S. Circuit Court, District of New Jersey, Oct. Sess., 1798*, RG 21 (Na-

Baldwin's trial afforded the Republican papers a field day. In stories which ranged from denunciatory accounts to droll commentaries, they stressed three themes, registering surprise and indignation that a man could be convicted on such a petty charge and accusing the Federalists of seeking to enforce conformity of opinion while expanding presidential prerogatives. Finally, they balanced their animosity for the tavernkeeper-turned-informer by expressing their sympathy for the victim of the information.

"Here's *Liberty* for you," jeered a Newark newspaper in reporting Baldwin's arrest.[76] "When we heard that Luther Baldwin was indicted for sedition," the New York *Argus* agreed, "we supposed that he had been guilty of something criminal. . . . We must confess that our astonishment has been excessive on hearing the peculiarity of the expressions for which so formal a trial was instituted." To this journal the prosecution again illustrated the "rage of faction." "When cognizance is taken of such a ridiculous expression," it concluded, every Republican could see "the extraordinary malignancy of the federal faction."

According to the *Argus*, presidential prerogatives under the Sedition Law resembled the sacrosanct privileges of a monarch. Royalists in Europe would be pleased to read an account of this curious trial as evidence that their cause "might yet succeed in this country." Many a Briton, the journal continued, would believe that the president was treated with as much respect as a king and that persons who spoke contemptuously of him would be punished as severely in the United States as speakers who insulted the king would be treated in England. The editor bluntly charged that "the federalists are resolved that if they cannot force the republicans to admire John Adams, they shall not speak what they think of him." Happily, he concluded, the Democratic-Republicans at least could think their thoughts to themselves without being controlled.[77]

Nothing about the case was overlooked; its every feature became grist for the Republican mill. The only power which the Federalists now lacked, the Newark *Centinel* asserted, was that of prosecuting and treading underfoot all those who refused "to be duped

---

tional Archives). I am indebted to Father William O'Brien, S.J., of Georgetown University, for calling my attention to this item. Baldwin's case is reported in the *Aurora*, Oct. 12; *Chronicle*, Nov. 15; *Oracle of the Day*, Oct. 26, 1799. Judge Cushing's wife mentions Lespenard's case in her letter to Abigail Adams, Oct. 9, 1798, Adams Papers, VIII, no. 97 (Mass. Hist. Soc.).

[76] *Chronicle*, Nov. 15, 1798.   [77] *Argus*, Oct. 12 and 15, 1799.

into their measures." [78] Other opposition newspapers pointed to the rise of the "useful profession of informers" and recommended the tavernkeeper in Newark to any person needing such services. This "voluntary informer," one paper reported, had testified against an intoxicated man whose only offense had been a mere expression, which injured no one's person or property.[79] Yet he was reported later to have declared publicly that Baldwin was a good citizen, an honest man, and a friend of his country, who meant no harm in what he had said.[80]

The *Argus* hinted at an explanation of the tavernkeeper's inconsistency by calling him a "wretched tool, who, for the sake of a little patronage, we need not add, a little pelf, would sacrifice a neighbour, and at the same time know him to be a good citizen, an honest man and a friend to his country." [81] A correspondent from Newark strengthened this hypothesis when he reported that "the *dram-seller*, the celebrated John Burnet," was being considered as the Federalist candidate for coroner. In an ironical letter, the writer, obviously a Republican, argued somewhat facetiously that since the tavernkeeper had risked so much for the president he ought to be rewarded with any office that the people of Newark could bestow on him. Not only had he turned informer; he had "nobly persevered in prosecuting the old fellow for daring to utter such a contemptuous expression of our beloved president, whom every one knows is one of the best of men, and thank God, we have shewn the cursed democrats that we will let none of them speak disrespectfully of any part of that dear man." [82]

Nor were the elements of low comedy in Baldwin's conviction overlooked. Indeed the contemporary writers used much more basic language than historians have usually done in describing the episode. Observing that the chief executive had been enroute to his seat at Quincy, the papers made the president's posterior the target of their remarks. The lusty *Argus* asked:

Can the most enthusiastic federalists and tories suppose that those who are opposed to them would feel any justification in firing at such a disgusting a target as the _____ of J. A. but we can recollect the day when many of the gentry would have had no objection, but would have been pleased could

[78] *Centinel of Freedom*, quoted in the *Aurora*, Oct. 12, 1799.
[79] *Argus*, Oct. 12, 1799.
[80] *Centinel of Freedom*, quoted in the *Aurora*, Oct. 12, 1799.
[81] *Argus*, Oct. 15, 1799.
[82] "Communication" from a Newark writer, *ibid*.

they have found an opportunity to practice a little in that way, as the popping at such an obnoxious character would have been the highest recommendation for a tory to the favor of a Henry Clinton or a Robinson.[83]

In commenting on the monarchical tendency of the prosecution, a Newark correspondent claimed that although a British subject might speak of the king's head Baldwin was punished "for speaking of the president's a—." [84] By November, 1799, however, Republican newspapers reverted to a more stilted prose and, while still making political capital from Baldwin's case, referred only to the president's posterior.

Continuing to heap ridicule on the Federalists for prosecuting "this *heinous joke*," [85] the opposition press stressed the pointed moral of the comic proceedings: *"Beware of the SEDITION LAW."* [86] To Baldwin, the martyr of the moment, they offered their sympathy for his expensive discovery "that joking may be very dangerous even to a free country." [87]

Though the Baldwin trial is only a comic footnote to the Federalists' stringent effort to enforce the Sedition Act during the presidential campaign between Jefferson and Adams, it nonetheless belongs among the cases which illustrate the possibilities of oppression in that statute. At the same time, it illustrates that attempts in America to suppress freedom of speech by legal means may boomerang against the suppressor and may create such powerful persuasions as legalistic protests, constitutional objections, and the sportive malice that can be developed through ridicule, irony, and ribald anatomical references.

[83] *Argus,* Oct. 15, 1799. Also see the *Times and Virginia Advertiser,* Nov. 2, 1799, for a Virginian's satirical remarks about avoiding references to Pickering's "hinder parts" because of Baldwin's fate.

[84] "Communication" from a Newark writer, *Argus,* Oct. 15, 1799.

[85] *Argus,* Nov. 15, 1799.   [86] *Chronicle,* Nov. 15, 1798.

[87] *Argus,* Nov. 15, 1799.

Part Three

THE REIGN OF WITCHES: ENFORCEMENT MACHINERY AND THE ELECTION OF 1800

CHAPTER XIII

William Duane, the Aurora, and the Alien and Sedition Laws

What's this but libelling against the senate?
—WILLIAM SHAKESPEARE, *Titus Andronicus*

BY THE spring of 1800 the Federalists had singled out three foreign-born Americans as the leading "scribblers" against Adams' administration. Thomas Cooper, born in England, and James T. Callender, born in Scotland, were naturalized citizens. The third, William Duane, claimed to be a native-born American because of his birth in colonial New York.

These three "foreign Emissaries," the *Philadelphia Gazette* announced on March 11, 1800, had been chosen by the Jacobins to direct the Republican publicity for the campaign of 1800. An article the next day declared that the trio would be guided by the "Chief Juggler," Thomas Jefferson, who had finally "obtained the entire management of the Jacobin puppets." Callender, one of the most prolific pamphleteers of the day and a writer for the Richmond *Examiner,* would direct the attack on the government in the South; Cooper would handle the western part of the United States; and Duane would be given the eastern division. To cope with these and other "intriguing, mischief-making foreigners," the *Connecticut Courant* proposed prompt execution of the Alien and Sedition Laws. If several hundred aliens had been deported, it argued, "and a few more Matthew Lyons had been shut up in prison for their seditious libels, we should not have had so many *Duanes, Burkes, Bees,* and

[a] host of other villians, filling the country with falsehoods, slanders, and factions." [1]

Following Bache's death during the yellow fever epidemic in September, 1798, the Philadelphia *Aurora* reappeared in November under the editorship of William Duane. Like his predecessor, the new editor spoke the language of the people and proved to be as able a critic, commentator, and controversialist as Bache had been. A master of invective, he wrote pungent prose in a hard-hitting style, which not only made for interesting articles but also enabled the *Aurora* to hold its position as the leading Republican organ in the United States. Indeed, his energetic attacks on the Adams administration soon involved him in a sedition prosecution like the one pending against Bache when he died.

Born in colonial New York of Irish parents, Duane resided in New York and Philadelphia for fourteen years before he returned with his mother to her native Ireland in 1774. For the next twenty-two years he lived in the British Empire, gaining so much renown as the liberal editor of the Calcutta *Indian World* that he was seized by the governor, deported without trial, and divested of his property without legal process because of his criticism of governmental officials of the East India Company. After a sojourn as parliamentary reporter for the London *General Advertiser*, Duane returned to Philadelphia, joining the *Aurora* as Bache's assistant in 1796. [2]

Only three months after the new editor assumed control in 1798, the Federalists brought their first charge against him. It was Duane's animosity toward the Alien Friends Act which set the stage for this legal conflict. Because of his Irish ancestry, he took an even more pronounced stand against that statute than Bache had done. [3] Secretary of State Timothy Pickering and the Federalist press immediately denounced the Republican editor as a United Irishman. [4] When a group of citizens and aliens residing in the nation's capital

[1] *Connecticut Courant,* July 29, 1799.

Although slightly longer, this chapter is substantially the same as the article which appeared in *The Pennsylvania Magazine of History and Biography,* 77 (1953), 123–155.

[2] Allen C. Clark, "William Duane," Columbia Historical Society, *Records* (Washington, D.C., 1906), IX, 19–21.

[3] In December, 1798, only a month after he began editing the *Aurora,* Duane observed that "the United Irishmen stand precisely in the same *odious circumstances* with relation to England that John Adams stood twenty years ago—they consider George III, an intolerable tyrant *now,* and he did *then.*"

[4] Pickering to the President, Phila., July 24, 1799, Pickering Papers, XI, 487 (Mass. Hist. Soc.). Duane always maintained that he was a native-born American, but eventually he took out naturalization papers to be on the safe side.

voted to send a petition to Congress requesting the repeal of the Alien Law, Duane and three recent arrivals from Ireland, Dr. James Reynolds, Robert Moore, and Samuel Cuming, were chosen to circulate some of the memorials for signatures in Philadelphia.

On the morning of Sunday, February 9, 1799, Duane and the others visited St. Mary's Catholic Church, where they posted small signs requesting "Natives of Ireland, who worship at this church . . . to remain in the yard after divine service, until they have affixed their signatures to a memorial for the repeal of the *Alien Bill.*" Two signs were tacked to the church walls near the entrance, and others were placed on the gates leading into the churchyard.[5] Some of the Federalist communicants objected to the posting of a "*Jacobin* paper" on church property and ripped the signs off. One of them reported to the priest that "a seditious meeting" was scheduled in the yard after service and circulated this word among some of the church members. During the service, however, there was no disturbance or noise, and when church let out, Reynolds, Moore, and Cuming had two memorials spread out on a tombstone waiting for signatures. A large number of people gathered around Dr. Reynolds, and several persons subscribed to the petition. When someone shouted, "Turn him out," one of the crowd pushed Reynolds, who pulled a gun to defend himself. The doctor was then knocked down, disarmed, and kicked, and the petitioning rally broke up.[6]

Porcupine's Gazette branded this episode as a *"United Irish Riot"* and cautioned Philadelphians that the *"day is now come"* when the United Irish, "a nefarious combination" favoring the Irish independence movement, constituted "a terror and torment to America." [7] Despite the lack of evidence that Duane, Moore, or Cuming participated in the Reynolds scuffle, they were later arrested with the doctor.[8] All four were charged with being evilly disposed per-

[5] Testimony of John Brown, "Trial of Duane, et al, for seditious riot," Wharton *State Trials*, 348. In this report, Wharton incorrectly cites the Alien Enemies Law as the one being petitioned against. *Ibid.*, 388n. It was the Alien Friends Act, however, that the petitioners opposed. See *Annals*, 5C, 3S (Feb. 12, 1799), 2884–2906.

[6] See the testimony of James Gallagher, John Connor, John Brown, and Lewis Ryan, and the statement of defense counsel Robert H. Dunkin, in Wharton, *State Trials*, 351–352, 349, 348, 354–355, and 359.

[7] *Albany Centinel*, Feb. 19, 1799; *Porcupine's Gazette*, Feb., 1799, reprinted in *Porcupine's Works*, X, 97.

[8] Two indictments were returned. One charged the quartet with seditious riot, and the other charged Reynolds with an assault on Gallagher with a deadly weapon, with intent to kill. The cases were tied together and therefore were

sons who willfully and maliciously stirred up a seditious riot by attempting to obtain signatures to the petition against the Alien Law, with intent to subvert the government of the United States.[9]

Cited as "Duane's case," the trial that followed might better have been called "Reynolds' case"; all of the evidence dealt with the doctor's actions. The fact that the proceedings are designated by Duane's name, however, suggests that the Federalists considered the editor the most important man in the group indicted. If they could convict Bache's successor as an accomplice and participant in the Reynolds "riot," they could fine and imprison him, along with the other offenders against "national dignity and decorum."

Joseph Hopkinson, composer of "Hail Columbia" and a recent appointee of President Adams to negotiate an Indian treaty, was selected as special state prosecutor, and Alexander J. Dallas, secretary of the Commonwealth of Pennsylvania, headed the defense counsel. Both sides agreed that the petition was a protest against the Alien Law, that it was unexceptional in itself, that some members of the congregation signed it and that others had wanted to, and that no violence occurred until the rush on Reynolds.[10]

Testimony revealed that it was not unusual in Ireland to post notices on church gates, that it was customary for the congregation to tend to public business after church, and that it was never considered a profanation of the church or an insult to the congregation, although the pastors were always consulted. In this instance, however, the petitioning group had failed to obtain the consent of the church authorities. This lack of consultation, the head priest testified, was not only an insult to himself and the board of trustees; he considered any meeting held after church without his consent to be "perfectly wrong." [11]

Matthew Clay, a member of Congress from Virginia, swore that

---

heard by the same jury. They are cited, however, as the "Trial of Duane, Reynolds, Moore and Cuming, for Seditious Riot," with no reference to the separate charge against Reynolds. See Wharton, *State Trials*, 347. The trial was held on Feb. 21, 1799, in the state Court of Oyer and Terminer for the County of Philadelphia.

[9] The presentment to the grand jury was drafted by Robert Wharton, the Federalist mayor of Philadelphia. It charged the four men with deliberately procuring an assembly of people with the determination of subverting the government of the United States. *Ibid.*, 363.

[10] Testimony of John Taggart, *ibid.*, 356; Lewis Ryan, *ibid.*, 355; James Gallagher, *ibid.*, 352; John Brown, *ibid.*, 348; and Thaddeus McCarney, *ibid.*, 361.

[11] Testimony of Rev. Mr. Carr and Rev. Leonard Neale of St. Mary's Church, *ibid.*, 353–354.

he had warned Reynolds of a plot to assassinate him and that the doctor had procured a gun to defend himself.[12] None of the other defendants carried weapons, and Reynolds did not produce his until pushed. There was no mention of misconduct on the part of Duane, Moore, or Cuming, and no proof that Duane was present when the scuffle took place. Indeed, the prosecutor did not mention Duane's name in his closing argument to the jury.[13]

Nonetheless, the case was an attempt to strike at the nation's most influential Republican editor. Moreover, it was an attempt to suppress the free exercise of the right of petition, at least when that right was practiced by aliens. Conceding that citizens have the right to petition for redress of grievances, Prosecutor Hopkinson declared that "aliens have no right whatever to petition, or to interfere in any respect with the government of this country—as the right of voting in elections is confined to our citizens, the right of petitioning is also—if aliens do not like the laws of this country, God knows there are ways and wishes enough for them to go back again." Following the same line of argument advanced by the nativists during the debates on the Naturalization Law of 1798, the state prosecutor contended that America's greatest evils arose from the admission of foreigners to political participation. "The introduction of this foreign leaven amongst us," he asserted, had "fermented the whole mass of the community" and finally "divided and rent" the country into contending political parties.[14]

In an aggressive defense speech, Dallas branded the trial as "a party case, a party question altogether," inspired by partisan hate. He called attention to the efforts of the Federalists to deprive the defendants of counsel, first by saying that they should not be allowed any and then by saying that if any lawyer stepped forward, he ought to be denounced. "According to the politics of the present day," he argued, "any man who wishes to exercise the right of free opinion . . . is marked out for party obloquy."

The petitioners had been called Jacobins, Dallas declared, but the peaceful exercise of the right of petitioning could not be Jacobinism. It was guaranteed by the Constitution, and no amount of denunciation could convert it into a criminal act. By no legal con-

[12] Wharton, *State Trials*, 359–360.

[13] *Ibid.*, 378–379. The prosecution introduced seven witnesses, but only John Brown swore that he saw Duane in the churchyard before the service was over. *Ibid.*, 348.

[14] For an insulting reference to Dallas' foreign birth, see Hopkinson's remarks. *Ibid.*, 379–380.

tortion could the defendants' expression of opinion against the Alien Law be twisted into an attempt or even an intention to overturn the Constitution and all law. "They never meant to oppose the [alien] law," he continued, "but in the mode provided by the constitution." Denying that there had been a riot, he justified Reynolds' action as self-defense, with no intent to murder.[15]

After a thirty-minute deliberation the jury acquitted the defendants. Thus the Federalists lost the first skirmish in their campaign to suppress Duane. At the same time they also failed in their attempt to strike at the Democratic-Republican party through the foreign-born in its ranks.[16] The jury had repudiated the arguments that aliens were not entitled to a lawful exercise of the right of petition as guaranteed in the Constitution.

Duane's release outraged Federalist editors, who attacked the Jeffersonian editor with increasing severity.[17] By midsummer of 1799 the Federalists were ready to launch a second attack on the obnoxious editor. On July 24 Duane discussed the role of British influence in American politics, asserting that "the high character for private and public virtue, which America achieved in her struggle against Britain has been tarnished by British intrigue." Moreover, he claimed to have documentary proof that British influence had had some success in the United States. The best evidence, he declared, was a letter in his possession in which President Adams deplored the effect of British influence in procuring the appointment "of an officer of the most confidential and important trust under the government." [18]

Citing a letter written by Secretary Pickering as further documentary evidence of the baleful British influence, Duane accused the leading Cabinet official of saying that in case of a war with Great Britain a foreign war was not the only one to be dreaded. This, Duane wrote, was the same as saying that Britain's adherents would oppose the American government in any conflict with England. Finally, he alleged that the British secret service had expended

[15] *Ibid.*, 364–367. Dallas was assisted by John Beckley and Robert H. Dunkin.

[16] Raymond Walters, *Alexander James Dallas, Lawyer, Politician, Financier, 1759–1817* (Philadelphia, 1943), 79.

[17] *Gazette of the United States*, March 2, 1799.

[18] *Aurora*, July 24, 1799. In 1792 Adams wrote his friend Tench Coxe that he suspected "much British influence in the appointment" of Thomas Pinckney as ambassador to England. Adams to Coxe, Quincy, May, 1792, Gibbs, *Memoirs of the Administrations of Washington and John Adams*, II, 424–425. In 1797 Adams dismissed Coxe as commissioner of revenue. Coxe then became a Republican stalwart, and it was through him that Duane received Adams' letter. See Hildreth, *The History of the United States*, V, 379–380.

$800,000 in the United States in 1798 to influence American policy. "These are facts," Duane concluded, "which no perfidious artifices can evade, nor impudence deny. . . . The people must endeavor to identify as well as they can the channels in which this corruption of Britain has circulated." [19]

In calling the president's attention to the article, Pickering assailed Duane's suggestion that Adams "had asserted the influence of the British Government in the affairs of our own—and insinuated that it was obtained by bribery." This was not the first time the editor had made this suggestion, the secretary said; the *Aurora* constantly poured forth "an uninterrupted stream of slander on the American Government." Pickering proposed to dam it up by a dual legal proceeding against the editor. He promised to direct the federal district attorney to institute a sedition prosecution against Duane, but he also mentioned that Duane might be banished from the United States as a dangerous alien. The secretary informed the president:

The editor of the *Aurora* pretends he is an *American Citizen,* saying that he was born in Vermont, but was, when a child, taken back with his parents to Ireland, where he was educated. But I understand the facts to be, that he went from America prior to our revolution, remained in the British dominions until after the peace, went to the British East Indies, where he committed or was charged with some crime, and returned to Great Britain, from whence, within three or four years past, he came to this country to stir up sedition and work other mischief.

Pickering therefore presumed that Duane was really a British subject who could be banished from the United States for his turbulence. Had the editor not set himself up as a captain of a company of volunteers whose distinguishing badge was a plume of cockneck feathers and a small black cockade with a large eagle? "He is doubtless a United Irishman," the secretary concluded, "and the company is probably formed, to oppose the authority of the Government; and in case of war and invasion by the French, to join them." [20]

[19] *Aurora,* July 24, 1799. Duane referred to Pickering's letter to James Monroe, American ambassador to France, on Sept. 12, 1795, in which the secretary vindicated Jay's Treaty and American neutrality and exhibited "the evils to flow from a war with Great Britain." At that time, he wrote that "it would be happy for us, if we could contemplate only a foreign war, in which all hearts and hands might be united." See Pickering to the President, Phila., July 24, 1799, Pickering Papers, XI, 487 (Mass. Hist. Soc.). This letter is reprinted in *Adams' Works,* IX, 3.

[20] Pickering to the President, July 24, 1799, Pickering Papers, XI, 487 (Mass. Hist. Soc.). Duane was a captain in the "Republican Greens." See the *Aurora,* July 24, 1799.

On the same day Pickering also sent Duane's offensive article to William Rawle, the federal district attorney in Philadelphia. "If the slander on the American Government," he wrote, "will justify a prosecution against the Editor or Author, be pleased to have it commenced." [21]

President Adams agreed that the *Aurora's* article was "imbued with rather more impudence than is common to that paper." "Is there any evil in the realms of actuality or possibility," he asked his secretary, "that the Aurora has not suggested of me?" Although he disdained any attempt to vindicate himself of any of that paper's lies, he thought Rawle would be unfit for his office if he did not think the passage libelous. "If he does not prosecute it," the president stated emphatically, "he will not do his duty." Adams also concurred that "the matchless effrontery of this Duane merits the execution of the alien law." "I am very willing," he confessed, "to try its strength upon him." [22]

On July 30, even before President Adams gave his approval for the twofold proceedings, Duane was arrested for seditious libel. On August 2 he was brought before District Judge Richard Peters and bound over until the October term of court.[23] In reporting his arrest, the editor swore that he had not published a fact which he could not prove. "Neither persecution," he promised, "nor any other peril to which *bad* men" might expose him would make him swerve from the cause of republicanism.

Pickering immediately notified President Adams of the instigation of the criminal suit against the editor for his charge that English secret service money had been distributed in the United States. Moreover, the secretary issued a standing order to the government prosecutor to survey the *Aurora* constantly "and to institute new prosecutions as often as he offends." Adams replied that Duane's trial for seditious libel "will bring out some whimsical things. At present I will say nothing. I have no apprehensions for myself or the public from the consequences." [24]

From Mount Vernon, too, came words of encouragement to Pickering. George Washington agreed that Federal officials should not remain silent "under the direct charge of bribery" by Duane. "The most dangerous consequences," he wrote, "would, in my opinion,

[21] Pickering to Rawle, July 24, Pickering Papers, XI, 486 (Mass. Hist. Soc.).

[22] Adams to Pickering, Quincy, Aug. 1, 1799, *Adams' Works*, IX, 5.

[23] *Gazette of the United States*, July 31 and Aug. 3, 1799. He was freed on $4,000 bail. Duane posted $2,000, and two sureties posted $1,000 each.

[24] Pickering to the President, Aug. 1, 1799, Pickering Papers, XI, 527 (Mass. Hist. Soc.); Adams to Pickering, Quincy, Aug. 16, 1799, *ibid.*, IX, 15.

have flowed from such silence, and therefore could not be overlooked." He approved the sedition prosecution against the editor, "for there seems to be no bounds to his attempts to destroy all confidence that the People might and (without sufficient proof of its demerits) ought, to have in their government; thereby dissolving it, and producing a disunion of the States." That civil war was the object of the *Aurora* and other Republican newspapers, Washington was firmly convinced.[25]

Since Duane was free on bail until the October term of court, the *Aurora* continued to appear regularly. The vigilant secretary of state, however, scrutinized each issue and handed several to the district attorney, who examined them for seditious material.[26] When the federal Circuit Court convened, therefore, Duane appeared not only to stand trial for his story about British influence, but also to face a second indictment which charged that he had violated the Sedition Law on August 3 with some offensive remarks about the conduct of federal troops.[27] Presiding at this session were Associate Justice Bushrod Washington of the United States Supreme Court and District Judge Richard Peters. The indictment based on Duane's allegation of British influence presented them with a ticklish problem. Although Duane was charged with libeling President Adams and the government, he claimed that he possessed one of the chief executive's letters which discussed that influence in American politics. The proceedings took a dramatic turn when the court expressed some doubt that the president had written such a letter, and the editor offered to stand trial instantly on that particular issue. "The Court and the District Attorney," he later wrote, "were for a moment, struck with astonishment, and a large concourse of people assembled to see the Editor of the Aurora hauled over the coals of the sedition ordeal, expressed their feelings by a sudden but impressive emotion of surprise and conviction."

On learning that Duane had an authenticated copy of the presi-

[25] Washington to Pickering, Mount Vernon, Aug. 4, 1799, Pickering Papers, XXV, 72 (Mass. Hist. Soc.). This letter is also printed in *Washington's Writings* (Fitzpatrick ed.), XXXVII, 322–324.

[26] Pickering to Rawle, Trenton, Sept. 22, 1799, Pickering Papers, XII, 82 (Mass. Hist. Soc.).

[27] *Aurora*, Oct. 22, 1799. Also see *Gazette of the United States*, Oct. 19, 1799. The court met on October 15 in Norristown because Philadelphia was besieged by yellow fever. For his criticism of the troops, Duane was dragged from his office and beaten by a group of officers and soldiers. See John Beckley to William Irvine, Phila., May 17, 1799, Irvine Papers, XIV, 86 (Hist. Soc. Pa.), who says that "club law has commenced here."

dent's letter, Judge Washington discussed whether or not it would be legal evidence and concluded that "it might possibly be admitted," even though it were "to be procured in evidence against Mr. Adams himself." Duane's counsel contended that the letter could not be refused. All his client had written, Dallas said, was that Mr. Adams had asserted that British influence had been exercised in American politics. Since the Sedition Law allowed the truth as a justification, the lawyer argued that Adams' authenticated letter containing this assertion was proof of the truth of Duane's statement.[28]

Nevertheless, Dallas asked for a postponement of the trial until the next term because of the absence of such material witnesses as Timothy Pickering, James Monroe, and Tench Coxe, who were needed to prove other parts of Duane's article. After a day's deliberation, the court agreed to postpone the trial on both indictments until June 11, 1800. Duane then was freed on $3,000 bail.[29]

Chagrined that the "whimsical things" brought out by the prosecution benefited Duane rather than President Adams,[30] Judge Peters "recommended" that the editor refrain from publishing either the indictments or the proceedings. If Duane violated this suggestion, the judge threatened "to take notice of it." [31] In the story discussing the postponement of his trial, the newspaperman abided by this ruling "out of respect to the constituted authorities." He was willing to remain silent on the charges, he said, until they were decided by the due course of law, trusting that the public would not consider "the finding of two bills upon ex parte evidence as a conviction. He solicits only a fair and liberal neutrality of opinion—*and no more*, until the matter is as fairly brought to legal issue."

At the same time, however, Duane indicated that the pending trial would not intimidate him. On the very day that he reported the postponement of his trial for the article on British influence, he repeated the charge in an editorial entitled "State of the Republic." "Where are we?" he asked rhetorically. "Precisely at that point

---

[28] *Aurora*, Nov. 1, 1800. The second indictment also charged Duane with seditious utterances because of his remarks about Pickering's letter to Monroe; see *Aurora*, May 12, 1800. Thus Pickering, who instituted the case with the president's approval, also was an interested party to this indictment.

[29] *Aurora*, Oct. 22, 1799. Also see the *Gazette of the United States*, Oct. 19, 1799.

[30] Richard Peters to Pickering, Oct. 23, 1799, Pickering Papers, XXV, 259 (Mass. Hist. Soc.).

[31] *Aurora*, Nov. 1, 1800.

when the fate of America is to be decided, by either of two descriptions of persons.

By the temper, steadfastness, and the wisdom of the people's servants.
or
By persons secretly combining and covertly usurping the public power—persons who are sapping the foundations of our freedom, prosperity, and national character, who daringly menace the constituted authorities to deter them from acts the most salutary, and necessary to the preservation of our peace and freedom.

Duane then repeated his charges of British influence. "It remains to be seen," he concluded, "whether this secretly working *faction* acting in concert with British agents and devoted solely to British Views are to prevail—or that the voice and will of America, speaking thro' its constitutional organs, and governed solely by American *views, will prevail to the utter exclusion of all and every foreign power,* whether that power acts by MENACE, by deceitful artifices, or by *corruption.*" [32]

Coming less than a week after the postponement of Duane's trial, this defiance must have galled the Federalists, yet they did not indict him for his restatement of his original charges. Indeed, Judge Peters confessed gloomily that he doubted if the postponed case would be tried, and William Cobbett confided that he had "every reason to believe, that it will *never come on.*" [33] Nor was the prosecution resumed. Instead, Duane finally informed his readers that the pending trial had been "withdrawn by order of the President." [34] The reason for this action by the federal authorities was obviously to prevent the circulation of the embarrassing letter in which Adams had asserted, in 1792, that he suspected "much British influence in the appointment" of Thomas Pinckney as ambassador to England. Rather than discomfit the chief executive, District Attorney Rawle withdrew the prosecution to await a more

---

[32] *Ibid.,* Oct. 22, 1799.

[33] Peters to Pickering, Oct. 23, 1799, Pickering Papers, XXV, 259 (Mass. Hist. Soc.); Memorandum by William Cobbett, undated, G. D. H. Cole, ed., *Letters from William Cobbett to Edward Thornton, Written in the Years 1797 to 1800* (London, 1937), 122.

[34] *Aurora,* Oct. 3, 1800, reprinted in *Porcupine's Works,* XII, 145. Also see Duane to a correspondent in Richmond [James T. Callender], April 17, 1800, Richmond *Examiner,* May 2, 1800. This letter is also printed by Worthington C. Ford, ed., "Letters of William Duane," Mass. Hist. Soc., *Proceedings,* 2d ser., 20 (1906), 260.

favorable time to suppress the increasingly objectionable editor.[35]

Disappointed with this turn of events, Federalist editors redoubled their denunciation of Duane, condemning the *Aurora* as "the great *'speaking trumpet of the devil,'*" and its editor as "the most scurrillous, illiberal and lying paragraphist, and conceited coxcomb" ever to disgrace America. Conversely, Republican papers hailed the *Aurora* for its detection and exposure of the enemies of civil liberty.[36]

As the election of 1800 neared, it became urgent that the Federalists should silence the chief opposition gazette, or at least discredit its constant attacks. The Republican press reported that a Federalist senator was supposed to have complained that "if the *Aurora* is not blown up, Jefferson will be elected in defiance of everything." [37] The coming campaign promised to be a difficult one for the Federalists, whose nominee for president, John Adams, had won over Jefferson by but three votes in 1796. In 1799, moreover, the Federalists had lost the gubernatorial race in Pennsylvania. This meant, of course, that the Keystone State was lost to them in 1800, unless the presidential electors were chosen by districts rather than by a state-wide vote. The Federalists in the Pennsylvania legislature therefore tried to change the state election law to provide for district elections.[38]

At the same time Senator James Ross, the defeated candidate for governor of Pennsylvania, introduced an electoral count bill in the United States Senate in a bold attempt to alter by law rather

[35] Schouler, *History of the United States,* I, 460. Adams' letter to Coxe, Quincy, May, 1792, is in Gibbs, *Administrations of Washington and Adams,* II, 424–425. Coxe forbade Duane to publish Adams' letter and Dallas made the same recommendation. The editor did not violate his promise to Coxe until the *Gazette of the United States* and *Porcupine's Gazette* accused him of forgery and falsehood in fabricating the letter. *Aurora,* Nov. 1, 1800. The appearance of this confidential letter occasioned an apology from President Adams to Thomas Pinckney. See the president's letter of Oct. 27, 1800, in Gibbs, *Administrations of Washington and Adams,* II, 425. For Coxe's reply to the president's innuendoes against him, see Coxe to Duane, *Aurora,* Nov. 1, 1800.

[36] *United States Oracle* (Portsmouth, N.H.), March 22, 1800; *Columbian Centinel,* Oct. 5, 1799; *Palladium* (Frankfort, Ky.), Dec. 19, 1799.

[37] *Palladium,* April 10, 1800.

[38] Harry Marlin Tinkcom, *The Republicans and Federalists in Pennsylvania, 1790–1801: A Study in National Stimulus and Local Response* (Harrisburg, Pa., 1950), 243–244. Although the Federalist candidate, Ross, lost the election, he carried thirteen counties and the city of Philadelphia, while McKean carried but twelve.

than by amendment the constitutional system of counting the presidential electoral vote. A thoroughly vicious measure, it would have established a "Grand Committee of Thirteen," consisting of six members elected by each house, and the chief justice of the Supreme Court. Since both the Senate and the House were controlled by Federalist majorities and all members of the Supreme Court were thorough Federalists, the committee would have been an adjunct of the Federalist party. Meeting in secret session, this body was to summon and examine men and papers, determine which electoral votes to count and which to disallow, throw out the illegal votes, and decide on who should be president according to their tally of the electoral vote. Their report was to be made on March 1, and there was to be no appeal from their decision.[39]

In noting the introduction of the Ross bill, the *Aurora* described its backers as "the party hostile to the popular interests," who wished "to destroy the popular authority and to engross every power which the people enjoy by the right and constitution in the hands of a few." Convinced that the measure was a scheme to control the election of 1800, three Republican senators furnished copies to Duane, who published the complete text on February 19, 1800. Asserting that the Federalists were bent on depriving the people of a fair election, the editor claimed that the bill had been drafted by a Federalist caucus without the knowledge of Charles Pinckney, Republican senator from South Carolina, who was on the Senate committee considering Ross's motion. The bill, Duane concluded, was "an offspring of this spirit of faction secretly working." [40]

The aroused Federalist senators were so chagrined at these charges that they sought a way to punish the editor for his audacity in publishing a report of their proceedings and commenting on their conduct. They finally hit upon the novel expedient of appointing a standing committee of privileges.[41] Although such a body had

[39] The Ross bill contained fourteen sections. It is printed in full in the *Aurora*, Feb. 19, 1800. Ross introduced his resolution on Jan. 23, 1800. See *Annals*, 6C, 1S, 29–32. Walters, *Dallas*, 92–93; Dumas Malone, *The Public Life of Thomas Cooper, 1783–1839* (New Haven, Conn., 1926), 113–116; and McMaster, *History of the People of the United States*, II, 462–465, give good sketches of this episode.

[40] *Aurora*, Jan. 27, 1800. Duane incorrectly reported that the bill had passed the Senate, when in reality it had only received its second reading; he later rectified this statement.

[41] Senator Jonathan Dayton of New Jersey, a brigadier general in the provisional army under the field command of Alexander Hamilton, proposed on Feb. 25, 1800, that the committee be established. *Annals*, 6C, 1S, 53. A straight party vote of 22 to 7 approved. Also see the *Aurora*, March 18, 1800.

never before existed, a five-man committee was established to determine whether or not Duane's publication of the bill was a breach of the Senate's privileges.[42] They were to find out by what authority he published the bill, and by what authority he stated that Pinckney had never been consulted. A blanket authorization also was granted to the committee to investigate "the origin of sundry assertions in the same paper" about the Senate.[43]

In discussing his motion, Senator Uriah Tracy took a lofty position, bluntly declaring that it was a crime to publish a bill while it was still before the Senate. Nor was the press at liberty to publish untruths respecting the official conduct of that body. Yet Duane's paper was guilty of both crimes, he charged. It not only published the Ross bill, but also asserted that it had passed the Senate, even though every senator knew that it was still before them and might yet be recommitted, amended, or rejected. Moreover, he continued, every senator knew that Pinckney had participated in the discussions of the Ross committee; even Duane had confessed his error. Yet the original falsehood, Tracy insisted, even though retracted, must have been "calculated to produce an effect upon the public mind."

Asserting that liberty of the press meant the right to publish only "truth and just political information," Tracy argued that it was as necessary to maintain the privileges of the Senate as it was to support the liberty of the press. The Constitution, he said, conferred on congressmen "several privileges" which were given so that Congress might execute its public duties. These privileges were established not for the particular advantage of senators and representatives, but "for the interest of the people." To maintain the privileges of the Senate, therefore, was to maintain "the liberty of the citizens, and the security of the Government." [44]

[42] *Annals,* 6C, 1S, 62. This committee included Dayton, Uriah Tracy of Connecticut, Henry Latimer of Delaware, and Nathaniel Chipman of Vermont—all Federalists—and John Brown, a Republican senator from Kentucky.

[43] *Ibid.,* 63. An amendment to this motion authorized the committee to investigate why Duane reported that the bill had already passed the Senate, when in reality it had received only its second reading. *Ibid.,* 68.

[44] *Ibid.,* 85–87. These are the privileges as defined in the Constitution: "Each House shall be the Judge of the Elections, Returns and Qualifications of its own Members . . . and may be authorized to compel the Attendance of absent Members, in such Manner, and under such Penalties as each House may provide. Each House may determine the Rules of its Proceedings, punish its Members for disorderly Behavior, and, with the Concurrence of two thirds, expel a Member." Art. I, Sec. 5. Senators and representatives "shall in all Cases, except Treason, Felony and Breach of the Peace, be privileged from Arrest dur-

These latter objects, the senator reasoned, should not be sacrificed to the licentiousness of the press. When the privileges of the Senate came into conflict with the liberty of the press, it became necessary to ascertain the limits of the privileges. Tracy denied that these applied only to conduct in the Senate chamber. The authority to punish interruptions of the Senate's deliberations, therefore, "must extend to remedy the evil wherever we may meet it, or otherwise our authority is inadequate to protect itself."

By pushing this line of argument to its limits, the Connecticut senator finally concluded that the Senate could not be questioned anywhere at any time by anyone. "If it is admitted that we have the right of protecting ourselves within these walls, from attacks made on us in our presence," he argued, "it follows of course that we are not to be slandered or questioned elsewhere." This *non sequitur* became the basis for immediate proceedings against Duane. That "daring editor" had circulated a defamatory article against the Senate, and "the right of self-preservation" made it mandatory that the Senate itself instantly contradict this assertion. But contradiction alone was not enough. "The slow and tardy steps of truth," Tracy announced, always are outdistanced by the "defamation and calumny of yesterday." Nor was an indictment and trial the solution. This procedure was so slow that the foul aspersions of the editor would continue to circulate, and the Senate, having been suspect so long, would sustain "a deep wound."

According to Senator Tracy, the only way to vindicate the reputation of the Senate and to promote respect for its dignity, which derived from the people, was for the Senate to punish the editor for his crime. He hinted that even if this could not be done, the inquiry might "lead us to discover some person whom we can punish." Perhaps some senator was in "a secret league to transmit intelligence which is confidentially entrusted to his care." He closed with a veiled threat to members who might be guilty of communicating the texts of bills to editors. Since the question of privilege was a new one, he informed them, it might be necessary to purge some senators before the Senate itself acquired a "right understanding" of its prerogatives.

After these drastic proposals, however, Tracy entered a disclaimer; "he did not mean to punish for publishing the transaction which took place in the senate, but to prevent misrepresentation and

---

ing their Attendance at the Session of their respective Houses, . . . and for any Speech or Debate in either House, they shall not be questioned in any other Place." Art. I, Sec. 6.

abuse." His whole speech, nevertheless, made it evident that he wanted to punish Duane without trial by jury for his publication of the Ross bill and for his comments on the reasons why he thought the Federalists supported it.[45]

The Democratic-Republican minority launched a vigorous opposition to Tracy's motion to investigate the *Aurora*. Since his name was mentioned in both Duane's article and in Tracy's motion, Senator Charles Pinckney thought it altogether proper that he should discuss the proposed conduct of the Senate. Not only did Tracy's motion involve a consideration of the privileges of Congress and freedom of the press, but it also raised the all-important questions of the constitutional right of the people to make observations on the conduct of Congress and their right to trial by jury if accused of any crime.

Pinckney argued that the privileges of Congress are defined in the Constitution. Nowhere was there any mention of the right of either house to order the appearance of a person charged with printing attacks on its public conduct and to imprison him at its will. Nor did Congress possess any inherent power to punish verbal or written attacks on, or misrepresentations of, its conduct. If it had that power, why had the Congress of 1798 made such offenses triable in federal courts under the Sedition Law? Although Pinckney deplored that law, he considered it less arbitrary than Tracy's motion, because it at least allowed the accused a trial by a jury of his peers rather than a trial by his immediate accusers.

Knowing the oppressive use that the British Parliament had made of undefined "inherent" privileges, the Republican senator continued, the founders of the Constitution had specified the few principles necessary to the undisturbed exercise of legislative duties in a free government. The prerogatives of Parliament, Pinckney declared, were utterly inadmissible in America. "Here the right to investigate the conduct of the Legislature, and of official men, is not only recognized and established, but the Constitution seems to require it as a duty, from the citizens." The people periodically delegated to their legislators the management of their public concerns, but the latter were always accountable for their conduct. "Public bodies are public property," he asserted, "and so indeed are public men." To determine their merits, the public had a right freely and frequently to examine their actions. The press was a two-way channel, which not only kept the public informed, but which also conveyed truth "to magistrates and rulers, who will frequently

[45] *Annals*, 6C, 1S, 86–88.

find things written, that their friends did not dare to advise them." To shackle the press, he argued, was to chain the public mind.

Although he lamented the invective in the papers of both parties, Pinckney could not see why the *Aurora* should be investigated for its remarks, when the *Gazette of the United States* was not examined for its even more violent abuse of the Senate when that body stopped enlistments of the army. If the criticism of that ultra-Federalist paper did no great violence to Tracy's concern for the dignity and reputation of the Senate, Pinckney hoped that the Connecticut senator also would consent to overlook the *Aurora's*. This seemed to him the best policy, for "in politics, as in religion, persecution seldom made converts." He concluded by calling for a postponement of Tracy's motion.[46]

If the *Aurora's* article was criminal, Senator William Cocke of Tennessee added, it could be punished under the Sedition Law. He had never heard, however, that it was a crime to print the Senate's transactions. That body had always printed its bills for its own use, he pointed out, and these circulated without any injunction of secrecy. Often they were sent into every state of the Union. Yet Tracy's motion inquired how the editor of the *Aurora* got to see the Ross bill. When the bill was read, he continued, the doors of the Senate gallery had been open to the public. Any spectator could have copied it in shorthand, or perhaps remembered it. Did the Federalists, he queried, propose to punish every man who repeated, printed, or published the public business of the Senate?[47]

The Federalists made no direct reply to these questions but marshaled their usual majority to override the Republican attempt to postpone Tracy's motion.[48] Senator Humphrey Marshall of Kentucky immediately proposed that the Senate should inquire into all breaches of its privileges by newspapers, whether they were of a Federalist or a Republican persuasion. If the Senate's concern for its honor and dignity was anything more than a political maneuver, he proposed that it consider the slander and calumny directed at it by the *Gazette of the United States*. This motion, however, was voted down, and further attempts to amend Tracy's proposition were refused.[49]

In a desperate effort to assure a jury trial to the accused editor,

[46] *Ibid.*, 72–84. Also see the *Gazette of the United States*, Feb. 13, 1800.

[47] *Annals*, 6C, 1S, 84.

[48] *Ibid.*, 92. The vote was 19 to 9. The proceedings are reported in the *Aurora*, March 18, 1800.

[49] *Annals*, 6C, 1S, 92–96; 103–104. The vote was 16 to 11. Also see Stevens T. Mason to Madison, Phila., March 7, 1800, Madison Papers, 21–73 (Lib. Cong.).

the Republicans tried to replace the original motion with one authorizing the committee on privileges to inquire whether the *Aurora* story was a seditious libel and, if so, whether the attorney general should be requested to prosecute Duane. As much as they despised the Sedition Law of 1798, the opposition party favored its use to the Senate's sitting as prosecutor, judge, and jury. This amendment, however, was lost by a straight party vote. The committee, headed by Senator Jonathan Dayton of New Jersey, then was instructed to investigate the *Aurora* and to report on measures to be taken against the editor.[50]

Condemning Duane without a hearing, the Federalist committee drafted a resolution which declared his article to be a "high breach of the privileges" of the Senate. By adopting this report, the Senate agreed that Duane had written a seditious libel, containing false, defamatory, scandalous, and malicious assertions tending to defame the Senate, to bring its members into contempt and disrespect, and to excite against them the hatred of the good people of the United States. This definition of sedition, however, varied somewhat from that of the statute of 1798. Instead of finding that Duane's words were written with "bad intent," the Senate found him guilty of writing words whose "bad tendency" they feared. Although Tracy had claimed that it was necessary to punish the editor in order to preserve the Senate from destruction, that event was obviously so remote that the only grounds on which he could be seized was that of the tendency of his words to bring about that event at some time in the future. The ex parte finding also obviated any inquiry into Duane's intent and made it unnecessary to examine him or any other witnesses before announcing a verdict of guilty.[51]

To Andrew Jackson, who had resigned his Senate seat early in 1798, Congressman W. C. C. Claiborne reported that the Senate's proceedings seemed "well calculated to reflect much disgrace on that Body." The Republican press generally deplored the Senate's steps as "star chamber proceedings," but the Federalist papers lauded its actions against the *Aurora*, "that prostitute of newspapers," that "mother of abominations." [52] On March 20, 1800, a month and a day after Duane's story appeared and two days after the com-

[50] *Annals*, 6C, 1S, 104–105. The vote was 19 to 8.

[51] *Ibid.*, 111–112. On March 18, 1800, a vote of 20 to 8 decided that the story was defamatory and malicious, but it dropped to 17 to 11 on whether the story was a high breach of privilege.

[52] See Claiborne to Jackson, Phila., March 20, 1800, Jackson Papers, III, 144 (Lib. Cong.); Richmond *Examiner,* May 2, 1800; and the *Gazette of the United States,* Dec. 1, 1800.

mittee on privileges found him guilty of seditious utterances, the Senate ordered him to appear on March 24 to defend his conduct.[53] For this occasion, the committee prepared a special form of proceedings. When the editor appeared, the president of the Senate, Thomas Jefferson, was to read the charge on which Duane had been found guilty of a "high breach of privileges." Before passing sentence, however, the Senate was to allow him to say anything he wished to "in excuse or extenuation" of his article. If he had no evidence to present, the sergeant at arms was to hold him in custody until the Senate decided on his sentence. If he had a defense, he was to offer his testimony to the Senate, then be released while that body deliberated his fate. When the upper chamber reached a decision, the sergeant at arms was to notify the editor, who was to appear to hear the verdict pronounced.[54]

During these maneuvers, Duane was not silent. Branding the Senate's action as a "monstrous attempt" to implicate and coerce him, he served notice that he would discuss that body's proceedings "with all freedom that the Constitution secures to the press." He stated that while he would respect the legal and constitutional acts of the Senate, he also owed duties to the Constitution itself and to the public rights involved in the case. No power, he wrote, could compel him to ignore these superior duties. "No terror—no force—no menace—no fear" could make him betray the rights which were at stake in the Senate's conduct.

Nor did Duane soft-pedal his attacks on the Federalists in general or those in the Senate in particular. On the very day that the Senate condemned his earlier remarks on the Ross bill as seditious, he printed another slashing attack on that measure. One of his correspondents also wrote that "in every part of the country and on every occasion wherein the subversion of our popular and free form of government can be contemned or injured, we find a party acting in unison, uniformly turbulent, intolerant, jealous of liberty, trembling at discussion, talking of order and regular government, and still launching into the most disorderly outrages and violence."

The Senate's summons was served on Duane on March 21, 1800, the day that the above article appeared. Vowing his determination to maintain his constitutional rights, the editor requested his readers

[53] *Annals*, 6C, 1S, 113. At that time, Duane was to have an "opportunity to make any proper defence for his conduct, in publishing the aforesaid false, defamatory, scandalous and malicious assertions, and pretended information." The committee's report also reprints the *Aurora*'s article of Feb. 19, 1800. *Ibid.*, 113–115. Also see the *Aurora*, March 21, 1800.

[54] *Annals*, 6C, 1S, 117.

"to suspend their opinion, and not to be led by mistaken zeal to say or do anything discreditable to the republican cause. . . . Wait with the patient firmness of men conscious of a good cause," he told them, "and if the enemies of our liberties should take any steps injurious to the public rights, hostile to the constitution, or dangerous to personal security and the rights of discussion, they will furnish new evidence of their views, and the people will remember them at the period when a new election will call for a consideration of men and measures." [55]

One day before his scheduled appearance, the editor informally engaged Alexander James Dallas, secretary of the Commonwealth of Pennsylvania, and Thomas Cooper, prominent Republican lawyer, as consultants. The three then planned Duane's legal moves, and Cooper, in an unusual letter to Jefferson, outlined their strategy to meet the attack by the body over which the vice-president officially presided. First, they planned to send a letter to Jefferson in his official capacity, requesting the Senate to allow Duane the assistance of counsel and compulsory process to summon witnesses. They hoped that these requests would be denied, so that he could take a strong stand against appearing before the Senate. Since time was short, however, they feared Duane would have to appear before the Senate had an opportunity to authorize or deny counsel. In that case, the editor was to appear and personally request legal assistance. If the Senate allowed aid, the counsel would first demand a postponement; once the case came up, they would deny the jurisdiction of the Senate. If this was overruled, they proposed to withdraw from the case, and Duane would be kept out of the reach of the Senate's process server. If, however, the editor should be found, his lawyers would seek a writ of habeas corpus to challenge the Senate's action. [56]

In accordance with these plans, Duane sent his letter to the Senate, but before action could be taken, he appeared in the Senate as ordered and repeated his request to be represented by counsel. The Senate agreed to allow assistance, but specified that defense counselors could be heard only in denial of any facts charged against him, or "in excuse and extenuation of his offence."

[55] *Aurora*, March 17, 18, 21, and 24, 1800.

[56] Thomas Cooper to Jefferson, March 23, 1800, Jefferson's Papers, CXXI, 20951 (Lib. Cong.). As early as March 20, the day the Senate ordered Duane's appearance, a congressman reported a rumor that the editor would not attend the Senate. See W. C. C. Claiborne to Andrew Jackson, March 20, 1800, Jackson Papers, III, 144 (Lib. Cong.).

The editor then was ordered to reappear on March 26 at noon.[57]

On March 25 Duane addressed identical letters to Dallas and Cooper asking them to appear officially as his counsel next day. He informed them that he had attended before the Senate as ordered, not from a conviction that it had power to command his presence, but from a sense of "delicacy and regard" for that body as one of the branches of the federal legislature. "I fear," he concluded, "the resolution inclosed will prevent me from deriving all the benefit from your assistance which I had a right to expect from your acknowledged abilities, and justice to my cause." [58]

With this letter, this case also took a dramatic turn. Both Dallas and Cooper refused to serve as Duane's counsel because the resolution authorizing their appearance excluded any inquiry into the jurisdiction of the Senate over such cases. By allowing arguments only in excuse or extenuation before imposing sentence, moreover, the Senate ruled out any justification of the offensive paragraphs by proving the truth of the facts which they contained. "I cannot suppose," Dallas informed Duane, "that you, or your counsel, would find it practicable to deny the existence of any fact, which the senate has already (doubtless upon sufficient evidence) examined and established; and the language of excuse, or extenuation, must always proceed with better grace, and more advantage from the penitent offender, than from a professional advocate." [59]

Cooper's refusal was even more emphatic. Since the Senate had prejudged all the material questions and dictated the defense methods of the accused, he thought that any counsel would be but "a tame and manacled assistant." Writing with a vehemence reminiscent of Duane's original criticism of the upper chamber, the lawyer wrote, "I will not degrade myself by submitting to appear before the senate with *their gag in my mouth*." [60]

Finding himself deprived of professional assistance because of the Senate's restrictions, Duane refused any further voluntary attendance before that body.[61] When he failed to appear on March 25, therefore, the Senate declared him guilty of contempt and issued a warrant for the sergeant at arms to take him into custody and

[57] *Annals,* 6C, 1S, 117–119. The letter is printed in the *Aurora,* March 25, 1800.

[58] Duane to Dallas, March 25, 1800, *Aurora,* March 27, 1800.

[59] Dallas to Duane, *ibid.*   [60] Cooper to Duane, *ibid.*

[61] Duane to the President of the Senate [Thomas Jefferson], *ibid.* This letter also is printed in the *Annals,* 6C, 1S, 122. For references to Duane's defiance, see Stevens T. Mason to Madison, April 2, 1800, Madison Papers, 21–77 (Lib. Cong.); and John Dawson to James Monroe, March 28, 1800, Monroe Papers (N.Y. Pub. Lib.).

hold him subject to its orders. The warrant, signed by Jefferson as presiding officer of the Senate, provided that all marshals, deputy marshals, and civil officers of the federal government, "and every other person," were required to aid and assist the sergeant at arms in seizing Duane.[62]

It soon became difficult to determine whether the Senate's proceedings against the defiant Duane more nearly resembled a comic opera or an earnest manhunt. On the day that the Senate issued its warrant, the editor went into hiding and dared that august body to capture him. Surmising that the editor was hiding at George Logan's estate outside Philadelphia, the *Gazette of the United States* committed its suspicions to rhyme:

> From the Senate D[uan]e flying,
> As advised by Mr. D[allas],
> Out to St[e]nt[o]n snugly lying,
> Bids defiance to the gallows.
>
> There with L[ogan], hatching treason,
> *Sowing seed* on his plantation,
> Brooding o'er Paine's Age of Reason,
> D[uan]e seeks for consolation.[63]

In a public letter Duane claimed that he had not left Philadelphia, but was living in his own house most of the time. Indeed, he asserted that he had appeared on parade with his militia corps.[64] After one of these bold appearances, the chagrined Federalists were reported to have collected $300 which they paid to twenty-two constables in an effort "to *ferret* out the obstinate democrat." [65] Yet he managed to evade the Senate's process server until Congress adjourned.[66]

[62] *Annals*, 6C, 1S, 124. Also see John Dawson to Madison, March 30, 1800, Madison Papers, 21–75 (Lib. Cong.).

[63] *Gazette of the United States*, April 18, 1800. Also see the *Philadelphia Gazette*, March 27 and 29, 1800.

[64] The "Republican Greens," Duane's military company, announced on April 13, 1800, that they would meet under the command of Lieutenant John Roney rather than Captain Duane. *Aurora*, April 13, 1800. Duane made his assertion in a letter to J.[ames] T. C.[allender], April 17, 1800, Richmond *Examiner*, May 2, 1800.

[65] See "Letter from a Gentleman in Philadelphia to his friend in New York," April 11, 1800, *American Citizen* (New York), April 19, 1800.

[66] Duane to J.[ames] T. C.[allender], April 17, 1800, Richmond *Examiner*, May 2, 1800. Governor James Monroe of Virginia seems to have been the only Republican leader who thought that Duane should have met the Senate challenge. "As it is," Monroe wrote, "they establish the principle and avoid the odium of

On the day that Duane went into hiding, the *Aurora* announced that Republicans were circulating a petition asking the Senate to reconsider its resolutions against the editor. The *Philadelphia Gazette* immediately condemned the circulation of the petition as an effort to array the people against the government. "A worthless fellow from a foreign nation," it declared, "aided by fellow exiles, has dared, in his own cause, to issue a proscription of the senate of the United States, in the shape of a petition. It remains to be seen whether our government, our safety, and our happiness are to be subverted by such men as the Irish and English fugitives—Duane and Cooper." [67]

While the Federalist press fulminated against subversives, Duane continued to write for his paper. [68] Tracing the Senate's proceedings to party spirit and personal enmity, the editor attributed his prosecution to his zeal and steadfastness in the cause of republicanism. He claimed that a group of Federalists had decided at a caucus held in Philadelphia that the success of their party in the approaching presidential election depended on the destruction of the *Aurora* and the defeat of its director. The Senate's action was part of a general program to break down that paper and ruin its editor. Nor was he the only victim, Duane pointed out. Sedition trials, he charged, had been prosecuted in various parts of the United States "to terrify printers into silence or servility." These cases were designed to show that "the danger of enquiry into the merits of public characters would be so great as to deter any man from discussion. . . ." "But men are still found," he vowed, "who dare to speak truth." [69]

When Duane learned that Jefferson had signed the Senate warrant, he hastened to explain that it was another Federalist trick, designed to embarrass the vice-president. Since Jefferson had no vote except in case of a tie, his signature did not indicate that he approved the warrant. The committee on privileges, Duane wrote, had proposed that Jefferson sign it, the majority had agreed,

---

his prosecution, thro the constitution. He suffers all they can inflict without exciting publick sympathy in his favor." Monroe to Jefferson, April 23, 1800, Jefferson Papers, CVI, 18268 (Lib. Cong.).

[67] *Philadelphia Gazette*, March 28, 1800.

[68] In the *Aurora*, March 28, 1800, he notified his readers that they could communicate with him within less than forty-eight hours by writing to him under seal.

[69] *Ibid.*, May 27, 1800. Duane declared that he was a defendant in nine law suits, some of them on facts for which he was "willing to perish if he does not prove."

so he had no choice but to sign. Yet he was no more accountable for the warrant for Duane's arrest "than for the Sedition Law, or Mr. Ross's law for regulating elections, &c., a measure expressly designed to prevent Mr. Jefferson being elected President of the United States." Yet if that bill passed, the editor observed, Jefferson would have to sign it.[70]

Although he could no longer report the debates on the Ross bill, Duane watched its progress. On April 1 he again denounced it as a party maneuver, and the next day he told how he had come into possession of three copies of the bill. He refused, however, to reveal his sources of information. When the House finally disagreed with the Senate's electoral count bill, Duane claimed that its rejection was another striking proof of the value of a "free and jealous spirit of investigation through the medium of the Press." Although the Federalists in the Senate had tried to overwhelm him by terror and oppression for revealing the party nature of the original bill, he argued, even the amended version was "too abominable to be countenanced by the House of Representatives." [71] Thus, the bill which had brought on the proceedings against the Republican editor expired while he was at large.

The Senate, however, still smarted from Duane's defiance. When a pro-*Aurora* remonstrance and petition from the citizens of Philadelphia was presented by Senator William Bingham on May 10, the Federalists moved to table it without a reading, but the vote resulted in an even split. Casting one of his few votes as presiding officer of the Senate, Jefferson broke the tie and the petition was read.[72] The petitioners regretted that the Senate had adopted doctrines and practices of the privileged legislative bodies of Europe, and they "dreaded the introduction of rights unlimited, and power unbounded, whether under the name of privilege, or prerogative, or implied authorities, or constructive powers." The Senate's action, they remonstrated, was really a second kind of Sedition Law, only

[70] *Aurora*, April 1, 1800. For Jefferson's comments on the bill as it finally passed the Senate, see his letter to L. W. Tazewell, Phila., April 10, 1800, Jefferson Papers (Mass. Hist. Soc.). This measure, Jefferson reported, was much worse than the version printed by Duane, for the Senate "struck out the clause limiting the powers of the electoral committee, and extended it to *all* subjects of enquiry."

[71] *Ibid.*, April 28, 1800. The rejection of the Ross bill by the House was due largely to John Marshall's moderation as the Federalist leader. See Theodore Sedgwick to Rufus King, Phila., May 11, 1800, *King's Correspondence*, III, 237–238.

[72] *Annals*, 6C, 1S, 180. Also see the *Aurora*, May 13, 1800. Although Senator Bingham, a Federalist, introduced the petition, he voted not to allow its reading.

worse. It allowed neither trial by jury, nor confrontation of witnesses. Accusers should not be the judge, the jury, and the punisher of the accused. Because they were persuaded that "the surest safeguard of the rights and liberties of the People is the freedom of that Press"—that "Bulwark of Republican Liberty"—the petitioners requested the Senate to reconsider its action against Duane.[73]

Rejecting this plea completely, the Senate concluded its session by requesting President Adams to instruct the proper law officer to prosecute Duane under the Sedition Law for his article of February 19, 1800.[74] The president willingly complied with this request. On May 16 he sent duplicate letters to Charles Lee, attorney general of the United States, and to Jared Ingersoll, the federal district attorney in Philadelphia, directing them to commence legal proceedings against the editor of the *Aurora*.[75]

While this action was pending, the Federalist press kept up a constant attack on the Republican editor. Although the usual line of condemnation was on Duane's Irish ancestry, the *Gazette of the United States* leveled the gun of anti-Semitism against him. "Duane," the paper assured its readers, "was once a Jew Cloathsman in London, from which place, and from which occupation, his *integrity* expelled him. . . . He passed in London under the name of Jew Aine." [76]

Not until October 17, 1800, was Duane indicted by the federal grand jury. The editor and his counsel, Dallas, appeared in court that day before Associate Justice William Paterson of the United States Supreme Court and Judge Peters. Dallas observed that the Senate had requested President Adams to institute these proceedings on the last day of its session when nearly all the persons whose testimony would substantiate the truth of Duane's charge had left Philadelphia. Without the evidence of several senators, Dallas con-

[73] *Aurora*, May 13, 1800. The text was first given in *ibid.*, March 28, 1800.

[74] *Annals*, 6C, 1S, 184 (May 14, 1800). The vote on this resolution, the Senate's last official act before adjournment, was 13 to 4. See the *Albany Register*, May 23, 1800. On May 14 the Senate refused to allow the reading of a second petition from Philadelphia citizens in favor of Duane.

[75] *Adams' Works*, IX, 56. Ingersoll succeeded Rawle, Bache's prosecutor, early in May, 1800. See the *Aurora*, May 9, 1800. While Duane was in hiding, a federal grand jury indicted him on April 14, 1800, for libeling the British minister to the United States, Robert Liston. See the *Aurora*, April 15, 1800, and the Richmond *Examiner*, May 2, 1800. Although this indictment was brought in the federal Circuit Court, it could hardly have been brought under the Sedition Law, as that measure protected only the president, Congress, and the government from adverse criticism.

[76] *Gazette of the United States*, July 16, 1800.

tinued, the editor could not prove the facts which the law allowed as a means of exonerating himself. This evidence was indispensable not only to the defendant; the importance of the case itself made a thorough investigation a matter of justice to the Senate as well as to the people themselves, who had taken a great interest in the earlier proceedings. Dallas then submitted an affidavit naming over twenty material witnesses and requested the district attorney to agree to a postponement.

Ingersoll acknowledged that the case needed careful investigation. "If the charges in this case were founded," he said, "the public ought to know it, for to a republican government nothing was so necessary as confidence in its Legislators, nothing more fatal than to deprive them of it thro' misrepresentation." In that case the district attorney promised to prosecute to the full extent of the law. If Duane's claims were unfounded—and Ingersoll thought they were—he deserved to be severely punished. Nonetheless, the prosecutor agreed to the postponement, stating that he did not want it alleged, as had been done in other sedition cases, that party considerations had a share in any case he conducted. After observing that the court was neither guided nor actuated by any party, Judge Paterson postponed the trial.[77]

Since the federal government had moved from Philadelphia to Washington in the summer of 1800, Ingersoll agreed to allow a mixed commission to go to the new capital to interview senators whose testimony the defense deemed material. The govenment prosecutor was to nominate two commissioners and Duane was to appoint two more. Any two of them could take evidence as long as there was one commissioner representing each party. To represent the government, Ingersoll named Charles Lee, attorney general of the United States, and Harrison Gray Otis, the Massachusetts congressman who had been so instrumental in securing the passage of the Alien and Sedition Laws. Lee declined, but Otis accepted.

Duane did not request the commission to function until February 15, 1801, when his counsel, A. J. Dallas, would be in Washington. Otis met once after that date with the defendant's commissioners. Although all the senatorial witnesses were summoned, only Humphrey Marshall of Kentucky attended. Since the Washington wit-

[77] *Aurora*, Oct. 20, 1800. These witnesses included Senators Tracy, Read, Bingham, and Latimer, who had favored the action of the committee on privileges, and Mason and Marshall, who had not. Congressmen Sedgwick and Gunn were also listed.

nesses were beyond the legal processes of the Circuit Court sitting in Philadelphia, they were not bound to answer the questions of the commission, which therefore adjourned to meet later. On that same day, however, Otis left Washington. Since the commission was joint, his departure prevented any further meetings. Duane's attempts to obtain evidence to support his charges against the Senate, therefore, were thwarted by Congressman Otis' sudden departure.[78]

Before the next Circuit Court convened in May, 1801, moreover, Jefferson had replaced Adams as president of the United States and the Sedition Law had expired. The new chief executive immediately asked Duane for a list of prosecutions of a public nature against him, observing that he would treat the Sedition Law as a nullity whenever he met it in his line of official functions. If the prosecution recommended by the Senate was based on that law, Jefferson promised to order a nolle prosequi. His respect for the Senate, however, would oblige him to ask the district attorney to consider whether there was any ground for a prosecution under an acknowledged law in any court. When Duane failed to submit a list of the public prosecutions pending against him, Jefferson concluded that either the trials were not scheduled for some time or that the editor had decided "to meet the investigation before a jury summoned by an impartial officer." In either event, he did not dismiss the case instituted by the Senate, because of Duane's failure to inform him of its status.[79]

When the Circuit Court met, therefore, the case against the *Aurora* was on the docket and was called up for prosecution. The editor's attorneys, Thomas Cooper and Mahlon Dickerson, observed that the efforts to secure defense evidence had been unsuccessful and asked for another postponement. They objected that the limited jurisdiction of the court sitting in Philadelphia did not afford the defendant compulsory process in Washington. This made it improbable that the editor could subpoena the senators implicated by his remarks, because they would not want to testify against themselves. Moreover, these witnesses were now scattered and would not return to Washington until the next session of Congress, which was scheduled to meet in December, 1801. But their chief ground for requesting a continuance was the plea that Duane's efforts to obtain evidence when all the necessary witnesses were in Washington had

[78] *Gazette of the United States,* May 18, 1801.

[79] Jefferson to Duane, May 23, 1801, *Jefferson's Writings* (Ford ed.), VIII, 5.

been defeated by the action of the prosecutor's agent, Congressman Otis.

Although reluctant to grant another postponement, the Circuit Court judges finally did so, but only on the condition that the case should be tried peremptorily at the October term. This, of course, ruled out the possibility of waiting until Congress convened before taking testimony from the widely dispersed senatorial witnesses. Judge Griffith declared that the continuance was not based on Duane's objection to the lack of compulsory process to obtain witnesses. Any editor who published a charge which brought the government into hatred and contempt should be prepared to prove it when he made the statement. "He acts at his *peril*," the judge declared; "he knows his authority." In short, he argued, a newspaperman should be well enough informed to know that a court cannot issue compulsory process outside its jurisdiction and "foresee the hardship, (if there be one)."

Nonetheless, Judge Griffith favored a continuance because of the "omission and acts of the prosecutor or agents of the prosecutor, who [now] insists on a trial." Duane's effort to obtain evidence, he concluded, "was rendered abortive by the acts of the commissioners named on the *part of the prosecutor*." "Had the defendant not relied upon the execution of the commission," presiding Judge Tilghman added, "he *might* possibly have used *other* means of procuring testimony, if he had any; and therefore ought now to have that opportunity." Although Otis' action was no doubt unintentional, the judge observed that its effect was the same as if done "with all the possible consequences of designed direliction [sic]." [80]

Duane hastened to inform the president that his trial had been continued until October, when it was "to be tried peremptorily!!!" [81] Jefferson pointed out that the postponement gave the editor time to explain what action he wanted the president to take in the case. Duane then requested a dismissal of the indictment for his remarks about the Ross bill. He explained that he had not expected the case to come up in 1801 because a trial under the Sedition Law would be a recognition of its validity, though he knew that the president

---

[80] *Gazette of the United States*, May 18, 1801. Judge Basset dissented from the ruling. This was the first session of the Circuit Court under the Judiciary Act of 1801, which relieved Supreme Court justices of riding circuit. All three judges were "midnight appointees" of President John Adams.

[81] Duane to Jefferson, Phila., May 10, 1801, Ford, "Letters of Duane," Mass. Hist. Soc., *Proceedings*, 2d ser., 20 (1906), 263.

considered it a nullity. If the case came to trial as scheduled, he would have to submit it to the discretion of the court. "Though no man," Duane wrote, could "doubt the truth of every tittle uttered" in his article on the electoral count bill, the government had since shifted from Philadelphia to Washington, and the witnesses had scattered. He had tried to secure evidence in the new capital to support his assertions about caucuses, but he had failed. Nor did he see any prospect of obtaining the kind of evidence the court demanded. Even if he could obtain the information, it would take all his time from his means of livelihood. Because of family considerations, therefore, Duane requested that the suit be dismissed.[82]

Jefferson complied quickly by discontinuing the prosecution under the Sedition Law. As he had decided earlier, he directed a new proceeding against Duane "on whatever other law might be in evidence against the offence" of criticizing the Senate. When this was done, the grand jury, of course, found no law against criticism of Congress other than the expired Sedition Law and refused to find an indictment.[83]

In a special message which he prepared for the Senate but never delivered, Jefferson explained that in taking his action he had endeavored

to do the duty of my station between the Senate and Citizen, to pursue for the former that legal vindication which was the object of their resolution, to cover the latter with whatsoever of protection the Constitution had guarded him & to secure to the press that degree of freedom in which it remained under the authority of the states, with whom alone the power is left of abridging that freedom, the General Government being expressly excluded from it.[84]

Occupying a new position in 1801, the leading opponent of the Sedition Law thus brought an end to the proceedings which had begun nearly a year and a half earlier, when he was forced by his position as presiding officer of the Senate to sign, against his

[82] Duane to Jefferson, June 10, 1801, *ibid.*, 267.

[83] Levi Lincoln to A. J. Dallas, Dept. of State, Washington, March 25, 1801, Jefferson Papers, CXI, 19057 (Lib. Cong.); Jefferson to Edward Livingston, Washington, D.C., Nov. 1, 1801, *Jefferson's Writings* (Ford ed.), VIII, 58n. Also see Gallatin to Jefferson, Nov. 12, 1801, Jefferson Papers, CXVII, 20275 (Lib. Cong.).

[84] Undated manuscript [1801], *Jefferson's Writings* (Ford ed.), VIII, 56n. Also see Jefferson to Gallatin, Nov. 12, 1801, *ibid.*, 57n. For a brief discussion of Jefferson's action, see W. C. Ford, "Jefferson and the Newspaper," Columbia Historical Society, *Records,* 8 (1905), 94–95.

better judgment, the warrant for Duane's arrest. Although Jefferson pleaded his regard for the Senate as the reason for instituting a new proceeding against Duane, the failure of the grand jury to find any legal basis for the Senate's complaint clearly branded the original action by the Federalist majority as a usurpation of authority and a direct attempt to punish Duane and the *Aurora* for their criticism of the disreputable Ross bill.

CHAPTER XIV

President Adams, Thomas Cooper, and Sedition

And now, Sir, what shall I say to you on the subject of "libels and satires? Lawless things, indeed!"—JOHN ADAMS to Timothy Pickering

THE Thomas·Cooper case, together with the proceedings against Duane and the trial of Callender, best illustrates the efforts of the Federalists to overawe Republican writers during the election of 1800. An English radical, Cooper had moved to the United States in 1794 during the conservative reaction in England to the French Revolution. He was a man with considerable talents in several fields. Trained as a lawyer, he owned a textile mill in Manchester and attained some renown as a chemist. After a visit to Paris in 1792, he was denounced in Parliament by Edmund Burke for his radicalism. In turn, Cooper penned a powerful reply which was a bold attack on the "privileged orders." Although he was in no personal danger in England, he was convinced that freedom of thought and speech were no longer possible there.

In 1794 the newly arrived immigrant settled in Northumberland County, Pennsylvania, and became a citizen of the United States. He lived part of this time with Dr. Joseph Priestley, the famed English scientist-clergyman. In relative obscurity, he practiced law, served unofficially as a physician, and did not become conspicuous in politics until 1799.[1] Cooper first aroused Federalist animosity

[1] For an excellent biography, see Dumas Malone, *The Public Life of Thomas*

while serving as editor of the Sunbury and Northumberland *Gazette* from April 20 through June 29, 1799. Dedicating this obscure country newspaper to political controversy, he wrote vigorous essays criticizing the Adams administration. It was his farewell editorial effort which marked him for future prosecution under the Sedition Law. Although he apologized for having "to fill up the vacant columns of the week," he did not discount the importance of the subject which he chose for discussion: the party cleavage in the United States. Neither did he offer excuses for the stand which he took in opposition to the Federalists. However praiseworthy their motives, their measures seemed to him "to stretch to the utmost the constitutional authority of our Executive, and to introduce the political evils of those European governments whose principles we have rejected."

To illustrate the policies of the administration which he opposed, Cooper used the device of supposing himself to be the president and then listed party measures he would follow if he wanted to increase executive power at the expense of the governed. This was, of course, but a thinly veiled attack on the president, and the Federalists did not overlook it in their scrutiny of Republican writings for seditious statements. Cooper declared that if he were a usurping president, he would first undermine the Constitution either by expanding its grants of power so as to encroach upon the rights reserved to the states or by explaining away the plain and obvious meaning of its words. State governments would be denounced as clogs in the wheels of the federal government and state officials accused of disaffection if they expressed opposition to the measures of the administration. After extending the powers of federal courts and officials, he would restrict the liberty of the press on the ground that free discussion of public characters was too dangerous for despotism to tolerate. His chief weapon would be laws against libel and sedition, which would serve as legal fences to protect the sanctity of government officials. He would have his party followers charge all who opposed the measures of his administration as enemies of their country; his partisans would brand such persons "as dangerous and seditious, as disturbers of the peace of society, and desirous of overturning the Constitution." Through such measures it would be possible to "suppress all political conversation."

Cooper, 1793–1839 (New Haven, 1926). This personal sketch is based on the first three chapters of Malone's book.

A shorter version of this chapter appeared in *The Mississippi Valley Historical Review*, 42 (1955), 438–465.

"The grand engine," however, "the most useful instrument of despotic ambition, would be a standing army . . . and a naval armament." This would be the principal means of accomplishing his purposes of expanding executive powers and of undermining the rights and influence of the people, because "in no instance whatever has a standing army, regularly maintained, failed of rendering the governing powers independent of the people." By making the militia idle, useless, and contemptible, a standing army would provide the partisans of the ruling party with arms, at the same time disarming and paralyzing its opponents. If no reason existed for the establishment and maintenance of a standing force, he would invent one—not for defense against invaders from without, but for use against the friends and principles of liberty from within. An army and a navy would gain him the support of the mercantile interests, would attract other supporters through offices and contracts, and would furnish the means of suppressing "a more active opposition to my views than I could safely submit to."

Cooper then softened his essay by disavowing any intention of accusing any man or set of men of attempting to aim at power independent of the people; but he concluded that President Adams had used violent language against the principles of freedom, the sovereignty of the people, and the rights of man. The Republican writer objected specifically to the Alien and Sedition Laws and to the increase in the size of the army and navy. He hoped that these measures would be steadily resisted by the American people "but opposed in the only justifiable way of opposition under a free government, by discussion in the first instance, and a change of persons by constitutional election if no other method will succeed." [2]

This farewell address of Cooper to the patrons of the *Gazette* was republished in the powerful Philadelphia *Aurora* on July 12, 1799, was reprinted in Cooper's *Political Essays* in 1799, and also was included in the second edition in February, 1800. The fact that the address was reprinted in the *Aurora* indicated Cooper's growing stature in the Republican ranks. To the Federalists he had become a "demagogue" worthy of the Sedition Law.

Secretary of State Pickering soon received a letter from Charles Hall, a Sunbury Federalist whom Adams had appointed in 1797 as

[2] Address to the Readers of the *Sunbury and Northumberland Gazette*, June 29, 1799, *ibid.* (2d ed.), 25–29. For a recent discussion of President Adams' attitude toward governmental power, see Koch, "Hamilton, Adams and the Pursuit of Power," *Review of Politics*, 16 (1954), 37–66, especially 62.

an agent to assist in arbitrating American and British debts.[3] Observing that Cooper's essay had been republished in the *Aurora*, Hall asserted that if it did as much mischief in Philadelphia as it had done among the uninformed people in central Pennsylvania it was a misfortune that it had ever met the public's view. Since it could not be suppressed, Hall had prepared a Federalist reply to correct its effects. He requested the secretary of state to insert it in one of the Philadelphia papers to offset the influence of Cooper's address. Convinced that Cooper was merely a tool of the Republicans, Hall described the political editorial as an attempt "to prepare the minds of the people for the Election." Equating oppositionist political activity with subversive machinations, the Sunbury Federalist informed Pickering that Cooper's address had been written with malicious motives "in enmity to the constitution and Government of the Country." He stated that Cooper alone was not responsible for circulating his malicious electioneering pamphlet. The famed Dr. Priestley had helped in getting the address printed and distributed in hand bill form, and this activity had been condemned by all Federalists in Sunbury—or as Hall expressed it, "by every friend of the Constitution." [4]

Impressed with Hall's rebuttal, Secretary Pickering promised to send it on to one of the Philadelphia papers for publication. "It is important," he wrote his informant, "that the observations should circulate as extensively as the poison for which they were intended as the antidote." For that reason he urged Hall to reprint his observations as a pamphlet to counteract further the Republican address, and promised not only to distribute it but also to see that Hall was reimbursed for his efforts.[5] Pickering also agreed that the Republicans' desire for political office, whether it was the governorship of Pennsylvania or the presidency of the United States, was positive proof that they were both seditious and turbulent. He was particularly incensed by Dr. Priestley's conduct. This alien, whom the secretary had once thought a persecuted Christian driven from England, was like the mass of "seditious, turbulent democrats." Not even the wisest government could make them contented, "un-

[3] The appointment is discussed in Charles Hall to President Adams, Sunbury, Pa., Aug. 8, 1797, Adams Papers, XIX, 77 (Mass. Hist. Soc.). Priestley recommended Cooper for this job in 1797.

[4] Hall to Pickering, Sunbury, July 26, 1799, Pickering Papers, XXV, 58–59 (Mass. Hist. Soc.).

[5] Pickering to Hall, Phila., Aug. 1, 1799, *ibid.*, XI, 528. Whether Pickering meant to pay these expenses from government funds, from Federalist contributions, or from his own pocket is not stated,

less they were placed at its head." To Hall he expressed the hope that William Rawle, district attorney for Pennsylvania, would prosecute both Cooper and Priestley. "I am sorry," Pickering concluded in a nativist strain, "that Cooper like Priestley has not remained an Alien. The indecency of these *strangers* thus meddling with our government, merits a severe animadversion."

Pickering immediately relayed Hall's information to President Adams and enclosed an issue of the *Aurora* containing Cooper's address. After describing the author as "a warm opposition man," he also noted that his attendance "at the *democratic* assembly on the 4th of July at Northumberland," coupled with his role in distributing Cooper's handbill, clearly demonstrated his indecency as well as "his discontented and turbulent Spirit." Although Priestley was an alien, Cooper had "taken care to get himself admitted to citizenship." It was regrettable, the secretary lamented, that both of these disturbers of "our internal tranquillity" could not be removed from the United States under the Alien Law.[6]

Replying in a letter devoted exclusively to the enforcement of the Alien and Sedition Laws, President Adams wrote that "libels and satires" were "Lawless things, indeed!" Convinced that "a meaner, a more artful, or a more malicious libel" than Cooper's address had not appeared, the president condemned it as seditious. "As far as it alludes to me," he added, "I despise it; but I have no doubt it is a libel against the whole government, and as such ought to be prosecuted." Adams interpreted Cooper's writing as the spiteful work of a disappointed office seeker. In 1797, he informed Pickering, Cooper had solicited the appointment as American agent to argue claims before the mixed commission arbitrating American and British debts. Priestley had also submitted a letter of recommendation. Both had apologized for Cooper's "reputation as a democrat," the president continued, "and gave intimation of a reformation." He wondered, however, how either should have thought it compatible with his duty to appoint "a stranger" in preference to one of "the great number of able natives, who wished for this trust." Did they think that the American people would be satisfied to entrust these important interests "to an Englishman, or any other foreigner?" Following his rule of never answering letters of solicitation or recommendation for offices, the president had not replied to either of his correspondents. Although Adams was willing to prosecute Cooper for sedition, he vetoed the use of the Alien Law

[6] Pickering to the President, Aug. 1, 1799 (private), *ibid.*, XI, 524. This letter also appears in *Adams' Works*, IX, 5–6.

against his old friend, Dr. Priestley, who he thought had been led into all his errors by Cooper.[7]

Despite the administration's willingness to use the Sedition Law at this time, Cooper was not indicted. Nevertheless, his farewell editorial had stirred President Adams and his family deeply. Quick to defend her husband's reputation, Mrs. Adams denounced "the Demo Cooper and the Demo philosopher," and her son, Thomas Bolyston Adams, agreed that the editorial was not only abominable but that Priestley's role in circulating it was also discreditable.[8] Although somewhat more restrained, the chief executive did not overlook the incident. To Benjamin Waterhouse, he confided the anecdote of Dr. Priestley's recommendation of Cooper, and his correspondent replied that the action must have been "folly in Dr. P. or something worse." [9] When "A True American" answered Cooper by publishing a defense of the president's policies in a Philadelphia newspaper, Mrs. Adams was sure that it was written by T. B. Adams to vindicate his father. To counteract Cooper's poison, she sent a copy to her sister and instructed her to have it republished in a Boston paper. Like her husband, the first lady deplored "impertinent paragraphs fabricated by busy bodies who are forever meddling with things they understand not." After the defense appeared in *J. Russell's Gazette* in Boston, she reported that she had been mistaken about the author; her son had not written it after all, nor did she know who the author was.[10]

A few days after the comments of "A True American" were published in Philadelphia, another anonymous answer to Cooper's ad-

[7] Adams to Pickering, Quincy, Aug. 13, 1799, *Adams' Works*, IX, 13. See Chapter IX for the proposed use of the Alien Law against Priestley.

[8] See T. B. Adams to Abigail Adams, Aug. 26, 1799, Adams Papers, VIII, 148 (Mass. Hist. Soc.), repeating his mother's phraseology, and his letter to Mrs. Adams, Rock Hall, Germantown, Sept. 16, 1799, *ibid.*, 150. From Prussia, John Quincy Adams wrote a letter severely lashing Cooper and Priestley as Jacobins, and T. B. Adams sent extracts to the *Gazette of the United States*. See T. B. Adams to Abigail Adams, Phila., Oct. 5, 1800, Adams Papers, VIII, 207 (Mass. Hist. Soc.).

[9] Benjamin Waterhouse to John Adams, Cambridge, Aug. 15, 1799, *ibid.*, XX, 216.

[10] Abigail to Mary Cranch, East Chester, N.Y., Nov. 1–3, and Nov. 26, 1799, Mitchell, *New Letters*, 212–213 and 216. "A True American's" answer to Cooper was probably written by Charles Hall of Sunbury and inserted in the Federalist press by Pickering. It appeared in the *Gazette of the United States*, Oct. 23, 1799; it was reprinted from Mrs. Adams' copy in *J. Russell's Gazette*, Nov. 18 and 21, 1799. Hall was a friend of T. B. Adams. See T. B. Adams to Abigail Adams, Phila., June 1, 1800, Adams Papers, VIII, 196 (Mass. Hist. Soc.).

dress appeared in the Reading *Weekly Advertiser.* Obviously based on information which could have come only from the president, this article asked if the Thomas Cooper who wrote the address was the same one who had requested the president to appoint him to an office in 1797. Had not this Cooper, while admitting that he had been a democrat in politics, assured Adams that his real political sentiments were agreeable to the president and government of the United States? Had not Dr. Priestley's letter also assured Adams of "the pliability of his friend Cooper's democratic principles?" The communication asserted that the president had rejected the application with disdain, expressing surprise that Priestley should think "that I would appoint any Englishman to that important office in preference to an American." Denouncing Cooper's address as a "cunning and insidious" production—"the offspring of disappointment and revenge"—the anonymous writer concluded by calling upon Cooper to answer his charges.[11]

Cooper quickly accepted the challenge. Early in November, 1799, exactly one week after the anonymous Reading letter appeared, he issued a handbill from Northumberland in which he admitted that he was the same Thomas Cooper who had applied to President Adams. But he denied that his address had been motivated by revenge, and he vigorously attacked the charge that he was a political hypocrite. He notified the public that he would not have stooped to answer "anonymous slander" had the Reading article not been based on information which "must have been originally derived from the president himself." Although he disapproved of the president's conduct, Cooper wrote, he thought well of his intentions and therefore could not believe him capable of misrepresentation. But someone in the administration must have furnished the information used by the "malignant writer" of the Reading statement.[12]

Because Cooper's later indictment for sedition was based upon

[11] Reading *Weekly Advertiser* (Pennsylvania), Oct. 26, 1799. This letter virtually paraphrased Adams' letter to Pickering concerning Cooper's application for appointment. Pickering probably wrote the letter or furnished the information to the writer, because he was the only man besides the president to have this data.

[12] The text of this handbill, written at Northumberland on Nov. 2, 1799, is given in full in *An Account of the Trial of Thomas Cooper, of Northumberland; on a charge of libel against the President of the United States; taken in short hand, with a preface, notes and appendix, by Thomas Cooper* (Phila., April, 1800), 3–7. In an erratum (*ibid.,* 64), Cooper denied that this account was printed for him. It was taken in shorthand by Joseph Gales. The pamphlet is referred to hereafter as *Cooper's Trial.*

this handbill, it is necessary to examine it in some detail. After quoting his and Priestley's letters to Adams, Cooper appealed to the public to decide whether his application letter was manly or vain and servile. "Do not these letters take for granted that I am a democrat, though not a disturber of all government; and that what I am I shall remain, even though it be deemed a *reasonable objection to my appointment?* Is this, or is this not, adhering to my principle, whatever become of my interest?" Although he saw no objection to taking any fair means to improve his position in America, he denied that even the "prudence of middle age" and the duty to provide for his family could make him sacrifice his principles. "It is not in the power of promises or threats, of wealth or poverty, to extinguish the political enthusiasm which has actuated my conduct for these twenty years."

Declaring that two years had elapsed between his letter to the president and his writing on American politics, the part-time editor denied that his polemical articles were undertaken to obtain revenge for the president's rejection of his application. Using the language later charged as seditious, Cooper wrote that he saw no impropriety in his original requests of Adams; "at that time he had just entered into office; he was hardly in the infancy of political mistake; even those who doubted his capacity, thought well of his intentions." Neither had the president yet sanctioned the abolition of trial by jury in the Alien Act, Cooper continued, or entrenched his public character behind the legal barriers of the Sedition Law. "Nor were we yet saddled with the expense of a permanent navy, or threatened under his auspices with the existence of a standing army. Our credit was not yet reduced so low as to borrow money at eight percent in time of peace, while the unnecessary violence of official expressions might justly have provoked a war." Cooper then criticized the president's co-operation with the British in the extradition of an impressed seaman who claimed to be an American citizen:

Mr. Adams had not yet . . . interfered as President of the United States to influence the decisions of a Court of Justice. A stretch of authority which the Monarch of Great Britain would have shrunk from; an interference without precedent, against law and against mercy! This melancholy case of *Jonathan Robbins*, a native citizen of America, forcibly impressed by the British and delivered up with the advice of Mr. Adams to the mock trial of a British court martial, had not yet astonished the republican citizens of this free country. A case too little known, but which the people ought to be fully apprized before the election, and they shall be.[13]

13 *Ibid.*, 6–7. The passages in quotes were the words selected as seditious.

A Northumberland Federalist immediately forwarded Cooper's handbill to President Adams, cautioning him that Cooper and Priestley were friends neither of Adams, the government, the Constitution, nor of the laws of the United States. Blasting the Republicans as "Jacobins, Democrats, [and] enemies to God and Man," he informed the chief magistrate that these wicked tools of faction "are continually busy to destroy all order, Society and tranquility."[14] When Mrs. Adams saw Cooper's abuse of the president, she was certain that the author had made himself liable to the penalty of the Sedition Law by his "Mad democratic Stile." Although Cooper's writings had obviously marked him as a candidate for prosecution, the authorities once again failed to move against him immediately.[15] To Mrs. Adams, the president's secretary offered a plausible explanation for this delay, observing that "such mad men as Cooper can never do injury to the Government; their mad zeal defeats their own purposes."[16] For another five months, therefore, Cooper wrote in behalf of the Jeffersonians, becoming so active in the preliminaries to the campaign of 1800 that the Federalists listed him as one of the top three Republican "scribblers." The *Philadelphia Gazette* warned that this "foreign Emissary" would be aided by Dr. Priestley, "that journeyman of discontent and sedition," in directing "the whole of the Jacobin interest of the western country."[17]

It was not Cooper's newspaper writings, however, which led directly to his prosecution under the Sedition Act. Instead it was his co-operation with Duane in defying the Senate which finally gave the impetus for his trial. After the Senate declared Duane guilty of a "high-handed breach of privileges" because of his criticism of its electoral bill, the editor requested Cooper and Dallas to serve as his counsel. To appear under the Senate's limitations, Cooper replied, would only tend to disgrace his client's cause as well as his own. Under such conditions, a gagged lawyer would become nothing more than the Senate's "manacled assistant." Cooper could not refrain from concluding his letters with an outspoken

[14] Bernard Hubley, Jr., to John Adams, Northumberland, Nov. 7, 1799, Adams Papers, XX, 245 (Mass. Hist. Soc.).

[15] Abigail Adams to Mary Cranch, Phila., Nov. 26, 1799, Mitchell, *New Letters*, 216. Although Cooper published his defense on Nov. 2, 1799, he was not indicted until April 12, 1800.

[16] William Smith Shaw to Abigail Adams, Dec. 2, 1799, Adams Papers (Mass. Hist. Soc.). Shaw was the president's nephew, who served as the chief executive's private secretary.

[17] "A Federal Republican," *Philadelphia Gazette*, March 12, 1800.

criticism of the Federalist attack on the Republican editor. "Where rights are undefined," this opponent of the Sedition Law proclaimed, "and power is unlimited—where the freedom of the press is actually attacked, under whatever intention of curbing its licentiousness, the melancholy period cannot be far distant when the citizen will be converted into a subject."[18]

The refusal of Cooper and Dallas to represent Duane gave the editor his excuse for not attending the Senate's proceedings. In attacking Duane for his defiance, the Federalists did not overlook his legal advisers. "Anti-Jacobin" described "Tom Cooper" as a canting English Jacobin bent on arousing the mob in Duane's favor. This infamous agitator could expect no mercy from the advocates of truth and justice in America. The editor of the *Gazette* agreed. Cooper's letter to the Senate was not only insulting to that body but was degrading to the American people. The Federalist editor refused to comment on its contents, however, because he hoped "that severer notice will be taken of its insolence."[19]

Nor was the editor of the *Gazette* disappointed. On April 9, 1800, exactly two weeks after this paper's call for "severer action," Thomas Cooper was arrested for seditious libel. Although Cooper's indictment is directly traceable to his refusal to act as Duane's counsel, District Attorney William Rawle singled out Cooper's handbill of November 2, 1799, written nearly five months earlier. Accusing Cooper of being "a person of wicked and turbulent disposition," the indictment charged that his defense against the anonymous letter published in the Reading paper was a false, scandalous, and malicious writing which he had wickedly and maliciously printed with the intent of defaming the president and exciting against him the hatred of the good people of the United States.[20]

On April 10, Cooper posted $1,000 bail for his appearance at court and Israel Israel, Republican sheriff of Philadelphia County, put up $1,000 more. On April 12, the indictment presented by Rawle was found a true bill by the grand jury. At his arraignment, Cooper pleaded not guilty and asked the court to issue subpoenas for President Adams, Secretary of State Pickering, Congressman John Davenport, Jacob Wagner, chief clerk in the State Department, and others.

[18] Cooper to Duane, Phila., March 25, 1800, *Aurora*, March 27, 1800.

[19] *Philadelphia Gazette*, March 27, 1800.

[20] "Proceedings in the Circuit Court of the United States . . . April 11, 1800," *Cooper's Trial*, 3. The most recent popular account of Cooper's case gives the high lights of the trial by quoting from the court record. See Clark Gavin, *Foul, False and Infamous: Famous Libel and Slander Cases of History* (New York, 1950), 69–104.

Dallas appeared as a friend of the court and assisted Cooper in his legal motions. The trial date was set for April 16.[21]

Associate Justice Samuel Chase, who had already handed down the most severe sentence imposed under the Sedition Law, shared the bench in this case with District Judge Richard Peters. On the trial date, Cooper asked if his subpoena had been served on the president, and Judge Chase replied that the court had prohibited the clerk from issuing the subpoena, on the ground that it was an improper step. Since the question had never before been decided, Cooper obtained permission to explain his reasons for requesting the president's testimony. In the first place, the Constitution contained no statement which exempts the president from court process. His chief reason for wanting the subpoena, however, was that he had become a defendant in a sedition case because of the president's disclosure of a confidential correspondence. The handbill for which he stood indicted was not a voluntary production, Cooper informed the court. It was a reply forced from him as a vindication of his own character in answer to a false attack on him based on information obtainable only from the president. Since the American republic was a government of equal rights and equal laws, he hoped that no man, including the president, would be elevated above the laws or hold privileges paramount to justice.

The presiding judge replied that the court's refusal to issue the subpoena was not based on presidential prerogative. But in a prosecution for a libel of the president, the chief executive could not be expected, and certainly not compelled, to appear. His libeler could not put him on the stand and ask him if he was guilty of maladministration. This was not only an improper request, Judge Chase ruled, but a "very indecent" one and the court refused to hear further argument on the point.[22]

The defendant then raised a question about the procurement of documentary evidence, such as certified copies of the addresses to, and the answers from, the president at the height of the XYZ crisis in 1798. Since some of the statements alleged to be seditious had

21 For Cooper's eleven-point plea of not guilty, see "Trial of Cooper," *Porcupine's Works*, XII, 3–4; *Cooper's Trial*, 9.

22 *Cooper's Trial*, 10. For criticism of this ruling as a violation of the right of the accused to be confronted with the witnesses against him, see "An Enquirer," April 29, 1800, *Poughkeepsie Journal*, reprinted in the *Albany Register*, May 16, 1800. Although the Republicans attacked Judge Chase's ruling in the Cooper case, they later denounced Marshall's action in the Burr trial when he issued a subpoena for Jefferson. See Beveridge, *Marshall*, III, 444–447. Marshall's reasoning paralleled Cooper's arguments.

been based on these writings, the defendant deemed them necessary to his defense. The district attorney, he said, had first agreed
to allow him to use Fenno's *Gazette of the United States* for the
official texts of these writings, but had reversed the ruling because
of his fear that the newspaper copies might not be faithful tran-
scripts of the originals. This meant that Cooper would now need
authenticated copies of these documents, and he asked a postponement while he tried to procure office copies. Judge Chase gave him
three days, setting the new trial date for April 19.[23]

When the court reconvened, the defendant reported that he had
been unable to obtain authenticated copies of the addresses or the
answers from the secretary of state or from the president. After
Pickering informed him that none of these writings were deposited
in the State Department,[24] Cooper applied to President Adams and
requested that the president's secretary furnish copies.[25] When the
president failed to answer, the defendant bought a book of the
addresses and answers and sent it to the chief executive's private
secretary to be checked against the originals. The secretary replied
that Cooper would not receive "any information concerning answers
to addresses" from the president's house.[26]

Claiming that it was unsafe to go to trial while his accuser withheld legal evidence which was material to his defense, the accused
editor asked that his trial be postponed until he could obtain the
necessary authenticated copies. After pointing out that the president
was not Cooper's prosecutor in this case, Judge Chase asserted
that the defendant should not have made statements without proof.
Writing about the president was risky business, and if Cooper had
made any mistakes he had to take the consequences. "If in making
those assertions you relied on the public [news] papers it was at
your own risk; and it was your own fault not to have had authentic
copies." At the same time, however, the judge ruled that no one

[23] *Cooper's Trial*, 11–12.

[24] Pickering to Cooper, Dept. of State, April 17, 1800, Pickering Papers,
XIII, 399 (Mass. Hist. Soc.). Cooper also requested the secretary to furnish information on ambassadorial appointments to be used in defense of one of the
statements in his handbill. See Cooper to Pickering, "Tuesday Evening," *ibid.*,
XXVI, 83. Pickering endorsed the letter, "April 15, 1800." Although the secretary
was subpoenaed and appeared, he was not called to testify. *Cooper's Trial*, 25.

[25] Cooper's undated request is filed with the Adams Papers, XX, 107–107a
(Mass. Hist. Soc.). It is also reprinted as Cooper to the President, April 17, 1800,
Cooper's Trial, 13. The addresses were compiled as *A Selection of the Patriotic
Addresses, to the President. . . . Together with the President's Answers* (Boston,
1798).

[26] William S. Shaw to Cooper, April 18, 1800, *Cooper's Trial*, 13.

had a right to obtain official copies. Even if they had been obtained, he continued, the court would have to determine their admissibility as evidence, just as it would have to determine whether or not newspapers could be accepted as evidence.[27]

Cooper was tried for a political crime in the nation's capital during a heated presidential campaign. Dramatically high-lighting the divergent views of the major parties on the role of public criticism in a popular form of government, his trial gained immediate national attention. Its political significance was illustrated by the attendance of most of the high-ranking Federalists. From the president's official family came four spectators—his private secretary and the secretaries of state, war, and navy. Indeed, Pickering, who had instigated the proceedings with the president's approval, sat on the bench with the judges. Congressman Robert Goodloe Harper was there to watch the operation of the Sedition Law's section two, which he had authored. Senators Uriah Tracy and Jacob Read of the Committee on Privileges attended to witness the trial of the lawyer who, only three weeks earlier, had refused to appear before the Senate with their gag in his mouth.[28]

William Rawle, prosecutor of the Whiskey Rebels and John Fries in the only two treason trials under the Constitution up to that time, conducted the government's case against Cooper and stressed the necessity of making an example of Cooper in order to deter others from misleading the people by false and defamatory publications. The people themselves had appointed the president to his high office, the prosecutor observed; to abuse him was to withdraw from him the popular confidence required for the proper conduct of government business. According to the government attorney, two factors aggravated Cooper's offense. Although most persons who published defamatory writings tried to avoid punishment by hiding behind fictitious signatures, Cooper boldly stood forth as author. Moreover, Rawle continued, the defendant's education had gained him a standing in a remote and uninformed part of the country, and he used these advantages to disseminate his "dangerous productions." This sort of criticism threatened the tranquillity and security of the nation, and it was mandatory that these erroneous opinions should be stamped out. "Government should not

[27] *Cooper's Trial,* 13–14. Jefferson implied that the federal marshal packed the jury against Cooper. Jefferson to Edmund Pendleton, Phila., April 19, 1800, Jefferson Papers, CVI, 18261 (Lib. Cong.).

[28] *Cooper's Trial,* 25, 64. Pickering and Harper were subpoenaed, but Cooper failed to introduce any oral testimony. *Ibid.,* 14, 25, 31.

encourage the idea, that they will not prosecute such atrocious conduct," he said, "for if this conduct should be allowed to pass over[,] the peace of the country would be endangered. Error leads to discontent, discontent to a fancied idea of oppression, and that to insurrection." The two rebellions which had already happened, said Rawle—who had prosecuted the insurgents on both occasions —afforded alarming proofs of this principle.[29]

Cooper, then, was prosecuted because his criticism tended to lead to insurrection against the government. The causation, according to Rawle, was indirect, but real. Having leaped from words to insurrection, Rawle found little difficulty in taking the short step from the "bad tendency" of Cooper's words to his "bad intent" in writing the words. Although Cooper denied any "bad intent," Rawle could not help suspecting him of the motives he disclaimed; he presumed that Cooper's "conduct must have arisen from the basest motives." [30] Since the words tended to undermine public confidence in the president, the intent must have been bad, and it was the duty of the jury to show that this kind of attack on the government was not to be made with impunity.[31]

The only government witness was John Buyers, justice of the peace at Sunbury. He testified that Cooper visited him on December 6, 1799, showed him the handbill of November 2, admitted writing it, and notified him that this information might save him trouble at another time. On cross-examination by Cooper, the justice of the peace admitted that they were in the habit of "frequently joking each other on political subjects." [32]

In conducting his own defense, Cooper claimed that the sedition statute furnished him two legal defenses for his remarks: first, they were true and therefore justified, no matter what his motives were; second, his motives were "honest and fair." Political accusations, he contended, could not bring the president into contempt if they related to an examination of his public conduct and if no improper motives were imputed to him. He concluded that by taking the text of his indictment from the context of the handbill, the government might be able to construe his remarks into improper imputations of the president's motives, even though the first paragraph,

[29] Ibid., 16. Also see Wharton, State Trials, 663.

[30] Cooper's Trial, 36, 15; Wharton, State Trials, 669, 662–663.

[31] Cooper's Trial, 41, 16; Wharton, State Trials, 663.

[32] Cooper's Trial, 17. President Adams later appointed Buyers as collector of excise, replacing T. Hamilton of Northumberland, a Federalist friend of Cooper. Cooper to Jefferson, Phila., March 17, 1801, Jefferson Papers, CX, 18983 (Lib. Cong.).

which was not included in the presentment, explained that Cooper questioned not the president's motives, but his actions. His defense therefore consisted of a detailed analysis of the essay as a whole and of the contention that his criticism was true and therefore legitimate.

The defendant claimed, moreover, that his handbill was an involuntary publication on his part. It had been issued in answer to a "base and cowardly slander" in the Reading *Weekly Advertiser,* which accused him of privately approving of measures which he publicly disapproved. To vindicate his moral and political character, Cooper said, he had appealed to the public. He was now "dragged . . . before this tribunal" to defend his vindication. Yet his handbill had originated not from motives of turbulence and malice, but from self-defense. His object had not been to attack the character of the president but to protect his own. Cooper's defense thus turned on the right of peaceful political opposition to the authorities, and he urged that his statements were nothing more than a legitimate expression of dissatisfaction with men and measures of the party in power.[33]

It was common knowledge, he added, that the United States was almost equally divided into two parties. Since the parties were mutually suspicious, a bias among the partisans of one side against the other could not fail to exist. This was bound to be so on a strictly political question, and it followed that a defendant under the Sedition Law was placed in a most difficult position, because the judges who presided at the trial and the marshal who selected the jury were political appointees of the president whose conduct had been attacked.[34]

Cooper readily agreed that confidence in the executive branch of the government was necessary to a certain degree, but the "new-fangled doctrine of infallibility" would suppress freedom of the press and the right of political opposition. Confidence in the executive should be based on measures that compel approbation. Public support could not be "exacted by the guarded provision of sedition laws, by attacks on the freedom of the press, by prosecutions, pains and penalties on those which boldly express truth, or who may honestly and innocently err in their political sentiments." Whether

---

[33] *Cooper's Trial,* 19–20.

[34] *Ibid.,* 18. Cooper said that although he had a right to presume a political bias on the part of the court and the jury, he was sure that the jury would "reverence as you ought the sacred obligation of the oath you have taken." In Pennsylvania federal juries were chosen by the federal marshals.

his opinions of the president's public conduct were right or wrong, Cooper thought they would have been better refuted by evidence and argument than by indictment. "Fines and imprisonment," he added prophetically, "will produce conviction neither in the mind of the sufferer nor of the public." He claimed that the people could not exercise their franchise on rational grounds if they were not left free to discuss the public characters of officials elected by and responsible to them. "How can they do it," he asked, "if these prosecutions in *terrorem* close all the avenues of information, and throw a veil over the grossest misconduct of our periodical rulers."

After his introductory remarks, Cooper then took up his specific charges against Adams' administration, defending his statement that the president in 1797 "was but in the infancy of political mistake." Was it a crime, he asked, to say that the president might be mistaken? He knew that in England the king could do no wrong, but he had never known that the president of the United States possessed the same attribute. He was also charged with saying "that even those who doubted his capacity thought well of his intentions." Was it criminal to doubt the capacity of the president? The word "capacity" was one of comparative meaning; obviously a man who had raised himself to the presidency was industrious and talented. Yet those who voted for Jefferson in 1796 "must have believed Mr. Adams of inferior capacity to that gentleman." Both he and at least one-half of the people of the United States had voted for Jefferson. If it was a crime to have spoken of his doubts of the president's capacity, Cooper said defiantly, "I fear I shall continue in this respect incorrigible." [35]

The defendant also attempted to prove the truth of his other charges, devoting considerable attention to the questions of a permanent navy and a standing army, the establishment of expensive embassies in autocratic European countries, the usurious interest rate of 8-per-cent paid on government loans, the president's violent expressions against France, and his action in the case of Jonathan Robbins. Cooper admitted that his discussion of the 8-per-cent interest rate was meant as censure of President Adams for his sanction of the measure. He thought the loan extravagant; not even in war had Great Britain offered such a high interest. He not only dreaded all loans, but more than that he abhorred a funding system and a national debt; above all, he disliked an 8-per-cent interest rate because it was an endorsement of usury by the government whose laws otherwise forbade it to individuals. "If thus to think be

[35] *Cooper's Trial*, 19–21.

a crime," Cooper concluded, "I must patiently abide the punishment." [36]

Considering Cooper's detailed analysis of his handbill and his courageous presentation of his case without counsel, it is difficult to avoid the conclusion that his argument was clearly more than a defense before the jury; it was also an appeal to the American people who would go to the polls that year to choose between Adams and Jefferson. At the same time that he defended his criticisms of the Federalist administration, he put on record, and subsequently published, a vigorous defense of freedom of speech and press and the right of political opposition, demonstrating by example his conviction that a free man has a perfect right to freely examine the conduct of elected officials and to campaign for their dismissal by the electorate.

Replying to Cooper's defense point by point, District Attorney Rawle called for the conviction of the defendant for his publishing the seditious writing with the deliberately malicious intention of injuring "the character of the President." Although the case was brought in the name of the *United States* versus *Cooper*, Rawle obviously regarded it as akin to a personal libel suit of a ruler against the ruled. The people of the United States had thought it proper to confide in President Adams as the man best qualified to judge of the propriety of measures most clearly designed to preserve the peace and promote the happiness of America. It was therefore incumbent upon the constituted authorities, headed by the president, to determine questions of governmental policy. Since he trusted in the wisdom and integrity of the present president, the government attorney informed the jury, he did not pretend to be a judge of such questions. On the other hand, Rawle assured them, Cooper was no more qualified to judge than he was. Momentous measures of public policy, he asserted, were too mysterious for ordinary citizens; the people could not know enough about the issues to understand them. "Those who are qualified and who have been appointed for the purpose, have judged for the nation," the prosecutor insisted, and it was criminal of Cooper "to raise surmises

[36] *Ibid.*, 26. Although Judge Chase declared that Cooper should use "proper evidence" to prove his assertions, he agreed that sedition trials differed from ordinary criminal cases. He therefore allowed a greater latitude in the introduction of evidence, although he preferred authenticated public documents. Cooper pointed out that if these documents were barred from him, he would stand convicted because denied access to the only legal proof of the truth of his assertions. Chase finally agreed that Cooper could read "anything and everything" he pleased. *Ibid.*, 21–22, 28.

and suspicions of the wisdom and design of measures of this kind, which he cannot know sufficient of to explain, or the people to understand." Indeed, the reprehensible nature of Cooper's remarks about the nation's highest characters was aggravated because they were deliberately propagated "among an ignorant people" in a remote part of the frontier country.

The political coloring of the prosecution was best illustrated by the remarks of the government's attorney concerning the Robbins case. Asserting that Cooper's appraisal of this case was warped by his "political prejudices," he contended that the Republicans would have opposed the president's action had it been the opposite of the course which they now denounced. "No conduct of the President however wise, no motives however pure, could screen him from the attacks of party spirit." According to Rawle, the display of seditious party spirit in Cooper's handbill was not his only crime. By taking advantage of the leniency of the Sedition Law and of the court, Cooper had compounded his original crime by committing additional sedition in arguing his "most extraordinary and unexampled" defense. From "the whole tenor of his present argument, as well as from his publication," the government prosecutor charged, it was evident "that his object is not so much to convince you Gentlemen of the jury, that his assertions are true, as to cast an unmerited reflection on the general character and conduct of the President." Thus, Cooper's attempt to defend and justify his views became additional proof of his bad intent. "The nature of his defense," the district attorney concluded, "evidently shows that he meant to justify his own conduct and language throughout." The defendant's statements of opinion were false, and they had been made with the criminal and malignant intent of persuading the public that Adams was unfit for the presidency.[37]

In his charge to the jury, Judge Chase was even more insistent upon Cooper's guilt than Rawle had been. "Since ours is a government founded on the opinions and confidence of the people," he said, it followed that

if a man attempts to destroy the confidence of the people in their officers, their supreme magistrate, and their legislature, he effectually saps the foundation of the government. A republican government can only be

[37] For the prosecutor's speech, see *ibid.*, 35–42. Comparing the federal sedition prosecution to civil proceedings in private suits at the state level, Rawle concluded that "there is no difference then between the defense that may be set up to an action of slander, or libel on a private person, and that which is permitted under the law whereon this indictment is grounded." *Ibid.*, 35–36.

destroyed in two ways; the introduction of luxury, or the licentiousness of the press. . . . The legislature of this country knowing this maxim, has thought proper to pass a law to check this licentiousness of the press.

Judge Chase's charge illustrated the ambiguity of the Sedition Law's provisions as to the burden of proof. He began by instructing the jury that the government had to prove two facts: first, that the defendant wrote the handbill, and second, that he published it with "bad intent." In his concluding remarks, however, he discussed the section which made the truth of the remarks a legal justification, no matter what the intentions of the writer. This provision placed the burden of proof squarely upon the defendant. Judge Chase's instructions made it clear that the accused was considered guilty until proved innocent, rather than innocent until proved guilty. "If you undertake to publish," he said, "without having proper evidence before you to justify your assertions, you do it at your own risk." [38] The writer "must prove every charge he has made . . . he must prove it to the marrow. If he asserts three things, and proves but one, he fails— If he proves but two, he fails in his defense, for he must prove the whole of his assertion to be true." [39] Although the government was supposed to prove that the words of the accused were false, scandalous, and malicious and uttered with intent to defame, the defendant had to prove that his words were true, thus reversing the burden of proof requirements in criminal cases. If he failed, the defendant's statements were presumed false as charged in the indictment, and the jury had only to decide on intent.

In this trial, however, the presiding judge relieved the jury of even that duty by flatly stating that bad intent had been proved. The fact that Cooper had shown his handbill to a justice of the peace and jokingly admitted that it was his was "outrageous," said Judge Chase. This action showed that Cooper "intended to dare and defy the government, and to provoke them, and his subsequent conduct satisfies my mind," the judge continued, "that such was his disposition. For he justified the publication in all its parts, and

[38] For Chase's complete charge, see *ibid.*, 42–50. This particular remark was made during the trial. *Ibid.*, 21.

[39] *Ibid.*, 49. Under this ruling, even if Cooper should prove that Adams had done everything charged against him or, as Judge Chase said, "though he should prove . . . that the President had interfered to influence the decisions of a court of justice that he delivered up Jonathan Robbins without precedent, against law and against mercy, this would not be sufficient, unless he proved at the same time, that Jonathan Robbins was a native American, and had been forcibly impressed, and compelled to serve on board a British ship of war."

declares it to be founded in truth." Thus Justice Chase agreed with the prosecutor that the very attempt of the accused to take advantage of the law's provision allowing the truth to be given in evidence was proof of Cooper's criminal intent.[40]

If there had been any doubts as to Cooper's criminal motives, the judge said that his defense had removed them: had he not boldly admitted that he intended "to censure the conduct of the President?" Even in passages which Cooper denied were reflections on the president's motives, the judge could detect a sting. Criticism of the president's conduct, he declared, implied a criticism of his intentions. Under this interpretation, criticism *per se* was criminal, if it was intended as criticism.

In one instance, Chase cast aside his judicial functions and took over Rawle's role of prosecutor. He informed the jury that the government attorney had neglected "a little circumstance" which the judge regarded as proof of Cooper's bad intent. In an allusion to Jonathan Robbins, Cooper had said that it was "a case too little known, but of which the people ought to be fully apprised before the election, and they *shall be*." This sentence, according to the presiding justice, proved that Cooper was "actuated by improper motives" because his "evident design" was "to arouse the people against the President so as to influence their minds against him on the next election." It proved that the charge against the president was "made with intent to bring the President into contempt and disrepute, and excite against him the hatred of the people of the United States." Not only were the remarks made with "bad intent," but they were false, scandalous, and malicious; any but the most ignorant knew that there could be no standing army in America. He concluded that once again Cooper had published untruths, knowing them to be untruths.

After this judicial condemnation of the defendant, Judge Chase instructed the members of the jury that they were to acquit Cooper if they thought that he had published his remarks without bad intent or if he had proved the truth of his assertions. These instructions, of course, showed judicial impartiality only on the surface, because the whole of the judge's charge had been spent in stressing the falsity of the assertions and the bad intent with which they had been made. The judge made a verdict of guilty almost inevitable when he confessed that he could not suppress his aversion to

[40] *Cooper's Trial*, 43–44; Thomas F. Carroll, "Freedom of Press in the Federalist Period—The Sedition Act," *Michigan Law Review*, 18 (1920), 615.

Cooper's "gross attack" upon the president. "Take this publication in all its parts," he told the jury, "and it is the boldest attempt I have known to poison the minds of the people. . . . This publication is evidently intended to mislead the ignorant, and inflame their minds against the President, and to influence their votes on the next election."

After a short deliberation, the jury pronounced Cooper guilty.[41] Their verdict amounted to a condemnation of Cooper for electioneering against Adams with "bad intent," that is, with the intent of electing Jefferson to succeed him in 1800.

In addressing Cooper before sentencing him, Chase again emphasized the political meaning of the trial. "Every person knows the political disputes which have existed amongst us. It is notorious that there are two parties in the country; you have stated this yourself. You have taken one side"—the side which Chase had the day before described as being "against the government"—"we do not pretend to say, that you have not a right to express your sentiments, only taking care not to injure the characters of those to whom you are opposed." Suspicious that Cooper's fine might be paid by "the party inimical to the government," Judge Chase stated that if that were to be done he "would go to the utmost extent of the power of the court" and assess a $2,000 fine. He added that while he did not wish to impose an oppressive sentence or to go beyond a person's ability to pay, he meant to restrain as far as he could "all such licentious attacks on the government of the country."

Cooper indignantly denied that he was or ever had been a party hack writer. "There is no party in this or any other country," he said, "that can offer me a temptation to prostitute my pen." He did not deny having party opinions and predilections for particular men and measures, but he denied acting upon "minor consideration." He belonged to the "great party of mankind" and had written what he sincerely "thought would conduce to the good of mankind." Concluding in a defiant mood, Cooper asserted that the court's comments on his motives were ill founded, and he challenged Judge Chase to correct his mistake insofar as it had been made from misapprehension or misinformation. District Judge Richard Peters, who had remained silent during the trial, now suggested that the question of party interest should not determine the severity of the sentence, but that the court should consider only the prisoner's ability to pay the fine imposed. To give time for resolving this disagreement

[41] *Cooper's Trial*, 46–50.

on the bench, Judge Chase adjourned the court. On April 24, Cooper was sentenced to six months in federal prison and assessed a $400 fine. When his term of imprisonment expired, he was to post a $2,000 surety bond for good behavior.[42]

Imprisonment did not silence Thomas Cooper. It soon became evident that the Federalists had another potential martyr on their hands, one who was determined to appeal his case to the "solemn tribunal of the Public." Only a week after he was sentenced, he wrote a preface to an account of his trial which was published in pamphlet form. In it he asked the public to reflect upon his "political trial" for a political crime and to decide whether the men who sanctioned the proceedings were fit subjects for re-election. The leading lesson that his trial taught, Cooper declared, was that the public should "hold their tongues, and restrain their pens, on the subject of politics." Not content with issuing this appeal, the prisoner also addressed a long letter to Judge Chase, which was widely circulated in the Jeffersonian journals. Condemning as a hardship and an absurdity the court's insistence on strict legal evidence in a political trial, Cooper also accused Chase of "improper conduct" in his charge to the jury. The Supreme Court justice, he said, had no right to argue the case against the defendant in a criminal trial, to notice and correct the omissions of the government's prosecutor, to dwell upon circumstances aggravating the alleged crime, or to let the jury perceive a bias in the mind of the court. Although these actions might have been applauded by the high-ranking Federalists attending the trial, Cooper thought the public would take another view.[43]

The events which preceded Cooper's trial, the court proceedings, his sentencing, and the subsequent events received considerable attention in both Federalist and Republican newspapers. The administration journals gave it fuller attention than did the *Aurora*, whose editor was still hiding out from the Senate's process server. Yet the *Aurora* did not avoid the issue completely. When General Stevens

---

[42] *Ibid.*, 50–52. Cooper was to post $1,000, and two sureties were to post $500 each. The standard accounts give May 1, 1800, as the date of sentencing, but April 24 is correct. See the *Gazette of the United States*, April 24, 1800, and the *Aurora*, April 25, 1800.

[43] Cooper to Chase, Prison of Philadelphia, May 1, 1800, *Cooper's Trial*, app. VI, 58–64. Even before his trial he foresaw that this insistence on strictly legal proof would work to the disadvantage of the accused. See his essay on the Sedition Law, *Political Essays* (2d ed., 1800), 10–11. During his trial he observed that such strictness would end "all political discussion in promiscuous society." *Cooper's Trial*, 21.

Thomson Mason, the Virginia senator, greeted Cooper with a fraternal hug after he had been sentenced, a Federalist paper accused him of shaking hands with the prisoner in "the very face of justice." The *Aurora* observed tartly that "the court ought not to be offended with the conduct of General Mason, as it was expressive of all the respect and veneration he feels for their honors." [44] Indeed, Senator Mason felt so strongly about Cooper's trial that he denounced it in a letter to Governor James Monroe of Virginia as a "cruel and abominable persecution." The courts in the Middle and New England states, he declared, were stretching the doctrines of treason and sedition to "a most extraordinary length." "They seemed determined to suppress all political enquiry," the Virginian concluded, "conscious that the conduct of their friend J.[ohn] A.[dams] cannot stand a fair scrutiny." [45]

Although the Republicans deplored Cooper's imprisonment, the Federalist papers made gleeful references to the "seditious convict," "the noted Cooper." The *Philadelphia Gazette* gloated over the difficulties of the "wight of Northumberland" but thought that he could console himself by taking advantage of his unexampled opportunities to ruminate upon liberty while deprived of it. [46] Pickering's private secretary, Joseph Dennie, former editor of the Federalist *Farmer's Weekly Museum* in Walpole, New Hampshire, and later editor of the literary *Port Folio* in Philadelphia, celebrated Cooper's conviction in a poetic dialogue entitled "Prison Eclogue." [47] In a discussion between Priestley and Cooper, Dennie represented Priestley as wondering why Cooper was the only Democratic-Republican writer in jail:

> I wonder more that *thou* art here alone.
> Sedition stalks so boldly through the State,
> Lampoons distract, and libels irritate.

[44] *Aurora*, reprinted in the Richmond *Examiner*, May 13, 1800.

[45] Mason to Monroe, April 29, 1800, Monroe Papers, VI, 958 (Lib. Cong.). The only treason trials under the Constitution up to that time had taken place in Pennsylvania. For the trial of the Whiskey Insurgents, see Wharton, *State Trials*, 102–184; for those of Fries and the Northampton Insurgents, see *ibid.*, 458–651.

[46] *Philadelphia Gazette*, May 8, 1800.

[47] Dennie was an ardent Federalist who wrote political and moral essays under the name of "The Lay Preacher." Because of his outstanding literary style and his services to the Federalist cause, he was invited to Philadelphia in 1799 as Pickering's private secretary. He also obtained an editorial position on the *Gazette of the United States*, long the semiofficial organ of the high Federalists. See George F. Whicher, "Joseph Dennie," *DAB*, V, 325.

Adjourn'ed the Senate, braving see Duane
Sneaks into town, and heads his Greens again;
The ribald, Callender can hardly meet
A prison's shelter (for the wretch must eat.) [48]

Dennie then had Cooper reply that he was not unhappy that the president had at last granted his application for a place. From his cell, which was furnished with a quill, Cooper reasoned, "I can blaspheme, or libel, as I will."

Shortly after Cooper was imprisoned, his Federalist friends of Northumberland and vicinity began circulating a petition which asked President Adams to pardon their neighbor. Cooper thanked them but said that he would not leave prison through the acceptance of a favor from the president. Referring to the statement which the chief executive made when Reverend Ogden presented the petition for the pardon of Congressman Matthew Lyon, Cooper asserted that he agreed with Mr. Adams that "repentance should precede forgiveness." He would refuse a presidential pardon "until I receive myself, & hear that Dr. *Priestley* has received a satisfactory acknowledgement from Mr. Adams, of the impropriety of his conduct to us." Commenting on the sudden conversion of the Federalists to moderation, Cooper warned that his pardon would be nothing more than a campaign trick and therefore reminded the administration that he would not be "the voluntary cats-paw of electioneering clemency." [49]

Thus he refused absolutely to accept any pardon or take any action which might be interpreted as a confession that he had committed a criminal act. He had intended to censure the conduct of the president before he was jailed, and he continued to censure it once he was behind bars. The dateline "Philadelphia Prison" marked a number of communiqués from Cooper exhorting the Republicans to greater efforts against the Federalists. Only a few days before his release from jail, the *Gazette of the United States* ridiculed Cooper

[48] The poem is reprinted in *Porcupine's Works*, XII, 112–118. Dennie's official title in the State Department was "Inspector of Records"; see the *Bee*, Oct. 16, 1799. For his extracurricular literary efforts while serving in this capacity, Dennie was ribbed unmercifully by the Republican press. The *Bee*, Nov. 13, 1799, listed some of his duties as follows: "Censor general of republican politics," "Inspector general of newspapers," "Poet Laureat to his infallibility," and "Biographical dauber and varnisher."

[49] Cooper to the editor, Prison of Philadelphia, May 10, 1800, *Aurora*, May 17, 1800.

for manufacturing columns for Duane's *Aurora* from the federal prison.[50]

When John Hall, the federal marshal, notified Cooper on October 8, 1800, that his term was up and that he could leave prison, the prisoner observed that he had not paid his fine but expected to do so that day. After Hall assured him that he could pay it when convenient, they left the jail together and met Israel Israel, the Republican sheriff of Philadelphia who had posted bond for Cooper when he was indicted. While still on the street, Cooper received from the postman the letter which he had expected; it contained a draft for $400 drawn on Abel Humphries at two months. Cooper remained with Hall while Israel took the draft to have Humphries discount it, but that obdurate Federalist refused to be a party to Cooper's release. After Stephen Girard had come to Israel's rescue by discounting the draft and refusing to charge any interest, Cooper paid the money to Hall.[51] After the fine was paid, he was bound over to good behavior for twelve months.[52]

Upon his release Cooper at once resumed his warfare with the Federalists. Although he had been unable to "repay insolence with Chastisement" while in prison, two days after he gained freedom he wrote the editor of the *Gazette of the United States* that he would do himself justice when he could do so without injury to the friends who were his sureties. Coming from a fellow lately arrived in the United States, the editor replied bitterly, Cooper's letter was "unparalleled impudence." More than that it was a threat by a "Foreign fugitive" against an American editor, a native of Pennsylvania. The letter, he continued, was a typical trick of the Jacobins to prevent exposure of their infamy. When the liberty of the press was used to expose Democrats, those lovers of liberty tried to intimidate Federalist editors with threats of vengeance. The editor pre-

[50] *Gazette of the United States*, Oct. 8, 1800. T. B. Adams informed the first lady that Cooper was using the pseudonym of "Constitutionalist" in the *Aurora*. See his letter to Abigail Adams, Phila., Oct. 5, 1800, Adams Papers, VIII, 207 (Mass. Hist. Soc.).

[51] The date of Cooper's release is given in Thomas Leiper to Jefferson, Phila., Oct. 9, 1800, Jefferson Papers (Mass. Hist. Soc.). For the details on the payment of the fine, see Cooper to Mahlon Dickerson, Columbia, S.C., March 13, 1830, "Letters of Dr. Thomas Cooper, 1825–1832," *American Historical Review*, 6 (1900–01), 733. Also see McMaster, *The Life and Times of Stephen Girard, Mariner and Merchant* (Philadelphia and London, 1918), I, 397–398, and House Report No. 244, 22C, 1S.

[52] Cooper to C. P. Wayne, editor, Oct. 10, 1800, *Gazette of the United States*, Oct. 11, 1800. He mentions that friends had posted surety.

dicted that if Jefferson and his supporters should win the election, "no Editor will risk the publication of Truth, when it is against *them;*—for if he do he will most assuredly risk assassination." He admonished all friends of good government to save the country from a Republican "reign of terror" by voting the Federalist ticket on October 15 when Pennsylvania went to the polls.[53]

Just as the Federalists continued to belabor Cooper for electioneering effect, so too did the Republicans point to his ordeal for political purposes. His emergence "from *Chase's* repository of republicans" was marked by two public celebrations in Philadelphia, where he was toasted as "the conspicuous victim of the sedition law, the friend of science, and the able advocate of universal liberty." Warmed by "the enlivening grape," the Democratic-Republicans also drank triumphant toasts to predictions that the coming election would end with "the packers of juries unkennelled" and result in "the United States administered by republicans, and as a republic forever." [54]

Cooper's trial vividly illustrated the views of the Federalists as to free speech and their conception of the role of the people in a republic. Both political parties agreed that the American government rested on the consent of the people. The Federalists, however, contended that the election of officials by the people served as a continuing vote of confidence in those leaders. Once these officers were chosen, they were the "constituted authorities" who ran public affairs until the next election. To find fault with the "authorities" whom the American people had chosen was to undermine public confidence in the government. By identifying the administration with the government, and the government with the Constitution, the Federalists concluded that criticism of their administration was an attempt to subvert the Constitution and to overthrow the government. It was arrogant, therefore, of Cooper or anyone else to criticize the president and to claim to be wiser than he in formulating

[53] "An American Republican" reported in the *Gazette of the United States,* Oct. 13, 1800, that the Jacobin ticket for Pennsylvania "was originally formed by a foreign Cooper, while in Goal [*sic*], and has undergone no alterations since it came from him." William Rawle, Cooper's prosecutor, headed the Philadelphia committee of correspondence directing the Federalist publicity campaign in the election of 1800. See his appeal to the voters in *ibid.,* Oct. 14, 1800. The foreman and two of the members of the federal grand jury which indicted Cooper were running on the Federalist ticket. See *ibid.,* Oct. 15, 1800. A member of the trial jury was also a Federalist candidate for the common council. *Ibid.* The grand jurors are listed in *Cooper's Trial,* app. I, 52, and the petit jurors in *ibid.,* 15.

[54] *Aurora,* Nov. 5, 1800; *Palladium,* Nov. 4, 1800.

public policy. Such criticism was not only in contempt of a superior who had been elevated by popular choice to the highest office in the land; it was contemptuous of the people themselves who had elected him. To bring the president into disrepute was criminal because the stability of the government depended on public confidence.

The Republicans of 1800 agreed that the American government rested on the people's consent, but they widened the concept of "public confidence" to coincide with that of "public opinion." Thus public officials could lose the confidence of the public as well as gain it. Public opinion was in a continuous process of formulation and could be constitutionally registered in speeches or in the press. The public could examine the conduct of the "constituted authorities" and could denounce it as well as praise it. The people were free to discuss the actions of their elected agents and to withdraw their confidence at the next election if they thought it proper.

Thomas Cooper's trial demonstrated that the Federalists, who claimed to be the founders and perpetual guardians of the Constitution, would deny to their political opponents, who wished to administer the government established by that charter, the means by which it had been adopted—peaceful persuasion. Although the federal Constitution had worked a revolution in American government, the Federalists now condemned as "revolutionary" a party which sought to gain control of the government by constitutional means. Thus the trial itself provides an outstanding example of the way in which they used the Sedition Act of 1798 as the instrument for suppressing political opposition to Federalist authority.[55]

[55] In a note to the letter of John Adams which endorsed the action against Cooper, Charles Francis Adams says, "There can be no doubt that this prosecution was a mistake. The fact of his having been a disappointed applicant for office would have been a far more effective instrument to rely upon, in order to neutralize his influence." *Adams' Works,* IX, 14n.

CHAPTER XV

Sedition in the Old Dominion: James T. Callender and The Prospect before Us

Take your choice . . . between Adams, war and
beggary, and Jefferson, peace and competency.
—JAMES T. CALLENDER

WRITING to Vice-President Jefferson early in 1800, Governor
James Monroe of Virginia predicted that "an attempt will be made
to carry the Sedition Law here, as an electioneering trick, in the
course of the summer." [1] In the midst of the bitterly contested presidential campaign between Adams and Jefferson, the Richmond
Examiner confirmed the governor's worst fears when it announced
in May that "the force of the SEDITION LAW has at length
reached Virginia." [2] The last proceeding instituted under that act
and the only one prosecuted in a Southern state, the trial of James
Thomson Callender was tied directly to the electoral contest between the Federalists and the Democratic-Republicans.

---

[1] Monroe to Jefferson, Richmond, May 25, 1800, Stanislaus Murray Hamilton,
ed., *The Writings of James Monroe* (New York and London, 1900), III (1796–
1802), 180.

This chapter is an expansion of an article which appeared in *The Journal of
Southern History*, 20 (1954), 157–182.

[2] Richmond *Examiner*, May 27, 1800, reprinted in the *Albany Register*, June
10, 1800.

Supreme Court Justice Samuel Chase, who presided at Callender's trial, made his circuit ride of 1800 a sustained effort to curb Democratic electioneering methods and writers. In the trial of Thomas Cooper, he had agreed with the government prosecutor that a conviction was necessary in order to set an example for the critics of the Adams administration. In the same month he presided at the second trial of John Fries for treason and so outraged the defense counsel, William Lewis, the foremost Federalist lawyer in Philadelphia, and Alexander Dallas, the leading Republican advocate, that they withdrew from the case, leaving Fries undefended. Less than a month after Chase sentenced Fries to be "hanged by the neck until dead," President Adams issued a full pardon.[3]

Callender's case was the most striking instance of judicial prosecution conducted by Justice Chase. In May, 1800, the "hanging judge," as the Republicans called him, swung onto the Southern Circuit, where he initiated the sedition proceeding against the Richmond writer. According to Chase, the principal object of the prosecution was to demonstrate that the laws of the United States could be enforced in the Old Dominion,[4] one of the two states whose legislatures had denounced the Alien and Sedition Laws as unconstitutional. Because it crystallized Republican hostility to the federal judiciary and later led directly to Chase's impeachment, this trial has come to be regarded as the most important of all the cases brought under the Sedition Law of 1798.[5]

Callender's writings had long been an irritant to the authorities. In 1792 he had published The Political Progress of Great Britain, which led to his indictment in Edinburgh in 1793. To escape his trial for seditious criticism of the government, he fled to the United States. The British authorities promptly outlawed him.[6] After his arrival in America, the Scottish immigrant continued his political writing, becoming a pronounced partisan of the Republicans. In 1797 he published an account of the election of 1796, which was

[3] Trial of Northampton Insurgents, Wharton, State Trials, 641.

[4] Richmond Examiner, June 6, 1800, reprinted in the Albany Register, June 17, 1800.

[5] "The Trial of James Thompson Callender, for a Seditious Libel" is reported in Wharton, State Trials, 688–721, and as Case 14,709 in The Federal Cases, XV, 239–260. The fullest discussion is in Frederick Trevor Hill, Decisive Battles of the Law (New York, 1906), 1–26. The most recent mention is in Claude G. Bowers, "Jefferson and Civil Liberties," Atlantic Monthly, 191 (Jan., 1953), 52–58.

[6] Thomas Bayly Howell and T. J. Howell, Cobbett's Complete Collection of State Trials and Proceedings for High Treason and Other Crimes and Misdemeanors from the Earliest Period . . . (London, 1809–1826), XXII, 79–84.

pro-Jeffersonian in tone and, like most political tracts of the time, vituperative in content.[7] It was his *History of the United States for 1796,* however, which marked him as one of the leading scandal-mongers and hence one of the outstanding pamphleteers of the day. In this work he not only accused Alexander Hamilton of corrupt financial dealings but also uncovered some of that statesman's more intimate personal affairs. To vindicate his public honor, the Federalist leader confessed his private transgressions in a pamphlet answering Callender's.[8]

By 1798 Callender had shifted to the Philadelphia *Aurora,* where he assisted B. F. Bache and William Duane in their assaults on Federalism. His new role, coupled with his pungent pamphleteering, marked him as a special target of the supporters of the Adams administration. Long before the introduction of either the alien or the sedition bills, the Federalist press demanded legal action against Callender. Reflecting the antiforeignism aroused by the diplomatic crisis with France, the *Gazette of the United States* condemned him as the foreign tool of domestic faction and called for the suppression of his writings; the times were too critical to permit vile Jacobin abuse of the administration. Urging the necessity of a sedition law to curb Callender's criticism, the newspaper queried:

In the name of justice and honor, how long are we to tolerate this scum of party filth and beggarly corruption, worked into a form somewhat like a man, to go thus with impunity? Do not the times approach when it must and ought to be dangerous for this wretch, or any other, thus to vilify our country and government, thus to treat with indignity and contempt the whole American people, to teach our enemies to despise us and cast forth unremitting calumny and venom on our constitutional authorities.

"In short," the Federalist organ concluded, Callender, who usually edited the *Aurora* in Bache's absence, had published "sufficient general slander on our country to entitle him to the benefit of the gallows." [9]

[7] *The American Annual Register, or Historical Memoirs of the United States for the Year 1796* (Philadelphia, Jan. 19, 1797).

[8] *The History of the United States for 1796; Including a Variety of Interesting Particulars Relative to the Federal Government Previous to That Period* (Philadelphia, 1797). For Hamilton's reply, see his *Observations on Certain Documents Contained in No. V and VI of "The History of the United States for the Year 1796," in Which the Charge of Speculation against Alexander Hamilton, Late Secretary of the Treasury Is Fully Refuted* (Philadelphia, 1797).

[9] "An American," *Gazette of the United States,* April 24, 1798, reprinted in the New York *Commercial Advertiser,* April 28, 1798.

The repressive measures passed by the Federalists and the acceleration of the newspaper attacks on him made Callender apprehensive of his continued safety in Philadelphia. To avoid the Alien Law, he became a naturalized citizen.[10] As the Sedition Act moved through Congress, he made preparations to leave the nation's capital. His fears were increased when Bache was arrested even before the enactment of the Sedition Law. On July 13, 1798, the day before President Adams signed that fateful act, a Federalist paper in Philadelphia announced that "Envoy Callender left this city on a tour to the westward"—destination unknown.[11]

Callender's destination, however, was the South, not the West. Leaving his four children with Thomas Leiper, a Republican leader in Pennsylvania, he fled to Virginia, where he sought refuge with Senator Stevens Thomson Mason.[12] In August the administration press circulated a report that the former assistant on the "seditious, disorganizing and infamous *Aurora*" had been picked up near Leesburg on suspicion of being a vagrant who had escaped from the Baltimore wheelbarrow gang.[13] When Senator Mason secured the writer's release by producing his naturalization papers and swearing to his good character, *Porcupine's Gazette* ran a denunciatory article on "Mason the Senator and Callender, the Runaway." [14] The *Aurora,* whose editor was then awaiting trial for sedition under a common law indictment, replied that "the whole crew of snivling tory scribblers seems to have resusitated upon the news that *Callender* has removed to Virginia." [15]

Fearing for his safety, Callender refrained from writing for several months after he fled Philadelphia. As opposition to the Sedition Law illustrated its growing unpopularity, the author decided that he might safely resume his political writings. He was certain that by the spring of 1799 "the public mind will be much riper than

---

[10] Jefferson to Madison, Phila., June 7, 1798, *Jefferson's Writings,* VIII, 267. Callender later wrote that in consequence of the Alien Act, "I have been menaced with prosecution and imprisonment, by David Call, that sorry understrapper of Federal usurpation." Callender, *The Prospect before Us,* quoted in Worthington Chauncey Ford, ed., *Thomas Jefferson and James Thomson Callender, 1798–1802* (Brooklyn, 1897), 9n.

[11] New York *Daily Advertiser,* July 17, 1798.

[12] Callender to Jefferson, Raspberry Plain, Sept. 22, 1798, Ford, *Jefferson and Callender,* 10. Also see Jefferson to Monroe, Washington, July 15, 1802, *Jefferson's Writings* (Bergh ed.), X, 331.

[13] *Alexandria Gazette* (Virginia), reprinted in the New York *Daily Advertiser,* Aug. 13, 1798.

[14] *Porcupine's Gazette,* reprinted in *Porcupine's Works,* IX, 215, 221.

[15] *Aurora,* Aug. 6, 1798.

it is at present for the admission of truth." For obvious reasons, however, he preferred to publish in Virginia rather than Philadelphia. "I think no judge in this state will, by that time, dare to raise a process of sedition." [16]

In 1799, therefore, Callender moved to Petersburg and joined the staff of the South's leading Republican paper, the Richmond *Examiner*, edited by Meriwether Jones. There he renewed his critical examination of the administration's policies, boosting the circulation of the Virginia journal to a new high.[17] His writings were immediately denounced as seditious by Richmond Federalists who met at the Swan Tavern to form an Anti-Callender Society, a vigilante organization dedicated to silencing the "miscreant." [18] The suspicions of the Federalist vigilantes were shared by Secretary of State Timothy Pickering. As a part of his efforts to apply the sedition statute during the election of 1800, he alerted the federal district attorney in Virginia to scrutinize the "audacious calumnies" in the *Examiner*. The "extreme violence" of this and other Republican newspapers, he wrote, called for "efficient measures to correct them by legal process." To him it was obvious that the Jeffersonian newspaper was "devoted to promote the views of France and of opposition to our own government." Pickering therefore instructed the government prosecutor, Thomas Nelson, to examine every issue of the *Examiner* and to prosecute the parties responsible for the publication of any libelous matter against the federal government or its officers.[19] A month later he reiterated his conviction that the

[16] Callender to Jefferson, Raspberry Plain, Sept. 22, 1798, Ford, *Jefferson and Callender*, 10, 14.

[17] Dumas Malone, "James Thomson Callender," *DAB*, III, 425; Callender to Jefferson, Richmond, Aug. 10, 1799, Ford, *Jefferson and Callender*, 15–16. Callender claimed that 150 new subscribers lifted circulation to more than 800 weekly.

[18] *Virginia Magazine of History and Biography*, 29 (1921), 175. This controversy over the attempt to run Callender out of town may be followed in the *Virginia Argus* (Richmond), Aug. 12, 13, and 17, 1799. For the associators' statement of policy, see *ibid.*, Aug. 12. Jefferson wrote that by meditating violence against Callender, the Federalists were setting an example of "club-law." "The Richmond associators . . . by their committee, have in the public papers avowed their purpose of taking out of the hands of the law the function of declaring who may or may not have free residence among us." The vice-president added that the law would decide if the election of a committee to run Callender out of town was an overt act which brought the associators within the pale of the law. Jefferson to Callender, Monticello, Sept. 6, 1799, *Writings* (Ford ed.), VII, 392–393.

[19] Pickering to Thomas Nelson, Phila., Aug. 12, 1799, Pickering Papers, XI, 611–612 (Mass. Hist. Soc.). Pickering gave the law a very loose construction.

journal was "a virulent *Jacobin,* or if you please, *French-devoted* paper in Richmond," the "champion, or the instrument, of the violent party." Its purpose, he declared, was "to oppose and vilify the federal government and probably to destroy it and dissolve the Union." [20]

While working for the *Examiner,* Callender compiled material for his best-known pamphlet, an electioneering blurb advocating the elevation of Virginia's favorite son to the presidency. In his booklet, *The Prospect before Us,* the author exceeded his promise to give the public "such a Tornado as no Govt [sic] ever got before." [21]

The reign of Mr. Adams [he wrote] has been one continued tempest of malignant passions. As President, he has *never* opened his lips, or lifted his pen without threatening and scolding; the grand object of his administration has been to exasperate the rage of contending parties to calumniate and destroy every man who differs from his opinions. . . . Adams and Washington have since been shaping a series of these paper jobbers into judges and ambassadors, as their whole courage lies in want of shame; these poltroons, without risking a manly and intelligible defence of their own measures, raise an affected yelp against the corruption of the French Directory, as if any corruption would be more venal, more notorious, more execrated than their own. The object of Mr. Adams was to recommend a

---

Although it protected only the president, the Congress, and the government from seditious criticism, he proposed to expand it in practice to protect all federal officers.

[20] Pickering to William Bingham, Trenton, Sept. 22, 1799, *ibid.,* XII, 96. Since the district attorney of Virginia resided in Yorktown, Pickering suggested that he deputize a Richmond Federalist "of approved talents and firmness" to maintain an on-the-spot check of the *Examiner.* At the recommendation of Supreme Court Justice Bushrod Washington, Pickering suggested Daniel Call as special assistant to Nelson. See Pickering to Nelson, *ibid.,* XI, 611–612; Call to George Washington, Richmond, Jan. 10, 1799, Washington Papers, CCXCIV (Lib. Cong.); and Call to Jefferson, Richmond, Aug. 26, 1799, Jefferson Papers (Mass. Hist. Soc.).

[21] Callender to Jefferson, Raspberry Plain, Nov. 19, 1798, Ford, *Jefferson and Callender,* 14. While preparing this pamphlet, Callender occasionally received encouragement from Jefferson; see Jefferson to Callender, Sept. 6, and Oct. 6, 1799, *Jefferson's Writings* (Ford ed.), VII, 392–393 and 393–394; Jefferson to George Jefferson, Oct. 24, 1800, and George Jefferson to Jefferson, Nov. 3, 1800, Jefferson Papers (Mass. Hist. Soc.). Jefferson later claimed that his donations to Callender were charities to one who solicited support, rather than proofs of his approbation of Callender's writings. See Jefferson to Monroe, July 15, 1802, *Jefferson's Writings* (Bergh ed.), X, 330–332. For an unsympathetic account of Jefferson's relations with Callender, see Ford, *Jefferson and Callender.* For a more generous appraisal, see Frank L. Mott, *Jefferson and the Press* (Baton Rouge, La., 1943), 32–37.

French war, professedly for the sake of supporting American commerce, but in reality for the sake of yoking us into an alliance with the British tyrant.

Callender also called Adams a "hoary headed incendiary" and inserted this electioneering advice:

You will then make your choice between paradise and perdition; you will choose between the man who has deserted and reversed all his principles, and that man whose own example strengthens all his laws, that man whose predictions, like those of Henry, had been converted into history. You will choose between that man whose life is unspotted by crime, and that man whose hands are reeking with the blood of the poor, friendless Connecticut sailor: I see the tear of indignation starting on your cheeks! You anticipate the name of John Adams. . . . Take your choice, then, between Adams, war and beggary, and Jefferson, peace and competency.[22]

It was neither District Attorney Nelson nor his assistant who called Pickering's attention to Callender's campaign contributions, but a vigilant Federalist place-seeker. Although the first volume of *The Prospect before Us* was not published until January, 1800, John B. Walton, an applicant for a federal appointment, reported to Pickering on December 23, 1799, that the book was in press. As the pamphlet contained many invectives against President Adams, the correspondent doubted that the author would circulate it in Philadelphia. Walton therefore promised to forward a copy to the secretary as soon as it was published. He despaired of crushing the Republican faction in Virginia and bringing them to justice, however, because both the courts and the legislature were "so crowded with Jacobines and French Partisans, that the attempt would be vain." To him it seemed that the political principles of James Madison, John Taylor, and William B. Giles, leaders of the Virginia Assembly, led to degeneracy and destruction.[23]

A month later Walton mailed a copy of Callender's book to the secretary of state and called for federal action against the author. The pamphlet was not only "too black and degrading" but also "too much patronized in this Country to be Suffered to go on in their abuse of Government." Callender was such a "dreadful ca-

---

[22] *U.S.* v. *Callender,* Wharton, *State Trials,* 688–690. Henry Adams, *History of the United States of America during the First Administration of Thomas Jefferson* (New York, 1880), I, 324, says that "so far as license was concerned, 'The Prospect Before Us' was a mild libel compared with Cobbett's, Coleman's, and Dennie's cataracts of abuse" against Jefferson.

[23] John B. Walton to Pickering, Richmond, Dec. 23, 1799, Pickering Papers, XXV, 321 (Mass. Hist. Soc.).

lamity," the Virginia correspondent informed Pickering, that the local Federalists would "think it a National blessing if the General Government or Executive would lend their ade [sic] and take him from us." [24]

Although Pickering received The Prospect early in 1800, Callender was not brought to trial until the election campaign reached a high point in June. By March, 1800, he had found four new outlets for his articles. In addition to the Examiner, his writings appeared in the Friend of the People and the National Magazine, both published in Richmond, and in the Petersburg Republican and the Staunton Scourge of Aristocracy. To Jefferson he reported that he was "now firing through five port holes, at once, which is enough for one hand." [25] Increasingly his material was reprinted in the nation's leading Democratic-Republican gazettes. Constantly painting the gloomy prospect before the nation if the Federalists were returned to office, he hammered away at his favorite theme: "Let us, by one grand effort," he urged the electorate, "snatch our country from that bottomless vortex of corruption and perdition which yawn before us." [26]

Despite Walton's prediction that Callender would fear to distribute his pamphlet in Philadelphia, copies of The Prospect before Us were sent to booksellers in the nation's capital, and the audacious author sent a copy to President Adams. When Mrs. Adams saw a copy, she denounced its "abuse and scandel [sic]," and classed "all the host of Callender's lies" with the libels of Thomas Cooper, who had just been convicted of sedition. Both were parties to the Republican campaign to win the election of 1800; the opposition, she declared, was determined to gain power even though that meant "the sacrifice of all that Good men hold dear and sacred." [27]

Writing in the New York Spectator, "Marcellus" endorsed this view. Pointing to Callender's advocacy of Jefferson's candidacy, this writer denounced The Prospect for its unrivaled "falsehood sedition and calumny." The object of Jefferson, "and of course the Jacobins at large," was the destruction of the Constitution. If the Virginian became president, "Marcellus" predicted, he would de-

24 Walton to Pickering, Jan. 19, 1800, ibid., XXVI, 16.

25 Callender to Jefferson, Richmond, March 14, 1800, Ford, Jefferson and Callender, 20.

26 J.[ames] T. C.[allender] to Duane, Richmond, April 27, 1800, Richmond Examiner, May 2, 1800.

27 Callender to Jefferson, Richmond, April 21, 1800, Jefferson Papers, CVI, 18262 (Lib. Cong.); Abigail Adams to Mary Cranch, Phila., May 5, 1800, Mitchell, New Letters, 251–252.

stroy the national debt, the funding system, and the whole scheme of federal finance. One of the chief losers would be crippled veterans of the Revolution, because the government would be without money to pay them. Moreover, Jefferson would appoint Jacobins to replace Federalists and this would lead directly to the destruction of the government. Either the Federalists in the Senate would block confirmation of Jefferson's appointees and the government would collapse, or the Senate would approve the jacobinic Democrats and they would destroy the government.[28]

In an effort to stifle Callender's contribution to this attempted subversion of the Constitution, the Federalists tried to suppress the sale of his pamphlet in Philadelphia. The author condemned the move as a "pitiful and illegal proceeding." "It seems that a message," he reported in the *Examiner,* "has been delivered by authority, to all the booksellers in Philadelphia, forbiding [sic] them to sell the work." Seemingly safe in his Virginia sanctuary, he added a specific challenge to the authorities: "If the author has afforded room for *an action,* do prosecute him. But do not take such pitiful *behind the door measures* in order to stop the circulation of truth." [29]

The Federalists quickly accepted Callender's defiant invitation. It was Justice Chase, however, rather than Secretary Pickering who set the trial in motion. The judge had long been of the opinion that "a licentious press is the bane of freedom, and the peril of Society." [30] While en route to Virginia on his first tour of the Southern Circuit, he held court in Maryland, where his friend, Luther Martin, the state attorney general, learned that he was going to Richmond and gave him a copy of Callender's book so that he might "amuse himself with it on the road, and afterwards make what use of it he pleased." Martin, sometimes called the "Federalist Bulldog," had underlined many passages which he thought were offensive and libelous.[31]

[28] *Spectator,* April 23 and 26, 1800.

[29] Richmond *Examiner,* May 9, 1800. When copies of Callender's *Prospect* failed to reach its subscribers, the editor observed that it usually occurred in "those counties where the Post-Masters were *aristocrats.*"

[30] Chase to James McHenry, Dec. 4, 1796, Bernard C. Steiner, ed., *The Life and Correspondence of James McHenry, Secretary of War under Washington and Adams* (Cleveland, 1907), 203.

[31] Testimony of Luther Martin, *Report of the Trial of the Honorable Samuel Chase . . . Taken in Short Hand, by Charles Evans . . .* (Baltimore, 1805), 63. Martin bought two of the books in New York and offered one to Supreme Court Justice Bushrod Washington. The judge, however, bought a personal copy. Also see the testimony of John Thompson Mason, *ibid.,* 43. This report is cited hereafter as the *Chase Trial.*

Judge Chase, whose temper was naturally "quick and warm," later said that "his indignation was strongly" excited "by Callender's atrocious and profligate libel." Before he left Baltimore he decided that *The Prospect before Us* was a violation of the Sedition Law. In a jocular conversation at Annapolis he remarked that he would take the book to Richmond and punish Callender, if Virginia was not "utterly depraved" or if a jury of honest men could be found there. Asserting that he was as great a friend to the liberty of the press as any man, he insisted that he would teach Virginia lawyers the difference between the liberty and the licentiousness of the press. Thus, when Chase headed for Virginia, he left with the determination "to enforce the laws of his country." En route to Richmond he showed *The Prospect* to James Triplett, who informed him that Callender had been arrested in Virginia once under the vagrant law. It was a pity, the judge replied, that they had not hanged the rascal.[32]

When Judge Chase arrived in Richmond on May 21, the political pot was boiling.[33] The *Virginia Federalist* had leveled a continual attack on Callender ever since his book had appeared, always referring to him as "a renegado, who, some years ago, narrowly escaped the gallows of his own country." [34] Callender replied in kind, accusing the Federalist editor of misquoting passages from the book and challenging him to prove his charges.[35] Seeking to link the pamphleteer directly with Jefferson, the Federalist organ announced early in May that Callender was staying at Monticello. On May 16 the *Examiner* denied this rumor and reported that Callender was residing in Petersburg. Thus when the grand jury met on May 23 to receive from Judge Chase the charge in which he spoke of offenses against the Sedition Law, they knew the whereabouts of Callender.[36]

[32] *The Answer and Pleas of Samuel Chase . . . to the Articles of Impeachment* (Washington City, 1805), 60; *Chase Trial,* 219–223, 63–64, 44.

[33] John Randolph later asserted that federal troops "were brought to Richmond and kept there during the trial of Callender"; see his speech as manager of the impeachment trial of Chase. *Chase Trial,* 260. See the *Virginia Magazine of History and Biography,* 29 (1921), 117, for a statement that there was "a regiment of regular infantry stationed in barracks in Richmond or Manchester. The officers, who appear to have been all Virginians, were Federalists to a man."

[34] *Virginia Federalist* (Richmond), April 9, 1800. A political controversy between Meriwether Jones, editor of the *Examiner,* and James Rind, editor of the *Federalist,* led to a duel in Richmond. Rind was slightly injured. See the *Albany Register,* May 9, 1800.

[35] Advertisement dated April 11, 1800, *Examiner,* April 29, 1800.

[36] *Examiner,* May 16 and June 6, 1800.

On May 24 the grand jury returned a presentment against Callender, and the district attorney drew up an indictment which the jury approved that evening.[37] Although the presentment referred to Callender as the author of *The Prospect before Us*, the indictment did not name the book. Instead, twenty offensive passages were extracted from it, and Callender was charged with maliciously designing to defame President Adams by writing and publishing the words with intent to bring him into contempt and to excite the hatred of the good people of the United States toward him. A second count also recited the twenty excerpts and charged the author with the separate offense of causing or procuring these false, scandalous, and malicious statements to be printed and published. Like all sedition indictments this one used the standard epithets to describe the accused as "a person of wicked, depraved, evil disposed, disquiet and turbulent mind and disposition." [38]

Although the case obviously involved a clash between state and national authority, Governor James Monroe made it clear that he would allow no interference in the orderly enforcement of the Sedition Law in the Old Dominion. In the period between Callender's indictment and his arrest, the governor wrote that he hoped "the people will behave with dignity on the occasion and give no pretext for comments to their discredit. If I could suppose the contrary I would take proper steps to aid in bringing him forth. I mean to prevent any popular meeting to the contrary." [39]

The *Examiner* also urged moderation as the guide in the pending legal controversy:

Let us now show our calumniators, by a perfect obedience to this law, which we believe not only to be unconstitutional, but inexpedient; that republicans, while they oppose by every constitutional effort, obnoxious systems of administration and unpopular laws, are always willing to be governed by the acts of a majority. Virginia . . . will patiently expect the return of reason, truth, and liberty; and with them, that confidence which should forever subsist throughout the United States. . . . Let us then be temperate—he who cannot submit to a few years of incarceration for the good of his country, degrades the Dignity of Man.[40]

[37] The grand jury presentment and the manuscript indictment, signed by Thomas Nelson, are in *U.S. v. James T. Callender*, U.S. Circuit Court, Virginia District, Ended Cases, 1800 (Va. State Lib.).

[38] *U.S. v. Callender*, Indictment, *Chase Trial*, app. IV, 48–53.

[39] Governor Monroe to Jefferson, Richmond, May 25, 1800, *Monroe's Writings*, III, 180.

[40] Richmond *Examiner*, May 27, 1800, reprinted in *Albany Register*, June 10, 1800.

The warrant for Callender's arrest was sworn out on May 24, but he was not apprehended immediately and Judge Chase expressed his fear "that we shall not be able to get the damned rascal in this court." [41] Three days later, however, Callender was arrested in Petersburg and brought before the Supreme Court justice, who released him on $400 bail pending trial.[42]

The Callender case gained notoriety even before it came to trial. When the Republican papers learned of Judge Chase's role in bringing about the indictment, they lashed him severely. His sudden departure from Philadelphia in May, the *Aurora* claimed, could now be explained. Duane reported that Luther Martin had given a copy of *The Prospect* to the judge, "who set off for *Richmond* to wreck vengeance on Callender. A jury conveniently *packed* by a federal *Marshal*," the *Aurora* continued, "has found a bill under the Sedition Law against *Callender*, and *Judge Chase* swears Callender must go into prison, for he cannot get the *official documents* to prove all he has published, though nobody doubts a word of what he has stated—as fair calculations." [43]

The people of Virginia, who had furnished Callender with refuge for two years, became his ardent champions. By virtue of their hatred of the Sedition Law, the state legislature twice had condemned that statute as unconstitutional. In keeping with the assertion in the Virginia Resolutions that the states possessed the right "to interpose for arresting the evil, and for maintaining within their respective limits the authorities, rights, and liberties appertaining to them," Governor Monroe asked Jefferson, author of the Kentucky Resolutions, if it would be "proper for the Executive to employ counsel to defend him [Callender], and supporting the law, give an eclat to a vindication of the principles of the State?" Even before the newspaperman's arrest, Jefferson replied that Callender "should be substantially defended, whether in the first stage by public interference"—that is, by state-employed counsel—"or private contributions." [44]

Both methods were utilized in Callender's behalf. The citizens of Caroline County, under the leadership of Colonel John Taylor

[41] Testimony of James Triplett, *Chase Trial*, 44.

[42] Testimony of William Marshall, clerk of the Virginia Circuit Court, *ibid.*, 64. Marshall was the brother of John Marshall, who had succeeded Pickering as secretary of state in Adams' Cabinet. For Marshall's order to D. M. Randolph, district marshal, see *U.S.* v. *Callender*, 1800 (Va. State Lib.).

[43] *Aurora*, June 2, 1800.

[44] Monroe to Jefferson, Richmond, May 25, 1800, *Monroe's Writings*, III, 180; Jefferson to Monroe, May 26, 1800, *Jefferson's Writings* (Ford ed.), IX, 136–137.

of Caroline, leader in the Virginia Assembly in 1800 and former United States senator, raised over $100 for the accused writer, who was "poor and has three infant children who live by his daily labor." The subscription paper declared that Callender's cause was "closely allied to the preservation of the Constitution, and to the freedom of public opinion; and that he ought to be comforted in his bonds." [45] The defense counsel also contributed their services. Philip Norborne Nicholas, attorney general of Virginia, William Wirt, clerk of the House of Delegates and the rising leader of the Virginia bar, and George Hay, son-in-law of Governor Monroe and later Nicholas' successor as attorney general, volunteered to defend Callender and, as Hay said, "the cause of the Constitution." [46]

On May 28 Callender pleaded not guilty to the charge, and his counsel filed an affidavit asking for a continuance of the trial till the November court term because of the absence of material witnesses and documents. Even if the persons and documents were readily available, his attorneys argued, they needed time to prepare a defense against the twenty charges contained in each of the two counts. Judge Chase repeated his statement, made during the Cooper trial, that every person who published an alleged libel ought always to have on hand the documents which would prove the truth of the assertions. [47] He therefore ruled that the affidavit was insufficient to procure a continuance, but he agreed to postpone the trial for five days. On June 2 the defendant was granted another day's postponement pending the arrival of William B. Giles.

Containing all the stuff of which drama is made, Callender's case excited tremendous interest. It promised to be a head-on clash between Republicans and Federalists, between bar and bench, between state and federal authority. On the day set for the newsman's

45 Boston *Independent Chronicle*, July 10, 1800, quoted by Beveridge, *Marshall*, III, 38–39.

46 *Chase Trial*, 37. Because of his belief that the Sedition Law was unconstitutional, Hay said that he had decided to defend any person who should be prosecuted in Virginia for a violation of that law. Hay had already written a powerful attack on the Sedition Act in January, 1799. See Hortensius [George Hay], *An Essay on the Liberty of the Press Respectfully Inscribed to the Republican Printers throughout the United States* (Philadelphia, printed 1799, Richmond, reprinted by Samuel Pleasants, Junior, 1803).

47 William Marshall, *Chase Trial*, 64. In this affidavit, Callender swore that Timothy Pickering, William B. Giles, Stevens T. Mason, William Gardner, Tench Coxe, Judge Bee, and General Blackburn were witnesses essential to his defense and set forth what he hoped to prove by each one. The affidavit was printed in the Richmond *Examiner*, June 4, 1800, and reprinted in the *Albany Register*, June 17, 1800. Also see Wharton, *State Trials*, 690–691.

appearance, the courtroom "was thronged with spectators from every quarter." [48] Before the trial began, the defense counsel again renewed their motion for a continuance until the next court's session. Hay argued that the court had declared Giles's testimony to be pertinent when it granted a delay the day before. But he relied chiefly on his contention that he and his associates had not had time to prepare a defense. The usual practice in Virginia on an indictment for a misdemeanor, he asserted, was for the accused to appear at the succeeding court, thus giving him time to ready a defense. He had known of the case for only seven days, Hay continued, and in that short period he had not had time to examine the doctrine of seditious libels on government officials. He was not ashamed, he said, to acknowledge his ignorance of the law of seditious libels because, fortunately for the people of Virginia, no case had required lawyers to study the subject. He urged that an immediate trial would be of no consequence to the United States government or to the good name of President Adams; the chief executive's reputation rested on the opinion of the people and could never be affected by the abuse of a single individual, especially "an obscure and friendless foreigner." [49]

The Sedition Law, according to Hay, was not intended to deal with abuse, erroneous deductions, or opinions, but only with "fact falsely and maliciously asserted." He argued that a statement of fact was the assertion of that which was susceptible of proof by "direct and positive evidence; everything else was opinion." Yet Callender had been indicted for political opinion. What sort of evidence, the lawyer asked, would be necessary to prove that the reign of Mr. Adams had been one continued tempest of malignant passions. This assertion was open to endless argument; it was one on which men of good sense and upright principles might well disagree. Yet if an assertion was incapable of being proved or disproved, "the privilege of giving the truth in evidence was a nullity. A jury of one party would not believe it when given; a jury of the other party would not require it to be given."

Judge Chase interrupted Callender's counsel to deny that the charges in the indictment were merely opinions and not facts falsely stated. Discarding judicial restraint, he bluntly branded Callender's book as false; the defendant's bad intentions seemed "sufficiently

[48] *Virginia Gazette*, June, 1800, reprinted in Ford, *Jefferson and Callender*, 23.
[49] Wharton, *State Trials*, 692–695. Although Callender was foreign born, he was a naturalized citizen. That he was neither friendless nor obscure is illustrated by his trial.

obvious" to the judge. "Must there be a departure from common sense," he asked, "to find a construction favorable to the traverser?" Hay's construction of the Sedition Law, the judge continued, "admits the publication, but denies its criminality. If the traverser certainly published that defamatory paper, read it and consider it. . . . The question here is, with what intent the traverser published these charges?" Despite Nicholas' protest that a verdict of guilty would not satisfy the public mind of Callender's guilt, especially if he were defended by unprepared counsel and deprived of the testimony of absent witnesses, Judge Chase ordered the marshal to call the jury. Although there is conflicting evidence as to whether or not the Supreme Court justice instructed the federal marshal to strike from the jury panel "any of those creatures or people called democrats," [50] the fact remains that the trial jury consisted exclusively of Federalists.[51]

In his introductory remarks to the jury, Thomas Nelson, the government prosecutor, clearly shifted the burden of proof from his own shoulders to those of the defense counsel. The jury had to find Callender guilty if, from an examination of the internal evidence of the pamphlet itself, they believed that it was not a free, candid, and wholly truthful discussion of constitutional subjects, real grievances, or political principles and opinions. Although he informed the jury that they could not convict if Callender's statements were true, he pointed out that the defense had to prove the truth of all the "facts and allegations" made by the accused. Nor did he think "the extremest ingenuity" could show that the statements could be given any other construction than that ascribed by the indictment.[52]

This was the clearest statement of presumptive guilt made by any district attorney prosecuting a case under the Sedition Law. The indictment which accused Callender of making seditious statements with bad intentions was presumed true until proved untrue

[50] John Heath, a member of the bar of the Richmond circuit, swore that he heard Judge Chase issue the instructions to the federal marshal, David M. Randolph. *Chase Trial,* 43–44. Randolph swore that he had never received such instructions from the judge. *Ibid.,* 68.

[51] William Marshall, clerk of the Circuit Court, swore that all of the trial jury were opposed to Callender "in political sentiments"; *ibid.,* 66. For the defense counsel's challenges to the array and to the individual jurors, see Wharton, *State Trials,* 695–697, and the court reporter's record of the trial sworn to by David Robertson in *Chase Trial,* 73–94. The jurors are listed in the Richmond *Examiner,* June 4, 1800.

[52] Wharton, *State Trials,* 697–698.

by the defendant. Instead of the government having to prove false-hood or "bad intent," the defense had to disprove the charges, and even the prosecutor doubted that the most ingenious person could do that. This concept that the accused was guilty until proved innocent can only be described as "guilt by accusation." It left only one fact to be proved by the prosecution—whether or not the accused was the author and publisher of the seditious libel.

District Attorney Nelson therefore first proposed to introduce witnesses to prove that Callender published *The Prospect before Us*, but Hay warned that some of them would incriminate themselves by their testimony. The Sedition Law applied to anyone who printed or aided and abetted the publication of seditious remarks. Judge Chase, however, brushed aside this objection by pledging that the government would not prosecute any of the witnesses introduced by the government attorney.[53]

After nine witnesses had testified that Callender had written and published the book,[54] Nelson proposed to introduce the book into evidence so that the charges in the indictment might be compared with the passages in *The Prospect before Us*. Hay immediately objected that the book could not be introduced in support of the indictment because it was nowhere mentioned in the two counts. Ever since the beginning of the "unhappy prosecutions for libels" in England, he contended, the invariable practice had been to describe by name the book from which libelous passages were extracted. Thus the publication of the book, even though it contained fifty offensive passages, was but one act and subject to but one prosecution. Under this rule, if the government tried to indict the accused for the same or any other passages in the same book, the decision of the jury and the court could be pleaded against being twice placed in jeopardy for the same offense. Since Callender's indictment contained but twenty extracts from the book, Hay feared that if the jury acquitted him on all of these, the prosecutor might go through the book again and scour out more passages and try him a second time for publishing the book. Or if the accused was convicted, he might be prosecuted for other passages from the same book as soon as he had completed his first sentence.

"It requires very little legal ability," Judge Chase replied, "to

---

[53] *Ibid.*, 698.

[54] For the testimony of William Duval, Henry Banks, William Burton, William A. Rind, Meriwether Jones, Thomas Nicholson, John Dixon, James Lyon, and Samuel Pleasants, see *ibid.*, 698–700. James Lyon, son of Congressman Matthew Lyon, was copublisher of Callender's book.

demonstrate that the title need not be recited; and it is equally easy to prove that the decision in this case may be pleaded in bar of any other prosecution for the same offense." He therefore ruled that the book could be introduced as evidence even though not mentioned in the indictment. Although he also ruled that any subsequent indictment could not be brought against the accused for any charge on which Callender was found guilty, the judge implied that the defendant could be tried for any other statements from his book.[55]

Before going through the twenty charges in the first count, Nelson again reminded the jury that "bad intent" was a necessary ingredient to the crime of seditious libel. In his discussion, however, the prosecutor confused malicious intent with wicked words and thus equated the "bad intent" of the speaker with the "bad tendency" of the words. "If the matter was libellous," he told them, "that is false, scandalous, and malicious, the intention must be wicked and criminal, and you must find him guilty." Instead of establishing four ingredients to prove criminality—that the words were false, scandalous, malicious, and uttered with "bad intent"—Nelson narrowed the number to three. If the jury thought that the words were false, scandalous, and malicious, they were instructed by the prosecutor to presume that the intent must have been "wicked and criminal." This, of course, was but another example of presumptive intent. Since it was up to the defendant to prove that his statements were not false, this amounted to telling the jury that the government had closed its case by proving that Callender published the statements.[56]

The prosecutor did not attempt to prove that the charges were false, scandalous, and malicious, and made with bad intent. Reading each of the twenty charges, Nelson from time to time told the jury that the defendant had to prove the truth of each and every charge or he was guilty. On the first charge, in which Callender

[55] Wharton, *State Trials*, 700–704. Wharton has this to say of the judge's ruling: "This position, notwithstanding the boisterous way in which it is laid down, is incorrect. There must be always at common law an exact recital of the alleged libellous matter, unless in the indictment itself the pleader excuses himself from so doing on the ground of the destruction of the instrument, or its possession by the defendant. See the authorities collected in *Wharton's Prec. of Indictment*, 545. *Ford* v. *Bennett*, 1 Ld., Ray, 415. R. V. Bear, 2 Salk., 417. At the same time, Mr. Hay's position, that the title must be set out, is not sustained by the authorities, though it is clear that in knocking it down, Judge Chase knocked down nearly the whole law of libels besides."

[56] Wharton, *Chase Trials*, 705. Wharton must have thought that this was the case because he does not even include the court record where Nelson discusses each of the twenty charges. See *ibid.*, 705. David Robertson's transcript of this evidence is contained in *Chase Trial*, 83–88.

asserted that "the reign of Mr. Adams has been one continued tempest of malignant passions," the prosecutor offered this conclusion:

Is this true? what evidence is there of its truth. If not true, with what intention has he published it? Was it not to excite the contempt and hatred of the people against him? His object cannot be misunderstood. Take the whole of this libel together; and you cannot hesitate to say, that it is false, scandalous and malicious.

In commenting on another charge, the district attorney made the flat statement that the burden of proof in sedition cases rested not upon the government but upon the defendant. "It is not necessary for me to *disprove*," he said; "they must *prove* the fact." Callender's statement "was certainly a libel," the district attorney concluded, "unless he can prove the truth thereof." [57]

Nelson pointed out that at least one of Callender's statements was not subject to proof. In discussing what would happen if Adams were elected in 1800 instead of Jefferson, the Republican writer had declared that even though "Mr. Adams were to make a treaty with France, yet such is the grossness of his prejudice, and so great is the violence of his passions that under his administration, America would be in constant danger of a second quarrel." This, said the Federalist prosecutor, was the same as saying to the citizens of the United States, "Do not re-elect the present president, for he will involve you in war." Since this was a prediction of things to come, the district attorney concluded that "you cannot say that this is true, therefore, it must be false, scandalous, and malicious."

In one instance, he denied that the truth of a statement was a defense against the charge of sedition, although the statute plainly said so, and he had so informed the jury. Callender had written that President Adams' system consisted of "a French war, an American navy, a large standing army, an additional load of taxes and all the other symptoms and consequences of debt and despotism." Nelson told the jury that it was unnecessary for him to inquire into the propriety or impropriety of such government measures as taxes, an army and navy, or war or peace,

because the book is evidently emitted with a malicious intention. If you were to think his words were true but published with a malicious intention to defame, you could not exculpate him; the conclusion of his climax

[57] *Chase Trial*, 84–85. Although he sometimes told the jury that it was up to them to decide if the statements were true or false, at other times he informed them that whether a statement was false or true, they had to have proof of its truth submitted to them. *Ibid.*, 87.

renders a misconception impossible; "*and all other consequences of debt and despotism.*" After such explicitly malignant terms, you cannot hesitate to say, that he is guilty—it is represented to you, that he [the president] will tax and oppress you, and exercise despotic, tyrannical powers over you. Are these terms used with any other intention, than what is stated in the indictment.

Like most Federalists, Nelson used the words "administration" and "government" interchangeably. The government of the United States was chosen by the people themselves, he said, and under the Adams administration there had been "unexampled prosperity and happiness." Since it was the best government that had been devised by mankind, it was more than he could understand how it was possible for the people not to be attached to it. Although the government attorney pointed out the right of every citizen to participate in elections and to withdraw his vote of confidence from any elected official, he asserted that this could be done only "at the constitutional periods of making new elections." Conceding that everyone could "even expatiate on the virtues of the new candidate," he branded Callender's language in endorsing Jefferson as "swollen and pompous." This right to endorse an opposition candidate, moreover, did not warrant a person in traducing and defaming the candidate who already held the presidential office. "Cannot a good thing be said of one individual," the prosecutor asked, "without saying black and damnable things of another? Is it necessary, in order to recommend one man, to the presidential office, that you should charge another with bringing on his country war and beggary. The whole forms a perfect chain of malice, falsehood and slander." [58]

The Callender case, however, is best remembered not for the government's plea but for Judge Chase's rulings against the defense. He frequently interrupted the defendant's counsel and finally drove them from the case. The first witness for Callender was John Taylor of Caroline, senator from Virginia until 1794 and, with Madison and Giles, leader in the Virginia Assembly in 1800. As soon as the Virginian was sworn, Judge Chase prevented his testifying by inquiring what the defense hoped to prove by the witness. When they replied that their examination of Taylor would prove that Adams had avowed to him principles that justified Callender's statement that the president was "a professed aristocrat," the judge demanded that

[58] Wharton, *State Trials*, 83–88. The prosecutor commented on nineteen of the twenty charges contained in the indictment. The eighteenth, the only one which he failed to discuss, stated that "every feature in the conduct of Mr. Adams forms a distinct and additional evidence, that he was determined at all events to embroil this country with France."

the defense counsel submit in writing the questions which they intended to ask the witness.[59] After Nicholas listed the questions, the judge ruled Taylor's evidence inadmissible.[60] The proposed line of questioning, he said, pertained to a charge that contained two points —that the president was an aristocrat and that he had proved serviceable to the British interest. To be admissable, Taylor's testimony would have to prove both points. "No evidence," the judge continued, "is admissable that does not go to justify the whole charge. . . . The offered testimony has no direct and proper application to the issue; it would deceive and mislead the jury; an argumentative justification of a trivial, unimportant part of a libel, would be urged before a jury as a substantial vindication of the whole." Chase maintained that admitting such testimony "would, by misleading the jury under such illegal testimony, destroy public treaties and public faith; and nothing would be more uncertain than law, were such an illegal excuse admitted in courts of law.[61]

When Nicholas suggested that it might be proper to prove one part of a specific charge by one witness and another part by other evidence, thereby substantiating the whole of the charge, Judge Chase replied that this recommendation by "the young gentleman was irregular and subversive of every principle of law . . . it was a popular argument, calculated to deceive the people, but very incorrect." Hay protested against this ruling so effectively that the judge requested the prosecutor to consent to admitting Taylor's evidence, but Nelson refused.[62]

After Hay and Nicholas had been squelched, Wirt attempted to

[59] The twelfth charge in the first court claimed that Callender had written that the president "was a professed aristocrat; he had proved faithful and servicable to the British interest."

[60] John Marshall, who witnessed this trial while serving as secretary of state in Adams' Cabinet, later testified that he had "never known questions reduced to writing in the first instance." At the time of this testimony he was chief justice of the Supreme Court on which Chase also sat. See his testimony in *Chase Trial*, 70.

[61] Wharton, *State Trials*, 707. In his impeachment trial, Chase said that "the term 'aristocrat' is one of these vague, indefinite terms, which admit not of precise meaning, and are not susceptible of proof." See *The Answer and Pleas of Samuel Chase . . . to the Articles of Impeachment* (1805), 43.

[62] Wharton, *State Trials*, 707–708. Judge Cyrus Griffin concurred in this ruling. Judge Chase admitted that he might be wrong, but stated that the record of the court proceedings could be made the basis for an appeal to the Supreme Court on a writ of error. If the defendant's counsel chose to do this, the judge said, he would be the first man to grant the appeal. John Marshall thought that Judge Chase's ruling was wrong. He testified that he knew of no criminal case in which the testimony of a witness was rejected because he was unable to prove all the defense. See *Chase Trial*, 70.

address the jury on the constitutionality of the Sedition Law, but the presiding judge twice interrupted him and finally ordered him to take his seat. Wirt's line of argument was also inadmissable, Judge Chase said, and he was prepared for such a move. "Hear my words: I wish the world to know them—my opinion is the result of mature reflection." He then read a long opinion denying the right of the jury to consider the constitutionality of the Sedition Law in deciding a case tried under it. After he informed the defense lawyers that they might advance arguments to show that he was mistaken in this ruling, Wirt made that attempt only to be told that his reasoning was "*a non sequitur,* sir." Nor was Hay more successful. Two interruptions by Judge Chase forced him to fold up his papers. Although the judge promised not to interrupt again, Hay refused to proceed and the defense counsel, for the second time in two months, withdrew from a case presided over by Justice Chase.[63]

From that moment on, the prospect before Callender was not good. The withdrawal of his attorneys meant, of course, that he went undefended. The district attorney had doubted that "the extremest ingenuity" could refute the accusation in the indictment, and Judge Chase's repeated interruptions gave no ingenious person a chance to disprove them. The judge's actions, therefore, fully sustained Nelson's doctrine of "guilt by accusation." As a matter of fact, Judge Chase had set the stage for this doctrine in the preliminary discussion over a continuance, when he declared that the book was false and that the intentions of its author were "sufficiently obvious."

In charging the jury, however, Judge Chase instructed them that the government must have proved that Callender wrote the book and that it contained false, scandalous, and malicious statements, published with intent to defame the president. In concluding his charge, he announced that it was his duty as a federal judge "to execute the laws of the United States with justice and impartiality, with firmness and decision." Thus, to his judicial functions of interpreting and construing the laws, he added that of executing them as well.[64]

[63] Wharton, *State Trials,* 708–712. Chase's frequent interruptions of the defense in Fries's trial for treason led to the withdrawal of his lawyers.

[64] *Ibid.,* 712–718, reprints the charge from Judge Chase's manuscript. Most of the charge reiterates Chase's reasons for refusing to allow the defense to address the jury on the constitutionality of the Sedition Law. It is a persuasive presentation of the doctrine of judicial review, utilizing most of the arguments advanced three years later by Chief Justice Marshall in *Marbury* v. *Madison.* It also contained an indirect condemnation of the arguments advanced in the Virginia Resolutions concerning the right of a state legislature to express an opinion on the constitutionality of federal legislation.

When the jury returned a verdict of guilty after deliberating two hours, the Supreme Court jurist declared that it was "pleasing to him, because it shewed that the laws of the United States could be enforced in Virginia, the principal object of this prosecution." [65] Before sentencing Callender, Judge Chase lectured him on the dangerous consequences of sowing "dissensions, discontent and discord among the people." "Mr. Adams," Justice Chase assured the convicted author, "was far from deserving the character which he had given him." Since Callender was a well-informed observer, the judge insisted, he must have known of President Adams' eminent services to his country and the length of time he had served it. Thus the enormity of the offense "was aggravated by its having been wilfully committed"; it seemed impossible that any rational man could believe Adams guilty of the "atrocious crimes" recited by Callender. "To believe such an accusation" was, he said, "an attack upon the people themselves; for . . . it was self evident that an intelligent stranger, who could read these severe charges and believe them, must unavoidably think that the people who had elected to so dignified a station so abandoned and infamous a character, must be depraved and wicked themselves." [66] Until he had read Callender's defamation of the chief magistrate, he had not thought there was so bad a man in the United States. [67] He was "extremely happy," he said, "that Callender was not a native American." [68]

For a foreigner who had found asylum in the United States to defame the president struck the federal judge as being "especially ungenerous." Chase assured the newspaperman that there was a very great difference between the liberty and the licentiousness of the press. An abusive press would destroy any government, particularly a republican form of government. By corrupting public opinion, it would undermine the morals of the people. "If calumny, defamation and falsehood were to be indiscriminately tolerated and encouraged," he argued, "it would reduce virtue to the level of vice, and no man, however upright in his conduct, could be secure from slander —there would be no encouragement to integrity." Although liberty

[65] Richmond *Examiner*, June 6, 1800, reprinted in the *Albany Register*, June 17, 1800. These are as near to the judge's exact words as the reporter could recall; he vouched that they had "the *exact meaning*" contained in the judge's observations.

[66] *Virginia Gazette*, June, 1800, reprinted in Ford, *Jefferson and Callender*, 23–24. Also see Robertson's transcript, *Chase Trial*, 94.

[67] Richmond *Examiner*, June 6, 1800, reprinted in the *Albany Register*, June 17, 1800. Also see Callender, *Prospect*, II, pt. ii, 86.

[68] Robertson's transcript, *Chase Trial*, 94.

of the press allowed "unrestrained but fair discussion of principles and conduct," it did not guarantee impunity to willful and malicious slanderers. There were but two ways of remedying the evils of bad laws and bad legislators: either petition the lawmakers to repeal their acts, or remove the representatives and replace them with better men. Instead of following these constitutional modes of redress, Callender had disobeyed the law of the land and, "avowedly for an electioneering purpose, had ascribed to Mr. Adams a worse character than the worst ministers of the worst of tyrants had—that he represented him in blacker colors than Sejanus himself." [69] As evidence of his "firmness and decision" in executing the laws, Judge Chase then sentenced Callender to nine months in jail, assessed a $200 fine, and bound him over on a $1,200 bond to good behavior for two years.[70] Appropriately enough, the last victim of the Sedition Law was to remain in prison until the day that that statute expired.[71]

In their campaign against the foreign-born writers whom they considered the leading Republican publicists, the Federalists succeeded in jailing Callender and Cooper. Coming soon after the Cooper case, the trial of Callender created a political tempest in the election year of 1800. The Republican press condemned Judge Chase as "ungenerous and relentless" and characterized "the precipitate manner" in which he handled the trial as "extremely reprehensible." [72] While disavowing any desire "to throw odium upon the jury," the *Examiner* insinuated that it was packed.[73] It would be admitted, the Republican paper asserted, that "a jury composed of George Wythe, Edmond Pendleton, John Taylor, William B. Giles,

[69] *Virginia Gazette,* June, 1800, reprinted in Ford, *Jefferson and Callender,* 24.

[70] Richmond *Examiner,* June 4, 1800, reprinted in the *Albany Register,* June 17, 1800. Callender was to post $600 for bond and two persons had to post $300 each. He was to remain in jail until his fine was paid and his security posted.

[71] Callender was found guilty on June 3, 1800, and the law expired on March 3, 1801. Judge Chase enclosed his opinion in the Callender case to President Adams and suggested that he should hand it to his private secretary for publication in the Boston papers. Samuel Chase to John Adams, Baltimore, June 21, 1800, Adams Papers, XXI, no. 103 (Mass. Hist. Soc.).

[72] *Examiner,* June 6, 1800, reprinted in the *Albany Register,* June 17, 1800. For a report that Chase's "arbitrary unlawyerlike conduct" converted a confirmed Federalist to Republicanism, see Garritt Minor to Joseph C. Cabell, Richmond, July 8, 1800, Cabell Papers (Univ. of Va.). The presiding judge's severe reprimands to the leading members of the Virginia bar have led one legal historian to comment on "Judge Chase's peculiar recklessness of manner during the trial." Wharton, *State Trials,* 718n.

[73] For testimony that every juror was a Federalist, see footnote 51.

James Madison, Wilson C. Nicholas, St. George Tucker, Richard Brent, John Tayler, Stephens T. Mason, John Page, Spencer Rhoan [sic], and a thousand other characters in Virginia equally respectable, and capable of forming correct political opinions would have found him NOT GUILTY." [74] Not so reserved in its condemnation, the *Aurora* blasted Judge Chase in an unfinished couplet:

> Cursed of thy father, scum of all that's base,
> Thy sight is odious and thy name is [Chase].[75]

Imprisonment did not halt Callender's pen. Finding himself a martyr to the Democratic-Republican cause, the newspaperman continued his attacks upon the Federalists, singling out Judge Chase and President Adams for special treatment. Describing the Supreme Court justice as "the most detestable and detested rascal in the state of Maryland," he argued that Chase conducted sedition trials as if he were the prosecuting attorney, with a fat fee in his pocket, rather than the presiding jurist.[76] When the judge wrote the prisoner that he planned to beat him after his release, Callender replied that "in case of an attack, I'll shoot him." [77]

Indeed, Chase's differentiation between liberty and licentiousness of the press made no impression on Callender. Shaking his forged fetters in the Federalists' faces, he lectured the administration on its responsibilities to the people. "Government," he declared, "exists but by the support of public opinion, and the press is the axis around which public opinion may be said to revolve." Convinced that "the insolence and abuse of liberty are preferable to the grovelling decorum, and the funereal silence of despotism," he converted his Richmond cell into a campaign publicity center.[78] Resolving to dedicate his life to the "Federal faction," he promised to give them "a cut and thrust volume per annum for some years to come." [79]

[74] Richmond *Examiner*, June 4, 1800, reprinted in the *Albany Register*, June 17, 1800.

[75] *Aurora*, Aug. 8, 1800.

[76] Callender, *Prospect*, II, pt. II, 47. Callender referred to Chase as "a wretch who, for his swindling correspondence with a Baltimore flour merchant, should have been flogged at the cart's tail, out of the seventy-five congress." For a reference to Chase's speculative activities during the Revolution, see E. S. Corwin, "Samuel Chase," *DAB*, IV, 35.

[77] Callender to Jefferson, Richmond Jail, Oct. 27, 1800, Ford, *Jefferson and Callender*, 30.

[78] Callender, *Prospect*, II, pt. II, 96, 36.

[79] Callender to Jefferson, Sept. 8 and 13, 1800, Ford, *Jefferson and Callender*, 25–26.

While still in prison, Callender published the second volume of
The Prospect before Us, as vehement an attack on the Federalists
as any of his earlier writings. Condemning the president as "that
scourge, that scorn, that outcast of America," he reached an abusive
low, blasting Adams in a chapter defiantly entitled "More Sedition."
"This federal gem," he wrote, "this apostle of the parsons of Connecticut, is not only a repulsive pedant, a gross hypocrite, and an
unprincipled oppressor, but . . . he is, in private life, one of the
most egregious fools upon the continent." A person without abilities and without virtues, this despicable attorney was incapable of
attracting either tenderness or esteem, Callender continued; he possessed "neither that innocence of sensibility, which incites us to
love, nor that omnipotence of intellect which commands us to admire." In his most generous estimate of the president, the Republican writer described him as a ruffian, "super-eminently entitled not
only to the laughter, but likewise to the curses of mankind." [80]

Although the Federalist newspapers hoped that Callender's conviction would deter others "from any attempts to violate the laws
of our country," [81] it obviously had no such effect on the prisoner.
During the election of 1800, his contributions continued to appear
in the *Examiner* and the *Virginia Argus* in Richmond and in the
Petersburg *Republican.*[82] Even the report of his trial became campaign literature. Only two days after Callender was sentenced, the
editor of the *Examiner* announced that he would try to procure a
transcript of the trial. From the shorthand notes of Daniel Robertson, a pamphlet report of the case was soon published.[83] This report, of course, served only to spread Callender's writings even more
widely than otherwise would have been the case. Thus, the attempt
to suppress "seditious criticism" of the authorities facilitated its
spread.[84]

[80] Callender, *Prospect,* II, pt. II, 76–77, 81. In this reference, which was
written after the election of Jefferson in 1800, Callender referred to Adams as
"the NOW blasted tyrant of America."

[81] *Virginia Gazette,* quoted by Ford, *Jefferson and Callender,* 23.

[82] Callender to Jefferson, Richmond Jail, Nov. 17, 1800, *ibid.,* 30.

[83] Wharton, *State Trials,* 688. Robertson's report is partially reproduced in
Chase Trial, 73–94.

[84] For the decision of Jefferson and his Cabinet to pardon Callender, see "Notes
on Procedures on Prosecutions under Sedition Act," March 9, 1801, Jefferson
Papers, CX, 18892 (Lib. Cong.), and *Jefferson's Writings* (Ford ed.), IX, xx.
The *Maryland Gazette,* March 26, 1801, reports Callender's pardon. The pardon
is recorded in the *Book of Pardons and Remissions, No. I (1793–1812),* Dept.
of State, March 16, 1801, 44–45, General Records of the Dept. of State, RG 59
(National Archives).

CHAPTER XVI

Two New England Prosecutions

The freedom of speech, to discuss and debate
  On the deeds of our servants who govern the State,
We'll never resign to sticklers for power,
  Though courtiers and sycophants frown and look sour.
                    —ANTHONY HASWELL

THE legal steps in Pennsylvania and Virginia against Duane, Cooper, and Callender were the most widely publicized proceedings under the Sedition Law in 1800, but they were not the only ones. New York witnessed three federal indictments, although only one case was finally tried. In New England, however, the Federalists created two minor martyrs for the Republicans when they indicted and convicted second-string editors in Connecticut and Vermont.

Anthony Haswell and Freedom of the Press: Sequel to Lyon's Case

The leading Democratic-Republican newspaper in Vermont at the end of the eighteenth century was Anthony Haswell's *Vermont Gazette* in Bennington. One of the few Jeffersonian journals in Federalist New England, it stood out like a fire in the Green Mountains on a dark night. Long an ardent supporter of the "immortal Jefferson," Haswell was a vigorous critic of President John Adams, his principles, and the policies of his administration. He opposed the enactment of the Alien and Sedition Laws by a Federalist-dominated Congress and their approval by the chief executive.

Only a month after the passage of the Sedition Act, he adopted a noncommittal method of contrasting it with the personal liberty guarantees of the Bill of Rights. Under the heading "Text from the Constitution," the editor printed the provisions of the Fifth and Sixth Amendments, and directly below these he gave the full text of the new statute as the "Comment by the 5th Congress at the second session." [1]

This audacity made him the target of criticism from the Federalist presses in Vermont. Three weeks after his censure of the congressional acts, he reported that he had been "and is threatened with prosecution under the sedition law; with tarring and feathering, pulling down his house, etc." With an air of bravado, he informed his opponents that he would neither court their visit nor shrink from their attack, but keep to his post conscientiously. [2]

When Congressman Matthew Lyon became the first victim of the Sedition Law a month later, Haswell condemned the trial as a "persecution" rather than a prosecution. Viewing it as an attack on American liberty and democratic principles, he became Lyon's most ardent champion in Vermont. At the time of the congressman's trial, the editor again reported the rumor that he was marked for Federalist prosecution. Scorning threats of physical violence, he pledged to give his patrons true and impartial statements and to detect the aim of despots when he could, even though "the gag or the bowstring appear among the displays of dignity." Describing himself as a sworn friend to lawful authority and the federal constitution, he denied affiliation with any party. He was, however, "warmly engaged in the cause of liberty; an enemy to lawless power, and foreign and domestic tyranny." [3]

After this statement of principles, Haswell launched an attack on the Federalist campaign in the Vermont congressional election which belied his disavowal of the party attachment. He accused the Federalists of dispatching riders throughout the state to circulate "a cordon of lies" against the Republican candidates. The freemen of the state, he reported, had been cautioned to beware of his *Gazette* because the editor "received french pay in quarterly remittances." Moreover, they had been warned that he would soon

[1] *Vermont Gazette*, Aug. 18, 1798, cited by John Spargo, *Anthony Haswell, Printer—Patriot—Ballader* (Rutland, 1925), 57. This account owes much to Mr. Spargo's excellent work.

[2] *Vermont Gazette*, Sept. 8, 1798, *ibid.*

[3] *Vermont Gazette*, Oct. 12, 1798, Spargo, *Haswell*, 57–58. Although the Federalists accused Haswell of receiving quarterly stipends from the French, he was in prison for debt on the Fourth of July, 1799. See Spargo, *Haswell*, 43–44.

be arrested for treason "and his press stopped by authority." Branding these Federalist assertions as falsehoods, Haswell challenged his accusers to prove them. Until they did, he concluded that theirs was a bad cause which aimed at despotism.

During Lyon's imprisonment, Haswell called attention to the severe manner in which federal Marshal Jabez Fitch treated the congressman. On January 3, 1799, a month before Lyon's sentence expired, Haswell's paper carried the advertisement for Lyon's lottery scheme to raise money for the fine and court costs. Addressed "to the enemies of political persecution in the western district of Vermont," this public notice asserted that their representative was held by "the oppressive hand of usurped power in a loathsome prison, deprived almost of the right of reason." All the indignities capable of a "hard-hearted savage" had been heaped upon him by the federal marshal, who had been elevated by the Federalists to a position where he could "satiate his barbarity on the misery of his victims." Yet even the expiration of Lyon's term of imprisonment would not guarantee his freedom unless he paid his "ransom" of nearly $1,100. The advertisement then described the lottery and concluded, "May we not hope that this amount may answer the desired purpose, and that our representative shall not languish a day in prison for want of money after the measure of Federal injustice is filled up?" [4]

In the same issue, Haswell also reprinted a paragraph from the Philadelphia *Aurora*, attacking the Adams administration for its dismissal of officeholders for their political principles. Entitled "British Influence," the paragraph charged that the administration had advertised its confidence in Tories by appointing to office "men who had fought against our independence, who had shared in the desolation of our homes, and the abuse of our wives and daughters." [5]

On Lyon's triumphant journey to Philadelphia following his release from prison in February, 1799, he stopped in Bennington, where Haswell delivered the welcoming speech congratulating the congressman on his return to freedom. Once again the editor condemned Lyon's trial as an "unprecedented and cruel persecution of our federal representative." Lyon was also serenaded by enthusi-

[4] The advertisement first appeared in the *Vermont Gazette*, Jan. 3, 1799, and was published in several subsequent issues. The text is given in *U.S. v. Haswell*, Wharton, *State Trials*, 684. Wharton's account also appears as Case No. 15,324, *Federal Cases*, XXVI, 218.

[5] *U.S. v. Haswell*, Wharton, *State Trials*, 685.

astic songs written by Haswell. The "Patriotic Exultation on Lyon's Release from the Federal Bastile" was sung, appropriately enough, to the tune of "The Joys of Scolding." When this ballad was printed as a broadside, Haswell added a stanza proclaiming that

> The freedom of speech, to discuss and debate
>   On the deeds of our servants who govern the State,
> We'll never resign to sticklers for power,
>   Though courtiers and sycophants frown and look sour.[6]

Thirteen months after Haswell first predicted his prosecution, and as a direct result of his exercise of the right of freedom of the press to favor Lyon and to oppose the Federalists, the Bennington editor became the second Vermont victim of the Sedition Law. On October 7, 1799, he was indicted for seditious utterances contained in Lyon's lottery advertisement and in the paragraph concerning Tories which he had reprinted from the *Aurora*.[7]

October 8, 1799, was a cold, wet, disagreeable day in Bennington. It did not brighten much for editor Haswell, who was ill, when two deputy marshals served the warrant for his arrest.[8] The writ did not specify the charge against the journalist; it simply ordered him to be brought before the court to answer an indictment returned by the grand jurors of the district. Hoping to avoid a trip in the chilling rain if he could be represented by counsel, Haswell asked the deputies what charges had been leveled against him. They either did not know or refused to divulge them, because he later wrote that they were as silent "as the midnight police officers of the French Bastile, the secret messengers of the Spanish Inquisition, or the Mutes of the Turkish bowstring for strangling." [9]

Less than an hour after his arrest, the Republican editor was on his way to Rutland to appear before the United States District Court.[10] The Vermont roads were muddy, the weather was cold and

---

[6] Broadside dated "Bennington, third day of Lyon's release, Feb. 12, 1799. No thanks to Power." Quoted by McMaster, *History of the People of the United States*, II, 401n. For Haswell's speech and other stanzas from the "Exultation," see Chapter XI.

[7] United States Circuit Court bail bond record, Vermont District, October term, 1799, held at Rutland, Vt. This document is reproduced as Plate XI in Spargo, *Haswell*, 55.

[8] These details are taken from Haswell's account of his arrest and trial, which he reported in the *Green Mountain Farmer* (Bennington), March 31, 1813. His arrest is reported in the New York *Spectator*, Oct. 19, 1799; the *Aurora*, Oct. 24, 1799; and the *Gazette of the United States*, Nov. 6, 1799.

[9] *Green Mountain Farmer*, March 31, 1813, cited by Spargo, *Haswell*, 59.

[10] New London *Bee*, Oct. 30, 1799.

wet, and Haswell was sick and "distressed." Covering the fifty-five miles in thirteen hours, the trio arrived at the Rutland tavern about one o'clock on the morning of the ninth, where Haswell was fortunate enough to meet Daniel Dyer, a friend from Clarendon who was willing to post bail. This offer, however, was vetoed by Marshal Fitch, whose unfair treatment of Lyon had been denounced in the advertisement for which Haswell stood indicted. The marshal not only refused to accept Dyer's money for bail, but he was vituperative to Haswell and made disparaging remarks about Israel Smith, the chief justice of Vermont whom Haswell hoped to obtain as counsel. The marshal clapped the editor in jail until he was called into court next morning.[11]

When he appeared before Associate Justice William Cushing of the United States Supreme Court on October 9, Haswell finally learned that he was charged with a "false malicious wicked and seditious libel" against the government of the United States. The first count was based on the assertions in the lottery advertisement and the second on the paragraph about Adams appointing Tories to office.[12]

Although Haswell willingly admitted the publication of these items, he pleaded not guilty to the charge of sedition. He denied writing the lottery advertisement, which he had simply inserted at commercial rates in the ordinary way. Two respectable citizens, Major Elias Buel, manager of the lottery, and James Lyon, clerk, would testify, if asked, that they wrote it and were responsible for it. The second count, he said, was a fair statement of undisputed facts and could not fall within the definition of seditious utterances. Haswell therefore asked that the case be dropped or that it be postponed until he had time to obtain counsel and prepare a defense.[13]

As he had in Lyon's case, District Attorney Charles Marsh insisted on an immediate trial. Since Haswell admitted publishing the two items and pleaded their truth, the prosecutor contended, he had confessed his guilt, because the doctrine of "the greater the truth the greater the libel" applied under the common law of criminal

[11] *Green Mountain Farmer*, March 31, 1813, cited by Spargo, *Haswell*, 59–60.

[12] Spargo, *Haswell*, 61, says that part of the indictment is in the handwriting of Nathaniel Chipman, Federalist senator from Vermont, who was one of Lyon's and Haswell's bitterest political enemies.

[13] *Green Mountain Farmer*, March 31, 1813, *ibid.*, 61–62. For references to Haswell's prosecution, see Jefferson to L. W. Tazewell, Phila., April 10, 1800, Jefferson Papers (Mass. Hist. Soc.), and Jefferson to Edmund Pendleton, Phila., April 19, 1800, Jefferson Papers, CVI, 18261 (Lib. Cong.).

libel. Judge Cushing reminded the government attorney, who should have known better, that the sedition statute allowed truth as a justification. He therefore postponed the case until the May, 1800, term of court and bound Haswell over to $2,000 bail.[14]

The editor returned to Bennington little knowing that he had barely missed a second indictment for sedition. During the summer of 1799, Haswell published a patriotic oration commemorating Independence Day, which Eziekiel Bacon had delivered in Williamstown, Massachusetts. The Federalists later showed their distaste for Bacon's efforts by burning his speech in front of Williams College.[15] When the pamphlet issued from Haswell's press, therefore, the Federalist district attorney drew up an indictment for presentation to the grand jury during the October term. Charging that Haswell was "a malicious and seditious person and of a depraved mind and wicked and diabolical disposition," the prosecutor argued that the editor had contrived to defame the United States government, the president, and Congress. He had tried to stir up sedition in the United States on the Fourth of July, when he did "with force and arms wickedly, knowingly and maliciously, write, print, utter and publish and did then and there cause and procure to be written uttered and publish'd of and concerning the said Government . . . President and Congress of the United States a certain scandalous and seditious writing or libel." Bacon's oration, the indictment continued, contained "scurrilous, feign and false and scandalous seditious and malicious matters." The grand jury which indicted Haswell for his publication of Lyon's lottery advertisement, however, refused to agree that his publication of a patriotic pamphlet was seditious.[16]

Vermont's Federalists rejoiced that "the editor of the Bennington petty vehicle of sedition" had been indicted for printing Lyon's lottery scheme. Denouncing Haswell's plea that the allegedly libelous matter had appeared in an advertisement, they exulted that the government had a law with which "to punish disorganizers." "If receiving pay for printing sedition could be pleaded in its justification," one Federalist wrote, "we fancy, that, not only little Tony [Haswell], but the Aurora men, and many others, coadjutors and

[14] *Bee*, Nov. 20, 1799, reports the postponement. Also see Spargo, *Haswell*, 62–63. Haswell posted $1,000 on October 10 and Daniel Dyer posted the same amount.

[15] Evans, *American Bibliography*, Item 35137, XX, 257.

[16] Spargo discovered this indictment in the archives of the United States District Court at Burlington, Vt. See Spargo, *Haswell*, 58, Plate XII.

fellow labourers in the Gallic vineyard, might escape the pains, and penalties" prescribed by the Sedition Law. "I hope the time is fast arriving, in which . . . the din of democracy is no longer heard in our land." [17]

Between October, 1799, and May, 1800, Haswell continued to publish his paper and to participate in community affairs. When Bennington turned out to mourn the death of George Washington, the town chose Haswell to deliver the oration in his memory.[18] Of necessity, however, much of his time was spent in trying to assemble legal evidence for his defense before the federal court. He corresponded with Matthew Lyon and others concerning the first count, and he wrote to William Duane for evidence bearing on the second. He also obtained a certified copy of the correspondence between Secretary of War James McHenry and General William Darke of the Virginia militia, relating to the Tory charge.

The May term of the Circuit Court was held on the eastern side of the Green Mountains in the Federalist stronghold of Windsor.[19] On April 29, 1800, the ballader of Bennington set out for his trial, but not before jotting down a few rhymed "reflections the morning of his departure for Windsor, to stand trial before the Circuit Court":

> What tho' in the toils a republican's caught
> And condemn'd to do penance in gaol,
> From his suffering or death shall conviction be wrought,
> And the efforts of tyranny fail.
>
> The dastard and tory who crouches for gain,
> And fawns on the puppets of power,
> Shall reflect that what has been may happen again,
> And his prospects all fail in an hour. . . .

[17] *Gazette of the United States,* Nov. 6, 1799, reprinting a story from the *Vergennes Gazette.* Several papers reported that the grand jury which indicted Haswell also brought charges against Judah P. Spooner, a former printer on Matthew Lyon's *Scourge of Aristocracy;* Dr. Shaw of Castleton; and a second indictment against Congressman Lyon. See Chapter IX.

[18] Anthony Haswell, *An Oration Delivered by Request of Temple Lodge, Bennington, Vermont, December 27th, 1799, Being the Anniversary Festival of St. John the Baptist; When a Procession of Citizens and Masons Was Formed in Honor of the Memory of General George Washington, from the Press of the Author.*

[19] Lyon refused to postpone his case in 1798 until the 1799 term because he feared the political bias against him on the eastern side of the mountains. His trial, therefore, took place in Rutland rather than Windsor.

And if truth is a libel—Alas! and Alas!
May the spirit of seventy-five,
Again be enkindled—A toast—let it pass!
For who would his freedom survive.[20]

The personnel involved in this sequel to Lyon's trial differed only in the new defendant. Judge William Paterson of the Supreme Court again presided and was assisted by Samuel Hitchcock, federal district judge. Charles Marsh again prosecuted as district attorney. Haswell was defended by Israel Smith, chief justice of Vermont, who had advised Lyon during his trial, and by David Fay, one of the Bennington lawyers whom Lyon had tried to obtain as counsel in 1798. On April 28, 1800, Haswell's lawyers petitioned for a further postponement of the trial to allow more time to procure the attendance of two material witnesses who resided outside the state of Vermont. They filed an affidavit stating that the testimony of General William Darke and James McHenry was necessary to prove that Tories had been appointed to federal office occasionally. To support their petition, they also submitted a second affidavit to show that one Vermont witness was ill and another detained by accident.[21]

The government prosecutor objected to a postponement on two grounds, claiming that the defendant had not used due diligence in gathering his witnesses. Moreover, even if McHenry and Darke were present and testified to the truth of the Tory charge, their evidence would be inadmissible because this prosecution was at common law and must be guided by the rule of "the greater the truth, the greater the libel." The judge, however, ruled that the indictment rested in part, at least, on the Sedition Law, which allowed testimony as to the truth of the assertions. On the other hand, he remarked that mere proof that old Tories had been occasionally employed by the government would not be a justification for the other comments in the sentence. Haswell would have to prove that the Tories who had been appointed by the Adams ad-

[20] *Vermont Gazette*, May 5, 1800, quoted by Spargo, *Haswell*, 69–70. This issue contained an apology for the scarcity of news. The editor promised a larger issue in the next weeks, unless "a modern federal mandate confine him, a la mode, where he is, or remove him farther from his family."

[21] *Vermont Gazette*, May 26, 1800, reprinted in the *Albany Register*, May 30, 1800. Haswell asserted that he failed to procure these two witnesses solely because he was unable "to obtain information on the mode of process necessary to compel their attendance." For the views of General Darke and Secretary McHenry, see the *Aurora*, Feb. 19, 1799. This interesting correspondence is summarized by Dauer, *The Adams Federalists*, 216–217.

ministration were the same men who shared personally in the desolation of American towns and in the abuse of American wives, sisters, and daughters. The justice nevertheless granted a four-day postponement to allow for the appearance of the Vermont witnesses whom the editor expected at any time.[22]

On May 5, 1800, Vermont's second sedition trial opened with the government attorney offering evidence to show that the passages in the indictment had been published in Haswell's *Vermont Gazette*. He asserted that these publications were seditious libels against the government of the United States generally, and on the Circuit Court and the federal marshal of the District of Vermont in particular. When Haswell printed them, the prosecutor contended, he intended to bring the government of the United States into contempt and disrepute and to excite against it the hatred of the good people of the United States.[23]

Haswell's attorneys replied that the advertisement reflected not on the government generally but only on the marshal and the jailer, who were specifically accused of holding Lyon by the oppressive hand of usurped power. The defendant also called witnesses to swear to the severity of Marshal Fitch's treatment of the Vermont representative. Lyon had been denied the use of pen, ink, and paper, unless he allowed his letters to be censored, and the jailer had noted down the names of Lyon's visitors for retaliatory use by the Federalists.

When the court authorized Haswell to address the jury in his own behalf, he denied that he was the real publisher of the statements contained in the advertisement. Although he admitted that he was the sole editor, printer, and publisher of the *Vermont Gazette*, he pointed out that the publication of the ad had been paid for by the manager and the clerk of Lyon's lottery. They were therefore

[22] *Vermont Gazette*, May 26, 1800; *U.S. v. Haswell*, Wharton, *State Trials*, 685. Marsh had advanced this argument at Haswell's arraignment in October, 1799, when Judge Cushing corrected him. Despite Judge Paterson's qualification, and a later statement by Haswell, this case seems to have been prosecuted under the federal Sedition Law. See Federal Case No. 15,324, *Federal Cases*, XXVI, 218–220. For Haswell's assertion that the action was "laid at Common Law by the U.S.," see his letter to John Adams, Bennington, Vt., June 3, 1800, Adams Papers, XXI, no. 22 (Mass. Hist. Soc.).

[23] *U.S. v. Haswell*, Wharton, *State Trials*, 685; *Vermont Gazette*, May 26, reprinted in the *Albany Register*, May 30, 1800. The fact that Haswell was charged with libeling the Circuit Court by publishing the lottery advertisement made Judges Paterson and Hitchcock parties to the prosecution because they had presided at Lyon's trial. It should be noted, however, that federal judges and marshals were not protected from critical remarks by the Sedition Law.

really responsible for its contents. He argued that if someone advertised a reward to any person meeting certain qualifications, the winner could only claim his prize from the advertiser, not from the printer. In the same way Major Buel and James Lyon were the real publishers of the lottery announcement. They were responsible men, the editor asserted, who avowed the publication and signed it with their names.[24]

Although this argument sounds logical, it could have no validity under the Sedition Law, which applied not only to those who uttered or wrote forbidden words but also to those who printed or published them. In one sense, too, it was a naïve argument. The local Federalists who brought the indictment obviously considered Haswell as bigger game than Buel and the younger Lyon. Because he edited the most important Republican paper in upper New England, his political influence in the election year of 1800 was more potent than that of either of the other men.[25]

Haswell's second argument was more to the point. Even if the jury decided that he was the publisher of the allegedly offensive words, he contended that no inference ought to be drawn from them unless it was clearly implied. He flatly denied that he, Buel, or Lyon meant to call into question the authority of the United States by anything printed in the advertisement. The words referred exclusively to the assumption of power and the extreme severity of Marshal Fitch and his agents.[26]

The exchange between Darke and McHenry, the defendant argued, plainly showed that "prominent old tories" had the confidence of the Adams administration. The paragraph which he reprinted from the Aurora used the word "Tories" in the popular sense of the term: they were men who had opposed American independence.[27]

Judge Paterson's charge to the jury was similar in its technicalities

[24] Manuscript defense read by Haswell, quoted by Wharton, State Trials, 685–686n.

[25] For an early example of the importance with which Haswell was regarded by the Federalists, see Porcupine's Gazette, Oct. 19, 1798.

[26] Wharton, State Trials, 685–686n. Haswell referred to the first part of the lottery announcement which read as follows: "Your representative [Matthew Lyon] is holden by an oppressive hand of usurped power in a loathsome prison . . . and suffering all the indignities which can be heaped upon him by a hard-hearted savage. . . . But in spite of Fitch [the marshal] and to their sorrow, time will pass away."

[27] Vermont Gazette, May 26, 1800, reprinted in the Albany Register, May 30, 1800.

to the one which he delivered in Lyon's case. He observed that the sedition statute had benignly altered the common law by allowing the truth of the words as a defense against conviction. The jury had to decide whether or not the evidence proved that the violent language in the advertisement was truly descriptive of Marshal Fitch's treatment of Lyon. If his justification did not come up to the charge, the defendant had failed in his defense.

In his examination of the evidence, the judge virtually reargued the government's case. "You must look critically at the tendency of the whole libel laid before you," he said, "and minutely scrutinize its parts." Thus, he stressed the "bad tendency" of the words rather than the "bad intent" of the speaker, reducing the test of criminality to the ancient English common law standard of finding fault with one's superiors.[28] Paterson then examined the phraseology of the advertisement to determine its tendency. Who was the man referred to as *"your representative"* in the beginning of the seditious piece? "Why, behold Matthew Lyon," he answered, "a seditious libeller of your government, a convict justly suffering the penalty of a mild law, that spares the lives of those who had aimed at the subversion of all lawful authority among you, hoping by unprecedented clemency, to have prevented base repetition of his crime, like that which you have now under consideration." [29]

The judge then asked the jury to consider what the advertisement meant by the "oppressive hand of usurped power." It did not refer to the federal marshal, but to "the constituted authorities of your country, the legislative, executive, and judicial powers of your free and happy country! A country whose blessings surpassing all others, must be preserved pure, by the exemplary punishment of those who utter dangerous and malignant publications like those submitted to your view." If Lyon was in a "loathsome dungeon," it was because that place was a proper one "to correct a turpitude darker than its deepest gloom." After quoting that part of the lottery announcement which complained that Lyon was "deprived almost of the light of heaven" in his cell, the judge marveled that the prisoner could talk of heaven, "after condemning and reviling . . . your constituted authorities, and after laboring to overturn your constitution, the boast of liberty." It was up to the jury, Justice Paterson directed, to preserve the Constitution "from the malicious

28 *U.S.* v. *Haswell*, Wharton, *State Trials*, 686.

29 For President Adams' praise of the leniency of the Sedition Law, see the president to the Vermont Assembly, Phila., Nov. 30, 1798, *Vermont Gazette*, Dec. 27, 1798. This letter is analyzed in Chapter XI.

attacks of unprincipled sedition." As to Haswell's contention that he was neither the author nor real publisher of the advertisement, the judge observed that it was not necessary that the defendant should have written the defamatory matter. "If it was issued in his paper," he concluded, "it is enough." [30]

On the second count, the presiding justice ruled that it was immaterial whether Haswell had proved that Tories had been appointed to government office or that McHenry's reply to Darke indicated that they were worthy of the confidence of the government, because this justification did not come up to the charge. To support his statement, the defendant would first have to prove by sworn testimony that the individual appointed was or had been a Tory and that he had been guilty of burning towns, desolating homes, and raping women. The editor, the judge ruled, must "identify the man holding commission, from whose hands the incendiary torch was wrested, who personally violated your females; or who personally discharged the murderous gun, that killed a citizen of America, or the proof is irrelevant." [31]

Finally, Judge Paterson practically demanded conviction when he concluded that Haswell had made no attempt to justify these statements. "If the jury, therefore, believe, beyond reasonable doubt, that the intent was defamatory, and the publication was made, they must convict." As in Lyon's trial, Judge Paterson again failed to mention the possibility of acquittal, although in his praise of the Sedition Law he did mention the provision making truth a justification. But his flat assertion that one part of Haswell's publication was not justified meant that the presumption of falsity had not been dispelled. The only question for the jury to decide was that of intent to defame the federal government. After a short deliberation, the jury returned a verdict of guilty. On May 9, 1800, the court sentenced the editor to two months in federal prison, fined him $200, and assessed court costs. [32]

Although Haswell requested confinement in Bennington, the judge left that matter to Marshal Fitch, who first imprisoned the editor in the Rutland jail. [33] On May 13, however, Haswell was shifted to

[30] *Green Mountain Farmer*, March 31, 1813, quoted by Spargo, *Haswell*, 76–77. Shortly after the trial, Haswell wrote out the judge's charge to the best of his recollection, but he did not publish it until 1813. Wharton made use of Haswell's papers in preparing the case of *U.S.* v. *Haswell* in his *State Trials*, 685, and as Case No. 15,324, *Federal Cases*, XXVI, 218.

[31] *Green Mountain Farmer*, March 31, 1813, quoted by Spargo, *Haswell*, 73.

[32] *U.S.* v. *Haswell*, Wharton, *State Trials*, 686; Spargo, *Haswell*, 78.

[33] Haswell to his wife, Rutland jail, May 11, 1800, cited by Spargo, *Haswell*, 80.

the Bennington jail, where he completed his sentence.[34] His incarceration, however, was no repetition of Lyon's. Since he served his sentence in his home town, his treatment was not so severe as Lyon's had been. His paper appeared regularly and featured weekly communiqués which kept his readers informed as to how he fared. Viewing his trial as persecution of a just cause by a bad administration, he readily accepted his role of martyrdom. Letters issued regularly from his cell, to be printed throughout the Republican press in the summer before the elections of 1800. Determined to make as much political capital from his imprisonment as he could, he quoted with approval the adage that the blood of martyrs was the seed of the church. The Federalist administration's "persecution" of Republican editors, he protested, was opening "a new era of martyrdom, a degree less bloody, but probably destined to be as prolific quite, in yielding a fresh harvest of rational liberty; and although woes crowd on so fast that one treads hard upon another's heels, the whole is for the furtherance of freedom, and must eventuate in the happiness of America." For that reason he reported that he would not exchange his cell, "with his consciousness of suffering in a virtuous cause, for the most elegant palace in the city of Washington." [35]

Despite these public pronouncements, however, the proud printer was soon reduced to poverty and forced to present a pitiable petition to the president requesting a pardon. Stressing his inability to support his wife and nine children while he was imprisoned, he added that the necessity of meeting medical expenses for a stricken son complicated the task of paying his fine and court costs. To avoid impending ruin for his family, he asked remission of his fine and release from prison, but President Adams took no action.[36]

Even during his confinement, the editor-ballader praised American liberty and contrasted it with despotic governments. In a poem written on the occasion of a fellow prisoner being confined in his cell, Haswell observed that

> In the realms that own a tyrant,
> Where release can seldom come,
> Tears may follow close confinement,
> Jail is like the final doom.

[34] Writ of Mittimus for Haswell dated Bennington, May 13, 1800, archives of the District Court, Burlington, *ibid.*, 82.

[35] *Albany Register,* May 23 and June 13, 1800.

[36] Haswell to John Adams, Bennington gaol, June 3, 1800, Adams Papers, XXI, no. 22 (Mass. Hist. Soc.).

But in this high favor'd nation,
Tho' the tyrant clanks his chain,
Yet the man of lowest station,
Soon can liberty obtain.[37]

On July 7 he notified the public that he would obtain his liberty two days later at ten o'clock. Looking forward to a "renovating life of freedom," he viewed his release as a "smiling period, swiftly approaching." Although he promised not to remain silent and chastised, he admitted that his criticism would be circumspect. In order to remain free he proposed "to elude the fangs of despotism with caution," "to expose the deformity of the monster, and to clip his talons as often as he had it in his power, when approachable with safety." [38]

This proposal met with the approval of Haswell's neighbors, who postponed the Fourth of July celebration in Bennington until his release. When he emerged from his prison cell, the editor received a hero's welcome. While a band struck up "Yankee Doodle," a crowd of nearly two thousand applauded his liberation, then placed him at the head of a triumphant parade through Bennington. As he had hoped, the discharge of cannon "and the acclamation of his neighbors and political friends" hailed him as a martyr to that freedom which he had fought for in the American Revolution.[39]

There is little doubt that the prosecutions of Lyon and Haswell weakened the Federalist cause in Vermont.[40] The Bennington editor summarized the role these trials played in the election of 1800 in one of his rhymes entitled "A Review of Past Scenes":

Not long ago it was the mode,
In John's administration,
To deem each democrat a rogue,
And jeer him like the nation;
But jeering could not quite complete,
Their system of derision,
They therefore bound them hands and feet,
And cast them into prison.

From old Virginia to Vermont,
Each state produced its victim,

[37] Spargo, *Haswell*, 84.

[38] *Vermont Gazette*, cited by *ibid.*, 86.

[39] These details are taken from a sketch of Haswell by Hiland Hall, governor of Vermont, in *Vermont Quarterly Gazette, A Historical Magazine* (Oct., 1861), 176–177. Also see Wharton, *State Trials*, 687n.

[40] When Lyon did not stand for election in 1800, he was succeeded by Israel Smith, who had defended him and Haswell.

And Judge and Jury bent upon't,
Indicted, tried and trick'd em,
There Lyon growl'd but growl'd in vain.
For John was hard of hearing,
And Haswell sung a lonesome strain,
Two months in durance bearing.

At length election came about,
And democrats were handy,
They plied their skill the land throughout,
Sing Yankee Doodle Dandy;
Then Thomas took the seat from John,
And dungeons lost their men, Sir,
Through Jefferson the grace was shewn,
Our press is free again, Sir!

John took his flight in darkest gloom,
With sixteen moon-shine judges,
Away as silent as the tomb,
Each useless creature trudges,
The alien and sedition law,
Neglected lay a dying,
While federal printers fill'd with awe,
We heard peccavi crying.[41]

Seditious Criticism in Connecticut: Charles Holt and the New London Bee

The most interesting of the eighteenth-century gazettes in Connecticut was the New London *Bee*, edited by Charles Holt from 1797 until 1802. "During its brief career," writes the historian of Connecticut newspapers, "the *Bee* imparted more information per issue on political matters of the day than could be found in any other Connecticut journal. It seldom descended to unpleasant personalities, preferring to laud deserving men than to revile vulnerable ones." [42] The *Bee* suffered one handicap, however; it had the misfortune of being the most active Jeffersonian journal in Connecticut, the most Federalist of all the states.[43]

[41] Spargo, *Haswell*, 144–146.

[42] Jarvis Means Morse, *Connecticut Newspapers in the Eighteenth Century* (New Haven, Conn., 1935), 25–27.

This section has appeared in *The Historian*, 18 (1955), 41–56.

[43] Connecticut was the only state not to have at least one Republican in its representation. Its members included the most extreme of the Federalists: Senators James Hillhouse and Uriah Tracy and Congressmen John Allen, Samuel Dana, Joshua Coit, Nathaniel Smith, Roger Griswold, William Edmond, and Chauncey Goodrich.

Established in 1797, the *Bee* rapidly established itself among Democratic-Republican papers in New England as second only to the powerful Boston *Independent Chronicle*.[44] Its success was indicated by the mounting severity of the attacks on it by its opponents. At first the Federalists treated the *Bee* with lofty contempt. Although "Diogenes" called attention to the newly founded Republican newspaper, he hardly thought it worthy of mention. "I presume," he wrote in the *Connecticut Courant*, the state's most influential Federalist publication, "the Bee never was heard of by ten men in the state, except now and then a democrat, fifteen miles from New London. . . . Who the printers are I do not know. I dare say they do not wish that many enquiries should be made about them." [45]

When the Federalists did stoop to notice Holt, they dismissed him as one of the lowest grade of Jacobin printers. He survived, the New York *Daily Advertiser* asserted, only because he copied stories from the Philadelphia *Aurora*, which the Federalists denounced as "the fountain of disorganization." The ideas of the "antipatriot Bache" were ground over and over through the democratic mills "till at length it creeps out of Holt's hopper perfect bran." Although the New York editor might have suggested a sedition indictment against the *Bee*, he did not call for its immediate suppression. Instead, he advised the government to prosecute the *Aurora* so that the lesser "muddy streams," such as Holt's, would dry up.[46]

By the end of 1798, however, the Federalists had changed their minds about the *Bee*, fearing that it carried its own sting. When the editors of the *Courant* discovered the names of some of Holt's subscribers, they threatened to expose them to public censure for such an unpatriotic practice. Increasingly the *Bee* was condemned as a partisan press which published only the Republican version of political issues.[47] To these attacks, Holt hotly replied that since "nine tenths of the newspapers in Connecticut are decidedly partial to *one side*, and keep the *other* totally out of sight," he made it

[44] Donald H. Stewart, Jeffersonian Journalism, 1790–1801 (doctoral dissertation, Columbia University, 1950), 1125. This prodigious project deserves wider circulation.

[45] *Connecticut Courant*, March 5, 1798, quoted by J. Eugene Smith, *One Hundred Years of the Hartford Courant* (New Haven, 1949), 74.

[46] New York *Daily Advertiser*, July 28, 1798.

[47] *Courant*, May 27, 1799, Smith, *Hartford Courant*, 74. For a Connecticut Yankee's denunciation of the *Bee* as "remarkable only for its . . . scandalous abuse of our federal administration," see the *Courant*, Aug. 19, 1799.

"the business of THE BEE to print on *the other.*" He agreed that an impartial printer should publish both sides of public questions, but added that a perusal of Connecticut journals, filled with addresses to President Adams, would "lead to a belief that the whole country are united in approbation of all the measures of government, without a dissenting voice—which is not the fact." There had been extensive opposition to the Alien and Sedition Laws as unconstitutional, arbitrary, and oppressive, he continued, but these had not been reported in the Federalist gazettes. "If my contemporary editors wish to see the columns of the Bee sometimes filled with pretexts of *monarchy* and *aristocracy,*" he suggested that they "set the example by giving a place to facts and arguments in favor of *democracy,* and I will follow it with pleasure." Until that time, his attitude would be firm, though temperate and respectful. "Whatever may serve the true republican interest and support the wholesome laws and constitution of my country," he concluded, "shall be my constant endeavor to collect and publish." [48]

Outraged by such defiance, the Federalists redoubled their attacks on the *Bee.* The Hartford *Courant* leveled its shrillest invective at Holt, labeling him as "that lying drone from New London," and Richard Alsop, one of the Hartford Wits, branded his paper as seditious.[49] By the fall of 1799 the *Bee* was characterized by a Federalist gazette as "a notorious Jacobin paper." Holt replied that Connecticut's "spirit of federalism has arrived at an alarming height." He was convinced that "a man cannot vote as he pleases, read what newspapers he pleases, or hardly *think* as he pleases, without being denounced by the hot heads of the federal party as a Jacobin, and enemy to his country, and every attempt made to injure him." [50]

Unawed by Federalist frowns, Holt continued to blast the leaders and policies of the administration, leveling his most withering criticism at the provisional army raised during the Half War with France. On May 8, 1799, he printed a letter from a Danbury reader who condemned the federal forces as a standing army. Where, this writer queried, were recruits to be found for such an army? He denied that young farmers would volunteer. They would risk their lives readily enough to ward off invasion or to crush intestine

48 *Bee,* Nov. 14, 1798. When Congress passed the Sedition Law, Holt reminded his correspondents to exercise caution in phrasing their communications. *Ibid.,* July 18, 1798.

49 *Courant,* Sept. 30, 1799; Smith, *Hartford Courant,* 74; Alsop to King, Middletown, Conn., May 4, 1799, Harrington, *Alsop,* 30–31.

50 *Otsego Herald* (Cooperstown, N.Y.), Oct. 10, 1799; *Bee,* Nov. 21, 1798.

tumults, but they would never "give their bare backs to the smiter under Prussian military discipline, or devote their valor to promote the views of ambition or to oppose their country and prosperity with a standing army." To repel foreign foes they would fight, but they would never spend their best days "in arms & vice, in order to glitter in regimentals, wear a sword, and lounge in idleness as drones, unpitied and pennyless." Why should they, the correspondent asked, when by their industry and economy, they might become fathers of families, and men of great respectability, and even wealth, as "husbandmen in the immense regions which are cultivating in the west." [51]

The Danbury writer reserved his strongest remarks against the recruiting service for General Alexander Hamilton, who, only two years before, had confessed publicly to adultery in order to clear himself of charges of public corruption.[52] Was this man, the correspondent questioned, a proper commander for American youth? "Are our young officers and soldiers to learn virtue from general Hamilton? Or like their general are they to be found in the bed of adultery?" "This is a serious consideration," the writer continued, "for the army, for fathers, brothers, husbands and sons." [53] Standing armies should be discouraged in the United States not only for the sake of morality but because the people considered them "as useless and burthensome, as idle and dissipated." The correspondent concluded that this information should be considered by Connecticut's citizens before they permitted their sons to enter into wars that might destroy "both you and them." Fettered presses, he said, had screened this information from the citizens.

Fearful that the authorities might overlook this criticism of administration policy, Barzillai Hudson and George Goodwin, editors of the *Connecticut Courant*, initiated the sedition suit against Holt by furnishing the federal district attorney with a copy of the *Bee* containing the obnoxious remarks. When the grand jury finally

[51] *Bee*, May 6, 1799, reprinted in the Richmond *Examiner*, and *Virginia Argus*, May 9, 1800. For a similar view of the army, expressed by a Cabinet official during the same year, see Secretary of the Treasury Wolcott's observation that "the state of idleness to which they are necessarily condemned tends to corrupt their principles." Wolcott to Fisher Ames, Phila., Dec. 29, 1799, Gibbs, *Administrations of Washington and Adams*, II, 317.

[52] Alexander Hamilton, *Observations on Certain Documents Contained in No. V and VI of "The History of the United States for the Year 1796."*

[53] *Bee*, May 6, 1799. The writer added that "in actual service, especially on the frontiers & among the female Indians officers are not always moral, or careful to provide for their amours."

charged the Republican editor on September 17, 1799, with seditious utterances, they based the indictment on the copy which the Federalist publishers had provided.[54] Describing Holt as "a wicked, malicious, seditious and ill-disposed person" who was "greatly disaffected to the government of the United States of America," the indictment accused him of seditiously contriving to stir up and excite discontent and seditions among the citizenry, with intent to defame the government, President Adams, and both houses of Congress. His critical article, the grand jury charged, was designed to excite an unlawful combination for opposing and resisting the laws establishing the army recruiting service. "To the evil and pernicious example of all others," Holt had deliberately published his essay "in open violation of law." Not only were his utterances in contempt of the government; they also disturbed "the peace and dignity of the said United States." [55]

On September 21 Holt was arrested in New London and taken before Chief Justice Oliver Ellsworth and District Judge Richard Law, who were holding Circuit Court in Hartford. After the editor pleaded not guilty, the court set his trial for April, 1800, when he was to answer for his publication of the letter from one of his Danbury subscribers.

The Republican press did not wait until the trial to blast the proceedings against Holt. Opposition editors quickly pointed to the role played by the publishers of the *Courant* in bringing about the indictment. Moreover, Goodwin had two brothers on the grand jury which charged Holt. Without elaborating on their usual theme of "British influence" and Federalist favors to "old Tories," they also claimed that the foreman of the grand jury, Amos Bull, had been a British commissary during the American Revolution.[56]

During the period from September, 1799, until April, 1800, Holt discussed the coming trial and predicted that after the latter date the *Bee* would have to be suspended "for a length of time not to be determined by the editor." [57] *Carey's Diary* also predicted that Holt would be fined and imprisoned even though others had re-

---

[54] *Carey's Diary* (Philadelphia), reprinted in *Aurora*, Jan. 17, 1800.

[55] *Bee*, May 21, 1800.

[56] The first mention of the indictment of "Holt the *Bee man*" is in Congressman Chauncey Goodrich's letter to Secretary of the Treasury Wolcott, Hartford, Sept. 28, 1799, Wolcott Papers, V, 81 (Conn. Hist. Soc.). It is also reported in the *Kentucky Gazette* (Lexington), Oct. 24, 1799, and the *Otsego Herald*, Oct. 10, 1799. The grand jury story is taken from *Carey's Diary*, reprinted in the *Aurora*, Jan. 17, 1800.

[57] Morse, *Connecticut Newspapers*, 26.

printed what he had published without being indicted. This Philadelphia paper pointed out that Holt had not only offended the political powers in Connecticut, but also had antagonized the "illuminati" by exposing their art and malevolence. For that he would be rewarded by all the anathemas, prayers, and influence that the pulpit, throne, and sword could turn against him.[58]

The pending trial did not dampen Holt's enthusiasm for the Republican party. When a new opposition journal, the *Republican Ledger*, was established in Portsmouth, New Hampshire, he hailed its appearance as "the signal of *approaching day.*" The *"dawning in the east,"* he hoped, would dispel the Federalist darkness. Since "nothing but the freedom of the press can preserve the liberties of the people from the artifices of its pretended friends," he viewed the circulation of free papers in the United States as "a happy omen." Three weeks later he celebrated the appearance of another Republican paper, Boston's *Constitutional Telegraphe*. Appearing in the bosom of New England conservatism, it joined the *Independent Chronicle* in Boston, the new patriotic Portsmouth paper, "a good, tho' lukewarm paper in Dedham," and a few others, he said, which were giving New England "more and more enlightenment on political subjects." Although Holt omitted his own gazette from the list of leading Democratic prints in the Northeast, the *Aurora* announced that the circulation of the *Bee* "rises under persecution." [59]

Early in April, 1800, however, Holt indicated that the upward flight of the *Bee* probably would cease with his trial for sedition. Rather than apologize for his original story, he preferred to close temporarily his editorial career in Connecticut with more criticism of some of the soldiers stationed near New London. Although his pending trial had led him to refrain from publishing the exploits of some of the "defenders of the country," he declared that his regard for truth emboldened him to record their outrages. He had not reported stories about the rowdy conduct of some of the soldiers—of "the insults and threats offered to peaceable inhabitants and helpless women in the neighborhood, and the alarm and disturbance excited by firing in the streets and under the windows at all hours of the night." An enemy occupation army, the editor

---

[58] *Carey's Diary*, reprinted in the *Aurora*, Jan. 17, 1800. This prediction was close to the mark. Not only was Holt fined and imprisoned, but his trial was held in the New Haven meetinghouse; see the Richmond *Examiner*, May 13, 1800.

[59] *Bee*, Sept. 18 and Oct. 9, 1799; *Aurora*, Nov. 23, 1799.

asserted, could not have caused more uneasiness. The people near the garrison at Fort Trumbull feared "their lives and property were in jeopardy from men whom they scruple not to call a band of disorganized, unprincipled and abandoned characters, a burden, a pest, and a terror to the citizens who are taxed for their support." To Holt it appeared that such conduct answered "no good purpose but that of exciting in the breasts of citizens a natural and just abhorrence for standing armies." [60]

On April 11, 1800, Holt appeared before Judge Bushrod Washington at the New Haven Circuit Court to defend himself against the charge of printing seditious words "tending to discourage the recruiting service" and to bring the government of the United States into contempt and disrepute by asserting that it maintained a standing army.[61] His lawyers, David Daggett and Stephen T. Hosmer, readily admitted the fact that the letter had been published in the *Bee*, but they argued that it did not violate the law. First of all, they attacked the constitutionality of the Sedition Law itself, giving the usual legal arguments against the act. They asserted that the Preamble to the Constitution "specifies the *objects*, not the *powers* of the general government." The people delegated certain powers to the federal government but those not delegated remained with the states. The Constitution conferred no power on Congress to pass a sedition statute, nor could the "sweeping clause" be extended to the case in question. Moreover, "it would be dangerous thus to extend it by construction." [62] Holt's counsel argued two other points in justification of the letter. The factual parts of the letter were true, they declared, and the parts on which the indictment was based did not amount to a breach of the law because they were matters of opinion.[63]

Although the district attorney, Pierpont Edwards, conceded the

[60] *Bee*, April 2, 1800. Holt reported two assaults on respectable young women by soldiers and named one of the assailants.

[61] Richmond *Examiner*, May 9 and 13, 1800. Although the Federalists bitterly resented the criticism of General Hamilton, his reputation was not protected by the Sedition Law. For Hamilton's earlier suggestion that the reputations of all government officials be protected from libels, see his letter to Dayton, 1799, *Hamilton's Works* (Lodge ed.), VIII, 521–522, discussed in Chapter VIII; for Hamilton's prosecution of the New York *Argus*, see Chapter XVII.

[62] *Spectator*, April 26, 1800. Also see the *Commercial Advertiser*, April 23, 1800. Neither of these papers gave the defense arguments in justification of the publication because, they claimed, "the warmest advocates of the prisoner, in private conversation, admitted that if the law is constitutional, the jury ought to find the prisoner guilty."

[63] Richmond *Examiner*, May 9, 1800.

truth of the statements about Hamilton's "amours," he contended
that Holt had published a malicious falsehood when he called the
army a standing force instead of a provisional one. The whole of
the criminality, therefore, was predicated upon the assertion that
the United States had a standing army. This statement, the prosecution charged, was an attempt to undermine the confidence of the
people in the government and to bring it into contempt and disrepute.[64]

As a matter of fact, the question of army recruiting was a secondary feature of the trial. In his preliminary remarks defending the
constitutionality of the Sedition Law, Prosecutor Edwards said
that the people established the Constitution for "certain general
or national purposes" and therefore delegated to Congress "certain
specific powers of high national consequence, such as the collection of duties, and the raising of armies for defense and protection." Since the power to raise forces for the general defense was
expressly delegated to Congress, Edwards continued, "it forms a
necessary consequence, that they must have the power to punish
any attempt to defeat the measures they had adopted for that
purpose." "Malicious attempts to defeat the operations of the law,
by bringing into contempt the government and the men who administer it, is universally admitted to be a great crime and justly
punishable. If so, then the government of the United States must
possess the same power to defend its measures, from such slanderous attempts, as every other government." Malicious falsehoods
against the government and its laws were calculated "to withdraw
from it the public confidence, render the laws odious to the people,
and thus defeat their operation." The United States could punish
these falsehoods in order to make its deliberations respected as the
public will. This power, the district attorney concluded, was more
necessary in a free government than in any other because it "rests
entirely on the confidence of the people. Deprive such a government
of the public confidence, and its energy is destroyed—its ends are
defeated." [65] According to the prosecutor, the only liberty abridged
by the Sedition Law was "the liberty of *lying maliciously*—a liberty
which none but rascals can wish to enjoy."

[64] Although the prosecutor argued that the *Bee's* story "tended" to discourage
the recruiting service, there is no indication that he offered any evidence that
the article actually discouraged recruitment.

[65] *Spectator*, April 26, 1800. Also see the *Commercial Advertiser*, April 23,
1800. It is clear from this statement of the law that any peaceful agitation for the
repeal of an odious law might be punished under the Sedition Law. This was the
position taken in the Peck case; see Chapter XVII.

In his "learned, candid and dispassionate charge" to the jury, Judge Washington made a verdict of guilty almost inevitable by striking down Holt's two defense arguments. "By a train of reasoning too powerful to be resisted," reported a New Haven correspondent, the Supreme Court justice upheld the constitutionality of the Sedition Act and proved Holt's "publication to be libellous, beyond even the possibility of a doubt." [66] A Federalist paper claimed that the government's case and the judge's charge were so impressive that "even the friends of the prisoner who had collected from Dan to Beersheba, to hear the trial, and afford aid and comfort to their brother, discovered some symptoms of conviction." The countenances of most of them fell, however, "and they appeared confounded." [67]

The jury retired overnight and returned a verdict of guilty on April 12, 1800. When Holt appeared for sentencing, Judge Washington lectured him on the tendency which "libels on a free government have to discredit and destroy the Government itself," and on the especially "heinous and aggravating circumstances which attended the publication of the libel" in the *Bee*. The court then imposed a three-month prison sentence and a $200 fine, but granted Holt's request that he be confined at New London.[68]

Although a Federalist paper praised the "humanity of the Judges" in assessing such mild punishment,[69] the Republican press quickly assailed the conviction. In any other times, the *Aurora* lamented, the prosecution would have excited astonishment. Even in 1800, when sedition trials were common occurrences, "the public were so interested in this audacious stretch of power, that the court was under the necessity of removing from its ordinary place of sitting to the *meeting house*, to complete in the house of God the work of—*religion and order*." [70]

[66] *Connecticut Journal* (New Haven), April 24, 1800. Also see *Gazette of the United States*, April 24, 1800.

[67] *Commercial Advertiser*, April 23, 1800; *Spectator*, April 26, 1800.

[68] *Connecticut Journal*, April 24, 1800. Holt later advertised "An Account of the Trial of Charles Holt, for Sedition, before the Circuit Court of the United States, at New Haven, on the 17th of April, 1800." See the *Bee*, Sept. 3, 1800. Although he registered the title on July 9, 1800, and promised that the pamphlet would be published shortly, it apparently never appeared in print. T. R. Harlow, Director of the Connecticut Historical Society, to the author, Jan. 6, 1953.

[69] *Commercial Advertiser*, April 23, 1800. Also see the *Spectator*, April 26, 1800. These papers "trusted" that in this one case a three-month jail sentence would not "dishonor" the Sedition Law, which allowed sentences up to two years and fines up to $2,000.

[70] *Aurora*, April 25, 1800.

If the report of the trial was true, the New York *American Citizen* commented, editors would have to obtain a dictionary containing all the terms applicable to a body of enlisted soldiers in order to keep clear of prosecutions. "It would require indeed a connoisseur in law terms," the paper continued, "to tell why the word *standing* was more seditious and libellous than the word *provisional.*" The editor was not without his own ideas on the definitions of these terms: some thought that the word "provisional" "was the only proper term to apply to men who did nothing but eat provisions. But during the American war," he concluded, "the army was properly called a standing army because they had to stand and face their enemies." [71]

William Duane, editor of the *Aurora,* compared the Holt case with that of Thomas Cooper, whose indictment also referred to the question of a standing army. In that trial, Justice Chase had explained to the jury that it was criminal to impute to the president the design of maintaining a standing army. Under the Constitution, the judge had declared, there could be no such thing as a standing army because that charter provides that army supplies can be voted no longer than two years. Since Congress can withhold these supplies, Chase ruled, all armies of the United States are provisional rather than permanent. [72] This was a judicial bit of sophistry, the *Aurora* concluded, which was a naked and ridiculous attempt to blind the public. In England, a country to which the judges were always referring for precedents, Parliament passed the mutiny bill every year. This was the only legitimate authority for maintaining the British army, and on that basis the American provisional army had twice the duration of the British standing army. The imperial army was maintained, Duane wrote, by the ascendancy of the British executive in Parliament. "By corruption, by family influence, by places, titles, and pensions," it secured a majority of the 558 members of Commons and of "250 senators or PEERS." What was done in England to maintain a standing army, the *Aurora* concluded, might be done anywhere "avaricious and vicious" men were found. [73]

That Holt's article was no blow to the provisional army may be

---

[71] *American Citizen* (New York), April 22, 1800, reprinted in the *Virginia Argus* (Richmond), May 2, 1800. Also see the Richmond *Examiner*, May 13, 1800.

[72] See *U.S.* v. *Cooper,* Wharton, *State Trials,* 676.

[73] *Aurora,* April 29, 1800. At the time this article appeared, Duane was hiding out from a Senate contempt citation.

shown easily. The tension with France had eased so much by 1800 that only a month after Holt's conviction President Adams signed a law providing for the disbanding of the provisional army on June 15, 1800. Congress was debating this law when Holt was convicted. It is clear that the editor was prosecuted in 1800 because his vigorous articles, in the words of the district attorney, tended to bring "into contempt the government and the men who administer it." The prosecution and conviction effectively silenced the troublesome Republican editor from April 2 until August 27 in the crucial election year of 1800.[74] Moreover, the editor was deprived of his means of livelihood at the same time that a fine was levied.[75]

While in prison, Holt suspended the publication of the *Bee*, except for a supplement issued in May. In expressing his regret that his paper could not appear regularly, he did not overlook the opportunity to jab at the Federalists. "It is impossible to continue" a newspaper, he wrote, while being held "a close prisoner in the common gaol of this city." [76] He informed his readers, however, that he planned to revive the *Bee* in an enlarged and improved form. The *Albany Register* urged "the friends of Liberty, not only in Connecticut, but in the neighboring states," to support Holt's paper when he was in a position to issue it again, predicting that if a few more such papers could be established in New England the principles of 1776 would triumph over "the new-fangled doctrines of *Aristocracy* which a combination of *Apostates* have been too successful in disseminating in those states." [77]

A month after Holt's release, the *Bee* was back in business. Chastised but unrepentant, the editor promised to serve his readers with equal zeal, though with more prudence than formerly. "Instructed so well in the doctrines and consequences of libels and seditions, he believes there is little danger of suffering for want of knowledge or

[74] See the *Bee*, May 21, 1800, for the report that Congress had authorized the disbanding of the army.

[75] Meriwether Jones, editor of the Richmond *Examiner*, proposed that a joint contribution be made by Republicans in Virginia to aid the families of his "persecuted fellow workers," Holt and Cooper, both of whom were convicted in the same month. As Holt had no children, Jones suggested that prior consideration be given Mrs. Cooper. Richmond *Examiner*, reprinted in the *Virginia Argus*, May 9, 1800.

[76] *Bee*, May 21, 1800. Jefferson "paid sums of money for the bee" when it was "staggering under the sedition law." Jefferson to Monroe, July 17, 1802, *Jefferson's Writings* (Ford ed.), VII, 167.

[77] *Albany Register*, June 3, 1800. As in the Lyon case, Senator Stevens T. Mason raised money to pay Holt's fine. See Mason to Jefferson, Raspberry Plain, July 11, 1800, Jefferson Papers, CVI, 18317–18318 (Lib. Cong.).

discretion on these points." Since he had been taught the value of liberty during his deprivation of it, he trusted that the sincerity of his attachment to the cause of freedom and justice would not be doubted. Once again he vowed that in the conduct of the *Bee* "a firm and undeviating course will therefore be pursued, in disseminating useful knowledge and cultivating and maintaining a reverence and love for our constitution and our liberties as secured by that important instrument."

Following his return to freedom, Holt not unnaturally made the Sedition Law his chief target. In his first issue he quoted "an ingenious writer's" attack on that Federalist enactment: "Those who are locking up the press . . . because it produces, at times, gross libels, ought to consider that the *sun* and the *Nile* produce monsters, and that it is something better for the world to bear a few inconveniences arising from general blessings, than to be wholly deprived of fire and water." Holt added that "*guilt* is more galled by *truth* than innocence by *lies;* and hence it has been said by a set of worthies that they do not care what falsehoods are published concerning them, but will never forgive one who meddles with facts!" [78]

In a thinly disguised criticism of the authorities, Holt wrote under the name of "Nathan Sleek," supposedly an exasperated Federalist who deplored the reappearance of the *Bee.* "I see . . . no good comes from those trials for sedition," Sleek protested; "I did hope that a little wholesome chastisement would reform your manners, or render you more cautious in your observations." Regretful that Judge Washington had not extracted "the jacobinical sting" from the *Bee,* Sleek was certain that Judge Samuel Chase, "that sworn enemy of free democrats . . . , would have made you a real example, to terrify democratic printers from insolently avowing opinions contrary to the ruling powers." "Punishment only hardens printers," the editor-as-irate-Federalist concluded; "they come out of jail holding their heads higher than if they had never been persecuted. Finally they assume the appearance of innocent men who have suffered wrongfully." [79]

Charles Holt never wrote truer words.

[78] *Bee,* Aug. 27, 1800. On October 1 the *Bee* reported that some Americans were emigrating to Canada to avoid the Alien and Sedition Laws.
[79] *Bee,* Sept. 3, 1800.

CHAPTER XVII

Sedition, Subversion, and Suppression: The New York Cases

In times like these in which we live, it will not
do to be over-scrupulous.—ALEXANDER HAMILTON

BOTH before and after the federal common law case against the
New York *Time Piece* in 1798, the administration checked closely on
Republican political publications in the Empire State for seditious
criticism. The final flurry of proceedings in New York involved
three comparatively little known cases—the conviction and pardon
of William Durrell, the indictment of Jedidiah Peck for circulating
a petition against the Alien and Sedition Laws, and the combined
federal-state measures against Mrs. Ann Greenleaf and David Frothingham of the New York *Argus*.

The Sedition and Pardon of William Durrell

Most of the victims of the sedition prosecutions during the administration of President Adams were Jeffersonian journalists who
criticized the Federalist program. William Durrell, publisher of an
obscure upstate New York weekly, had the double distinction of
being the first editor arrested after the enactment of the sedition
statute and the only Republican pardoned for his offensive remarks.
It also appears that his case, unlike the other federal cases, was tried
under the common law doctrine of seditious libels rather than under
the Sedition Law of 1798.

As editor of the *Mount Pleasant Register,* Durrell reprinted from the *New Windsor Gazette* of June 5, 1798, a paragraph which was critical of the president. When a copy reached Timothy Pickering, the ever-vigilant secretary of state carefully marked the passage. Enclosing it to Richard Harison, federal district attorney for New York, he instructed the government prosecutor, a loyal Federalist, to determine whether the obnoxious paragraph contained libelous matter. If he should decide that it did, he was to institute a prosecution against the editor of the *New Windsor Gazette* and another against Durrell for his reprinting the article.[1]

Although these instructions were written more than two weeks before the Sedition Law went into effect, Durrell was not arrested until July 17, three days after President Adams had signed that measure. Taken into custody in the name of the president for a libel against the chief magistrate of the nation, Durrell was released on $4,000 bail, a large sum for a country printer.[2] Endorsing this action as "VERY GOOD," the leading upstate Federalist organ added "*so they go*," recalling that both Benjamin Franklin Bache, editor of the Philadelphia *Aurora,* and John Daly Burk, director of the New York *Time Piece,* were already under common law indictments for seditious libels against President Adams.[3]

Although the trial dangled over the editor's head for nearly two years, the consequences of this legal threat were immediate. Fearful that his inability "to discriminate" might lead him inadvertently to publish an offensive article, Durrell immediately discontinued the publication of his country journal. Thus the pending prosecution reduced him to poverty even before his indictment.[4]

It was not until the autumn of 1799 that Durrell was formally indicted for publishing the "false scandalous malicious and defamotry [*sic*] Libel of and concerning John Adams." Unfortunately, the historical investigator, like President Adams, cannot gratify his desire

[1] Pickering to Harison, June 28, 1798, Pickering Papers, VIII, 604 (Mass. Hist. Soc.), and *Domestic Letters (1797–1798)*, X, 437, RG 59 (National Archives).

This section was published in *The New York Historical Society Quarterly*, 40 (1956).

[2] *Mount Pleasant Register*, July 24, 1798, reprinted in the *Albany Gazette,* Aug. 14, 1798; *Time Piece,* Aug. 8, 1798. Durrell had to post $2,000 for his appearance and two sureties had to post $1,000 each. The editor of the New Windsor paper was not arrested.

[3] *Albany Centinel,* Aug. 14, 1798.

[4] "Sworn Petition for Clemency," *U.S.* v. *William Durrell,* April 5, 1800, *Minute Book, 1790–1808,* Eastern Circuit of the New York District, 176, RG 21 (National Archives).

for "more Information of the Nature of the Libell"; both the indictment and the news item for which Durrell was arrested have been
lost, leaving no record of the objectionable remarks. Nor do the minutes of the court proceedings specify whether the editor was indicted
at common law or under the Sedition Act of 1798. It is more than
probable, however, that he was not charged under the sedition statute, because his offense occurred nearly a month before the passage
of that law. To have indicted him under this measure, therefore,
would have constituted a clear violation of the ex post facto provision of the Constitution. Durrell must have been charged under the
common law of seditious libel. In such cases, unlike those tried
under the Sedition Law, the truth of the critical remarks could not
be offered as a defense, and the province of the jury was narrowed
to deciding, not whether the words were false, scandalous, and
malicious, but simply whether the accused had published the critical
opinions.[5]

On September 5, 1799 Durrell pleaded not guilty before the United
States Circuit Court. After District Attorney Harison requested the
postponement of the trial, the editor's bail was reduced to $3,000,
and he was released until the next circuit held in New York City.[6]
This delay in the trial, Durrell later complained, reduced his hard-
hit printing business to a minimum, thus operating as a "severe
punishment independent of the inconvenience and expence of attending the several Courts." Indeed, the unemployed printer's pre-
cipitous progress to poverty was climaxed in the autumn of 1799
when the sheriff of Westchester County foreclosed on Durrell's real
and personal property, forcing him to borrow the furniture with
which he, his wife, and five children kept house.[7]

During the election year of 1800 the Federalists increasingly resorted to sedition prosecutions as a political weapon against Republican writers. When the case of the inconspicuous upstate printer
came up in the spring of 1800, therefore, it attracted little attention

[5] Durrell was indicted on Sept. 4, 1799. See *Minute Book, 1790–1808*, 146.
These proceedings, however, do not specify the libelous matter. The other
records of the federal courts for the Southern District of New York in the
National Archives do not contain Durrell's indictment or case papers, nor are
these to be found in the records remaining in the office of the Clerk of the
Court for the Southern District. Pertinent copies of the *Mount Pleasant Register*
and the *New Windsor Gazette* do not exist. See Evans, *American Bibliography*,
XII, item 32156, 129, and Brigham, *American Newspapers, 1690–1820*, I, 605.

[6] *U.S. v. Durrell*, Sept. 5, 1799, *Minute Book, 1790–1808*, 146–147, RG 21
(National Archives).

[7] "Sworn Petition for Clemency," April 5, 1800, *ibid.*, 176–177.

compared with the coverage given the proceedings against such prominent Jeffersonian publicists as William Duane, Thomas Cooper, and James T. Callender. Moreover, the trial was a routine affair, lacking the dramatic qualities which high-lighted these widely publicized prosecutions. The only evidence introduced by the government, for instance, was the *Mount Pleasant Register* containing the offensive criticism. Without hearing any defense testimony, the presiding judge, Associate Justice Bushrod Washington of the United States Supreme Court, read his charge to the jury, which shortly returned a verdict of guilty.[8]

On April 5 the convicted editor presented a pitiable plea for clemency, setting forth his ignorance of the fact that republication of objectionable criticism was, like original publication, a criminal offense. Although he did not admit the illegality of the article which he had published, he agreed that it was an improper item which he would have rejected had he read it "with but common attention." He ascribed his difficulty to a personal grudge held by the informer whose affidavit provided the basis for the charge against him. The issue of the *New Windsor Gazette* from which he had copied the fateful words, Durrell swore, had been presented to his office by this unidentified person with the premeditated intent of bringing him into difficulty with the law. His enemy, moreover, had since boasted that "he was the sole cause of that publication." [9]

Turning from this rather disingenuous argument, the editor attempted to buttress his request for clemency with a plea of poverty. Pointing to the discontinuance of his newspaper, he observed that he had been out of business for nearly two years; a jail sentence, therefore, would deprive his family of their sole source of support—the labor of his hands—thus compounding "the distresses of the innocent and helpless." After this impassioned plea, Judge Washington and District Judge John Sloss Hobart postponed a decision on punishment, but four days later they sentenced Durrell to four months in jail and a fifty-dollar fine. He was to remain in prison until the fine was paid; upon his release he was to post a $2,000 security for his good behavior for two years.[10]

[8] Only two witnesses were sworn. John T. Bainbridge identified the *Register* in which the libel appeared. Mordeca Hale is also listed as a prosecution witness, but the nature of his testimony is not given. *U.S. v. Durrell*, April 4, 1800, *ibid.*, 172–173.

[9] "Sworn Petition for Clemency," April 5, 1800, *ibid.*, 176–177.

[10] Durrell was sentenced on April 9, 1800, *ibid.*, 186–187. For brief accounts of the trial, see the *Commercial Advertiser*, April 17, 1800; *Spectator*, April 19,

"It is remarkable," the Republican press observed, "that the original publisher of the *Libel* has not been taken notice of, while the person who only republished it, is shut up in prison, and deprived of the means of supporting his family, who are incapable of helping themselves." [11] This was no exaggeration, and the prosecutor and the federal judges prevailed upon Pickering and the president to pardon Durrell.

The day after the editor began his sentence, Harison wrote the secretary of state that Durrell "appears to be very poor at present, has a large family to maintain, and has a considerable Time since discontinued his news paper." Moreover, the editor met the conditions laid down by the president in Congressman Lyon's case that "penitence precede pardon." "He pretends also that the Libell was inadvertently copied from another Paper," Harison pointed out, "and that it would not have been published in his, if he had been fully apprised of it's Nature." As Durrell's offense related only to the president personally and not to his administration or to the government, the federal judges who sentenced him had hinted to the prosecutor that "it might be worthy of Consideration whether a Remission of all the Sentence except what relates to the Security for future conduct, might not operate beneficially." The unemployed editor scarcely seemed an object for example to other editors, and the prosecutor obviously thought that leniency would be more expedient politically than punishment.[12]

Impressed by the prosecutor's opinion and "the Intimations of the Judges," President Adams decided on magnanimity, but not without some reluctance. "I wish," he wrote Pickering, ". . . that I had more Information of the Nature of the Libell." Although he refused to grant a full pardon, he directed the secretary to release Durrell from "all the Sentence, except what relates to the Security for future good Behaviour." In accordance with this authorization, Pickering forwarded Durrell's partial pardon to Harison on April 22, 1800.[13]

1800; *American Citizen* (New York), April 18 and 21, 1800; *Virginia Argus*, May 2, 1800; and Milton Wheaton Hamilton, *The Country Printer, New York State, 1785–1830* (New York, 1936), 175.

[11] *American Citizen*, April 21, 1800.

[12] Harison to Pickering, New York, April 10, 1800, Pickering Papers, XXVI, 77 (Mass. Hist. Soc.).

[13] Adams to Pickering, Phila., April 21, 1800, *Miscellaneous Letters, Jan.–Dec., 1800*, RG 59 (National Archives); Pickering to Harison, Phila., April 22, 1800, Pickering Papers, XIII, 406 (Mass. Hist. Soc.).

After serving less than two weeks of his four-month sentence, Durrell became the only seditious culprit to be released from fine and imprisonment by a presidential pardon.[14] His security for future good conduct, however, remained in force as a reminder that he was bound not to repeat his criticisms of President Adams without risking the loss of his $2,000 security. This seems to have been enough to insure the continued silence of the impoverished printer.

The Sedition Law and the Right of Petition: The Peck Case

More than any indictment under the Sedition Act of 1798, other than that of Congressman Matthew Lyon, the criminal proceedings against Jedidiah Peck reveal the extreme to which the repression of political opinion could be pushed under that law. At the time of his arrest in 1799, Peck was a member of the New York Assembly. His sole sedition consisted of circulating a petition which favored the repeal of the Alien and Sedition Laws. The attempt of the Federalists to prosecute him for exercising a right guaranteed by the First Amendment illustrated the immediate political purposes to which the Sedition Law could be put.

A soldier in the Revolution, Peck later settled in the frontier county of Otsego, New York, in 1790, where he became a jack-of-all-trades. Although he was a skillful millwright, he could also "survey your farm in the day time, exhort and pray in your family at night, and talk on politics the rest . . . of the time." Despite the lack of a formal education, he was a man of native sagacity whose writings show familiarity not only with the Bible but with ancient and modern history, the classics, and philosophy.[15] By virtue of his persistent efforts to establish a free common school system, he is best remembered as the father of the public school system in New York.[16]

---

[14] Book of Pardons and Remissions, No. I, 1794–1812, 31–32, RG 59 (National Archives). Also see the American Citizen, May 5, 1800.

[15] Jabez D. Hammond, The History of Political Parties in . . . New York . . . to 1840 (Albany, 1842), I, 124; Throop Wilder, "Jedidiah Peck, Statesman, Soldier, Preacher," New York History, 22 (1941), 293. Wilder says that Peck cited Pascal, Paine, Montesquieu, Rousseau, and Quintillian.

This section is a more substantially documented account than my article in New York History, 35 (1954), 63–72.

[16] See Sherman Williams, "Jedidiah Peck, the Father of the Public School System of the State of New York," N.Y. State Hist. Assoc., Quarterly Journal, 1 (1920), 219–240. Peck was a member of the state Assembly from 1798 until 1804, when he was elected to the state Senate (1804–1808). He also served as a member of the state Council of Appointment.

Peck entered politics as a frontier Federalist and was soon in conflict with the aristocratic leaders of the party in Otsego County. Writing under the name of "Plough Jogger," he led a revolt within the Federalist party for a greater voice in the rank and file. In 1796 he ran for the state Assembly against General Jacob Morris, son of one of the signers of the Declaration of Independence and nephew of the confirmed Federalist, Gouverneur Morris. During this unsuccessful campaign, Peck made political capital out of his own lack of a formal education. "I dare say," he wrote in a letter to one of the lawyers who opposed him, "you cannot only prove by your old books, that despotic government is best; but that courts of inquisition, are the best to keep the dull rebels in awe, to govern the swinish multitude, to teach block-heads, and that ignorance is the mother of devotion." [17]

Although Peck was a firm believer in the ability of the common man to participate in governmental affairs, he did not identify himself with the Republican party in these early campaigns. [18] Nor did he oppose Judge William Cooper, the country squire who dominated the Federalist party in central New York. Instead, he presided at a meeting which voted unanimously to support the judge's re-election to Congress. Although sustaining another defeat in the election of 1797, Peck was still in good enough standing with the Federalists to be appointed an associate judge of the Otsego County Court of Common Pleas over which Judge Cooper presided. Peck's political fortunes now took an upturn and in 1798 he was elected to the state Assembly. [19]

In the first flush of national feeling during the Half War with France, Peck presided over a meeting of local citizens who sent to President John Adams a laudatory address denouncing the French Directory and calling for defense measures. [20] In the state legislature,

[17] Jedidiah Peck, *The Political Wars of Otsego County; or the Downfall of Jacobinism* (Cooperstown, 1796), 90, quoted by James Arthur Frost, *Life on the Upper Susquehanna, 1763–1860* (New York, 1951), 47. The next three paragraphs rely heavily on Frost's excellent sketch of the conflict between the Federalists, led by Judge Cooper, and the Republicans, who rallied behind Peck after 1799.

[18] Hammond, *Political Parties in New York*, I, 115, says: "Strictly speaking, the federal party in that county [Otsego] could hardly be said at that time to have had any opposition." Also see Francis Whiting Halsey, *The Old New York Frontier, 1614–1800* (New York, 1901), 365–368.

[19] *Otsego Herald* (Cooperstown), Sept. 15, 1796, and April 27, 1797, quoted by Frost, *Upper Susquehanna*, 47; Hammond, *Political Parties in New York*, I, 115.

[20] *Otsego Herald*, May 31, 1798.

however, Peck did not always vote with the Federalists. With eight or ten other members who had been elected as Federalists, he voted with his party on the matter of political appointments and "personal questions." But on questions involving measures and principles, the same ideals which had led him to revolt against aristocratic leadership in the Federalist party led him to vote usually on the democratic side.[21] The regular Federalists lashed at Peck as a "trimmer" and accused him of going over to the "French party." [22]

The Sedition Law could only alienate a man who believed that the people are competent to choose and criticize their rulers. Judge Peck, who had fought for that principle from within the Federalist party, continued to do so in the Assembly. When the legislature debated the Kentucky and Virginia Resolutions in February, 1799, Peck not only opposed the Federalist moves to reject them but also favored a resolve declaring the Alien and Sedition Laws unconstitutional. Although the Federalists adopted a resolution which stated that only the judiciary could decide on the constitutionality of laws, Peck voted for the Republican motion which asserted that the right of expressing an opinion on the constitutionality of all laws belonged not only to the judicial branch "but also to the people, both as private individuals and as legislators." This resolve disclaimed "the servile idea" that it was improper for the Assembly to adopt resolutions applauding or disapproving the acts of Congress or any branch of the federal government.[23]

When the motion censuring both the Alien and Sedition Laws failed, Peck voted for two resolutions which separately declared the laws unconstitutional.[24] At the same session he moved farther from the Federalists when he supported a Republican measure which would have provided for the election of presidential electors by the people rather than by the state legislature.

Incensed with Peck's apostasy, the Federalists retaliated on March 9, 1799, when they secured his removal as judge of the Court of Common Pleas. This dismissal was unlike other cases of removal, for the cause of removal does not appear on the minutes of the Council of Appointment. Nor was Peck allowed to appear and defend himself against the undisclosed charge that was lodged against him.

[21] Hammond, *Political Parties in New York*, I, 123.

[22] *Otsego Herald*, Sept. 6, 1798.

[23] *Journal of the Assembly of the State of New York at Their Twenty Second Session, 1798–1799* (Feb. 16, 1799), 120. The Federalists, who controlled the Assembly, declared that such an assertion had a "direct tendency to destroy the independence of the general government." *Ibid.*, 123.

[24] *Ibid.*, 121–122.

That the Federalists had read Peck out of the party appeared evident when the aristocratic leadership, including Judge Cooper, lined up against him in his campaign for re-election. Less than two months later, however, Peck was returned to the Assembly by a triumphant majority, and organized the frontier democracy under the banner of Jefferson's Democratic-Republican party.[25]

It was Peck's animosity for the Alien and Sedition Laws which gave the Otsego County Federalists their opportunity to suppress the man they could not defeat at the polls. General John Armstrong, author of the Newburgh Letters after the Revolution and himself a Federalist until the extreme laws of 1798,[26] wrote a severe petition to Congress advocating the repeal of the Alien and Sedition Laws. Copies of this petition were sent to Peck, who had opposed the laws in the state legislature and who now gladly circulated them among his neighbors for signatures. "He always had his saddle bags with him," wrote one of his neighbors, "filled with political papers and scraps, that he distributed wherever he went from home." [27]

Condemning the obnoxious congressional measures as "a Series of Evils equally diffusive and calamitous, equally general and destructive," Peck's petition predicted that they would lead to a foreign war, a violated Constitution, and a divided people. Originated in mistake and prosecuted in error, the Federalist program had become the foundation of a "System of Alarm, of Suspicion, of Tyranny, and of Expense." Although the petition lashed the Alien Friends Act as ungenerous, unjust, unnecessary, and unconstitutional, it reserved its sharpest slaps for the Sedition Law. "The former is directed at Foreigners; the latter is levelled at ourselves. The former tyrannizes over Men, who in general have been born and bred under oppression. But it is the superlative Wickedness of the latter to convert Freemen into Slaves." [28]

[25] Hammond, *Political Parties in New York*, I, 122–123, 127; Frost, *Upper Susquehanna*, 48; and Halsey, *The Old New York Frontier*, 367.

[26] De Alva Stanwood Alexander, *A Political History of the State of New York* (New York, 1906), I, 89. Armstrong was not then known as the author. In 1800, the general was chosen United States senator.

[27] Levi Beardsley, *Reminiscences . . . Early Settlement of Otsego County* (New York, 1852), 72.

[28] Portions of the petition are printed in Irving Mark and Eugene L. Schwaab, *The Faith of Our Fathers* (New York, 1952), 11–12. Parts are also recited in the indictment in the case of *U.S.* v. *Jedidiah Peck*, in *Records of the U.S. Circuit Court*, Southern District of N.Y., Sept. 4, 1799, RG 21 (National Archives). There is a broadside, which contains the complete text, in the Wolcott Papers, XV, 60 (Conn. Hist. Soc.).

In the opinion of Judge Cooper, then a Federalist congressman, the mere circulation of the petition was seditious. Denouncing Peck as an "agent of the disafected [sic]," the distraught judge, fearing that there was "a want of Energy to silence those wretches," was exercised that the remote parts of the nation were "kept in constant dissatisfaction with the General Government by the industry of its enemies." To prove his conviction that "the Public tranquillity is a Consideration not to be neglected," the congressman inserted an advertisement in the local paper bluntly warning his constituents that persons circulating the petition were liable to two years in federal prison and a $2,000 fine. After informing the public that Peck had wickedly imported the petition into Otsego County, Cooper mailed a copy to District Judge John Sloss Hobart, insisting that the assemblyman should be prosecuted under the Sedition Law.[29] The federal judge relayed the information to District Attorney Harison, who had received an order from Secretary of State Pickering in 1799 to step up prosecutions for sedition.[30] When Harison recommended action against Peck, the grand jury which indicted Durrell and Mrs. Ann Greenleaf, proprietor of the New York *Argus*, presented the state legislator for his "evil and pernicious Example" to others. The indictment ran in the usual form, accusing Peck of wickedly and maliciously circulating "with Force and Arms" a false, scandalous, and malicious petition to Congress in "open violation of law . . . and against the Peace and dignity of the United States." [31]

Following Peck's arrest at Burlington late in September, 1799, the Federalist press jubilantly reported that the "influential jacobin" had been taken into custody.[32] The Republican *Register* of Albany, on the other hand, denounced "that powerful state engine, the Sedition Law of Congress," and traced the indictment to the political wars in Otsego County. "The influence which Mr. Peck has acquired

[29] William Cooper to Oliver Wolcott, Cooperstown, Aug. 20 and Sept. 16, 1799, Wolcott Papers, XV, 43, 59 (Conn. Hist. Soc.); William Cooper, "CAUTION," Cooperstown, April 18, 1799, *Albany Centinel*, April 23, 1799.

[30] Pickering to Harison, Aug. 12, 1799, Pickering Papers, XI, 599 (Mass. Hist. Soc.); Lyman H. Butterfield, "Judge William Cooper (1754–1809): A Sketch of his Character and Accomplishment," *New York History*, 30 (1949), 400; and Hammond, *Political Parties in New York*, I, 131–132. Cooper served in Congress from 1799 until 1801 and consistently voted against attempts to repeal these laws.

[31] Manuscript indictment, *U.S. v. Jedidiah Peck*, Sept. 4, 1799, RG 21 (National Archives).

[32] For Peck's arrest, see the *Albany Register*, Oct. 1, 1799, quoted in the *Bee*, Oct. 16, 1799. For the Federalist reaction, see the *Gazette of the United States*, Oct. 9, 1799.

in Otsego . . . ," the paper declared, "has without doubt become dangerous in the views of the faction in that county." Moreover, his conviction, whether instigated by "the lower grade of spies and delators, or the more dignified automaton of faction," would deprive his constituents of his services "at an interesting crisis."

The paper charged that Peck had alienated the Federalists by moving several resolutions, "the success of which, by re-investing the people with their most important elective rights, would have given a death blow to the political consequences" of the dominant party. Defending the Republican legislator as "a man who has the virtue and firmness to resist the encroachments of power, and to point out to his fellow citizens the necessity and the objects of reform," the *Register* concluded that the Federalist effort to crush Peck was "an attempt truly worthy of the satellites of aristocracy." [33]

Peck's five days' journey as a prisoner from Cooperstown to New York City in the fall of 1799 became a triumphant processional rather than the march of a doomed man. One historian has written:

A hundred missionaries in the cause of democracy, stationed between New-York and Cooperstown could not have done so much for the republican cause as this journey of Judge Peck. . . . It was nothing less than the public exhibition of a suffering martyr for the freedom of speech and the press, and the right of petitioning, to the view of the citizens of the various places through which the marshal travelled with his prisoner.[34]

Republican newspapers reported that Peck was "taken from his home at midnight, manacled, and dragged from his home," because he dared ask his neighbors to petition Congress to repeal the offensive Sedition Law. "The rule of George Third," declared another, "was gracious and loving compared to such tyranny." [35]

Although he was arrested in 1799, the "Plough Jogger's" trial was not scheduled until April, 1800, the month in which he was up for re-election.

While his trial was pending, Peck continued to represent his constituents in the General Assembly. In the session which began on January 28 and ended on April 8, 1800, the Republicans chose him to introduce a bill to divide the state into districts for the choice of presidential electors by the people rather than by the legislature.

[33] Quoted in the *Bee*, Oct. 16, 1799.
[34] Hammond, *Political Parties in New York*, I, 132.
[35] Quoted by Alexander, *Political History of New York*, I, 89. Alexander says that "in the wildest delirium of revolutionary days, when patriots were refusing to drink tea, and feeding it to the fishes, New York had not been more deeply stirred than now."

The Federalists not only opposed this measure as unconstitutional but argued that the people, because of their lack of knowledge, were not as capable for this task as the legislators. Peck headed the Republican speakers, who defended the right of the people to choose the electors.[36]

In reporting the debates on this bill, the New York *American Citizen* attacked the Federalist position that the people could not be trusted as much as the legislators in selecting electors. "If this was true, and the sentiment generally prevailed, this country would instantly be under the most [un]qualified monarchy or aristocracy." Without mentioning Peck's pending trial, the paper asked this question:

Would not the federal judges do more honor to the cause of republicanism, if, while they are pointing out the bad effects of libels in a free representative government, they would mention the above as the most pernicious libel that was ever promulgated against any people. If the people be not capacitated to perform the business of election, what political purpose are they competent to? None at all, there is an end to republican government. But if any of the public agents are libelled, and thereby brought into contempt there is still among the mass of the community, those who are worthy of public confidence, that have not been brought into contempt. The sedition law protects the agents of the people, and that too possibly, when their actions bring them into disrespect, and contempt, and leaves the rights and sovereignty of the people unprotected.[37]

During the 1800 session of the Assembly, Peck's case came before the April term of the Circuit Court sitting in New York City. His trial was postponed, however, because all the witnesses, both for the prosecution and for the defense, lived nearly two hundred miles from the city and did not attend.[38]

By that time, too, the Federalists realized their blunder in arresting the popular Republican leader. Indeed, the Otsego Federalists feared making the minister a martyr, as his conviction could only strengthen his prospects in the April election. "The Friends of Government in general who live near Mr. Peck," the government prosecutor wrote Pickering, "seem to think that his consequence

---

[36] Hammond, *Political Parties in New York*, I, 133–134.

[37] *American Citizen*, reprinted in the *Aurora*, April 29, 1800. The *Citizen* was the successor to the New York *Argus* (*Greenleaf's New Daily Advertiser*), which had been forced out of business on the eve of the election of 1800 by a twofold federal-state sedition proceeding.

[38] Cooper to Wolcott, Cooperstown, Aug. 20, 1799, Wolcott Papers, XV, 43 (Conn. Hist. Soc.).

would be augmented by the measures, which might be taken for his punishment." For this reason, and the considerable expense which the procuring of witnesses would involve on any future occasion, the district attorney was "disposed to think that more Good will flow from suspending the Prosecution, than from the Pursuit of it." Keeping the trial hanging over his head would keep him "under greater Restraint . . . than he would be under after he had submitted to the Consequences of a Trial." Finally, he was really not big enough game to bother with. "He was only an instrument," Harison concluded, "in the Hands of more important and designing Persons." [39]

Pickering laid Harison's letter before President Adams, who instructed the secretary to inform the district attorney to use his own discretion in the Peck prosecution. For all practical purposes, the sedition proceedings against Peck were dropped. This action was taken only on the grounds of expediency, however, and the trial could be called up any time the district attorney thought that the advantages of prosecution outweighed those of suspension. [40]

As the local Federalists had feared, the charge against Peck strengthened his vote-getting power. For the first time since he had run for the Assembly, the "Plough Jogger" headed the list of candidates chosen from Otsego County. [41]

Commenting on the election victory of the Republicans in New York State, the *Albany Register* discussed the emergence of political parties as recognized instruments of political action. The *Register* observed that when the Republicans

remember how often their honest endeavours to convince the people of their danger have been stigmatized as the ebullitions of faction, of party malice, and disappointed ambition, let them reflect that the victory which has crowned their exertions proves the stigma to have been unjust, and compensates for all the slander, persecution and tyranny to which they have been subjected; and let them ever bear in remembrance, that it is not always wrong, as the crouching sticklers for *passive obedience* and *non-resistance* pretend, to form a party against men to whom the powers of government may have been committed. In a free country, let no man be afraid or ashamed to avow that he belongs to a party, if conscious that the views of his party are consistent with public liberty. "I am not," (says a celebrated defender of English liberty), "ashamed

[39] Harison to Pickering, New York, April 10, 1800, Pickering Papers, XXVI, 77–78 (Mass. Hist. Soc.).

[40] Pickering to Harison, Phila., April 22, 1800, *ibid.*, XIII, 406.

[41] *Otsego Herald*, May 15, 1800; *Albany Register*, May 30, 1800.

of the appellation of party when the phrase is rightly understood; for without parties, cemented by union of sound principles, evil men and evil principles cannot be successfully resisted." [42]

Jedidiah Peck could certainly agree with these sentiments. His steadfast assertion of republican principles and his practical application of his basic civil rights mark him out as a too-little-known defender of the rights of free speech and peaceful petitioning.

The Suppression of the New York Argus

Following the demise of the *Time Piece,* the New York *Argus* was the only Republican newspaper in New York City. In 1798 it ranked next to the Philadelphia *Aurora* and the Boston *Independent Chronicle* as a leading Jeffersonian journal. Established and edited by Thomas Greenleaf, the paper enlarged its influence by printing a country edition entitled *Greenleaf's New York Journal and Patriotic Register,* which condensed the week's news and circulated widely outside the metropolitan area.

Shortly after his inauguration in 1797, President Adams listed the *Argus* as one of the three leading opposition journals which, he predicted, would soon acquit him of the crime of receiving their praise.[43] When the paper became critical of Adams' defense program in 1797–1798, it was only a short step from thinking its praise a crime to charging that its criticism was seditious. Nor were the New York Federalist papers backward in making the charge. The *Commercial Advertiser* declared that the sedition bill had one good effect even before President Adams signed it, citing Greenleaf's promise of July 13 "scrupulously to regulate his conduct by it in the future." If he did so, the *Advertiser* asserted, there was no need to distribute the *Argus,* because "when the sting is destroyed it would be folly to continue the vile attempts to wound." [44]

When liberty poles made their appearance in upstate New York, the *Advertiser* held the *Argus* largely responsible for such "wooden Gods of sedition." [45] A correspondent reported seeing "poles of rebel-

---

[42] *Albany Register,* May 30, 1800.

[43] John Adams to Abigail Adams, Phila., April 24, 1797, C. F. Adams, *Letters of John Adams Addressed to His Wife,* 254.

The portions of this section relating to Alexander Hamilton have appeared in a longer article in *The Review of Politics,* 16 (1954), 305–333.

[44] *Commercial Advertiser,* July 14, 1798.

[45] For a denunciation of liberty poles as an example of "wild democracy's misrule," see the *Albany Centinel,* Aug. 10, 1798.

lion" at Newburgh, New Windsor, Montgomery, Warbridge, Goshen, Florida, Warwick, Blooming Grove, and Fish-kill. "The sedition and stamp acts, added to their long riveted enmity to the constitution, are the chief cause of this display of democratic fever," the paper declared. It admitted, however, that it had no evidence that "this combination of knaves and fools" had any intention of opposing the execution of the laws by force. The people who erected the poles had been misled by the Democratic-Republican papers published by the "stupid faction" at Newburgh and Goshen. Moreover, the only New York City newspaper to circulate in these counties was Greenleaf's country edition, the *Patriotic Register*. This was "a striking proof of its *utility*," the *Advertiser* concluded. As an afterthought it sneered: "Blessed Democracy." [46]

One of the upstate Federalist papers suggested that the Republicans should stop the seditious publications of Bache and Greenleaf "and make a conflagration of those they now have." [47] It was not the Federalists, however, but yellow fever which forced both the *Aurora* and the *Argus* to suspend operation in September, 1798. Like Bache, Greenleaf died in the epidemic of that year, and like Bache's widow, Mrs. Greenleaf revived her husband's paper, which the Federalists continued to attack. Deploring the existence of the *Argus* and other seditious newspapers, one of the *General Advertiser's* correspondents suggested that the government subsidize official newspapers for distribution in areas served solely by opposition prints in order to counteract their influence. [48]

Secretary of State Pickering, however, proposed to use a weapon closer at hand. As a part of the Federalist program of sedition prosecutions against the leading Republican papers prior to the election of 1800, he instructed District Attorney Richard Harison to examine the *Argus* daily for "audacious calumnies against the government." Branding the paper as seditious because of its "opposition to our

[46] *Commercial Advertiser*, Aug. 11, 1798, reprinted in the *Albany Centinel*, Aug. 17, 1798. The *Aurora*, July 18, 1798, reported this inscription on the Newburgh pole:

1776

Liberty   Justice
The Constitution Inviolate
No British Alliance
No Sedition Bill

[47] Story dated Hudson, N.Y., Aug. 7, 1798, reprinted in the *Albany Centinel*, Aug. 10, 1798.

[48] *General Advertiser*, May 16, 1799.

own government," he directed the district attorney to prosecute it for any libel on the government or any of its officers.[49]

Accordingly, Harison subscribed to the *Argus* at public expense, and after scanning its pages during the fall of 1799 he secured an indictment against Mrs. Greenleaf reminiscent of those against David Brown, Jedidiah Peck, and William Duane. Her offenses involved advocacy of the right to erect liberty poles, denunciation of the Alien and Sedition Acts, and accusations that the "federal Government was corrupt and inimical to the preservation of Liberty," subsidizing at least five Federalist editors to pillory those seeking "to keep alive that jealousy and watchfulness so essential to the preservation of civil Liberty." [50] Mrs. Greenleaf's trial, however, was postponed until April, 1800, because of her illness and a yellow fever epidemic in New York.[51]

While the *Argus* was reeling under the federal sedition indictment, a state libel prosecution instituted by Alexander Hamilton aimed a knockout blow at the paper, forcing Mrs. Greenleaf to sell it before her trial came on in 1800. Even though Hamilton's charge was not prosecuted under the Sedition Law, it deserves attention in any discussion of the enforcement of that law. First, the state case brought by Hamilton and the sedition prosecution pending against the *Argus* killed the Republican paper, just before the all-important contest between Jefferson and Adams. Moreover, the action was brought by Major General Hamilton on the ground that the libelous comments which the *Argus* directed against him threatened the overturn of the government of the United States. Third, it is a practical illustration of Hamilton's belief in the necessity of criminal prosecutions of outspoken critics of elected and appointed officials. Finally, like all sedition cases, it was strictly a political trial from start to finish.

On November 6, 1799, Mrs. Greenleaf's paper reprinted an article which had appeared in several Republican journals. The story featured an extract from a Philadelphia letter which charged that

[49] Pickering to Harison, Phila., Aug. 12, 1799, Pickering Papers, XI, 599 (Mass. Hist. Soc.).

[50] Mrs. Greenleaf was the only female accused of being a wicked and malicious person seeking to stir up sedition "with Force and Arms." Her offensive articles appeared on Feb. 9 and Aug. 13, 1799. For her indictment, see *U.S.* v. *Ann Greenleaf*, Sept. 4, 1799, RG 21 (National Archives).

[51] For Mrs. Greenleaf's illness as a reason for postponement, see the deposition of Louis Roy, Sept. 5, 1799, *Court Minute Book, 1790–1808*, 147, RG 21 (National Archives); and Harison to Pickering, April 10, 1800, Pickering Papers, XXVI, 78 (Mass. Hist. Soc.).

Hamilton was at the bottom of an effort to suppress the Philadelphia *Aurora*, by purchasing it. In the presence of several persons, the letter asserted, Mrs. Benjamin Franklin Bache had been offered $6,000 in part payment. Two impartial persons were to determine the purchase price, and the remainder was to be paid when she gave up the paper. Declaring that she could not dishonor her husband's memory or her children's future fame by such baseness, Bache's widow refused the offer. The letter reported her as saying, that when she parted with her paper "it should be to Republicans only." [52]

In an editorial commentary on the letter, the reprinted article asked how Hamilton expected to raise $20,000, the estimated price of the *Aurora*. In 1797, the story pointed out, he had pleaded his relative poverty in order to clear himself of a charge of speculation while secretary of the treasury, claiming that he could not raise $1,000 at that time.[53] The paper suggested that if Hamilton could not raise the money personally, there were two other sources available: a subscription might be taken up among "an association of orderly federalists," [54] or British secret service money might be utilized. It was sure that a word to Robert Liston, the British minister to the United States, "would do the business at once." He "could not politely refuse to join" in view of the *Aurora*'s offensive stories about "British influence" among the Federalists. By whatever means the Federalists might raise the money, their ownership of the *Aurora*, the story admitted, would shield them from irritating criticism which "the mildness of the sedition law as yet suffers the *Aurora* to bestow on them." [55]

On the day that the *Argus* reprinted this story, Hamilton called it to the attention of the attorney general of New York. If this had been merely another personal attack, General Hamilton wrote, he would have followed his usual example of "repaying hatred with contempt." It was not personal reputation, however, but "public motives" which demanded that he resort to the laws to punish his

---

[52] *Constitutional Telegraphe* (Boston), reprinted in the *Argus*, Nov. 6, 1799.

[53] Callender charged Hamilton with speculation in *The History of the United States for 1796*. For Hamilton's reply, see his *Observations on . . . 'The History . . . for 1796.'* This is commonly called the Reynolds Affair pamphlet because of Hamilton's confession to adultery with Mrs. Reynolds in order to vindicate his public honor. For his plea of relative poverty, see the pamphlet, *Hamilton's Works* (Lodge ed.), VI, 467.

[54] This was a sarcastic dig at the Federalists, who had organized a vigilante group of "associators" in Richmond to run Callender out of town. See Chapter XV.

[55] *Constitutional Telegraphe*, reprinted in the *Argus*, Nov. 6, 1799.

calumniators. This was necessary, he continued, because the designs of the Republicans, "the faction opposed to the government," were "to overturn our government, and, with it the great pillars of social security and happiness, in this country." These designs had been worked into a system which now made them formidable. One principal means of bringing about the overturn of the government, Hamilton charged, was to circulate "audacious falsehoods" in an attempt to destroy the confidence of the people in those who were conspicuous supporters of the government.

Hamilton was convinced that this means had been only too successful in overthrowing other governments and that it was likely to have "very fatal consequences" for the American government, unless immediately counteracted. Because criticism of the government's adherents would lead to its overturn, it became a public duty for the state attorney general to punish the critics. The attack on him, General Hamilton insisted, "demanded peculiar attention. A bolder calumny; one more absolutely destitute of foundation, was never propagated." Its "dangerous tendency," he said, needed no comment, but he commented on it anyway. According to his interpretation, it was calculated "to inspire the belief that the independence and liberty of the press are endangered by the intrigues of ambitious citizens aided by foreign gold." The Federalist leader therefore requested a criminal prosecution of the publishers of the *Argus*.[56]

This letter clearly shows that Hamilton's case and the federal sedition proceedings against the Republican newspaper rested on the same basic assumption. Both the general, who classified himself as a "conspicuous supporter of the government," and Pickering, the "Scourge of Jacobinism," charged that the *Argus* was in opposition to the government. Hamilton's insistence upon a criminal prosecution against the paper because of its "audacious falsehoods" against him was almost a restatement of Pickering's demand that it should be prosecuted for sedition because of its "audacious calumnies against the government." Indeed, if the Sedition Law had been revised to protect the reputations of all government officials, as General Hamilton had suggested ten months earlier, he could have initiated a federal prosecution. In the absence of an expanded sedi-

[56] Hamilton to Joseph Hoffman, attorney general, Nov. 6, 1799, "Trial of David Frothingham for a Libel on General Hamilton, New York Oyer and Terminer, 1799," Wharton, *State Trials*, 649–650n. The letter was originally published in the *Gazette and General Advertiser*, Nov. 8, 1799. It is undated, and consequently misplaced, in both editions of Hamilton's works. See *Works* (Lodge ed.), VIII, 536–537, and *ibid.* (Hamilton ed.), VI, 413–414.

tion law, however, Hamilton resorted to a state proceeding based on "public motives," claiming that the tendency of the remarks against him was so dangerous to the federal government that it was necessary to counteract them immediately by state action. In reality, of course, Hamilton brought a criminal suit for a private defamatory libel, but he justified his action not so much on the ground of defending his personal reputation as on that of saving the nation from a fatal overturn.

In accordance with Hamilton's request, the assistant attorney general of New York, Cadwallader D. Colden, called at the *Argus* office on November 7 and informed Mrs. Greenleaf of the intended prosecution. Although she claimed that the offensive article was reprinted from the Boston *Telegraphe* and plainly labeled, the state's attorney pointed out that under the Sedition Law the *Argus* was responsible for its republication. After examining the article, David Frothingham, the foreman of Mrs. Greenleaf's paper, said that he supposed that he was responsible for what appeared in the *Argus*. He specifically denied having any part in the composition of the article, however, and again claimed that it was a reprint.[57]

In its report of Colden's visit, the *Argus* raised the question as to why Hamilton had selected it for prosecution. Why, it asked, had he passed over the original source and attacked those who neither knew the authors nor could ascertain them? If the prosecution was caused by the paper's republicanism, the editor vowed that "we shall suffer with a firmness worthy of the cause we have endeavoured to support." Whatever the motive for prosecution, the paper affirmed its good intentions in discharging its duty to its country and to republicanism. The situation of printers, it concluded, was dangerous when "*terror* is pronounced to be the order of the day, and the liberty of the press is menaced with coercion."

Since Mrs. Greenleaf was under indictment for sedition, the state's attorney's office decided to arrest David Frothingham for publication of the letter which outraged Hamilton. On November 9 the journeyman-foreman was taken into custody and placed on bail pending trial. The *Argus* quickly identified the state proceeding against it with the prosecution under the Sedition Law and denounced it as part of a system of persecution against all printers "*who dare support the cause of freedom and the rights of man.*" A Republican newspaper, it asserted, was bound to have a host of enemies in a city where old Tories of Revolutionary days still lived, where commerce attracted herds of British clerks, and where all

[57] Testimony of Colden, Frothingham's Trial, Wharton, *State Trials*, 648–649.

the other papers were Federalist in sentiment. While the Federalist party had hailed the Sedition Law "with loud, reiterated applauses," the Republican printers had viewed it as the "PRECURSOR of persecution." The editor announced that four prosecutions had been started against the *Argus* since that law had been passed.[58]

Hamilton's action in instigating the suit against the lone Jeffersonian newspaper in New York City exposed him to further Republican criticism. "The heart of this man must be formed of peculiar stuff," the *Aurora* commented. His prosecution against Mrs. Greenleaf's paper was based upon a mere suggestion contained in a public letter. In reality, the Philadelphia editor wrote, there had been attempts in 1799 to destroy the *Aurora* by buying it out of business; several persons had tried to alter its politics or suppress it altogether. Some of these persons, he continued, were "*sycophants* of certain political characters." Although the *Aurora* had remained silent about these attempts, they had become known, and an Eastern paper had printed a letter which asserted that Mrs. Bache had been offered $6,000 and that Hamilton was at the bottom of this effort to purchase the paper. "That the sum was offered is a fact which cannot be denied," the editor of the *Aurora* declared. It was also true that reports, both before and after the offer, had said that Hamilton was anxious about this business. "Although the fact is not to be carried home to him by positive evidence," the *Aurora* concluded, "yet there is the strongest reason to believe that he did take part in certain transactions calculated to destroy this paper." [59]

In its report of Frothingham's arrest, the *Argus* denounced "the pomposity and egotism" of Hamilton for his public announcement of his intention to prosecute. His move, the paper declared, could only prejudice the mind of the jury who tried the case. The Federalist leader had flatly accused the Republicans of being "the underminer of the basis of 'Social Security and Happiness.'" Mrs. Greenleaf charged that the Federalists, while posing as lovers of good order and supporters of the government, were endeavoring to terrify every independent printer in the United States whose paper was devoted "not to the CREATURES OF THE PEOPLE, BUT TO THE PEOPLE THEMSELVES." [60]

Hamilton was repeatedly held up as a hypocrite because he justified the prosecution as a means of maintaining the "social security and happiness" of the republic rather than as a means of protecting himself from political criticism. "A hypocrit [*sic*]," the *Argus* asserted, "generally boasts of his merit and his good deeds in public.

[58] *Argus*, Nov. 9 and 11, 1799.   [59] *Aurora*, Nov. 11, 1799.
[60] *Argus*, Nov. 11, 1799.

He appears to do meritorious acts merely for the purpose of exciting applause and not for the gratification of self-approbation." [61] The paper accused Hamilton of being one of the worst types of offenders against "social security and happiness" because of his confessed unchastity.[62]

Three days before Frothingham's trial, the *Argus* proposed "A Query for Federalists:" "What are the best means to suppress a paper by?" The editor suggested that goading a printer with prosecutions was a better plan than buying up his establishment. If the Federalists should succeed in suppressing the free utterances of political opinions and observations on the conduct of the servants of the people, there would be no freedom of the press. Doubting the infallibility of man, the editor was sure that public trustees did not become perfect upon being placed in office.[63]

On November 21, 1799, Frothingham was tried before the New York Court of Oyer and Terminer. Judge Radcliffe presided, sitting with Richard Varick, the mayor, and Richard Harison, the recorder. The judge was a former Federalist assemblyman. Harison, who was also federal district attorney for the New York District, was then preparing the sedition case against Mrs. Greenleaf. Colonel Richard Varick, another leading Federalist in the legal profession, had served a dozen years as recorder and mayor of New York. Frothingham was prosecuted by Josiah Hoffman, a "vehement and voluble" Federalist who, until his appointment as attorney general by Governor John Jay, had been the leader of his party in the state Assembly. Hoffman was assisted in the prosecution by Colden, his law partner, whom the Federalist Council of Appointment had selected as state's attorney for the counties surrounding New York City.[64]

[61] *Argus*, Nov. 19, 1799. The *Aurora* asserted that Hamilton was not as sturdy a supporter of the government as he claimed. "He has lately found out that he cannot rule Mr. Adams," it stated. See *Aurora*, Nov. 13, 1799. Hamilton and the Cabinet had failed to prevent the sailing of the second mission to France after Adams ordered its departure in October, 1799. For Hamilton's severe denunciation of this action, see his *Letter from Alexander Hamilton concerning the Public Conduct of John Adams, Esq., President of the United States* (New York, 1800), 23–41, especially 28–33 and 36. The pamphlet was so critical of Adams that one of the victims of the Sedition Law tried to have Hamilton prosecuted for seditious libel. See Dumas Malone, "The Threatened Prosecution of Alexander Hamilton under the Sedition Act by Thomas Cooper," *American Historical Review*, 29 (1923–24), 76–81.

[62] *Argus*, Nov. 21, 1799, and *passim* after Nov. 6, 1799.

[63] *Argus*, Nov. 18, 1799.

[64] Fox, *The Decline of Aristocracy in the Politics of New York*, 14–15. In his chapter on "The Few, the Rich, and the Well Born," Fox characterizes Varick as one who "sustained the dignity of the old Federalist directorate and added to

The political character of the trial was indicated also by Frothingham's selection of Brockholst and Edward Livingston as his defense counsel. Brockholst Livingston, a leading Republican advocate in New York, wrote occasional pieces for the *Argus*.[65] His brother, Edward Livingston, outstanding congressional opponent of the Alien and Sedition Laws, helped to prepare the defense but did not argue the case.[66]

Since New York's Constitution contained no guarantee of freedom of speech or of the press until 1821, Frothingham's case was tried under the common law doctrine of libel which derived from colonial days. Under this doctrine, the truth of the libel was no justification; truth or falsity had nothing to do with libel. If the writing or printing, or even a picture, tended to expose a man to hatred, contempt, or ridicule, the accused was guilty of libel. The exclusion of truth as a defense meant that convictions were even easier to obtain in criminal cases at the state level than they were under the Sedition Law, which allowed truth as a justification.

Frothingham pleaded not guilty to the indictment, which charged him with publishing a libel designed "to injure the name and reputation of General Hamilton, to expose him to public hatred and contempt, and to cause it to be believed that he was opposed to the Republican Government of the United States." The libel was alleged to be threefold. First, it asserted that Hamilton was at the bottom of attempts to buy the *Aurora* and that Mrs. Bache refused to sell because Hamilton or his agents would use it to injure Republicanism. Second, it insinuated and was intended to cause it to be suggested that the general had corruptly speculated while secretary of the treasury. Third, it implied that General Hamilton was in collusion with Liston to purchase the *Aurora* with British secret service money and that this partnership with His Majesty's minister was to answer corrupt purposes of the British monarch.[67]

---

the prestige of his class." Hoffman, Harison, and Colden had been Loyalists during the American Revolution.

[65] One of these led to a challenge from a Federalist in 1798. In the duel that followed, Livingston shot and killed his opponent. See Charles Havens Hunt, *Life of Edward Livingston* (New York, 1864), 54.

[66] Two years later Edward Livingston replaced Varick as mayor. Brockholst Livingston was elevated to the United States Supreme Court by Jefferson in 1806.

[67] Indictment, Frothingham's Trial, Wharton, *State Trials*, 649. There is a photostatic copy of the true bill indictment in the Hamilton Papers (N.Y. Pub. Lib.). The jury foreman, William Bayard, was a long-time friend of the general's; it was at his house that Hamilton died after his duel with Burr.

To prove that Frothingham had published the article, Attorney General Hoffman offered the evidence of Assistant Attorney General Colden, who was also the assistant prosecutor of Frothingham. Colden described his trip to the *Argus* office at Hamilton's request. Since Mrs. Greenleaf was a widow, he had promised that he would not indict her if she would point out the real editor of the paper. He testified that Mrs. Greenleaf had declared that Frothingham was accountable for whatever appeared in her paper. Although Frothingham had not admitted that he was the editor or proprietor of the *Argus*, he had said that he "expected" that he was responsible. But he had denied having had a hand in the composition of the article complained of, asserting that it was reprinted from another paper.[68] This argument, however, was no defense, as the republication of the article constituted a new libel.

The only other witness to appear during the trial was Hamilton. The attorney general offered the general's evidence in order to explain the innuendoes as charged in the indictment and to show that every part of them was false. Livingston objected to Hamilton's testifying on either of the points. However absurd the doctrine, he said, the common law was well settled that the truth of the matter could not be given in evidence on an indictment for libeling an individual. Since the question of the truth or falsity of the libel was not before the jury, testimony on its falsity should be excluded unless evidence of its truth was also admitted. If the court, however, allowed testimony on both truth and falsity then the issue would be a question for the jury to decide.

Nor, said Livingston, should Hamilton be allowed to explain the innuendoes contained in the indictment. If these did not arise naturally from the passage, no oral testimony should be received to explain them. In any event, Hamilton should not be the one to explain them; he was not a disinterested witness. The attorney general had already informed the jury that the witness considered his reputation dearer than life or property and that the plaintiff's reputation depended to a great extent on their verdict. Moreover, the witness could not help being passionately interested in any questions that would have to be put to him on innuendoes. He had instituted the prosecution by an intemperate letter ordering the attorney general to "commence it immediately." Livingston conceded that in criminal prosecutions injured parties were admitted as witnesses, but he claimed that this was an unusual case in which the witness had insisted upon a prosecution in order to sustain his reputation.

[68] Wharton, *State Trials*, 650.

He therefore asked the court to exclude Hamilton's testimony.[69]

The court agreed that since the law barred the defendant from giving the truth of the publication as a defense, it would be improper for Hamilton to offer evidence of its falsity. At the same time, however, the judges ruled that the general was a competent witness to explain the innuendoes. Although he spent most of his time in discussing the methods he had used to disprove the charges of speculation against him while he was secretary of the treasury, he testified that the *Argus* article libeled him by insinuating that he was hostile to the republican form of government. He also denied that he had been concerned in any offer to purchase Mrs. Bache's paper, even though "he considered the Aurora . . . a paper hostile to the government of the United States." [70]

Before turning to a discussion of the libel itself, Brockholst Livingston opened the defense argument with an attempt to show that Frothingham was not responsible for the appearance of the article. He offered to prove that the defendant was neither editor nor proprietor of the *Argus;* he was only an eight-dollar-a-week journeyman. When the state prosecutor objected that the journeyman had confessed himself responsible, the defense counsel claimed that Frothingham's expressions were not a confession. To shield Mrs. Greenleaf, he had said that he expected that he was responsible. Livingston also argued that his client was not legally accountable because no journeyman had ever been prosecuted for publishing a libel. If one could be punished, a paper might be suppressed easily. When a libel appeared, not only the editor but all his employees might be held liable, sent to jail, and their paper allowed to expire. The testimony which he wished to submit would show the defendant's innocence. After refusing to admit any testimony regarding Frothingham's position on the *Argus,* the court also rejected any evidence which attempted to disprove the imputation of malice by showing that the article was copied from another paper.

Frothingham's counsel then set up two defenses, contending that the publication was no libel and that, even if it were, the defendant was not answerable for it. He was sure that Hamilton's name was secure from any attack such as that made in the article. Indeed, he was astonished that the general would stoop to notice it. Conviction of Frothingham could not add to Hamilton's fame or good

[69] *Argus,* Dec. 9, 1799. This issue and that of Dec. 13, 1799, give the most voluminous report of the trial. Wharton made no use of them in preparing his sketch.

[70] *Argus,* Dec. 9, 1799. Also see Wharton, *State Trials,* 651n.

name, nor would an acquittal detract from it. The defense counsel then made a rebuttal of the allegations in the indictment in an attempt to show that the article was not a malicious defamation tending to blacken Hamilton's reputation by exposing him to public hatred and ridicule.

The most prominent charge was that Hamilton was at the bottom of an attempt to suppress the *Aurora* by purchasing it. There was nothing criminal in this statement, Livingston argued; newspapers were a form of private property that could be bought and sold. Ever since the death of the editor and publisher of the *Aurora*, Benjamin Franklin Bache, during the yellow fever epidemic of 1798, it had been known that the paper was on the market. Livingston knew of nothing which would prevent Hamilton's becoming a bidder. If the general made the purchase, he might suppress the paper altogether and use the types for other purposes, just as the present owner could. Indeed, if the *Aurora* was really hostile to the government of the United States, as Hamilton had testified, it would even be praiseworthy of him to suppress it by legal means. If he succeeded, "it would be another feather in his cap, and entitle him to the thanks instead of the ridicule and hatred of his fellow citizens." Livingston concluded that suppression of a newspaper by legal means was a private, not a criminal, matter.[71]

Moreover, the article had not charged that Hamilton or his agents had used any illegal means. The offer to purchase the *Aurora* was both fair and honorable and could not detract from Hamilton's reputation. The arrangements were eminently equitable—$6,000 down and the rest to be paid after an impartial evaluation of the paper's worth.

The indictment also charged that Hamilton was libeled by Mrs. Bache's statement that the paper would go to republicans only; this insinuated that he was antirepublican. The plaintiff, Livingston said, seemed to regard it as a crime that a man living in a republic was not a republican. Yet the letter did not charge Hamilton with being an antirepublican; that was one of the innuendoes which he spelled out from it. The letter merely stated that Mrs. Bache rejected the purchase offer and gave her reasons. Even if the charge had been made, Livingston continued, it would not have been criminal. As long as a man abided by the laws, he could believe that monarchy was a stronger protector of personal liberty and property than a democratic or republican government. He could publicly avow these views and even urge that the Constitution should be amended to

[71] *Argus*, Dec. 9, 1799.

change the title of the chief executive from president to king and to make the succession hereditary. If a public man advocated these measures and his constituents disagreed, they could refuse to re-elect him, but he could not be punished otherwise.

Livingston concluded that the obvious meaning of the word "republican" as used in the letter was that of a party label.[72] It was notorious that the United States contained two political parties. The Federal party favored the administration and the Republican party opposed it. In this sense, Livingston argued, Hamilton could have no objections to being called "an antirepublican"; it was simply another way of saying that he was a good Federalist. Livingston claimed, therefore, that there was nothing libelous in this assertion.

In another place in his argument, the defense counsel struck at the political bias of prosecutions for libels of public men. He did not deny that the newspapers were full of attacks on personal character, but he contended that the only way to suppress libels on individuals in an age of a rabid party press was to direct proceedings against calumniators regardless of party. "Calumny against the Vice President," he pointed out, "has not yet attracted the notice or called forth the sympathy or indignation of any attorney general. While libels against him were permitted and encouraged, the federalists, as they were pleased to call themselves, must expect while human nature continued what it is, the same kind of treatment by way of retaliation."[73]

Since it was neither criminal to suppress the *Aurora* by legal private means or to call a man "an antirepublican," Livingston discussed the article's conjectures as to how the purchase money was to be raised. According to the indictment, the letter implied that Hamilton would purchase the *Aurora* with money which he had obtained through speculation while he was secretary of the treasury. Livingston pointed out, however, that the article had not stated who was to pay the purchase price; it had only stated some hypothetical methods of raising the money. Nor had it suggested that Hamilton should contribute any money at all unless he subscribed to a fund raised by "orderly federalists." Even if he did this, it would be a worthy investment of funds, one which might lead to a division of profits based on the amount invested.

Moreover, Livingston continued, "as good federalists, they might have thought it a praiseworthy deed, to aid in suppressing a paper

[72] The word "Republican" was printed with a capital rather than in lower case in the *Argus* article of Nov. 6, 1799.
[73] *Argus*, Dec. 9, 1799.

which many of them considered as the vehicle of sedition, and as injurious to the views of their party." Even if a subscription actually had been raised, rather than merely conjectured, the participants would not have been punishable, nor would their participation have derogated from their reputation.

The last resource suggested for the purchase was British secret service money. State Prosecutor Hoffman interpreted this hypothetical statement as an accusation of a formidable combination between Hamilton and Liston to overturn the government of the United States through corrupt use of British gold. This implication, Livingston declared, was an innuendo which could be conjured up only by a prosecutor given to stretching words beyond all sensible meaning. He claimed that Liston or any other Englishman could establish a newspaper in the United States and that some had done so.[74] Nor did the article in the *Argus* state that the paper which would replace the *Aurora*, if Hamilton succeeded in purchasing it, would be employed for purposes inimical to the interests of the United States. On the contrary, the article made it clear that any such successor to the *Aurora* would be controlled by the Federalists who prided themselves on their attachment to the Adams administration of the federal government.[75]

At the end of five hours of testimony and argument, Judge Radcliffe submitted the case to the jury. Speaking for the court, he cautioned them against party spirit "in a case so apt to excite it." Explaining the proceeding in terms of personal reputation, the judge made no reference whatsoever to Hamilton's assertion that the newspaper attack on him as a conspicuous supporter of the government tended to its overturn, although this had been the point which Hamilton stressed as his reason for bringing the suit.

In his charge to the jury, the judge again cited the common law definition of defamatory libel as the standard by which to judge the criminality of the offensive article. If a writing tended to expose a man to hatred, contempt, or ridicule, whether it was true or false, the publisher was guilty of libel. Moreover, "words might mean more than they expressed"; innuendoes were sometimes necessary to explain their whole or true meaning. By innuendoes, which were sup-

[74] *Porcupine's Gazette*, edited by William Cobbett, was the most conspicuous example. Liston offered to make Cobbett a stipendiary of the British government while he edited this paper but the editor refused. See Cole, *Letters from William Cobbett*, xxiv, xxxvii. Cole calls Cobbett "an unpaid agent, or rather one who lived by his writings without any sort of subsidy."

[75] *Argus*, Dec. 9, 1799.

ported by Hamilton's testimony, the indictment had been interpreted
to mean that the general "was not a Republican," that he had speculated corruptly, and that he had received money from the British
king for purposes inimical to the republican form of government
adopted by the United States and guaranteed by the Constitution
to the States.

The judge informed the jury that it simply had to decide two
things: was the *Argus* article designed to expose Hamilton to the
hatred and contempt of his fellow citizens; if so, did Frothingham
publish it? To reach its conclusions, the jury would have to decide
whether the innuendoes alleged in the indictment were such as
men of common understanding would give the article. The court
then made an acquittal almost impossible by announcing its unanimous opinion that the innuendoes were just, that the matter was
libelous, and that Frothingham, even though only a journeyman,
was liable for its publication. The court was explicit on this last point:
"There could be no doubt as to the distinct manner in which he
had assumed all responsibility." [76]

This condemnation of the defendant by the bench made a verdict
of guilty virtually inevitable. After only three hours' deliberation
the jury agreed with the judge as to Frothingham's guilt, but it
recommended clemency. [77]

During the interim between Frothingham's trial on November
21 and his sentencing on December 3, a New Yorker predicted that
"from the well known *moderation* of our Mayor, &c there can be
very little doubt of Mr. Frothingham being treated as severely as
is consistent with party prudence." [78] In an effort to capitalize on
the jury's recommendation of clemency, Frothingham submitted a
petition setting forth his reasons for asking for a mitigated sentence.
He swore that he was not the editor or publisher of the *Argus*, that
he received eight dollars a week for assisting in carrying on that
paper, that the offensive article had appeared in several other papers
before being copied by the *Argus*, and that he did not know its
author or consider it a libel on Hamilton or anyone else. He neither
knew Hamilton nor bore any malice toward him; indeed, he had
never seen him until the day of the trial. Moreover, he had never
written a single line against Hamilton in his life. Finally, he added

[76] Wharton, *State Trials*, 651. Also see the *Gazette and General Advertiser*,
Nov. 25, 1799.

[77] *Spectator*, Nov. 23, 1799; *Aurora*, Nov. 25 and Dec. 6, 1799; *Argus*, Dec.
4, 1799.

[78] Letter to the editor, dated New York, Nov. 22, 1799, *Aurora*, Nov. 25, 1799.

a personal item: his salary of eight dollars a week was the sole support of his wife and six children.

Attorney General Hoffman opposed any mitigation of sentence, arguing that the *Argus* had aggravated the offense by its articles since November 6 and that the sentence should reflect it. Livingston objected that by Colden's admission the prosecution considered Frothingham responsible only for the letter printed November 6. The defendant was neither editor nor publisher of the paper and had just sworn that he had never written anything against Hamilton. Moreover, if he were liable for these subsequent publications, and they were to add to the severity of his sentence, he might be indicted for them later and thus be punished twice for the same offense.

Overruling these objections, the court directed the attorney general to read the later articles. Frothingham then filled out a second affidavit swearing that he had not written anything for, or caused anything to be inserted in, the *Argus* subsequent to November 6. If any of these articles were supposed to reflect on Hamilton they were published without his agency directly or indirectly.[79]

Despite the jury's recommendation of clemency and the defendant's petitions for mercy, the court showed neither. "If he has a wife and children," Judge Radcliffe said before delivering sentence, "he ought to have thought of them before he violated the laws of the country." If the defendant had submitted any evidence of the truth of the libel, he added, it would have gone a long way to mitigate the sentence. At the same time, however, he admitted that the law did not permit truth to be submitted as a justification of the libel. The fact that Frothingham was a journeyman rather than editor or publisher was no reason to mitigate the sentence. Indeed, the judge claimed that the paper had "teemed" with equally malicious and virulent libels since the original publication; this could hardly be grounds for clemency.

The judge also maintained that the prosecution had nothing whatsoever to do with the liberty of the press; it was concerned only with its licentiousness. Malicious reports could destroy the best reputations in the world, and could render good government odious. "In every well regulated society," he said, "there must be laws to prevent the licentiousness of the press—all well disposed people must approve the salutary restraint." Those who did not were simply depraved. It was not necessary that the judges should inquire as to whether the libel actually affected the reputation of the plaintiff.

[79] Sworn affidavit of David Frothingham, *Greenleaf's New York Journal and Patriotic Register*, Dec. 14, 1799.

"Every such slander," he concluded, "must be supposed to have some effect, and the best established character for virtue and integrity, might not always be able to resist a continual repetition of such attacks."

On December 3, Frothingham was sentenced to four months' imprisonment and assessed a fine of $100. He was to remain in jail until the fine was paid. Moreover, he would not be released until he posted a $2,000 bond as a guarantee of his good behavior for two years after the expiration of his sentence.[80]

The Federalist *Gazette of the United States* moaned that the fine was much too lenient, although it had no complaint about the prison term.[81] The *Argus* and the *Aurora,* on the other hand, deplored the severity of the sentence. "Be it remembered," they said, "that the jury recommended Frothingham to the clemency of the court— How kindly has it complied." The *Argus* attacked the trial as a political one from beginning to end and charged that the jury was, with only a few exceptions, composed of true Federalists. It hinted, too, that even the judgment seat might be polluted by prejudice in times of high party passions. "When the unpopular measures of government have produced a degree of opposition in their subjects," the paper declared, "bad rulers have endeavoured to destroy contradiction and complaint by embracing every opportunity to persecute their opponents." A short time later, however, the *Argus* paid mock deference to the decision in a simple advertisement: "Wanted, a foreman of respectability." [82]

Frothingham's prosecution at Hamilton's insistence was a part of the Federalists' twofold legal proceedings against the *Argus.* Although Colden testified that he did not wish to prosecute Ann Greenleaf because she was a widow, neither Hamilton nor the federal authorities showed such chivalry. Indeed, District Attorney Richard Harison, one of the judges in Frothingham's trial, had secured an indictment against Mrs. Greenleaf for sedition even before Frothingham's arrest. Whatever the object of the combined federal-state prosecutions, their effect was to suppress the third most powerful Republican paper in the United States and the only Jeffersonian journal in New York City at that time. Under these relentless legal attacks, Mrs. Greenleaf was forced to sell the *Argus* and the *Patriotic Register,* whose circulation among the "ignorant"

[80] *Gazette and General Advertiser,* Dec. 5, 1799. Also see Wharton, *State Trials,* 651, who incorrectly gives the amount of the fine as $500.

[81] *Gazette of the United States,* Dec. 23, 1799.

[82] *Argus,* Dec. 4, 13, and 18, 1799; *Aurora,* Dec. 6, 1799.

rural voters so alarmed the Federalists, but she made sure that her successors were Republicans. Even though her papers were succeeded immediately by two new Republican gazettes, the *American Citizen* and the *Republican Watchtower*, Mrs. Greenleaf's long-established journals ceased publication under duress only two months before the New York elections in May, 1800.[83]

Mrs. Greenleaf was scheduled for trial before the April, 1800, term of Circuit Court, which was to be presided over by Justice Bushrod Washington and District Judge John Sloss Hobart, formerly Federalist senator from New York. The frequent prosecutions for sedition in 1800 led the federal district attorney to question the political expediency of prosecuting either Mrs. Greenleaf or Jedidiah Peck. He was sure that any severity against the widow of Greenleaf "would without doubt be censured more extensively, if in Consequence of it she should be subjected to any Punishment which might operate as an Example."

Harison therefore wrote to Pickering suggesting his doubts about pressing the prosecution against Ann Greenleaf. He did not overlook the fact that she had discontinued her paper and could no longer repeat her attacks on the administration. Indeed, it had been so long since the original prosecution was started that the offense, which "was not of a very heinous Nature," "has since been forgotten." Since the defendant and her friends were ready "to acknowledge the Clemency of Government," Harison asked Pickering to instruct him whether or not the proceedings should be dropped.[84]

The secretary of state laid Harison's letter before President Adams who agreed that the reasons urged were "quite sufficient for me to consent and indeed to direct a Nolle Prosequi." Pickering sent this directive to the district attorney, who then dropped the prosecution against the ex-proprietor of the *Argus*.[85]

Nonetheless, these proceedings played a considerable role in the

[83] Brigham, *American Newspapers, 1690–1820*, I, 610. David Denniston bought the papers on March 8, 1800, and immediately established the *American Citizen* as the Republican successor to the *Argus;* the *Republican Watchtower* replaced the *Patriotic Register.* For Federalist alarm at the circulation of Greenleaf's papers, especially among the "ignorant" rural voters, see the *Commercial Advertiser,* July 14 and Aug. 11, 1798; the *Albany Centinel,* Aug. 10, 1798; and the *Gazette and General Advertiser,* May 16, 1799.

[84] Harison to Pickering, April 10, 1800, Pickering Papers, XXVI, 78 (Mass. Hist. Soc.).

[85] Adams to Pickering, Phila., April 21, 1800, *Department of State Miscellaneous Letters, Jan.–Dec., 1800,* RG 59 (National Archives); and Pickering to Harison, Phila., April 22, 1800, Pickering Papers, XIII, 406 (Mass. Hist. Soc.).

Federalists' attempt to defeat Jefferson in 1800. Despite their efforts, they failed to turn the Republican tide in New York. The May elections returned a majority of Republican state legislators, who, under the law then prevailing, would choose the presidential electors.[86] That the Empire State Federalists were desperately fearful of Jefferson's triumph is shown by their response to the Republican victory in their state. Again it was Hamilton who took the lead in forming a plan to alter the mode of choosing presidential electors and thus to return New York to the Federalist column. His extraordinary letter of May 7, 1800, written five days after the election of the new legislature, shows that he was willing to go even farther in his post-election attempts to thwart Jefferson's elevation than he had been prior to the state election, when he had launched the prosecution against the *Argus*.

To Governor Jay, he repeated his belief that "the anti-federal party" was composed of incongruous materials, "all tending to mischief—some of them to the OVERTHROW of the GOVERNMENT, by stripping it of its due energies; others of them, to a REVOLUTION, after the manner of BONAPARTE." Hamilton informed the governor that if the new state legislature was to meet without further Federalist action, "the very high probability is that this will bring *Jefferson* into the chief magistry." To prevent this, he proposed a measure that was not without "weighty objections," but which was absolutely necessary. He suggested that the governor should call a special session of the "lame-duck" legislature, which was Federalist dominated, and jam through a bill providing for the choice of presidential electors in districts by popular vote. "In times like these in which we live, it will not do to be overscrupulous," he assured the governor. While the step would be unusual, he thought it "*legal* and *constitutional*." Moreover, it would achieve its object: "This," he concluded, ". . . will insure a majority of votes in the United States for a Federal candidate."[87]

Hamilton's justification of this proposal was much the same as his justification of the prosecution of the *Argus*. Both were motivated by political necessity. He hoped that if such action was taken, the motive for it would be publicly avowed. The governor

---

[86] For an analysis of the election in New York, see Charles A. Beard, *Economic Origins of Jeffersonian Democracy* (New York, 1915), 366–372, 382–387.

[87] Hamilton to Jay, May 7, 1800, *Hamilton's Works* (Lodge ed.), VIII, 549–551. Lodge censures this proposal as "one entirely unworthy of Hamilton. It was due to his anger and disgust at the result of the election in New York." *Ibid.*, 551n.

should inform the legislators that, "without their interposition, the executive authority of the general government would be transferred to hands hostile to the system heretofore pursued with so much success, and dangerous to the peace, happiness, and order of the country." Hamilton agreed that any such political maneuver would be condemned by the Republicans but he was sure that "the measure will not fail to be approved by all the federal party." Because of its obvious party purpose, Jay repudiated this bald-faced proposal.

During the excitement following the XYZ affair, Hamilton supported the Alien and Sedition Laws and advocated their vigorous enforcement. When he failed to obtain an expanded sedition law to protect all federal officials whatsoever, he resorted to the state courts to prosecute the opposition press. His role in the suppression of the New York *Argus* stamped him as an advocate of the doctrine that an administration may utilize seditious libel prosecutions against its opponents. When the Federalists faced the prospect of becoming the dissenting minority, he tried to block majority rule by altering the electoral processes in order to keep his party in power. Although Hamilton is generally depicted as a defender of civil liberties who, with Marshall, opposed the Federalist alien and sedition system, it is only too evident that he was ready, willing, and able, in one case at least, to stifle democratic dissent.[88]

The prosecution of New York newspapers for sedition shows a perfect score as far as suppression goes. Durrell's *Mount Pleasant Register* expired two years before Durrell was tried, and the more influential city papers, the *Time Piece* and the *Argus*, collapsed before the date scheduled for the trials of their editors. If, as Professor Channing claims, "the presidential election of 1800 turned entirely upon the election in New York," [89] it looks very much as if the cases brought against Democratic-Republican journals in the Empire State were part of the Federalist campaign against Jefferson.

[88] See Chapter VIII, pp. 152–155.
[89] Channing, *History of the United States*, IV, 236.

CHAPTER XVIII

The Sedition Law, Free Speech, and the American Political Process

The influence of discussion has presided at the creation of intellectual freedom.—WALTER BAGEHOT

POPULAR government rests on the right of the public to choose between opposing views. Since an informed public opinion is vital to republican government, freedom of expression is necessary for the formation of that opinion. If people cannot communicate their thoughts to one another without running the risk of prosecution, no other liberty can be secure, because freedom of speech and of the press are essential to any meaning of liberty.

The years between 1798 and 1801 afford the first instance under the Constitution in which American political leaders faced the problem of defining the role of public criticism in a representative government. During this period of changing political ideas, the basic pattern of the American political process emerged, and the essential features of the American civil liberties tradition were formulated. The failure of repressive measures to silence criticism of elected officials re-emphasized the new and revolutionary political principle which had been the basis of the War of Independence: the idea that government rests upon the consent of the governed.

The view which the law takes of the offense of publishing and uttering seditious words depends upon the attitude it holds concerning the relation of the rulers to the people. Are the people the superiors of the rulers, or are the rulers the superiors of the people? The first view holds that sovereignty resides with the people and not with the government. The so-called rulers are the elected agents and servants of the people, who may discuss questions relating not only to government policy but also to punishment or dismissal of dishonest, inadequate, or unpopular agents. If anyone disagrees with the faultfinding, he may advocate the cause of the agents. The most that can happen is the replacement of the agent with another more to the people's liking.[1]

The criminal law of seditious libel which emerged in England during the seventeenth and eighteenth centuries developed at a time when the accepted view made the rulers the superiors of the people.[2] By virtue of their exalted positions, the rulers were considered the wise and good guides of the country. Authority, therefore, had to be approached with proper decorum. Mistakes might be pointed out in respectful petitions, but whether the rulers were mistaken or not, no censure could be leveled against them. The people could not make adverse comments in conversation, in clandestine pamphlets or, later, in newspapers. The only lawful method of presenting grievances was through their lawful representatives in the legislature, who might be petitioned in an orderly and digni- fied manner.[3]

This view made words punishable, because to find fault with the government tended to undermine the respect of the people for it and to reduce its dignity and authority. The "bad tendency" test, moreover, presumed that criticism tended to overthrow the state. There was no need to prove any intention on the part of the defendant to produce disaffection or to excite an insurrection; it was enough if he intended to publish the blame. The law of seditious libel was thus the product of the view that the govern- ment was master.[4]

---

[1] Sir James Fitzjames Stephen, *A History of the Criminal Law of England* (London, 1883), II, 299–300.

Portions of this chapter were published in *The William and Mary Quarterly*, 3d ser., 9 (1952), 497–511.

[2] Williams S. Holdsworth, *A History of English Law* (London, 1903–1938), VIII, 378.

[3] *Ibid.*, 337–338. Also see George Chase, ed., *Blackstone's Commentaries*, 3d ed. (New York, 1894), bk. IV, ch. vii, 915–918; Chafee, *Free Speech in the United States*, 3–35; Henry Schofield, "Freedom of the Press in the United States," *Essays on Constitutional Law and Equity* (Boston, 1921), II, 510.

[4] Holdsworth, *History of English Law*, VIII, 341. This commentator defines

It was to this English common law concept that the Federalists turned for their model. Even so, they attempted to adapt the authoritarian practice to the basic realities of popular government by working out a compromise between the rights of the authorities and the rights of the people. An aristocratic party which deplored political democracy, they based their defense of the right of authorities to freedom from public criticism, paradoxically enough, on the fact that the American government rested on the consent of the governed. They contended that the election of officials by the people demonstrated the confidence which the people had in those officers. Once those officials had been elevated by the people to the highest offices in the land, they became the "constituted authorities" who ran things until the next election. Thus, the Federalists exalted the officeholder above the mass of the citizens. It was a greater offense to criticize one of the rulers than it was to criticize one of the people themselves, because the rulers partook of the majesty of the whole people.

The Federalist theory of government, moreover, held that the right of political participation was not the province of all men but the prerogative of a chosen few. As Jay put it, "those who own the country are the most fit persons to participate in the government of it." The Sedition Law was consistent with the Federalist concept of an elite ruling class. Thinking that the stability of American society depended on "the few, the rich, and the well born," they opposed any criticism which might threaten their positions as rulers by undermining public confidence in their administration. Because they had been in power since the adoption of the Constitution, they looked upon themselves as the peculiar guardians of the nation's welfare. By identifying their administration with the government, and the government with the Constitution, the Federalists concluded that criticism of their administration was an attempt to subvert the Constitution and to overthrow the government.

The Republicans agreed that the government of the United States rested on the people, but they widened the concept of "public confidence" to coincide with "public opinion." Elected officials could lose the confidence of the people as well as gain it. To continue to merit public confidence, their measures had to meet

---

seditious libel as "the intentional publication of a writing which reflected on the government." This is the substance of Coke's case, *De Libellis famosis* (1606), which Stephen calls "the nearest approach to a definition of the crime with which I am acquainted."

public approval. Public opinion was not a cyclical phenomenon which appeared every two years to be registered at the polls. It was in continuous process of formulation and could be conveyed constitutionally in speeches or in the press. The people did not vote themselves out of further political participation by the act of voting in elected officials. They were free to examine the conduct of the authorities; they could denounce it as well as praise it. They did not have to wait until election time to withdraw their confidence from an agent whom they decided was unworthy of it.

The Republicans based their arguments against the Sedition Law on the ground that it destroyed "the responsibility of public servants and public measures to the people." Madison specifically condemned the law, because it exposed the United States, "which acquired the honour of taking the lead among nations towards perfecting political principles," to the disgrace of retreating "towards the exploded doctrine that the administrators of the Government are the masters and not the servants of the people." [5]

Although the Federalists asserted that the Sedition Law was declaratory of the English common law, they also announced that it mitigated the rigors of the law as expounded by Blackstone. It made the intent of the speaker, as well as the tendency of his words, an essential element in the crime of seditious libel. Moreover, it allowed truth as a justification and made the jury the judge of the criminality of the utterances. Of what value to the accused were these three procedural safeguards?

The interpretation which the courts put on the truth provision made it worse than useless as an aid to the defendant. Under the rulings handed down by the judges of the Supreme Court on circuit, this supposed safeguard actually reversed the normal criminal law presumption of innocence. Instead of the government's having to prove that the words of the accused were false, scandalous, and malicious, the defendant had to prove that they were true. As Judge Samuel Chase put it, the accused had to prove all of his statements "to the marrow. If he asserts three things and proves but two," the jurist said, "he fails in his defense, for he must prove the whole of his assertions to be true." This is a clear illustration of the doctrine of presumptive guilt; in practice, the courts presumed the defendant guilty until he proved himself innocent.

Moreover, the accused was required not only to prove the truth of every word in every statement but, in one instance, to prove

[5] Address of the General Assembly to the People of the Commonwealth of Virginia, Jan. 23, 1799, *Madison's Writings* (Hunt ed.), VI, 338.

an entire count in an indictment by the same witness. Even though the statement contained more than one point, the defendant could not introduce different witnesses to prove different points. According to Judge Chase, this practice would have been "irregular and subversive of every principle of law." [6]

The court also refused to distinguish between a false statement of facts and erroneous opinions. Indeed, the expression of any opinion on future events could be condemned as false under the interpretation given section three of the law. Although the prosecutor could no more prove the falsity of a prediction than the defendant could prove its truth, the statement was considered false because the defendant had failed to carry the burden of proof.

What was the effect of the clause requiring that bad intent should be proved? In every case, the government prosecutors and the judges presumed the bad intent of the speaker from the bad tendency of the words. Moreover, it was the tendency of the words to find fault with elected officials which was penalized and not the intent to cause violence. Although the Vermont and New York indictments used the words "with force and arms," these were merely legal epithets thrown into the indictment. There was no effort to prove that Congressman Lyon, editor Haswell, Assemblyman Peck, or Mrs. Greenleaf intended to use force and violence or even that the tendency of their criticism was to bring about ruptures of the public peace. Lyon's prosecution was based on the "force and arms" concept, even though he was running for re-election himself. By presuming the bad intent of the speaker from the bad tendency of the words, the courts narrowed the legal test of criminality to the pre-Revolutionary common law test; persons were punished if the tendency of their words was to undermine public confidence in the elected officials and thus to render it less likely that they might be re-elected.[7]

Finally, the function of the trial jury was reduced almost to that of a rubber stamp. It is evident from the replies of grand juries to charges from federal judges, and from the verdicts of the trial juries, that both were Federalist-dominated, if not made up exclusively of Federalists. The rigor with which the trial judges restricted challenges of jurors by defense attorneys virtually prevented any examination for political bias and led to extensive criticism of the courts. Congressman Matthew Lyon, the first victim

[6] For Chief Justice John Marshall's disagreements, see *Chase Trial,* 70.

[7] For an outstanding analysis of "intent" and "tendency," see Chafee, *Free Speech in the United States,* 23–25.

of the law, claimed that all of his trial jurors were chosen from towns which were hostile to him. The Callender case, however, is the only one in which it can be proved positively that the trial jury was Federalist to a man. Whether the juries were deliberately packed or not, they were usually chosen by the federal marshal, who was a Federalist and who became the keeper of the prisoner upon conviction. In no event can the juries be called impartial. Indeed, Beveridge observes that "the juries were nothing more than machines that registered the will, opinion, or even inclination of the national judges and the United States district attorneys. In short, in these prosecutions, trial by jury in any real sense was not to be had." [8]

Under the Sedition Law, the jury was to decide on the criminality of the utterance; one of its vital functions was to decide on the intent of the speaker. The proper duty of the court in sedition cases was to aid the jury in reaching a decision, by instructing it on what the law was in one set of circumstances or in another. The judges were given no power to pass on the facts of publication or intent.[9] In practice, however, they determined the intent of the defendant.

In the trial of Thomas Cooper, Judge Chase ruled that the defendant's effort to prove the truth of his publication demonstrated his bad intent. The defendant's attempt to utilize the legal defense allowed by the Sedition Law, the judge declared, "showed that he intended to dare and defy the Government, and to provoke them, and his subsequent conduct satisfies my mind that such was his disposition. For he justifies the publication, and declares it to be formed in truth. It is proved to be his publication."

Thus the judge ruled, and directed the jury to find, that Cooper had published the words and that he had done so with wicked intent. "It is the boldest attempt I have known to poison the minds

[8] Beveridge, *Marshall*, III, 42. He also asserts that "in many States the United States Marshals selected what persons they pleased as members of the grand juries and trial juries. These officers of the National courts were, without exception, Federalists; in many cases Federalist politicians. When making up juries they selected only persons of the same manner of thinking as that of the marshals and judges themselves."

Also see Anderson, "Alien and Sedition Laws," Amer. Hist. Assoc., *Annual Report for 1912*, 125–126; Warren, *The Supreme Court in United States History*, rev. ed. (Boston, 1937), I, 164–168, and the Papers of George Bancroft Relating to the Administration of John Adams (N.Y. Pub. Lib.).

[9] Carroll, "Freedom of Speech and of the Press in the Federalist Period: The Sedition Act," *Michigan Law Review*, 18 (1920), 644n.

of the people," he told the jury. It was poison not because it incited the people to force and violence but because it criticized President John Adams in an election year, tending to defeat his campaign against Thomas Jefferson. In short, the instructions of the judges made verdicts of guilty virtually inevitable.[10]

To summarize, then, the clause on truth was nullified by the courts; the right of the jury to decide the criminality of the writing was usurped by the presiding judges; and the test of intent was reduced to the seventeenth-century common law test of bad tendency. Without these procedural safeguards, the Sedition Law was almost a duplicate of the English common law of seditious libel. Since intent was presumed from tendency, the test of criminality became the same: the tendency of the words to bring rulers into disrepute.

The evidence is conclusive that the Sedition Law, as enforced, reduced the limits of speech and press in the United States to those set by the English common law in the days before the American Revolution. This was the standard advocated by the Federalists who enacted the law, and it was the standard applied by the Federalist judges who interpreted the law.

The basic question, then, is this: is the pre-Revolutionary rule the guide to the liberties protected by the First Amendment? Is the bad-tendency test compatible with free and open discussion of public affairs by the people? Formulated in an age of authority, the common law doctrine of seditious utterances was antirepublican to the core. When Blackstone wrote his *Commentaries* in 1769, he was trying to describe the law as it then existed. Although prior censorship had expired seventy-five years before he wrote, the British government continued to institute numerous sedition prosecutions.[11] Blackstone discussed the importance of a free press in a free state, but he insisted that liberty of the press meant only that no restraints could be laid upon writings prior to their publication.[12]

---

[10] The two leading legal writers on the Sedition Law have observed that the summing up of the judges to the juries "left nothing for honest jurors to do but return verdicts of guilty." See *ibid.*, 641, and Henry Schofield, "Freedom of the Press," *Essays on Constitutional Law*, II, 534.

[11] Wilkes's famous case had been before the English public for six years when Blackstone's work appeared. In the next year, the ministers of George III began the even more important prosecutions of the printers of Junius' letters. Sir Thomas Erskine May, *The Constitutional History of England, since the Accession of George the Third, 1760–1860, with a Supplementary Chapter, 1861–1871* (New York, 1889), II, 113–114.

[12] *Blackstone's Commentaries*, bk. IV, ch. vii, 915–918.

In stressing the sovereignty of the legislature, Blackstone emphasized the supremacy of the government over the subject. Whatever liberties the people possessed were conferred by the government. They had no "inalienable right" to liberty of the press; that had been created automatically when Parliament failed to extend the Licensing Act of 1695. So long as the writings were not censored before being printed, the press was free. Blackstone's definition, however, legalized suppression any time after the moment of publication; the most vital or the most harmless discussion of public policy could be punished if it was obnoxious to the authorities. Common law asserted the right of the state to punish those who wrote true statements about public magistrates if they tended to expose them to public hatred, contempt, and ridicule. Such statements were punishable because "the direct tendency of these libels is the breach of the public peace, by stirring up the objects of them to revenge, and perhaps to bloodshed." In criminal proceedings, truth was no defense. It was the provocation to action, and not the falsity of the statement, which was punished. The tendency to disturb the public peace was the measure of criminality. Moreover, the common law presumed that the tendency of all libel was bad. It placed the judges of the King's Bench in a position to condemn any writings which had a tendency to excite and move the people to change the existing order of things.[13] Sir James Fitzjames Stephen has observed that the practical enforcement of the law of seditious libel in England "was wholly inconsistent with any serious public discussion of political affairs." As long as it was recognized as the law of the land, any political discussion existed only by sufferance of the government.[14]

This was the model to which the Federalists turned in 1798. Not only did they define the First Amendment by the pre-Revolutionary English common law, but they also urged the necessity of imitating the repressive alien and sedition legislation which Great Britain had passed to combat the social and political forces unleashed by the French Revolution. Although England enforced these measures as wartime precautions, the Federalists insisted on the need for a similar policy whether war came or not. Indeed, the Sedition Law

[13] For Blackstone's reference to the role of the expiration of the Licensing Act in the establishment of liberty of the press, see *Commentaries*, 915–918. For a discussion of why Parliament failed to extend the act, see Thomas Babington Macaulay, *The History of England From the Accession of James II* (New York, 1856), IV, 488–490.

[14] Stephen, *History of the Criminal Law*, II, 348. Not until 1843 did England admit truth as a defense in criminal libel suits, and then it was allowed only in rebuttal. See Lord Campbell's Act, 6 and 7 Victoria, C. 96, s.6.

was to expire not at the end of the diplomatic impasse with France but with the end of President Adams' term of office. By following the British precedents, the Federalists subscribed to the authoritarian view that the government is the master, not the servant, of the people.

The American Revolution culminated in the formulation and establishment in the United States of a form of government which rested on the will of the governed. Growing out of the natural-rights philosophy of the seventeenth and eighteenth centuries, this revolutionary theory of government was founded on the principle that governments are instituted to secure, among other things, the liberties of the individual. A written Constitution established a limited government, which was barred from invading these "inalienable rights."

The meaning of the First Amendment did not crystallize in 1791, when the Bill of Rights was added to the Constitution. Not until the years from 1798 to 1801, when the Sedition Act was debated and enforced, did the limits of liberty of speech and of the press become an issue which focused attention squarely on its definition as a part of the American experiment in self-government.[15] The first thing to be kept in mind in determining the meaning of the First Amendment is that it was added by the people as a further bulwark guarding civil liberties in the United States from governmental interference.[16] Moreover, the rights protected by the proviso were those prevailing not in England but in the United States.[17]

One of the political catalysts of the American Revolution was the effort of the British to subdue the popular press in colonial America. This attempt was twofold. Under the Stamp Act of 1765, a prohibitive tax was placed on the paper used by the presses. Had this law been executed, it would have forced the inexpensive press out of circulation, thus suppressing colonial discussion of politics in the popular papers. A second method used to crush colonial opposition to ministerial policies was an accelerated use of the law

[15] Chafee, *Free Speech in the United States*, 29.

[16] Schofield, "Freedom of the Press," *Essays on Constitutional Law*, II, 569, says that the constitutional declarations of liberty of speech and of the press are the original work of the American people in the sphere of law and government.

In Number 84 of *The Federalist*, Hamilton argued that the Constitution conferred no power by which restrictions might be imposed on the press.

[17] Albert J. Beveridge, "The Effect of the French Revolution on England and America," *Chicago Legal News*, 53 (1920), 103.

of seditious libel.[18] Indeed, when George III issued his proclamation of rebellion against the American colonies, he gave as its official title "A Proclamation, By the King, for Suppressing Rebellion and Sedition." [19]

There are several important pronouncements prior to the debates of 1798 which indicate that liberty of the press in the post-Revolutionary United States meant more than the English common law rule. Many of the colonial publications on political affairs were considered seditious and even treasonable under the common law and its loose administration by the king's judges.[20] That one of the objects of the American Revolution was to abolish the common law restriction on liberty of the press, especially on political discussion, is illustrated by one of the addresses framed by the First Continental Congress in 1774. In a letter addressed to the inhabitants of Quebec, Congress enumerated five rights basic to a free government. One of these was liberty of the press. "Besides the advancement of truth, science, morality, and arts in general," its importance consisted "in its diffusion of liberal sentiments on the administration of Government, its ready communication of thought between subjects, and the consequential promotion of union among them, whereby oppressive officers are shamed or intimidated into more honourable and just modes of conducting affairs." [21]

This statement of liberty of the press specifically denies the right of the government to censure remarks because of their tendency to bring magistrates into public shame and contempt. Indeed, it asserts the opposite right of criticizing administrative officials chosen by the "free and full consent" of the governed.

[18] Clyde Augustus Duniway, *The Development of Freedom of the Press in Massachusetts* (New York, 1906), 124–136; Arthur M. Schlesinger, "The Colonial Newspapers and the Stamp Act," *New England Quarterly*, 8 (1935), 63–83. Also see Edmund S. and Helen M. Morgan, *The Stamp Act Crisis: Prologue to Revolution* (Chapel Hill, 1953), 187, and Chafee, *Free Speech in the United States*, 21. For the increased use of the law of seditious libel in England during the pre-Revolutionary period, see May, *Constitutional History of England*, II, 110, 114.

[19] Peter Force, *American Archives* (Washington, 1840), 4th ser., III, 240–241. The proclamation was issued Aug. 23, 1775.

[20] Bradley Chapin, "The American Revolution as Lese Majesty," *Pennsylvania Magazine of History and Biography*, 79 (July, 1955), 310–330. Also see Chapin, "The Law of Treason during the American Revolution, 1765–1783" (doctoral dissertation, Cornell University, 1951).

[21] "Letter Addressed to the Inhabitants of the Province of Quebec," Oct. 26, 1774, W. C. Ford, ed., *Journal of the Continental Congress* (Washington, 1904), I, 108.

The Declaration of Independence, of course, was the classic repudiation of the idea that the government was the master of the people. The Virginia Act for Establishing Religious Freedom, written by the author of the Declaration, is another Revolutionary document which sets forth a philosophical justification of the right of a person to intellectual freedom.[22] The Preamble includes a declaration for individual liberty not only in religion but also in civil affairs:

To suffer the civil magistrate to intrude his powers into the field of opinion and to restrain the profession or propagation of principles on supposition of their ill tendency, is a dangerous falacy [sic], which at once destroys all religious liberty, because he being of course judge of that tendency, will make his opinions the rule of judgment, and approve or condemn the sentiment of others only as they shall square with or differ from his own; that it is time enough for the rightful purposes of government for its officers to interfere when principles break out into overt acts against peace and good order; and finally, that truth is great and will prevail if left to herself; that she is the proper and sufficient antagonist to error, and has nothing to fear from the conflict unless by human interposition disarmed of her natural weapons, free argument and debate; errors ceasing to be dangerous when it is permitted freely to contradict them.[23]

The basic doctrine of this bill, which Jefferson always ranked next to the Declaration of Independence, was its rejection of the bad tendency test in the field of opinion. In a line which was deleted when the bill passed, Jefferson stated "that the opinions of men are not the object of civil government, nor under its jurisdiction." Even without this line, however, the Virginia Act for Establishing Religious Freedom announced the right of an individual to choose his beliefs, religious or political, free from compulsion.

The fact that the rights of free speech and of a free press are linked with the rights of conscience, assembly, and petition in the First Amendment throws much light on the meaning of the guarantees added to the Constitution at the insistence of the American people. Whereas the First Amendment secures the separation of church and state, England had a state-supported church. Moreover, the right of assembly was severely restricted in England at the time the Bill of Rights was ratified in the United States.[24] The

[22] Although the bill did not become law until 1785, it was written in 1777 and was printed as early as 1779. For a facsimile of the 1779 text, see Julian P. Boyd and others, eds., The Papers of Thomas Jefferson (Princeton, 1950), II, 304.

[23] Jefferson Papers (Boyd ed.), II, 546.

[24] Philip A. Brown, The French Revolution in English History (London, 1918).

First Amendment certainly did not follow the English example in the field of religion and assembly. As Madison emphasized in the congressional debates over the rights incorporated in the First Amendment, "The freedom of the press and rights of conscience, those choicest privileges of the people, are unguarded in the British Constitution." Although any invasion of them by the government always was resisted in Parliament by able advocates, he observed that the Magna Charta did not contain any provision for the security of rights "respecting which the people of America are most alarmed." [25] The First Amendment can no more be considered an endorsement of the English common law definition of freedom of the press than it can be interpreted as an adoption of English practices in the field of religion and assembly.

Indeed, Madison based his explanation of the First Amendment in 1799 on the essential difference "between the nature of the British Government and the nature of the American Governments." In England, Parliament was omnipotent; in the United States, "the People, not the Government, possess the absolute sovereignty." In the United States, the legislatures are not omnipotent, nor are the magistrates infallible. "The nature of governments elective, limited, and responsible in all their branches," Madison continued, "may well be supposed to require a greater freedom of animadversion than might be tolerated" by one that is composed of an hereditary king and upper house, neither elected by, nor responsible to, the people, and an omnipotent lower house. [26]

There is other contemporary evidence which indicates that freedom of speech and of the press in the United States was viewed as a liberal protection guaranteeing free discussion of public matters. In his essay on the press, Benjamin Franklin asserted that "if by the *Liberty of the Press* were understood merely the Liberty of discussing the Propriety of Public Measures and political opinions, let us have as much of it as you please." [27]

One of the strongest statements on the American meaning of the liberty of the press was contained in the reply of the Federalist envoys to France in answer to Talleyrand's protest against remarks in the American press critical of the Directory. "The genius of the

[25] *Annals,* IC, 434. For a thorough discussion of *The Birth of the Bill of Rights, 1776–1791,* see the excellent study by Robert Allen Rutland.

[26] Report on the Virginia Resolutions, 1799–1800 session, Virginia State Assembly, *Madison's Writings* (Hunt ed.), VI, 387–388.

[27] "The Court of the Press," Sept. 12, 1789, *Franklin's Writings* (Smyth ed.), X, 38. For an analysis of this essay and Harper's interpretation, see Chapter VIII.

Constitution," wrote Pinckney, Marshall, and Gerry in a passage which their fellow Federalists ignored, "and the opinion of the people of the United States, cannot be overruled by those who administer the Government. Among those principles deemed sacred in America," they continued, "among those sacred rights considered as forming the bulwark of their liberty, which the Government contemplates with awful reverence and would approach only with the most cautious circumspection, there is no one of which the importance is more deeply impressed on the public mind than the liberty of the press." [28]

All these statements went much farther than the Blackstonian theory which held that liberty of the press prevented only government censorship. Although they all agreed that the absence of censorship was an important part of that freedom, they also asserted the right of the people to participate in free and full discussion of public affairs. They were declarations based on American experience, not on British precedents. They rejected the authoritarian view that the rulers are the superiors of the people.

In his *History of the Criminal Law of England,* Stephen asserted that to those who believe that the people are the masters of the government, "and who carry it out to all its consequences, there can be no such offence as sedition. There may indeed be breaches of the peace which may destroy or threaten life, limb, or property, and there may be incitements to such offences, but," he maintained, "no imaginable censure of the government, short of censure which has an immediate tendency to produce such a breach of the peace, ought to be regarded as criminal." Although Stephen considered this statement too extreme for England in view of her historical development, this is the view expounded by the American people in the Declaration of Independence, fought for in the American Revolution, and established in the state and federal constitutions. In short, the English common law crime of sedition and the American principle of popular government cannot coexist.[29]

In every case in which the law was enforced, a political crime was punished for the same reason that all political crimes have ever been punished—for expressions of discontent with the authorities. As Professor Henry Schofield has pointed out, the sedition

[28] "Envoys to the French Minister of Exterior Affairs," *Annals,* 5C, 3449.

[29] Stephen, *History of Criminal Law of England,* II, 300; Schofield, "Freedom of the Press," *Essays on Constitutional Law,* II, 535, 520–521. For a lucid discussion of *Freedom of the Press,* see the recent book by William L. Chenery (New York, 1955).

cases clearly demonstrated "the great danger . . . that men will be fined and imprisoned, under the guise of being punished for their bad motives, or bad intent and ends, simply because the powers that be do not agree with their opinions, and spokesmen of minorities may be terrorized and silenced when they are most needed by the community and most useful to it, and when they stand most in need of the protection of the law against a hostile, arrogant majority." [30]

Calling the Sedition Law the greatest and most fatal error of the Federalist party, Charles Francis Adams, the grandson and biographer of John Adams, noted that republican government cannot function without free discussion. "It cannot be denied," he wrote, "that the attempt to punish individuals for mere expressions of opinion of public measures and public men, to subject them perhaps to fine and imprisonment, and certainly to heavy and burdensome charges in their defense, for exercising a latitude of speech however extreme, in the heat and excitement attending the political conflicts of a free country, verged too closely upon an abridgment of the liberty of speech and of the press to be quite reconcilable to the theory of free institutions." [31]

The Alien and Sedition Laws played a prominent role in shaping the American tradition of civil liberties. Based on the concept that the government was master, these laws provoked a public response which clearly demonstrated that the people occupied that position. The severity of the Sedition Law failed to prevent the "overthrow" of the Adams administration by the Jeffersonian "disorganizers." Indeed, the law furnished a ready text which the Democratic-Republicans used to incite the American people to legal "insurgency" at the polls; the election resulted in the repudiation of the party which tried to protect itself behind the Sedition Law. It elevated to power a party whose leaders stressed the concept that freedom of opinion is an essential part of an all-encompassing freedom of the mind; for Jefferson and Madison the First Freedom occupied a high, preferred position as the only effectual guardian of every other right. To them, as to the United States Supreme Court later, the defeat of the Federalists illustrated the common understanding that the First Amendment abolished the English common law crime of seditious libel, of which the Sedition Law was merely declaratory.[32]

[30] Schofield, *Essays*, II, 540.
[31] Adams, *Life and Works of John Adams*, I, 560–561.
[32] In *U.S.* v. *Hudson and Goodwin*, 7 Cranch 32 (1812), the Supreme Court

The adherence of the people to the Republicans marked the beginning of a new political era. As John Adams himself pointed out, the election resulted in the "revolution of 1801":[33] the Age of Federalism was at an end. Public opinion had never been without its influence on the conduct of government but it had been grudgingly acknowledged by the Federalists. It now became the basis of American democratic development. As early as 1794, Madison had stated concisely what has since become the traditional American view: "If we advert to the nature of Republican Government, we shall find that the censorial power is in the people over the Government, and not in the Government over the people." [34]

The sharp and lasting defeat administered to the Federalists at the beginning of the nineteenth century made a deep impression on the party leaders of that century. Not until the entry of the United States into World War I did Congress again impose restrictions on utterances and publications and thus encroach on the civil liberties tradition founded on the resentment against the laws of 1798.[35] The Sedition Act of 1918, however, was a wartime measure which was repealed in 1921. The first peacetime sedition statute was not passed until 1940, when Congress enacted the Alien Registration Act, commonly called the Smith Act.

With these two exceptions, the United States has preferred to abide by the principles enunciated by Jefferson in his first inaugural address. Referring to the election of 1800 as a "contest of opinion" which had been decided by "the voice of the nation," the new president reasserted the right of the people "to think freely and to

---

rejected the argument that the United States possessed common law jurisdiction over the crime of seditious libel and ruled that crimes against the United States must be established by statutes. The court specifically stated that "although this question is brought up now for the first time to be decided by this Court, we consider it as having been long since settled in *public opinion*. In no other case for many years has this jurisdiction been asserted; and the general acquiescence of legal men shews the prevalence of opinion in favor of the negative of the proposition." The italics are mine.

The reaction against the federal statute of 1798 also had its effect on state prosecutions for seditious libel, rendering them less and less frequent until they ceased altogether. Edward S. Corwin, "Freedom of Speech and Press under the First Amendment: A Résumé," *Yale Law Journal*, 30 (1920), 48, reprinted in American Association of Law Schools, *Select Essays in Constitutional Law*, II, 1063.

[33] *Adams' Works*, X, 162.   [34] *Annals*, 3C, 2S (Nov. 27, 1794), 934.

[35] Robert E. Cushman, "Alien and Sedition Laws," *Encyclopedia of Social Sciences* (New York, 1930), I, 635. Also see Chafee, *Free Speech in the United States, passim.*

speak and to write what they think." Although he stoutly defended the right of the majority to rule, he cautioned that its will "to be rightful must be reasonable. The minority," he declared, "possess their equal rights, which equal law must protect, and to violate would be oppression." In a passage which condemned the Sedition Law without naming it, he restated the fundamental principle of the American experiment in popular government:

If there be any among us who would wish to dissolve this Union or to change its republican form, let them stand undisturbed as monuments of the safety with which error of opinion may be tolerated where reason is left free to combat it. I know, indeed, that some honest men fear that a republican government can not be strong, that this Government is not strong enough; but would the honest patriot, in the full tide of successful experiment, abandon a government which has so far kept us free and firm on the theoretic and visionary fear that this Government, the world's best hope, may by possibility want energy to preserve itself? I trust not. I believe this, on the contrary, the strongest Government on earth. I believe it the only one where every man, at the call of the law, would fly to the standard of the law, and would meet invasions of the public order as his own personal concern. Sometimes it is said that man can not be trusted with the government of himself. Can he, then, be trusted with the government of others? Or have we found angels in the forms of kings to govern him? Let history answer this question.[36]

The American experiment in self-government, which was conceived in liberty, was dedicated to the proposition that public discussion is a political duty; that men may disagree on public issues; that the opportunity to speak their minds on supposed grievances affords the best means of deciding on proper remedies; that in the marketplace, or on the battleground, of opinions, the people will be able to distinguish truth from error; and that the sounder principles and measures will prevail. Without free speech and a free press, representative government is not truly representative. Without them, popular government cannot function.

[36] Richardson, *Messages*, I, 322.

Postscript

In times of change and danger when there is a quick-sand of fear under men's reasoning, a sense of continuity with generations gone before can stretch like a lifeline across the scary present.—JOHN DOS PASSOS

The Alien and Sedition Laws

1. *An Act supplementary to and to amend the act, intituled "An act to establish an uniform rule of naturalization; and to repeal the act heretofore passed on that subject."*

Section 1. *Be it enacted by the Senate and House of Representatives of the United States of America in Congress assembled,* That no alien shall be admitted to become a citizen of the United States, or of any state, unless in the manner prescribed by the act, intituled "An act to establish an uniform rule of naturalization; and to repeal the act heretofore passed on that subject," he shall have declared his intention to become a citizen of the United States, five years, at least, before his admission, and shall, at the time of his application to be admitted, declare and prove, to the satisfaction of the court having jurisdiction in the case, that he has resided within the United States fourteen years, at least, and within the state or territory where, or for which such court is at the time held, five years, at least, besides conforming to the other declarations, renunciations and proofs, by the said act required any thing therein to the contrary hereof notwithstanding: *Provided,* that any alien, who was residing within the limits, and under the jurisdiction of the United States, before the twenty-ninth day of January, one thousand seven hundred and ninety-five, may, within one year after the passing of this act—and any alien who shall have made the declaration of his intention to become a citizen of the United States, in conformity to the provisions of the act, intituled "An act to establish an uniform rule of naturalization, and to repeal the act heretofore passed on that subject," may, within four years after having made the declaration aforesaid, be admitted to become a citizen, in the manner prescribed by the said act, upon his making proof that he has resided five years, at least, within the limits, and under the jurisdiction of the United States: *And provided also,* that no alien, who shall be a native, citizen, denizen or subject of any nation or state with whom the United States shall be at war, at the time of his application, shall be then admitted to become a citizen of the United States.

Sec. 2. *And be it further enacted,* That it shall be the duty of the clerk, or other recording officer of the court before whom a declaration has been, or shall be made, by any alien, of his intention to become a citizen of the United States, to certify and transmit to the office of the Secretary of State of the United States, to be there filed and recorded, an abstract of such declaration, in which, when hereafter made, shall be a suitable description of the name, age, nation, residence and occupation, for the time being, of the alien; such certificate to be made in all cases, where the declaration has been or shall be made, before the passing of this act, within three months thereafter; and in all other cases, within two months after the declaration shall be received by the court. And in all cases hereafter arising, there shall be paid to the clerk, or recording officer as aforesaid, to defray the expense of such abstract and certificate, a fee of two dollars; and the clerk or officer to whom such fee shall be paid or tendered, who shall refuse or neglect to make and certify an abstract, as aforesaid, shall forfeit and pay the sum of ten dollars.

Sec. 3. *And be it further enacted,* That in all cases of naturalization heretofore permitted or which shall be permitted, under the laws of the United States, a certificate shall be made to, and filed in the office of the Secretary of State, containing a copy of the record respecting the alien, and the decree or order of admission by the court before whom the proceedings thereto have been, or shall be had: And it shall be the duty of the clerk or other recording officer of such court, to make and transmit such certificate, in all cases which have already occurred, within three months after the passing of this act; and in all future cases, within two months from and after the naturalization of an alien shall be granted by any court competent thereto:—And in all future cases, there shall be paid to such clerk or recording officer the sum of two dollars, as a fee for such certificate, before the naturalization prayed for, shall be allowed. And the clerk or recording officer, whose duty it shall be, to make and transmit the certificate aforesaid, who shall be convicted of a wilful neglect therein, shall forfeit and pay the sum of ten dollars, for each and every offence.

Sec. 4. *And be it further enacted,* That all white persons, aliens, (accredited foreign ministers, consuls, or agents, their families and domestics, excepted) who, after the passing of this act, shall continue to reside, or who shall arrive, or come to reside in any port or place within the territory of the United States, shall be reported, if free, and of the age of twenty-one years, by themselves, or being under the age of twenty-one years, or holden in service, by their parent, guardian, master or mistress in whose care they shall be, to the clerk of the district court of the district, if living within ten miles of the port or place, in which their residence or arrival shall be, and otherwise, to the collector of such port or place, or some officer or other person there, or nearest thereto, who shall be authorized by the President of the United States, to register aliens: And report, as aforesaid, shall be made in all cases of residence, within six months from and after the passing of this act, and in all after cases, within forty-eight hours after the first arrival or coming into the territory of the United States, and shall ascertain the sex, place of birth, age, nation, place of allegiance or citizenship, condition or occupation, and place of actual or intended residence within the United States, of the alien or aliens reported, and by whom the report is made. And it shall be the duty of the clerk, or other officer, or person authorized, who shall receive such report, to record the same in a book to be kept for that purpose, and to grant to the person making the report, and to each individual concerned therein, whenever required, a certificate of such report and registry; and whenever such report and registry shall be made to, and by any officer or person authorized, as aforesaid, other than the clerk of the district court, it shall be the duty of such officer, or other person, to certify and transmit, within three months thereafter, a transcript of such registry, to the said clerk of the district court of the district in which the same shall happen; who shall file the same in his office, and shall enter and transcribe the same in a book to be kept by him for that purpose. And the clerk, officer or other person authorized to register aliens, shall be entitled to receive, for each report and registry of one individual or family of individuals, the sum of fifty cents and for every certificate of a report and registry the sum of fifty cents, to be paid by the person making or requiring the same, respectively. And the clerk of the district court, to whom a return of the registry of any alien, shall have been made, as aforesaid, and the successor of such clerk, and of any other officer or person authorized to register aliens, who shall hold any former registry, shall and may grant certificates thereof, to the same effect as the original register might do. And the clerk of each district court shall, during one year from the passing of this act, make monthly returns to the department of State, of all aliens registered and returned, as aforesaid, in his office.

Sec. 5. *And be it further enacted,* That every alien who shall continue to reside, or who shall arrive, as aforesaid, of whom a report is required as aforesaid, who shall refuse or neglect to make such report, and to receive a certificate thereof, shall forfeit and pay the sum of two dollars; and any justice of the peace, or other civil magistrate, who has authority to require surety of the peace, shall and may, on complaint to him made thereof, cause such alien to be brought before him, there to give surety of the peace and good behaviour during his residence within the United States, or for such term as the justice or other magistrate shall deem reasonable, and until a report and registry of such alien shall be made, and a certificate thereof, received as aforesaid; and in failure of such surety, such alien shall and may be committed to the common gaol, and shall be there held, until the order which the justice or magistrate shall and may reasonably make, in the premises, shall be performed. And every person, whether alien, or other, having the care of any alien or aliens, under the age of twenty-one years, or of any white alien holden in service, who shall refuse and neglect to make report thereof, as aforesaid, shall forfeit the sum of two dollars, for each and every such minor or servant, monthly, and every month, until a report and registry, and a certificate thereof, shall be had, as aforesaid.

Sec. 6. *And be it further enacted,* That in respect to every alien, who shall come to reside within the United States after the passing of this act, the time of registry of such alien shall be taken to be the time when the term of residence within the limits, and under the jurisdiction of the United States, shall have commenced, in case of an application by such alien, to be admitted a citizen of the United States; and a certificate of such registry shall be required, in proof of the term of residence, by the court to whom such application shall and may be made.

Sec. 7. *And be it further enacted,* That all and singular the penalties established by this act, shall and may be recovered in the name, and to the use of any person, who will inform and sue for the same, before any judge, justice, or court, having jurisdiction in such case, and to the amount of such penalty, respectively.

Approved, June 18, 1798. (*Statutes at Large,* I, 566–569).

2. *An Act concerning Aliens.*

Section 1. *Be it enacted by the Senate and House of Representatives of the United States of America in Congress assembled,* That it shall be lawful for the President of the United States at any time during the continuance of this act, to *order* all such *aliens* as he shall judge dangerous to the peace and safety of the United States, or shall have reasonable grounds to suspect are concerned in any treasonable or secret machinations against the government thereof, to depart out of the territory of the United States, within such time as shall be expressed in such order, which order shall be served on such alien by delivering him a copy thereof, or leaving the same at his usual abode, and returned to the office of the Secretary of State, by the marshal or other person to whom the same shall be directed. And in case any alien, so ordered to depart, shall be found at large within the United States after the time limited in such order for his departure, and not having obtained a *license* from the President to reside therein, or having obtained such *license* shall not have conformed thereto, every such alien shall, on conviction thereof, be imprisoned for a term not exceeding three years, and shall never after be admitted to become a citizen of the United States. *Provided always, and be it further enacted,* that if any alien so ordered to depart shall prove to the satisfaction of the President, by evidence to be taken before such person or persons as the President shall direct, who are for that purpose hereby authorized to administer oaths, that no injury or danger to the United States will arise from suffering such alien to reside therein, the President may grant a *license* to such alien to remain within the United States for such time as he shall judge proper, and at such place as he may designate. And the President may also require of such alien to enter into a bond to the United States, in such penal sum as he may direct, with one or more sufficient sureties to the satisfaction of the person authorized by the President to take the same, conditioned for the good behavior of such alien during his residence in the United States, and not violating his license, which license the President may revoke, whenever he shall think proper.

Sec. 2. *And be it further enacted,* That it shall be lawful for the President of the United States, whenever he may deem it necessary for the public safety, to order to be removed out of the territory thereof, any alien who may or shall be in prison in pursuance of this act; and to cause to be arrested and sent out of the United States such of those aliens as shall have been ordered to depart therefrom and shall not have obtained a license as aforesaid, in all cases where, in the opinion of the President, the public safety requires a speedy removal. And if any alien so removed or sent out of the United States by the President shall voluntarily return thereto, unless by permission of the President of the United States, such alien on conviction thereof, shall be imprisoned so long as, in the opinion of the President, the public safety may require.

Sec. 3. *And be it further enacted,* That every master or commander of any ship or vessel which shall come into any port of the United States after the first day of July next, shall immediately on his arrival make report in writing to the collector or other chief officer of the customs of such port, of all aliens, if any, on board his vessel, specifying their names, age, the place of nativity, the country from which they shall have come, the nation to which they belong and owe allegiance, their occupation and a description of their persons, as far as he shall be informed thereof, and on failure, every such master and commander shall forfeit and pay three hundred dollars, for the payment whereof on default of such master or commander, such vessel shall also be holden, and may by such collector or other officer of the customs be detained. And it shall be the duty of such collector or other officer of the customs, forthwith to transmit to the office of the department of state true copies of all such returns.

Sec. 4. *And be it further enacted,* That the circuit and district courts of the United States, shall respectively have cognizance of all crimes and offences against this act. And all marshals and other officers of the United States are required to execute all precepts and orders of the President of the United States issued in pursuance or by virtue of this act.

Sec. 5. *And be it further enacted,* That it shall be lawful for any alien who may be ordered to be removed from the United States, by virtue of this act, to take with him such part of his goods, chattels, or other property, as he may find convenient; and all property left in the United States by any alien, who may be removed, as aforesaid, shall be, and remain subject to his order and disposal, in the same manner as if this act had not been passed.

Sec. 6. *And be it further enacted,* That this act shall continue and be in force for and during the term of two years from the passing thereof. Approved, June 25, 1798. (*Statutes at Large,* I, 570–572).

3. *An Act respecting Alien Enemies.*

Section 1. *Be it enacted by the Senate and House of Representatives of the United States of America in Congress assembled,* That whenever there shall be a declared war between the United States and any foreign nation or government, or any invasion or predatory incursion shall be perpetrated, attempted, or threatened against the territory of the United States, by any foreign nation or government, and the President of the United States shall make public proclamation of the event, all natives, citizens, denizens, or subjects of the hostile nation or government, being males of the age of fourteen years and upwards, who shall be within the United States, and not actually naturalized, shall be liable to be apprehended, restrained, secured and removed, as alien enemies. And the President of the United States shall be, and he is hereby authorized, in any event, as aforesaid, by his proclamation thereof, or other public act, to direct the conduct to be observed, on the part of the United States, towards the aliens who shall become liable, as aforesaid; the manner and degree of the restraint to which they shall be subject, and in what cases, and upon what security their residence shall be permitted, and to provide for the removal of those, who, not being permitted to reside within the United States, shall refuse or neglect to depart therefrom; and to establish any other regulations which shall be found necessary in the premises and for the public safety: Provided, that aliens resident within the United States, who shall become liable as enemies, in the manner aforesaid, and who shall not be chargeable with actual hostility, or other crime against the public safety, shall be allowed, for the recovery, disposal, and removal of their goods and effects, and for their departure, the full time which is, or shall be stipulated by any treaty, where any shall have been between the United States, and the hostile nation or government, of which they shall be natives, citizens, denizens or subjects: and where no such treaty shall have existed, the President of the United States may ascertain and declare such reasonable time as may be consistent with the public safety, and according to the dictates of humanity and national hospitality.

Sec. 2. *And be it further enacted,* That after any proclamation shall be made as aforesaid, it shall be the duty of the several courts of the United States, and of each state, having criminal jurisdiction, and of the several judges and justices of the courts of the United States, and they shall be, and are hereby respectively, authorized upon complaint, against any alien or alien enemies, as aforesaid, who shall be resident and at large within such jurisdiction or district, to the danger of the public peace or safety, and contrary to the tenor or intent of such proclamation, or other regulations which the President of the United States shall and may establish in the premises, to cause such alien or aliens to be duly apprehended and convened before such court, judge or justice; and after a full examination and hearing on such complaint, and sufficient cause therefor appearing, shall and may order such alien or aliens to be removed out of the territory of the United States, or to give sureties of their good behaviour, or to be otherwise restrained, conformably to the proclamation or regulations which shall and may be established as aforesaid, and may imprison, or otherwise secure such alien or aliens, until the order which shall and may be made, as aforesaid, shall be performed.

Sec. 3. *And be it further enacted,* That it shall be the duty of the marshal of the district in which any alien enemy shall be apprehended, who by the President of the United States, or by order of any court, judge or justice, as aforesaid, shall be required to depart, and to be removed, as aforesaid, to provide therefor, and to execute such order, by himself or his deputy, or other discreet person or persons to be employed by him, by causing a removal of such alien out of the territory of the United States; and for such removal the marshal shall have the warrant of the President of the United States, or of the court, judge or justice ordering the same, as the case may be.

Approved, July 6, 1798. (*Statutes at Large,* I, 577–578).

4. An Act in addition to the act, entitled "An act for the punishment of certain crimes against the United States."

Section 1. *Be it enacted by the Senate and House of Representatives of the United States of America, in Congress assembled,* That if any persons shall unlawfully combine or conspire together, with intent to oppose any measure or measures of the government of the United States, which are or shall be directed by proper authority, or to impede the operation of any law of the United States, or to intimidate or prevent any person holding a place or office in or under the government of the United States, from undertaking, performing or executing his trust or duty; and if any person or persons, with intent as aforesaid, shall counsel, advise or attempt to procure any insurrection, riot, unlawful assembly, or combination, whether such conspiracy, threatening, counsel, advice, or attempt shall have the proposed effect or not, he or they shall be deemed guilty of a high misdemeanor, and on conviction, before any court of the United States having jurisdiction thereof, shall be punished by a fine not exceeding five thousand dollars, and by imprisonment during a term not less than six months nor exceeding five years; and further, at the discretion of the court may be holden to find sureties for his good behaviour in such sum, and for such time, as the said court may direct.

Sec. 2. *And be it further enacted,* That if any person shall write, print, utter or publish, or shall cause or procure to be written, printed, uttered or published, or shall knowingly and willingly assist or aid in writing, printing, uttering or publishing any false, scandalous and malicious writing or writings against the government of the United States, or either house of the Congress of the United States, or the President of the United States, with intent to defame the said government, or either house of the said Congress, or the said President, or to bring them, or either of them, into contempt or disrepute; or to excite against them, or either or any of them, the hatred of the good people of the United States, or to stir up sedition within the United States, or to excite any unlawful combinations therein, for opposing or resisting any law of the United States, or any act of the President of the United States, done in pursuance of any such law, or of the powers in him vested by the constitution of the United States, or to resist, oppose, or defeat any such law or act, or to aid, encourage or abet any hostile designs of any foreign nation against the United States, their people or government, then such person, being thereof convicted before any court of the United States having jurisdiction thereof, shall be punished by a fine not exceeding two thousand dollars, and by imprisonment not exceeding two years.

Sec. 3. *And be it further enacted and declared,* That if any person shall be prosecuted under this act, for the writing or publishing any libel aforesaid, it shall be lawful for the defendant, upon the trial of the cause, to give evidence in his defence, the truth of the matter contained in the publication charged as a libel. And the jury who shall try the cause, shall have a right to determine the law and the fact, under the direction of the court, as in other cases.

Sec. 4. *And be it further enacted,* That this act shall continue and be in force until the third day of March, one thousand eight hundred and one, and no longer: *Provided,* that the expiration of the act shall not prevent or defeat a prosecution and punishment of any offence against the law, during the time it shall be in force.

Approved, July 14, 1798. (*Statutes at Large,* I, 596–597).

Bibliographical Note

THE sources of this study are so widely scattered in manuscript and in print that even a selective bibliography would quickly degenerate into little more than an indiscriminate list of references under various classified headings. I have, of course, examined the predictable manuscript collections—and more than a few of the unpredictable ones; the depositories are listed in the preface. As all investigators must, I also have plowed through masses of monographic material and biographical studies. Footnote citations give complete bibliographical information on sources pertinent to this work.

The only purpose of this note, therefore, is to single out some of the items which have been most useful in writing this book. The opening of the Adams Family Papers at the Massachusetts Historical Society in 1954 was itself a historic event, but the manuscripts contain little information for this study which was not already available in other sources. For the most part, the papers covering the period from 1796 to 1801 supplement and corroborate material long available in Charles Francis Adams' surprisingly comprehensive edition of the *Works of John Adams*. It should be pointed out, however, that one of the letterbooks of President Adams could not be located at the time I used the Adams Papers. Stewart Mitchell's edition of the *New Letters of Abigail Adams, 1788–1801* (Boston, 1947) contains some extremely interesting material.

Of vastly greater importance are the Papers of Timothy Pickering at the Massachusetts Historical Society. The key man in the administration's enforcement of the Alien and Sedition Laws, Pickering corresponded with the district attorneys throughout the United States and was in touch with most of the leading Federalists. An excellent, annotated *Historical*

Index to the Pickering Papers, published in the Massachusetts Historical Society *Collections,* 6th ser., vol. VIII (Boston, 1896), is an indispensable guide to those manuscripts. Pickering's official correspondence is contained in the General Records of the Department of State (Records Group 59) at the National Archives. Among the most useful volumes are Domestic Letters, X–XI; Instructions to Ministers and Consuls, 1797–1801; and Miscellaneous Letters, 1800.

The enactment of the alien and sedition legislation can be traced in the *Debates and Proceedings in the Congress of the United States, 1789–1825* (Washington, 1834–56), which are cited throughout this volume as the *Annals.* The texts of the laws may be found in *The Statutes at Large of the United States, 1789–1873* (Boston, 1845–73), I, 566, 570, 577, 596. A basic source not only for the enactment but also for the enforcement of the laws is the party press. More than fifty newspapers were examined with care, and dozens of others checked. The most thorough coverage of national politics is to be found in Fenno's *Gazette of the United States* and in Bache's *Aurora,* both of Philadelphia, but the partisan presses of Boston, New York, Baltimore, and Richmond give excellent regional news. All researchers in early American journalism are indebted to Clarence S. Brigham for his *History and Bibliography of American Newspapers, 1690–1820* (Worcester, 1947, two vols.).

Francis Wharton has edited the *State Trials of the United States during the Administrations of Washington and Adams . . .* (Philadelphia, 1849). These include the federal prosecutions of Callender, Cooper, Haswell, and Lyon; the Pennsylvania case against Duane and others for seditious riot in Philadelphia; and the New York prosecution of Frothingham for libeling Hamilton. The Records of the United States Circuit Courts (Records Group 21) at the National Archives contain a District of New Jersey Minute Book for 1798 (on microfilm), which lists the proceedings against Lespenard, Clark, and Baldwin. The Archives also has the records of the District of New York concerning Durrell, Peck, and Mrs. Greenleaf. The manuscript records of the District of Virginia relating to *United States* v. *Callender* are in the Virginia State Library, Richmond.

Although this volume is based largely on primary materials, I have relied heavily on secondary works in certain areas. My footnote references indicate my indebtedness to Frank Maloy Anderson's pioneering work on "The Enforcement of the Alien and Sedition Laws" in the American Historical Association's *Annual Report for 1912;* his article is the starting point for specialized work in this field. Prior to the publication of Manning J. Dauer's book on *The Adams Federalists* (Baltimore, 1953), I used his doctoral dissertation, "The Basis for the Support for John Adams in the Federalist Party" (University of Illinois, 1933). John Spencer Bassett, *The Federalist System, 1789–1801* (vol. IX in *The American Nation Series,* New York and London, 1906), was not as helpful as was Claude G. Bowers, *Jefferson and Hamilton, The Struggle for Democracy in America* (Boston and New York, 1925), nor was Nathan Schachner's recent work on *The Founding Fathers* (New York, 1954) as useful as his biography of *Thomas Jefferson* (New York, 1951, two vols.).

The only previous monographic study of the legislation is John C. Miller, *Crisis in Freedom: The Alien and Sedition Laws* (Boston, 1951). It is a brief, popular survey which stresses readability over analysis. Marshall Smelser has written two excellent articles on the period: "The Jacobin Phrenzy: Federalism and the Menace of Liberty, Equality, and Fraternity," *Review of Politics*, 13 (Oct., 1951); and "George Washington and the Alien and Sedition Laws," *American Historical Review*, 59 (Jan., 1954).

The historical background of the legal concept of seditious libel is handled beautifully in Sir William S. Holdsworth's *History of English Law* (London, 1903–1938, twelve vols.), but my chief debt is to Zechariah Chafee's brilliant interpretation of *Free Speech in the United States* (Cambridge, 1948). Two articles are basic to an understanding of the legislation: Thomas F. Carroll, "Freedom of Speech and of the Press in the Federalist Period: The Sedition Act," *Michigan Law Review*, 18 (May, 1920); and Henry Schofield, "Freedom of the Press in the United States," *Essays on Constitutional Law and Equity* (Boston, 1921). Least reliable is William Winslow Crosskey, whose devil theory of constitutional development is discussed fully in his *Politics and the Constitution in the History of the United States* (Chicago, 1953, two vols.).

Index

Act Concerning Aliens, *see* Alien Friends Law

Adams, Abigail, 72; advocates federal sedition bill, 97; approves alien friends bill, 53; condemns Jefferson, 191; denounces Boston *Independent Chronicle*, 97, 248; denounces Callender, 341, Cooper, 312, 315, Priestley, 315; deplores *Aurora's* impudence, 97, 191; favors suppression of Republican newspapers, 191; importance of her letters as reflections of President Adams' attitudes, 96n; labels Republicans as "French party," 96; on addresses to president, 9; on Republican presses as instruments of faction, 96; on Republicans as traitors, 15-16; praises arrests of Bache and Burk, 212; prophecy on her husband's inaugural day, 5; proposes that Mass. enact a sedition law, 249; subscribes to "bad tendency" test, 191

Adams, Abijah: convicted of seditious libel, 254; indicted for criticism of Massachusetts' rejection of Virginia Resolutions, 253

Adams, Charles Francis: labels Cooper's prosecution a mistake, 333n; on Sedition Law and free press, 431

Adams, John: and case against Baldwin, 270; announces Marshall's return from XYZ mission, 4; anti-alien sentiments of, 162; appoints first mission to France, 6; approves sedition prosecution of Cooper, 311, of Duane, 284; calls special session of Congress, 1797, 6; complies with Senate request to prosecute Duane, 301; contemplates deportation proceedings against Cobbett, 175; defends his approval of Sedition Law, 152; discusses enforcement of Alien Friends Law, 159; efforts of administration to link Jefferson to treasonable correspondence plot, 195, 195-196n; favors strict construction of Alien Friends Law, 163; importance of his public addresses in nurturing alien and sedition legislation, 20; inherits difficulties with France from Washington's administration, 5; interprets Alien Law strictly, 175; labels political opponents as French partisans, 18; notifies Congress of failure of first mission to France, 6; on *Aurora's* praise, 190; on British influence in American politics, 282n, 285; on criticism by Boston *Independent Chronicle*, 247-248; on deportation proceedings against Moreau, 170; on "diplomatic skill of France," 16; on domestic faction, 18-19; on faction in Virginia, 18;

447